# Fearless Critic

## Praise for the restaurant guides

"Pulls no punches...even icons get goosed."

–*Austin American-Statesman*

"Deft, unblushing prose...good friends to the honest diner, they call it as they see it."

–T. Susan Chang,
Food & Travel Correspondent,
*Boston Globe*

"Exceptionally experienced restaurantgoers...knowledgeable and enthusiastic about eating well."

–*Yale Daily News*

"Immensely useful, written with panache, as respectful of 'Roadfood' as of 'fine-dining'...one of the most compelling restaurant guides we've seen."

–Jane and Michael Stern,
Authors, *Roadfood;*
columnists, *Gourmet*

"Not just a useful book—a pleasure to read. The only people who won't find it a pleasure are the owners of some of the really bad restaurants it warns us about."

D1498838

"Scathing and scintillating."

–*New Haven Register*

# Also from Fearless Critic

The Wine Trials: 100 wines under $15 that beat $50
to $150 bottles in brown-bag blind tastings
*by Robin Goldstein*

Fearless Critic Austin Restaurant Guide, 2nd Edition

Fearless Critic Houston Restaurant Guide

Fearless Critic New Haven Restaurant Guide,
3rd Edition

# Fearless Critic

## Washington DC Area Restaurant Guide

WWW.FEARLESSCRITIC.COM

# First edition, 2009/2010

Printed in the United States of America

10 9 8 7 6 5 4 3 2 1

ISBN 978-09740143-8-8

# Fearless Critic

## Washington DC Area Restaurant Guide

# Fearless Critics

**Robin Goldstein,** Editor-in-Chief
**Alexis Herschkowitsch,** Associate Publisher
**Erin McReynolds,** Managing Editor
**Rebecca Markovits,** Editor
**Kent Wang,** Chief Technology Officer
**Justin Yu,** Executive Chef
**Nat Davis,** Wine Director

**Justine Chiou,** Fearless Critic
**Sandra Di Capua,** Fearless Critic
**Christina Dahlman,** Fearless Critic
**Misha Govshteyn,** Fearless Critic
**Coco Krumme,** Fearless Critic
**Whitney Satin,** Fearless Critic

## Associate editors

Mary Wegmann
Misha Sobolevsky

## Contributing editors

Mariela Alfonzo, Andrea Armeni, Cecily Baskir, Nikia Bergan, Tyler
Cowen, Barry Goldstein, Amber Husbands, Cormac Miller, David
Menschel, Brittany Prelogar, Gina Reinhardt, Hal Stubbs, Lu Stubbs,
Susan Stubbs, Julia Travis

## Special thanks

Margarita Barcenas, Steve Bercu, Tom Bowen, LeVette Brocks, Adam
Brownstein, Ed Cavazos, Brian DiMarco, Frazer Dobson, Julian Faulkner,
Andrew Gajkowski, Sam Herman, Adele Herman, Elizabeth Jordan,
Evelyn Julian, Jeff Kaplan, Greg Khalil, Sidney Kwiram, Jill Lewis, Marisa
Love, Jenny Mandel, Missy Mikol, Doug Mote, Angela Pedowitz, Tamar
Perez, Sherry Pleas, Craig Popelars, Wade Norris, Ben Rosenblum,
Danny Rosenblum, David Rosenblum, Murray Rosenblum, Walter
Schmamp, Giuliano Stiglitz, Jenny Wang, Walter Weintz, Stuart White,
Peter Workman, and the rest of the staff at Workman Publishing.

# Contents

# Fearless Critics

## Robin Goldstein
is the founder and editor-in-chief of the Fearless Critic series and author of *The Wine Trials* and five restaurant guides. He has also written for more than 30 *Fodor's* travel guides, from Italy to Hong Kong. Robin has an A.B. in neuroscience and philosophy from Harvard University, a J.D. from Yale Law School, a certificate in cooking from the French Culinary Institute, and a WSET advanced wine and spirits certificate.

## Alexis Herschkowitsch
is the associate publisher of the Fearless Critic series. She has written and edited for *The Wine Trials,* several *Fearless Critic* guides, and five *Fodor's* guides to Mexico, El Salvador, and Thailand. Alexis has a B.A. from the University of Texas at Austin and a WSET advanced wine and spirits certificate.

## Erin McReynolds
is the managing editor of the Fearless Critic series. She has worked in the restaurant industry for 10 years. She has an M.F.A. in Creative Writing from Queens University of Charlotte and a B.A. from California State University, Fullerton.

## Justine Chiou
is an avid cook and an even more avid eater. She is convinced that she has an invincible stomach and can consume more bacon in one sitting than anyone else she knows. She has an A.B. in history and literature from Harvard University.

## Christina Dahlman
spends much of her time cooking, eating, or thinking about her next meal. She has worked in law and policy consulting, and has an A.B. in philosophy from Harvard University, as well as a certificate in mind, brain, and behavior.

## Sandra Di Capua
has been a researcher and recipe tester for Joan Nathan's cookbook, *In Search of the Foods of the Jews of France*. She has an A.B. in romance studies from Harvard University.

## Coco Krumme
grew up in the food mecca of Berkeley, California, where her mother and the Cheeseboard were her first food educators. She has a B.A. from Yale University.

## Whitney Satin
is a baking addict. She volunteers for Food and Friends, which provides meals to people in the DC area living with HIV/AIDS, cancer, and other debilitating illnesses. She has an A.B. in Social Studies from Harvard University.

*Fearless Critics are not allowed to participate in the evaluations of any restaurants with which they are or every have been associated.*

# Preface

Haven't you heard the news? DC's Chinatown has been condemned. There's no good food there anymore, they say. It's a wasteland.

In the wee hours of the morning, a couple of cooks from Minibar skulk out the door of Café Atlantico and turn up 7th Street. The last guest has left their eight-seat temple to molecular gastronomy. The counters are wiped down; the nitrogen tanks have been sealed up for the night, the sodium alginate and calcium chloride put away.

The two men walk away, away from the channels of power and influence. They walk past the hulking Verizon Center. They walk from silk and steel toward the smells of sewage, from two-hundred-dollar darkness toward a block of Blade Runner neon.

They walk quickly, these men, these men that have learned to make human beings breathe like dragons, these men that have been anointed as philosopher-kings by America's culinary televangelists—and, yes, by the congregation, too, by the food bloggers who are photographing and twittering each little plate as if terrified by the unavoidable mortality of an olive-oil bon-bon—terrified that when its skin cracks and it releases its oil, its gustatory memory might be lost in time, as the Rutger Hauer character might say, like tears in rain.

Finally, the two cooks arrive at a storefront that looks like an icon of Chinatown's condemnation. It is the "New Big Wong," and all that's advertised on its windows is a stir-fry lunch, fried rice, five bucks or so.

It is there that the men descend from darkness into pools of fluorescent light—and there, the feast begins: with a jellyfish salad, with a live Dungeness crab from the tank, with a Cantonese roast duck that has been hanging from the ceiling by its neck—ritually hacked, for these men, into crunchy, transcendent tenderness.

In the words of Radiohead: This is really happening. The wizards of America's New Culinary Order are dining at the New Big Wong.

You should be, too. Go to Shaw, where your beautiful Ethiopian waitress will snort-giggle with appreciation when you tell her you want your kitfo raw. *Raw beef!* When the cab driver at the next table laughs at you—he's eating spaghetti and meatballs—you explain to him that you're consuming raw or undercooked meats, poultry, seafood, shellfish, or eggs in hopes of increasing your risk of foodborne illness.

Go to Falls Church, go to Hyattsville, go to Annandale, where the best Korean restaurants in America require no reservations; their strip parking lots are wide open. You don't *really* want the pig's-blood sausage, do you? Nobody likes *that*. It's *their* thing. *Their* Korea. Yet it's been here for a while now. We just weren't paying attention. Washigton, DC was turning into one of the greatest culinary world's fairs ever assembled—and we weren't even paying attention.

The wizened wizard of this gastro-temple peeks around the corner from her kitchen, watching your table intently until you take a bite. Eventually, she accepts it: *you're really eating the soondae.* A smile spreads across her face, the corners of her eyes crinkled in appreciation. It lasts just a moment, but it is a truly modern moment. Then she ducks back into the kitchen and gets back to the work of remaking America.

This is really happening.

# The Fearless Critic system

Welcome to a new kind of restaurant guide. We've written, edited, and fact-checked 500 full-page reviews that rigorously rate more than 875 places to eat (including local minichains) in the greater Washington, DC area, including the Maryland and Virginia suburbs out to (and occasionally beyond) the Beltway. And as you might guess, the authors are very, very full.

The Fearless Critic's "brutally honest" philosophy can be summed up in one sentence: our duty is to the readers, not the restaurants. We do not accept advertising from dining establishments, chefs, or restaurateurs. We visit all restaurants incognito and pay for our own meals. We visit most establishments several times, and most of our reviews are informed by years of repeat visits by our Fearless Critic Council, a team of local food nerds who visit and evaluate each other's restaurants without identifying themselves.

In order to qualify for inclusion in this book, an establishment must serve food. Of course, we haven't included every restaurant in the DC area; there are several thousand of them. We've focused on the restaurants that we thought it most important to review, whether for positive or negative reasons. This meant omitting many restaurants, including many restaurants that, for people who live in the immediate neighborhood, might be relevant. We've visited many more restaurants than we wrote up, and we've chosen to include only the places that we thought would be most relevant for readers given our space constraints. As a general rule, in order to be included, a restaurant must be relevant: either good, famous, or centrally located, but not necessarily all of the above.

We're also sure, however, that we have also unwittingly omitted many true out-of-the-way gems, and for that we apologize in advance (and encourage you to let us know about them at **fearless@fearlesscritic.com**, so that they might be included in the next edition). But we hope that we'll also turn you on to a lot of little places with which you might not be familiar, and we hope we've done a generally good job covering many of the eateries worth knowing about in and around the District. We have also included several restaurants in the suburbs that, by our judgment, are notable enough to be included.

If you're not already familiar with our philosophy, as you'll see once you start reading, the Fearless Critic style is relentlessly opinionated— something you might not be used to when you read a restaurant review. We're happy to wax poetic if we love a place, but as First Amendment fans, we're also not afraid to tell you if a place is overpriced, rude, or just plain bad. (That said, whenever possible, we try to be entertaining while doing it.) Our goal is to evaluate the restaurants—good or bad—so you don't have to; we hope to help you decide where to eat, and also where *not* to eat.

Our book is ultimately a reference guide, so we focus more on evaluation of food and feel than we do on chefs' names and pedigrees. We're more restaurant inspectors than restaurant promoters, and we aim for a punchy evaluation of a restaurant's strengths and weaknesses that ends with a clear judgment and recommendation.

Your hard-earned dollars matter a lot to us, and we hope that the money you've spent on this book will save you untold sums in the future by preventing you from wasting hundreds of dollars on potentially bad, boring meals. Therein, we believe, lies much of the usefulness of food criticism.

So, welcome to a new kind of restaurant review, and a new kind of restaurant guide to the nation's capital. We hope you'll be a convert.

# The rating scale

After the Fearless Critics evaluate each establishment incognito, we all get together and assign two numerical ratings to each establishment.

**Food rating (1 to 10):** This is strictly a measure of whether the food on offer is appetizing or objectionable, insipid or delicious. We close our eyes to reputation, price, and puffery when we taste, so don't be surprised to find a greasy spoon outscoring a historic, upscale, sit-down establishment, for one simple reason: the food just tastes better. Markets, bakeries, sweets shops, and ice cream shops, since they're not primarily in the business of serving meals, are ineligible for this rating. Be forewarned that we use the whole 10-point scale, and this is the area where we're most severely critical, so if you're in the if-you-don't-have-something-nice-to-say-then-don't-say-anything school of thought, please take the ratings with a grain of salt. We hope that fanatical foodies will appreciate our rigor and honesty. A food score above 8 constitutes a recommendation; a 9 or above is a high recommendation.

**Feel rating (1 to 10):** Many guides rate the service and décor at a restaurant, but rather than counting the number of pieces of silverware on the table or the number of minutes and seconds before the food arrives, we ask ourselves a simple question: does being here make us happy? The most emphatic "yes" inspires the highest rating. We don't give out points for tablecloths or tuxedos. We reward warm lighting, comfortable accomodations, a finely realized theme, and a strong sense of place. If it's a place steeped in history, or just an eminently classic DC joint (think Ben's Chili Bowl), we give bonus points for that, because it's certainly part of the "feel." The dim glow of candles, dark wood, and old White House paraphernalia at your local dive might just garner more accolades than the proliferation of accoutrements at a stuffy so-called "fine dining" restaurant.

Also figured into the "feel" rating is the question of whether you'll love or loathe the prospect of interacting with the people who stand between you and your meal. We don't expect the burger flipper at a greasy spoon to start spouting off elaborate wine adjectives, but if a restaurant's staff is unusually helpful and caring, or extraordinarily enthusiastic and knowledgeable about what's coming out of the kitchen, then the "feel" rating will reflect that. On the flip side, if the staff is consistently indifferent or condescending—or seems to have gone on strike—then points will be deducted from the experience rating of the restaurant, which happens as often at high-priced places as it does at corner take-out joints. Consider this a nonviolent revolution in the food-review world. Viva.

**The math:** There's no grade inflation here. For the city as a whole, ratings are curved around 5.5, but since we've left quite a few low-rated, out-of-the-way establishments out of the book (because we don't think it's helpful to readers to review them), the average food rating in the book is approximately 6.8, and the average feel rating is approximately 7.1. Let yourself get used to our system, and don't be scared off by a restaurant with a grade in the 6's. Only 134 (27.8%) of the 482 rated restaurants in the book (the other 18 were in unrated categories) scored an 8 or above, and only 23 (4.7%) scored a 9 or above. Only four restaurants in the book (0.8%) were awarded a food score of 9.5 or above: Komi, CityZen, 2 Amys Pizza, and Minibar.

# The other stuff on the page

**Average dinner price:** This dollar value is a guide to how much, on average, you should expect to spend per person on a full dinner at the restaurant, including one alcoholic beverage, tax, and a 20% tip (for table-service establishments; we encourage you to tip at coffeeshops and take-out joints too, but we don't figure it into the meal price). This is an imperfect science, but we go by what the average person tends to order at each place. At simple take-out places, this might be just a sandwich and a soda; at more elaborate sit-down restaurants, we usually figure in the cost of an appetizer (one for every person) and dessert (one for every two people). If the restaurant pushes bottled water or side dishes on you, we figure that in, too. For alcoholic drinks, too, we are guided by what people generally tend to order. At Pizzeria Paradiso, it's a beer. At Oyamel, it's a margarita. At Bobby Van's, it's a third of a bottle of a low-to-mid-priced wine. Keep in mind that at the higher-end restaurants, you will generally spend considerably less than the quoted price if you go for lunch, or if you order non-alcoholic drinks instead. Only restaurants that serve meals are eligible for price estimates; this excludes dessert-and-coffee places, markets, and so on.

**Genre:** Every establishment in *The Fearless Critic* is associated with one or more culinary genres. Our "Lists" section includes a cross-referenced guide to all restaurants by genre. Most genres—e.g. Indian or pizza—are self-explanatory, but some require clarification: **American** covers traditional meat-and-potatoes fare, bar food, burgers, greasy spoons, and such, but **steakhouses** have their own category, as does **Southern** cuisine, which includes soul food, fried chicken, Cajun, and Louisiana Creole cooking. **New American** is fast becoming an over-broad catch-all, but we haven't come up with a better term to describe the upmarket American culinary category that draws upon diverse world ingredients and techniques. New American also encompasses the market-to-table and haute nostalgic restaurants that have become fashionable lately. The **Latin American** category includes Central American, South American, Dominican, and Puerto Rican, but not

Mexican or Cuban, which have their own categories. **Caribbean** is focused on the islands of the West Indies (e.g. Jamaica, Trinidad). **Baked goods** can be sweet or savory. **Groceries** can include unprepared foods of any type.

**Establishment type:** We have divided eating establishments into several categories. The largest category is **casual restaurant,** which means a place with waiter service at tables but a generally laid-back atmosphere without much fuss. An **upmarket restaurant** is a place with more elegant, trendy, or special-occasion ambitions. The **counter service** category includes cafeterias, self-service places, and also establishments where you place an order at a counter but it is then brought out to your table. We see a **bar** as an establishment that's fundamentally about serving drinks at heart, but it must serve food to be included (although the kitchen often closes before the doors). **Café** means a place whose primary business is the provision of coffee or tea, but it must serve food of some sort to be included in the book. We've also included several notable **markets** in the DC area, most of (but not all of) which also serve certain varieties of prepared foods that can be eaten straightaway. The **wine bar** scene has taken off in the past couple of years, but we only include establishments that have some commitment to a real food program.

**Address:** We have included addresses and neighborhood designations for up to three locations, although, where feasible, we have indexed additional locations in the Lists section of the book. For chains with more than three locations, you should consult our web site, **fearlesscritic.com**, for a listing of all DC-area locations.

**Special features:** These appear in the middle column of information. **Breakfast** and **Brunch** generally mean that a restaurant has a special menu, or separate portion of the menu, geared toward those meals, not just that the place is open in the morning. By **date-friendly,** we mean establishments that we find particularly romantic in some way—and that doesn't necessarily mean tuxedoed waiters or high prices. We look for warm lighting, good vibes, and a sense of easy fun. **Delivery** can be limited to a certain geographical range or minimum order. **Good wines** needn't mean a long list, but it must be well chosen and well priced—you'd be surprised how rare that is. **Kid-friendly** doesn't just mean a couple of high chairs in the corner; it means a place where the little ones will actually be happy, whether for culinary reasons or for the availability of special activities or play areas. The **live music** designation includes establishments that have it only on certain days or nights, so call ahead if it's atmospherically important to you. **Outdoor dining** can mean anything from a couple of sidewalk tables to a sprawling beer garden. **Wi-Fi** has to be free to qualify—this is the 21st century, after all. We are particularly careful when choosing which establishments to flag as **veg-friendly**. The designation is not limited to vegetarian-only places, but we look for menus where vegetarians will not just be accommodated—they'll actually have an ample selection.

# Brutally honest

As you might guess from the name of the book, *The Fearless Critic* is brutally honest. One of our Contributing Editors calls it "in-your-face" restaurant reviewing. One newspaper called it "scathing." Some people have suggested that our style is rude to restaurants. But we consider it rude for some restaurants to serve tasteless food at high prices, or to subject patrons to a disaffected attitude. And we're here to help you.

How is one to choose between two places if both are portrayed in dizzying, worshipful prose? And how frustrating is it to find out that at least one of them was a waste of your time and money? If you're celebrating a special occasion, as one often does by dining out, the sting of disappointment after a bad meal is that much more acute. What's *definitely* rude—and costly—is for an unsuspecting patron to dine on the strength of a sugar-coated review, only to discover the truth the hard way, with friends or date in tow. In short, our duty is to our readers, not to the restaurants.

Our goal is to save you the cost, disappointment, and possible discomfort of a bland, overpriced meal—and to point you preemptively in the direction of something better. Helping you choose, every time you eat out, is what makes this endeavor worthwhile for us. And so, within these pages, we tell you exactly what we'd tell a good friend if she called us up and asked what we *really* thought of a place.

This unapologetic approach may take a moment to get used to. But in the end, we believe opinionated commentary to be the highest possible compliment to the local dining scene. That is to say, the food here is definitely worth talking about.

We don't expect you to agree with everything we say—sometimes, we don't even agree with each other—but we do hope you can appreciate our conviction that, in food writing, opinion is better expressed openly than buried between the lines. We believe that, over the course of a book of 500 reviews, we will earn your trust. And whether you concur or dissent, we would love to hear from you; we'd like nothing better than to inspire more relentlessly opinionated diners in and around DC. Visit us at **fearlesscritic.com** to post your own opinions, or your thoughts on ours.

# Fearless Critic quirks

**Cooking times:** as you might notice within these pages, we prefer most cuts of meat rare or medium-rare, and we prefer our fish and fowl moist and juicy rather than dry and more fully cooked. Specifically, our reviews often comment on whether or not establishments are willing to serve a dish as rare as requested. Although we understand that there are many people who like their meat more cooked than we do, our complaint isn't with restaurants that serve meat medium or medium-well by default; it's with restaurants that refuse to serve meat rare *even upon request*. Still, people who like their meat cooked medium or more should take our comments with a grain of salt.

**Seasoning:** speaking of a grain of salt, we complain from time to time about undersalted dishes. Our position is that there is no such thing as salting "to taste" in the professional kitchen. As a matter of chemistry, a certain amount of salt is necessary to bring out the complexity in most savory flavors: meats, fishes, soups, sauces, and so on. If you don't believe us, try this experiment, suggested by Italian food guru Marcella Hazan: pour two half-glasses of red wine, dump some salt into one of them, swirl them both around, and smell both glasses. The salt really brings out the bouquet (you won't want to drink it, though...).

Undersalting is one of the most common ways that an otherwise well-executed dish can fall completely flat. This problem can usually be corrected with the salt shaker (unless the food is deep-fried, in which case it's too late). But we think a dish should come to the table properly seasoned and ready to eat, not left in the final stages of preparation. (This is why we're so baffled by the peppermill service—how are you supposed to know if a dish needs pepper before you've tasted it? And if it does, why didn't the chef already add the proper amound?) If you want your meal with less salt than normal, you can ask for it, and the restaurant should honor the request. Otherwise, forcing the customer to finish that process is as absurd as plopping a salad down in front of a customer with a whole carrot and a peeler.

Most top chefs around the world would agree that proper seasoning is a matter of necessity, not opinion. At a seminar given by famed chef Jacques Pépin, an audience member asked him whether or not the classic French recipe that he was preparing would "work" with less salt. Responded Pépin: "If you have dietary restrictions, then let me know, and I will underseason your food—at your own risk. But I'm your chef, not your doctor." Amen.

**"Mains":** you won't find the word "entrée" in *The Fearless Critic*. The word is inherently ambiguous, and particularly confusing to foreigners, as the French word "entrée" means "starter" or "appetizer." We're not sure how "entrée" came to mean a main course in the United States, but here we say "main course," or "main," if that's what we mean.

**The *Fearless Critic* style guide:** we don't italicize foreign words in this book, nor do we capitalize dish names unless they're invented by the restaurant. We're minimalists.

# Fearless feedback

The heart and soul of this endeavor is our firm belief that the world of restaurant reviewing can only be improved by opening outspoken channels of communication between restaurants and their customers. We hope that the honest articulation of our opinions and dining experiences will encourage you to do the same—if you have a bad meal, or a great one, *tell the restaurant*. Tell them what was right and what was wrong. It can only help. And tell us; we've set up an interactive space at **fearlesscritic.com**, where readers can express agreement or dissent of any sort. The commentary found on the site is moderated only to keep out spammers, not to edit readers' opinions. It doesn't require registration, and you can even post anonymously. Please, read some reviews, go try some restaurants, and then log on and let us know what you think. Our critics will do their best to respond to posts from time to time. We look forward to hearing from you.

# The fine print

This entire book is a work of opinion, and should be understood as such. Any and all judgments rendered upon restaurants within these pages, regardless of tense, are intended as statements of pure opinion. Facts have been thoroughly checked with the restaurants in person, via telephone, and on the restaurants' web sites; we have gone to the utmost lengths to ensure that every fact is correct, and that every ingredient in every dish is properly referenced. Any factual errors that nonetheless remain are purely unintentional. That said, menus and plates (not to mention hours of operation) change so frequently at restaurants that any printed book, however new, cannot help but be a bit behind the times. Check in at **fearlesscritic.com** for new reviews, updates, discussion boards, and more.

# About Fearless Critic Media

Fearless Critic Media is a lean, fiercely independent publishing house founded by Robin Goldstein in 2006 and dedicated to providing useful information in an engaging format. In conjunction with its partner, Workman Publishing Company, Fearless Critic Media publishes relentlessly opinionated, irreverent food and wine books. Look for *The Wine Trial*s, our blind-tasting guide to wine under $15, in bookstores and food and wine shops nationwide. Other Fearless Critic books include the *Fearless Critic Austin Restaurant Guide, 2nd Edition* and the *Fearless Critic Houston Restaurant Guide*, which can be bought at barnesandnoble.com, amazon.com, bookstores, and retail stores. For all the latest book and distribution information, see **fearlesscritic.com**. Fearless Critic books are distributed by **Workman Publishing Company (workman.com)**.

# Fearless Critic

**Lists**

# Most delicious

These are DC's **top 100 kitchens** judged from a **pure food** perspective. Ties are ordered by feel rating.

| Rank | | Food | Cuisine | Location | Type | Price |
|------|---|------|---------|----------|------|-------|
| 1 | Komi | 9.7 | New American | Dupont | Upmarket | $140 |
| 2 | CityZen | 9.6 | New American | Southwest DC | Upmarket | $120 |
| 3 | 2 Amys Pizza | 9.6 | Pizza | Cleveland Park | Casual | $35 |
| 4 | Minibar | 9.5 | New American | Penn Quarter | Upmarket | $160 |
| 5 | Makoto | 9.4 | Japanese | Palisades | Upmarket | $80 |
| 6 | Westend Bistro | 9.4 | New American | West End | Upmarket | $65 |
| 7 | Obelisk | 9.3 | Italian | Dupont | Upmarket | $110 |
| 8 | Vermilion | 9.2 | New American | Old Town | Upmarket | $65 |
| 9 | Poste Moderne Brasserie | 9.2 | New American | Penn Quarter | Upmarket | $80 |
| 10 | Adour | 9.1 | French | Downtown | Upmarket | $125 |
| 11 | Hank's Oyster Bar | 9.1 | Seafood | Multiple locations | Upmarket | $45 |
| 12 | Citronelle | 9.1 | New American | Georgetown | Upmarket | $210 |
| 13 | Marvin | 9.1 | Southern | U Street | Upmarket | $45 |
| 14 | Tosca | 9.1 | Italian | Downtown | Upmarket | $75 |
| 15 | Oe Gad Gib | 9.0 | Korean | Annandale, VA | Casual | $20 |
| 16 | Al Crostino | 9.0 | Italian | U Street | Upmarket | $55 |
| 17 | Posto | 9.0 | Italian, Pizza | Logan Circle | Upmarket | $55 |
| 18 | Vidalia | 9.0 | Southern | Dupont | Upmarket | $70 |
| 19 | Seoul Soondae | 9.0 | Korean | Annandale, VA | Casual | $15 |
| 20 | Hai Duong | 9.0 | Vietnamese | Falls Church, VA | Casual | $15 |
| 21 | Ray's Hell-Burger | 9.0 | American | Multiple locations | Counter | $15 |
| 22 | Teddy's Roti Shop | 9.0 | Caribbean | Takoma Park, MD | Counter | $15 |
| 23 | Thanh Tong | 9.0 | Vietnamese | Falls Church, VA | Casual | $15 |
| 24 | Bistro Bis | 8.9 | French | Capitol Hill | Upmarket | $70 |
| 25 | Annan-Gol | 8.9 | Korean | Annandale, VA | Casual | $20 |
| 26 | Roger Miller Restaurant | 8.9 | Cameroonian | Silver Spring, MD | Casual | $30 |
| 27 | Pesce | 8.9 | Seafood | Dupont | Upmarket | $60 |
| 28 | Gamasot | 8.9 | Korean | Springfield, VA | Casual | $15 |
| 29 | Oriental East | 8.9 | Chinese | Silver Spring, MD | Casual | $40 |
| 30 | Hong Kong Palace | 8.9 | Chinese | Falls Church, VA | Casual | $15 |
| 31 | Restaurant Eve | 8.8 | New American | Old Town | Upmarket | $150 |
| 32 | Gooldaegee | 8.8 | Korean | Annandale, VA | Casual | $20 |
| 33 | Al Tiramisú | 8.8 | Italian | Dupont | Upmarket | $55 |
| 34 | Central Michel Richard | 8.8 | French | Penn Quarter | Upmarket | $70 |
| 35 | Marcel's | 8.8 | French | West End | Upmarket | $90 |
| 36 | The Source | 8.8 | New American | Penn Quarter | Upmarket | $120 |
| 37 | Palena | 8.8 | New American | Cleveland Park | Upmarket | $100 |
| 38 | Light House Tofu | 8.8 | Korean | Multiple locations | Casual | $15 |
| 39 | Shashemene | 8.8 | Ethiopian | Shaw | Casual | $25 |
| 40 | Corduroy | 8.8 | New American | Mt. Vernon Square | Upmarket | $70 |
| 41 | China Garden | 8.8 | Chinese | Arlington, VA | Casual | $20 |
| 42 | Etete | 8.8 | Ethiopian | Shaw | Casual | $30 |
| 43 | Cho Cu Sai Gon | 8.8 | Chinese | Falls Church, VA | Casual | $20 |
| 44 | New Big Wong | 8.8 | Chinese | Chinatown | Casual | $25 |
| 45 | Taberna del Alabardero | 8.7 | Spanish | Farragut | Upmarket | $75 |
| 46 | BLT Steak | 8.7 | Steakhouse | Farragut | Upmarket | $95 |
| 47 | Eamonn's | 8.7 | Seafood, Irish | Old Town | Casual | $20 |
| 48 | Ngoc Anh | 8.7 | Vietnamese | Falls Church, VA | Casual | $25 |
| 49 | Dduk Sarang | 8.7 | Korean | Annandale, VA | Casual | $15 |
| 50 | Tabeer | 8.7 | Pakistani | Hyattsville, MD | Casual | $25 |
| 51 | Com Tam Saigon | 8.7 | Vietnamese | Falls Church, VA | Casual | $10 |
| 52 | Granja de Oro | 8.7 | Latin American | Adams Morgan | Counter | $20 |
| 53 | Café du Parc | 8.6 | French | Downtown | Upmarket | $60 |
| 54 | Nora | 8.6 | New American | Dupont | Upmarket | $80 |

| 55 | Montmartre | 8.6 | French | Capitol Hill | Upmarket | $60 |
|---|---|---|---|---|---|---|
| 56 | Rasika | 8.6 | Indian | Penn Quarter | Upmarket | $70 |
| 57 | Liberty Tavern | 8.6 | American | Arlington, VA | Casual | $40 |
| 58 | Meaza | 8.6 | Ethiopian | Falls Church, VA | Casual | $20 |
| 59 | Bob's Noodle 66 | 8.6 | Taiwanese | Rockville, MD | Casual | $15 |
| 60 | El Charrito Caminante | 8.6 | Mexican | Arlington, VA | Counter | $15 |
| 61 | China Star | 8.6 | Chinese | Fairfax, VA | Casual | $15 |
| 62 | Kabob Palace | 8.6 | Middle Eastern | Arlington, VA | Counter | $20 |
| 63 | Zaytinya | 8.5 | Middle Eastern | Chinatown | Upmarket | $65 |
| 64 | To Sok Jip | 8.5 | Korean | Annandale, VA | Casual | $15 |
| 65 | Urbana | 8.5 | New American | Dupont | Upmarket | $55 |
| 66 | Bobby Van's Steakhouse | 8.5 | Steakhouse | Multiple locations | Upmarket | $95 |
| 67 | Oohhs & Aahhs | 8.5 | Southern | Shaw | Counter | $25 |
| 68 | The Oval Room | 8.5 | New American | Farragut | Upmarket | $75 |
| 69 | Sushi-Ko | 8.5 | Japanese | Multiple locations | Upmarket | $60 |
| 70 | Great Wall Szechuan | 8.5 | Chinese | Logan Circle | Casual | $25 |
| 71 | Costa Verde | 8.5 | Peruvian | Arlington, VA | Casual | $30 |
| 72 | El Pollo Rico | 8.5 | Latin American | Multiple locations | Counter | $10 |
| 73 | Prime Rib | 8.5 | Steakhouse | Farragut | Upmarket | $90 |
| 74 | Buck's Fishing & Camping | 8.4 | Southern | Upper NW | Upmarket | $60 |
| 75 | Brasserie Beck | 8.4 | Belgian | Downtown | Upmarket | $55 |
| 76 | Dino | 8.4 | Italian | Cleveland Park | Upmarket | $50 |
| 77 | Proof | 8.4 | New American | Penn Quarter | Wine bar | $55 |
| 78 | Restaurant Eve (Bistro) | 8.4 | New American | Old Town | Upmarket | $60 |
| 79 | Kaz Sushi Bistro | 8.4 | Japanese | Downtown | Upmarket | $55 |
| 80 | Sakana | 8.4 | Japanese | Dupont | Casual | $35 |
| 81 | Ray's the Steaks | 8.4 | Steakhouse | Arlington, VA | Upmarket | $45 |
| 82 | Nava Thai | 8.4 | Thai | Wheaton, MD | Casual | $25 |
| 83 | A & J Restaurant | 8.4 | Chinese | Multiple locations | Casual | $30 |
| 84 | Pollo Granjero | 8.4 | Latin American | Multiple locations | Counter | $15 |
| 85 | Bistrot du Coin | 8.3 | French | Dupont | Casual | $50 |
| 86 | Zola | 8.3 | New American | Penn Quarter | Upmarket | $60 |
| 87 | Hook | 8.3 | Seafood | Georgetown | Upmarket | $80 |
| 88 | Thai X-ing | 8.3 | Thai | Shaw | Casual | $30 |
| 89 | Rainbow Restaurant | 8.3 | Ghanaian | Gaithersburg, MD | Casual | $20 |
| 90 | Kotobuki | 8.3 | Japanese | Palisades | Casual | $25 |
| 91 | Smith & Wollensky | 8.3 | Steakhouse | Farragut | Upmarket | $85 |
| 92 | Thai Market | 8.3 | Thai | Silver Spring, MD | Counter | $20 |
| 93 | Founding Farmers | 8.2 | American | Farragut | Upmarket | $50 |
| 94 | Irene's Pupusas | 8.2 | Salvadoran | Multiple locations | Casual | $25 |
| 95 | Pizzeria Paradiso | 8.2 | Pizza | Multiple locations | Casual | $30 |
| 96 | Mogotillo | 8.2 | Salvadoran | Takoma Park, MD | Casual | $20 |
| 97 | Ray's the Classics | 8.2 | Steakhouse | Silver Spring, MD | Upmarket | $45 |
| 98 | Tackle Box | 8.2 | Seafood | Georgetown | Casual | $25 |
| 99 | Taquería Nacional | 8.2 | Mexican | Penn Quarter | Counter | $15 |
| 100 | Myanmar | 8.2 | Burmese | Falls Church, VA | Casual | $30 |

# Good vibes

**Fearless Critic's feel rating** measures the enjoyment we get from the atmosphere and people. Here are the **top 50**. Ties are ordered by food rating.

| Rank | | Feel | Cuisine | Location | Type | Price |
|---|---|---|---|---|---|---|
| 1 | Inn at Little Washington | 9.8 | New American | Washington, VA | Upmarket | $250 |
| 2 | Afterwords Café | 9.7 | American | Dupont | Café | $35 |
| 3 | Busboys & Poets | 9.7 | American | Multiple locations | Casual | $25 |
| 4 | Restaurant Eve | 9.6 | New American | Old Town | Upmarket | $150 |
| 5 | Tabard Inn | 9.6 | American | Dupont | Upmarket | $55 |
| 6 | Marrakesh | 9.6 | Moroccan | Mt. Vernon Square | Upmarket | $50 |
| 7 | L'Auberge Chez François | 9.6 | French | Great Falls, VA | Upmarket | $110 |
| 8 | W Domku | 9.5 | Scandinavian | Petworth | Casual | $40 |
| 9 | Round Robin Bar | 9.5 | American | Downtown | Bar | $40 |
| 10 | Little Fountain Café | 9.5 | New American | Adams Morgan | Upmarket | $45 |
| 11 | Cashion's Eat Place | 9.4 | New American | Adams Morgan | Upmarket | $60 |
| 12 | Park Café | 9.4 | New American | Capitol Hill | Upmarket | $60 |
| 13 | Café Saint-Ex | 9.4 | French | U Street | Casual | $40 |
| 14 | Oe Gad Gib | 9.3 | Korean | Annandale, VA | Casual | $20 |
| 15 | Café du Parc | 9.3 | French | Downtown | Upmarket | $60 |
| 16 | Nora | 9.3 | New American | Dupont | Upmarket | $80 |
| 17 | Bistrot du Coin | 9.3 | French | Dupont | Casual | $50 |
| 18 | Zola | 9.3 | New American | Penn Quarter | Upmarket | $60 |
| 19 | Quarry House Tavern | 9.3 | American | Silver Spring, MD | Casual | $25 |
| 20 | Firefly | 9.3 | New American | Dupont | Upmarket | $60 |
| 21 | Blue Duck Tavern | 9.3 | New American | West End | Upmarket | $80 |
| 22 | The Majestic | 9.3 | New American | Old Town | Upmarket | $50 |
| 23 | Leopold's Kafe | 9.3 | Austrian | Georgetown | Casual | $40 |
| 24 | Brickskeller | 9.3 | American | Dupont | Bar | $15 |
| 25 | Montmartre | 9.2 | French | Capitol Hill | Upmarket | $60 |
| 26 | Buck's Fishing & Camping | 9.2 | Southern | Upper NW | Upmarket | $60 |
| 27 | Founding Farmers | 9.2 | American | Farragut | Upmarket | $50 |
| 28 | Ben's Chili Bowl | 9.2 | American | Multiple locations | Counter | $15 |
| 29 | Morrison-Clark Inn | 9.2 | Southern | Downtown | Upmarket | $60 |
| 30 | Oyamel | 9.2 | Mexican | Penn Quarter | Upmarket | $60 |
| 31 | CityZen | 9.1 | New American | Southwest DC | Upmarket | $120 |
| 32 | Obelisk | 9.1 | Italian | Dupont | Upmarket | $110 |
| 33 | Adour | 9.1 | French | Downtown | Upmarket | $125 |
| 34 | Hank's Oyster Bar | 9.1 | Seafood | Multiple locations | Upmarket | $45 |
| 35 | Gooldaegee | 9.1 | Korean | Annandale, VA | Casual | $20 |
| 36 | Brasserie Beck | 9.1 | Belgian | Downtown | Upmarket | $55 |
| 37 | Cork | 9.1 | New American | Logan Circle | Wine bar | $40 |
| 38 | Ceiba | 9.1 | Nuevo Latino | Downtown | Upmarket | $60 |
| 39 | Java House | 9.1 | Middle Eastern | Dupont | Counter | $10 |
| 40 | Commissary | 9.1 | American | Logan Circle | Casual | $30 |
| 41 | Citronelle | 9.0 | New American | Georgetown | Upmarket | $210 |
| 42 | Marvin | 9.0 | Southern | U Street | Upmarket | $45 |
| 43 | Al Tiramisú | 9.0 | Italian | Dupont | Upmarket | $55 |
| 44 | Central Michel Richard | 9.0 | French | Penn Quarter | Upmarket | $70 |
| 45 | Marcel's | 9.0 | French | West End | Upmarket | $90 |
| 46 | Rasika | 9.0 | Indian | Penn Quarter | Upmarket | $70 |
| 47 | Bourbon | 9.0 | American | Multiple locations | Bar | $35 |
| 48 | Commonwealth | 9.0 | British | Columbia Heights | Casual | $40 |
| 49 | Coppi's Organic | 9.0 | Italian, Pizza | U Street | Upmarket | $50 |
| 50 | Tallula | 9.0 | New American | Arlington, VA | Upmarket | $55 |

# By genre

Places to eat **listed by culinary concept, ranked by food rating.** Unranked establishments (e.g. grocery stores) appear at the bottom of the list if they're relevant.

## Afghan

| | | | | |
|---|---|---|---|---|
| 8.6 | Kabob Palace | Arlington, VA | Counter | $20 |
| 7.8 | Afghan Grill | Cleveland Park | Casual | $40 |
| 6.3 | Faryab | Bethesda, MD | Casual | $25 |

## American *includes traditional American food, bar food, burgers, and greasy-spoon fare. For creative American, California-influenced or Asian-influenced American, or market-to-table cuisine, see "New American." For steakhouses, Southern cuisine, sandwiches, or baked goods, see those genres.*

| | | | | |
|---|---|---|---|---|
| 9.0 | Ray's Hell-Burger | Multiple locations | Counter | $15 |
| 8.6 | Liberty Tavern | Arlington, VA | Casual | $40 |
| 8.2 | Founding Farmers | Farragut | Upmarket | $50 |
| 8.2 | Ray's the Classics | Silver Spring, MD | Upmarket | $45 |
| 8.1 | Quarry House Tavern | Silver Spring, MD | Casual | $25 |
| 8.1 | Ben's Chili Bowl | Multiple locations | Counter | $15 |
| 8.1 | Bourbon | Multiple locations | Bar | $35 |
| 8.1 | C.F. Folks | Dupont | Casual | $20 |
| 8.0 | Afterwords Café | Dupont | Café | $35 |
| 8.0 | Houston's | Rockville, MD | Upmarket | $55 |
| 8.0 | Weenie Beanie | Arlington, VA | Counter | $5 |
| 7.9 | Mitsitam Native Foods Café | Southwest DC | Counter | $35 |
| 7.6 | Tabard Inn | Dupont | Upmarket | $55 |
| 7.6 | Round Robin Bar | Downtown | Bar | $40 |
| 7.6 | Matchbox | Chinatown | Casual | $35 |
| 7.5 | Busboys & Poets | Multiple locations | Casual | $25 |
| 7.5 | Ulah Bistro | U Street | Upmarket | $45 |
| 7.4 | Five Guys | Multiple locations | Counter | $10 |
| 7.2 | Jimmy T's | Capitol Hill | Casual | $25 |
| 7.1 | District Chophouse | Penn Quarter | Casual | $45 |
| 7.1 | The Caucus Room | Penn Quarter | Upmarket | $90 |
| 7.0 | Cassatt's | Arlington, VA | Casual | $25 |
| 7.0 | Good Stuff Eatery | Capitol Hill | Counter | $15 |
| 6.9 | Old Ebbitt Grill | Downtown | Casual | $40 |
| 6.9 | Annie's Paramount | Dupont | Casual | $35 |
| 6.9 | Tunnicliff's Tavern | Capitol Hill | Casual | $40 |
| 6.9 | Whitlow's on Wilson | Arlington, VA | Casual | $35 |
| 6.8 | Trusty's | Capitol Hill | Casual | $35 |
| 6.7 | Bookbinder's Old Town | Old Town | Upmarket | $80 |
| 6.7 | Harry's Tap Room | Multiple locations | Casual | $50 |
| 6.6 | Capitol City Brewery | Multiple locations | Casual | $35 |
| 6.6 | Chop't | Multiple locations | Counter | $10 |
| 6.5 | Open City | Woodley Park | Café | $40 |
| 6.5 | Café Olé | Upper NW | Casual | $30 |
| 6.5 | Pete's Diner | Capitol Hill | Casual | $25 |
| 6.5 | Capital Grille | Multiple locations | Upmarket | $85 |
| 6.4 | Martin's Tavern | Georgetown | Casual | $35 |
| 6.2 | Café Saint-Ex | U Street | Casual | $40 |
| 6.2 | Rosemary's Thyme Bistro | Dupont | Casual | $40 |
| 6.2 | Stoney's Bar & Grill | Logan Circle | Casual | $40 |
| 6.0 | Cococabana Bar & Grill | Hyattsville, MD | Casual | $30 |
| 6.0 | Finn & Porter | Multiple locations | Upmarket | $75 |
| 5.9 | Asylum | Dupont | Bar | $25 |
| 5.9 | Eli's | Dupont | Casual | $20 |

## American *continued*

| | | | | |
|---|---|---|---|---|
| 5.8 | The Big Hunt | Dupont | Bar | $20 |
| 5.8 | Charlie Palmer Steak | Capitol Hill | Upmarket | $110 |
| 5.6 | Johnny Rockets | Multiple locations | Casual | $25 |
| 5.5 | Local 16 | U Street | Upmarket | $40 |
| 5.1 | Tryst | Adams Morgan | Café | $25 |
| 5.1 | Clyde's | Multiple locations | Casual | $40 |
| 5.0 | Skye Lounge | Farragut | Casual | $40 |
| 4.9 | Gordon Biersch | Multiple locations | Casual | $35 |
| 4.8 | Pour House | Capitol Hill | Casual | $35 |
| 4.6 | The Tombs | Georgetown | Bar | $25 |
| 4.6 | Veranda | Logan Circle | Casual | $40 |
| 4.3 | Café Luna | Dupont | Casual | $35 |
| 4.3 | Hard Times Café | Multiple locations | Casual | $20 |
| 4.3 | J. Paul's | Georgetown | Casual | $45 |
| 4.2 | Luna Grill & Diner | Multiple locations | Casual | $30 |
| 4.1 | Diner | Adams Morgan | Casual | $25 |
| 4.0 | Brickskeller | Dupont | Bar | $15 |
| 4.0 | Commissary | Logan Circle | Casual | $30 |
| 3.8 | Logan Tavern | Logan Circle | Casual | $35 |
| 3.8 | The Front Page | Dupont | Casual | $35 |
| 3.8 | Union Pub | Capitol Hill | Casual | $25 |
| | Sweetgreen | Georgetown | Counter | |

## Austrian

| | | | | |
|---|---|---|---|---|
| 7.6 | Leopold's Kafe | Georgetown | Casual | $40 |

## Baked goods

| | | | | |
|---|---|---|---|---|
| 7.9 | El Dorado | Hyattsville, MD | Counter | $10 |
| 7.7 | Bethesda Bagels | Bethesda, MD | Counter | $10 |
| 7.3 | Coco Sala | Downtown | Upmarket | $50 |
| 7.3 | Patisserie Poupon | Georgetown | Café | $35 |
| 7.2 | Firehook | Multiple locations | Counter | $10 |
| 7.0 | Cakelove and Love Café | Multiple locations | Café | $10 |
| 6.7 | Bagels & Baguettes | Capitol Hill | Café | $10 |
| 6.7 | Bean Counter | Georgetown | Café | $15 |
| 6.2 | Le Bon Café | Capitol Hill | Café | $20 |
| 5.8 | Sticky Fingers Bakery | Columbia Heights | Counter | $10 |
| 4.9 | Java Green | Farragut | Café | $20 |
| 4.8 | ACKC Cocoa Bar | Multiple locations | Café | $10 |
| 4.5 | Camille's Sidewalk Café | Multiple locations | Café | $25 |
| | Dolcezza | Multiple locations | Counter | |
| | M. E. Swing | Foggy Bottom | Café | |
| | Marvelous Market | Multiple locations | Market | |

## Balkan

| | | | | |
|---|---|---|---|---|
| 8.1 | Cosmopolitan Bakery | Alexandria, VA | Café | $25 |

## Barbecue

| | | | | |
|---|---|---|---|---|
| 7.3 | Urban Bar-B-Que Company | Multiple locations | Counter | $25 |
| 6.9 | Red Hot & Blue | Multiple locations | Casual | $15 |
| 6.3 | Old Glory Bar-B-Que | Georgetown | Casual | $30 |
| 6.1 | Kenny's BBQ | Capitol Hill | Counter | $20 |
| 5.6 | Rocklands | Multiple locations | Casual | $15 |

## Belgian

| | | | | |
|---|---|---|---|---|
| 9.1 | Marvin | U Street | Upmarket | $45 |
| 8.4 | Brasserie Beck | Downtown | Upmarket | $55 |
| 7.0 | Belga Café | Capitol Hill | Casual | $30 |
| 6.0 | Granville Moore's Brickyard | Northeast DC | Casual | $40 |

## Brazilian

| | | | | |
|---|---|---|---|---|
| 6.7 | Fogo de Chão | Downtown | Upmarket | $80 |
| 5.1 | Grill from Ipanema | Adams Morgan | Casual | $45 |

## British

| | | | | |
|---|---|---|---|---|
| 8.0 | Commonwealth | Columbia Heights | Casual | $40 |

## Burmese

| | | | | |
|---|---|---|---|---|
| 8.2 | Myanmar | Falls Church, VA | Casual | $30 |
| 6.5 | Mandalay | Silver Spring, MD | Casual | $25 |
| 6.0 | Burma | Chinatown | Casual | $25 |

## Cafés

| | | | | |
|---|---|---|---|---|
| 8.1 | ching ching CHA | Georgetown | Café | $25 |
| 8.1 | Bread Line | Farragut | Café | $15 |
| 8.1 | Cosmopolitan Bakery | Alexandria, VA | Café | $25 |
| 8.0 | Afterwords Café | Dupont | Café | $35 |
| 7.3 | Patisserie Poupon | Georgetown | Café | $35 |
| 7.2 | Café Berlin | Capitol Hill | Café | $35 |
| 7.2 | Bread & Chocolate | Multiple locations | Café | $15 |
| 7.0 | Cakelove and Love Café | Multiple locations | Café | $10 |
| 6.7 | Bagels & Baguettes | Capitol Hill | Café | $10 |
| 6.7 | Bean Counter | Georgetown | Café | $15 |
| 6.5 | Open City | Woodley Park | Café | $40 |
| 6.5 | Café Bonaparte | Georgetown | Café | $45 |
| 6.2 | Le Bon Café | Capitol Hill | Café | $20 |
| 6.2 | Teaism | Multiple locations | Café | $20 |
| 5.7 | La Crêperie | Arlington, VA | Café | $15 |
| 5.6 | Banana Café & Piano Bar | Capitol Hill | Café | $30 |
| 5.1 | Tryst | Adams Morgan | Café | $25 |
| 4.9 | Java Green | Farragut | Café | $20 |
| 4.8 | ACKC Cocoa Bar | Multiple locations | Café | $10 |
| 4.5 | Camille's Sidewalk Café | Multiple locations | Café | $25 |
| 3.1 | Wellness Café | Capitol Hill | Café | $20 |
| | M. E. Swing | Foggy Bottom | Café | |

## Cameroonian

| | | | | |
|---|---|---|---|---|
| 8.9 | Roger Miller Restaurant | Silver Spring, MD | Casual | $30 |

## Caribbean

| | | | | |
|---|---|---|---|---|
| 9.0 | Teddy's Roti Shop | Takoma Park, MD | Counter | $15 |
| 7.7 | Sweet Mango Café | Petworth | Casual | $25 |
| 6.5 | Negril | Multiple locations | Counter | $15 |
| 5.7 | The Islander Caribbean | U Street | Casual | $25 |

## Chinese

| | | | | |
|---|---|---|---|---|
| 8.9 | Oriental East | Silver Spring, MD | Casual | $40 |
| 8.9 | Hong Kong Palace | Falls Church, VA | Casual | $15 |
| 8.8 | China Garden | Arlington, VA | Casual | $20 |
| 8.8 | Cho Cu Sai Gon | Falls Church, VA | Casual | $20 |
| 8.8 | New Big Wong | Chinatown | Casual | $25 |
| 8.6 | Bob's Noodle 66 | Rockville, MD | Casual | $15 |
| 8.6 | China Star | Fairfax, VA | Casual | $15 |
| 8.5 | Great Wall Szechuan | Logan Circle | Casual | $25 |
| 8.4 | A & J Restaurant | Multiple locations | Casual | $30 |
| 8.2 | Li Ho | Chinatown | Casual | $10 |
| 8.1 | ching ching CHA | Georgetown | Café | $25 |
| 7.8 | Full Kee | Multiple locations | Casual | $25 |
| 7.7 | Peking Gourmet Inn | Falls Church, VA | Casual | $35 |
| 7.4 | Shanghai Village | Bethesda, MD | Casual | $35 |

## Chinese _continued_

| 7.3 | Chinatown Express | Chinatown | Casual | $25 |
|-----|-------------------|-----------|--------|-----|
| 6.4 | Mark's Duck House | Falls Church, VA | Casual | $30 |
| 6.0 | Kanlaya | Chinatown | Casual | $30 |
| 5.7 | Sunflower Vegetarian | Falls Church, VA | Casual | $20 |
| 5.3 | Yuan Fu | Rockville, MD | Casual | $25 |
| 5.3 | Eat First | Chinatown | Casual | $20 |
| 5.1 | Asian Spice | Chinatown | Casual | $40 |
| 4.7 | Hunan Dynasty | Capitol Hill | Casual | $25 |
| 4.6 | Mr. Chen's | Woodley Park | Casual | $25 |
| 4.5 | Meiwah | Multiple locations | Casual | $45 |
| 4.5 | Tony Cheng's Seafood | Chinatown | Casual | $35 |
| 4.0 | Tai Shan | Chinatown | Casual | $15 |
| 3.8 | Wok & Roll | Chinatown | Casual | $20 |
| 3.7 | Harmony Café | Georgetown | Casual | $15 |

## Cuban

| 6.2 | Cubano's | Silver Spring, MD | Casual | $35 |
|-----|----------|-------------------|--------|-----|
| 5.6 | Banana Café & Piano Bar | Capitol Hill | Café | $30 |
| 5.0 | Lima | Downtown | Upmarket | $55 |

## Ethiopian

| 8.8 | Shashemene | Shaw | Casual | $25 |
|-----|-----------|------|--------|-----|
| 8.8 | Etete | Shaw | Casual | $30 |
| 8.6 | Meaza | Falls Church, VA | Casual | $20 |
| 8.1 | Queen Makeda | Shaw | Casual | $30 |
| 7.9 | Langano | Silver Spring, MD | Casual | $25 |
| 7.8 | Dukem | Shaw | Casual | $25 |
| 7.5 | Meskerem | Adams Morgan | Casual | $25 |
| 7.1 | Axum | Shaw | Casual | $25 |
| 7.1 | Harar Mesob | Arlington, VA | Casual | $25 |
| 6.8 | Madjet | Shaw | Casual | $23 |
| 3.6 | Zed's Ethiopian Restaurant | Georgetown | Casual | $30 |

## French

| 9.1 | Adour | Downtown | Upmarket | $125 |
|-----|-------|----------|----------|------|
| 9.1 | Citronelle | Georgetown | Upmarket | $210 |
| 8.9 | Bistro Bis | Capitol Hill | Upmarket | $70 |
| 8.8 | Central Michel Richard | Penn Quarter | Upmarket | $70 |
| 8.8 | Marcel's | West End | Upmarket | $90 |
| 8.6 | Café du Parc | Downtown | Upmarket | $60 |
| 8.6 | Montmartre | Capitol Hill | Upmarket | $60 |
| 8.3 | Bistrot du Coin | Dupont | Casual | $50 |
| 8.0 | Two Quail | Mt. Vernon Square | Upmarket | $60 |
| 8.0 | Lavandou | Cleveland Park | Upmarket | $65 |
| 8.0 | La Baguette | Dupont | Counter | $15 |
| 7.5 | La Chaumière | Georgetown | Upmarket | $60 |
| 7.2 | Bread & Chocolate | Multiple locations | Café | $15 |
| 6.9 | Bastille | Old Town | Upmarket | $55 |
| 6.9 | Petits Plats | Woodley Park | Casual | $45 |
| 6.5 | Café Bonaparte | Georgetown | Café | $45 |
| 6.2 | Café Saint-Ex | U Street | Casual | $40 |
| 6.0 | L'Auberge Chez François | Great Falls, VA | Upmarket | $110 |
| 6.0 | La Ferme | Chevy Chase, MD | Upmarket | $60 |
| 5.9 | Bistro Français | Georgetown | Casual | $40 |
| 5.7 | La Crêperie | Arlington, VA | Café | $15 |
| 5.5 | Napoleon Bistro | Adams Morgan | Upmarket | $60 |
| 5.4 | La Madeleine | Multiple locations | Counter | $30 |
| 4.9 | Brasserie Monte Carlo | Bethesda, MD | Casual | $45 |

## German

| 7.2 | Café Berlin | Capitol Hill | Café | $35 |

## Ghanaian

| 8.3 | Rainbow Restaurant | Gaithersburg, MD | Casual | $20 |

## Ghanian

| 7.8 | Akosombo | Mt. Vernon Square | Casual | $15 |

## Greek

| 9.7 | Komi | Dupont | Upmarket | $140 |
| 7.5 | Taverna the Greek Islands | Silver Spring, MD | Casual | $35 |
| 7.2 | Stoupsy's | Farragut | Counter | $5 |
| 7.1 | Greek Deli | Farragut | Counter | $15 |
| 6.4 | Zorba's Café | Dupont | Counter | $25 |
| 6.3 | Astor Mediterranean | Multiple locations | Casual | $20 |
| 5.6 | Byblos | Cleveland Park | Casual | $25 |
| 4.6 | Veranda | Logan Circle | Casual | $40 |

## Groceries

| Daruma Japanese Market | Bethesda, MD | Counter |
| Dean & Deluca | Georgetown | Market |
| Eastern Market | Capitol Hill | Market |
| Harris Teeter | Multiple locations | Market |
| The Italian Store | Arlington, VA | Counter |
| Maine Avenue Fish Market | Southwest DC | Market |
| Marvelous Market | Multiple locations | Market |
| Mediterranean Bakery | Alexandria, VA | Counter |
| Trader Joe's | Multiple locations | Market |
| Whole Foods Market | Multiple locations | Market |

## Ice cream

| The Dairy Godmother | Alexandria, VA | Counter |
| Dickey's Frozen Custard | Multiple locations | Counter |
| Dolcezza | Multiple locations | Counter |
| Max's Best Ice Cream | Glover Park | Counter |
| Sweetgreen | Georgetown | Counter |
| Thomas Sweet | Georgetown | Counter |

## Indian

| 8.6 | Rasika | Penn Quarter | Upmarket | $70 |
| 8.1 | Bombay Club | Farragut | Upmarket | $45 |
| 8.0 | Passage to India | Bethesda, MD | Casual | $40 |
| 7.6 | Amma Vegetarian Kitchen | Multiple locations | Casual | $20 |
| 7.4 | Bombay Bistro | Multiple locations | Casual | $25 |
| 7.2 | Heritage India | Multiple locations | Casual | $40 |
| 7.2 | Bombay Curry Company | Alexandria, VA | Casual | $20 |
| 7.2 | Mayur Kabab House | Chinatown | Casual | $20 |
| 7.1 | Jyoti | Adams Morgan | Casual | $25 |
| 7.1 | Udupi Palace | Takoma Park, MD | Casual | $20 |
| 6.7 | White Tiger | Capitol Hill | Casual | $35 |
| 6.4 | Nirvana | Farragut | Casual | $35 |
| 6.3 | Tandoor Grill | Capitol Hill | Casual | $30 |
| 6.2 | Indique | Cleveland Park | Upmarket | $40 |
| 6.0 | Aatish on the Hill | Capitol Hill | Casual | $30 |
| 5.6 | Bombay Restaurant | Silver Spring, MD | Casual | $30 |
| 4.9 | Aditi Indian Cuisine | Multiple locations | Casual | $35 |
| 4.7 | Aroma | Multiple locations | Casual | $25 |
| 4.4 | Naan & Beyond | Multiple locations | Counter | $25 |

## Irish

| 8.7 | Eamonn's | Old Town | Casual | $20 |
| 6.8 | Fadó | Chinatown | Bar | $27 |

## Italian

| 9.3 | Obelisk | Dupont | Upmarket | $110 |
| 9.1 | Tosca | Downtown | Upmarket | $75 |
| 9.0 | Al Crostino | U Street | Upmarket | $55 |
| 9.0 | Posto | Logan Circle | Upmarket | $55 |
| 8.8 | Al Tiramisú | Dupont | Upmarket | $55 |
| 8.4 | Dino | Cleveland Park | Upmarket | $50 |
| 8.0 | Coppi's Organic | U Street | Upmarket | $50 |
| 7.8 | Pasta Mia | Adams Morgan | Casual | $25 |
| 7.7 | Mia's Pizza | Bethesda, MD | Casual | $25 |
| 7.4 | Sorriso | Cleveland Park | Casual | $40 |
| 7.3 | Spezie | Farragut | Upmarket | $80 |
| 7.2 | Cucina Vivace | Arlington, VA | Upmarket | $55 |
| 7.1 | Faccia Luna | Multiple locations | Casual | $40 |
| 6.9 | Bistro Italiano | Penn Quarter | Casual | $25 |
| 6.6 | Sette Osteria | Dupont | Casual | $40 |
| 6.6 | Amici Miei | Potomac, MD | Casual | $50 |
| 6.5 | Tragara | Bethesda, MD | Upmarket | $80 |
| 6.2 | Rosemary's Thyme Bistro | Dupont | Casual | $40 |
| 6.2 | Etrusco | Dupont | Upmarket | $60 |
| 6.2 | Murali | Arlington, VA | Upmarket | $50 |
| 6.1 | Teatro Goldoni | Farragut | Upmarket | $90 |
| 6.1 | Café Milano | Georgetown | Upmarket | $75 |
| 6.1 | Primi Piatti | Foggy Bottom | Upmarket | $70 |
| 6.0 | Cococabana Bar & Grill | Hyattsville, MD | Casual | $30 |
| 5.9 | Sesto Senso | Dupont | Upmarket | $55 |
| 5.8 | Filomena | Georgetown | Casual | $50 |
| 5.7 | Circa | Dupont | Casual | $40 |
| 5.7 | Bertucci's | Multiple locations | Casual | $35 |
| 5.3 | Il Mulino | Downtown | Upmarket | $80 |
| 4.8 | Trattoria Alberto | Capitol Hill | Casual | $45 |
| 4.6 | La Tomate | Dupont | Upmarket | $45 |
| 4.6 | Veranda | Logan Circle | Casual | $40 |
| 4.5 | Paolo's | Georgetown | Casual | $40 |
| 4.3 | Café Luna | Dupont | Casual | $35 |
| 4.2 | Luna Grill & Diner | Multiple locations | Casual | $30 |
| 3.7 | I Ricchi | Dupont | Upmarket | $80 |
| 3.7 | Olazzo | Multiple locations | Upmarket | $45 |
| 3.6 | Dupont Italian Kitchen | Dupont | Casual | $40 |
| 3.6 | Prego Delly | Capitol Hill | Counter | $25 |
| 2.7 | Buca di Beppo | Dupont | Casual | $30 |

## Japanese

| 9.4 | Makoto | Palisades | Upmarket | $80 |
| 8.5 | Sushi-Ko | Multiple locations | Upmarket | $60 |
| 8.4 | Kaz Sushi Bistro | Downtown | Upmarket | $55 |
| 8.4 | Sakana | Dupont | Casual | $35 |
| 8.3 | Kotobuki | Palisades | Casual | $25 |
| 7.8 | Tako Grill | Bethesda, MD | Casual | $45 |
| 7.0 | Yee Hwa | Downtown | Casual | $40 |
| 7.0 | Tachibana | Tysons Corner, VA | Casual | $45 |
| 6.6 | Kyoto | Capitol Hill | Casual | $30 |
| 6.6 | Nooshi | Farragut | Casual | $25 |
| 5.9 | Kanpai | Arlington, VA | Casual | $30 |
| 5.7 | Tono Sushi | Woodley Park | Casual | $40 |
| 5.6 | Thai Chef | Dupont | Casual | $40 |
| 5.5 | Matuba | Arlington, VA | Casual | $20 |
| 4.6 | Uni | Dupont | Casual | $40 |

## Japanese *continued*

| | | | |
|---|---|---|---|
| 4.5 | Meiwah | Multiple locations | Casual | $45 |
| 4.2 | Sushi-Go-Round & Tapas | Chinatown | Casual | $45 |
| | Daruma Japanese Market | Bethesda, MD | Counter | |

## Korean

| | | | |
|---|---|---|---|
| 9.0 | Oe Gad Gib | Annandale, VA | Casual | $20 |
| 9.0 | Seoul Soondae | Annandale, VA | Casual | $15 |
| 8.9 | Annan-Gol | Annandale, VA | Casual | $20 |
| 8.9 | Gamasot | Springfield, VA | Casual | $15 |
| 8.8 | Gooldaegee | Annandale, VA | Casual | $20 |
| 8.8 | Light House Tofu | Multiple locations | Casual | $15 |
| 8.7 | Dduk Sarang | Annandale, VA | Casual | $15 |
| 8.5 | To Sok Jip | Annandale, VA | Casual | $15 |
| 7.0 | Yee Hwa | Downtown | Casual | $40 |
| 6.3 | Mandu | Dupont | Casual | $40 |

## Latin American *includes South American, Central American, Caribbean*

| | | | |
|---|---|---|---|
| 8.7 | Granja de Oro | Adams Morgan | Counter | $20 |
| 8.5 | El Pollo Rico | Multiple locations | Counter | $10 |
| 8.4 | Pollo Granjero | Multiple locations | Counter | $15 |
| 8.0 | Don Pollo | Hyattsville, MD | Counter | $15 |
| 7.9 | El Dorado | Hyattsville, MD | Counter | $10 |
| 7.7 | Crisp & Juicy | Multiple locations | Counter | $10 |
| 7.5 | Pollo Campero | Multiple locations | Counter | $10 |
| 7.4 | Super Pollo | Arlington, VA | Counter | $10 |
| 7.1 | Julia's Empanadas | Multiple locations | Counter | $5 |
| 7.0 | Chi-Cha Lounge | U Street | Casual | $30 |
| 5.6 | Banana Café & Piano Bar | Capitol Hill | Café | $30 |

## Malaysian

| | | | |
|---|---|---|---|
| 7.1 | Malaysia Kopitiam | Dupont | Casual | $25 |
| 6.9 | Straits of Malaya | Dupont | Casual | $35 |

## Markets

| | | |
|---|---|---|
| Dean & Deluca | Georgetown | Market |
| Eastern Market | Capitol Hill | Market |
| Harris Teeter | Multiple locations | Market |
| Maine Avenue Fish Market | Southwest DC | Market |
| Marvelous Market | Multiple locations | Market |
| Trader Joe's | Multiple locations | Market |
| Whole Foods Market | Multiple locations | Market |

## Mexican

| | | | |
|---|---|---|---|
| 8.6 | El Charrito Caminante | Arlington, VA | Counter | $15 |
| 8.2 | Mogotillo | Takoma Park, MD | Casual | $20 |
| 8.2 | Taquería Nacional | Penn Quarter | Counter | $15 |
| 8.0 | Oyamel | Penn Quarter | Upmarket | $60 |
| 8.0 | Taquería Distrito Federal | Multiple locations | Casual | $20 |
| 7.6 | Guajillo | Arlington, VA | Casual | $35 |
| 7.5 | La Sandía | Tysons Corner, VA | Upmarket | $50 |
| 7.3 | Mixtec | Adams Morgan | Casual | $25 |
| 7.2 | Taquería El Poblano | Multiple locations | Casual | $15 |
| 7.0 | Las Placitas | Capitol Hill | Casual | $40 |
| 6.6 | Chevys Fresh Mex | Multiple locations | Casual | $30 |
| 6.5 | Alero | Multiple locations | Casual | $40 |
| 6.0 | Cococabana Bar & Grill | Hyattsville, MD | Casual | $30 |
| 6.0 | Tortilla Café | Capitol Hill | Casual | $20 |
| 5.9 | El Tamarindo | Adams Morgan | Casual | $40 |
| 5.9 | Burrito Brothers | Multiple locations | Counter | $20 |
| 5.8 | Rosa Mexicano | Penn Quarter | Upmarket | $55 |

## Mexican *continued*

| | | | |
|---|---|---|---|
| 5.2 | La Loma | Capitol Hill | Casual | $30 |
| 2.9 | Austin Grill | Multiple locations | Casual | $30 |
| 2.8 | California Tortilla | Multiple locations | Counter | $10 |
| 2.2 | Lauriol Plaza | Adams Morgan | Casual | $35 |

## Middle Eastern

| | | | |
|---|---|---|---|
| 8.6 | Kabob Palace | Arlington, VA | Counter | $20 |
| 8.5 | Zaytinya | Chinatown | Upmarket | $65 |
| 8.1 | Fresh Med | Cleveland Park | Counter | $20 |
| 8.0 | Kabob Bazaar | Arlington, VA | Casual | $20 |
| 7.5 | Lebanese Taverna | Multiple locations | Casual | $40 |
| 7.4 | Neyla | Georgetown | Upmarket | $70 |
| 7.1 | Tabaq Bistro | U Street | Upmarket | $45 |
| 7.0 | Mama Ayesha's | Adams Morgan | Casual | $40 |
| 7.0 | Moby Dick | Multiple locations | Casual | $25 |
| 6.8 | Bacchus of Lebanon | Bethesda, MD | Upmarket | $60 |
| 6.6 | Java House | Dupont | Counter | $10 |
| 6.5 | Café Olé | Upper NW | Casual | $30 |
| 6.3 | Astor Mediterranean | Multiple locations | Casual | $20 |
| 6.3 | DC Café | Dupont | Counter | $25 |
| 5.9 | Old City Café & Bakery | Adams Morgan | Counter | $10 |
| 5.7 | Couscous Café | Dupont | Counter | $10 |
| 5.6 | Byblos | Cleveland Park | Casual | $25 |
| 5.4 | Amsterdam Falafel Shop | Adams Morgan | Counter | $10 |
| 5.0 | Skye Lounge | Farragut | Casual | $40 |
| 4.3 | Skewers | Dupont | Casual | $30 |
| 1.4 | Prince Café | Multiple locations | Casual | $25 |
| | Mediterranean Bakery | Alexandria, VA | Counter | |

## Moroccan

| | | | |
|---|---|---|---|
| 8.0 | Taste of Morocco | Arlington, VA | Casual | $35 |
| 6.7 | Marrakesh | Mt. Vernon Square | Upmarket | $50 |
| 5.7 | Couscous Café | Dupont | Counter | $10 |
| 5.0 | Marrakesh Palace | Dupont | Upmarket | $45 |

## New American

| | | | |
|---|---|---|---|
| 9.7 | Komi | Dupont | Upmarket | $140 |
| 9.6 | CityZen | Southwest DC | Upmarket | $120 |
| 9.5 | Minibar | Penn Quarter | Upmarket | $160 |
| 9.4 | Westend Bistro | West End | Upmarket | $65 |
| 9.2 | Vermilion | Old Town | Upmarket | $65 |
| 9.2 | Poste Moderne Brasserie | Penn Quarter | Upmarket | $80 |
| 9.1 | Citronelle | Georgetown | Upmarket | $210 |
| 9.0 | Vidalia | Dupont | Upmarket | $70 |
| 8.8 | Restaurant Eve | Old Town | Upmarket | $150 |
| 8.8 | Central Michel Richard | Penn Quarter | Upmarket | $70 |
| 8.8 | The Source | Penn Quarter | Upmarket | $120 |
| 8.8 | Palena | Cleveland Park | Upmarket | $100 |
| 8.8 | Corduroy | Mt. Vernon Square | Upmarket | $70 |
| 8.6 | Nora | Dupont | Upmarket | $80 |
| 8.5 | Zaytinya | Chinatown | Upmarket | $65 |
| 8.5 | Urbana | Dupont | Upmarket | $55 |
| 8.5 | The Oval Room | Farragut | Upmarket | $75 |
| 8.4 | Buck's Fishing & Camping | Upper NW | Upmarket | $60 |
| 8.4 | Proof | Penn Quarter | Wine bar | $55 |
| 8.4 | Restaurant Eve (Bistro) | Old Town | Upmarket | $60 |
| 8.3 | Zola | Penn Quarter | Upmarket | $60 |
| 8.0 | Inn at Little Washington | Washington, VA | Upmarket | $250 |
| 8.0 | 2941 Restaurant | Falls Church, VA | Upmarket | $100 |
| 7.9 | Cashion's Eat Place | Adams Morgan | Upmarket | $60 |
| 7.9 | Firefly | Dupont | Upmarket | $60 |

## New American *continued*

| | | | |
|---|---|---|---|
| 7.9 | Farrah Olivia | Old Town | Upmarket | $65 |
| 7.9 | Black's Bar & Kitchen | Bethesda, MD | Upmarket | $75 |
| 7.9 | 1789 | Georgetown | Upmarket | $100 |
| 7.8 | Blue Duck Tavern | West End | Upmarket | $80 |
| 7.8 | Tallula | Arlington, VA | Upmarket | $55 |
| 7.8 | Bardeo | Cleveland Park | Wine bar | $35 |
| 7.8 | Café Atlántico | Penn Quarter | Upmarket | $75 |
| 7.7 | The Majestic | Old Town | Upmarket | $50 |
| 7.7 | Agraria | Georgetown | Upmarket | $60 |
| 7.6 | Park Café | Capitol Hill | Upmarket | $60 |
| 7.6 | Mendocino Grille | Georgetown | Wine bar | $60 |
| 7.6 | Equinox | Penn Quarter | Upmarket | $75 |
| 7.5 | Cork | Logan Circle | Wine bar | $40 |
| 7.4 | Ardeo | Cleveland Park | Upmarket | $65 |
| 7.4 | Jackson 20 | Old Town | Upmarket | $65 |
| 7.4 | DISH + drinks | Foggy Bottom | Upmarket | $55 |
| 7.3 | Coco Sala | Downtown | Upmarket | $50 |
| 7.3 | Vinoteca | U Street | Wine bar | $45 |
| 7.3 | Bourbon Steak | Georgetown | Upmarket | $115 |
| 7.3 | DC Coast | Downtown | Upmarket | $75 |
| 7.1 | Kemble Park Tavern | Palisades | Upmarket | $60 |
| 7.1 | PS 7's | Chinatown | Upmarket | $60 |
| 7.1 | Tabaq Bistro | U Street | Upmarket | $45 |
| 7.1 | Nicaro | Rockville, MD | Upmarket | $75 |
| 7.0 | Mio | Downtown | Upmarket | $70 |
| 7.0 | Rustico | Alexandria, VA | Casual | $40 |
| 7.0 | Nage | Dupont | Upmarket | $60 |
| 6.9 | Carlyle | Arlington, VA | Casual | $40 |
| 6.9 | Circle Bistro | West End | Upmarket | $70 |
| 6.8 | The Lafayette Room | Farragut | Upmarket | $85 |
| 6.7 | Persimmon | Chevy Chase, MD | Upmarket | $75 |
| 6.6 | Evening Star Café | Alexandria, VA | Upmarket | $55 |
| 6.5 | Veritas Wine Bar | Dupont | Wine bar | $40 |
| 6.5 | Evolve | Adams Morgan | Upmarket | $40 |
| 6.3 | Peacock Café | Georgetown | Upmarket | $60 |
| 6.3 | Station 9 | U Street | Upmarket | $45 |
| 6.1 | Chef Geoff's | Multiple locations | Upmarket | $50 |
| 5.9 | Grapeseed | Bethesda, MD | Wine bar | $75 |
| 5.9 | 15 Ria | Logan Circle | Upmarket | $60 |
| 5.8 | Hudson | West End | Upmarket | $65 |
| 5.8 | Vegetate | Mt. Vernon Square | Upmarket | $45 |
| 5.7 | Sonoma | Capitol Hill | Wine bar | $65 |
| 5.6 | Little Fountain Café | Adams Morgan | Upmarket | $45 |
| 5.6 | Darlington House | Dupont | Upmarket | $65 |
| 5.3 | Boulevard Woodgrill | Arlington, VA | Casual | $45 |
| 5.2 | Beacon Bar & Grill | Dupont | Casual | $45 |
| 5.1 | Pomegranate Bistro | Potomac, MD | Upmarket | $60 |
| 4.8 | 701 | Penn Quarter | Upmarket | $70 |
| 3.9 | Sequoia | Georgetown | Upmarket | $50 |

## New Zealand

| | | | |
|---|---|---|---|
| 7.0 | Cassatt's | Arlington, VA | Casual | $25 |

## Nuevo Latino

| | | | |
|---|---|---|---|
| 7.8 | Café Atlántico | Penn Quarter | Upmarket | $75 |
| 7.0 | Ceiba | Downtown | Upmarket | $60 |
| 5.0 | Lima | Downtown | Upmarket | $55 |
| 3.5 | Café Citron | Dupont | Casual | $35 |

## Pakistani

| | | | |
|---|---|---|---|
| 8.7 | Tabeer | Hyattsville, MD | Casual | $25 |
| 7.2 | Mayur Kabab House | Chinatown | Casual | $20 |

## Pan-Asian

| | | | |
|---|---|---|---|
| 7.4 | TenPenh | Downtown | Upmarket | $70 |
| 7.1 | Oya | Penn Quarter | Upmarket | $75 |
| 6.7 | Zengo | Chinatown | Upmarket | $65 |
| 6.6 | Nooshi | Farragut | Casual | $25 |
| 6.2 | Teaism | Multiple locations | Café | $20 |
| 5.9 | Maté | Georgetown | Casual | $45 |
| 5.5 | Bangkok Joe's | Georgetown | Casual | $45 |
| 5.2 | Spices | Cleveland Park | Casual | $35 |
| 5.1 | Singapore Bistro | Farragut | Casual | $25 |
| 5.1 | Asian Spice | Chinatown | Casual | $40 |
| 5.0 | Café Asia | Multiple locations | Casual | $30 |
| 4.8 | Mie N Yu | Georgetown | Upmarket | $55 |
| 4.8 | Fusion Grill | Capitol Hill | Upmarket | $55 |
| 4.8 | Asia Nine | Penn Quarter | Casual | $35 |
| 4.4 | Raku | Multiple locations | Upmarket | $35 |
| 4.2 | Sushi-Go-Round & Tapas | Chinatown | Casual | $45 |
| 4.0 | Tony Cheng's Mongolian | Chinatown | Casual | $35 |
| 3.7 | Ping by Charlie Chiang's | Arlington, VA | Casual | $45 |

## Peruvian

| | | | |
|---|---|---|---|
| 8.5 | Costa Verde | Arlington, VA | Casual | $30 |
| 7.1 | El Chalán | Farragut | Casual | $45 |

## Pizza

| | | | |
|---|---|---|---|
| 9.6 | 2 Amys Pizza | Cleveland Park | Casual | $35 |
| 9.0 | Posto | Logan Circle | Upmarket | $55 |
| 8.5 | Urbana | Dupont | Upmarket | $55 |
| 8.2 | Pizzeria Paradiso | Multiple locations | Casual | $30 |
| 8.1 | RedRocks | Columbia Heights | Casual | $35 |
| 8.0 | Coppi's Organic | U Street | Upmarket | $50 |
| 8.0 | Vace | Multiple locations | Counter | $30 |
| 7.7 | Mia's Pizza | Bethesda, MD | Casual | $25 |
| 7.6 | Matchbox | Chinatown | Casual | $35 |
| 7.4 | Sorriso | Cleveland Park | Casual | $40 |
| 7.3 | Café Pizzaiolo | Multiple locations | Casual | $35 |
| 7.1 | Faccia Luna | Multiple locations | Casual | $40 |
| 6.9 | Ella's Pizza | Chinatown | Casual | $40 |
| 6.9 | Comet Ping Pong | Upper NW | Casual | $35 |
| 6.6 | Sette Osteria | Dupont | Casual | $40 |
| 6.4 | Al's Pizza | Purcellville, VA | Counter | $20 |
| 5.7 | Bertucci's | Multiple locations | Casual | $35 |
| 5.7 | Armand's | Multiple locations | Casual | $25 |
| 5.3 | Alberto's Stone Oven Pizza | Multiple locations | Counter | $5 |
| 3.5 | Jumbo Slice | Adams Morgan | Counter | $5 |
| | The Italian Store | Arlington, VA | Counter | |

## Polish

| | | | |
|---|---|---|---|
| 7.7 | W Domku | Petworth | Casual | $40 |

## Portuguese

| | | | |
|---|---|---|---|
| 7.9 | Tavira | Chevy Chase, MD | Upmarket | $60 |

## Salvadoran

| | | | |
|---|---|---|---|
| 8.6 | El Charrito Caminante | Arlington, VA | Counter | $15 |
| 8.2 | Irene's Pupusas | Multiple locations | Casual | $25 |

## Salvadoran *continued*

| 8.2 | Mogotillo | Takoma Park, MD | Casual | $20 |
| 8.1 | Pupusería San Miguel | Columbia Heights | Casual | $10 |
| 7.9 | La Casita | Multiple locations | Casual | $10 |
| 7.9 | El Dorado | Hyattsville, MD | Counter | $10 |
| 7.0 | Las Placitas | Capitol Hill | Casual | $40 |
| 6.0 | Tortilla Café | Capitol Hill | Casual | $20 |
| 5.9 | El Tamarindo | Adams Morgan | Casual | $40 |

## Sandwiches

| 8.1 | Bread Line | Farragut | Café | $15 |
| 8.0 | Vace | Multiple locations | Counter | $30 |
| 8.0 | La Baguette | Dupont | Counter | $15 |
| 7.7 | Café Tu-O-Tu | Georgetown | Counter | $15 |
| 7.7 | Bethesda Bagels | Bethesda, MD | Counter | $10 |
| 7.6 | Deli City | Northeast DC | Counter | $15 |
| 7.5 | Earl's Sandwiches | Arlington, VA | Counter | $15 |
| 7.4 | Potbelly Sandwich Works | Multiple locations | Counter | $10 |
| 7.3 | Patisserie Poupon | Georgetown | Café | $35 |
| 7.3 | Café Pizzaiolo | Multiple locations | Casual | $35 |
| 7.1 | Greek Deli | Farragut | Counter | $15 |
| 7.0 | Cakelove and Love Café | Multiple locations | Café | $10 |
| 6.8 | La Prima | Multiple locations | Counter | $20 |
| 6.7 | Bagels & Baguettes | Capitol Hill | Café | $10 |
| 6.4 | Zorba's Café | Dupont | Counter | $25 |
| 6.2 | Le Bon Café | Capitol Hill | Café | $20 |
| 5.9 | Eli's | Dupont | Casual | $20 |
| 5.8 | Sticky Fingers Bakery | Columbia Heights | Counter | $10 |
| 5.4 | La Madeleine | Multiple locations | Counter | $30 |
| 5.1 | The Brown Bag | Multiple locations | Counter | $15 |
| 4.9 | Java Green | Farragut | Café | $20 |
| 4.5 | Camille's Sidewalk Café | Multiple locations | Café | $25 |
| 3.6 | Prego Delly | Capitol Hill | Counter | $25 |
| 3.1 | Wellness Café | Capitol Hill | Café | $20 |
|  | Dickey's Frozen Custard | Multiple locations | Counter |  |
|  | The Italian Store | Arlington, VA | Counter |  |

## Scandinavian

| 7.7 | W Domku | Petworth | Casual | $40 |

## Seafood

| 9.1 | Hank's Oyster Bar | Multiple locations | Upmarket | $45 |
| 8.9 | Pesce | Dupont | Upmarket | $60 |
| 8.7 | Eamonn's | Old Town | Casual | $20 |
| 8.3 | Hook | Georgetown | Upmarket | $80 |
| 8.2 | Tackle Box | Georgetown | Casual | $25 |
| 7.9 | BlackSalt | Palisades | Upmarket | $45 |
| 7.9 | Black's Bar & Kitchen | Bethesda, MD | Upmarket | $75 |
| 7.8 | Johnny's Half Shell | Capitol Hill | Upmarket | $65 |
| 7.7 | The Wharf Seafood | Southwest DC | Counter | $25 |
| 7.4 | Mar de Plata | Multiple locations | Casual | $50 |
| 7.4 | Oceanaire Seafood Room | Downtown | Upmarket | $82 |
| 7.3 | DC Coast | Downtown | Upmarket | $75 |
| 7.3 | Kinkead's | Foggy Bottom | Upmarket | $75 |
| 7.0 | McCormick & Schmick's | Multiple locations | Upmarket | $60 |
| 7.0 | Nage | Dupont | Upmarket | $60 |
| 6.8 | Starfish Café | Capitol Hill | Casual | $55 |
| 6.3 | Grillfish | West End | Upmarket | $45 |
| 3.9 | Tony & Joe's Seafood Place | Georgetown | Upmarket | $55 |
|  | Maine Avenue Fish Market | Southwest DC | Market |  |

## Southern *includes soul food, Cajun, Creole*

| | | | | |
|---|---|---|---|---|
| 9.1 | Marvin | U Street | Upmarket | $45 |
| 9.0 | Vidalia | Dupont | Upmarket | $70 |
| 8.5 | Oohhs & Aahhs | Shaw | Counter | $25 |
| 8.4 | Buck's Fishing & Camping | Upper NW | Upmarket | $60 |
| 8.0 | Morrison-Clark Inn | Downtown | Upmarket | $60 |
| 8.0 | Crème | U Street | Casual | $45 |
| 8.0 | Georgia Brown's | Downtown | Upmarket | $55 |
| 7.6 | Deli City | Northeast DC | Counter | $15 |
| 7.2 | Florida Avenue Grill | U Street | Casual | $15 |
| 7.2 | Cantina Marina | Southwest DC | Casual | $35 |
| 7.1 | Acadiana | Mt. Vernon Square | Upmarket | $60 |
| 6.0 | The Red and the Black | Northeast DC | Bar | $25 |

## Spanish

| | | | | |
|---|---|---|---|---|
| 8.7 | Taberna del Alabardero | Farragut | Upmarket | $75 |
| 7.4 | Mar de Plata | Multiple locations | Casual | $50 |
| 7.3 | Jaleo | Multiple locations | Upmarket | $50 |
| 5.7 | La Tasca | Multiple locations | Casual | $40 |

## Steakhouse

| | | | | |
|---|---|---|---|---|
| 8.7 | BLT Steak | Farragut | Upmarket | $95 |
| 8.5 | Bobby Van's Steakhouse | Multiple locations | Upmarket | $95 |
| 8.5 | Prime Rib | Farragut | Upmarket | $90 |
| 8.4 | Ray's the Steaks | Arlington, VA | Upmarket | $45 |
| 8.3 | Smith & Wollensky | Farragut | Upmarket | $85 |
| 8.2 | Ray's the Classics | Silver Spring, MD | Upmarket | $45 |
| 7.9 | Morton's | Multiple locations | Upmarket | $100 |
| 7.8 | Ruth's Chris Steakhouse | Multiple locations | Upmarket | $90 |
| 7.5 | Sam & Harry's | Dupont | Upmarket | $85 |
| 7.1 | District Chophouse | Penn Quarter | Casual | $45 |
| 7.1 | The Caucus Room | Penn Quarter | Upmarket | $90 |
| 7.0 | The Palm | Multiple locations | Upmarket | $95 |
| 6.9 | Annie's Paramount | Dupont | Casual | $35 |
| 6.9 | Fleming's | Tysons Corner, VA | Upmarket | $90 |
| 6.7 | Bookbinder's Old Town | Old Town | Upmarket | $80 |
| 6.7 | Fogo de Chão | Downtown | Upmarket | $80 |
| 6.5 | Capital Grille | Multiple locations | Upmarket | $85 |
| 5.8 | Charlie Palmer Steak | Capitol Hill | Upmarket | $110 |

## Sudanese

| | | | | |
|---|---|---|---|---|
| 7.5 | El Khartoum | Shaw | Counter | $20 |

## Sweet drinks

| | | | | |
|---|---|---|---|---|
| 4.8 | ACKC Cocoa Bar | Multiple locations | Café | $10 |
| 4.5 | Camille's Sidewalk Café | Multiple locations | Café | $25 |
| 3.1 | Wellness Café | Capitol Hill | Café | $20 |

## Taiwanese

| | | | | |
|---|---|---|---|---|
| 8.6 | Bob's Noodle 66 | Rockville, MD | Casual | $15 |

## Thai

| | | | | |
|---|---|---|---|---|
| 8.4 | Nava Thai | Wheaton, MD | Casual | $25 |
| 8.3 | Thai X-ing | Shaw | Casual | $30 |
| 8.3 | Thai Market | Silver Spring, MD | Counter | $20 |
| 7.5 | Thai Square | Arlington, VA | Casual | $35 |
| 7.2 | Bangkok 54 | Arlington, VA | Casual | $35 |
| 7.0 | Regent Thai | Dupont | Casual | $35 |
| 6.8 | Thai Tanic | Logan Circle | Casual | $30 |
| 6.8 | Po Siam | Alexandria, VA | Casual | $30 |

## Thai *continued*

| | | | |
|---|---|---|---|
| 6.0 | Kanlaya | Chinatown | Casual | $30 |
| 5.9 | Mai Thai | Multiple locations | Casual | $35 |
| 5.9 | Tara Thai | Multiple locations | Casual | $25 |
| 5.9 | Thaiphoon | Multiple locations | Casual | $40 |
| 5.6 | Thai Chef | Dupont | Casual | $40 |
| 5.1 | Old Siam | Capitol Hill | Casual | $25 |
| 4.4 | Rice | Logan Circle | Upmarket | $30 |
| 4.0 | Thai Roma | Capitol Hill | Casual | $35 |
| 3.2 | Sala Thai | Multiple locations | Casual | $25 |

## Turkish

| | | | |
|---|---|---|---|
| 7.7 | Café Tu-O-Tu | Georgetown | Counter | $15 |
| 7.4 | Café Divan | Glover Park | Casual | $35 |

## Vietnamese

| | | | |
|---|---|---|---|
| 9.0 | Hai Duong | Falls Church, VA | Casual | $15 |
| 9.0 | Thanh Tong | Falls Church, VA | Casual | $15 |
| 8.8 | Cho Cu Sai Gon | Falls Church, VA | Casual | $20 |
| 8.7 | Ngoc Anh | Falls Church, VA | Casual | $25 |
| 8.7 | Com Tam Saigon | Falls Church, VA | Casual | $10 |
| 7.4 | Nam-Viet | Multiple locations | Casual | $30 |
| 7.2 | Pho Xe Lua | Falls Church, VA | Casual | $15 |
| 7.1 | Saigon Saigon | Arlington, VA | Casual | $25 |
| 5.5 | Green Papaya | Bethesda, MD | Upmarket | $35 |
| 4.3 | Vietnam Georgetown | Georgetown | Casual | $30 |

## Wine bars

| | | | |
|---|---|---|---|
| 8.4 | Proof | Penn Quarter | Wine bar | $55 |
| 7.8 | Bardeo | Cleveland Park | Wine bar | $35 |
| 7.6 | Mendocino Grille | Georgetown | Wine bar | $60 |
| 7.5 | Cork | Logan Circle | Wine bar | $40 |
| 7.3 | Vinoteca | U Street | Wine bar | $45 |
| 6.5 | Veritas Wine Bar | Dupont | Wine bar | $40 |
| 5.9 | Grapeseed | Bethesda, MD | Wine bar | $75 |
| 5.7 | Sonoma | Capitol Hill | Wine bar | $65 |

# By location

Places to eat **listed by neighborhood, suburb, or town, ranked by food rating.**

## Adams Morgan

| | | Cuisine | Type | Price |
|---|---|---|---|---|
| 8.7 | Granja de Oro | Latin American | Counter | $20 |
| 8.4 | Pollo Granjero | Latin American | Counter | $15 |
| 8.1 | Bourbon | American | Bar | $35 |
| 7.9 | Cashion's Eat Place | New American | Upmarket | $60 |
| 7.8 | Pasta Mia | Italian | Casual | $25 |
| 7.5 | Meskerem | Ethiopian | Casual | $25 |
| 7.3 | Mixtec | Mexican | Casual | $25 |
| 7.1 | Jyoti | Indian | Casual | $25 |
| 7.1 | Julia's Empanadas | Latin American | Counter | $5 |
| 7.0 | Mama Ayesha's | Middle Eastern | Casual | $40 |
| 6.5 | Evolve | New American | Upmarket | $40 |
| 6.3 | Astor Mediterranean | Middle Eastern, Greek | Casual | $20 |
| 5.9 | El Tamarindo | Mexican, Salvadoran | Casual | $40 |
| 5.9 | Old City Café & Bakery | Middle Eastern | Counter | $10 |
| 5.6 | Little Fountain Café | New American | Upmarket | $45 |
| 5.5 | Napoleon Bistro | French | Upmarket | $60 |
| 5.4 | Amsterdam Falafel Shop | Middle Eastern | Counter | $10 |
| 5.3 | Alberto's Stone Oven Pizza | Pizza | Counter | $5 |
| 5.1 | Tryst | American | Café | $25 |
| 5.1 | Grill from Ipanema | Brazilian | Casual | $45 |
| 4.1 | Diner | American | Casual | $25 |
| 3.5 | Jumbo Slice | Pizza | Counter | $5 |
| 2.2 | Lauriol Plaza | Mexican | Casual | $35 |
| 1.4 | Prince Café | Middle Eastern | Casual | $25 |
| | Harris Teeter | Groceries | Market | |

## Alexandria Old Town

| | | | | |
|---|---|---|---|---|
| 9.2 | Vermilion | New American | Upmarket | $65 |
| 9.1 | Hank's Oyster Bar | Seafood | Upmarket | $45 |
| 8.8 | Restaurant Eve | New American | Upmarket | $150 |
| 8.7 | Eamonn's | Seafood, Irish | Casual | $20 |
| 8.4 | Restaurant Eve (Bistro) | New American | Upmarket | $60 |
| 7.9 | Farrah Olivia | New American | Upmarket | $65 |
| 7.7 | The Majestic | New American | Upmarket | $50 |
| 7.4 | Jackson 20 | New American | Upmarket | $65 |
| 7.4 | Five Guys | American | Counter | $10 |
| 7.2 | Firehook | Baked goods | Counter | $10 |
| 7.2 | Bread & Chocolate | French | Café | $15 |
| 7.1 | Faccia Luna | Italian, Pizza | Casual | $40 |
| 6.9 | Bastille | French | Upmarket | $55 |
| 6.7 | Bookbinder's Old Town | Steakhouse, American | Upmarket | $80 |
| 5.9 | Mai Thai | Thai | Casual | $35 |
| 5.7 | La Tasca | Spanish | Casual | $40 |
| 5.7 | Bertucci's | Italian, Pizza | Casual | $35 |
| 5.4 | La Madeleine | French, Sandwiches | Counter | $30 |
| 4.3 | Hard Times Café | American | Casual | $20 |
| 2.9 | Austin Grill | Mexican | Casual | $30 |
| | Whole Foods Market | Groceries | Market | |

## Alexandria, VA

| | | | | |
|---|---|---|---|---|
| 8.1 | Cosmopolitan Bakery | Balkan | Café | $25 |
| 7.4 | Potbelly Sandwich Works | Sandwiches | Counter | $10 |
| 7.4 | Five Guys | American | Counter | $10 |

## Alexandria, VA *continued*

| | | | | |
|-----|------|------|------|-----|
| 7.3 | Café Pizzaiolo | Pizza, Sandwiches | Casual | $35 |
| 7.2 | Bombay Curry Company | Indian | Casual | $20 |
| 7.2 | Taquería El Poblano | Mexican | Casual | $15 |
| 7.0 | Rustico | New American | Casual | $40 |
| 6.9 | Red Hot & Blue | Barbecue | Casual | $15 |
| 6.8 | Po Siam | Thai | Casual | $30 |
| 6.6 | Evening Star Café | New American | Upmarket | $55 |
| 6.0 | Finn & Porter | American | Upmarket | $75 |
| 5.6 | Rocklands | Barbecue | Casual | $15 |
| 5.1 | Clyde's | American | Casual | $40 |
| 4.8 | ACKC Cocoa Bar | Sweet drinks, Baked goods | Café | $10 |
| 2.8 | California Tortilla | Mexican | Counter | $10 |
| | The Dairy Godmother | Ice cream | Counter | |
| | Mediterranean Bakery | Middle Eastern, Groceries | Counter | |
| | Trader Joe's | Groceries | Market | |

## Annandale, VA

| | | | | |
|-----|------|------|------|-----|
| 9.0 | Oe Gad Gib | Korean | Casual | $20 |
| 9.0 | Seoul Soondae | Korean | Casual | $15 |
| 8.9 | Annan-Gol | Korean | Casual | $20 |
| 8.8 | Gooldaegee | Korean | Casual | $20 |
| 8.8 | Light House Tofu | Korean | Casual | $15 |
| 8.7 | Dduk Sarang | Korean | Casual | $15 |
| 8.5 | To Sok Jip | Korean | Casual | $15 |
| 8.4 | A & J Restaurant | Chinese | Casual | $30 |
| 7.4 | Five Guys | American | Counter | $10 |

## Arlington, VA

| | | | | |
|-----|------|------|------|-----|
| 9.0 | Ray's Hell-Burger | American | Counter | $15 |
| 8.8 | China Garden | Chinese | Casual | $20 |
| 8.6 | Liberty Tavern | American | Casual | $40 |
| 8.6 | El Charrito Caminante | Mexican, Salvadoran | Counter | $15 |
| 8.6 | Kabob Palace | Middle Eastern, Afghan | Counter | $20 |
| 8.5 | Costa Verde | Peruvian | Casual | $30 |
| 8.5 | El Pollo Rico | Latin American | Counter | $10 |
| 8.4 | Ray's the Steaks | Steakhouse | Upmarket | $45 |
| 8.0 | Weenie Beanie | American | Counter | $5 |
| 8.0 | Kabob Bazaar | Middle Eastern | Casual | $20 |
| 8.0 | Taste of Morocco | Moroccan | Casual | $35 |
| 7.9 | Morton's | Steakhouse | Upmarket | $100 |
| 7.8 | Tallula | New American | Upmarket | $55 |
| 7.8 | Ruth's Chris Steakhouse | Steakhouse | Upmarket | $90 |
| 7.7 | Crisp & Juicy | Latin American | Counter | $10 |
| 7.6 | Guajillo | Mexican | Casual | $35 |
| 7.5 | Busboys & Poets | American | Casual | $25 |
| 7.5 | Lebanese Taverna | Middle Eastern | Casual | $40 |
| 7.5 | Earl's Sandwiches | Sandwiches | Counter | $15 |
| 7.5 | Thai Square | Thai | Casual | $35 |
| 7.4 | Potbelly Sandwich Works | Sandwiches | Counter | $10 |
| 7.4 | Five Guys | American | Counter | $10 |
| 7.4 | Nam-Viet | Vietnamese | Casual | $30 |
| 7.4 | Super Pollo | Latin American | Counter | $10 |
| 7.3 | Jaleo | Spanish | Upmarket | $50 |
| 7.3 | Café Pizzaiolo | Pizza, Sandwiches | Casual | $35 |
| 7.2 | Bangkok 54 | Thai | Casual | $35 |
| 7.2 | Cucina Vivace | Italian | Upmarket | $55 |
| 7.2 | Taquería El Poblano | Mexican | Casual | $15 |
| 7.1 | Faccia Luna | Italian, Pizza | Casual | $40 |
| 7.1 | Harar Mesob | Ethiopian | Casual | $25 |
| 7.1 | Saigon Saigon | Vietnamese | Casual | $25 |
| 7.0 | Cassatt's | American, New Zealand | Casual | $25 |

## Arlington, VA *continued*

| | | | |
|---|---|---|---|
| 7.0 | McCormick & Schmick's | Seafood | Upmarket | $60 |
| 7.0 | Cakelove and Love Café | Baked goods, Sandwiches | Café | $10 |
| 7.0 | Moby Dick | Middle Eastern | Casual | $25 |
| 6.9 | Whitlow's on Wilson | American | Casual | $35 |
| 6.9 | Carlyle | New American | Casual | $40 |
| 6.9 | Red Hot & Blue | Barbecue | Casual | $15 |
| 6.7 | Harry's Tap Room | American | Casual | $50 |
| 6.6 | Capitol City Brewery | American | Casual | $35 |
| 6.6 | Chevys Fresh Mex | Mexican | Casual | $30 |
| 6.3 | Astor Mediterranean | Middle Eastern, Greek | Casual | $20 |
| 6.2 | Murali | Italian | Upmarket | $50 |
| 5.9 | Thaiphoon | Thai | Casual | $40 |
| 5.9 | Kanpai | Japanese | Casual | $30 |
| 5.7 | La Tasca | Spanish | Casual | $40 |
| 5.7 | Bertucci's | Italian, Pizza | Casual | $35 |
| 5.7 | Armand's | Pizza | Casual | $25 |
| 5.7 | La Crêperie | French | Café | $15 |
| 5.6 | Rocklands | Barbecue | Casual | $15 |
| 5.5 | Matuba | Japanese | Casual | $20 |
| 5.3 | Boulevard Woodgrill | New American | Casual | $45 |
| 5.0 | Café Asia | Pan-Asian | Casual | $30 |
| 4.7 | Aroma | Indian | Casual | $25 |
| 4.3 | Hard Times Café | American | Casual | $20 |
| 4.2 | Luna Grill & Diner | American, Italian | Casual | $30 |
| 3.7 | Ping by Charlie Chiang's | Pan-Asian | Casual | $45 |
| 3.2 | Sala Thai | Thai | Casual | $25 |
| 2.8 | California Tortilla | Mexican | Counter | $10 |
| | Dickey's Frozen Custard | Sandwiches, Ice cream | Counter | |
| | Harris Teeter | Groceries | Market | |
| | The Italian Store | Pizza, Sandwiches | Counter | |
| | Marvelous Market | Groceries, Baked goods | Market | |
| | Whole Foods Market | Groceries | Market | |

## Bethesda, MD

| | | | |
|---|---|---|---|
| 8.0 | Passage to India | Indian | Casual | $40 |
| 8.0 | Vace | Sandwiches, Pizza | Counter | $30 |
| 7.9 | Black's Bar & Kitchen | New American, Seafood | Upmarket | $75 |
| 7.9 | Morton's | Steakhouse | Upmarket | $100 |
| 7.8 | Ruth's Chris Steakhouse | Steakhouse | Upmarket | $90 |
| 7.8 | Tako Grill | Japanese | Casual | $45 |
| 7.7 | Mia's Pizza | Italian, Pizza | Casual | $25 |
| 7.7 | Bethesda Bagels | Sandwiches, Baked goods | Counter | $10 |
| 7.5 | Lebanese Taverna | Middle Eastern | Casual | $40 |
| 7.4 | Potbelly Sandwich Works | Sandwiches | Counter | $10 |
| 7.4 | Shanghai Village | Chinese | Casual | $35 |
| 7.4 | Five Guys | American | Counter | $10 |
| 7.3 | Jaleo | Spanish | Upmarket | $50 |
| 7.0 | McCormick & Schmick's | Seafood | Upmarket | $60 |
| 7.0 | Moby Dick | Middle Eastern | Casual | $25 |
| 6.8 | Bacchus of Lebanon | Middle Eastern | Upmarket | $60 |
| 6.5 | Tragara | Italian | Upmarket | $80 |
| 6.3 | Faryab | Afghan | Casual | $25 |
| 5.9 | Grapeseed | New American | Wine bar | $75 |
| 5.9 | Tara Thai | Thai | Casual | $25 |
| 5.7 | Bertucci's | Italian, Pizza | Casual | $35 |
| 5.5 | Green Papaya | Vietnamese | Upmarket | $35 |
| 5.4 | La Madeleine | French, Sandwiches | Counter | $30 |
| 5.1 | The Brown Bag | Sandwiches | Counter | $15 |
| 4.9 | Brasserie Monte Carlo | French | Casual | $45 |
| 4.4 | Raku | Pan-Asian | Upmarket | $35 |
| 4.3 | Hard Times Café | American | Casual | $20 |
| 3.7 | Olazzo | Italian | Upmarket | $45 |

## Bethesda, MD *continued*

| | | | |
|---|---|---|---|
| 3.2 | Sala Thai | Thai | Casual | $25 |
| 2.9 | Austin Grill | Mexican | Casual | $30 |
| 2.8 | California Tortilla | Mexican | Counter | $10 |
| | Daruma Japanese Market | Japanese, Groceries | Counter | |
| | Dolcezza | Ice cream, Baked goods | Counter | |
| | Trader Joe's | Groceries | Market | |
| | Whole Foods Market | Groceries | Market | |

## Capitol Hill

| | | | | |
|---|---|---|---|---|
| 8.9 | Bistro Bis | French | Upmarket | $70 |
| 8.6 | Montmartre | French | Upmarket | $60 |
| 7.8 | Johnny's Half Shell | Seafood | Upmarket | $65 |
| 7.6 | Park Café | New American | Upmarket | $60 |
| 7.4 | Five Guys | American | Counter | $10 |
| 7.2 | Café Berlin | German | Café | $35 |
| 7.2 | Jimmy T's | American | Casual | $25 |
| 7.2 | Firehook | Baked goods | Counter | $10 |
| 7.0 | Belga Café | Belgian | Casual | $30 |
| 7.0 | Good Stuff Eatery | American | Counter | $15 |
| 7.0 | Las Placitas | Mexican, Salvadoran | Casual | $40 |
| 6.9 | Tunnicliff's Tavern | American | Casual | $40 |
| 6.8 | Starfish Café | Seafood | Casual | $55 |
| 6.8 | Trusty's | American | Casual | $35 |
| 6.7 | White Tiger | Indian | Casual | $35 |
| 6.7 | Bagels & Baguettes | Sandwiches, Baked goods | Café | $10 |
| 6.6 | Kyoto | Japanese | Casual | $30 |
| 6.6 | Capitol City Brewery | American | Casual | $35 |
| 6.5 | Pete's Diner | American | Casual | $25 |
| 6.3 | Tandoor Grill | Indian | Casual | $30 |
| 6.2 | Le Bon Café | Baked goods, Sandwiches | Café | $20 |
| 6.1 | Kenny's BBQ | Barbecue | Counter | $20 |
| 6.0 | Tortilla Café | Salvadoran, Mexican | Casual | $20 |
| 6.0 | Aatish on the Hill | Indian | Casual | $30 |
| 5.9 | Burrito Brothers | Mexican | Counter | $20 |
| 5.8 | Charlie Palmer Steak | Steakhouse, American | Upmarket | $110 |
| 5.7 | Sonoma | New American | Wine bar | $65 |
| 5.7 | Armand's | Pizza | Casual | $25 |
| 5.6 | Banana Café & Piano Bar | Cuban, Latin American | Café | $30 |
| 5.6 | Johnny Rockets | American | Casual | $25 |
| 5.2 | La Loma | Mexican | Casual | $30 |
| 5.1 | Old Siam | Thai | Casual | $25 |
| 4.8 | Fusion Grill | Pan-Asian | Upmarket | $55 |
| 4.8 | Trattoria Alberto | Italian | Casual | $45 |
| 4.8 | Pour House | American | Casual | $35 |
| 4.7 | Hunan Dynasty | Chinese | Casual | $25 |
| 4.0 | Thai Roma | Thai | Casual | $35 |
| 3.8 | Union Pub | American | Casual | $25 |
| 3.6 | Prego Delly | Sandwiches, Italian | Counter | $25 |
| 3.1 | Wellness Café | Sandwiches, Sweet drinks | Café | $20 |
| | Eastern Market | Groceries | Market | |
| | Harris Teeter | Groceries | Market | |
| | Marvelous Market | Groceries, Baked goods | Market | |

## Chevy Chase, MD

| | | | | |
|---|---|---|---|---|
| 8.5 | Sushi-Ko | Japanese | Upmarket | $60 |
| 7.9 | Tavira | Portuguese | Upmarket | $60 |
| 7.2 | Bread & Chocolate | French | Café | $15 |
| 6.7 | Persimmon | New American | Upmarket | $75 |
| 6.0 | La Ferme | French | Upmarket | $60 |
| 5.1 | Clyde's | American | Casual | $40 |
| 4.5 | Meiwah | Chinese, Japanese | Casual | $45 |

## Chinatown

| | | | |
|---|---|---|---|
| 8.8 | New Big Wong | Chinese | Casual | $25 |
| 8.5 | Zaytinya | Middle Eastern | Upmarket | $65 |
| 8.2 | Li Ho | Chinese | Casual | $10 |
| 7.8 | Full Kee | Chinese | Casual | $25 |
| 7.6 | Matchbox | American, Pizza | Casual | $35 |
| 7.4 | Potbelly Sandwich Works | Sandwiches | Counter | $10 |
| 7.4 | Five Guys | American | Counter | $10 |
| 7.3 | Chinatown Express | Chinese | Casual | $25 |
| 7.2 | Firehook | Baked goods | Counter | $10 |
| 7.2 | Mayur Kabab House | Pakistani, Indian | Casual | $20 |
| 7.1 | PS 7's | New American | Upmarket | $60 |
| 6.9 | Ella's Pizza | Pizza | Casual | $40 |
| 6.8 | Fadó | Irish | Bar | $27 |
| 6.7 | Zengo | Pan-Asian | Upmarket | $65 |
| 6.6 | Chop't | American | Counter | $10 |
| 6.0 | Burma | Burmese | Casual | $25 |
| 6.0 | Kanlaya | Thai, Chinese | Casual | $30 |
| 5.7 | La Tasca | Spanish | Casual | $40 |
| 5.3 | Eat First | Chinese | Casual | $20 |
| 5.1 | Clyde's | American | Casual | $40 |
| 5.1 | Asian Spice | Chinese, Pan-Asian | Casual | $40 |
| 4.5 | Tony Cheng's Seafood | Chinese | Casual | $35 |
| 4.2 | Sushi-Go-Round & Tapas | Pan-Asian, Japanese | Casual | $45 |
| 4.0 | Tai Shan | Chinese | Casual | $15 |
| 4.0 | Tony Cheng's Mongolian | Pan-Asian | Casual | $35 |
| 3.8 | Wok & Roll | Chinese | Casual | $20 |
| 2.8 | California Tortilla | Mexican | Counter | $10 |

## Cleveland Park

| | | | |
|---|---|---|---|
| 9.6 | 2 Amys Pizza | Pizza | Casual | $35 |
| 8.8 | Palena | New American | Upmarket | $100 |
| 8.4 | Dino | Italian | Upmarket | $50 |
| 8.1 | Fresh Med | Middle Eastern | Counter | $20 |
| 8.0 | Lavandou | French | Upmarket | $65 |
| 8.0 | Vace | Sandwiches, Pizza | Counter | $30 |
| 7.8 | Bardeo | New American | Wine bar | $35 |
| 7.8 | Afghan Grill | Afghan | Casual | $40 |
| 7.4 | Ardeo | New American | Upmarket | $65 |
| 7.4 | Sorriso | Italian, Pizza | Casual | $40 |
| 7.4 | Nam-Viet | Vietnamese | Casual | $30 |
| 7.2 | Firehook | Baked goods | Counter | $10 |
| 6.5 | Alero | Mexican | Casual | $40 |
| 6.2 | Indique | Indian | Upmarket | $40 |
| 5.6 | Byblos | Greek, Middle Eastern | Casual | $25 |
| 5.2 | Spices | Pan-Asian | Casual | $35 |
| 2.8 | California Tortilla | Mexican | Counter | $10 |

## Columbia Heights

| | | | |
|---|---|---|---|
| 8.1 | RedRocks | Pizza | Casual | $35 |
| 8.1 | Pupusería San Miguel | Salvadoran | Casual | $10 |
| 8.0 | Commonwealth | British | Casual | $40 |
| 8.0 | Taquería Distrito Federal | Mexican | Casual | $20 |
| 7.5 | Pollo Campero | Latin American | Counter | $10 |
| 7.4 | Potbelly Sandwich Works | Sandwiches | Counter | $10 |
| 7.4 | Five Guys | American | Counter | $10 |
| 7.1 | Julia's Empanadas | Latin American | Counter | $5 |
| 5.8 | Sticky Fingers Bakery | Baked goods, Sandwiches | Counter | $10 |

## Downtown

| | | | |
|---|---|---|---|
| 9.1 | Adour | French | Upmarket | $125 |
| 9.1 | Tosca | Italian | Upmarket | $75 |

## Downtown *continued*

| | | | |
|------|------|------|------|
| 8.6 | Café du Parc | French | Upmarket | $60 |
| 8.5 | Bobby Van's Steakhouse | Steakhouse | Upmarket | $95 |
| 8.4 | Brasserie Beck | Belgian | Upmarket | $55 |
| 8.4 | Kaz Sushi Bistro | Japanese | Upmarket | $55 |
| 8.0 | Morrison-Clark Inn | Southern | Upmarket | $60 |
| 8.0 | Georgia Brown's | Southern | Upmarket | $55 |
| 7.9 | Morton's | Steakhouse | Upmarket | $100 |
| 7.8 | Ruth's Chris Steakhouse | Steakhouse | Upmarket | $90 |
| 7.6 | Round Robin Bar | American | Bar | $40 |
| 7.4 | TenPenh | Pan-Asian | Upmarket | $70 |
| 7.4 | Potbelly Sandwich Works | Sandwiches | Counter | $10 |
| 7.4 | Oceanaire Seafood Room | Seafood | Upmarket | $82 |
| 7.4 | Five Guys | American | Counter | $10 |
| 7.3 | Coco Sala | New American | Upmarket | $50 |
| 7.3 | DC Coast | Seafood, New American | Upmarket | $75 |
| 7.2 | Firehook | Baked goods | Counter | $10 |
| 7.0 | Ceiba | Nuevo Latino | Upmarket | $60 |
| 7.0 | Mio | New American | Upmarket | $70 |
| 7.0 | Yee Hwa | Korean, Japanese | Casual | $40 |
| 6.9 | Old Ebbitt Grill | American | Casual | $40 |
| 6.7 | Fogo de Chão | Brazilian, Steakhouse | Upmarket | $80 |
| 6.6 | Capitol City Brewery | American | Casual | $35 |
| 6.6 | Chop't | American | Counter | $10 |
| 6.1 | Chef Geoff's | New American | Upmarket | $50 |
| 6.0 | Finn & Porter | American | Upmarket | $75 |
| 5.3 | Il Mulino | Italian | Upmarket | $80 |
| 5.1 | The Brown Bag | Sandwiches | Counter | $15 |
| 5.0 | Lima | Nuevo Latino, Cuban | Upmarket | $55 |
| 4.5 | Camille's Sidewalk Café | Sandwiches, Baked goods | Café | $25 |
| 4.4 | Naan & Beyond | Indian | Counter | $25 |
| | Marvelous Market | Groceries, Baked goods | Market | |

## Dulles International Airport

| | | | |
|------|------|------|------|
| 7.4 | Potbelly Sandwich Works | Sandwiches | Counter | $10 |
| 7.4 | Five Guys | American | Counter | $10 |
| 6.7 | Harry's Tap Room | American | Casual | $50 |
| 4.9 | Gordon Biersch | American | Casual | $35 |
| 2.8 | California Tortilla | Mexican | Counter | $10 |

## Dupont

| | | | |
|------|------|------|------|
| 9.7 | Komi | New American, Greek | Upmarket | $140 |
| 9.3 | Obelisk | Italian | Upmarket | $110 |
| 9.1 | Hank's Oyster Bar | Seafood | Upmarket | $45 |
| 9.0 | Vidalia | Southern, New American | Upmarket | $70 |
| 8.9 | Pesce | Seafood | Upmarket | $60 |
| 8.8 | Al Tiramisú | Italian | Upmarket | $55 |
| 8.6 | Nora | New American | Upmarket | $80 |
| 8.5 | Urbana | New American, Pizza | Upmarket | $55 |
| 8.4 | Sakana | Japanese | Casual | $35 |
| 8.3 | Bistrot du Coin | French | Casual | $50 |
| 8.2 | Pizzeria Paradiso | Pizza | Casual | $30 |
| 8.1 | C.F. Folks | American | Casual | $20 |
| 8.0 | Afterwords Café | American | Café | $35 |
| 8.0 | La Baguette | French, Sandwiches | Counter | $15 |
| 7.9 | Firefly | New American | Upmarket | $60 |
| 7.8 | Ruth's Chris Steakhouse | Steakhouse | Upmarket | $90 |
| 7.6 | Tabard Inn | American | Upmarket | $55 |
| 7.5 | Sam & Harry's | Steakhouse | Upmarket | $85 |
| 7.4 | Mar de Plata | Spanish, Seafood | Casual | $50 |
| 7.4 | Potbelly Sandwich Works | Sandwiches | Counter | $10 |
| 7.4 | Five Guys | American | Counter | $10 |

## Dupont *continued*

| | | | |
|---|---|---|---|
| 7.2 | Heritage India | Indian | Casual | $40 |
| 7.2 | Firehook | Baked goods | Counter | $10 |
| 7.1 | Malaysia Kopitiam | Malaysian | Casual | $25 |
| 7.1 | Julia's Empanadas | Latin American | Counter | $5 |
| 7.0 | The Palm | Steakhouse | Upmarket | $95 |
| 7.0 | Regent Thai | Thai | Casual | $35 |
| 7.0 | Moby Dick | Middle Eastern | Casual | $25 |
| 7.0 | Nage | New American, Seafood | Upmarket | $60 |
| 6.9 | Annie's Paramount | American, Steakhouse | Casual | $35 |
| 6.9 | Straits of Malaya | Malaysian | Casual | $35 |
| 6.6 | Java House | Middle Eastern | Counter | $10 |
| 6.6 | Sette Osteria | Italian, Pizza | Casual | $40 |
| 6.6 | Chop't | American | Counter | $10 |
| 6.5 | Veritas Wine Bar | New American | Wine bar | $40 |
| 6.5 | Alero | Mexican | Casual | $40 |
| 6.4 | Zorba's Café | Greek, Sandwiches | Counter | $25 |
| 6.3 | Mandu | Korean | Casual | $40 |
| 6.3 | DC Café | Middle Eastern | Counter | $25 |
| 6.2 | Rosemary's Thyme Bistro | American, Italian | Casual | $40 |
| 6.2 | Etrusco | Italian | Upmarket | $60 |
| 6.2 | Teaism | Pan-Asian | Café | $20 |
| 5.9 | Mai Thai | Thai | Casual | $35 |
| 5.9 | Sesto Senso | Italian | Upmarket | $55 |
| 5.9 | Thaiphoon | Thai | Casual | $40 |
| 5.9 | Asylum | American | Bar | $25 |
| 5.9 | Eli's | Sandwiches, American | Casual | $20 |
| 5.8 | The Big Hunt | American | Bar | $20 |
| 5.7 | Circa | Italian | Casual | $40 |
| 5.7 | Couscous Café | Moroccan, Middle Eastern | Counter | $10 |
| 5.7 | Bertucci's | Italian, Pizza | Casual | $35 |
| 5.6 | Darlington House | New American | Upmarket | $65 |
| 5.6 | Thai Chef | Thai, Japanese | Casual | $40 |
| 5.6 | Johnny Rockets | American | Casual | $25 |
| 5.3 | Alberto's Stone Oven Pizza | Pizza | Counter | $5 |
| 5.2 | Beacon Bar & Grill | New American | Casual | $45 |
| 5.0 | Marrakesh Palace | Moroccan | Upmarket | $45 |
| 4.6 | La Tomate | Italian | Upmarket | $45 |
| 4.6 | Uni | Japanese | Casual | $40 |
| 4.4 | Raku | Pan-Asian | Upmarket | $35 |
| 4.3 | Skewers | Middle Eastern | Casual | $30 |
| 4.3 | Café Luna | American, Italian | Casual | $35 |
| 4.2 | Luna Grill & Diner | American, Italian | Casual | $30 |
| 4.0 | Brickskeller | American | Bar | $15 |
| 3.8 | The Front Page | American | Casual | $35 |
| 3.7 | I Ricchi | Italian | Upmarket | $80 |
| 3.6 | Dupont Italian Kitchen | Italian | Casual | $40 |
| 3.5 | Café Citron | Nuevo Latino | Casual | $35 |
| 3.2 | Sala Thai | Thai | Casual | $25 |
| 2.7 | Buca di Beppo | Italian | Casual | $30 |
| | Marvelous Market | Groceries, Baked goods | Market | |

## Fairfax, VA

| | | | |
|---|---|---|---|
| 8.6 | China Star | Chinese | Casual | $15 |
| 7.8 | Ruth's Chris Steakhouse | Steakhouse | Upmarket | $90 |
| 7.4 | Five Guys | American | Counter | $10 |
| 7.4 | Bombay Bistro | Indian | Casual | $25 |
| 7.0 | Moby Dick | Middle Eastern | Casual | $25 |
| 6.9 | Red Hot & Blue | Barbecue | Casual | $15 |
| 2.8 | California Tortilla | Mexican | Counter | $10 |
| | Trader Joe's | Groceries | Market | |
| | Whole Foods Market | Groceries | Market | |

## Falls Church, VA

| | | | | |
|---|---|---|---|---|
| 9.0 | Hai Duong | Vietnamese | Casual | $15 |
| 9.0 | Thanh Tong | Vietnamese | Casual | $15 |
| 8.9 | Hong Kong Palace | Chinese | Casual | $15 |
| 8.8 | Cho Cu Sai Gon | Chinese, Vietnamese | Casual | $20 |
| 8.7 | Ngoc Anh | Vietnamese | Casual | $25 |
| 8.7 | Com Tam Saigon | Vietnamese | Casual | $10 |
| 8.6 | Meaza | Ethiopian | Casual | $20 |
| 8.2 | Myanmar | Burmese | Casual | $30 |
| 8.0 | 2941 Restaurant | New American | Upmarket | $100 |
| 7.8 | Full Kee | Chinese | Casual | $25 |
| 7.7 | Peking Gourmet Inn | Chinese | Casual | $35 |
| 7.7 | Crisp & Juicy | Latin American | Counter | $10 |
| 7.5 | Pollo Campero | Latin American | Counter | $10 |
| 7.4 | Five Guys | American | Counter | $10 |
| 7.2 | Pho Xe Lua | Vietnamese | Casual | $15 |
| 6.9 | Red Hot & Blue | Barbecue | Casual | $15 |
| 6.6 | Chevys Fresh Mex | Mexican | Casual | $30 |
| 6.4 | Mark's Duck House | Chinese | Casual | $30 |
| 5.9 | Tara Thai | Thai | Casual | $25 |
| 5.7 | Sunflower Vegetarian | Chinese | Casual | $20 |
| 1.4 | Prince Café | Middle Eastern | Casual | $25 |
| | Trader Joe's | Groceries | Market | |
| | Whole Foods Market | Groceries | Market | |

## Farragut

| | | | | |
|---|---|---|---|---|
| 8.7 | Taberna del Alabardero | Spanish | Upmarket | $75 |
| 8.7 | BLT Steak | Steakhouse | Upmarket | $95 |
| 8.5 | The Oval Room | New American | Upmarket | $75 |
| 8.5 | Prime Rib | Steakhouse | Upmarket | $90 |
| 8.3 | Smith & Wollensky | Steakhouse | Upmarket | $85 |
| 8.2 | Founding Farmers | American | Upmarket | $50 |
| 8.1 | Bombay Club | Indian | Upmarket | $45 |
| 8.1 | Bread Line | Sandwiches | Café | $15 |
| 7.4 | Potbelly Sandwich Works | Sandwiches | Counter | $10 |
| 7.3 | Spezie | Italian | Upmarket | $80 |
| 7.2 | Firehook | Baked goods | Counter | $10 |
| 7.2 | Stoupsy's | Greek | Counter | $5 |
| 7.1 | El Chalán | Peruvian | Casual | $45 |
| 7.1 | Greek Deli | Greek, Sandwiches | Counter | $15 |
| 7.0 | McCormick & Schmick's | Seafood | Upmarket | $60 |
| 6.8 | The Lafayette Room | New American | Upmarket | $85 |
| 6.6 | Nooshi | Pan-Asian, Japanese | Casual | $25 |
| 6.4 | Nirvana | Indian | Casual | $35 |
| 6.2 | Teaism | Pan-Asian | Café | $20 |
| 6.1 | Teatro Goldoni | Italian | Upmarket | $90 |
| 5.1 | Singapore Bistro | Pan-Asian | Casual | $25 |
| 5.0 | Skye Lounge | Middle Eastern, American | Casual | $40 |
| 5.0 | Café Asia | Pan-Asian | Casual | $30 |
| 4.9 | Java Green | Sandwiches, Baked goods | Café | $20 |
| 4.7 | Aroma | Indian | Casual | $25 |
| 4.4 | Naan & Beyond | Indian | Counter | $25 |
| | Dickey's Frozen Custard | Sandwiches, Ice cream | Counter | |

## Foggy Bottom

| | | | | |
|---|---|---|---|---|
| 7.4 | DISH + drinks | New American | Upmarket | $55 |
| 7.4 | Potbelly Sandwich Works | Sandwiches | Counter | $10 |
| 7.3 | Kinkead's | Seafood | Upmarket | $75 |
| 6.8 | La Prima | Sandwiches | Counter | $20 |
| 6.6 | Chop't | American | Counter | $10 |
| 6.1 | Primi Piatti | Italian | Upmarket | $70 |
| 5.9 | Burrito Brothers | Mexican | Counter | $20 |

## Foggy Bottom *continued*

| 5.7 | Bertucci's | Italian, Pizza | Casual | $35 |
| 5.6 | Johnny Rockets | American | Casual | $25 |
| 5.1 | The Brown Bag | Sandwiches | Counter | $15 |
| | M. E. Swing | Baked goods | Café | |
| | Marvelous Market | Groceries, Baked goods | Market | |
| | Trader Joe's | Groceries | Market | |

## Gaithersburg, MD

| 8.3 | Rainbow Restaurant | Ghanaian | Casual | $20 |
| 7.5 | Pollo Campero | Latin American | Counter | $10 |
| 7.0 | Moby Dick | Middle Eastern | Casual | $25 |
| 6.9 | Red Hot & Blue | Barbecue | Casual | $15 |
| 6.6 | Chevys Fresh Mex | Mexican | Casual | $30 |
| 5.9 | Tara Thai | Thai | Casual | $25 |
| | Trader Joe's | Groceries | Market | |
| | Whole Foods Market | Groceries | Market | |

## Georgetown

| 9.1 | Citronelle | New American, French | Upmarket | $210 |
| 8.3 | Hook | Seafood | Upmarket | $80 |
| 8.2 | Pizzeria Paradiso | Pizza | Casual | $30 |
| 8.2 | Tackle Box | Seafood | Casual | $25 |
| 8.1 | ching ching CHA | Chinese | Café | $25 |
| 7.9 | Morton's | Steakhouse | Upmarket | $100 |
| 7.9 | 1789 | New American | Upmarket | $100 |
| 7.7 | Agraria | New American | Upmarket | $60 |
| 7.7 | Café Tu-O-Tu | Turkish, Sandwiches | Counter | $15 |
| 7.6 | Leopold's Kafe | Austrian | Casual | $40 |
| 7.6 | Mendocino Grille | New American | Wine bar | $60 |
| 7.6 | Amma Vegetarian Kitchen | Indian | Casual | $20 |
| 7.5 | La Chaumière | French | Upmarket | $60 |
| 7.4 | Neyla | Middle Eastern | Upmarket | $70 |
| 7.4 | Five Guys | American | Counter | $10 |
| 7.3 | Bourbon Steak | New American | Upmarket | $115 |
| 7.3 | Patisserie Poupon | Baked goods, Sandwiches | Café | $35 |
| 7.0 | Moby Dick | Middle Eastern | Casual | $25 |
| 6.7 | Bean Counter | Baked goods | Café | $15 |
| 6.5 | Café Bonaparte | French | Café | $45 |
| 6.4 | Martin's Tavern | American | Casual | $35 |
| 6.3 | Peacock Café | New American | Upmarket | $60 |
| 6.3 | Old Glory Bar-B-Que | Barbecue | Casual | $30 |
| 6.1 | Café Milano | Italian | Upmarket | $75 |
| 5.9 | Bistro Français | French | Casual | $40 |
| 5.9 | Maté | Pan-Asian | Casual | $45 |
| 5.8 | Filomena | Italian | Casual | $50 |
| 5.7 | Armand's | Pizza | Casual | $25 |
| 5.6 | Johnny Rockets | American | Casual | $25 |
| 5.5 | Bangkok Joe's | Pan-Asian | Casual | $45 |
| 5.4 | La Madeleine | French, Sandwiches | Counter | $30 |
| 5.1 | Clyde's | American | Casual | $40 |
| 4.9 | Aditi Indian Cuisine | Indian | Casual | $35 |
| 4.8 | Mie N Yu | Pan-Asian | Upmarket | $55 |
| 4.6 | The Tombs | American | Bar | $25 |
| 4.5 | Paolo's | Italian | Casual | $40 |
| 4.3 | Vietnam Georgetown | Vietnamese | Casual | $30 |
| 4.3 | J. Paul's | American | Casual | $45 |
| 3.9 | Tony & Joe's Seafood Place | Seafood | Upmarket | $55 |
| 3.9 | Sequoia | New American | Upmarket | $50 |
| 3.7 | Harmony Café | Chinese | Casual | $15 |
| 3.6 | Zed's Ethiopian Restaurant | Ethiopian | Casual | $30 |
| 1.4 | Prince Café | Middle Eastern | Casual | $25 |

### Georgetown *continued*

| | | | |
|---|---|---|---|
| Dean & Deluca | Groceries | Market | |
| Dolcezza | Ice cream, Baked goods | Counter | |
| Marvelous Market | Groceries, Baked goods | Market | |
| Sweetgreen | American, Ice cream | Counter | |
| Thomas Sweet | Ice cream | Counter | |
| Whole Foods Market | Groceries | Market | |

### Germantown, MD

| | | | | |
|---|---|---|---|---|
| 7.9 | La Casita | Salvadoran | Casual | $10 |

### Glover Park

| | | | | |
|---|---|---|---|---|
| 8.5 | Sushi-Ko | Japanese | Upmarket | $60 |
| 8.1 | Bourbon | American | Bar | $35 |
| 7.4 | Café Divan | Turkish | Casual | $35 |
| 7.2 | Heritage India | Indian | Casual | $40 |
| 5.6 | Rocklands | Barbecue | Casual | $15 |
| | Max's Best Ice Cream | Ice cream | Counter | |

### Great Falls, VA

| | | | | |
|---|---|---|---|---|
| 6.0 | L'Auberge Chez François | French | Upmarket | $110 |

### Hyattsville, MD

| | | | | |
|---|---|---|---|---|
| 8.7 | Tabeer | Pakistani | Casual | $25 |
| 8.2 | Irene's Pupusas | Salvadoran | Casual | $25 |
| 8.0 | Don Pollo | Latin American | Counter | $15 |
| 7.9 | El Dorado | Salvadoran | Counter | $10 |
| 6.0 | Cococabana Bar & Grill | Italian, Mexican, American | Casual | $30 |

### Logan Circle

| | | | | |
|---|---|---|---|---|
| 9.0 | Posto | Italian, Pizza | Upmarket | $55 |
| 8.5 | Great Wall Szechuan | Chinese | Casual | $25 |
| 7.5 | Cork | New American | Wine bar | $40 |
| 7.4 | Mar de Plata | Spanish, Seafood | Casual | $50 |
| 6.8 | Thai Tanic | Thai | Casual | $30 |
| 6.2 | Stoney's Bar & Grill | American | Casual | $40 |
| 5.9 | 15 Ria | New American | Upmarket | $60 |
| 5.1 | The Brown Bag | Sandwiches | Counter | $15 |
| 4.8 | ACKC Cocoa Bar | Sweet drinks, Baked goods | Café | $10 |
| 4.6 | Veranda | Greek, Italian, American | Casual | $40 |
| 4.4 | Rice | Thai | Upmarket | $30 |
| 4.4 | Raku | Pan-Asian | Upmarket | $35 |
| 4.0 | Commissary | American | Casual | $30 |
| 3.8 | Logan Tavern | American | Casual | $35 |
| | Whole Foods Market | Groceries | Market | |

### Mt. Vernon Square

| | | | | |
|---|---|---|---|---|
| 8.8 | Corduroy | New American | Upmarket | $70 |
| 8.0 | Two Quail | French | Upmarket | $60 |
| 7.8 | Akosombo | Ghanian | Casual | $15 |
| 7.5 | Busboys & Poets | American | Casual | $25 |
| 7.1 | Acadiana | Southern | Upmarket | $60 |
| 6.7 | Marrakesh | Moroccan | Upmarket | $50 |
| 5.8 | Vegetate | New American | Upmarket | $45 |

### Nationals Park

| | | | | |
|---|---|---|---|---|
| 8.1 | Ben's Chili Bowl | American | Counter | $15 |
| 7.4 | Five Guys | American | Counter | $10 |
| 6.9 | Red Hot & Blue | Barbecue | Casual | $15 |
| 4.3 | Hard Times Café | American | Casual | $20 |

## Northeast DC

| | | | |
|---|---|---|---|
| 7.6 | Deli City | Southern, Sandwiches | Counter | $15 |
| 6.0 | The Red and the Black | Southern | Bar | $25 |
| 6.0 | Granville Moore's Brickyard | Belgian | Casual | $40 |

## Palisades

| | | | |
|---|---|---|---|
| 9.4 | Makoto | Japanese | Upmarket | $80 |
| 8.3 | Kotobuki | Japanese | Casual | $25 |
| 7.9 | BlackSalt | Seafood | Upmarket | $45 |
| 7.1 | Kemble Park Tavern | New American | Upmarket | $60 |
| | Marvelous Market | Groceries, Baked goods | Market | |

## Penn Quarter

| | | | |
|---|---|---|---|
| 9.5 | Minibar | New American | Upmarket | $160 |
| 9.2 | Poste Moderne Brasserie | New American | Upmarket | $80 |
| 8.8 | Central Michel Richard | French, New American | Upmarket | $70 |
| 8.8 | The Source | New American | Upmarket | $120 |
| 8.6 | Rasika | Indian | Upmarket | $70 |
| 8.4 | Proof | New American | Wine bar | $55 |
| 8.3 | Zola | New American | Upmarket | $60 |
| 8.2 | Taquería Nacional | Mexican | Counter | $15 |
| 8.0 | Oyamel | Mexican | Upmarket | $60 |
| 7.8 | Café Atlántico | Nuevo Latino | Upmarket | $75 |
| 7.6 | Equinox | New American | Upmarket | $75 |
| 7.4 | Potbelly Sandwich Works | Sandwiches | Counter | $10 |
| 7.3 | Jaleo | Spanish | Upmarket | $50 |
| 7.2 | Firehook | Baked goods | Counter | $10 |
| 7.1 | District Chophouse | Steakhouse, American | Casual | $45 |
| 7.1 | Oya | Pan-Asian | Upmarket | $75 |
| 7.1 | The Caucus Room | Steakhouse, American | Upmarket | $90 |
| 7.0 | McCormick & Schmick's | Seafood | Upmarket | $60 |
| 6.9 | Bistro Italiano | Italian | Casual | $25 |
| 6.5 | Capital Grille | Steakhouse, American | Upmarket | $85 |
| 6.2 | Teaism | Pan-Asian | Café | $20 |
| 5.8 | Rosa Mexicano | Mexican | Upmarket | $55 |
| 4.9 | Gordon Biersch | American | Casual | $35 |
| 4.8 | 701 | New American | Upmarket | $70 |
| 4.8 | Asia Nine | Pan-Asian | Casual | $35 |
| 4.5 | Camille's Sidewalk Café | Sandwiches, Baked goods | Café | $25 |
| 2.9 | Austin Grill | Mexican | Casual | $30 |

## Petworth

| | | | |
|---|---|---|---|
| 8.0 | Taquería Distrito Federal | Mexican | Casual | $20 |
| 7.7 | W Domku | Scandinavian, Polish | Casual | $40 |
| 7.7 | Sweet Mango Café | Caribbean | Casual | $25 |

## Potomac, MD

| | | | |
|---|---|---|---|
| 6.6 | Amici Miei | Italian | Casual | $50 |
| 5.1 | Pomegranate Bistro | New American | Upmarket | $60 |
| 2.8 | California Tortilla | Mexican | Counter | $10 |

## Purcellville, VA

| | | | |
|---|---|---|---|
| 6.4 | Al's Pizza | Pizza | Counter | $20 |

## Reagan National Airport

| | | | |
|---|---|---|---|
| 7.4 | Potbelly Sandwich Works | Sandwiches | Counter | $10 |
| 7.4 | Five Guys | American | Counter | $10 |
| 4.9 | Gordon Biersch | American | Casual | $35 |
| 2.8 | California Tortilla | Mexican | Counter | $10 |

## Rockville, MD

| | | | | |
|---|---|---|---|---|
| 8.8 | Light House Tofu | Korean | Casual | $15 |
| 8.6 | Bob's Noodle 66 | Taiwanese, Chinese | Casual | $15 |
| 8.4 | A & J Restaurant | Chinese | Casual | $30 |
| 8.0 | Houston's | American | Upmarket | $55 |
| 7.7 | Crisp & Juicy | Latin American | Counter | $10 |
| 7.4 | Five Guys | American | Counter | $10 |
| 7.4 | Bombay Bistro | Indian | Casual | $25 |
| 7.3 | Urban Bar-B-Que Company | Barbecue | Counter | $25 |
| 7.1 | Nicaro | New American | Upmarket | $75 |
| 7.0 | Moby Dick | Middle Eastern | Casual | $25 |
| 5.9 | Tara Thai | Thai | Casual | $25 |
| 5.7 | La Tasca | Spanish | Casual | $40 |
| 5.7 | Armand's | Pizza | Casual | $25 |
| 5.6 | Rocklands | Barbecue | Casual | $15 |
| 5.4 | La Madeleine | French, Sandwiches | Counter | $30 |
| 5.3 | Yuan Fu | Chinese | Casual | $25 |
| 4.9 | Gordon Biersch | American | Casual | $35 |
| 4.3 | Hard Times Café | American | Casual | $20 |
| 2.9 | Austin Grill | Mexican | Casual | $30 |
| 2.8 | California Tortilla | Mexican | Counter | $10 |
| | Trader Joe's | Groceries | Market | |
| | Whole Foods Market | Groceries | Market | |

## Shaw

| | | | | |
|---|---|---|---|---|
| 8.8 | Shashemene | Ethiopian | Casual | $25 |
| 8.8 | Etete | Ethiopian | Casual | $30 |
| 8.5 | Oohhs & Aahhs | Southern | Counter | $25 |
| 8.3 | Thai X-ing | Thai | Casual | $30 |
| 8.1 | Queen Makeda | Ethiopian | Casual | $30 |
| 7.8 | Dukem | Ethiopian | Casual | $25 |
| 7.5 | El Khartoum | Sudanese | Counter | $20 |
| 7.1 | Axum | Ethiopian | Casual | $25 |
| 6.8 | Madjet | Ethiopian | Casual | $23 |
| 6.5 | Negril | Caribbean | Counter | $15 |

## Silver Spring, MD

| | | | | |
|---|---|---|---|---|
| 8.9 | Roger Miller Restaurant | Cameroonian | Casual | $30 |
| 8.9 | Oriental East | Chinese | Casual | $40 |
| 8.3 | Thai Market | Thai | Counter | $20 |
| 8.2 | Irene's Pupusas | Salvadoran | Casual | $25 |
| 8.2 | Ray's the Classics | Steakhouse, American | Upmarket | $45 |
| 8.1 | Quarry House Tavern | American | Casual | $25 |
| 7.9 | La Casita | Salvadoran | Casual | $10 |
| 7.9 | Langano | Ethiopian | Casual | $25 |
| 7.7 | Crisp & Juicy | Latin American | Counter | $10 |
| 7.5 | Taverna the Greek Islands | Greek | Casual | $35 |
| 7.4 | Potbelly Sandwich Works | Sandwiches | Counter | $10 |
| 7.4 | Five Guys | American | Counter | $10 |
| 7.3 | Urban Bar-B-Que Company | Barbecue | Counter | $25 |
| 7.0 | Cakelove and Love Café | Baked goods, Sandwiches | Café | $10 |
| 7.0 | Moby Dick | Middle Eastern | Casual | $25 |
| 6.5 | Mandalay | Burmese | Casual | $25 |
| 6.5 | Negril | Caribbean | Counter | $15 |
| 6.2 | Cubano's | Cuban | Casual | $35 |
| 5.7 | Armand's | Pizza | Casual | $25 |
| 5.6 | Bombay Restaurant | Indian | Casual | $30 |
| 3.7 | Olazzo | Italian | Upmarket | $45 |
| 2.9 | Austin Grill | Mexican | Casual | $30 |
| 2.8 | California Tortilla | Mexican | Counter | $10 |
| | Trader Joe's | Groceries | Market | |
| | Whole Foods Market | Groceries | Market | |

## Southwest DC

| | | | | |
|---|---|---|---|---|
| 9.6 | CityZen | New American | Upmarket | $120 |
| 7.9 | Mitsitam Native Foods Café | American | Counter | $35 |
| 7.7 | The Wharf Seafood | Seafood | Counter | $25 |
| 7.4 | Potbelly Sandwich Works | Sandwiches | Counter | $10 |
| 7.2 | Cantina Marina | Southern | Casual | $35 |
| | Maine Avenue Fish Market | Groceries, Seafood | Market | |

## Springfield, VA

| | | | | |
|---|---|---|---|---|
| 8.9 | Gamasot | Korean | Casual | $15 |
| 5.7 | Bertucci's | Italian, Pizza | Casual | $35 |
| 2.9 | Austin Grill | Mexican | Casual | $30 |
| | Trader Joe's | Groceries | Market | |
| | Whole Foods Market | Groceries | Market | |

## Takoma Park, MD

| | | | | |
|---|---|---|---|---|
| 9.0 | Teddy's Roti Shop | Caribbean | Counter | $15 |
| 8.4 | Pollo Granjero | Latin American | Counter | $15 |
| 8.2 | Mogotillo | Salvadoran, Mexican | Casual | $20 |
| 7.1 | Udupi Palace | Indian | Casual | $20 |

## Tysons Corner, VA

| | | | | |
|---|---|---|---|---|
| 7.9 | Morton's | Steakhouse | Upmarket | $100 |
| 7.8 | Ruth's Chris Steakhouse | Steakhouse | Upmarket | $90 |
| 7.5 | Lebanese Taverna | Middle Eastern | Casual | $40 |
| 7.5 | La Sandía | Mexican | Upmarket | $50 |
| 7.4 | Five Guys | American | Counter | $10 |
| 7.2 | Firehook | Baked goods | Counter | $10 |
| 7.0 | The Palm | Steakhouse | Upmarket | $95 |
| 7.0 | McCormick & Schmick's | Seafood | Upmarket | $60 |
| 7.0 | Cakelove and Love Café | Baked goods, Sandwiches | Café | $10 |
| 7.0 | Moby Dick | Middle Eastern | Casual | $25 |
| 7.0 | Tachibana | Japanese | Casual | $45 |
| 6.9 | Fleming's | Steakhouse | Upmarket | $90 |
| 6.8 | La Prima | Sandwiches | Counter | $20 |
| 6.5 | Capital Grille | Steakhouse, American | Upmarket | $85 |
| 5.7 | Bertucci's | Italian, Pizza | Casual | $35 |
| 5.4 | La Madeleine | French, Sandwiches | Counter | $30 |
| 5.1 | Clyde's | American | Casual | $40 |
| 4.9 | Gordon Biersch | American | Casual | $35 |
| | Marvelous Market | Groceries, Baked goods | Market | |

## U Street

| | | | | |
|---|---|---|---|---|
| 9.1 | Marvin | Southern, Belgian | Upmarket | $45 |
| 9.0 | Al Crostino | Italian | Upmarket | $55 |
| 8.1 | Ben's Chili Bowl | American | Counter | $15 |
| 8.0 | Coppi's Organic | Italian, Pizza | Upmarket | $50 |
| 8.0 | Crème | Southern | Casual | $45 |
| 7.5 | Busboys & Poets | American | Casual | $25 |
| 7.5 | Ulah Bistro | American | Upmarket | $45 |
| 7.3 | Vinoteca | New American | Wine bar | $45 |
| 7.2 | Florida Avenue Grill | Southern | Casual | $15 |
| 7.1 | Tabaq Bistro | Middle Eastern | Upmarket | $45 |
| 7.0 | Chi-Cha Lounge | Latin American | Casual | $30 |
| 7.0 | Cakelove and Love Café | Baked goods, Sandwiches | Café | $10 |
| 6.5 | Alero | Mexican | Casual | $40 |
| 6.3 | Station 9 | New American | Upmarket | $45 |
| 6.2 | Café Saint-Ex | French, American | Casual | $40 |
| 5.7 | The Islander Caribbean | Caribbean | Casual | $25 |
| 5.5 | Local 16 | American | Upmarket | $40 |
| 3.2 | Sala Thai | Thai | Casual | $25 |

## Union Station

| | | | |
|---|---|---|---|
| | Union Station Food Court | | Counter | |

## Upper NW

| | | | | |
|---|---|---|---|---|
| 8.4 | Buck's Fishing & Camping | Southern, New American | Upmarket | $60 |
| 7.4 | Potbelly Sandwich Works | Sandwiches | Counter | $10 |
| 6.9 | Comet Ping Pong | Pizza | Casual | $35 |
| 6.5 | Café Olé | Middle Eastern, American | Casual | $30 |
| 6.1 | Chef Geoff's | New American | Upmarket | $50 |
| 5.9 | Tara Thai | Thai | Casual | $25 |
| 1.4 | Prince Café | Middle Eastern | Casual | $25 |
| | Marvelous Market | Groceries, Baked goods | Market | |
| | Whole Foods Market | Groceries | Market | |

## Vienna, VA

| | | | | |
|---|---|---|---|---|
| 7.6 | Amma Vegetarian Kitchen | Indian | Casual | $20 |
| 5.9 | Tara Thai | Thai | Casual | $25 |
| 4.9 | Aditi Indian Cuisine | Indian | Casual | $35 |
| | Whole Foods Market | Groceries | Market | |

## Washington, VA

| | | | | |
|---|---|---|---|---|
| 8.0 | Inn at Little Washington | New American | Upmarket | $250 |

## West End

| | | | | |
|---|---|---|---|---|
| 9.4 | Westend Bistro | New American | Upmarket | $65 |
| 8.8 | Marcel's | French | Upmarket | $90 |
| 7.8 | Blue Duck Tavern | New American | Upmarket | $80 |
| 7.2 | Bread & Chocolate | French | Café | $15 |
| 6.9 | Circle Bistro | New American | Upmarket | $70 |
| 6.3 | Grillfish | Seafood | Upmarket | $45 |
| 5.8 | Hudson | New American | Upmarket | $65 |
| 4.5 | Meiwah | Chinese, Japanese | Casual | $45 |

## Wheaton, MD

| | | | | |
|---|---|---|---|---|
| 8.5 | El Pollo Rico | Latin American | Counter | $10 |
| 8.4 | Nava Thai | Thai | Casual | $25 |
| 7.5 | Pollo Campero | Latin American | Counter | $10 |

## Woodley Park

| | | | | |
|---|---|---|---|---|
| 7.5 | Lebanese Taverna | Middle Eastern | Casual | $40 |
| 6.9 | Petits Plats | French | Casual | $45 |
| 6.5 | Open City | American | Café | $40 |
| 5.7 | Tono Sushi | Japanese | Casual | $40 |
| 4.6 | Mr. Chen's | Chinese | Casual | $25 |

# By special feature

Ranked by food rating.

| | Breakfast | Cuisine | Location | Type | Price |
|---|---|---|---|---|---|
| 9.2 | Poste Moderne Brasserie | New American | Penn Quarter | Upmarket | $80 |
| 9.1 | Adour | French | Downtown | Upmarket | $125 |
| 9.0 | Hai Duong | Vietnamese | Falls Church, VA | Casual | $15 |
| 8.9 | Bistro Bis | French | Capitol Hill | Upmarket | $70 |
| 8.9 | Gamasot | Korean | Springfield, VA | Casual | $15 |
| 8.6 | Café du Parc | French | Downtown | Upmarket | $60 |
| 8.6 | Kabob Palace | Middle Eastern | Arlington, VA | Counter | $20 |
| 8.5 | Urbana | New American | Dupont | Upmarket | $55 |
| 8.5 | Oohhs & Aahhs | Southern | Shaw | Counter | $25 |
| 8.3 | Thai Market | Thai | Silver Spring, MD | Counter | $20 |
| 8.2 | Founding Farmers | American | Farragut | Upmarket | $50 |
| 8.2 | Taquería Nacional | Mexican | Penn Quarter | Counter | $15 |
| 8.1 | Ben's Chili Bowl | American | Multiple locations | Counter | $15 |
| 8.1 | Pupusería San Miguel | Salvadoran | Columbia Heights | Casual | $10 |
| 8.1 | Bread Line | Sandwiches | Farragut | Café | $15 |
| 8.1 | Cosmopolitan Bakery | Balkan | Alexandria, VA | Café | $25 |
| 8.0 | Afterwords Café | American | Dupont | Café | $35 |
| 8.0 | Morrison-Clark Inn | Southern | Downtown | Upmarket | $60 |
| 8.0 | La Baguette | French, Sandwiches | Dupont | Counter | $15 |
| 8.0 | Taquería Distrito Federal | Mexican | Multiple locations | Casual | $20 |
| 8.0 | Weenie Beanie | American | Arlington, VA | Counter | $5 |
| 7.9 | Firefly | New American | Dupont | Upmarket | $60 |
| 7.9 | La Casita | Salvadoran | Multiple locations | Casual | $10 |
| 7.9 | El Dorado | Salvadoran | Hyattsville, MD | Counter | $10 |
| 7.8 | Blue Duck Tavern | New American | West End | Upmarket | $80 |
| 7.8 | Johnny's Half Shell | Seafood | Capitol Hill | Upmarket | $65 |
| 7.7 | Café Tu-O-Tu | Turkish, Sandwiches | Georgetown | Counter | $15 |
| 7.7 | The Wharf Seafood | Seafood | Southwest DC | Counter | $25 |
| 7.7 | Bethesda Bagels | Sandwiches | Bethesda, MD | Counter | $10 |
| 7.6 | Tabard Inn | American | Dupont | Upmarket | $55 |
| 7.6 | Leopold's Kafe | Austrian | Georgetown | Casual | $40 |
| 7.6 | Deli City | Southern | Northeast DC | Counter | $15 |
| 7.5 | Busboys & Poets | American | Multiple locations | Casual | $25 |
| 7.5 | Earl's Sandwiches | Sandwiches | Arlington, VA | Counter | $15 |
| 7.4 | Jackson 20 | New American | Old Town | Upmarket | $65 |
| 7.4 | DISH + drinks | New American | Foggy Bottom | Upmarket | $55 |
| 7.4 | Potbelly Sandwich Works | Sandwiches | Multiple locations | Counter | $10 |
| 7.3 | Patisserie Poupon | Baked goods | Georgetown | Café | $35 |
| 7.3 | Mixtec | Mexican | Adams Morgan | Casual | $25 |
| 7.2 | Florida Avenue Grill | Southern | U Street | Casual | $15 |
| 7.2 | Pho Xe Lua | Vietnamese | Falls Church, VA | Casual | $15 |
| 7.2 | Jimmy T's | American | Capitol Hill | Casual | $25 |
| 7.2 | Firehook | Baked goods | Multiple locations | Counter | $10 |
| 7.2 | Stoupsy's | Greek | Farragut | Counter | $5 |
| 7.2 | Bread & Chocolate | French | Multiple locations | Café | $15 |
| 7.1 | Greek Deli | Greek, Sandwiches | Farragut | Counter | $15 |
| 7.0 | Cassatt's | American | Arlington, VA | Casual | $25 |
| 7.0 | Nage | New American | Dupont | Upmarket | $60 |
| 6.9 | Old Ebbitt Grill | American | Downtown | Casual | $40 |
| 6.8 | The Lafayette Room | New American | Farragut | Upmarket | $85 |
| 6.8 | La Prima | Sandwiches | Multiple locations | Counter | $20 |

## Breakfast *continued*

| | | | | | |
|---|---|---|---|---|---|
| 6.7 | Bagels & Baguettes | Sandwiches | Capitol Hill | Café | $10 |
| 6.7 | Bean Counter | Baked goods | Georgetown | Café | $15 |
| 6.6 | Java House | Middle Eastern | Dupont | Counter | $10 |
| 6.5 | Open City | American | Woodley Park | Café | $40 |
| 6.5 | Café Bonaparte | French | Georgetown | Café | $45 |
| 6.5 | Pete's Diner | American | Capitol Hill | Casual | $25 |
| 6.4 | Martin's Tavern | American | Georgetown | Casual | $35 |
| 6.2 | Le Bon Café | Baked goods | Capitol Hill | Café | $20 |
| 6.2 | Teaism | Pan-Asian | Multiple locations | Café | $20 |
| 6.0 | Tortilla Café | Salvadoran | Capitol Hill | Casual | $20 |
| 5.9 | El Tamarindo | Mexican | Adams Morgan | Casual | $40 |
| 5.9 | 15 Ria | New American | Logan Circle | Upmarket | $60 |
| 5.8 | Hudson | New American | West End | Upmarket | $65 |
| 5.8 | Sticky Fingers Bakery | Baked goods | Columbia Heights | Counter | $10 |
| 5.7 | Couscous Café | Moroccan | Dupont | Counter | $10 |
| 5.6 | Johnny Rockets | American | Multiple locations | Casual | $25 |
| 5.4 | La Madeleine | French, Sandwiches | Multiple locations | Counter | $30 |
| 5.2 | Beacon Bar & Grill | New American | Dupont | Casual | $45 |
| 5.1 | Tryst | American | Adams Morgan | Café | $25 |
| 5.1 | The Brown Bag | Sandwiches | Multiple locations | Counter | $15 |
| 4.9 | Java Green | Sandwiches | Farragut | Café | $20 |
| 4.5 | Camille's Sidewalk Café | Sandwiches | Multiple locations | Café | $25 |
| 4.3 | Café Luna | American, Italian | Dupont | Casual | $35 |
| 4.2 | Luna Grill & Diner | American, Italian | Multiple locations | Casual | $30 |
| 4.1 | Diner | American | Adams Morgan | Casual | $25 |
| 4.0 | Commissary | American | Logan Circle | Casual | $30 |
| | Dean & Deluca | Groceries | Georgetown | Market | |
| | Dickey's Frozen Custard | Sandwiches | Multiple locations | Counter | |
| | Eastern Market | Groceries | Capitol Hill | Market | |
| | M. E. Swing | Baked goods | Foggy Bottom | Café | |
| | Maine Avenue Fish Market | Groceries, Seafood | Southwest DC | Market | |
| | Marvelous Market | Groceries | Multiple locations | Market | |
| | Trader Joe's | Groceries | Multiple locations | Market | |
| | Whole Foods Market | Groceries | Multiple locations | Market | |

## Brunch

| | | | | | |
|---|---|---|---|---|---|
| 9.2 | Vermilion | New American | Old Town | Upmarket | $65 |
| 9.2 | Poste Moderne Brasserie | New American | Penn Quarter | Upmarket | $80 |
| 9.1 | Hank's Oyster Bar | Seafood | Multiple locations | Upmarket | $45 |
| 9.1 | Marvin | Southern, Belgian | U Street | Upmarket | $45 |
| 8.9 | Bistro Bis | French | Capitol Hill | Upmarket | $70 |
| 8.9 | Oriental East | Chinese | Silver Spring, MD | Casual | $40 |
| 8.8 | China Garden | Chinese | Arlington, VA | Casual | $20 |
| 8.6 | Montmartre | French | Capitol Hill | Upmarket | $60 |
| 8.6 | Liberty Tavern | American | Arlington, VA | Casual | $40 |
| 8.5 | Urbana | New American | Dupont | Upmarket | $55 |
| 8.4 | Brasserie Beck | Belgian | Downtown | Upmarket | $55 |
| 8.3 | Hook | Seafood | Georgetown | Upmarket | $80 |
| 8.1 | Bourbon | American | Multiple locations | Bar | $35 |
| 8.1 | RedRocks | Pizza | Columbia Heights | Casual | $35 |
| 8.0 | Afterwords Café | American | Dupont | Café | $35 |
| 8.0 | Morrison-Clark Inn | Southern | Downtown | Upmarket | $60 |
| 8.0 | Oyamel | Mexican | Penn Quarter | Upmarket | $60 |
| 8.0 | Commonwealth | British | Columbia Heights | Casual | $40 |
| 8.0 | Crème | Southern | U Street | Casual | $45 |
| 8.0 | Georgia Brown's | Southern | Downtown | Upmarket | $55 |
| 8.0 | Weenie Beanie | American | Arlington, VA | Counter | $5 |
| 7.9 | Cashion's Eat Place | New American | Adams Morgan | Upmarket | $60 |
| 7.9 | Firefly | New American | Dupont | Upmarket | $60 |
| 7.9 | Farrah Olivia | New American | Old Town | Upmarket | $65 |
| 7.9 | BlackSalt | Seafood | Palisades | Upmarket | $45 |
| 7.9 | Black's Bar & Kitchen | New American | Bethesda, MD | Upmarket | $75 |

## Brunch *continued*

| | | | | | |
|---|---|---|---|---|---|
| 7.8 | Blue Duck Tavern | New American | West End | Upmarket | $80 |
| 7.8 | Tallula | New American | Arlington, VA | Upmarket | $55 |
| 7.8 | Café Atlántico | Nuevo Latino | Penn Quarter | Upmarket | $75 |
| 7.7 | Agraria | New American | Georgetown | Upmarket | $60 |
| 7.6 | Tabard Inn | American | Dupont | Upmarket | $55 |
| 7.6 | Park Café | New American | Capitol Hill | Upmarket | $60 |
| 7.6 | Guajillo | Mexican | Arlington, VA | Casual | $35 |
| 7.5 | Busboys & Poets | American | Multiple locations | Casual | $25 |
| 7.5 | Ulah Bistro | American | U Street | Upmarket | $45 |
| 7.5 | La Sandía | Mexican | Tysons Corner, VA | Upmarket | $50 |
| 7.4 | Ardeo | New American | Cleveland Park | Upmarket | $65 |
| 7.4 | Jackson 20 | New American | Old Town | Upmarket | $65 |
| 7.3 | Coco Sala | New American | Downtown | Upmarket | $50 |
| 7.3 | Vinoteca | New American | U Street | Wine bar | $45 |
| 7.3 | Jaleo | Spanish | Multiple locations | Upmarket | $50 |
| 7.3 | Mixtec | Mexican | Adams Morgan | Casual | $25 |
| 7.2 | Heritage India | Indian | Multiple locations | Casual | $40 |
| 7.2 | Taquería El Poblano | Mexican | Multiple locations | Casual | $15 |
| 7.2 | Bread & Chocolate | French | Multiple locations | Café | $15 |
| 7.1 | Kemble Park Tavern | New American | Palisades | Upmarket | $60 |
| 7.1 | Tabaq Bistro | Middle Eastern | U Street | Upmarket | $45 |
| 7.1 | Acadiana | Southern | Mt. Vernon Square | Upmarket | $60 |
| 7.1 | District Chophouse | Steakhouse | Penn Quarter | Casual | $45 |
| 7.1 | Nicaro | New American | Rockville, MD | Upmarket | $75 |
| 7.0 | Nage | New American | Dupont | Upmarket | $60 |
| 6.9 | Old Ebbitt Grill | American | Downtown | Casual | $40 |
| 6.9 | Bastille | French | Old Town | Upmarket | $55 |
| 6.9 | Annie's Paramount | American | Dupont | Casual | $35 |
| 6.9 | Tunnicliff's Tavern | American | Capitol Hill | Casual | $40 |
| 6.9 | Petits Plats | French | Woodley Park | Casual | $45 |
| 6.9 | Whitlow's on Wilson | American | Arlington, VA | Casual | $35 |
| 6.9 | Carlyle | New American | Arlington, VA | Casual | $40 |
| 6.8 | Fadó | Irish | Chinatown | Bar | $27 |
| 6.8 | The Lafayette Room | New American | Farragut | Upmarket | $85 |
| 6.7 | Persimmon | New American | Chevy Chase, MD | Upmarket | $75 |
| 6.7 | White Tiger | Indian | Capitol Hill | Casual | $35 |
| 6.7 | Bagels & Baguettes | Sandwiches | Capitol Hill | Café | $10 |
| 6.7 | Harry's Tap Room | American | Multiple locations | Casual | $50 |
| 6.6 | Sette Osteria | Italian, Pizza | Dupont | Casual | $40 |
| 6.6 | Evening Star Café | New American | Alexandria, VA | Upmarket | $55 |
| 6.5 | Café Bonaparte | French | Georgetown | Café | $45 |
| 6.5 | Alero | Mexican | Multiple locations | Casual | $40 |
| 6.5 | Café Olé | Middle Eastern | Upper NW | Casual | $30 |
| 6.4 | Martin's Tavern | American | Georgetown | Casual | $35 |
| 6.4 | Mark's Duck House | Chinese | Falls Church, VA | Casual | $30 |
| 6.3 | Peacock Café | New American | Georgetown | Upmarket | $60 |
| 6.3 | Station 9 | New American | U Street | Upmarket | $45 |
| 6.3 | Old Glory Bar-B-Que | Barbecue | Georgetown | Casual | $30 |
| 6.2 | Café Saint-Ex | French, American | U Street | Casual | $40 |
| 6.2 | Rosemary's Thyme Bistro | American, Italian | Dupont | Casual | $40 |
| 6.2 | Stoney's Bar & Grill | American | Logan Circle | Casual | $40 |
| 6.1 | Chef Geoff's | New American | Multiple locations | Upmarket | $50 |
| 6.0 | La Ferme | French | Chevy Chase, MD | Upmarket | $60 |
| 5.9 | Bistro Français | French | Georgetown | Casual | $40 |
| 5.9 | Asylum | American | Dupont | Bar | $25 |
| 5.9 | 15 Ria | New American | Logan Circle | Upmarket | $60 |
| 5.9 | Eli's | Sandwiches | Dupont | Casual | $20 |
| 5.8 | Rosa Mexicano | Mexican | Penn Quarter | Upmarket | $55 |
| 5.8 | Hudson | New American | West End | Upmarket | $65 |
| 5.8 | Filomena | Italian | Georgetown | Casual | $50 |
| 5.7 | Circa | Italian | Dupont | Casual | $40 |
| 5.6 | Darlington House | New American | Dupont | Upmarket | $65 |

## Brunch _continued_

| 5.5 | Napoleon Bistro | French | Adams Morgan | Upmarket | $60 |
|---|---|---|---|---|---|
| 5.3 | Boulevard Woodgrill | New American | Arlington, VA | Casual | $45 |
| 5.2 | Beacon Bar & Grill | New American | Dupont | Casual | $45 |
| 5.1 | Clyde's | American | Multiple locations | Casual | $40 |
| 5.1 | Grill from Ipanema | Brazilian | Adams Morgan | Casual | $45 |
| 4.9 | Brasserie Monte Carlo | French | Bethesda, MD | Casual | $45 |
| 4.9 | Gordon Biersch | American | Multiple locations | Casual | $35 |
| 4.9 | Java Green | Sandwiches | Farragut | Café | $20 |
| 4.8 | Mie N Yu | Pan-Asian | Georgetown | Upmarket | $55 |
| 4.8 | Pour House | American | Capitol Hill | Casual | $35 |
| 4.6 | The Tombs | American | Georgetown | Bar | $25 |
| 4.6 | Veranda | Greek, Italian | Logan Circle | Casual | $40 |
| 4.5 | Paolo's | Italian | Georgetown | Casual | $40 |
| 4.3 | Café Luna | American, Italian | Dupont | Casual | $35 |
| 4.3 | J. Paul's | American | Georgetown | Casual | $45 |
| 4.2 | Luna Grill & Diner | American, Italian | Multiple locations | Casual | $30 |
| 3.9 | Tony & Joe's Seafood Place | Seafood | Georgetown | Upmarket | $55 |
| 3.9 | Sequoia | New American | Georgetown | Upmarket | $50 |
| 3.8 | Logan Tavern | American | Logan Circle | Casual | $35 |
| 3.8 | The Front Page | American | Dupont | Casual | $35 |
| 3.6 | Dupont Italian Kitchen | Italian | Dupont | Casual | $40 |
| 2.9 | Austin Grill | Mexican | Multiple locations | Casual | $30 |

## Date-friendly

| 9.7 | Komi | New American | Dupont | Upmarket | $140 |
|---|---|---|---|---|---|
| 9.6 | CityZen | New American | Southwest DC | Upmarket | $120 |
| 9.5 | Minibar | New American | Penn Quarter | Upmarket | $160 |
| 9.4 | Makoto | Japanese | Palisades | Upmarket | $80 |
| 9.4 | Westend Bistro | New American | West End | Upmarket | $65 |
| 9.3 | Obelisk | Italian | Dupont | Upmarket | $110 |
| 9.2 | Vermilion | New American | Old Town | Upmarket | $65 |
| 9.2 | Poste Moderne Brasserie | New American | Penn Quarter | Upmarket | $80 |
| 9.1 | Adour | French | Downtown | Upmarket | $125 |
| 9.1 | Hank's Oyster Bar | Seafood | Multiple locations | Upmarket | $45 |
| 9.1 | Citronelle | New American | Georgetown | Upmarket | $210 |
| 9.1 | Marvin | Southern, Belgian | U Street | Upmarket | $45 |
| 9.0 | Oe Gad Gib | Korean | Annandale, VA | Casual | $20 |
| 9.0 | Al Crostino | Italian | U Street | Upmarket | $55 |
| 9.0 | Posto | Italian, Pizza | Logan Circle | Upmarket | $55 |
| 8.9 | Bistro Bis | French | Capitol Hill | Upmarket | $70 |
| 8.9 | Annan-Gol | Korean | Annandale, VA | Casual | $20 |
| 8.9 | Gamasot | Korean | Springfield, VA | Casual | $15 |
| 8.8 | Restaurant Eve | New American | Old Town | Upmarket | $150 |
| 8.8 | Gooldaegee | Korean | Annandale, VA | Casual | $20 |
| 8.8 | Al Tiramisú | Italian | Dupont | Upmarket | $55 |
| 8.8 | Central Michel Richard | French | Penn Quarter | Upmarket | $70 |
| 8.8 | Marcel's | French | West End | Upmarket | $90 |
| 8.8 | The Source | New American | Penn Quarter | Upmarket | $120 |
| 8.8 | Palena | New American | Cleveland Park | Upmarket | $100 |
| 8.7 | Taberna del Alabardero | Spanish | Farragut | Upmarket | $75 |
| 8.6 | Café du Parc | French | Downtown | Upmarket | $60 |
| 8.6 | Nora | New American | Dupont | Upmarket | $80 |
| 8.6 | Rasika | Indian | Penn Quarter | Upmarket | $70 |
| 8.6 | Liberty Tavern | American | Arlington, VA | Casual | $40 |
| 8.5 | Zaytinya | Middle Eastern | Chinatown | Upmarket | $65 |
| 8.5 | Urbana | New American | Dupont | Upmarket | $55 |
| 8.4 | Buck's Fishing & Camping | Southern | Upper NW | Upmarket | $60 |
| 8.4 | Brasserie Beck | Belgian | Downtown | Upmarket | $55 |
| 8.4 | Proof | New American | Penn Quarter | Wine bar | $55 |
| 8.4 | Restaurant Eve (Bistro) | New American | Old Town | Upmarket | $60 |
| 8.3 | Bistrot du Coin | French | Dupont | Casual | $50 |
| 8.3 | Zola | New American | Penn Quarter | Upmarket | $60 |

| 8.3 | Hook | Seafood | Georgetown | Upmarket | $80 |
|-----|------|---------|------------|----------|-----|
| 8.2 | Founding Farmers | American | Farragut | Upmarket | $50 |
| 8.2 | Pizzeria Paradiso | Pizza | Multiple locations | Casual | $30 |
| 8.1 | Quarry House Tavern | American | Silver Spring, MD | Casual | $25 |
| 8.1 | Bourbon | American | Multiple locations | Bar | $35 |
| 8.1 | ching ching CHA | Chinese | Georgetown | Café | $25 |
| 8.1 | RedRocks | Pizza | Columbia Heights | Casual | $35 |
| 8.0 | Inn at Little Washington | New American | Washington, VA | Upmarket | $250 |
| 8.0 | Afterwords Café | American | Dupont | Café | $35 |
| 8.0 | Morrison-Clark Inn | Southern | Downtown | Upmarket | $60 |
| 8.0 | Oyamel | Mexican | Penn Quarter | Upmarket | $60 |
| 8.0 | Commonwealth | British | Columbia Heights | Casual | $40 |
| 8.0 | Coppi's Organic | Italian, Pizza | U Street | Upmarket | $50 |
| 8.0 | Crème | Southern | U Street | Casual | $45 |
| 8.0 | Georgia Brown's | Southern | Downtown | Upmarket | $55 |
| 8.0 | Two Quail | French | Mt. Vernon Square | Upmarket | $60 |
| 8.0 | Lavandou | French | Cleveland Park | Upmarket | $65 |
| 7.9 | Cashion's Eat Place | New American | Adams Morgan | Upmarket | $60 |
| 7.9 | Firefly | New American | Dupont | Upmarket | $60 |
| 7.9 | Farrah Olivia | New American | Old Town | Upmarket | $65 |
| 7.9 | Black's Bar & Kitchen | New American | Bethesda, MD | Upmarket | $75 |
| 7.9 | Tavira | Portuguese | Chevy Chase, MD | Upmarket | $60 |
| 7.8 | Blue Duck Tavern | New American | West End | Upmarket | $80 |
| 7.8 | Johnny's Half Shell | Seafood | Capitol Hill | Upmarket | $65 |
| 7.8 | Bardeo | New American | Cleveland Park | Wine bar | $35 |
| 7.7 | W Domku | Scandinavian | Petworth | Casual | $40 |
| 7.7 | The Majestic | New American | Old Town | Upmarket | $50 |
| 7.7 | Agraria | New American | Georgetown | Upmarket | $60 |
| 7.7 | Café Tu-O-Tu | Turkish, Sandwiches | Georgetown | Counter | $15 |
| 7.6 | Tabard Inn | American | Dupont | Upmarket | $55 |
| 7.6 | Round Robin Bar | American | Downtown | Bar | $40 |
| 7.6 | Park Café | New American | Capitol Hill | Upmarket | $60 |
| 7.6 | Leopold's Kafe | Austrian | Georgetown | Casual | $40 |
| 7.6 | Mendocino Grille | New American | Georgetown | Wine bar | $60 |
| 7.6 | Equinox | New American | Penn Quarter | Upmarket | $75 |
| 7.5 | Busboys & Poets | American | Multiple locations | Casual | $25 |
| 7.5 | Cork | New American | Logan Circle | Wine bar | $40 |
| 7.5 | La Chaumière | French | Georgetown | Upmarket | $60 |
| 7.5 | Meskerem | Ethiopian | Adams Morgan | Casual | $25 |
| 7.5 | Ulah Bistro | American | U Street | Upmarket | $45 |
| 7.4 | Mar de Plata | Spanish, Seafood | Multiple locations | Casual | $50 |
| 7.4 | TenPenh | Pan-Asian | Downtown | Upmarket | $70 |
| 7.4 | Ardeo | New American | Cleveland Park | Upmarket | $65 |
| 7.3 | Coco Sala | New American | Downtown | Upmarket | $50 |
| 7.3 | Vinoteca | New American | U Street | Wine bar | $45 |
| 7.2 | Café Berlin | German | Capitol Hill | Café | $35 |
| 7.2 | Cantina Marina | Southern | Southwest DC | Casual | $35 |
| 7.1 | Kemble Park Tavern | New American | Palisades | Upmarket | $60 |
| 7.1 | PS 7's | New American | Chinatown | Upmarket | $60 |
| 7.1 | Tabaq Bistro | Middle Eastern | U Street | Upmarket | $45 |
| 7.0 | Ceiba | Nuevo Latino | Downtown | Upmarket | $60 |
| 7.0 | Mio | New American | Downtown | Upmarket | $70 |
| 7.0 | Belga Café | Belgian | Capitol Hill | Casual | $30 |
| 7.0 | Cassatt's | American | Arlington, VA | Casual | $25 |
| 7.0 | Good Stuff Eatery | American | Capitol Hill | Counter | $15 |
| 7.0 | Rustico | New American | Alexandria, VA | Casual | $40 |
| 6.9 | Old Ebbitt Grill | American | Downtown | Casual | $40 |
| 6.9 | Bistro Italiano | Italian | Penn Quarter | Casual | $25 |
| 6.9 | Petits Plats | French | Woodley Park | Casual | $45 |
| 6.9 | Straits of Malaya | Malaysian | Dupont | Casual | $35 |
| 6.7 | Marrakesh | Moroccan | Mt. Vernon Square | Upmarket | $50 |
| 6.7 | Persimmon | New American | Chevy Chase, MD | Upmarket | $75 |

## Date-friendly *continued*

| | | | | | |
|---|---|---|---|---|---|
| 6.5 | Café Bonaparte | French | Georgetown | Café | $45 |
| 6.5 | Veritas Wine Bar | New American | Dupont | Wine bar | $40 |
| 6.5 | Café Olé | Middle Eastern | Upper NW | Casual | $30 |
| 6.4 | Martin's Tavern | American | Georgetown | Casual | $35 |
| 6.3 | Peacock Café | New American | Georgetown | Upmarket | $60 |
| 6.3 | Station 9 | New American | U Street | Upmarket | $45 |
| 6.2 | Café Saint-Ex | French, American | U Street | Casual | $40 |
| 6.2 | Indique | Indian | Cleveland Park | Upmarket | $40 |
| 6.2 | Etrusco | Italian | Dupont | Upmarket | $60 |
| 6.2 | Cubano's | Cuban | Silver Spring, MD | Casual | $35 |
| 6.0 | L'Auberge Chez François | French | Great Falls, VA | Upmarket | $110 |
| 6.0 | La Ferme | French | Chevy Chase, MD | Upmarket | $60 |
| 6.0 | Granville Moore's Brickyard | Belgian | Northeast DC | Casual | $40 |
| 5.9 | Bistro Français | French | Georgetown | Casual | $40 |
| 5.8 | The Big Hunt | American | Dupont | Bar | $20 |
| 5.8 | Hudson | New American | West End | Upmarket | $65 |
| 5.8 | Filomena | Italian | Georgetown | Casual | $50 |
| 5.7 | La Tasca | Spanish | Multiple locations | Casual | $40 |
| 5.6 | Little Fountain Café | New American | Adams Morgan | Upmarket | $45 |
| 5.5 | Local 16 | American | U Street | Upmarket | $40 |
| 5.5 | Napoleon Bistro | French | Adams Morgan | Upmarket | $60 |
| 5.1 | Tryst | American | Adams Morgan | Café | $25 |
| 5.0 | Marrakesh Palace | Moroccan | Dupont | Upmarket | $45 |
| 4.9 | Brasserie Monte Carlo | French | Bethesda, MD | Casual | $45 |
| 4.8 | Mie N Yu | Pan-Asian | Georgetown | Upmarket | $55 |
| 4.8 | ACKC Cocoa Bar | Sweet drinks | Multiple locations | Café | $10 |
| 4.6 | The Tombs | American | Georgetown | Bar | $25 |
| 4.5 | Paolo's | Italian | Georgetown | Casual | $40 |
| 4.4 | Rice | Thai | Logan Circle | Upmarket | $30 |
| 4.0 | Brickskeller | American | Dupont | Bar | $15 |
| 3.9 | Tony & Joe's Seafood Place | Seafood | Georgetown | Upmarket | $55 |
| 3.9 | Sequoia | New American | Georgetown | Upmarket | $50 |
| | Dolcezza | Ice cream | Multiple locations | Counter | |
| | Max's Best Ice Cream | Ice cream | Glover Park | Counter | |

## Delivery

| | | | | | |
|---|---|---|---|---|---|
| 8.9 | Roger Miller Restaurant | Cameroonian | Silver Spring, MD | Casual | $30 |
| 8.9 | Hong Kong Palace | Chinese | Falls Church, VA | Casual | $15 |
| 8.8 | New Big Wong | Chinese | Chinatown | Casual | $25 |
| 8.6 | China Star | Chinese | Fairfax, VA | Casual | $15 |
| 8.5 | Sushi-Ko | Japanese | Multiple locations | Upmarket | $60 |
| 8.5 | Costa Verde | Peruvian | Arlington, VA | Casual | $30 |
| 8.5 | El Pollo Rico | Latin American | Multiple locations | Counter | $10 |
| 8.2 | Tackle Box | Seafood | Georgetown | Casual | $25 |
| 8.1 | Queen Makeda | Ethiopian | Shaw | Casual | $30 |
| 8.1 | Fresh Med | Middle Eastern | Cleveland Park | Counter | $20 |
| 8.1 | Bread Line | Sandwiches | Farragut | Café | $15 |
| 8.1 | Cosmopolitan Bakery | Balkan | Alexandria, VA | Café | $25 |
| 8.0 | La Baguette | French, Sandwiches | Dupont | Counter | $15 |
| 8.0 | Taquería Distrito Federal | Mexican | Multiple locations | Casual | $20 |
| 7.9 | Tavira | Portuguese | Chevy Chase, MD | Upmarket | $60 |
| 7.9 | Langano | Ethiopian | Silver Spring, MD | Casual | $25 |
| 7.7 | Café Tu-O-Tu | Turkish, Sandwiches | Georgetown | Counter | $15 |
| 7.7 | Bethesda Bagels | Sandwiches | Bethesda, MD | Counter | $10 |
| 7.6 | Equinox | New American | Penn Quarter | Upmarket | $75 |
| 7.6 | Amma Vegetarian Kitchen | Indian | Multiple locations | Casual | $20 |
| 7.5 | Taverna the Greek Islands | Greek | Silver Spring, MD | Casual | $35 |
| 7.5 | Thai Square | Thai | Arlington, VA | Casual | $35 |
| 7.5 | El Khartoum | Sudanese | Shaw | Counter | $20 |
| 7.4 | Potbelly Sandwich Works | Sandwiches | Multiple locations | Counter | $10 |
| 7.4 | Super Pollo | Latin American | Arlington, VA | Counter | $10 |
| 7.3 | Café Pizzaiolo | Pizza, Sandwiches | Multiple locations | Casual | $35 |

| 7.3 | Urban Bar-B-Que Company | Barbecue | Multiple locations | Counter | $25 |
|---|---|---|---|---|---|
| 7.2 | Bangkok 54 | Thai | Arlington, VA | Casual | $35 |
| 7.2 | Heritage India | Indian | Multiple locations | Casual | $40 |
| 7.2 | Bombay Curry Company | Indian | Alexandria, VA | Casual | $20 |
| 7.2 | Mayur Kabab House | Pakistani, Indian | Chinatown | Casual | $20 |
| 7.1 | Jyoti | Indian | Adams Morgan | Casual | $25 |
| 7.1 | Harar Mesob | Ethiopian | Arlington, VA | Casual | $25 |
| 7.0 | Mama Ayesha's | Middle Eastern | Adams Morgan | Casual | $40 |
| 7.0 | Regent Thai | Thai | Dupont | Casual | $35 |
| 7.0 | Cakelove and Love Café | Baked goods | Multiple locations | Café | $10 |
| 6.9 | Bistro Italiano | Italian | Penn Quarter | Casual | $25 |
| 6.9 | Straits of Malaya | Malaysian | Dupont | Casual | $35 |
| 6.8 | Thai Tanic | Thai | Logan Circle | Casual | $30 |
| 6.8 | Po Siam | Thai | Alexandria, VA | Casual | $30 |
| 6.8 | La Prima | Sandwiches | Multiple locations | Counter | $20 |
| 6.6 | Chop't | American | Multiple locations | Counter | $10 |
| 6.4 | Nirvana | Indian | Farragut | Casual | $35 |
| 6.3 | Tandoor Grill | Indian | Capitol Hill | Casual | $30 |
| 6.3 | Old Glory Bar-B-Que | Barbecue | Georgetown | Casual | $30 |
| 6.0 | Granville Moore's Brickyard | Belgian | Northeast DC | Casual | $40 |
| 6.0 | Kanlaya | Thai, Chinese | Chinatown | Casual | $30 |
| 6.0 | Aatish on the Hill | Indian | Capitol Hill | Casual | $30 |
| 5.9 | Mai Thai | Thai | Multiple locations | Casual | $35 |
| 5.9 | Tara Thai | Thai | Multiple locations | Casual | $25 |
| 5.9 | Eli's | Sandwiches | Dupont | Casual | $20 |
| 5.8 | Sticky Fingers Bakery | Baked goods | Columbia Heights | Counter | $10 |
| 5.7 | Couscous Café | Moroccan | Dupont | Counter | $10 |
| 5.7 | Tono Sushi | Japanese | Woodley Park | Casual | $40 |
| 5.7 | Bertucci's | Italian, Pizza | Multiple locations | Casual | $35 |
| 5.7 | Armand's | Pizza | Multiple locations | Casual | $25 |
| 5.6 | Thai Chef | Thai, Japanese | Dupont | Casual | $40 |
| 5.6 | Byblos | Greek | Cleveland Park | Casual | $25 |
| 5.3 | Alberto's Stone Oven Pizza | Pizza | Multiple locations | Counter | $5 |
| 5.3 | Eat First | Chinese | Chinatown | Casual | $20 |
| 5.2 | Spices | Pan-Asian | Cleveland Park | Casual | $35 |
| 5.1 | Pomegranate Bistro | New American | Potomac, MD | Upmarket | $60 |
| 5.1 | Singapore Bistro | Pan-Asian | Farragut | Casual | $25 |
| 5.1 | Asian Spice | Chinese, Pan-Asian | Chinatown | Casual | $40 |
| 5.1 | Old Siam | Thai | Capitol Hill | Casual | $25 |
| 5.0 | Café Asia | Pan-Asian | Multiple locations | Casual | $30 |
| 4.9 | Aditi Indian Cuisine | Indian | Multiple locations | Casual | $35 |
| 4.8 | ACKC Cocoa Bar | Sweet drinks | Multiple locations | Café | $10 |
| 4.8 | Fusion Grill | Pan-Asian | Capitol Hill | Upmarket | $55 |
| 4.7 | Hunan Dynasty | Chinese | Capitol Hill | Casual | $25 |
| 4.6 | Mr. Chen's | Chinese | Woodley Park | Casual | $25 |
| 4.6 | Uni | Japanese | Dupont | Casual | $40 |
| 4.5 | Meiwah | Chinese, Japanese | Multiple locations | Casual | $45 |
| 4.5 | Camille's Sidewalk Café | Sandwiches | Multiple locations | Café | $25 |
| 4.4 | Rice | Thai | Logan Circle | Upmarket | $30 |
| 4.4 | Naan & Beyond | Indian | Multiple locations | Counter | $25 |
| 4.3 | Café Luna | American, Italian | Dupont | Casual | $35 |
| 4.2 | Luna Grill & Diner | American, Italian | Multiple locations | Casual | $30 |
| 4.2 | Sushi-Go-Round & Tapas | Pan-Asian | Chinatown | Casual | $45 |
| 4.0 | Commissary | American | Logan Circle | Casual | $30 |
| 4.0 | Tai Shan | Chinese | Chinatown | Casual | $15 |
| 4.0 | Thai Roma | Thai | Capitol Hill | Casual | $35 |
| 3.8 | Logan Tavern | American | Logan Circle | Casual | $35 |
| 3.8 | Wok & Roll | Chinese | Chinatown | Casual | $20 |
| 3.7 | Ping by Charlie Chiang's | Pan-Asian | Arlington, VA | Casual | $45 |
| 3.6 | Dupont Italian Kitchen | Italian | Dupont | Casual | $40 |
| 3.2 | Sala Thai | Thai | Multiple locations | Casual | $25 |
| | Dickey's Frozen Custard | Sandwiches | Multiple locations | Counter | |

## Delivery *continued*

| | | | |
|---|---|---|---|
| Dolcezza | Ice cream | Multiple locations | Counter |
| Marvelous Market | Groceries | Multiple locations | Market |

## Good wine list

| | | | | | |
|---|---|---|---|---|---|
| 9.7 | Komi | New American | Dupont | Upmarket | $140 |
| 9.6 | CityZen | New American | Southwest DC | Upmarket | $120 |
| 9.5 | Minibar | New American | Penn Quarter | Upmarket | $160 |
| 9.3 | Obelisk | Italian | Dupont | Upmarket | $110 |
| 9.2 | Vermilion | New American | Old Town | Upmarket | $65 |
| 9.2 | Poste Moderne Brasserie | New American | Penn Quarter | Upmarket | $80 |
| 9.1 | Adour | French | Downtown | Upmarket | $125 |
| 9.1 | Citronelle | New American | Georgetown | Upmarket | $210 |
| 9.1 | Tosca | Italian | Downtown | Upmarket | $75 |
| 9.0 | Posto | Italian, Pizza | Logan Circle | Upmarket | $55 |
| 8.9 | Bistro Bis | French | Capitol Hill | Upmarket | $70 |
| 8.8 | Restaurant Eve | New American | Old Town | Upmarket | $150 |
| 8.8 | Al Tiramisú | Italian | Dupont | Upmarket | $55 |
| 8.8 | Marcel's | French | West End | Upmarket | $90 |
| 8.8 | The Source | New American | Penn Quarter | Upmarket | $120 |
| 8.8 | Corduroy | New American | Mt. Vernon Square | Upmarket | $70 |
| 8.7 | Taberna del Alabardero | Spanish | Farragut | Upmarket | $75 |
| 8.6 | Café du Parc | French | Downtown | Upmarket | $60 |
| 8.5 | Urbana | New American | Dupont | Upmarket | $55 |
| 8.5 | The Oval Room | New American | Farragut | Upmarket | $75 |
| 8.4 | Dino | Italian | Cleveland Park | Upmarket | $50 |
| 8.4 | Proof | New American | Penn Quarter | Wine bar | $55 |
| 8.4 | Restaurant Eve (Bistro) | New American | Old Town | Upmarket | $60 |
| 8.3 | Bistrot du Coin | French | Dupont | Casual | $50 |
| 8.3 | Hook | Seafood | Georgetown | Upmarket | $80 |
| 8.0 | Inn at Little Washington | New American | Washington, VA | Upmarket | $250 |
| 8.0 | Coppi's Organic | Italian, Pizza | U Street | Upmarket | $50 |
| 8.0 | 2941 Restaurant | New American | Falls Church, VA | Upmarket | $100 |
| 7.9 | Cashion's Eat Place | New American | Adams Morgan | Upmarket | $60 |
| 7.9 | Black's Bar & Kitchen | New American | Bethesda, MD | Upmarket | $75 |
| 7.9 | 1789 | New American | Georgetown | Upmarket | $100 |
| 7.8 | Blue Duck Tavern | New American | West End | Upmarket | $80 |
| 7.8 | Bardeo | New American | Cleveland Park | Wine bar | $35 |
| 7.8 | Café Atlántico | Nuevo Latino | Penn Quarter | Upmarket | $75 |
| 7.6 | Leopold's Kafe | Austrian | Georgetown | Casual | $40 |
| 7.6 | Equinox | New American | Penn Quarter | Upmarket | $75 |
| 7.5 | Cork | New American | Logan Circle | Wine bar | $40 |
| 7.4 | Ardeo | New American | Cleveland Park | Upmarket | $65 |
| 7.3 | Vinoteca | New American | U Street | Wine bar | $45 |
| 7.3 | Café Pizzaiolo | Pizza, Sandwiches | Multiple locations | Casual | $35 |
| 7.1 | Oya | Pan-Asian | Penn Quarter | Upmarket | $75 |
| 6.0 | L'Auberge Chez François | French | Great Falls, VA | Upmarket | $110 |
| 5.9 | Grapeseed | New American | Bethesda, MD | Wine bar | $75 |
| 5.8 | Charlie Palmer Steak | Steakhouse | Capitol Hill | Upmarket | $110 |
| 5.7 | Sonoma | New American | Capitol Hill | Wine bar | $65 |
| 4.8 | 701 | New American | Penn Quarter | Upmarket | $70 |
| | Dean & Deluca | Groceries | Georgetown | Market | |
| | Harris Teeter | Groceries | Multiple locations | Market | |
| | The Italian Store | Pizza, Sandwiches | Arlington, VA | Counter | |
| | Marvelous Market | Groceries | Multiple locations | Market | |
| | Trader Joe's | Groceries | Multiple locations | Market | |
| | Whole Foods Market | Groceries | Multiple locations | Market | |

## Kid-friendly

| | | | | | |
|---|---|---|---|---|---|
| 9.6 | 2 Amys Pizza | Pizza | Cleveland Park | Casual | $35 |
| 9.1 | Hank's Oyster Bar | Seafood | Multiple locations | Upmarket | $45 |
| 9.0 | Oe Gad Gib | Korean | Annandale, VA | Casual | $20 |

| 9.0 | Ray's Hell-Burger | American | Multiple locations | Counter | $15 |
| 8.9 | Annan-Gol | Korean | Annandale, VA | Casual | $20 |
| 8.9 | Oriental East | Chinese | Silver Spring, MD | Casual | $40 |
| 8.8 | Gooldaegee | Korean | Annandale, VA | Casual | $20 |
| 8.8 | China Garden | Chinese | Arlington, VA | Casual | $20 |
| 8.7 | Eamonn's | Seafood, Irish | Old Town | Casual | $20 |
| 8.7 | Granja de Oro | Latin American | Adams Morgan | Counter | $20 |
| 8.6 | Liberty Tavern | American | Arlington, VA | Casual | $40 |
| 8.6 | Bob's Noodle 66 | Taiwanese, Chinese | Rockville, MD | Casual | $15 |
| 8.6 | El Charrito Caminante | Mexican | Arlington, VA | Counter | $15 |
| 8.5 | Oohhs & Aahhs | Southern | Shaw | Counter | $25 |
| 8.5 | Costa Verde | Peruvian | Arlington, VA | Casual | $30 |
| 8.5 | El Pollo Rico | Latin American | Multiple locations | Counter | $10 |
| 8.4 | Buck's Fishing & Camping | Southern | Upper NW | Upmarket | $60 |
| 8.4 | Sakana | Japanese | Dupont | Casual | $35 |
| 8.4 | Ray's the Steaks | Steakhouse | Arlington, VA | Upmarket | $45 |
| 8.4 | Pollo Granjero | Latin American | Multiple locations | Counter | $15 |
| 8.3 | Rainbow Restaurant | Ghanaian | Gaithersburg, MD | Casual | $20 |
| 8.2 | Founding Farmers | American | Farragut | Upmarket | $50 |
| 8.2 | Irene's Pupusas | Salvadoran | Multiple locations | Casual | $25 |
| 8.2 | Pizzeria Paradiso | Pizza | Multiple locations | Casual | $30 |
| 8.2 | Tackle Box | Seafood | Georgetown | Casual | $25 |
| 8.2 | Li Ho | Chinese | Chinatown | Casual | $10 |
| 8.1 | Ben's Chili Bowl | American | Multiple locations | Counter | $15 |
| 8.1 | C.F. Folks | American | Dupont | Casual | $20 |
| 8.1 | RedRocks | Pizza | Columbia Heights | Casual | $35 |
| 8.0 | Afterwords Café | American | Dupont | Café | $35 |
| 8.0 | Morrison-Clark Inn | Southern | Downtown | Upmarket | $60 |
| 8.0 | Oyamel | Mexican | Penn Quarter | Upmarket | $60 |
| 8.0 | Crème | Southern | U Street | Casual | $45 |
| 8.0 | Georgia Brown's | Southern | Downtown | Upmarket | $55 |
| 8.0 | Passage to India | Indian | Bethesda, MD | Casual | $40 |
| 8.0 | La Baguette | French, Sandwiches | Dupont | Counter | $15 |
| 8.0 | Weenie Beanie | American | Arlington, VA | Counter | $5 |
| 8.0 | Kabob Bazaar | Middle Eastern | Arlington, VA | Casual | $20 |
| 8.0 | Taste of Morocco | Moroccan | Arlington, VA | Casual | $35 |
| 7.9 | La Casita | Salvadoran | Multiple locations | Casual | $10 |
| 7.9 | El Dorado | Salvadoran | Hyattsville, MD | Counter | $10 |
| 7.8 | Tallula | New American | Arlington, VA | Upmarket | $55 |
| 7.8 | Johnny's Half Shell | Seafood | Capitol Hill | Upmarket | $65 |
| 7.8 | Full Kee | Chinese | Multiple locations | Casual | $25 |
| 7.8 | Tako Grill | Japanese | Bethesda, MD | Casual | $45 |
| 7.7 | W Domku | Scandinavian | Petworth | Casual | $40 |
| 7.7 | Peking Gourmet Inn | Chinese | Falls Church, VA | Casual | $35 |
| 7.7 | Café Tu-O-Tu | Turkish, Sandwiches | Georgetown | Counter | $15 |
| 7.7 | Mia's Pizza | Italian, Pizza | Bethesda, MD | Casual | $25 |
| 7.7 | Crisp & Juicy | Latin American | Multiple locations | Counter | $10 |
| 7.6 | Tabard Inn | American | Dupont | Upmarket | $55 |
| 7.6 | Leopold's Kafe | Austrian | Georgetown | Casual | $40 |
| 7.6 | Amma Vegetarian Kitchen | Indian | Multiple locations | Casual | $20 |
| 7.6 | Deli City | Southern | Northeast DC | Counter | $15 |
| 7.5 | Meskerem | Ethiopian | Adams Morgan | Casual | $25 |
| 7.5 | La Sandía | Mexican | Tysons Corner, VA | Upmarket | $50 |
| 7.5 | Pollo Campero | Latin American | Multiple locations | Counter | $10 |
| 7.4 | Café Divan | Turkish | Glover Park | Casual | $35 |
| 7.4 | Potbelly Sandwich Works | Sandwiches | Multiple locations | Counter | $10 |
| 7.4 | Shanghai Village | Chinese | Bethesda, MD | Casual | $35 |
| 7.4 | Five Guys | American | Multiple locations | Counter | $10 |
| 7.4 | Bombay Bistro | Indian | Multiple locations | Casual | $25 |
| 7.3 | Coco Sala | New American | Downtown | Upmarket | $50 |
| 7.3 | Café Pizzaiolo | Pizza, Sandwiches | Multiple locations | Casual | $35 |
| 7.2 | Florida Avenue Grill | Southern | U Street | Casual | $15 |

## Kid-friendly *continued*

| | | | | | |
|---|---|---|---|---|---|
| 7.2 | Cantina Marina | Southern | Southwest DC | Casual | $35 |
| 7.2 | Heritage India | Indian | Multiple locations | Casual | $40 |
| 7.2 | Bombay Curry Company | Indian | Alexandria, VA | Casual | $20 |
| 7.2 | Taquería El Poblano | Mexican | Multiple locations | Casual | $15 |
| 7.1 | Kemble Park Tavern | New American | Palisades | Upmarket | $60 |
| 7.1 | District Chophouse | Steakhouse | Penn Quarter | Casual | $45 |
| 7.1 | Greek Deli | Greek, Sandwiches | Farragut | Counter | $15 |
| 7.1 | Udupi Palace | Indian | Takoma Park, MD | Casual | $20 |
| 7.0 | Cassatt's | American | Arlington, VA | Casual | $25 |
| 7.0 | Good Stuff Eatery | American | Capitol Hill | Counter | $15 |
| 7.0 | Rustico | New American | Alexandria, VA | Casual | $40 |
| 7.0 | Cakelove and Love Café | Baked goods | Multiple locations | Café | $10 |
| 7.0 | Yee Hwa | Korean, Japanese | Downtown | Casual | $40 |
| 6.9 | Old Ebbitt Grill | American | Downtown | Casual | $40 |
| 6.9 | Straits of Malaya | Malaysian | Dupont | Casual | $35 |
| 6.9 | Whitlow's on Wilson | American | Arlington, VA | Casual | $35 |
| 6.9 | Ella's Pizza | Pizza | Chinatown | Casual | $40 |
| 6.9 | Carlyle | New American | Arlington, VA | Casual | $40 |
| 6.9 | Red Hot & Blue | Barbecue | Multiple locations | Casual | $15 |
| 6.8 | Thai Tanic | Thai | Logan Circle | Casual | $30 |
| 6.7 | White Tiger | Indian | Capitol Hill | Casual | $35 |
| 6.7 | Fogo de Chão | Brazilian | Downtown | Upmarket | $80 |
| 6.7 | Harry's Tap Room | American | Multiple locations | Casual | $50 |
| 6.6 | Java House | Middle Eastern | Dupont | Counter | $10 |
| 6.6 | Chevys Fresh Mex | Mexican | Multiple locations | Casual | $30 |
| 6.6 | Amici Miei | Italian | Potomac, MD | Casual | $50 |
| 6.5 | Café Olé | Middle Eastern | Upper NW | Casual | $30 |
| 6.5 | Negril | Caribbean | Multiple locations | Counter | $15 |
| 6.4 | Martin's Tavern | American | Georgetown | Casual | $35 |
| 6.4 | Nirvana | Indian | Farragut | Casual | $35 |
| 6.4 | Mark's Duck House | Chinese | Falls Church, VA | Casual | $30 |
| 6.3 | Astor Mediterranean | Middle Eastern | Multiple locations | Casual | $20 |
| 6.3 | Station 9 | New American | U Street | Upmarket | $45 |
| 6.3 | Tandoor Grill | Indian | Capitol Hill | Casual | $30 |
| 6.3 | Old Glory Bar-B-Que | Barbecue | Georgetown | Casual | $30 |
| 6.3 | Faryab | Afghan | Bethesda, MD | Casual | $25 |
| 6.2 | Café Saint-Ex | French, American | U Street | Casual | $40 |
| 6.2 | Rosemary's Thyme Bistro | American, Italian | Dupont | Casual | $40 |
| 6.2 | Cubano's | Cuban | Silver Spring, MD | Casual | $35 |
| 6.0 | Kanlaya | Thai, Chinese | Chinatown | Casual | $30 |
| 5.9 | Mai Thai | Thai | Multiple locations | Casual | $35 |
| 5.9 | Kanpai | Japanese | Arlington, VA | Casual | $30 |
| 5.8 | Rosa Mexicano | Mexican | Penn Quarter | Upmarket | $55 |
| 5.8 | Filomena | Italian | Georgetown | Casual | $50 |
| 5.8 | Sticky Fingers Bakery | Baked goods | Columbia Heights | Counter | $10 |
| 5.7 | Couscous Café | Moroccan | Dupont | Counter | $10 |
| 5.7 | Bertucci's | Italian, Pizza | Multiple locations | Casual | $35 |
| 5.7 | Sunflower Vegetarian | Chinese | Falls Church, VA | Casual | $20 |
| 5.7 | Armand's | Pizza | Multiple locations | Casual | $25 |
| 5.6 | Rocklands | Barbecue | Multiple locations | Casual | $15 |
| 5.6 | Johnny Rockets | American | Multiple locations | Casual | $25 |
| 5.6 | Bombay Restaurant | Indian | Silver Spring, MD | Casual | $30 |
| 5.5 | Matuba | Japanese | Arlington, VA | Casual | $20 |
| 5.3 | Boulevard Woodgrill | New American | Arlington, VA | Casual | $45 |
| 5.3 | Yuan Fu | Chinese | Rockville, MD | Casual | $25 |
| 5.2 | Spices | Pan-Asian | Cleveland Park | Casual | $35 |
| 5.1 | Clyde's | American | Multiple locations | Casual | $40 |
| 5.0 | Marrakesh Palace | Moroccan | Dupont | Upmarket | $45 |
| 4.9 | Brasserie Monte Carlo | French | Bethesda, MD | Casual | $45 |
| 4.9 | Aditi Indian Cuisine | Indian | Multiple locations | Casual | $35 |
| 4.8 | ACKC Cocoa Bar | Sweet drinks | Multiple locations | Café | $10 |
| 4.5 | Paolo's | Italian | Georgetown | Casual | $40 |

## Kid-friendly *continued*

| 4.3 | Hard Times Café | American | Multiple locations | Casual | $20 |
|---|---|---|---|---|---|
| 4.2 | Luna Grill & Diner | American, Italian | Multiple locations | Casual | $30 |
| 4.0 | Commissary | American | Logan Circle | Casual | $30 |
| 4.0 | Tai Shan | Chinese | Chinatown | Casual | $15 |
| 3.9 | Tony & Joe's Seafood Place | Seafood | Georgetown | Upmarket | $55 |
| 3.9 | Sequoia | New American | Georgetown | Upmarket | $50 |
| 3.8 | The Front Page | American | Dupont | Casual | $35 |
| 3.7 | Ping by Charlie Chiang's | Pan-Asian | Arlington, VA | Casual | $45 |
| 3.7 | Olazzo | Italian | Multiple locations | Upmarket | $45 |
| 2.9 | Austin Grill | Mexican | Multiple locations | Casual | $30 |
| 2.8 | California Tortilla | Mexican | Multiple locations | Counter | $10 |
| 2.7 | Buca di Beppo | Italian | Dupont | Casual | $30 |
| | The Dairy Godmother | Ice cream | Alexandria, VA | Counter | |
| | Dean & Deluca | Groceries | Georgetown | Market | |
| | Dickey's Frozen Custard | Sandwiches | Multiple locations | Counter | |
| | Eastern Market | Groceries | Capitol Hill | Market | |
| | The Italian Store | Pizza, Sandwiches | Arlington, VA | Counter | |
| | Maine Avenue Fish Market | Groceries, Seafood | Southwest DC | Market | |
| | Max's Best Ice Cream | Ice cream | Glover Park | Counter | |
| | Mediterranean Bakery | Middle Eastern | Alexandria, VA | Counter | |
| | Sweetgreen | American, Ice cream | Georgetown | Counter | |
| | Thomas Sweet | Ice cream | Georgetown | Counter | |
| | Union Station Food Court | | Union Station | Counter | |

## Live music *of any kind, from jazz piano to rock, even occasionally*

| 9.1 | Marvin | Southern, Belgian | U Street | Upmarket | $45 |
|---|---|---|---|---|---|
| 8.8 | Marcel's | French | West End | Upmarket | $90 |
| 8.8 | Shashemene | Ethiopian | Shaw | Casual | $25 |
| 8.8 | Etete | Ethiopian | Shaw | Casual | $30 |
| 8.7 | Taberna del Alabardero | Spanish | Farragut | Upmarket | $75 |
| 8.6 | Meaza | Ethiopian | Falls Church, VA | Casual | $20 |
| 8.5 | Prime Rib | Steakhouse | Farragut | Upmarket | $90 |
| 8.3 | Hook | Seafood | Georgetown | Upmarket | $80 |
| 8.3 | Smith & Wollensky | Steakhouse | Farragut | Upmarket | $85 |
| 8.2 | Irene's Pupusas | Salvadoran | Multiple locations | Casual | $25 |
| 8.2 | Tackle Box | Seafood | Georgetown | Casual | $25 |
| 8.2 | Myanmar | Burmese | Falls Church, VA | Casual | $30 |
| 8.1 | Queen Makeda | Ethiopian | Shaw | Casual | $30 |
| 8.1 | Bombay Club | Indian | Farragut | Upmarket | $45 |
| 8.0 | Afterwords Café | American | Dupont | Café | $35 |
| 8.0 | Crème | Southern | U Street | Casual | $45 |
| 8.0 | Georgia Brown's | Southern | Downtown | Upmarket | $55 |
| 8.0 | Taquería Distrito Federal | Mexican | Multiple locations | Casual | $20 |
| 8.0 | Kabob Bazaar | Middle Eastern | Arlington, VA | Casual | $20 |
| 8.0 | Taste of Morocco | Moroccan | Arlington, VA | Casual | $35 |
| 7.9 | Black's Bar & Kitchen | New American | Bethesda, MD | Upmarket | $75 |
| 7.9 | Tavira | Portuguese | Chevy Chase, MD | Upmarket | $60 |
| 7.9 | Langano | Ethiopian | Silver Spring, MD | Casual | $25 |
| 7.9 | 1789 | New American | Georgetown | Upmarket | $100 |
| 7.8 | Johnny's Half Shell | Seafood | Capitol Hill | Upmarket | $65 |
| 7.8 | Dukem | Ethiopian | Shaw | Casual | $25 |
| 7.6 | Tabard Inn | American | Dupont | Upmarket | $55 |
| 7.5 | Busboys & Poets | American | Multiple locations | Casual | $25 |
| 7.5 | Lebanese Taverna | Middle Eastern | Multiple locations | Casual | $40 |
| 7.5 | Taverna the Greek Islands | Greek | Silver Spring, MD | Casual | $35 |
| 7.4 | Neyla | Middle Eastern | Georgetown | Upmarket | $70 |
| 7.4 | Potbelly Sandwich Works | Sandwiches | Multiple locations | Counter | $10 |
| 7.3 | Coco Sala | New American | Downtown | Upmarket | $50 |
| 7.3 | Vinoteca | New American | U Street | Wine bar | $45 |
| 7.3 | Kinkead's | Seafood | Foggy Bottom | Upmarket | $75 |
| 7.3 | Chinatown Express | Chinese | Chinatown | Casual | $25 |
| 7.2 | Bangkok 54 | Thai | Arlington, VA | Casual | $35 |

## Live music *continued*

| | | | | | |
|---|---|---|---|---|---|
| 7.2 | Mayur Kabab House | Pakistani, Indian | Chinatown | Casual | $20 |
| 7.2 | Taquería El Poblano | Mexican | Multiple locations | Casual | $15 |
| 7.1 | Nicaro | New American | Rockville, MD | Upmarket | $75 |
| 7.1 | Axum | Ethiopian | Shaw | Casual | $25 |
| 7.0 | Mio | New American | Downtown | Upmarket | $70 |
| 7.0 | Cassatt's | American | Arlington, VA | Casual | $25 |
| 6.9 | Whitlow's on Wilson | American | Arlington, VA | Casual | $35 |
| 6.9 | Comet Ping Pong | Pizza | Upper NW | Casual | $35 |
| 6.8 | Fadó | Irish | Chinatown | Bar | $27 |
| 6.8 | Starfish Café | Seafood | Capitol Hill | Casual | $55 |
| 6.8 | The Lafayette Room | New American | Farragut | Upmarket | $85 |
| 6.8 | Bacchus of Lebanon | Middle Eastern | Bethesda, MD | Upmarket | $60 |
| 6.7 | Marrakesh | Moroccan | Mt. Vernon Square | Upmarket | $50 |
| 6.7 | Zengo | Pan-Asian | Chinatown | Upmarket | $65 |
| 6.6 | Evening Star Café | New American | Alexandria, VA | Upmarket | $55 |
| 6.5 | Evolve | New American | Adams Morgan | Upmarket | $40 |
| 6.5 | Negril | Caribbean | Multiple locations | Counter | $15 |
| 6.3 | Station 9 | New American | U Street | Upmarket | $45 |
| 6.3 | Old Glory Bar-B-Que | Barbecue | Georgetown | Casual | $30 |
| 6.2 | Cubano's | Cuban | Silver Spring, MD | Casual | $35 |
| 6.1 | Chef Geoff's | New American | Multiple locations | Upmarket | $50 |
| 6.1 | Teatro Goldoni | Italian | Farragut | Upmarket | $90 |
| 6.0 | La Ferme | French | Chevy Chase, MD | Upmarket | $60 |
| 6.0 | The Red and the Black | Southern | Northeast DC | Bar | $25 |
| 6.0 | Cococabana Bar & Grill | Italian, Mexican | Hyattsville, MD | Casual | $30 |
| 5.9 | Maté | Pan-Asian | Georgetown | Casual | $45 |
| 5.9 | Asylum | American | Dupont | Bar | $25 |
| 5.8 | Hudson | New American | West End | Upmarket | $65 |
| 5.8 | Vegetate | New American | Mt. Vernon Square | Upmarket | $45 |
| 5.7 | La Tasca | Spanish | Multiple locations | Casual | $40 |
| 5.7 | The Islander Caribbean | Caribbean | U Street | Casual | $25 |
| 5.7 | La Crêperie | French | Arlington, VA | Café | $15 |
| 5.6 | Banana Café & Piano Bar | Cuban | Capitol Hill | Café | $30 |
| 5.5 | Green Papaya | Vietnamese | Bethesda, MD | Upmarket | $35 |
| 5.1 | Tryst | American | Adams Morgan | Café | $25 |
| 5.1 | Singapore Bistro | Pan-Asian | Farragut | Casual | $25 |
| 5.1 | Clyde's | American | Multiple locations | Casual | $40 |
| 5.1 | Grill from Ipanema | Brazilian | Adams Morgan | Casual | $45 |
| 5.0 | Skye Lounge | Middle Eastern | Farragut | Casual | $40 |
| 4.9 | Brasserie Monte Carlo | French | Bethesda, MD | Casual | $45 |
| 4.8 | Fusion Grill | Pan-Asian | Capitol Hill | Upmarket | $55 |
| 4.8 | Pour House | American | Capitol Hill | Casual | $35 |
| 4.8 | 701 | New American | Penn Quarter | Upmarket | $70 |
| 4.6 | The Tombs | American | Georgetown | Bar | $25 |
| 4.6 | La Tomate | Italian | Dupont | Upmarket | $45 |
| 4.6 | Veranda | Greek, Italian | Logan Circle | Casual | $40 |
| 4.5 | Paolo's | Italian | Georgetown | Casual | $40 |
| 4.3 | Skewers | Middle Eastern | Dupont | Casual | $30 |
| 4.3 | Café Luna | American, Italian | Dupont | Casual | $35 |
| 4.2 | Sushi-Go-Round & Tapas | Pan-Asian | Chinatown | Casual | $45 |
| 4.0 | Tai Shan | Chinese | Chinatown | Casual | $15 |
| 3.9 | Tony & Joe's Seafood Place | Seafood | Georgetown | Upmarket | $55 |
| 3.8 | Wok & Roll | Chinese | Chinatown | Casual | $20 |
| 3.5 | Café Citron | Nuevo Latino | Dupont | Casual | $35 |
| 3.2 | Sala Thai | Thai | Multiple locations | Casual | $25 |
| | Dolcezza | Ice cream | Multiple locations | Counter | |

## Outdoor dining *of any kind, from sidewalk tables to a big backyard patio*

| | | | | | |
|---|---|---|---|---|---|
| 9.6 | 2 Amys Pizza | Pizza | Cleveland Park | Casual | $35 |
| 9.2 | Poste Moderne Brasserie | New American | Penn Quarter | Upmarket | $80 |
| 9.1 | Hank's Oyster Bar | Seafood | Multiple locations | Upmarket | $45 |
| 9.1 | Marvin | Southern, Belgian | U Street | Upmarket | $45 |

## **Outdoor dining** *continued*

| 9.0 | Hai Duong | Vietnamese | Falls Church, VA | Casual | $15 |
|-----|-----------|------------|------------------|--------|-----|
| 8.9 | Bistro Bis | French | Capitol Hill | Upmarket | $70 |
| 8.9 | Roger Miller Restaurant | Cameroonian | Silver Spring, MD | Casual | $30 |
| 8.9 | Oriental East | Chinese | Silver Spring, MD | Casual | $40 |
| 8.9 | Hong Kong Palace | Chinese | Falls Church, VA | Casual | $15 |
| 8.8 | Marcel's | French | West End | Upmarket | $90 |
| 8.8 | The Source | New American | Penn Quarter | Upmarket | $120 |
| 8.8 | Palena | New American | Cleveland Park | Upmarket | $100 |
| 8.8 | Etete | Ethiopian | Shaw | Casual | $30 |
| 8.7 | Taberna del Alabardero | Spanish | Farragut | Upmarket | $75 |
| 8.7 | BLT Steak | Steakhouse | Farragut | Upmarket | $95 |
| 8.7 | Eamonn's | Seafood, Irish | Old Town | Casual | $20 |
| 8.7 | Granja de Oro | Latin American | Adams Morgan | Counter | $20 |
| 8.6 | Café du Parc | French | Downtown | Upmarket | $60 |
| 8.6 | Montmartre | French | Capitol Hill | Upmarket | $60 |
| 8.6 | Liberty Tavern | American | Arlington, VA | Casual | $40 |
| 8.6 | Meaza | Ethiopian | Falls Church, VA | Casual | $20 |
| 8.6 | Kabob Palace | Middle Eastern | Arlington, VA | Counter | $20 |
| 8.5 | Zaytinya | Middle Eastern | Chinatown | Upmarket | $65 |
| 8.5 | Bobby Van's Steakhouse | Steakhouse | Multiple locations | Upmarket | $95 |
| 8.5 | The Oval Room | New American | Farragut | Upmarket | $75 |
| 8.4 | Brasserie Beck | Belgian | Downtown | Upmarket | $55 |
| 8.4 | Dino | Italian | Cleveland Park | Upmarket | $50 |
| 8.4 | Proof | New American | Penn Quarter | Wine bar | $55 |
| 8.4 | Sakana | Japanese | Dupont | Casual | $35 |
| 8.3 | Thai X-ing | Thai | Shaw | Casual | $30 |
| 8.3 | Smith & Wollensky | Steakhouse | Farragut | Upmarket | $85 |
| 8.2 | Taquería Nacional | Mexican | Penn Quarter | Counter | $15 |
| 8.1 | Bourbon | American | Multiple locations | Bar | $35 |
| 8.1 | C.F. Folks | American | Dupont | Casual | $20 |
| 8.1 | RedRocks | Pizza | Columbia Heights | Casual | $35 |
| 8.1 | Bombay Club | Indian | Farragut | Upmarket | $45 |
| 8.1 | Bread Line | Sandwiches | Farragut | Café | $15 |
| 8.0 | Inn at Little Washington | New American | Washington, VA | Upmarket | $250 |
| 8.0 | Afterwords Café | American | Dupont | Café | $35 |
| 8.0 | Morrison-Clark Inn | Southern | Downtown | Upmarket | $60 |
| 8.0 | Oyamel | Mexican | Penn Quarter | Upmarket | $60 |
| 8.0 | Commonwealth | British | Columbia Heights | Casual | $40 |
| 8.0 | Georgia Brown's | Southern | Downtown | Upmarket | $55 |
| 8.0 | 2941 Restaurant | New American | Falls Church, VA | Upmarket | $100 |
| 8.0 | La Baguette | French, Sandwiches | Dupont | Counter | $15 |
| 8.0 | Taquería Distrito Federal | Mexican | Multiple locations | Casual | $20 |
| 8.0 | Kabob Bazaar | Middle Eastern | Arlington, VA | Casual | $20 |
| 8.0 | Don Pollo | Latin American | Hyattsville, MD | Counter | $15 |
| 7.9 | Cashion's Eat Place | New American | Adams Morgan | Upmarket | $60 |
| 7.9 | Farrah Olivia | New American | Old Town | Upmarket | $65 |
| 7.9 | Black's Bar & Kitchen | New American | Bethesda, MD | Upmarket | $75 |
| 7.9 | Morton's | Steakhouse | Multiple locations | Upmarket | $100 |
| 7.9 | Langano | Ethiopian | Silver Spring, MD | Casual | $25 |
| 7.8 | Blue Duck Tavern | New American | West End | Upmarket | $80 |
| 7.8 | Tallula | New American | Arlington, VA | Upmarket | $55 |
| 7.8 | Johnny's Half Shell | Seafood | Capitol Hill | Upmarket | $65 |
| 7.8 | Bardeo | New American | Cleveland Park | Wine bar | $35 |
| 7.8 | Café Atlántico | Nuevo Latino | Penn Quarter | Upmarket | $75 |
| 7.8 | Afghan Grill | Afghan | Cleveland Park | Casual | $40 |
| 7.8 | Dukem | Ethiopian | Shaw | Casual | $25 |
| 7.7 | W Domku | Scandinavian | Petworth | Casual | $40 |
| 7.7 | Agraria | New American | Georgetown | Upmarket | $60 |
| 7.7 | Café Tu-O-Tu | Turkish, Sandwiches | Georgetown | Counter | $15 |
| 7.7 | Mia's Pizza | Italian, Pizza | Bethesda, MD | Casual | $25 |
| 7.7 | The Wharf Seafood | Seafood | Southwest DC | Counter | $25 |
| 7.7 | Sweet Mango Café | Caribbean | Petworth | Casual | $25 |

| 7.7 | Crisp & Juicy | Latin American | Multiple locations | Counter | $10 |
|---|---|---|---|---|---|
| 7.6 | Tabard Inn | American | Dupont | Upmarket | $55 |
| 7.6 | Leopold's Kafe | Austrian | Georgetown | Casual | $40 |
| 7.6 | Mendocino Grille | New American | Georgetown | Wine bar | $60 |
| 7.6 | Equinox | New American | Penn Quarter | Upmarket | $75 |
| 7.6 | Matchbox | American, Pizza | Chinatown | Casual | $35 |
| 7.6 | Guajillo | Mexican | Arlington, VA | Casual | $35 |
| 7.5 | Cork | New American | Logan Circle | Wine bar | $40 |
| 7.5 | Lebanese Taverna | Middle Eastern | Multiple locations | Casual | $40 |
| 7.5 | Taverna the Greek Islands | Greek | Silver Spring, MD | Casual | $35 |
| 7.5 | Earl's Sandwiches | Sandwiches | Arlington, VA | Counter | $15 |
| 7.4 | TenPenh | Pan-Asian | Downtown | Upmarket | $70 |
| 7.4 | Ardeo | New American | Cleveland Park | Upmarket | $65 |
| 7.4 | Jackson 20 | New American | Old Town | Upmarket | $65 |
| 7.4 | Neyla | Middle Eastern | Georgetown | Upmarket | $70 |
| 7.4 | Potbelly Sandwich Works | Sandwiches | Multiple locations | Counter | $10 |
| 7.4 | Sorriso | Italian, Pizza | Cleveland Park | Casual | $40 |
| 7.4 | Super Pollo | Latin American | Arlington, VA | Counter | $10 |
| 7.3 | Vinoteca | New American | U Street | Wine bar | $45 |
| 7.3 | Bourbon Steak | New American | Georgetown | Upmarket | $115 |
| 7.3 | Jaleo | Spanish | Multiple locations | Upmarket | $50 |
| 7.3 | Patisserie Poupon | Baked goods | Georgetown | Café | $35 |
| 7.3 | Kinkead's | Seafood | Foggy Bottom | Upmarket | $75 |
| 7.3 | Urban Bar-B-Que Company | Barbecue | Multiple locations | Counter | $25 |
| 7.3 | Chinatown Express | Chinese | Chinatown | Casual | $25 |
| 7.2 | Café Berlin | German | Capitol Hill | Café | $35 |
| 7.2 | Cantina Marina | Southern | Southwest DC | Casual | $35 |
| 7.2 | Cucina Vivace | Italian | Arlington, VA | Upmarket | $55 |
| 7.2 | Mayur Kabab House | Pakistani, Indian | Chinatown | Casual | $20 |
| 7.2 | Bread & Chocolate | French | Multiple locations | Café | $15 |
| 7.1 | Kemble Park Tavern | New American | Palisades | Upmarket | $60 |
| 7.1 | PS 7's | New American | Chinatown | Upmarket | $60 |
| 7.1 | Tabaq Bistro | Middle Eastern | U Street | Upmarket | $45 |
| 7.1 | Acadiana | Southern | Mt. Vernon Square | Upmarket | $60 |
| 7.1 | Jyoti | Indian | Adams Morgan | Casual | $25 |
| 7.1 | Nicaro | New American | Rockville, MD | Upmarket | $75 |
| 7.1 | Faccia Luna | Italian, Pizza | Multiple locations | Casual | $40 |
| 7.1 | Greek Deli | Greek, Sandwiches | Farragut | Counter | $15 |
| 7.1 | Harar Mesob | Ethiopian | Arlington, VA | Casual | $25 |
| 7.1 | Saigon Saigon | Vietnamese | Arlington, VA | Casual | $25 |
| 7.0 | Belga Café | Belgian | Capitol Hill | Casual | $30 |
| 7.0 | Cassatt's | American | Arlington, VA | Casual | $25 |
| 7.0 | Mama Ayesha's | Middle Eastern | Adams Morgan | Casual | $40 |
| 7.0 | Good Stuff Eatery | American | Capitol Hill | Counter | $15 |
| 7.0 | Las Placitas | Mexican | Capitol Hill | Casual | $40 |
| 7.0 | Rustico | New American | Alexandria, VA | Casual | $40 |
| 7.0 | McCormick & Schmick's | Seafood | Multiple locations | Upmarket | $60 |
| 7.0 | Chi-Cha Lounge | Latin American | U Street | Casual | $30 |
| 7.0 | Regent Thai | Thai | Dupont | Casual | $35 |
| 6.9 | Bastille | French | Old Town | Upmarket | $55 |
| 6.9 | Tunnicliff's Tavern | American | Capitol Hill | Casual | $40 |
| 6.9 | Petits Plats | French | Woodley Park | Casual | $45 |
| 6.9 | Straits of Malaya | Malaysian | Dupont | Casual | $35 |
| 6.9 | Whitlow's on Wilson | American | Arlington, VA | Casual | $35 |
| 6.9 | Ella's Pizza | Pizza | Chinatown | Casual | $40 |
| 6.9 | Carlyle | New American | Arlington, VA | Casual | $40 |
| 6.9 | Red Hot & Blue | Barbecue | Multiple locations | Casual | $15 |
| 6.9 | Comet Ping Pong | Pizza | Upper NW | Casual | $35 |
| 6.8 | Starfish Café | Seafood | Capitol Hill | Casual | $55 |
| 6.8 | Trusty's | American | Capitol Hill | Casual | $35 |
| 6.8 | Bacchus of Lebanon | Middle Eastern | Bethesda, MD | Upmarket | $60 |
| 6.7 | Persimmon | New American | Chevy Chase, MD | Upmarket | $75 |

## Outdoor dining *continued*

| | | | | |
|---|---|---|---|---|
| 6.7 | White Tiger | Indian | Capitol Hill | Casual | $35 |
| 6.7 | Bookbinder's Old Town | Steakhouse | Old Town | Upmarket | $80 |
| 6.7 | Bagels & Baguettes | Sandwiches | Capitol Hill | Café | $10 |
| 6.7 | Bean Counter | Baked goods | Georgetown | Café | $15 |
| 6.7 | Harry's Tap Room | American | Multiple locations | Casual | $50 |
| 6.6 | Java House | Middle Eastern | Dupont | Counter | $10 |
| 6.6 | Sette Osteria | Italian, Pizza | Dupont | Casual | $40 |
| 6.6 | Evening Star Café | New American | Alexandria, VA | Upmarket | $55 |
| 6.6 | Chevys Fresh Mex | Mexican | Multiple locations | Casual | $30 |
| 6.6 | Amici Miei | Italian | Potomac, MD | Casual | $50 |
| 6.5 | Open City | American | Woodley Park | Café | $40 |
| 6.5 | Café Bonaparte | French | Georgetown | Café | $45 |
| 6.5 | Veritas Wine Bar | New American | Dupont | Wine bar | $40 |
| 6.5 | Alero | Mexican | Multiple locations | Casual | $40 |
| 6.5 | Café Olé | Middle Eastern | Upper NW | Casual | $30 |
| 6.5 | Pete's Diner | American | Capitol Hill | Casual | $25 |
| 6.5 | Evolve | New American | Adams Morgan | Upmarket | $40 |
| 6.4 | Martin's Tavern | American | Georgetown | Casual | $35 |
| 6.4 | Zorba's Café | Greek, Sandwiches | Dupont | Counter | $25 |
| 6.3 | Peacock Café | New American | Georgetown | Upmarket | $60 |
| 6.3 | Mandu | Korean | Dupont | Casual | $40 |
| 6.3 | Astor Mediterranean | Middle Eastern | Multiple locations | Casual | $20 |
| 6.3 | Grillfish | Seafood | West End | Upmarket | $45 |
| 6.3 | Tandoor Grill | Indian | Capitol Hill | Casual | $30 |
| 6.3 | Old Glory Bar-B-Que | Barbecue | Georgetown | Casual | $30 |
| 6.3 | DC Café | Middle Eastern | Dupont | Counter | $25 |
| 6.2 | Café Saint-Ex | French, American | U Street | Casual | $40 |
| 6.2 | Rosemary's Thyme Bistro | American, Italian | Dupont | Casual | $40 |
| 6.2 | Indique | Indian | Cleveland Park | Upmarket | $40 |
| 6.2 | Etrusco | Italian | Dupont | Upmarket | $60 |
| 6.2 | Cubano's | Cuban | Silver Spring, MD | Casual | $35 |
| 6.2 | Stoney's Bar & Grill | American | Logan Circle | Casual | $40 |
| 6.2 | Le Bon Café | Baked goods | Capitol Hill | Café | $20 |
| 6.2 | Murali | Italian | Arlington, VA | Upmarket | $50 |
| 6.2 | Teaism | Pan-Asian | Multiple locations | Café | $20 |
| 6.1 | Chef Geoff's | New American | Multiple locations | Upmarket | $50 |
| 6.1 | Teatro Goldoni | Italian | Farragut | Upmarket | $90 |
| 6.1 | Café Milano | Italian | Georgetown | Upmarket | $75 |
| 6.1 | Primi Piatti | Italian | Foggy Bottom | Upmarket | $70 |
| 6.1 | Kenny's BBQ | Barbecue | Capitol Hill | Counter | $20 |
| 6.0 | L'Auberge Chez François | French | Great Falls, VA | Upmarket | $110 |
| 6.0 | La Ferme | French | Chevy Chase, MD | Upmarket | $60 |
| 6.0 | Granville Moore's Brickyard | Belgian | Northeast DC | Casual | $40 |
| 6.0 | Kanlaya | Thai, Chinese | Chinatown | Casual | $30 |
| 6.0 | Tortilla Café | Salvadoran | Capitol Hill | Casual | $20 |
| 5.9 | Old City Café & Bakery | Middle Eastern | Adams Morgan | Counter | $10 |
| 5.9 | 15 Ria | New American | Logan Circle | Upmarket | $60 |
| 5.9 | Kanpai | Japanese | Arlington, VA | Casual | $30 |
| 5.8 | The Big Hunt | American | Dupont | Bar | $20 |
| 5.8 | Rosa Mexicano | Mexican | Penn Quarter | Upmarket | $55 |
| 5.8 | Hudson | New American | West End | Upmarket | $65 |
| 5.8 | Sticky Fingers Bakery | Baked goods | Columbia Heights | Counter | $10 |
| 5.7 | Circa | Italian | Dupont | Casual | $40 |
| 5.7 | Sonoma | New American | Capitol Hill | Wine bar | $65 |
| 5.7 | Couscous Café | Moroccan | Dupont | Counter | $10 |
| 5.7 | The Islander Caribbean | Caribbean | U Street | Casual | $25 |
| 5.7 | Tono Sushi | Japanese | Woodley Park | Casual | $40 |
| 5.7 | Sunflower Vegetarian | Chinese | Falls Church, VA | Casual | $20 |
| 5.7 | Armand's | Pizza | Multiple locations | Casual | $25 |
| 5.7 | La Crêperie | French | Arlington, VA | Café | $15 |
| 5.6 | Little Fountain Café | New American | Adams Morgan | Upmarket | $45 |
| 5.6 | Darlington House | New American | Dupont | Upmarket | $65 |

## Outdoor dining *continued*

| | | | | | |
|---|---|---|---|---|---|
| 5.6 | Rocklands | Barbecue | Multiple locations | Casual | $15 |
| 5.6 | Banana Café & Piano Bar | Cuban | Capitol Hill | Café | $30 |
| 5.6 | Byblos | Greek | Cleveland Park | Casual | $25 |
| 5.5 | Local 16 | American | U Street | Upmarket | $40 |
| 5.5 | Napoleon Bistro | French | Adams Morgan | Upmarket | $60 |
| 5.5 | Bangkok Joe's | Pan-Asian | Georgetown | Casual | $45 |
| 5.5 | Green Papaya | Vietnamese | Bethesda, MD | Upmarket | $35 |
| 5.4 | Amsterdam Falafel Shop | Middle Eastern | Adams Morgan | Counter | $10 |
| 5.4 | La Madeleine | French, Sandwiches | Multiple locations | Counter | $30 |
| 5.3 | Il Mulino | Italian | Downtown | Upmarket | $80 |
| 5.3 | Boulevard Woodgrill | New American | Arlington, VA | Casual | $45 |
| 5.2 | La Loma | Mexican | Capitol Hill | Casual | $30 |
| 5.2 | Beacon Bar & Grill | New American | Dupont | Casual | $45 |
| 5.1 | Pomegranate Bistro | New American | Potomac, MD | Upmarket | $60 |
| 5.1 | Grill from Ipanema | Brazilian | Adams Morgan | Casual | $45 |
| 5.1 | Asian Spice | Chinese, Pan-Asian | Chinatown | Casual | $40 |
| 5.1 | Old Siam | Thai | Capitol Hill | Casual | $25 |
| 5.1 | The Brown Bag | Sandwiches | Multiple locations | Counter | $15 |
| 5.0 | Marrakesh Palace | Moroccan | Dupont | Upmarket | $45 |
| 5.0 | Lima | Nuevo Latino | Downtown | Upmarket | $55 |
| 5.0 | Skye Lounge | Middle Eastern | Farragut | Casual | $40 |
| 4.9 | Brasserie Monte Carlo | French | Bethesda, MD | Casual | $45 |
| 4.9 | Gordon Biersch | American | Multiple locations | Casual | $35 |
| 4.9 | Java Green | Sandwiches | Farragut | Café | $20 |
| 4.8 | ACKC Cocoa Bar | Sweet drinks | Multiple locations | Café | $10 |
| 4.8 | Fusion Grill | Pan-Asian | Capitol Hill | Upmarket | $55 |
| 4.8 | Trattoria Alberto | Italian | Capitol Hill | Casual | $45 |
| 4.8 | Pour House | American | Capitol Hill | Casual | $35 |
| 4.8 | 701 | New American | Penn Quarter | Upmarket | $70 |
| 4.8 | Asia Nine | Pan-Asian | Penn Quarter | Casual | $35 |
| 4.7 | Aroma | Indian | Multiple locations | Casual | $25 |
| 4.6 | La Tomate | Italian | Dupont | Upmarket | $45 |
| 4.6 | Veranda | Greek, Italian | Logan Circle | Casual | $40 |
| 4.5 | Paolo's | Italian | Georgetown | Casual | $40 |
| 4.5 | Camille's Sidewalk Café | Sandwiches | Multiple locations | Café | $25 |
| 4.4 | Rice | Thai | Logan Circle | Upmarket | $30 |
| 4.4 | Raku | Pan-Asian | Multiple locations | Upmarket | $35 |
| 4.4 | Naan & Beyond | Indian | Multiple locations | Counter | $25 |
| 4.3 | Skewers | Middle Eastern | Dupont | Casual | $30 |
| 4.3 | Café Luna | American, Italian | Dupont | Casual | $35 |
| 4.3 | Hard Times Café | American | Multiple locations | Casual | $20 |
| 4.3 | Vietnam Georgetown | Vietnamese | Georgetown | Casual | $30 |
| 4.2 | Luna Grill & Diner | American, Italian | Multiple locations | Casual | $30 |
| 4.2 | Sushi-Go-Round & Tapas | Pan-Asian | Chinatown | Casual | $45 |
| 4.0 | Commissary | American | Logan Circle | Casual | $30 |
| 4.0 | Tai Shan | Chinese | Chinatown | Casual | $15 |
| 4.0 | Thai Roma | Thai | Capitol Hill | Casual | $35 |
| 3.9 | Tony & Joe's Seafood Place | Seafood | Georgetown | Upmarket | $55 |
| 3.9 | Sequoia | New American | Georgetown | Upmarket | $50 |
| 3.8 | Logan Tavern | American | Logan Circle | Casual | $35 |
| 3.8 | The Front Page | American | Dupont | Casual | $35 |
| 3.8 | Union Pub | American | Capitol Hill | Casual | $25 |
| 3.7 | Ping by Charlie Chiang's | Pan-Asian | Arlington, VA | Casual | $45 |
| 3.7 | Olazzo | Italian | Multiple locations | Upmarket | $45 |
| 3.6 | Dupont Italian Kitchen | Italian | Dupont | Casual | $40 |
| 3.6 | Zed's Ethiopian Restaurant | Ethiopian | Georgetown | Casual | $30 |
| 3.6 | Prego Delly | Sandwiches, Italian | Capitol Hill | Counter | $25 |
| 3.1 | Wellness Café | Sandwiches | Capitol Hill | Café | $20 |
| 2.9 | Austin Grill | Mexican | Multiple locations | Casual | $30 |
| 2.2 | Lauriol Plaza | Mexican | Adams Morgan | Casual | $35 |
| | The Dairy Godmother | Ice cream | Alexandria, VA | Counter | |
| | Dean & Deluca | Groceries | Georgetown | Market | |

## Outdoor dining *continued*

| | | | |
|---|---|---|---|
| The Italian Store | Pizza, Sandwiches | Arlington, VA | Counter |
| M. E. Swing | Baked goods | Foggy Bottom | Café |
| Maine Avenue Fish Market | Groceries, Seafood | Southwest DC | Market |
| Marvelous Market | Groceries | Multiple locations | Market |
| Sweetgreen | American, Ice cream | Georgetown | Counter |

## Wi-Fi

| | | | | | |
|---|---|---|---|---|---|
| 9.1 | Adour | French | Downtown | Upmarket | $125 |
| 9.0 | Teddy's Roti Shop | Caribbean | Takoma Park, MD | Counter | $15 |
| 8.9 | Bistro Bis | French | Capitol Hill | Upmarket | $70 |
| 8.9 | Roger Miller Restaurant | Cameroonian | Silver Spring, MD | Casual | $30 |
| 8.8 | Etete | Ethiopian | Shaw | Casual | $30 |
| 8.7 | BLT Steak | Steakhouse | Farragut | Upmarket | $95 |
| 8.6 | Café du Parc | French | Downtown | Upmarket | $60 |
| 8.6 | Nora | New American | Dupont | Upmarket | $80 |
| 8.6 | Liberty Tavern | American | Arlington, VA | Casual | $40 |
| 8.5 | Bobby Van's Steakhouse | Steakhouse | Multiple locations | Upmarket | $95 |
| 8.5 | Oohhs & Aahhs | Southern | Shaw | Counter | $25 |
| 8.5 | Costa Verde | Peruvian | Arlington, VA | Casual | $30 |
| 8.4 | Brasserie Beck | Belgian | Downtown | Upmarket | $55 |
| 8.3 | Hook | Seafood | Georgetown | Upmarket | $80 |
| 8.3 | Thai X-ing | Thai | Shaw | Casual | $30 |
| 8.1 | Ben's Chili Bowl | American | Multiple locations | Counter | $15 |
| 8.1 | RedRocks | Pizza | Columbia Heights | Casual | $35 |
| 8.1 | Bombay Club | Indian | Farragut | Upmarket | $45 |
| 8.1 | Bread Line | Sandwiches | Farragut | Café | $15 |
| 8.0 | Morrison-Clark Inn | Southern | Downtown | Upmarket | $60 |
| 8.0 | Commonwealth | British | Columbia Heights | Casual | $40 |
| 8.0 | Passage to India | Indian | Bethesda, MD | Casual | $40 |
| 7.9 | Firefly | New American | Dupont | Upmarket | $60 |
| 7.9 | Black's Bar & Kitchen | New American | Bethesda, MD | Upmarket | $75 |
| 7.8 | Blue Duck Tavern | New American | West End | Upmarket | $80 |
| 7.8 | Tallula | New American | Arlington, VA | Upmarket | $55 |
| 7.8 | Bardeo | New American | Cleveland Park | Wine bar | $35 |
| 7.7 | W Domku | Scandinavian | Petworth | Casual | $40 |
| 7.7 | Agraria | New American | Georgetown | Upmarket | $60 |
| 7.7 | Café Tu-O-Tu | Turkish, Sandwiches | Georgetown | Counter | $15 |
| 7.7 | Mia's Pizza | Italian, Pizza | Bethesda, MD | Casual | $25 |
| 7.7 | Sweet Mango Café | Caribbean | Petworth | Casual | $25 |
| 7.6 | Tabard Inn | American | Dupont | Upmarket | $55 |
| 7.6 | Round Robin Bar | American | Downtown | Bar | $40 |
| 7.6 | Park Café | New American | Capitol Hill | Upmarket | $60 |
| 7.6 | Equinox | New American | Penn Quarter | Upmarket | $75 |
| 7.5 | Busboys & Poets | American | Multiple locations | Casual | $25 |
| 7.5 | Ulah Bistro | American | U Street | Upmarket | $45 |
| 7.5 | Lebanese Taverna | Middle Eastern | Multiple locations | Casual | $40 |
| 7.4 | Café Divan | Turkish | Glover Park | Casual | $35 |
| 7.4 | Mar de Plata | Spanish, Seafood | Multiple locations | Casual | $50 |
| 7.4 | TenPenh | Pan-Asian | Downtown | Upmarket | $70 |
| 7.4 | DISH + drinks | New American | Foggy Bottom | Upmarket | $55 |
| 7.3 | Vinoteca | New American | U Street | Wine bar | $45 |
| 7.3 | Café Pizzaiolo | Pizza, Sandwiches | Multiple locations | Casual | $35 |
| 7.3 | Chinatown Express | Chinese | Chinatown | Casual | $25 |
| 7.2 | Florida Avenue Grill | Southern | U Street | Casual | $15 |
| 7.2 | Cantina Marina | Southern | Southwest DC | Casual | $35 |
| 7.2 | Heritage India | Indian | Multiple locations | Casual | $40 |
| 7.2 | Cucina Vivace | Italian | Arlington, VA | Upmarket | $55 |
| 7.2 | Mayur Kabab House | Pakistani, Indian | Chinatown | Casual | $20 |
| 7.2 | Bread & Chocolate | French | Multiple locations | Café | $15 |
| 7.1 | District Chophouse | Steakhouse | Penn Quarter | Casual | $45 |
| 7.0 | Mio | New American | Downtown | Upmarket | $70 |
| 7.0 | Rustico | New American | Alexandria, VA | Casual | $40 |

| 7.0 | Nage | New American | Dupont | Upmarket | $60 |
|---|---|---|---|---|---|
| 6.9 | Tunnicliff's Tavern | American | Capitol Hill | Casual | $40 |
| 6.9 | Whitlow's on Wilson | American | Arlington, VA | Casual | $35 |
| 6.9 | Fleming's | Steakhouse | Tysons Corner, VA | Upmarket | $90 |
| 6.9 | Red Hot & Blue | Barbecue | Multiple locations | Casual | $15 |
| 6.8 | Trusty's | American | Capitol Hill | Casual | $35 |
| 6.8 | Bacchus of Lebanon | Middle Eastern | Bethesda, MD | Upmarket | $60 |
| 6.7 | Bean Counter | Baked goods | Georgetown | Café | $15 |
| 6.6 | Java House | Middle Eastern | Dupont | Counter | $10 |
| 6.6 | Evening Star Café | New American | Alexandria, VA | Upmarket | $55 |
| 6.5 | Open City | American | Woodley Park | Café | $40 |
| 6.5 | Tragara | Italian | Bethesda, MD | Upmarket | $80 |
| 6.5 | Negril | Caribbean | Multiple locations | Counter | $15 |
| 6.4 | Mark's Duck House | Chinese | Falls Church, VA | Casual | $30 |
| 6.2 | Indique | Indian | Cleveland Park | Upmarket | $40 |
| 6.2 | Stoney's Bar & Grill | American | Logan Circle | Casual | $40 |
| 6.2 | Le Bon Café | Baked goods | Capitol Hill | Café | $20 |
| 6.1 | Teatro Goldoni | Italian | Farragut | Upmarket | $90 |
| 6.0 | The Red and the Black | Southern | Northeast DC | Bar | $25 |
| 6.0 | Burma | Burmese | Chinatown | Casual | $25 |
| 6.0 | Finn & Porter | American | Multiple locations | Upmarket | $75 |
| 5.9 | El Tamarindo | Mexican | Adams Morgan | Casual | $40 |
| 5.9 | Old City Café & Bakery | Middle Eastern | Adams Morgan | Counter | $10 |
| 5.9 | 15 Ria | New American | Logan Circle | Upmarket | $60 |
| 5.8 | The Big Hunt | American | Dupont | Bar | $20 |
| 5.8 | Hudson | New American | West End | Upmarket | $65 |
| 5.8 | Filomena | Italian | Georgetown | Casual | $50 |
| 5.8 | Sticky Fingers Bakery | Baked goods | Columbia Heights | Counter | $10 |
| 5.7 | Couscous Café | Moroccan | Dupont | Counter | $10 |
| 5.7 | Bertucci's | Italian, Pizza | Multiple locations | Casual | $35 |
| 5.7 | Armand's | Pizza | Multiple locations | Casual | $25 |
| 5.7 | La Crêperie | French | Arlington, VA | Café | $15 |
| 5.5 | Local 16 | American | U Street | Upmarket | $40 |
| 5.5 | Napoleon Bistro | French | Adams Morgan | Upmarket | $60 |
| 5.4 | Amsterdam Falafel Shop | Middle Eastern | Adams Morgan | Counter | $10 |
| 5.2 | Beacon Bar & Grill | New American | Dupont | Casual | $45 |
| 5.1 | Tryst | American | Adams Morgan | Café | $25 |
| 5.1 | Singapore Bistro | Pan-Asian | Farragut | Casual | $25 |
| 5.0 | Marrakesh Palace | Moroccan | Dupont | Upmarket | $45 |
| 4.9 | Gordon Biersch | American | Multiple locations | Casual | $35 |
| 4.9 | Java Green | Sandwiches | Farragut | Café | $20 |
| 4.9 | Aditi Indian Cuisine | Indian | Multiple locations | Casual | $35 |
| 4.8 | ACKC Cocoa Bar | Sweet drinks | Multiple locations | Café | $10 |
| 4.8 | Fusion Grill | Pan-Asian | Capitol Hill | Upmarket | $55 |
| 4.8 | Pour House | American | Capitol Hill | Casual | $35 |
| 4.6 | The Tombs | American | Georgetown | Bar | $25 |
| 4.6 | Veranda | Greek, Italian | Logan Circle | Casual | $40 |
| 4.5 | Meiwah | Chinese, Japanese | Multiple locations | Casual | $45 |
| 4.5 | Camille's Sidewalk Café | Sandwiches | Multiple locations | Café | $25 |
| 4.3 | Skewers | Middle Eastern | Dupont | Casual | $30 |
| 4.3 | Café Luna | American, Italian | Dupont | Casual | $35 |
| 4.2 | Sushi-Go-Round & Tapas | Pan-Asian | Chinatown | Casual | $45 |
| 4.0 | Commissary | American | Logan Circle | Casual | $30 |
| 4.0 | Thai Roma | Thai | Capitol Hill | Casual | $35 |
| 3.8 | The Front Page | American | Dupont | Casual | $35 |
| 3.8 | Wok & Roll | Chinese | Chinatown | Casual | $20 |
| 3.8 | Union Pub | American | Capitol Hill | Casual | $25 |
| 3.5 | Jumbo Slice | Pizza | Adams Morgan | Counter | $5 |
| 1.4 | Prince Café | Middle Eastern | Multiple locations | Casual | $25 |
| | Dolcezza | Ice cream | Multiple locations | Counter | |
| | M. E. Swing | Baked goods | Foggy Bottom | Café | |
| | Marvelous Market | Groceries | Multiple locations | Market | |

# Vegetarian-friendly guide

Places to eat that are **unusually strong in vegetarian options**. This doesn't just mean that there are salads or veggie pastas available; it means that vegetarians will really be happy with the selection at these places. Ranked by **food rating** unless otherwise noted.

## All vegetarian-friendly establishments

| | | | | | |
|---|---|---|---|---|---|
| 9.6 | 2 Amys Pizza | Pizza | Cleveland Park | Casual | $35 |
| 9.1 | Tosca | Italian | Downtown | Upmarket | $75 |
| 9.0 | Al Crostino | Italian | U Street | Upmarket | $55 |
| 9.0 | Posto | Italian, Pizza | Logan Circle | Upmarket | $55 |
| 8.8 | Al Tiramisú | Italian | Dupont | Upmarket | $55 |
| 8.8 | Light House Tofu | Korean | Multiple locations | Casual | $15 |
| 8.8 | Shashemene | Ethiopian | Shaw | Casual | $25 |
| 8.8 | Etete | Ethiopian | Shaw | Casual | $30 |
| 8.6 | Rasika | Indian | Penn Quarter | Upmarket | $70 |
| 8.6 | Meaza | Ethiopian | Falls Church, VA | Casual | $20 |
| 8.6 | Bob's Noodle 66 | Taiwanese, Chinese | Rockville, MD | Casual | $15 |
| 8.5 | Zaytinya | Middle Eastern | Chinatown | Upmarket | $65 |
| 8.5 | To Sok Jip | Korean | Annandale, VA | Casual | $15 |
| 8.5 | Urbana | New American | Dupont | Upmarket | $55 |
| 8.4 | Proof | New American | Penn Quarter | Wine bar | $55 |
| 8.4 | Sakana | Japanese | Dupont | Casual | $35 |
| 8.3 | Thai Market | Thai | Silver Spring, MD | Counter | $20 |
| 8.2 | Founding Farmers | American | Farragut | Upmarket | $50 |
| 8.2 | Pizzeria Paradiso | Pizza | Multiple locations | Casual | $30 |
| 8.1 | Ben's Chili Bowl | American | Multiple locations | Counter | $15 |
| 8.1 | Queen Makeda | Ethiopian | Shaw | Casual | $30 |
| 8.1 | ching ching CHA | Chinese | Georgetown | Café | $25 |
| 8.1 | RedRocks | Pizza | Columbia Heights | Casual | $35 |
| 8.1 | Bombay Club | Indian | Farragut | Upmarket | $45 |
| 8.1 | Fresh Med | Middle Eastern | Cleveland Park | Counter | $20 |
| 8.1 | Bread Line | Sandwiches | Farragut | Café | $15 |
| 8.0 | Afterwords Café | American | Dupont | Café | $35 |
| 8.0 | Coppi's Organic | Italian, Pizza | U Street | Upmarket | $50 |
| 8.0 | Passage to India | Indian | Bethesda, MD | Casual | $40 |
| 8.0 | Vace | Sandwiches, Pizza | Multiple locations | Counter | $30 |
| 8.0 | La Baguette | French, Sandwiches | Dupont | Counter | $15 |
| 8.0 | Kabob Bazaar | Middle Eastern | Arlington, VA | Casual | $20 |
| 8.0 | Taste of Morocco | Moroccan | Arlington, VA | Casual | $35 |
| 7.9 | Black's Bar & Kitchen | New American | Bethesda, MD | Upmarket | $75 |
| 7.9 | Langano | Ethiopian | Silver Spring, MD | Casual | $25 |
| 7.8 | Blue Duck Tavern | New American | West End | Upmarket | $80 |
| 7.8 | Bardeo | New American | Cleveland Park | Wine bar | $35 |
| 7.8 | Pasta Mia | Italian | Adams Morgan | Casual | $25 |
| 7.8 | Afghan Grill | Afghan | Cleveland Park | Casual | $40 |
| 7.8 | Dukem | Ethiopian | Shaw | Casual | $25 |
| 7.8 | Tako Grill | Japanese | Bethesda, MD | Casual | $45 |
| 7.7 | Peking Gourmet Inn | Chinese | Falls Church, VA | Casual | $35 |
| 7.7 | Café Tu-O-Tu | Turkish, Sandwiches | Georgetown | Counter | $15 |
| 7.7 | Mia's Pizza | Italian, Pizza | Bethesda, MD | Casual | $25 |
| 7.7 | Bethesda Bagels | Sandwiches | Bethesda, MD | Counter | $10 |
| 7.6 | Matchbox | American, Pizza | Chinatown | Casual | $35 |

| 7.6 | Amma Vegetarian Kitchen | Indian | Multiple locations | Casual | $20 |
|---|---|---|---|---|---|
| 7.5 | Busboys & Poets | American | Multiple locations | Casual | $25 |
| 7.5 | Cork | New American | Logan Circle | Wine bar | $40 |
| 7.5 | Meskerem | Ethiopian | Adams Morgan | Casual | $25 |
| 7.5 | Lebanese Taverna | Middle Eastern | Multiple locations | Casual | $40 |
| 7.5 | Taverna the Greek Islands | Greek | Silver Spring, MD | Casual | $35 |
| 7.4 | Café Divan | Turkish | Glover Park | Casual | $35 |
| 7.4 | TenPenh | Pan-Asian | Downtown | Upmarket | $70 |
| 7.4 | Ardeo | New American | Cleveland Park | Upmarket | $65 |
| 7.4 | Neyla | Middle Eastern | Georgetown | Upmarket | $70 |
| 7.4 | Potbelly Sandwich Works | Sandwiches | Multiple locations | Counter | $10 |
| 7.4 | Sorriso | Italian, Pizza | Cleveland Park | Casual | $40 |
| 7.4 | Bombay Bistro | Indian | Multiple locations | Casual | $25 |
| 7.3 | Coco Sala | New American | Downtown | Upmarket | $50 |
| 7.3 | Vinoteca | New American | U Street | Wine bar | $45 |
| 7.3 | Patisserie Poupon | Baked goods | Georgetown | Café | $35 |
| 7.3 | Café Pizzaiolo | Pizza, Sandwiches | Multiple locations | Casual | $35 |
| 7.2 | Heritage India | Indian | Multiple locations | Casual | $40 |
| 7.2 | Firehook | Baked goods | Multiple locations | Counter | $10 |
| 7.2 | Bombay Curry Company | Indian | Alexandria, VA | Casual | $20 |
| 7.2 | Bread & Chocolate | French | Multiple locations | Café | $15 |
| 7.1 | Oya | Pan-Asian | Penn Quarter | Upmarket | $75 |
| 7.1 | Jyoti | Indian | Adams Morgan | Casual | $25 |
| 7.1 | Axum | Ethiopian | Shaw | Casual | $25 |
| 7.1 | Faccia Luna | Italian, Pizza | Multiple locations | Casual | $40 |
| 7.1 | Greek Deli | Greek, Sandwiches | Farragut | Counter | $15 |
| 7.1 | Harar Mesob | Ethiopian | Arlington, VA | Casual | $25 |
| 7.1 | Udupi Palace | Indian | Takoma Park, MD | Casual | $20 |
| 7.1 | Malaysia Kopitiam | Malaysian | Dupont | Casual | $25 |
| 7.1 | Julia's Empanadas | Latin American | Multiple locations | Counter | $5 |
| 7.0 | Good Stuff Eatery | American | Capitol Hill | Counter | $15 |
| 7.0 | Las Placitas | Mexican | Capitol Hill | Casual | $40 |
| 7.0 | Cakelove and Love Café | Baked goods | Multiple locations | Café | $10 |
| 7.0 | Moby Dick | Middle Eastern | Multiple locations | Casual | $25 |
| 6.9 | Straits of Malaya | Malaysian | Dupont | Casual | $35 |
| 6.9 | Ella's Pizza | Pizza | Chinatown | Casual | $40 |
| 6.9 | Comet Ping Pong | Pizza | Upper NW | Casual | $35 |
| 6.8 | Thai Tanic | Thai | Logan Circle | Casual | $30 |
| 6.8 | Madjet | Ethiopian | Shaw | Casual | $23 |
| 6.8 | Bacchus of Lebanon | Middle Eastern | Bethesda, MD | Upmarket | $60 |
| 6.8 | La Prima | Sandwiches | Multiple locations | Counter | $20 |
| 6.7 | Marrakesh | Moroccan | Mt. Vernon Square | Upmarket | $50 |
| 6.7 | White Tiger | Indian | Capitol Hill | Casual | $35 |
| 6.7 | Bagels & Baguettes | Sandwiches | Capitol Hill | Café | $10 |
| 6.7 | Bean Counter | Baked goods | Georgetown | Café | $15 |
| 6.6 | Java House | Middle Eastern | Dupont | Counter | $10 |
| 6.6 | Sette Osteria | Italian, Pizza | Dupont | Casual | $40 |
| 6.6 | Amici Miei | Italian | Potomac, MD | Casual | $50 |
| 6.6 | Chop't | American | Multiple locations | Counter | $10 |
| 6.5 | Open City | American | Woodley Park | Café | $40 |
| 6.5 | Café Bonaparte | French | Georgetown | Café | $45 |
| 6.5 | Veritas Wine Bar | New American | Dupont | Wine bar | $40 |
| 6.5 | Café Olé | Middle Eastern | Upper NW | Casual | $30 |
| 6.5 | Pete's Diner | American | Capitol Hill | Casual | $25 |
| 6.4 | Zorba's Café | Greek, Sandwiches | Dupont | Counter | $25 |
| 6.4 | Nirvana | Indian | Farragut | Casual | $35 |
| 6.4 | Al's Pizza | Pizza | Purcellville, VA | Counter | $20 |
| 6.3 | Peacock Café | New American | Georgetown | Upmarket | $60 |
| 6.3 | Mandu | Korean | Dupont | Casual | $40 |
| 6.3 | Astor Mediterranean | Middle Eastern | Multiple locations | Casual | $20 |
| 6.3 | Tandoor Grill | Indian | Capitol Hill | Casual | $30 |
| 6.3 | DC Café | Middle Eastern | Dupont | Counter | $25 |

| 6.3 | Faryab | Afghan | Bethesda, MD | Casual | $25 |
| 6.2 | Rosemary's Thyme Bistro | American, Italian | Dupont | Casual | $40 |
| 6.2 | Indique | Indian | Cleveland Park | Upmarket | $40 |
| 6.2 | Le Bon Café | Baked goods | Capitol Hill | Café | $20 |
| 6.2 | Teaism | Pan-Asian | Multiple locations | Café | $20 |
| 6.1 | Café Milano | Italian | Georgetown | Upmarket | $75 |
| 6.0 | Burma | Burmese | Chinatown | Casual | $25 |
| 6.0 | Kanlaya | Thai, Chinese | Chinatown | Casual | $30 |
| 6.0 | Aatish on the Hill | Indian | Capitol Hill | Casual | $30 |
| 5.9 | Grapeseed | New American | Bethesda, MD | Wine bar | $75 |
| 5.9 | Mai Thai | Thai | Multiple locations | Casual | $35 |
| 5.9 | Asylum | American | Dupont | Bar | $25 |
| 5.9 | Old City Café & Bakery | Middle Eastern | Adams Morgan | Counter | $10 |
| 5.8 | Vegetate | New American | Mt. Vernon Square | Upmarket | $45 |
| 5.8 | Sticky Fingers Bakery | Baked goods | Columbia Heights | Counter | $10 |
| 5.7 | Circa | Italian | Dupont | Casual | $40 |
| 5.7 | Couscous Café | Moroccan | Dupont | Counter | $10 |
| 5.7 | Bertucci's | Italian, Pizza | Multiple locations | Casual | $35 |
| 5.7 | Sunflower Vegetarian | Chinese | Falls Church, VA | Casual | $20 |
| 5.7 | Armand's | Pizza | Multiple locations | Casual | $25 |
| 5.7 | La Crêperie | French | Arlington, VA | Café | $15 |
| 5.6 | Little Fountain Café | New American | Adams Morgan | Upmarket | $45 |
| 5.6 | Byblos | Greek | Cleveland Park | Casual | $25 |
| 5.6 | Bombay Restaurant | Indian | Silver Spring, MD | Casual | $30 |
| 5.5 | Napoleon Bistro | French | Adams Morgan | Upmarket | $60 |
| 5.5 | Bangkok Joe's | Pan-Asian | Georgetown | Casual | $45 |
| 5.4 | Amsterdam Falafel Shop | Middle Eastern | Adams Morgan | Counter | $10 |
| 5.4 | La Madeleine | French, Sandwiches | Multiple locations | Counter | $30 |
| 5.3 | Alberto's Stone Oven Pizza | Pizza | Multiple locations | Counter | $5 |
| 5.3 | Yuan Fu | Chinese | Rockville, MD | Casual | $25 |
| 5.2 | Spices | Pan-Asian | Cleveland Park | Casual | $35 |
| 5.1 | Tryst | American | Adams Morgan | Café | $25 |
| 5.1 | Pomegranate Bistro | New American | Potomac, MD | Upmarket | $60 |
| 5.0 | Marrakesh Palace | Moroccan | Dupont | Upmarket | $45 |
| 5.0 | Café Asia | Pan-Asian | Multiple locations | Casual | $30 |
| 4.9 | Brasserie Monte Carlo | French | Bethesda, MD | Casual | $45 |
| 4.9 | Gordon Biersch | American | Multiple locations | Casual | $35 |
| 4.9 | Java Green | Sandwiches | Farragut | Café | $20 |
| 4.9 | Aditi Indian Cuisine | Indian | Multiple locations | Casual | $35 |
| 4.8 | ACKC Cocoa Bar | Sweet drinks | Multiple locations | Café | $10 |
| 4.8 | Asia Nine | Pan-Asian | Penn Quarter | Casual | $35 |
| 4.7 | Aroma | Indian | Multiple locations | Casual | $25 |
| 4.6 | Mr. Chen's | Chinese | Woodley Park | Casual | $25 |
| 4.5 | Paolo's | Italian | Georgetown | Casual | $40 |
| 4.5 | Camille's Sidewalk Café | Sandwiches | Multiple locations | Café | $25 |
| 4.4 | Naan & Beyond | Indian | Multiple locations | Counter | $25 |
| 4.3 | Café Luna | American, Italian | Dupont | Casual | $35 |
| 4.2 | Luna Grill & Diner | American, Italian | Multiple locations | Casual | $30 |
| 4.1 | Diner | American | Adams Morgan | Casual | $25 |
| 4.0 | Commissary | American | Logan Circle | Casual | $30 |
| 4.0 | Tai Shan | Chinese | Chinatown | Casual | $15 |
| 4.0 | Thai Roma | Thai | Capitol Hill | Casual | $35 |
| 3.7 | Ping by Charlie Chiang's | Pan-Asian | Arlington, VA | Casual | $45 |
| 3.7 | I Ricchi | Italian | Dupont | Upmarket | $80 |
| 3.7 | Olazzo | Italian | Multiple locations | Upmarket | $45 |
| 3.7 | Harmony Café | Chinese | Georgetown | Casual | $15 |
| 3.6 | Dupont Italian Kitchen | Italian | Dupont | Casual | $40 |
| 3.6 | Zed's Ethiopian Restaurant | Ethiopian | Georgetown | Casual | $30 |
| 3.5 | Café Citron | Nuevo Latino | Dupont | Casual | $35 |
| 3.5 | Jumbo Slice | Pizza | Adams Morgan | Counter | $5 |
| 3.2 | Sala Thai | Thai | Multiple locations | Casual | $25 |
| 3.1 | Wellness Café | Sandwiches | Capitol Hill | Café | $20 |

## All vegetarian-friendly establishments *continued*

| | | | |
|---|---|---|---|
| The Dairy Godmother | Ice cream | Alexandria, VA | Counter |
| Daruma Japanese Market | Japanese, Groceries | Bethesda, MD | Counter |
| Dean & Deluca | Groceries | Georgetown | Market |
| Dickey's Frozen Custard | Sandwiches | Multiple locations | Counter |
| Dolcezza | Ice cream | Multiple locations | Counter |
| Harris Teeter | Groceries | Multiple locations | Market |
| The Italian Store | Pizza, Sandwiches | Arlington, VA | Counter |
| M. E. Swing | Baked goods | Foggy Bottom | Café |
| Marvelous Market | Groceries | Multiple locations | Market |
| Max's Best Ice Cream | Ice cream | Glover Park | Counter |
| Mediterranean Bakery | Middle Eastern | Alexandria, VA | Counter |
| Sweetgreen | American, Ice cream | Georgetown | Counter |
| Thomas Sweet | Ice cream | Georgetown | Counter |
| Trader Joe's | Groceries | Multiple locations | Market |
| Union Station Food Court | | Union Station | Counter |
| Whole Foods Market | Groceries | Multiple locations | Market |

## Vegetarian-friendly with top feel ratings

| | | | | | |
|---|---|---|---|---|---|
| 9.7 | Afterwords Café | American | Dupont | Café | $35 |
| 9.7 | Busboys & Poets | American | Multiple locations | Casual | $25 |
| 9.6 | Marrakesh | Moroccan | Mt. Vernon Square | Upmarket | $50 |
| 9.5 | Little Fountain Café | New American | Adams Morgan | Upmarket | $45 |
| 9.3 | Blue Duck Tavern | New American | West End | Upmarket | $80 |
| 9.2 | Founding Farmers | American | Farragut | Upmarket | $50 |
| 9.2 | Ben's Chili Bowl | American | Multiple locations | Counter | $15 |
| 9.1 | Cork | New American | Logan Circle | Wine bar | $40 |
| 9.1 | Java House | Middle Eastern | Dupont | Counter | $10 |
| 9.1 | Commissary | American | Logan Circle | Casual | $30 |
| 9.0 | Al Tiramisú | Italian | Dupont | Upmarket | $55 |
| 9.0 | Rasika | Indian | Penn Quarter | Upmarket | $70 |
| 9.0 | Coppi's Organic | Italian, Pizza | U Street | Upmarket | $50 |
| 9.0 | Peking Gourmet Inn | Chinese | Falls Church, VA | Casual | $35 |
| 9.0 | Open City | American | Woodley Park | Café | $40 |
| 9.0 | Tryst | American | Adams Morgan | Café | $25 |
| 8.9 | Zaytinya | Middle Eastern | Chinatown | Upmarket | $65 |
| 8.9 | Queen Makeda | Ethiopian | Shaw | Casual | $30 |
| 8.8 | 2 Amys Pizza | Pizza | Cleveland Park | Casual | $35 |
| 8.8 | Coco Sala | New American | Downtown | Upmarket | $50 |
| 8.8 | Vinoteca | New American | U Street | Wine bar | $45 |
| 8.8 | Café Bonaparte | French | Georgetown | Café | $45 |
| 8.7 | To Sok Jip | Korean | Annandale, VA | Casual | $15 |
| 8.7 | Rosemary's Thyme Bistro | American, Italian | Dupont | Casual | $40 |
| 8.7 | Circa | Italian | Dupont | Casual | $40 |
| 8.7 | Paolo's | Italian | Georgetown | Casual | $40 |
| 8.6 | Passage to India | Indian | Bethesda, MD | Casual | $40 |
| 8.6 | Café Tu-O-Tu | Turkish, Sandwiches | Georgetown | Counter | $15 |
| 8.6 | Café Divan | Turkish | Glover Park | Casual | $35 |
| 8.5 | Proof | New American | Penn Quarter | Wine bar | $55 |
| 8.5 | Meskerem | Ethiopian | Adams Morgan | Casual | $25 |
| 8.5 | Veritas Wine Bar | New American | Dupont | Wine bar | $40 |
| 8.5 | Café Citron | Nuevo Latino | Dupont | Casual | $35 |
| 8.4 | TenPenh | Pan-Asian | Downtown | Upmarket | $70 |
| 8.3 | Urbana | New American | Dupont | Upmarket | $55 |
| 8.3 | Sette Osteria | Italian, Pizza | Dupont | Casual | $40 |
| 8.3 | Diner | American | Adams Morgan | Casual | $25 |
| 8.2 | Pizzeria Paradiso | Pizza | Multiple locations | Casual | $30 |
| 8.2 | Bardeo | New American | Cleveland Park | Wine bar | $35 |
| 8.2 | Pasta Mia | Italian | Adams Morgan | Casual | $25 |
| 8.2 | Ardeo | New American | Cleveland Park | Upmarket | $65 |
| 8.0 | Al Crostino | Italian | U Street | Upmarket | $55 |
| 8.0 | Meaza | Ethiopian | Falls Church, VA | Casual | $20 |
| 8.0 | ching ching CHA | Chinese | Georgetown | Café | $25 |

## Vegetarian-friendly with top feel ratings *continued*

| | | | | | |
|---|---|---|---|---|---|
| 8.0 | Black's Bar & Kitchen | New American | Bethesda, MD | Upmarket | $75 |
| 8.0 | Matchbox | American, Pizza | Chinatown | Casual | $35 |
| 8.0 | Neyla | Middle Eastern | Georgetown | Upmarket | $70 |
| 8.0 | Patisserie Poupon | Baked goods | Georgetown | Café | $35 |
| 8.0 | Zorba's Café | Greek, Sandwiches | Dupont | Counter | $25 |
| 8.0 | Indique | Indian | Cleveland Park | Upmarket | $40 |
| 8.0 | Dupont Italian Kitchen | Italian | Dupont | Casual | $40 |
| 7.9 | Good Stuff Eatery | American | Capitol Hill | Counter | $15 |
| 7.8 | RedRocks | Pizza | Columbia Heights | Casual | $35 |
| 7.8 | Las Placitas | Mexican | Capitol Hill | Casual | $40 |
| 7.8 | Café Olé | Middle Eastern | Upper NW | Casual | $30 |
| 7.8 | Peacock Café | New American | Georgetown | Upmarket | $60 |
| 7.7 | Pomegranate Bistro | New American | Potomac, MD | Upmarket | $60 |
| 7.7 | Marrakesh Palace | Moroccan | Dupont | Upmarket | $45 |
| 7.6 | Posto | Italian, Pizza | Logan Circle | Upmarket | $55 |
| 7.6 | Lebanese Taverna | Middle Eastern | Multiple locations | Casual | $40 |
| 7.6 | Straits of Malaya | Malaysian | Dupont | Casual | $35 |
| 7.6 | Nirvana | Indian | Farragut | Casual | $35 |
| 7.6 | Grapeseed | New American | Bethesda, MD | Wine bar | $75 |
| 7.6 | Vegetate | New American | Mt. Vernon Square | Upmarket | $45 |
| 7.5 | Light House Tofu | Korean | Multiple locations | Casual | $15 |
| 7.5 | Sakana | Japanese | Dupont | Casual | $35 |
| 7.5 | Potbelly Sandwich Works | Sandwiches | Multiple locations | Counter | $10 |
| 7.5 | Sorriso | Italian, Pizza | Cleveland Park | Casual | $40 |
| 7.5 | Ella's Pizza | Pizza | Chinatown | Casual | $40 |
| 7.5 | White Tiger | Indian | Capitol Hill | Casual | $35 |
| 7.5 | Pete's Diner | American | Capitol Hill | Casual | $25 |
| 7.5 | Napoleon Bistro | French | Adams Morgan | Upmarket | $60 |
| 7.4 | Mia's Pizza | Italian, Pizza | Bethesda, MD | Casual | $25 |
| 7.4 | Oya | Pan-Asian | Penn Quarter | Upmarket | $75 |
| 7.4 | Mai Thai | Thai | Multiple locations | Casual | $35 |
| 7.4 | Couscous Café | Moroccan | Dupont | Counter | $10 |
| 7.3 | Mandu | Korean | Dupont | Casual | $40 |
| 7.3 | Brasserie Monte Carlo | French | Bethesda, MD | Casual | $45 |
| 7.3 | Ping by Charlie Chiang's | Pan-Asian | Arlington, VA | Casual | $45 |
| 7.1 | Heritage India | Indian | Multiple locations | Casual | $40 |
| 7.0 | Shashemene | Ethiopian | Shaw | Casual | $25 |
| 7.0 | Afghan Grill | Afghan | Cleveland Park | Casual | $40 |
| 7.0 | Café Pizzaiolo | Pizza, Sandwiches | Multiple locations | Casual | $35 |
| 7.0 | Firehook | Baked goods | Multiple locations | Counter | $10 |
| 7.0 | Jyoti | Indian | Adams Morgan | Casual | $25 |
| 7.0 | Bagels & Baguettes | Sandwiches | Capitol Hill | Café | $10 |
| 7.0 | Bean Counter | Baked goods | Georgetown | Café | $15 |
| 7.0 | Astor Mediterranean | Middle Eastern | Multiple locations | Casual | $20 |
| 7.0 | Le Bon Café | Baked goods | Capitol Hill | Café | $20 |
| 7.0 | Teaism | Pan-Asian | Multiple locations | Café | $20 |
| 7.0 | Burma | Burmese | Chinatown | Casual | $25 |
| 7.0 | Kanlaya | Thai, Chinese | Chinatown | Casual | $30 |
| 7.0 | ACKC Cocoa Bar | Sweet drinks | Multiple locations | Café | $10 |
| 7.0 | Aroma | Indian | Multiple locations | Casual | $25 |

## Vegetarian-friendly and date-friendly

| | | | | | |
|---|---|---|---|---|---|
| 9.0 | Al Crostino | Italian | U Street | Upmarket | $55 |
| 9.0 | Posto | Italian, Pizza | Logan Circle | Upmarket | $55 |
| 8.8 | Al Tiramisú | Italian | Dupont | Upmarket | $55 |
| 8.6 | Rasika | Indian | Penn Quarter | Upmarket | $70 |
| 8.5 | Zaytinya | Middle Eastern | Chinatown | Upmarket | $65 |
| 8.5 | Urbana | New American | Dupont | Upmarket | $55 |
| 8.4 | Proof | New American | Penn Quarter | Wine bar | $55 |
| 8.2 | Founding Farmers | American | Farragut | Upmarket | $50 |
| 8.2 | Pizzeria Paradiso | Pizza | Multiple locations | Casual | $30 |
| 8.1 | ching ching CHA | Chinese | Georgetown | Café | $25 |

## Vegetarian-friendly and date-friendly *continued*

| | | | | | |
|---|---|---|---|---|---|
| 8.1 | RedRocks | Pizza | Columbia Heights | Casual | $35 |
| 8.0 | Afterwords Café | American | Dupont | Café | $35 |
| 8.0 | Coppi's Organic | Italian, Pizza | U Street | Upmarket | $50 |
| 7.9 | Black's Bar & Kitchen | New American | Bethesda, MD | Upmarket | $75 |
| 7.8 | Blue Duck Tavern | New American | West End | Upmarket | $80 |
| 7.8 | Bardeo | New American | Cleveland Park | Wine bar | $35 |
| 7.7 | Café Tu-O-Tu | Turkish, Sandwiches | Georgetown | Counter | $15 |
| 7.5 | Busboys & Poets | American | Multiple locations | Casual | $25 |
| 7.5 | Cork | New American | Logan Circle | Wine bar | $40 |
| 7.5 | Meskerem | Ethiopian | Adams Morgan | Casual | $25 |
| 7.4 | TenPenh | Pan-Asian | Downtown | Upmarket | $70 |
| 7.4 | Ardeo | New American | Cleveland Park | Upmarket | $65 |
| 7.3 | Coco Sala | New American | Downtown | Upmarket | $50 |
| 7.3 | Vinoteca | New American | U Street | Wine bar | $45 |
| 7.0 | Good Stuff Eatery | American | Capitol Hill | Counter | $15 |
| 6.9 | Straits of Malaya | Malaysian | Dupont | Casual | $35 |
| 6.7 | Marrakesh | Moroccan | Mt. Vernon Square | Upmarket | $50 |
| 6.5 | Café Bonaparte | French | Georgetown | Café | $45 |
| 6.5 | Veritas Wine Bar | New American | Dupont | Wine bar | $40 |
| 6.5 | Café Olé | Middle Eastern | Upper NW | Casual | $30 |
| 6.3 | Peacock Café | New American | Georgetown | Upmarket | $60 |
| 6.2 | Indique | Indian | Cleveland Park | Upmarket | $40 |
| 5.6 | Little Fountain Café | New American | Adams Morgan | Upmarket | $45 |
| 5.5 | Napoleon Bistro | French | Adams Morgan | Upmarket | $60 |
| 5.1 | Tryst | American | Adams Morgan | Café | $25 |
| 5.0 | Marrakesh Palace | Moroccan | Dupont | Upmarket | $45 |
| 4.9 | Brasserie Monte Carlo | French | Bethesda, MD | Casual | $45 |
| 4.8 | ACKC Cocoa Bar | Sweet drinks | Multiple locations | Café | $10 |
| 4.5 | Paolo's | Italian | Georgetown | Casual | $40 |
| | Dolcezza | Ice cream | Multiple locations | Counter | |
| | Max's Best Ice Cream | Ice cream | Glover Park | Counter | |

## Vegetarian-friendly and kid-friendly

| | | | | | |
|---|---|---|---|---|---|
| 9.6 | 2 Amys Pizza | Pizza | Cleveland Park | Casual | $35 |
| 8.6 | Bob's Noodle 66 | Taiwanese, Chinese | Rockville, MD | Casual | $15 |
| 8.4 | Sakana | Japanese | Dupont | Casual | $35 |
| 8.2 | Founding Farmers | American | Farragut | Upmarket | $50 |
| 8.2 | Pizzeria Paradiso | Pizza | Multiple locations | Casual | $30 |
| 8.1 | Ben's Chili Bowl | American | Multiple locations | Counter | $15 |
| 8.1 | RedRocks | Pizza | Columbia Heights | Casual | $35 |
| 8.0 | Afterwords Café | American | Dupont | Café | $35 |
| 8.0 | Passage to India | Indian | Bethesda, MD | Casual | $40 |
| 8.0 | La Baguette | French, Sandwiches | Dupont | Counter | $15 |
| 8.0 | Kabob Bazaar | Middle Eastern | Arlington, VA | Casual | $20 |
| 8.0 | Taste of Morocco | Moroccan | Arlington, VA | Casual | $35 |
| 7.8 | Tako Grill | Japanese | Bethesda, MD | Casual | $45 |
| 7.7 | Peking Gourmet Inn | Chinese | Falls Church, VA | Casual | $35 |
| 7.7 | Café Tu-O-Tu | Turkish, Sandwiches | Georgetown | Counter | $15 |
| 7.7 | Mia's Pizza | Italian, Pizza | Bethesda, MD | Casual | $25 |
| 7.6 | Amma Vegetarian Kitchen | Indian | Multiple locations | Casual | $20 |
| 7.5 | Meskerem | Ethiopian | Adams Morgan | Casual | $25 |
| 7.4 | Café Divan | Turkish | Glover Park | Casual | $35 |
| 7.4 | Potbelly Sandwich Works | Sandwiches | Multiple locations | Counter | $10 |
| 7.4 | Bombay Bistro | Indian | Multiple locations | Casual | $25 |
| 7.3 | Coco Sala | New American | Downtown | Upmarket | $50 |
| 7.3 | Café Pizzaiolo | Pizza, Sandwiches | Multiple locations | Casual | $35 |
| 7.2 | Heritage India | Indian | Multiple locations | Casual | $40 |
| 7.2 | Bombay Curry Company | Indian | Alexandria, VA | Casual | $20 |
| 7.1 | Greek Deli | Greek, Sandwiches | Farragut | Counter | $15 |
| 7.1 | Udupi Palace | Indian | Takoma Park, MD | Casual | $20 |
| 7.0 | Good Stuff Eatery | American | Capitol Hill | Counter | $15 |
| 7.0 | Cakelove and Love Café | Baked goods | Multiple locations | Café | $10 |

| 6.9 | Straits of Malaya | Malaysian | Dupont | Casual | $35 |
|---|---|---|---|---|---|
| 6.9 | Ella's Pizza | Pizza | Chinatown | Casual | $40 |
| 6.8 | Thai Tanic | Thai | Logan Circle | Casual | $30 |
| 6.7 | White Tiger | Indian | Capitol Hill | Casual | $35 |
| 6.6 | Java House | Middle Eastern | Dupont | Counter | $10 |
| 6.6 | Amici Miei | Italian | Potomac, MD | Casual | $50 |
| 6.5 | Café Olé | Middle Eastern | Upper NW | Casual | $30 |
| 6.4 | Nirvana | Indian | Farragut | Casual | $35 |
| 6.3 | Astor Mediterranean | Middle Eastern | Multiple locations | Casual | $20 |
| 6.3 | Tandoor Grill | Indian | Capitol Hill | Casual | $30 |
| 6.3 | Faryab | Afghan | Bethesda, MD | Casual | $25 |
| 6.2 | Rosemary's Thyme Bistro | American, Italian | Dupont | Casual | $40 |
| 6.0 | Kanlaya | Thai, Chinese | Chinatown | Casual | $30 |
| 5.9 | Mai Thai | Thai | Multiple locations | Casual | $35 |
| 5.8 | Sticky Fingers Bakery | Baked goods | Columbia Heights | Counter | $10 |
| 5.7 | Couscous Café | Moroccan | Dupont | Counter | $10 |
| 5.7 | Bertucci's | Italian, Pizza | Multiple locations | Casual | $35 |
| 5.7 | Sunflower Vegetarian | Chinese | Falls Church, VA | Casual | $20 |
| 5.7 | Armand's | Pizza | Multiple locations | Casual | $25 |
| 5.6 | Bombay Restaurant | Indian | Silver Spring, MD | Casual | $30 |
| 5.3 | Yuan Fu | Chinese | Rockville, MD | Casual | $25 |
| 5.2 | Spices | Pan-Asian | Cleveland Park | Casual | $35 |
| 5.0 | Marrakesh Palace | Moroccan | Dupont | Upmarket | $45 |
| 4.9 | Brasserie Monte Carlo | French | Bethesda, MD | Casual | $45 |
| 4.9 | Aditi Indian Cuisine | Indian | Multiple locations | Casual | $35 |
| 4.8 | ACKC Cocoa Bar | Sweet drinks | Multiple locations | Café | $10 |
| 4.5 | Paolo's | Italian | Georgetown | Casual | $40 |
| 4.2 | Luna Grill & Diner | American, Italian | Multiple locations | Casual | $30 |
| 4.0 | Commissary | American | Logan Circle | Casual | $30 |
| 4.0 | Tai Shan | Chinese | Chinatown | Casual | $15 |
| 3.7 | Ping by Charlie Chiang's | Pan-Asian | Arlington, VA | Casual | $45 |
| 3.7 | Olazzo | Italian | Multiple locations | Upmarket | $45 |
| | The Dairy Godmother | Ice cream | Alexandria, VA | Counter | |
| | Dean & Deluca | Groceries | Georgetown | Market | |
| | Dickey's Frozen Custard | Sandwiches | Multiple locations | Counter | |
| | The Italian Store | Pizza, Sandwiches | Arlington, VA | Counter | |
| | Max's Best Ice Cream | Ice cream | Glover Park | Counter | |
| | Mediterranean Bakery | Middle Eastern | Alexandria, VA | Counter | |
| | Sweetgreen | American, Ice cream | Georgetown | Counter | |
| | Thomas Sweet | Ice cream | Georgetown | Counter | |
| | Union Station Food Court | | Union Station | Counter | |

## Vegetarian-friendly delivery

| 8.1 | Queen Makeda | Ethiopian | Shaw | Casual | $30 |
|---|---|---|---|---|---|
| 8.1 | Fresh Med | Middle Eastern | Cleveland Park | Counter | $20 |
| 8.1 | Bread Line | Sandwiches | Farragut | Café | $15 |
| 8.0 | La Baguette | French, Sandwiches | Dupont | Counter | $15 |
| 7.9 | Langano | Ethiopian | Silver Spring, MD | Casual | $25 |
| 7.7 | Café Tu-O-Tu | Turkish, Sandwiches | Georgetown | Counter | $15 |
| 7.7 | Bethesda Bagels | Sandwiches | Bethesda, MD | Counter | $10 |
| 7.6 | Amma Vegetarian Kitchen | Indian | Multiple locations | Casual | $20 |
| 7.5 | Taverna the Greek Islands | Greek | Silver Spring, MD | Casual | $35 |
| 7.4 | Potbelly Sandwich Works | Sandwiches | Multiple locations | Counter | $10 |
| 7.3 | Café Pizzaiolo | Pizza, Sandwiches | Multiple locations | Casual | $35 |
| 7.2 | Heritage India | Indian | Multiple locations | Casual | $40 |
| 7.2 | Bombay Curry Company | Indian | Alexandria, VA | Casual | $20 |
| 7.1 | Jyoti | Indian | Adams Morgan | Casual | $25 |
| 7.1 | Harar Mesob | Ethiopian | Arlington, VA | Casual | $25 |
| 7.0 | Cakelove and Love Café | Baked goods | Multiple locations | Café | $10 |
| 6.9 | Straits of Malaya | Malaysian | Dupont | Casual | $35 |
| 6.8 | Thai Tanic | Thai | Logan Circle | Casual | $30 |
| 6.8 | La Prima | Sandwiches | Multiple locations | Counter | $20 |

## Vegetarian-friendly delivery *continued*

| | | | | | |
|---|---|---|---|---|---|
| 6.6 | Chop't | American | Multiple locations | Counter | $10 |
| 6.4 | Nirvana | Indian | Farragut | Casual | $35 |
| 6.3 | Tandoor Grill | Indian | Capitol Hill | Casual | $30 |
| 6.0 | Kanlaya | Thai, Chinese | Chinatown | Casual | $30 |
| 6.0 | Aatish on the Hill | Indian | Capitol Hill | Casual | $30 |
| 5.9 | Mai Thai | Thai | Multiple locations | Casual | $35 |
| 5.8 | Sticky Fingers Bakery | Baked goods | Columbia Heights | Counter | $10 |
| 5.7 | Couscous Café | Moroccan | Dupont | Counter | $10 |
| 5.7 | Bertucci's | Italian, Pizza | Multiple locations | Casual | $35 |
| 5.7 | Armand's | Pizza | Multiple locations | Casual | $25 |
| 5.6 | Byblos | Greek | Cleveland Park | Casual | $25 |
| 5.3 | Alberto's Stone Oven Pizza | Pizza | Multiple locations | Counter | $5 |
| 5.2 | Spices | Pan-Asian | Cleveland Park | Casual | $35 |
| 5.1 | Pomegranate Bistro | New American | Potomac, MD | Upmarket | $60 |
| 5.0 | Café Asia | Pan-Asian | Multiple locations | Casual | $30 |
| 4.9 | Aditi Indian Cuisine | Indian | Multiple locations | Casual | $35 |
| 4.8 | ACKC Cocoa Bar | Sweet drinks | Multiple locations | Café | $10 |
| 4.6 | Mr. Chen's | Chinese | Woodley Park | Casual | $25 |
| 4.5 | Camille's Sidewalk Café | Sandwiches | Multiple locations | Café | $25 |
| 4.4 | Naan & Beyond | Indian | Multiple locations | Counter | $25 |
| 4.3 | Café Luna | American, Italian | Dupont | Casual | $35 |
| 4.2 | Luna Grill & Diner | American, Italian | Multiple locations | Casual | $30 |
| 4.0 | Commissary | American | Logan Circle | Casual | $30 |
| 4.0 | Tai Shan | Chinese | Chinatown | Casual | $15 |
| 4.0 | Thai Roma | Thai | Capitol Hill | Casual | $35 |
| 3.7 | Ping by Charlie Chiang's | Pan-Asian | Arlington, VA | Casual | $45 |
| 3.6 | Dupont Italian Kitchen | Italian | Dupont | Casual | $40 |
| 3.2 | Sala Thai | Thai | Multiple locations | Casual | $25 |
| | Dickey's Frozen Custard | Sandwiches | Multiple locations | Counter | |
| | Dolcezza | Ice cream | Multiple locations | Counter | |
| | Marvelous Market | Groceries | Multiple locations | Market | |

# What's still open?

**This is our late-night guide to DC food.** These places claim to stay open as follows; still, we recommend calling first, as the hours sometimes aren't honored on slow nights.

## Weekday food after 10pm

| | | | | | |
|---|---|---|---|---|---|
| 9.1 | Marvin | Southern, Belgian | U Street | Upmarket | $45 |
| 9.1 | Tosca | Italian | Downtown | Upmarket | $75 |
| 9.0 | Posto | Italian, Pizza | Logan Circle | Upmarket | $55 |
| 8.9 | Bistro Bis | French | Capitol Hill | Upmarket | $70 |
| 8.9 | Annan-Gol | Korean | Annandale, VA | Casual | $20 |
| 8.9 | Roger Miller Restaurant | Cameroonian | Silver Spring, MD | Casual | $30 |
| 8.9 | Gamasot | Korean | Springfield, VA | Casual | $15 |
| 8.8 | Gooldaegee | Korean | Annandale, VA | Casual | $20 |
| 8.8 | Al Tiramisú | Italian | Dupont | Upmarket | $55 |
| 8.8 | Central Michel Richard | French | Penn Quarter | Upmarket | $70 |
| 8.8 | Light House Tofu | Korean | Multiple locations | Casual | $15 |
| 8.8 | Shashemene | Ethiopian | Shaw | Casual | $25 |
| 8.8 | Corduroy | New American | Mt. Vernon Square | Upmarket | $70 |
| 8.8 | Etete | Ethiopian | Shaw | Casual | $30 |
| 8.7 | Taberna del Alabardero | Spanish | Farragut | Upmarket | $75 |
| 8.7 | BLT Steak | Steakhouse | Farragut | Upmarket | $95 |
| 8.7 | Eamonn's | Seafood, Irish | Old Town | Casual | $20 |
| 8.6 | Rasika | Indian | Penn Quarter | Upmarket | $70 |
| 8.6 | Meaza | Ethiopian | Falls Church, VA | Casual | $20 |
| 8.6 | Kabob Palace | Middle Eastern | Arlington, VA | Counter | $20 |
| 8.5 | Zaytinya | Middle Eastern | Chinatown | Upmarket | $65 |
| 8.5 | To Sok Jip | Korean | Annandale, VA | Casual | $15 |
| 8.5 | Sushi-Ko | Japanese | Multiple locations | Upmarket | $60 |
| 8.5 | Prime Rib | Steakhouse | Farragut | Upmarket | $90 |
| 8.4 | Brasserie Beck | Belgian | Downtown | Upmarket | $55 |
| 8.4 | Proof | New American | Penn Quarter | Wine bar | $55 |
| 8.4 | Sakana | Japanese | Dupont | Casual | $35 |
| 8.3 | Bistrot du Coin | French | Dupont | Casual | $50 |
| 8.3 | Hook | Seafood | Georgetown | Upmarket | $80 |
| 8.3 | Smith & Wollensky | Steakhouse | Farragut | Upmarket | $85 |
| 8.2 | Founding Farmers | American | Farragut | Upmarket | $50 |
| 8.2 | Irene's Pupusas | Salvadoran | Multiple locations | Casual | $25 |
| 8.2 | Pizzeria Paradiso | Pizza | Multiple locations | Casual | $30 |
| 8.2 | Mogotillo | Salvadoran | Takoma Park, MD | Casual | $20 |
| 8.2 | Li Ho | Chinese | Chinatown | Casual | $10 |
| 8.1 | Quarry House Tavern | American | Silver Spring, MD | Casual | $25 |
| 8.1 | Ben's Chili Bowl | American | Multiple locations | Counter | $15 |
| 8.1 | Bourbon | American | Multiple locations | Bar | $35 |
| 8.1 | Queen Makeda | Ethiopian | Shaw | Casual | $30 |
| 8.1 | RedRocks | Pizza | Columbia Heights | Casual | $35 |
| 8.1 | Bombay Club | Indian | Farragut | Upmarket | $45 |
| 8.0 | Afterwords Café | American | Dupont | Café | $35 |
| 8.0 | Oyamel | Mexican | Penn Quarter | Upmarket | $60 |
| 8.0 | Coppi's Organic | Italian, Pizza | U Street | Upmarket | $50 |
| 8.0 | Crème | Southern | U Street | Casual | $45 |
| 8.0 | Taquería Distrito Federal | Mexican | Multiple locations | Casual | $20 |
| 7.9 | Cashion's Eat Place | New American | Adams Morgan | Upmarket | $60 |
| 7.9 | Langano | Ethiopian | Silver Spring, MD | Casual | $25 |
| 7.8 | Blue Duck Tavern | New American | West End | Upmarket | $80 |

| 7.8 | Bardeo | New American | Cleveland Park | Wine bar | $35 |
|-----|--------|--------------|----------------|----------|-----|
| 7.8 | Ruth's Chris Steakhouse | Steakhouse | Multiple locations | Upmarket | $90 |
| 7.8 | Afghan Grill | Afghan | Cleveland Park | Casual | $40 |
| 7.8 | Full Kee | Chinese | Multiple locations | Casual | $25 |
| 7.7 | W Domku | Scandinavian | Petworth | Casual | $40 |
| 7.7 | Peking Gourmet Inn | Chinese | Falls Church, VA | Casual | $35 |
| 7.6 | Round Robin Bar | American | Downtown | Bar | $40 |
| 7.6 | Leopold's Kafe | Austrian | Georgetown | Casual | $40 |
| 7.6 | Matchbox | American, Pizza | Chinatown | Casual | $35 |
| 7.5 | Busboys & Poets | American | Multiple locations | Casual | $25 |
| 7.5 | Cork | New American | Logan Circle | Wine bar | $40 |
| 7.5 | La Chaumière | French | Georgetown | Upmarket | $60 |
| 7.5 | Meskerem | Ethiopian | Adams Morgan | Casual | $25 |
| 7.5 | Ulah Bistro | American | U Street | Upmarket | $45 |
| 7.5 | Lebanese Taverna | Middle Eastern | Multiple locations | Casual | $40 |
| 7.5 | Thai Square | Thai | Arlington, VA | Casual | $35 |
| 7.5 | El Khartoum | Sudanese | Shaw | Counter | $20 |
| 7.4 | Café Divan | Turkish | Glover Park | Casual | $35 |
| 7.4 | TenPenh | Pan-Asian | Downtown | Upmarket | $70 |
| 7.4 | Ardeo | New American | Cleveland Park | Upmarket | $65 |
| 7.4 | Jackson 20 | New American | Old Town | Upmarket | $65 |
| 7.4 | Neyla | Middle Eastern | Georgetown | Upmarket | $70 |
| 7.3 | Coco Sala | New American | Downtown | Upmarket | $50 |
| 7.3 | Vinoteca | New American | U Street | Wine bar | $45 |
| 7.3 | Bourbon Steak | New American | Georgetown | Upmarket | $115 |
| 7.3 | DC Coast | Seafood | Downtown | Upmarket | $75 |
| 7.3 | Kinkead's | Seafood | Foggy Bottom | Upmarket | $75 |
| 7.3 | Mixtec | Mexican | Adams Morgan | Casual | $25 |
| 7.3 | Chinatown Express | Chinese | Chinatown | Casual | $25 |
| 7.2 | Heritage India | Indian | Multiple locations | Casual | $40 |
| 7.2 | Mayur Kabab House | Pakistani, Indian | Chinatown | Casual | $20 |
| 7.1 | Kemble Park Tavern | New American | Palisades | Upmarket | $60 |
| 7.1 | Tabaq Bistro | Middle Eastern | U Street | Upmarket | $45 |
| 7.1 | Acadiana | Southern | Mt. Vernon Square | Upmarket | $60 |
| 7.1 | District Chophouse | Steakhouse | Penn Quarter | Casual | $45 |
| 7.1 | Oya | Pan-Asian | Penn Quarter | Upmarket | $75 |
| 7.1 | Jyoti | Indian | Adams Morgan | Casual | $25 |
| 7.1 | Axum | Ethiopian | Shaw | Casual | $25 |
| 7.1 | Harar Mesob | Ethiopian | Arlington, VA | Casual | $25 |
| 7.1 | Julia's Empanadas | Latin American | Multiple locations | Counter | $5 |
| 7.0 | Ceiba | Nuevo Latino | Downtown | Upmarket | $60 |
| 7.0 | Good Stuff Eatery | American | Capitol Hill | Counter | $15 |
| 7.0 | Las Placitas | Mexican | Capitol Hill | Casual | $40 |
| 7.0 | Rustico | New American | Alexandria, VA | Casual | $40 |
| 7.0 | Chi-Cha Lounge | Latin American | U Street | Casual | $30 |
| 6.9 | Old Ebbitt Grill | American | Downtown | Casual | $40 |
| 6.9 | Annie's Paramount | American | Dupont | Casual | $35 |
| 6.9 | Tunnicliff's Tavern | American | Capitol Hill | Casual | $40 |
| 6.9 | Straits of Malaya | Malaysian | Dupont | Casual | $35 |
| 6.9 | Whitlow's on Wilson | American | Arlington, VA | Casual | $35 |
| 6.9 | Carlyle | New American | Arlington, VA | Casual | $40 |
| 6.8 | Trusty's | American | Capitol Hill | Casual | $35 |
| 6.8 | Madjet | Ethiopian | Shaw | Casual | $23 |
| 6.7 | Marrakesh | Moroccan | Mt. Vernon Square | Upmarket | $50 |
| 6.6 | Java House | Middle Eastern | Dupont | Counter | $10 |
| 6.6 | Sette Osteria | Italian, Pizza | Dupont | Casual | $40 |
| 6.6 | Capitol City Brewery | American | Multiple locations | Casual | $35 |
| 6.6 | Nooshi | Pan-Asian | Farragut | Casual | $25 |
| 6.5 | Open City | American | Woodley Park | Café | $40 |
| 6.5 | Café Bonaparte | French | Georgetown | Café | $45 |
| 6.5 | Veritas Wine Bar | New American | Dupont | Wine bar | $40 |
| 6.5 | Alero | Mexican | Multiple locations | Casual | $40 |

| 6.5 | Evolve | New American | Adams Morgan | Upmarket | $40 |
|---|---|---|---|---|---|
| 6.4 | Martin's Tavern | American | Georgetown | Casual | $35 |
| 6.4 | Zorba's Café | Greek, Sandwiches | Dupont | Counter | $25 |
| 6.4 | Mark's Duck House | Chinese | Falls Church, VA | Casual | $30 |
| 6.3 | Peacock Café | New American | Georgetown | Upmarket | $60 |
| 6.3 | Astor Mediterranean | Middle Eastern | Multiple locations | Casual | $20 |
| 6.3 | Station 9 | New American | U Street | Upmarket | $45 |
| 6.3 | Old Glory Bar-B-Que | Barbecue | Georgetown | Casual | $30 |
| 6.3 | DC Café | Middle Eastern | Dupont | Counter | $25 |
| 6.2 | Café Saint-Ex | French, American | U Street | Casual | $40 |
| 6.2 | Rosemary's Thyme Bistro | American, Italian | Dupont | Casual | $40 |
| 6.2 | Indique | Indian | Cleveland Park | Upmarket | $40 |
| 6.2 | Stoney's Bar & Grill | American | Logan Circle | Casual | $40 |
| 6.2 | Murali | Italian | Arlington, VA | Upmarket | $50 |
| 6.1 | Café Milano | Italian | Georgetown | Upmarket | $75 |
| 6.1 | Primi Piatti | Italian | Foggy Bottom | Upmarket | $70 |
| 6.0 | The Red and the Black | Southern | Northeast DC | Bar | $25 |
| 6.0 | Granville Moore's Brickyard | Belgian | Northeast DC | Casual | $40 |
| 6.0 | Cococabana Bar & Grill | Italian, Mexican | Hyattsville, MD | Casual | $30 |
| 6.0 | Finn & Porter | American | Multiple locations | Upmarket | $75 |
| 5.9 | Bistro Français | French | Georgetown | Casual | $40 |
| 5.9 | Mai Thai | Thai | Multiple locations | Casual | $35 |
| 5.9 | Sesto Senso | Italian | Dupont | Upmarket | $55 |
| 5.9 | Maté | Pan-Asian | Georgetown | Casual | $45 |
| 5.9 | Thaiphoon | Thai | Multiple locations | Casual | $40 |
| 5.9 | El Tamarindo | Mexican | Adams Morgan | Casual | $40 |
| 5.9 | Asylum | American | Dupont | Bar | $25 |
| 5.9 | Old City Café & Bakery | Middle Eastern | Adams Morgan | Counter | $10 |
| 5.9 | Kanpai | Japanese | Arlington, VA | Casual | $30 |
| 5.8 | The Big Hunt | American | Dupont | Bar | $20 |
| 5.8 | Rosa Mexicano | Mexican | Penn Quarter | Upmarket | $55 |
| 5.8 | Hudson | New American | West End | Upmarket | $65 |
| 5.8 | Filomena | Italian | Georgetown | Casual | $50 |
| 5.7 | Circa | Italian | Dupont | Casual | $40 |
| 5.7 | La Tasca | Spanish | Multiple locations | Casual | $40 |
| 5.7 | Tono Sushi | Japanese | Woodley Park | Casual | $40 |
| 5.6 | Darlington House | New American | Dupont | Upmarket | $65 |
| 5.6 | Thai Chef | Thai, Japanese | Dupont | Casual | $40 |
| 5.6 | Banana Café & Piano Bar | Cuban | Capitol Hill | Café | $30 |
| 5.5 | Local 16 | American | U Street | Upmarket | $40 |
| 5.5 | Napoleon Bistro | French | Adams Morgan | Upmarket | $60 |
| 5.5 | Bangkok Joe's | Pan-Asian | Georgetown | Casual | $45 |
| 5.4 | Amsterdam Falafel Shop | Middle Eastern | Adams Morgan | Counter | $10 |
| 5.3 | Il Mulino | Italian | Downtown | Upmarket | $80 |
| 5.3 | Alberto's Stone Oven Pizza | Pizza | Multiple locations | Counter | $5 |
| 5.3 | Boulevard Woodgrill | New American | Arlington, VA | Casual | $45 |
| 5.3 | Eat First | Chinese | Chinatown | Casual | $20 |
| 5.2 | La Loma | Mexican | Capitol Hill | Casual | $30 |
| 5.2 | Spices | Pan-Asian | Cleveland Park | Casual | $35 |
| 5.2 | Beacon Bar & Grill | New American | Dupont | Casual | $45 |
| 5.1 | Tryst | American | Adams Morgan | Café | $25 |
| 5.1 | Singapore Bistro | Pan-Asian | Farragut | Casual | $25 |
| 5.1 | Clyde's | American | Multiple locations | Casual | $40 |
| 5.1 | Grill from Ipanema | Brazilian | Adams Morgan | Casual | $45 |
| 5.1 | Asian Spice | Chinese, Pan-Asian | Chinatown | Casual | $40 |
| 5.1 | Old Siam | Thai | Capitol Hill | Casual | $25 |
| 5.0 | Marrakesh Palace | Moroccan | Dupont | Upmarket | $45 |
| 5.0 | Lima | Nuevo Latino | Downtown | Upmarket | $55 |
| 5.0 | Skye Lounge | Middle Eastern | Farragut | Casual | $40 |
| 5.0 | Café Asia | Pan-Asian | Multiple locations | Casual | $30 |
| 4.9 | Gordon Biersch | American | Multiple locations | Casual | $35 |
| 4.8 | Mie N Yu | Pan-Asian | Georgetown | Upmarket | $55 |

## Weekday food after 10pm *continued*

| | | | | | |
|---|---|---|---|---|---|
| 4.8 | Fusion Grill | Pan-Asian | Capitol Hill | Upmarket | $55 |
| 4.8 | Trattoria Alberto | Italian | Capitol Hill | Casual | $45 |
| 4.8 | Pour House | American | Capitol Hill | Casual | $35 |
| 4.8 | 701 | New American | Penn Quarter | Upmarket | $70 |
| 4.8 | Asia Nine | Pan-Asian | Penn Quarter | Casual | $35 |
| 4.7 | Hunan Dynasty | Chinese | Capitol Hill | Casual | $25 |
| 4.6 | The Tombs | American | Georgetown | Bar | $25 |
| 4.6 | La Tomate | Italian | Dupont | Upmarket | $45 |
| 4.6 | Mr. Chen's | Chinese | Woodley Park | Casual | $25 |
| 4.6 | Veranda | Greek, Italian | Logan Circle | Casual | $40 |
| 4.5 | Paolo's | Italian | Georgetown | Casual | $40 |
| 4.5 | Meiwah | Chinese, Japanese | Multiple locations | Casual | $45 |
| 4.5 | Tony Cheng's Seafood | Chinese | Chinatown | Casual | $35 |
| 4.4 | Rice | Thai | Logan Circle | Upmarket | $30 |
| 4.3 | Skewers | Middle Eastern | Dupont | Casual | $30 |
| 4.3 | Hard Times Café | American | Multiple locations | Casual | $20 |
| 4.3 | J. Paul's | American | Georgetown | Casual | $45 |
| 4.2 | Luna Grill & Diner | American, Italian | Multiple locations | Casual | $30 |
| 4.2 | Sushi-Go-Round & Tapas | Pan-Asian | Chinatown | Casual | $45 |
| 4.1 | Diner | American | Adams Morgan | Casual | $25 |
| 4.0 | Brickskeller | American | Dupont | Bar | $15 |
| 4.0 | Commissary | American | Logan Circle | Casual | $30 |
| 4.0 | Tai Shan | Chinese | Chinatown | Casual | $15 |
| 4.0 | Tony Cheng's Mongolian | Pan-Asian | Chinatown | Casual | $35 |
| 3.8 | Logan Tavern | American | Logan Circle | Casual | $35 |
| 3.8 | The Front Page | American | Dupont | Casual | $35 |
| 3.8 | Wok & Roll | Chinese | Chinatown | Casual | $20 |
| 3.8 | Union Pub | American | Capitol Hill | Casual | $25 |
| 3.7 | Ping by Charlie Chiang's | Pan-Asian | Arlington, VA | Casual | $45 |
| 3.7 | Harmony Café | Chinese | Georgetown | Casual | $15 |
| 3.6 | Dupont Italian Kitchen | Italian | Dupont | Casual | $40 |
| 3.6 | Zed's Ethiopian Restaurant | Ethiopian | Georgetown | Casual | $30 |
| 3.5 | Café Citron | Nuevo Latino | Dupont | Casual | $35 |
| 3.5 | Jumbo Slice | Pizza | Adams Morgan | Counter | $5 |
| 3.2 | Sala Thai | Thai | Multiple locations | Casual | $25 |
| 2.2 | Lauriol Plaza | Mexican | Adams Morgan | Casual | $35 |
| 1.4 | Prince Café | Middle Eastern | Multiple locations | Casual | $25 |
| | Harris Teeter | Groceries | Multiple locations | Market | |
| | Thomas Sweet | Ice cream | Georgetown | Counter | |

## Weekday food after 11pm

| | | | | | |
|---|---|---|---|---|---|
| 9.1 | Marvin | Southern, Belgian | U Street | Upmarket | $45 |
| 8.9 | Annan-Gol | Korean | Annandale, VA | Casual | $20 |
| 8.8 | Gooldaegee | Korean | Annandale, VA | Casual | $20 |
| 8.8 | Shashemene | Ethiopian | Shaw | Casual | $25 |
| 8.8 | Etete | Ethiopian | Shaw | Casual | $30 |
| 8.7 | BLT Steak | Steakhouse | Farragut | Upmarket | $95 |
| 8.6 | Meaza | Ethiopian | Falls Church, VA | Casual | $20 |
| 8.6 | Kabob Palace | Middle Eastern | Arlington, VA | Counter | $20 |
| 8.5 | Zaytinya | Middle Eastern | Chinatown | Upmarket | $65 |
| 8.3 | Bistrot du Coin | French | Dupont | Casual | $50 |
| 8.2 | Irene's Pupusas | Salvadoran | Multiple locations | Casual | $25 |
| 8.2 | Mogotillo | Salvadoran | Takoma Park, MD | Casual | $20 |
| 8.2 | Li Ho | Chinese | Chinatown | Casual | $10 |
| 8.1 | Quarry House Tavern | American | Silver Spring, MD | Casual | $25 |
| 8.1 | Ben's Chili Bowl | American | Multiple locations | Counter | $15 |
| 8.1 | Bourbon | American | Multiple locations | Bar | $35 |
| 8.1 | Queen Makeda | Ethiopian | Shaw | Casual | $30 |
| 8.0 | Afterwords Café | American | Dupont | Café | $35 |
| 8.0 | Oyamel | Mexican | Penn Quarter | Upmarket | $60 |
| 7.9 | Langano | Ethiopian | Silver Spring, MD | Casual | $25 |
| 7.8 | Full Kee | Chinese | Multiple locations | Casual | $25 |

## Weekday food after 11pm *continued*

| | | | | |
|---|---|---|---|---|
| 7.6 | Round Robin Bar | American | Downtown | Bar | $40 |
| 7.5 | Busboys & Poets | American | Multiple locations | Casual | $25 |
| 7.5 | Cork | New American | Logan Circle | Wine bar | $40 |
| 7.5 | Meskerem | Ethiopian | Adams Morgan | Casual | $25 |
| 7.5 | Ulah Bistro | American | U Street | Upmarket | $45 |
| 7.5 | El Khartoum | Sudanese | Shaw | Counter | $20 |
| 7.3 | Vinoteca | New American | U Street | Wine bar | $45 |
| 7.3 | Mixtec | Mexican | Adams Morgan | Casual | $25 |
| 7.2 | Mayur Kabab House | Pakistani, Indian | Chinatown | Casual | $20 |
| 7.1 | Axum | Ethiopian | Shaw | Casual | $25 |
| 7.1 | Julia's Empanadas | Latin American | Multiple locations | Counter | $5 |
| 7.0 | Rustico | New American | Alexandria, VA | Casual | $40 |
| 7.0 | Chi-Cha Lounge | Latin American | U Street | Casual | $30 |
| 6.9 | Old Ebbitt Grill | American | Downtown | Casual | $40 |
| 6.9 | Annie's Paramount | American | Dupont | Casual | $35 |
| 6.9 | Tunnicliff's Tavern | American | Capitol Hill | Casual | $40 |
| 6.9 | Whitlow's on Wilson | American | Arlington, VA | Casual | $35 |
| 6.8 | Trusty's | American | Capitol Hill | Casual | $35 |
| 6.8 | Madjet | Ethiopian | Shaw | Casual | $23 |
| 6.5 | Open City | American | Woodley Park | Café | $40 |
| 6.5 | Veritas Wine Bar | New American | Dupont | Wine bar | $40 |
| 6.5 | Alero | Mexican | Multiple locations | Casual | $40 |
| 6.4 | Martin's Tavern | American | Georgetown | Casual | $35 |
| 6.4 | Zorba's Café | Greek, Sandwiches | Dupont | Counter | $25 |
| 6.3 | Old Glory Bar-B-Que | Barbecue | Georgetown | Casual | $30 |
| 6.3 | DC Café | Middle Eastern | Dupont | Counter | $25 |
| 6.2 | Café Saint-Ex | French, American | U Street | Casual | $40 |
| 6.2 | Stoney's Bar & Grill | American | Logan Circle | Casual | $40 |
| 6.1 | Café Milano | Italian | Georgetown | Upmarket | $75 |
| 6.0 | The Red and the Black | Southern | Northeast DC | Bar | $25 |
| 6.0 | Granville Moore's Brickyard | Belgian | Northeast DC | Casual | $40 |
| 6.0 | Cococabana Bar & Grill | Italian, Mexican | Hyattsville, MD | Casual | $30 |
| 5.9 | Bistro Français | French | Georgetown | Casual | $40 |
| 5.9 | Maté | Pan-Asian | Georgetown | Casual | $45 |
| 5.9 | El Tamarindo | Mexican | Adams Morgan | Casual | $40 |
| 5.9 | Asylum | American | Dupont | Bar | $25 |
| 5.8 | The Big Hunt | American | Dupont | Bar | $20 |
| 5.8 | Rosa Mexicano | Mexican | Penn Quarter | Upmarket | $55 |
| 5.8 | Hudson | New American | West End | Upmarket | $65 |
| 5.8 | Filomena | Italian | Georgetown | Casual | $50 |
| 5.7 | Circa | Italian | Dupont | Casual | $40 |
| 5.7 | La Tasca | Spanish | Multiple locations | Casual | $40 |
| 5.5 | Local 16 | American | U Street | Upmarket | $40 |
| 5.4 | Amsterdam Falafel Shop | Middle Eastern | Adams Morgan | Counter | $10 |
| 5.3 | Alberto's Stone Oven Pizza | Pizza | Multiple locations | Counter | $5 |
| 5.3 | Eat First | Chinese | Chinatown | Casual | $20 |
| 5.1 | Tryst | American | Adams Morgan | Café | $25 |
| 5.1 | Clyde's | American | Multiple locations | Casual | $40 |
| 5.0 | Lima | Nuevo Latino | Downtown | Upmarket | $55 |
| 5.0 | Skye Lounge | Middle Eastern | Farragut | Casual | $40 |
| 4.9 | Gordon Biersch | American | Multiple locations | Casual | $35 |
| 4.8 | Pour House | American | Capitol Hill | Casual | $35 |
| 4.8 | Asia Nine | Pan-Asian | Penn Quarter | Casual | $35 |
| 4.6 | The Tombs | American | Georgetown | Bar | $25 |
| 4.6 | Veranda | Greek, Italian | Logan Circle | Casual | $40 |
| 4.5 | Paolo's | Italian | Georgetown | Casual | $40 |
| 4.3 | Skewers | Middle Eastern | Dupont | Casual | $30 |
| 4.3 | J. Paul's | American | Georgetown | Casual | $45 |
| 4.1 | Diner | American | Adams Morgan | Casual | $25 |
| 4.0 | Brickskeller | American | Dupont | Bar | $15 |
| 4.0 | Tai Shan | Chinese | Chinatown | Casual | $15 |
| 3.5 | Café Citron | Nuevo Latino | Dupont | Casual | $35 |

## Weekday food after 11pm *continued*

| | | | | |
|---|---|---|---|---|
| 3.5 | Jumbo Slice | Pizza | Adams Morgan | Counter | $5 |
| 1.4 | Prince Café | Middle Eastern | Multiple locations | Casual | $25 |
| | Thomas Sweet | Ice cream | Georgetown | Counter | |

## Weekday food after midnight

| | | | | |
|---|---|---|---|---|
| 9.1 | Marvin | Southern, Belgian | U Street | Upmarket | $45 |
| 8.8 | Gooldaegee | Korean | Annandale, VA | Casual | $20 |
| 8.8 | Shashemene | Ethiopian | Shaw | Casual | $25 |
| 8.8 | Etete | Ethiopian | Shaw | Casual | $30 |
| 8.6 | Meaza | Ethiopian | Falls Church, VA | Casual | $20 |
| 8.3 | Bistrot du Coin | French | Dupont | Casual | $50 |
| 8.2 | Irene's Pupusas | Salvadoran | Multiple locations | Casual | $25 |
| 8.2 | Mogotillo | Salvadoran | Takoma Park, MD | Casual | $20 |
| 8.2 | Li Ho | Chinese | Chinatown | Casual | $10 |
| 8.1 | Quarry House Tavern | American | Silver Spring, MD | Casual | $25 |
| 8.1 | Ben's Chili Bowl | American | Multiple locations | Counter | $15 |
| 8.1 | Bourbon | American | Multiple locations | Bar | $35 |
| 8.1 | Queen Makeda | Ethiopian | Shaw | Casual | $30 |
| 8.0 | Afterwords Café | American | Dupont | Café | $35 |
| 7.9 | Langano | Ethiopian | Silver Spring, MD | Casual | $25 |
| 7.8 | Full Kee | Chinese | Multiple locations | Casual | $25 |
| 7.6 | Round Robin Bar | American | Downtown | Bar | $40 |
| 7.5 | Cork | New American | Logan Circle | Wine bar | $40 |
| 7.5 | Ulah Bistro | American | U Street | Upmarket | $45 |
| 7.5 | El Khartoum | Sudanese | Shaw | Counter | $20 |
| 7.3 | Vinoteca | New American | U Street | Wine bar | $45 |
| 7.1 | Axum | Ethiopian | Shaw | Casual | $25 |
| 7.1 | Julia's Empanadas | Latin American | Multiple locations | Counter | $5 |
| 7.0 | Chi-Cha Lounge | Latin American | U Street | Casual | $30 |
| 6.9 | Old Ebbitt Grill | American | Downtown | Casual | $40 |
| 6.9 | Annie's Paramount | American | Dupont | Casual | $35 |
| 6.9 | Tunnicliff's Tavern | American | Capitol Hill | Casual | $40 |
| 6.9 | Whitlow's on Wilson | American | Arlington, VA | Casual | $35 |
| 6.8 | Trusty's | American | Capitol Hill | Casual | $35 |
| 6.4 | Martin's Tavern | American | Georgetown | Casual | $35 |
| 6.3 | Old Glory Bar-B-Que | Barbecue | Georgetown | Casual | $30 |
| 6.3 | DC Café | Middle Eastern | Dupont | Counter | $25 |
| 6.2 | Café Saint-Ex | French, American | U Street | Casual | $40 |
| 6.2 | Stoney's Bar & Grill | American | Logan Circle | Casual | $40 |
| 6.1 | Café Milano | Italian | Georgetown | Upmarket | $75 |
| 6.0 | The Red and the Black | Southern | Northeast DC | Bar | $25 |
| 6.0 | Cococabana Bar & Grill | Italian, Mexican | Hyattsville, MD | Casual | $30 |
| 5.9 | Bistro Français | French | Georgetown | Casual | $40 |
| 5.9 | Maté | Pan-Asian | Georgetown | Casual | $45 |
| 5.9 | El Tamarindo | Mexican | Adams Morgan | Casual | $40 |
| 5.9 | Asylum | American | Dupont | Bar | $25 |
| 5.8 | The Big Hunt | American | Dupont | Bar | $20 |
| 5.5 | Local 16 | American | U Street | Upmarket | $40 |
| 5.4 | Amsterdam Falafel Shop | Middle Eastern | Adams Morgan | Counter | $10 |
| 5.3 | Alberto's Stone Oven Pizza | Pizza | Multiple locations | Counter | $5 |
| 5.3 | Eat First | Chinese | Chinatown | Casual | $20 |
| 5.1 | Tryst | American | Adams Morgan | Café | $25 |
| 5.0 | Lima | Nuevo Latino | Downtown | Upmarket | $55 |
| 4.8 | Pour House | American | Capitol Hill | Casual | $35 |
| 4.6 | The Tombs | American | Georgetown | Bar | $25 |
| 4.6 | Veranda | Greek, Italian | Logan Circle | Casual | $40 |
| 4.1 | Diner | American | Adams Morgan | Casual | $25 |
| 4.0 | Brickskeller | American | Dupont | Bar | $15 |
| 4.0 | Tai Shan | Chinese | Chinatown | Casual | $15 |
| 3.5 | Jumbo Slice | Pizza | Adams Morgan | Counter | $5 |
| 1.4 | Prince Café | Middle Eastern | Multiple locations | Casual | $25 |

## Weekday food after 1am

| 9.1 | Marvin | Southern, Belgian | U Street | Upmarket | $45 |
|---|---|---|---|---|---|
| 8.8 | Gooldaegee | Korean | Annandale, VA | Casual | $20 |
| 8.8 | Shashemene | Ethiopian | Shaw | Casual | $25 |
| 8.6 | Meaza | Ethiopian | Falls Church, VA | Casual | $20 |
| 8.2 | Irene's Pupusas | Salvadoran | Multiple locations | Casual | $25 |
| 8.1 | Ben's Chili Bowl | American | Multiple locations | Counter | $15 |
| 8.1 | Bourbon | American | Multiple locations | Bar | $35 |
| 8.1 | Queen Makeda | Ethiopian | Shaw | Casual | $30 |
| 7.8 | Full Kee | Chinese | Multiple locations | Casual | $25 |
| 7.5 | El Khartoum | Sudanese | Shaw | Counter | $20 |
| 7.3 | Vinoteca | New American | U Street | Wine bar | $45 |
| 7.1 | Axum | Ethiopian | Shaw | Casual | $25 |
| 7.1 | Julia's Empanadas | Latin American | Multiple locations | Counter | $5 |
| 7.0 | Chi-Cha Lounge | Latin American | U Street | Casual | $30 |
| 6.9 | Annie's Paramount | American | Dupont | Casual | $35 |
| 6.9 | Tunnicliff's Tavern | American | Capitol Hill | Casual | $40 |
| 6.9 | Whitlow's on Wilson | American | Arlington, VA | Casual | $35 |
| 6.8 | Trusty's | American | Capitol Hill | Casual | $35 |
| 6.4 | Martin's Tavern | American | Georgetown | Casual | $35 |
| 6.3 | Old Glory Bar-B-Que | Barbecue | Georgetown | Casual | $30 |
| 6.3 | DC Café | Middle Eastern | Dupont | Counter | $25 |
| 6.2 | Café Saint-Ex | French, American | U Street | Casual | $40 |
| 6.0 | The Red and the Black | Southern | Northeast DC | Bar | $25 |
| 6.0 | Cococabana Bar & Grill | Italian, Mexican | Hyattsville, MD | Casual | $30 |
| 5.9 | Bistro Français | French | Georgetown | Casual | $40 |
| 5.9 | Maté | Pan-Asian | Georgetown | Casual | $45 |
| 5.9 | El Tamarindo | Mexican | Adams Morgan | Casual | $40 |
| 5.8 | The Big Hunt | American | Dupont | Bar | $20 |
| 5.5 | Local 16 | American | U Street | Upmarket | $40 |
| 5.4 | Amsterdam Falafel Shop | Middle Eastern | Adams Morgan | Counter | $10 |
| 5.3 | Alberto's Stone Oven Pizza | Pizza | Multiple locations | Counter | $5 |
| 5.1 | Tryst | American | Adams Morgan | Café | $25 |
| 5.0 | Lima | Nuevo Latino | Downtown | Upmarket | $55 |
| 4.8 | Pour House | American | Capitol Hill | Casual | $35 |
| 4.6 | The Tombs | American | Georgetown | Bar | $25 |
| 4.1 | Diner | American | Adams Morgan | Casual | $25 |
| 4.0 | Brickskeller | American | Dupont | Bar | $15 |
| 4.0 | Tai Shan | Chinese | Chinatown | Casual | $15 |
| 3.5 | Jumbo Slice | Pizza | Adams Morgan | Counter | $5 |
| 1.4 | Prince Café | Middle Eastern | Multiple locations | Casual | $25 |

## Weekday food after 2am

| 8.8 | Gooldaegee | Korean | Annandale, VA | Casual | $20 |
|---|---|---|---|---|---|
| 7.5 | El Khartoum | Sudanese | Shaw | Counter | $20 |
| 6.3 | DC Café | Middle Eastern | Dupont | Counter | $25 |
| 5.9 | Bistro Français | French | Georgetown | Casual | $40 |
| 5.4 | Amsterdam Falafel Shop | Middle Eastern | Adams Morgan | Counter | $10 |
| 5.3 | Alberto's Stone Oven Pizza | Pizza | Multiple locations | Counter | $5 |
| 4.1 | Diner | American | Adams Morgan | Casual | $25 |
| 3.5 | Jumbo Slice | Pizza | Adams Morgan | Counter | $5 |
| 1.4 | Prince Café | Middle Eastern | Multiple locations | Casual | $25 |

## Weekend food after 10pm

| 9.6 | 2 Amys Pizza | Pizza | Cleveland Park | Casual | $35 |
|---|---|---|---|---|---|
| 9.4 | Westend Bistro | New American | West End | Upmarket | $65 |
| 9.2 | Vermilion | New American | Old Town | Upmarket | $65 |
| 9.2 | Poste Moderne Brasserie | New American | Penn Quarter | Upmarket | $80 |
| 9.1 | Citronelle | New American | Georgetown | Upmarket | $210 |
| 9.1 | Marvin | Southern, Belgian | U Street | Upmarket | $45 |
| 9.1 | Tosca | Italian | Downtown | Upmarket | $75 |
| 9.0 | Posto | Italian, Pizza | Logan Circle | Upmarket | $55 |

## Weekend food after 10pm *continued*

| | | | | | |
|---|---|---|---|---|---|
| 9.0 | Vidalia | Southern | Dupont | Upmarket | $70 |
| 9.0 | Seoul Soondae | Korean | Annandale, VA | Casual | $15 |
| 9.0 | Ray's Hell-Burger | American | Multiple locations | Counter | $15 |
| 8.9 | Bistro Bis | French | Capitol Hill | Upmarket | $70 |
| 8.9 | Annan-Gol | Korean | Annandale, VA | Casual | $20 |
| 8.9 | Roger Miller Restaurant | Cameroonian | Silver Spring, MD | Casual | $30 |
| 8.9 | Pesce | Seafood | Dupont | Upmarket | $60 |
| 8.9 | Gamasot | Korean | Springfield, VA | Casual | $15 |
| 8.9 | Oriental East | Chinese | Silver Spring, MD | Casual | $40 |
| 8.9 | Hong Kong Palace | Chinese | Falls Church, VA | Casual | $15 |
| 8.8 | Gooldaegee | Korean | Annandale, VA | Casual | $20 |
| 8.8 | Al Tiramisú | Italian | Dupont | Upmarket | $55 |
| 8.8 | Central Michel Richard | French | Penn Quarter | Upmarket | $70 |
| 8.8 | Marcel's | French | West End | Upmarket | $90 |
| 8.8 | The Source | New American | Penn Quarter | Upmarket | $120 |
| 8.8 | Light House Tofu | Korean | Multiple locations | Casual | $15 |
| 8.8 | Shashemene | Ethiopian | Shaw | Casual | $25 |
| 8.8 | Corduroy | New American | Mt. Vernon Square | Upmarket | $70 |
| 8.8 | China Garden | Chinese | Arlington, VA | Casual | $20 |
| 8.8 | Etete | Ethiopian | Shaw | Casual | $30 |
| 8.7 | Taberna del Alabardero | Spanish | Farragut | Upmarket | $75 |
| 8.7 | BLT Steak | Steakhouse | Farragut | Upmarket | $95 |
| 8.7 | Eamonn's | Seafood, Irish | Old Town | Casual | $20 |
| 8.7 | Granja de Oro | Latin American | Adams Morgan | Counter | $20 |
| 8.6 | Café du Parc | French | Downtown | Upmarket | $60 |
| 8.6 | Nora | New American | Dupont | Upmarket | $80 |
| 8.6 | Montmartre | French | Capitol Hill | Upmarket | $60 |
| 8.6 | Rasika | Indian | Penn Quarter | Upmarket | $70 |
| 8.6 | Liberty Tavern | American | Arlington, VA | Casual | $40 |
| 8.6 | Meaza | Ethiopian | Falls Church, VA | Casual | $20 |
| 8.6 | China Star | Chinese | Fairfax, VA | Casual | $15 |
| 8.6 | Kabob Palace | Middle Eastern | Arlington, VA | Counter | $20 |
| 8.5 | Zaytinya | Middle Eastern | Chinatown | Upmarket | $65 |
| 8.5 | To Sok Jip | Korean | Annandale, VA | Casual | $15 |
| 8.5 | Urbana | New American | Dupont | Upmarket | $55 |
| 8.5 | The Oval Room | New American | Farragut | Upmarket | $75 |
| 8.5 | Sushi-Ko | Japanese | Multiple locations | Upmarket | $60 |
| 8.5 | Great Wall Szechuan | Chinese | Logan Circle | Casual | $25 |
| 8.5 | Prime Rib | Steakhouse | Farragut | Upmarket | $90 |
| 8.4 | Brasserie Beck | Belgian | Downtown | Upmarket | $55 |
| 8.4 | Dino | Italian | Cleveland Park | Upmarket | $50 |
| 8.4 | Proof | New American | Penn Quarter | Wine bar | $55 |
| 8.4 | Sakana | Japanese | Dupont | Casual | $35 |
| 8.4 | Ray's the Steaks | Steakhouse | Arlington, VA | Upmarket | $45 |
| 8.4 | Nava Thai | Thai | Wheaton, MD | Casual | $25 |
| 8.4 | Pollo Granjero | Latin American | Multiple locations | Counter | $15 |
| 8.3 | Bistrot du Coin | French | Dupont | Casual | $50 |
| 8.3 | Zola | New American | Penn Quarter | Upmarket | $60 |
| 8.3 | Hook | Seafood | Georgetown | Upmarket | $80 |
| 8.3 | Kotobuki | Japanese | Palisades | Casual | $25 |
| 8.3 | Smith & Wollensky | Steakhouse | Farragut | Upmarket | $85 |
| 8.2 | Founding Farmers | American | Farragut | Upmarket | $50 |
| 8.2 | Irene's Pupusas | Salvadoran | Multiple locations | Casual | $25 |
| 8.2 | Pizzeria Paradiso | Pizza | Multiple locations | Casual | $30 |
| 8.2 | Mogotillo | Salvadoran | Takoma Park, MD | Casual | $20 |
| 8.2 | Tackle Box | Seafood | Georgetown | Casual | $25 |
| 8.2 | Li Ho | Chinese | Chinatown | Casual | $10 |
| 8.1 | Quarry House Tavern | American | Silver Spring, MD | Casual | $25 |
| 8.1 | Ben's Chili Bowl | American | Multiple locations | Counter | $15 |
| 8.1 | Bourbon | American | Multiple locations | Bar | $35 |
| 8.1 | Queen Makeda | Ethiopian | Shaw | Casual | $30 |
| 8.1 | RedRocks | Pizza | Columbia Heights | Casual | $35 |

## **Weekend food after 10pm** *continued*

| | | | | | |
|---|---|---|---|---|---|
| 8.1 | Bombay Club | Indian | Farragut | Upmarket | $45 |
| 8.0 | Afterwords Café | American | Dupont | Café | $35 |
| 8.0 | Oyamel | Mexican | Penn Quarter | Upmarket | $60 |
| 8.0 | Commonwealth | British | Columbia Heights | Casual | $40 |
| 8.0 | Coppi's Organic | Italian, Pizza | U Street | Upmarket | $50 |
| 8.0 | Crème | Southern | U Street | Casual | $45 |
| 8.0 | Georgia Brown's | Southern | Downtown | Upmarket | $55 |
| 8.0 | Two Quail | French | Mt. Vernon Square | Upmarket | $60 |
| 8.0 | Houston's | American | Rockville, MD | Upmarket | $55 |
| 8.0 | Taquería Distrito Federal | Mexican | Multiple locations | Casual | $20 |
| 8.0 | Kabob Bazaar | Middle Eastern | Arlington, VA | Casual | $20 |
| 8.0 | Taste of Morocco | Moroccan | Arlington, VA | Casual | $35 |
| 8.0 | Don Pollo | Latin American | Hyattsville, MD | Counter | $15 |
| 7.9 | Cashion's Eat Place | New American | Adams Morgan | Upmarket | $60 |
| 7.9 | Firefly | New American | Dupont | Upmarket | $60 |
| 7.9 | BlackSalt | Seafood | Palisades | Upmarket | $45 |
| 7.9 | Black's Bar & Kitchen | New American | Bethesda, MD | Upmarket | $75 |
| 7.9 | Langano | Ethiopian | Silver Spring, MD | Casual | $25 |
| 7.9 | 1789 | New American | Georgetown | Upmarket | $100 |
| 7.8 | Blue Duck Tavern | New American | West End | Upmarket | $80 |
| 7.8 | Tallula | New American | Arlington, VA | Upmarket | $55 |
| 7.8 | Bardeo | New American | Cleveland Park | Wine bar | $35 |
| 7.8 | Café Atlántico | Nuevo Latino | Penn Quarter | Upmarket | $75 |
| 7.8 | Ruth's Chris Steakhouse | Steakhouse | Multiple locations | Upmarket | $90 |
| 7.8 | Afghan Grill | Afghan | Cleveland Park | Casual | $40 |
| 7.8 | Full Kee | Chinese | Multiple locations | Casual | $25 |
| 7.8 | Tako Grill | Japanese | Bethesda, MD | Casual | $45 |
| 7.7 | W Domku | Scandinavian | Petworth | Casual | $40 |
| 7.7 | The Majestic | New American | Old Town | Upmarket | $50 |
| 7.7 | Peking Gourmet Inn | Chinese | Falls Church, VA | Casual | $35 |
| 7.7 | Agraria | New American | Georgetown | Upmarket | $60 |
| 7.7 | Mia's Pizza | Italian, Pizza | Bethesda, MD | Casual | $25 |
| 7.7 | Sweet Mango Café | Caribbean | Petworth | Casual | $25 |
| 7.6 | Round Robin Bar | American | Downtown | Bar | $40 |
| 7.6 | Leopold's Kafe | Austrian | Georgetown | Casual | $40 |
| 7.6 | Mendocino Grille | New American | Georgetown | Wine bar | $60 |
| 7.6 | Equinox | New American | Penn Quarter | Upmarket | $75 |
| 7.6 | Matchbox | American, Pizza | Chinatown | Casual | $35 |
| 7.6 | Guajillo | Mexican | Arlington, VA | Casual | $35 |
| 7.5 | Busboys & Poets | American | Multiple locations | Casual | $25 |
| 7.5 | Cork | New American | Logan Circle | Wine bar | $40 |
| 7.5 | La Chaumière | French | Georgetown | Upmarket | $60 |
| 7.5 | Meskerem | Ethiopian | Adams Morgan | Casual | $25 |
| 7.5 | Ulah Bistro | American | U Street | Upmarket | $45 |
| 7.5 | Lebanese Taverna | Middle Eastern | Multiple locations | Casual | $40 |
| 7.5 | La Sandía | Mexican | Tysons Corner, VA | Upmarket | $50 |
| 7.5 | Thai Square | Thai | Arlington, VA | Casual | $35 |
| 7.5 | El Khartoum | Sudanese | Shaw | Counter | $20 |
| 7.4 | Café Divan | Turkish | Glover Park | Casual | $35 |
| 7.4 | TenPenh | Pan-Asian | Downtown | Upmarket | $70 |
| 7.4 | Ardeo | New American | Cleveland Park | Upmarket | $65 |
| 7.4 | Jackson 20 | New American | Old Town | Upmarket | $65 |
| 7.4 | Neyla | Middle Eastern | Georgetown | Upmarket | $70 |
| 7.4 | Sorriso | Italian, Pizza | Cleveland Park | Casual | $40 |
| 7.4 | Shanghai Village | Chinese | Bethesda, MD | Casual | $35 |
| 7.4 | Nam-Viet | Vietnamese | Multiple locations | Casual | $30 |
| 7.4 | Bombay Bistro | Indian | Multiple locations | Casual | $25 |
| 7.3 | Coco Sala | New American | Downtown | Upmarket | $50 |
| 7.3 | Vinoteca | New American | U Street | Wine bar | $45 |
| 7.3 | Bourbon Steak | New American | Georgetown | Upmarket | $115 |
| 7.3 | DC Coast | Seafood | Downtown | Upmarket | $75 |
| 7.3 | Kinkead's | Seafood | Foggy Bottom | Upmarket | $75 |

## **Weekend food after 10pm** *continued*

| 7.3 | Mixtec | Mexican | Adams Morgan | Casual | $25 |
|-----|--------|---------|--------------|--------|-----|
| 7.3 | Chinatown Express | Chinese | Chinatown | Casual | $25 |
| 7.2 | Florida Avenue Grill | Southern | U Street | Casual | $15 |
| 7.2 | Café Berlin | German | Capitol Hill | Café | $35 |
| 7.2 | Bangkok 54 | Thai | Arlington, VA | Casual | $35 |
| 7.2 | Heritage India | Indian | Multiple locations | Casual | $40 |
| 7.2 | Cucina Vivace | Italian | Arlington, VA | Upmarket | $55 |
| 7.2 | Mayur Kabab House | Pakistani, Indian | Chinatown | Casual | $20 |
| 7.1 | Kemble Park Tavern | New American | Palisades | Upmarket | $60 |
| 7.1 | PS 7's | New American | Chinatown | Upmarket | $60 |
| 7.1 | Tabaq Bistro | Middle Eastern | U Street | Upmarket | $45 |
| 7.1 | Acadiana | Southern | Mt. Vernon Square | Upmarket | $60 |
| 7.1 | District Chophouse | Steakhouse | Penn Quarter | Casual | $45 |
| 7.1 | Oya | Pan-Asian | Penn Quarter | Upmarket | $75 |
| 7.1 | Jyoti | Indian | Adams Morgan | Casual | $25 |
| 7.1 | Axum | Ethiopian | Shaw | Casual | $25 |
| 7.1 | Harar Mesob | Ethiopian | Arlington, VA | Casual | $25 |
| 7.1 | Saigon Saigon | Vietnamese | Arlington, VA | Casual | $25 |
| 7.1 | Malaysia Kopitiam | Malaysian | Dupont | Casual | $25 |
| 7.1 | Julia's Empanadas | Latin American | Multiple locations | Counter | $5 |
| 7.0 | Ceiba | Nuevo Latino | Downtown | Upmarket | $60 |
| 7.0 | Mio | New American | Downtown | Upmarket | $70 |
| 7.0 | Belga Café | Belgian | Capitol Hill | Casual | $30 |
| 7.0 | Mama Ayesha's | Middle Eastern | Adams Morgan | Casual | $40 |
| 7.0 | Good Stuff Eatery | American | Capitol Hill | Counter | $15 |
| 7.0 | Las Placitas | Mexican | Capitol Hill | Casual | $40 |
| 7.0 | Rustico | New American | Alexandria, VA | Casual | $40 |
| 7.0 | Chi-Cha Lounge | Latin American | U Street | Casual | $30 |
| 7.0 | Regent Thai | Thai | Dupont | Casual | $35 |
| 7.0 | Moby Dick | Middle Eastern | Multiple locations | Casual | $25 |
| 7.0 | Tachibana | Japanese | Tysons Corner, VA | Casual | $45 |
| 6.9 | Old Ebbitt Grill | American | Downtown | Casual | $40 |
| 6.9 | Annie's Paramount | American | Dupont | Casual | $35 |
| 6.9 | Tunnicliff's Tavern | American | Capitol Hill | Casual | $40 |
| 6.9 | Petits Plats | French | Woodley Park | Casual | $45 |
| 6.9 | Straits of Malaya | Malaysian | Dupont | Casual | $35 |
| 6.9 | Whitlow's on Wilson | American | Arlington, VA | Casual | $35 |
| 6.9 | Ella's Pizza | Pizza | Chinatown | Casual | $40 |
| 6.9 | Fleming's | Steakhouse | Tysons Corner, VA | Upmarket | $90 |
| 6.9 | Carlyle | New American | Arlington, VA | Casual | $40 |
| 6.9 | Circle Bistro | New American | West End | Upmarket | $70 |
| 6.9 | Comet Ping Pong | Pizza | Upper NW | Casual | $35 |
| 6.8 | Fadó | Irish | Chinatown | Bar | $27 |
| 6.8 | Starfish Café | Seafood | Capitol Hill | Casual | $55 |
| 6.8 | Trusty's | American | Capitol Hill | Casual | $35 |
| 6.8 | Thai Tanic | Thai | Logan Circle | Casual | $30 |
| 6.8 | Madjet | Ethiopian | Shaw | Casual | $23 |
| 6.7 | Marrakesh | Moroccan | Mt. Vernon Square | Upmarket | $50 |
| 6.7 | White Tiger | Indian | Capitol Hill | Casual | $35 |
| 6.7 | Bookbinder's Old Town | Steakhouse | Old Town | Upmarket | $80 |
| 6.7 | Fogo de Chão | Brazilian | Downtown | Upmarket | $80 |
| 6.6 | Java House | Middle Eastern | Dupont | Counter | $10 |
| 6.6 | Sette Osteria | Italian, Pizza | Dupont | Casual | $40 |
| 6.6 | Evening Star Café | New American | Alexandria, VA | Upmarket | $55 |
| 6.6 | Capitol City Brewery | American | Multiple locations | Casual | $35 |
| 6.6 | Chevys Fresh Mex | Mexican | Multiple locations | Casual | $30 |
| 6.6 | Nooshi | Pan-Asian | Farragut | Casual | $25 |
| 6.5 | Open City | American | Woodley Park | Café | $40 |
| 6.5 | Café Bonaparte | French | Georgetown | Café | $45 |
| 6.5 | Veritas Wine Bar | New American | Dupont | Wine bar | $40 |
| 6.5 | Alero | Mexican | Multiple locations | Casual | $40 |
| 6.5 | Capital Grille | Steakhouse | Multiple locations | Upmarket | $85 |

## Weekend food after 10pm *continued*

| | | | | | |
|---|---|---|---|---|---|
| 6.5 | Evolve | New American | Adams Morgan | Upmarket | $40 |
| 6.5 | Tragara | Italian | Bethesda, MD | Upmarket | $80 |
| 6.4 | Martin's Tavern | American | Georgetown | Casual | $35 |
| 6.4 | Zorba's Café | Greek, Sandwiches | Dupont | Counter | $25 |
| 6.4 | Mark's Duck House | Chinese | Falls Church, VA | Casual | $30 |
| 6.3 | Peacock Café | New American | Georgetown | Upmarket | $60 |
| 6.3 | Mandu | Korean | Dupont | Casual | $40 |
| 6.3 | Astor Mediterranean | Middle Eastern | Multiple locations | Casual | $20 |
| 6.3 | Grillfish | Seafood | West End | Upmarket | $45 |
| 6.3 | Station 9 | New American | U Street | Upmarket | $45 |
| 6.3 | Tandoor Grill | Indian | Capitol Hill | Casual | $30 |
| 6.3 | Old Glory Bar-B-Que | Barbecue | Georgetown | Casual | $30 |
| 6.3 | DC Café | Middle Eastern | Dupont | Counter | $25 |
| 6.3 | Faryab | Afghan | Bethesda, MD | Casual | $25 |
| 6.2 | Café Saint-Ex | French, American | U Street | Casual | $40 |
| 6.2 | Rosemary's Thyme Bistro | American, Italian | Dupont | Casual | $40 |
| 6.2 | Indique | Indian | Cleveland Park | Upmarket | $40 |
| 6.2 | Stoney's Bar & Grill | American | Logan Circle | Casual | $40 |
| 6.2 | Murali | Italian | Arlington, VA | Upmarket | $50 |
| 6.2 | Teaism | Pan-Asian | Multiple locations | Café | $20 |
| 6.1 | Teatro Goldoni | Italian | Farragut | Upmarket | $90 |
| 6.1 | Café Milano | Italian | Georgetown | Upmarket | $75 |
| 6.1 | Primi Piatti | Italian | Foggy Bottom | Upmarket | $70 |
| 6.0 | The Red and the Black | Southern | Northeast DC | Bar | $25 |
| 6.0 | Granville Moore's Brickyard | Belgian | Northeast DC | Casual | $40 |
| 6.0 | Cococabana Bar & Grill | Italian, Mexican | Hyattsville, MD | Casual | $30 |
| 6.0 | Kanlaya | Thai, Chinese | Chinatown | Casual | $30 |
| 6.0 | Aatish on the Hill | Indian | Capitol Hill | Casual | $30 |
| 6.0 | Finn & Porter | American | Multiple locations | Upmarket | $75 |
| 5.9 | Bistro Français | French | Georgetown | Casual | $40 |
| 5.9 | Grapeseed | New American | Bethesda, MD | Wine bar | $75 |
| 5.9 | Mai Thai | Thai | Multiple locations | Casual | $35 |
| 5.9 | Sesto Senso | Italian | Dupont | Upmarket | $55 |
| 5.9 | Maté | Pan-Asian | Georgetown | Casual | $45 |
| 5.9 | Tara Thai | Thai | Multiple locations | Casual | $25 |
| 5.9 | Thaiphoon | Thai | Multiple locations | Casual | $40 |
| 5.9 | El Tamarindo | Mexican | Adams Morgan | Casual | $40 |
| 5.9 | Asylum | American | Dupont | Bar | $25 |
| 5.9 | Old City Café & Bakery | Middle Eastern | Adams Morgan | Counter | $10 |
| 5.9 | Kanpai | Japanese | Arlington, VA | Casual | $30 |
| 5.8 | The Big Hunt | American | Dupont | Bar | $20 |
| 5.8 | Rosa Mexicano | Mexican | Penn Quarter | Upmarket | $55 |
| 5.8 | Charlie Palmer Steak | Steakhouse | Capitol Hill | Upmarket | $110 |
| 5.8 | Hudson | New American | West End | Upmarket | $65 |
| 5.8 | Filomena | Italian | Georgetown | Casual | $50 |
| 5.7 | Circa | Italian | Dupont | Casual | $40 |
| 5.7 | La Tasca | Spanish | Multiple locations | Casual | $40 |
| 5.7 | Sonoma | New American | Capitol Hill | Wine bar | $65 |
| 5.7 | The Islander Caribbean | Caribbean | U Street | Casual | $25 |
| 5.7 | Tono Sushi | Japanese | Woodley Park | Casual | $40 |
| 5.7 | Bertucci's | Italian, Pizza | Multiple locations | Casual | $35 |
| 5.7 | Armand's | Pizza | Multiple locations | Casual | $25 |
| 5.7 | La Crêperie | French | Arlington, VA | Café | $15 |
| 5.6 | Little Fountain Café | New American | Adams Morgan | Upmarket | $45 |
| 5.6 | Darlington House | New American | Dupont | Upmarket | $65 |
| 5.6 | Thai Chef | Thai, Japanese | Dupont | Casual | $40 |
| 5.6 | Banana Café & Piano Bar | Cuban | Capitol Hill | Café | $30 |
| 5.6 | Johnny Rockets | American | Multiple locations | Casual | $25 |
| 5.5 | Local 16 | American | U Street | Upmarket | $40 |
| 5.5 | Napoleon Bistro | French | Adams Morgan | Upmarket | $60 |
| 5.5 | Bangkok Joe's | Pan-Asian | Georgetown | Casual | $45 |
| 5.5 | Matuba | Japanese | Arlington, VA | Casual | $20 |

## Weekend food after 10pm *continued*

| | | | | | |
|---|---|---|---|---|---|
| 5.4 | Amsterdam Falafel Shop | Middle Eastern | Adams Morgan | Counter | $10 |
| 5.3 | Il Mulino | Italian | Downtown | Upmarket | $80 |
| 5.3 | Alberto's Stone Oven Pizza | Pizza | Multiple locations | Counter | $5 |
| 5.3 | Boulevard Woodgrill | New American | Arlington, VA | Casual | $45 |
| 5.3 | Yuan Fu | Chinese | Rockville, MD | Casual | $25 |
| 5.3 | Eat First | Chinese | Chinatown | Casual | $20 |
| 5.2 | La Loma | Mexican | Capitol Hill | Casual | $30 |
| 5.2 | Spices | Pan-Asian | Cleveland Park | Casual | $35 |
| 5.2 | Beacon Bar & Grill | New American | Dupont | Casual | $45 |
| 5.1 | Tryst | American | Adams Morgan | Café | $25 |
| 5.1 | Singapore Bistro | Pan-Asian | Farragut | Casual | $25 |
| 5.1 | Clyde's | American | Multiple locations | Casual | $40 |
| 5.1 | Grill from Ipanema | Brazilian | Adams Morgan | Casual | $45 |
| 5.1 | Asian Spice | Chinese, Pan-Asian | Chinatown | Casual | $40 |
| 5.1 | Old Siam | Thai | Capitol Hill | Casual | $25 |
| 5.0 | Marrakesh Palace | Moroccan | Dupont | Upmarket | $45 |
| 5.0 | Lima | Nuevo Latino | Downtown | Upmarket | $55 |
| 5.0 | Skye Lounge | Middle Eastern | Farragut | Casual | $40 |
| 5.0 | Café Asia | Pan-Asian | Multiple locations | Casual | $30 |
| 4.9 | Brasserie Monte Carlo | French | Bethesda, MD | Casual | $45 |
| 4.9 | Gordon Biersch | American | Multiple locations | Casual | $35 |
| 4.8 | Mie N Yu | Pan-Asian | Georgetown | Upmarket | $55 |
| 4.8 | ACKC Cocoa Bar | Sweet drinks | Multiple locations | Café | $10 |
| 4.8 | Fusion Grill | Pan-Asian | Capitol Hill | Upmarket | $55 |
| 4.8 | Trattoria Alberto | Italian | Capitol Hill | Casual | $45 |
| 4.8 | Pour House | American | Capitol Hill | Casual | $35 |
| 4.8 | 701 | New American | Penn Quarter | Upmarket | $70 |
| 4.8 | Asia Nine | Pan-Asian | Penn Quarter | Casual | $35 |
| 4.7 | Hunan Dynasty | Chinese | Capitol Hill | Casual | $25 |
| 4.6 | The Tombs | American | Georgetown | Bar | $25 |
| 4.6 | La Tomate | Italian | Dupont | Upmarket | $45 |
| 4.6 | Mr. Chen's | Chinese | Woodley Park | Casual | $25 |
| 4.6 | Veranda | Greek, Italian | Logan Circle | Casual | $40 |
| 4.6 | Uni | Japanese | Dupont | Casual | $40 |
| 4.5 | Paolo's | Italian | Georgetown | Casual | $40 |
| 4.5 | Meiwah | Chinese, Japanese | Multiple locations | Casual | $45 |
| 4.5 | Tony Cheng's Seafood | Chinese | Chinatown | Casual | $35 |
| 4.4 | Rice | Thai | Logan Circle | Upmarket | $30 |
| 4.4 | Raku | Pan-Asian | Multiple locations | Upmarket | $35 |
| 4.3 | Skewers | Middle Eastern | Dupont | Casual | $30 |
| 4.3 | Hard Times Café | American | Multiple locations | Casual | $20 |
| 4.3 | Vietnam Georgetown | Vietnamese | Georgetown | Casual | $30 |
| 4.3 | J. Paul's | American | Georgetown | Casual | $45 |
| 4.2 | Luna Grill & Diner | American, Italian | Multiple locations | Casual | $30 |
| 4.2 | Sushi-Go-Round & Tapas | Pan-Asian | Chinatown | Casual | $45 |
| 4.1 | Diner | American | Adams Morgan | Casual | $25 |
| 4.0 | Brickskeller | American | Dupont | Bar | $15 |
| 4.0 | Commissary | American | Logan Circle | Casual | $30 |
| 4.0 | Tai Shan | Chinese | Chinatown | Casual | $15 |
| 4.0 | Tony Cheng's Mongolian | Pan-Asian | Chinatown | Casual | $35 |
| 3.9 | Tony & Joe's Seafood Place | Seafood | Georgetown | Upmarket | $55 |
| 3.9 | Sequoia | New American | Georgetown | Upmarket | $50 |
| 3.8 | Logan Tavern | American | Logan Circle | Casual | $35 |
| 3.8 | The Front Page | American | Dupont | Casual | $35 |
| 3.8 | Wok & Roll | Chinese | Chinatown | Casual | $20 |
| 3.8 | Union Pub | American | Capitol Hill | Casual | $25 |
| 3.7 | Ping by Charlie Chiang's | Pan-Asian | Arlington, VA | Casual | $45 |
| 3.7 | Olazzo | Italian | Multiple locations | Upmarket | $45 |
| 3.7 | Harmony Café | Chinese | Georgetown | Casual | $15 |
| 3.6 | Dupont Italian Kitchen | Italian | Dupont | Casual | $40 |
| 3.6 | Zed's Ethiopian Restaurant | Ethiopian | Georgetown | Casual | $30 |
| 3.5 | Café Citron | Nuevo Latino | Dupont | Casual | $35 |

## Weekend food after 10pm *continued*

| | | | | |
|---|---|---|---|---|
| 3.5 | Jumbo Slice | Pizza | Adams Morgan | Counter | $5 |
| 3.2 | Sala Thai | Thai | Multiple locations | Casual | $25 |
| 2.9 | Austin Grill | Mexican | Multiple locations | Casual | $30 |
| 2.7 | Buca di Beppo | Italian | Dupont | Casual | $30 |
| 2.2 | Lauriol Plaza | Mexican | Adams Morgan | Casual | $35 |
| 1.4 | Prince Café | Middle Eastern | Multiple locations | Casual | $25 |
| | Harris Teeter | Groceries | Multiple locations | Market | |
| | Thomas Sweet | Ice cream | Georgetown | Counter | |

## Weekend food after 11pm

| | | | | |
|---|---|---|---|---|
| 9.1 | Marvin | Southern, Belgian | U Street | Upmarket | $45 |
| 9.0 | Posto | Italian, Pizza | Logan Circle | Upmarket | $55 |
| 9.0 | Seoul Soondae | Korean | Annandale, VA | Casual | $15 |
| 8.9 | Annan-Gol | Korean | Annandale, VA | Casual | $20 |
| 8.9 | Roger Miller Restaurant | Cameroonian | Silver Spring, MD | Casual | $30 |
| 8.8 | Gooldaegee | Korean | Annandale, VA | Casual | $20 |
| 8.8 | Shashemene | Ethiopian | Shaw | Casual | $25 |
| 8.8 | Etete | Ethiopian | Shaw | Casual | $30 |
| 8.7 | BLT Steak | Steakhouse | Farragut | Upmarket | $95 |
| 8.7 | Eamonn's | Seafood, Irish | Old Town | Casual | $20 |
| 8.6 | Meaza | Ethiopian | Falls Church, VA | Casual | $20 |
| 8.6 | Kabob Palace | Middle Eastern | Arlington, VA | Counter | $20 |
| 8.5 | Zaytinya | Middle Eastern | Chinatown | Upmarket | $65 |
| 8.4 | Brasserie Beck | Belgian | Downtown | Upmarket | $55 |
| 8.4 | Proof | New American | Penn Quarter | Wine bar | $55 |
| 8.3 | Bistrot du Coin | French | Dupont | Casual | $50 |
| 8.3 | Smith & Wollensky | Steakhouse | Farragut | Upmarket | $85 |
| 8.2 | Founding Farmers | American | Farragut | Upmarket | $50 |
| 8.2 | Irene's Pupusas | Salvadoran | Multiple locations | Casual | $25 |
| 8.2 | Pizzeria Paradiso | Pizza | Multiple locations | Casual | $30 |
| 8.2 | Mogotillo | Salvadoran | Takoma Park, MD | Casual | $20 |
| 8.2 | Li Ho | Chinese | Chinatown | Casual | $10 |
| 8.1 | Quarry House Tavern | American | Silver Spring, MD | Casual | $25 |
| 8.1 | Ben's Chili Bowl | American | Multiple locations | Counter | $15 |
| 8.1 | Bourbon | American | Multiple locations | Bar | $35 |
| 8.1 | Queen Makeda | Ethiopian | Shaw | Casual | $30 |
| 8.1 | RedRocks | Pizza | Columbia Heights | Casual | $35 |
| 8.0 | Afterwords Café | American | Dupont | Café | $35 |
| 8.0 | Oyamel | Mexican | Penn Quarter | Upmarket | $60 |
| 8.0 | Coppi's Organic | Italian, Pizza | U Street | Upmarket | $50 |
| 8.0 | Crème | Southern | U Street | Casual | $45 |
| 7.9 | Langano | Ethiopian | Silver Spring, MD | Casual | $25 |
| 7.8 | Bardeo | New American | Cleveland Park | Wine bar | $35 |
| 7.8 | Full Kee | Chinese | Multiple locations | Casual | $25 |
| 7.7 | W Domku | Scandinavian | Petworth | Casual | $40 |
| 7.7 | Agraria | New American | Georgetown | Upmarket | $60 |
| 7.7 | Sweet Mango Café | Caribbean | Petworth | Casual | $25 |
| 7.6 | Round Robin Bar | American | Downtown | Bar | $40 |
| 7.6 | Leopold's Kafe | Austrian | Georgetown | Casual | $40 |
| 7.6 | Matchbox | American, Pizza | Chinatown | Casual | $35 |
| 7.5 | Busboys & Poets | American | Multiple locations | Casual | $25 |
| 7.5 | Cork | New American | Logan Circle | Wine bar | $40 |
| 7.5 | Meskerem | Ethiopian | Adams Morgan | Casual | $25 |
| 7.5 | Ulah Bistro | American | U Street | Upmarket | $45 |
| 7.5 | El Khartoum | Sudanese | Shaw | Counter | $20 |
| 7.4 | Neyla | Middle Eastern | Georgetown | Upmarket | $70 |
| 7.3 | Coco Sala | New American | Downtown | Upmarket | $50 |
| 7.3 | Vinoteca | New American | U Street | Wine bar | $45 |
| 7.3 | Mixtec | Mexican | Adams Morgan | Casual | $25 |
| 7.2 | Florida Avenue Grill | Southern | U Street | Casual | $15 |
| 7.2 | Mayur Kabab House | Pakistani, Indian | Chinatown | Casual | $20 |
| 7.1 | Kemble Park Tavern | New American | Palisades | Upmarket | $60 |

## Weekend food after 11pm *continued*

| | | | | |
|---|---|---|---|---|
| 7.1 | Tabaq Bistro | Middle Eastern | U Street | Upmarket | $45 |
| 7.1 | Oya | Pan-Asian | Penn Quarter | Upmarket | $75 |
| 7.1 | Jyoti | Indian | Adams Morgan | Casual | $25 |
| 7.1 | Axum | Ethiopian | Shaw | Casual | $25 |
| 7.1 | Julia's Empanadas | Latin American | Multiple locations | Counter | $5 |
| 7.0 | Rustico | New American | Alexandria, VA | Casual | $40 |
| 7.0 | Chi-Cha Lounge | Latin American | U Street | Casual | $30 |
| 6.9 | Old Ebbitt Grill | American | Downtown | Casual | $40 |
| 6.9 | Annie's Paramount | American | Dupont | Casual | $35 |
| 6.9 | Tunnicliff's Tavern | American | Capitol Hill | Casual | $40 |
| 6.9 | Whitlow's on Wilson | American | Arlington, VA | Casual | $35 |
| 6.9 | Carlyle | New American | Arlington, VA | Casual | $40 |
| 6.8 | Trusty's | American | Capitol Hill | Casual | $35 |
| 6.8 | Madjet | Ethiopian | Shaw | Casual | $23 |
| 6.6 | Sette Osteria | Italian, Pizza | Dupont | Casual | $40 |
| 6.6 | Capitol City Brewery | American | Multiple locations | Casual | $35 |
| 6.5 | Open City | American | Woodley Park | Café | $40 |
| 6.5 | Café Bonaparte | French | Georgetown | Café | $45 |
| 6.5 | Veritas Wine Bar | New American | Dupont | Wine bar | $40 |
| 6.5 | Alero | Mexican | Multiple locations | Casual | $40 |
| 6.5 | Evolve | New American | Adams Morgan | Upmarket | $40 |
| 6.4 | Martin's Tavern | American | Georgetown | Casual | $35 |
| 6.4 | Zorba's Café | Greek, Sandwiches | Dupont | Counter | $25 |
| 6.4 | Mark's Duck House | Chinese | Falls Church, VA | Casual | $30 |
| 6.3 | Old Glory Bar-B-Que | Barbecue | Georgetown | Casual | $30 |
| 6.3 | DC Café | Middle Eastern | Dupont | Counter | $25 |
| 6.2 | Café Saint-Ex | French, American | U Street | Casual | $40 |
| 6.2 | Rosemary's Thyme Bistro | American, Italian | Dupont | Casual | $40 |
| 6.2 | Stoney's Bar & Grill | American | Logan Circle | Casual | $40 |
| 6.1 | Café Milano | Italian | Georgetown | Upmarket | $75 |
| 6.0 | The Red and the Black | Southern | Northeast DC | Bar | $25 |
| 6.0 | Granville Moore's Brickyard | Belgian | Northeast DC | Casual | $40 |
| 6.0 | Cococabana Bar & Grill | Italian, Mexican | Hyattsville, MD | Casual | $30 |
| 5.9 | Bistro Français | French | Georgetown | Casual | $40 |
| 5.9 | Maté | Pan-Asian | Georgetown | Casual | $45 |
| 5.9 | El Tamarindo | Mexican | Adams Morgan | Casual | $40 |
| 5.9 | Asylum | American | Dupont | Bar | $25 |
| 5.9 | Old City Café & Bakery | Middle Eastern | Adams Morgan | Counter | $10 |
| 5.8 | The Big Hunt | American | Dupont | Bar | $20 |
| 5.8 | Rosa Mexicano | Mexican | Penn Quarter | Upmarket | $55 |
| 5.8 | Hudson | New American | West End | Upmarket | $65 |
| 5.8 | Filomena | Italian | Georgetown | Casual | $50 |
| 5.7 | Circa | Italian | Dupont | Casual | $40 |
| 5.7 | La Tasca | Spanish | Multiple locations | Casual | $40 |
| 5.7 | The Islander Caribbean | Caribbean | U Street | Casual | $25 |
| 5.6 | Darlington House | New American | Dupont | Upmarket | $65 |
| 5.6 | Johnny Rockets | American | Multiple locations | Casual | $25 |
| 5.5 | Local 16 | American | U Street | Upmarket | $40 |
| 5.5 | Napoleon Bistro | French | Adams Morgan | Upmarket | $60 |
| 5.5 | Bangkok Joe's | Pan-Asian | Georgetown | Casual | $45 |
| 5.4 | Amsterdam Falafel Shop | Middle Eastern | Adams Morgan | Counter | $10 |
| 5.3 | Il Mulino | Italian | Downtown | Upmarket | $80 |
| 5.3 | Alberto's Stone Oven Pizza | Pizza | Multiple locations | Counter | $5 |
| 5.3 | Boulevard Woodgrill | New American | Arlington, VA | Casual | $45 |
| 5.3 | Eat First | Chinese | Chinatown | Casual | $20 |
| 5.2 | La Loma | Mexican | Capitol Hill | Casual | $30 |
| 5.1 | Tryst | American | Adams Morgan | Café | $25 |
| 5.1 | Singapore Bistro | Pan-Asian | Farragut | Casual | $25 |
| 5.1 | Clyde's | American | Multiple locations | Casual | $40 |
| 5.1 | Grill from Ipanema | Brazilian | Adams Morgan | Casual | $45 |
| 5.1 | Asian Spice | Chinese, Pan-Asian | Chinatown | Casual | $40 |
| 5.1 | Old Siam | Thai | Capitol Hill | Casual | $25 |

## Weekend food after 11pm *continued*

| | | | | | |
|---|---|---|---|---|---|
| 5.0 | Marrakesh Palace | Moroccan | Dupont | Upmarket | $45 |
| 5.0 | Lima | Nuevo Latino | Downtown | Upmarket | $55 |
| 5.0 | Skye Lounge | Middle Eastern | Farragut | Casual | $40 |
| 5.0 | Café Asia | Pan-Asian | Multiple locations | Casual | $30 |
| 4.9 | Gordon Biersch | American | Multiple locations | Casual | $35 |
| 4.8 | Mie N Yu | Pan-Asian | Georgetown | Upmarket | $55 |
| 4.8 | Pour House | American | Capitol Hill | Casual | $35 |
| 4.8 | 701 | New American | Penn Quarter | Upmarket | $70 |
| 4.8 | Asia Nine | Pan-Asian | Penn Quarter | Casual | $35 |
| 4.6 | The Tombs | American | Georgetown | Bar | $25 |
| 4.6 | La Tomate | Italian | Dupont | Upmarket | $45 |
| 4.6 | Veranda | Greek, Italian | Logan Circle | Casual | $40 |
| 4.5 | Paolo's | Italian | Georgetown | Casual | $40 |
| 4.5 | Tony Cheng's Seafood | Chinese | Chinatown | Casual | $35 |
| 4.3 | Skewers | Middle Eastern | Dupont | Casual | $30 |
| 4.3 | J. Paul's | American | Georgetown | Casual | $45 |
| 4.2 | Luna Grill & Diner | American, Italian | Multiple locations | Casual | $30 |
| 4.1 | Diner | American | Adams Morgan | Casual | $25 |
| 4.0 | Brickskeller | American | Dupont | Bar | $15 |
| 4.0 | Commissary | American | Logan Circle | Casual | $30 |
| 4.0 | Tai Shan | Chinese | Chinatown | Casual | $15 |
| 4.0 | Tony Cheng's Mongolian | Pan-Asian | Chinatown | Casual | $35 |
| 3.9 | Tony & Joe's Seafood Place | Seafood | Georgetown | Upmarket | $55 |
| 3.8 | Logan Tavern | American | Logan Circle | Casual | $35 |
| 3.8 | The Front Page | American | Dupont | Casual | $35 |
| 3.8 | Wok & Roll | Chinese | Chinatown | Casual | $20 |
| 3.6 | Dupont Italian Kitchen | Italian | Dupont | Casual | $40 |
| 3.5 | Café Citron | Nuevo Latino | Dupont | Casual | $35 |
| 3.5 | Jumbo Slice | Pizza | Adams Morgan | Counter | $5 |
| 2.9 | Austin Grill | Mexican | Multiple locations | Casual | $30 |
| 2.2 | Lauriol Plaza | Mexican | Adams Morgan | Casual | $35 |
| 1.4 | Prince Café | Middle Eastern | Multiple locations | Casual | $25 |
| | Thomas Sweet | Ice cream | Georgetown | Counter | |

## Weekend food after midnight

| | | | | | |
|---|---|---|---|---|---|
| 9.1 | Marvin | Southern, Belgian | U Street | Upmarket | $45 |
| 9.0 | Seoul Soondae | Korean | Annandale, VA | Casual | $15 |
| 8.9 | Roger Miller Restaurant | Cameroonian | Silver Spring, MD | Casual | $30 |
| 8.8 | Gooldaegee | Korean | Annandale, VA | Casual | $20 |
| 8.8 | Shashemene | Ethiopian | Shaw | Casual | $25 |
| 8.8 | Etete | Ethiopian | Shaw | Casual | $30 |
| 8.6 | Meaza | Ethiopian | Falls Church, VA | Casual | $20 |
| 8.4 | Proof | New American | Penn Quarter | Wine bar | $55 |
| 8.3 | Bistrot du Coin | French | Dupont | Casual | $50 |
| 8.2 | Irene's Pupusas | Salvadoran | Multiple locations | Casual | $25 |
| 8.2 | Mogotillo | Salvadoran | Takoma Park, MD | Casual | $20 |
| 8.2 | Li Ho | Chinese | Chinatown | Casual | $10 |
| 8.1 | Quarry House Tavern | American | Silver Spring, MD | Casual | $25 |
| 8.1 | Ben's Chili Bowl | American | Multiple locations | Counter | $15 |
| 8.1 | Bourbon | American | Multiple locations | Bar | $35 |
| 8.1 | Queen Makeda | Ethiopian | Shaw | Casual | $30 |
| 8.1 | RedRocks | Pizza | Columbia Heights | Casual | $35 |
| 8.0 | Afterwords Café | American | Dupont | Café | $35 |
| 7.9 | Langano | Ethiopian | Silver Spring, MD | Casual | $25 |
| 7.8 | Full Kee | Chinese | Multiple locations | Casual | $25 |
| 7.6 | Round Robin Bar | American | Downtown | Bar | $40 |
| 7.6 | Matchbox | American, Pizza | Chinatown | Casual | $35 |
| 7.5 | Busboys & Poets | American | Multiple locations | Casual | $25 |
| 7.5 | Cork | New American | Logan Circle | Wine bar | $40 |
| 7.5 | Meskerem | Ethiopian | Adams Morgan | Casual | $25 |
| 7.5 | Ulah Bistro | American | U Street | Upmarket | $45 |
| 7.5 | El Khartoum | Sudanese | Shaw | Counter | $20 |

## Weekend food after midnight *continued*

| 7.3 | Vinoteca | New American | U Street | Wine bar | $45 |
|---|---|---|---|---|---|
| 7.3 | Mixtec | Mexican | Adams Morgan | Casual | $25 |
| 7.2 | Florida Avenue Grill | Southern | U Street | Casual | $15 |
| 7.1 | Axum | Ethiopian | Shaw | Casual | $25 |
| 7.1 | Julia's Empanadas | Latin American | Multiple locations | Counter | $5 |
| 7.0 | Chi-Cha Lounge | Latin American | U Street | Casual | $30 |
| 6.9 | Old Ebbitt Grill | American | Downtown | Casual | $40 |
| 6.9 | Annie's Paramount | American | Dupont | Casual | $35 |
| 6.9 | Tunnicliff's Tavern | American | Capitol Hill | Casual | $40 |
| 6.9 | Whitlow's on Wilson | American | Arlington, VA | Casual | $35 |
| 6.8 | Trusty's | American | Capitol Hill | Casual | $35 |
| 6.6 | Sette Osteria | Italian, Pizza | Dupont | Casual | $40 |
| 6.5 | Open City | American | Woodley Park | Café | $40 |
| 6.5 | Café Bonaparte | French | Georgetown | Café | $45 |
| 6.5 | Evolve | New American | Adams Morgan | Upmarket | $40 |
| 6.4 | Martin's Tavern | American | Georgetown | Casual | $35 |
| 6.3 | Old Glory Bar-B-Que | Barbecue | Georgetown | Casual | $30 |
| 6.3 | DC Café | Middle Eastern | Dupont | Counter | $25 |
| 6.2 | Café Saint-Ex | French, American | U Street | Casual | $40 |
| 6.2 | Stoney's Bar & Grill | American | Logan Circle | Casual | $40 |
| 6.1 | Café Milano | Italian | Georgetown | Upmarket | $75 |
| 6.0 | The Red and the Black | Southern | Northeast DC | Bar | $25 |
| 6.0 | Granville Moore's Brickyard | Belgian | Northeast DC | Casual | $40 |
| 6.0 | Cococabana Bar & Grill | Italian, Mexican | Hyattsville, MD | Casual | $30 |
| 5.9 | Bistro Français | French | Georgetown | Casual | $40 |
| 5.9 | Maté | Pan-Asian | Georgetown | Casual | $45 |
| 5.9 | El Tamarindo | Mexican | Adams Morgan | Casual | $40 |
| 5.9 | Asylum | American | Dupont | Bar | $25 |
| 5.9 | Old City Café & Bakery | Middle Eastern | Adams Morgan | Counter | $10 |
| 5.8 | The Big Hunt | American | Dupont | Bar | $20 |
| 5.8 | Hudson | New American | West End | Upmarket | $65 |
| 5.7 | Circa | Italian | Dupont | Casual | $40 |
| 5.7 | La Tasca | Spanish | Multiple locations | Casual | $40 |
| 5.6 | Johnny Rockets | American | Multiple locations | Casual | $25 |
| 5.5 | Local 16 | American | U Street | Upmarket | $40 |
| 5.4 | Amsterdam Falafel Shop | Middle Eastern | Adams Morgan | Counter | $10 |
| 5.3 | Alberto's Stone Oven Pizza | Pizza | Multiple locations | Counter | $5 |
| 5.3 | Eat First | Chinese | Chinatown | Casual | $20 |
| 5.1 | Tryst | American | Adams Morgan | Café | $25 |
| 5.1 | Clyde's | American | Multiple locations | Casual | $40 |
| 5.0 | Lima | Nuevo Latino | Downtown | Upmarket | $55 |
| 5.0 | Skye Lounge | Middle Eastern | Farragut | Casual | $40 |
| 4.9 | Gordon Biersch | American | Multiple locations | Casual | $35 |
| 4.8 | Pour House | American | Capitol Hill | Casual | $35 |
| 4.6 | The Tombs | American | Georgetown | Bar | $25 |
| 4.6 | Veranda | Greek, Italian | Logan Circle | Casual | $40 |
| 4.5 | Paolo's | Italian | Georgetown | Casual | $40 |
| 4.3 | J. Paul's | American | Georgetown | Casual | $45 |
| 4.1 | Diner | American | Adams Morgan | Casual | $25 |
| 4.0 | Brickskeller | American | Dupont | Bar | $15 |
| 4.0 | Tai Shan | Chinese | Chinatown | Casual | $15 |
| 3.8 | Wok & Roll | Chinese | Chinatown | Casual | $20 |
| 3.6 | Dupont Italian Kitchen | Italian | Dupont | Casual | $40 |
| 3.5 | Café Citron | Nuevo Latino | Dupont | Casual | $35 |
| 3.5 | Jumbo Slice | Pizza | Adams Morgan | Counter | $5 |
| 1.4 | Prince Café | Middle Eastern | Multiple locations | Casual | $25 |

## Weekend food after 1am

| 9.1 | Marvin | Southern, Belgian | U Street | Upmarket | $45 |
|---|---|---|---|---|---|
| 9.0 | Seoul Soondae | Korean | Annandale, VA | Casual | $15 |
| 8.8 | Gooldaegee | Korean | Annandale, VA | Casual | $20 |
| 8.8 | Shashemene | Ethiopian | Shaw | Casual | $25 |

## Weekend food after 1am *continued*

| | | | | | |
|---|---|---|---|---|---|
| 8.6 | Meaza | Ethiopian | Falls Church, VA | Casual | $20 |
| 8.4 | Proof | New American | Penn Quarter | Wine bar | $55 |
| 8.2 | Irene's Pupusas | Salvadoran | Multiple locations | Casual | $25 |
| 8.1 | Quarry House Tavern | American | Silver Spring, MD | Casual | $25 |
| 8.1 | Ben's Chili Bowl | American | Multiple locations | Counter | $15 |
| 8.1 | Bourbon | American | Multiple locations | Bar | $35 |
| 8.1 | Queen Makeda | Ethiopian | Shaw | Casual | $30 |
| 8.0 | Afterwords Café | American | Dupont | Café | $35 |
| 7.9 | Langano | Ethiopian | Silver Spring, MD | Casual | $25 |
| 7.8 | Full Kee | Chinese | Multiple locations | Casual | $25 |
| 7.5 | Busboys & Poets | American | Multiple locations | Casual | $25 |
| 7.5 | Meskerem | Ethiopian | Adams Morgan | Casual | $25 |
| 7.5 | Ulah Bistro | American | U Street | Upmarket | $45 |
| 7.5 | El Khartoum | Sudanese | Shaw | Counter | $20 |
| 7.3 | Vinoteca | New American | U Street | Wine bar | $45 |
| 7.3 | Mixtec | Mexican | Adams Morgan | Casual | $25 |
| 7.2 | Florida Avenue Grill | Southern | U Street | Casual | $15 |
| 7.1 | Axum | Ethiopian | Shaw | Casual | $25 |
| 7.1 | Julia's Empanadas | Latin American | Multiple locations | Counter | $5 |
| 7.0 | Chi-Cha Lounge | Latin American | U Street | Casual | $30 |
| 6.9 | Annie's Paramount | American | Dupont | Casual | $35 |
| 6.9 | Tunnicliff's Tavern | American | Capitol Hill | Casual | $40 |
| 6.9 | Whitlow's on Wilson | American | Arlington, VA | Casual | $35 |
| 6.8 | Trusty's | American | Capitol Hill | Casual | $35 |
| 6.4 | Martin's Tavern | American | Georgetown | Casual | $35 |
| 6.3 | Old Glory Bar-B-Que | Barbecue | Georgetown | Casual | $30 |
| 6.3 | DC Café | Middle Eastern | Dupont | Counter | $25 |
| 6.2 | Café Saint-Ex | French, American | U Street | Casual | $40 |
| 6.2 | Stoney's Bar & Grill | American | Logan Circle | Casual | $40 |
| 6.0 | The Red and the Black | Southern | Northeast DC | Bar | $25 |
| 6.0 | Granville Moore's Brickyard | Belgian | Northeast DC | Casual | $40 |
| 6.0 | Cococabana Bar & Grill | Italian, Mexican | Hyattsville, MD | Casual | $30 |
| 5.9 | Bistro Français | French | Georgetown | Casual | $40 |
| 5.9 | Maté | Pan-Asian | Georgetown | Casual | $45 |
| 5.9 | El Tamarindo | Mexican | Adams Morgan | Casual | $40 |
| 5.9 | Old City Café & Bakery | Middle Eastern | Adams Morgan | Counter | $10 |
| 5.8 | The Big Hunt | American | Dupont | Bar | $20 |
| 5.7 | La Tasca | Spanish | Multiple locations | Casual | $40 |
| 5.5 | Local 16 | American | U Street | Upmarket | $40 |
| 5.4 | Amsterdam Falafel Shop | Middle Eastern | Adams Morgan | Counter | $10 |
| 5.3 | Alberto's Stone Oven Pizza | Pizza | Multiple locations | Counter | $5 |
| 5.3 | Eat First | Chinese | Chinatown | Casual | $20 |
| 5.1 | Tryst | American | Adams Morgan | Café | $25 |
| 5.1 | Clyde's | American | Multiple locations | Casual | $40 |
| 5.0 | Lima | Nuevo Latino | Downtown | Upmarket | $55 |
| 5.0 | Skye Lounge | Middle Eastern | Farragut | Casual | $40 |
| 4.8 | Pour House | American | Capitol Hill | Casual | $35 |
| 4.6 | The Tombs | American | Georgetown | Bar | $25 |
| 4.1 | Diner | American | Adams Morgan | Casual | $25 |
| 4.0 | Brickskeller | American | Dupont | Bar | $15 |
| 4.0 | Tai Shan | Chinese | Chinatown | Casual | $15 |
| 3.5 | Jumbo Slice | Pizza | Adams Morgan | Counter | $5 |
| 1.4 | Prince Café | Middle Eastern | Multiple locations | Casual | $25 |

## Weekend food after 2am

| | | | | | |
|---|---|---|---|---|---|
| 9.1 | Marvin | Southern, Belgian | U Street | Upmarket | $45 |
| 8.8 | Gooldaegee | Korean | Annandale, VA | Casual | $20 |
| 8.8 | Shashemene | Ethiopian | Shaw | Casual | $25 |
| 8.1 | Ben's Chili Bowl | American | Multiple locations | Counter | $15 |
| 8.1 | Bourbon | American | Multiple locations | Bar | $35 |
| 8.1 | Queen Makeda | Ethiopian | Shaw | Casual | $30 |
| 8.0 | Afterwords Café | American | Dupont | Café | $35 |

## Weekend food after 2am *continued*

| | | | | | |
|---|---|---|---|---|---|
| 7.5 | El Khartoum | Sudanese | Shaw | Counter | $20 |
| 7.3 | Vinoteca | New American | U Street | Wine bar | $45 |
| 7.3 | Mixtec | Mexican | Adams Morgan | Casual | $25 |
| 7.2 | Florida Avenue Grill | Southern | U Street | Casual | $15 |
| 7.1 | Axum | Ethiopian | Shaw | Casual | $25 |
| 7.1 | Julia's Empanadas | Latin American | Multiple locations | Counter | $5 |
| 7.0 | Chi-Cha Lounge | Latin American | U Street | Casual | $30 |
| 6.9 | Annie's Paramount | American | Dupont | Casual | $35 |
| 6.9 | Tunnicliff's Tavern | American | Capitol Hill | Casual | $40 |
| 6.8 | Trusty's | American | Capitol Hill | Casual | $35 |
| 6.4 | Martin's Tavern | American | Georgetown | Casual | $35 |
| 6.3 | Old Glory Bar-B-Que | Barbecue | Georgetown | Casual | $30 |
| 6.3 | DC Café | Middle Eastern | Dupont | Counter | $25 |
| 6.2 | Café Saint-Ex | French, American | U Street | Casual | $40 |
| 6.0 | Granville Moore's Brickyard | Belgian | Northeast DC | Casual | $40 |
| 5.9 | Bistro Français | French | Georgetown | Casual | $40 |
| 5.9 | Maté | Pan-Asian | Georgetown | Casual | $45 |
| 5.9 | El Tamarindo | Mexican | Adams Morgan | Casual | $40 |
| 5.9 | Old City Café & Bakery | Middle Eastern | Adams Morgan | Counter | $10 |
| 5.8 | The Big Hunt | American | Dupont | Bar | $20 |
| 5.5 | Local 16 | American | U Street | Upmarket | $40 |
| 5.4 | Amsterdam Falafel Shop | Middle Eastern | Adams Morgan | Counter | $10 |
| 5.3 | Alberto's Stone Oven Pizza | Pizza | Multiple locations | Counter | $5 |
| 5.1 | Tryst | American | Adams Morgan | Café | $25 |
| 5.1 | Clyde's | American | Multiple locations | Casual | $40 |
| 5.0 | Lima | Nuevo Latino | Downtown | Upmarket | $55 |
| 5.0 | Skye Lounge | Middle Eastern | Farragut | Casual | $40 |
| 4.8 | Pour House | American | Capitol Hill | Casual | $35 |
| 4.6 | The Tombs | American | Georgetown | Bar | $25 |
| 4.1 | Diner | American | Adams Morgan | Casual | $25 |
| 4.0 | Brickskeller | American | Dupont | Bar | $15 |
| 4.0 | Tai Shan | Chinese | Chinatown | Casual | $15 |
| 3.5 | Jumbo Slice | Pizza | Adams Morgan | Counter | $5 |
| 1.4 | Prince Café | Middle Eastern | Multiple locations | Casual | $25 |

# Top tastes

Aquavit, W Domku
Barbecued shrimp and asiago cheese grits, Johnny's Half Shell
Bottle of beer, Brickskeller
Bottomless mimosas and Bloody Marys, Nage
Bourbon list, Bourbon
Bourbon stout, District Chophouse & Brewery
Carrot pappardelle with rabbit ragú, Tosca
Chao long (rice porridge), Hai Duong
Chesapeake Bay oysters, Maine Avenue Fish Market
Chicken and waffles, Marvin
Chicken ravioli with tomato cream sauce, Pasta Mia
Cocktails in the courtyard, The Inn at Little Washington
Coffee (fresh-roasted) on the patio, Java House
Cotton candy eel, Minibar
Crab cakes, C.F. Folks
Croque madame, Granville Moore's Brickyard
Croquetas de jamón, Taberna del Alabardero
Cuttlefish, Oe Gad Gib
Death by Chocolate cake, Afterwords Café
Derek tibs, Etete
Diablo burger, Ray's Hell-Burger
Dim sum, Oriental East
Empanada at 1am, Julia's Empanadas
Fava beans and pancetta, Black's Bar & Kitchen
Fish and chips, Eamonn's A Dublin Chipper
Fried chicken, Oohhs & Aahhs
Fried green tomato BLT, Café Saint-Ex
Fried oyster po' boy, Hank's Oyster Bar
Gin and tonic (with house-made tonic), Central Michel Richard
Glass of wine, Bardeo
Gnocchi in gorgonzola sauce, Al Crostino
Gnome's water, Tallula
Goat biryani, Tabeer
Goat curry roti, Teddy's Roti Shop
Goat pepper soup, Roger Miller Restaurant
Grilled baby octopus, Tako Grill
Grits, Georgia Brown's
Half-smoke, Weenie Beanie
Hanger steak, Ray's the Steaks
Katsikaki (roasted goat shoulder), Komi
Kitfo (Ethiopian steak tartare), Shashemene
Korean barbecue, Gooldaegee (Honey Pig)
Lobster burger, Citronelle
Ma po tofu, Great Wall Szechuan House
Mala pig blood with tofu in hot pot, China Star
Margarita with salt foam, Oyamel
Masala dosa, Amma Vegetarian Kitchen

Mint julep, Round Robin Bar at the Willard Hotel
Mixed grill, Peruvian style, Granja de Oro
Moules frites, Café du Parc
New-style sashimi, Sushi-Ko
Oysters, The Wharf Seafood at the Maine Street Fish Market
Parker house rolls, CityZen
Peking duck, Peking Gourmet Inn
Pizza margherita, 2 Amys Pizza
Pork belly barbecue, Annan-Gol
Pork buns, Li Ho
Porterhouse for two, BLT Steak
Prime rib, Prime Rib
Pumpkin frozen custard, The Dairy Godmother
Pupusa revuelta, Irene's Pupusas
Roast chicken, Pollo Granjero
Roast duck, Cantonese style, New Big Wong
Roasted rabbit loin in Framboise beer, Brasserie Beck
Salty oat cookie, Teaism
Scallops on lentils, Marcel's
Seared foie gras, Adour
Seasonal infused liquors, Poste Moderne Brasserie
Seco de res, Costa Verde
Seolleongtang (beef bone porridge), Dduk Sarang
Soondae, Seoul Soondae
Steak frites, Bistrot du Coin
Stiegl (Austrian beer) on draught, Leopold's Kafe
Swordfish sliders, Coco Sala
Tacos de lengua, El Charrito Caminante
Thousand-year egg, A & J Restaurant
Toro (fatty tuna) sushi, Makoto
Tuna carpaccio, Westend Bistro by Eric Ripert
We want the funk, give up the funk, Founding Farmers
Whole grilled branzino, Pesce

# Fearless Critic

## Reviews

# A & J Restaurant

Tasty Chinese that goes beyond Chinese-
American—hooray for that

**8.4** Food   **6.7** Feel

## Chinese

Casual restaurant   **$30** Price

Mon–Fri 11:30am–9pm
Sat–Sun 10am–9pm

**Bar** None
**Credit cards** None
**Reservations** Not accepted

**Annandale, VA**
4316 Markham St.
(703) 813-8181

**Rockville, MD**
1319 Rockville Pike
(301) 251-7878

Even if somebody in your party speaks Mandarin, expect the staff at A & J to be strict about circling. The rule has been instituted to avoid confusion: if a dish isn't circled on the paper menu, you don't get it, and verbal ordering is not allowed, even in Chinese. If any kind of "secret menu" exists at A & J, it takes a lot more than native fluency to tease it out.

Which is fine by us: after all, the normal menu is so good that it's hard to imagine any necessary amendments. In addition to traditional dim sum offerings—available not only at lunch but throughout the day—A & J serves a number of Northern dim sum dishes, which tend to be heartier than their Southern counterparts.

Take, for example, the scallion pancake. Whereas the dish in its most familiar form is served forth as a limp and rather precious object, the A & J version is at least half an inch thick, and must be ordered as a stand-alone plate (cong yu bing). Also not to be missed are guo tie: finger-thick logs of pork, scallions, and spice, rolled into a flour pancake and pan-fried to wonderful goldenness; the result is something akin to a flauta. A serving size of eight seems excessive only before you have your first taste. Afterwards, eight is hardly enough.

The non-Northern specialties at A & J are less spectacular. Steamed dumplings come in a number of varieties (pork, beef, vegetable) and are on par with what you'd see in other above-average dim sum joints. Noodles deliver as expected, although they, along with the soups, are improved with a spoonful from the jar of pickled red chili peppers that sits on every table.

And no visit is complete without the thousand-year egg: the A & J version of this spice-aged, blackened duck egg is smoky and cold, and it's served in a ring of (much younger) scrambled tofu with sesame oil and salt—one of the more delicious homages to the soybean we've seen in the past thousand years or so. –CK

# Aatish on the Hill

**6.0** Food   **5.2** Feel

An Indian joint that's trying to be fancy but would be better advised to stick to the basics

## Indian

Casual restaurant   **$30** Price

www.aatishonhill.com

Mon–Thu 11:30am–2:30pm, 5pm–10pm; Fri–Sat 11:30am–2:30pm, 5pm–10:30pm; Sun 5pm–10pm

**Bar** Beer, wine, liquor
**Credit cards** Visa, MC, AmEx
**Reservations** Accepted
Delivery, veg-friendly

**Capitol Hill**
609 Pennsylvania Ave. SE
(202) 544-0931

An erstwhile maligned hill spot (dissed for its shabby décor), Aatish has put cloths on its tables and fanned napkins in its glasses and tried to perk up its service. But the pink walls with cracking paint remain, the lighting is too dim, and the restaurant has not shed its endearing, if absent-minded, demeanor. Still, for a decent Indian meal without too many frills, Aatish is not a bad bet.

Billed as "Pakistani Tandoori Charcoal Cuisine," Aatish offers a range of northern-Indian-style dishes beyond tandoor. Some of the best options are the lamb curries, which feature fragrant meat and creamy compositions. Matter queema, for instance, blends spicy cooked lamb with a pea-and-potato curry whose woodsy flavor complements the meat. The vindaloo is sweet, if slightly oily.

On the vegetarian side, okra is a standout dish, with a restrained compromise between crispness and mush. There is some crunch to the curry, but plenty of smoothness as well, and the spicy tomato-based sauce does wonders to integrate the dish.

Many of Aatish's other offerings, however, are standard. The tandoori chicken fails to impress: the meat is moist enough, but the bird is under-spiced and tastes as if it could have been prepared in a conventional oven. Dal consists of whole split lentils floating in juice, rather than a blended dish cooked into a softer curry. And naan is pretty standard—soft and a little burnt on top—but nothing special.

There are also some quirks on Aatish's menu. We are, for example, not entirely sure what to make of the sliced maraschino cherries and peas sprinkled on top of basmati rice. Mixed vegetables are very heavy on the corn and, as a result, strangely sweet. Sometimes the restaurant's quirks are positive, though: pickles are unconventional but excellent, including well-brined cubes of lemon, cauliflower, and carrot.

Given a choice between the reliably mediocre offerings of other Indian restaurants on the Hill, and the hodgepodge possibilities of Aatish, we'd choose the latter. We can live with the creepy pink walls and maraschino cherries. –CK

# Acadiana

Mardi Gras it's not, but there's some enjoyable
Louisiana-themed food at this chainish spot

**7.1** Food

**7.5** Feel

## Southern

Upmarket restaurant

**$60** Price

www.acadianarestaurant.com

Mon–Thu 11:30am–2:30pm,
5:30pm–10:30pm; Fri
11:30am–2:30pm, 5:30pm–
11pm; Sat 5:30pm–11pm; Sun
11am–2:30pm, 5:30pm–
9:30pm

**Bar** Beer, wine, liquor
**Credit cards** Visa, MC, AmEx
**Reservations** Accepted
Outdoor dining

**Mt. Vernon Square**
901 New York Ave. NW
(202) 408-8848

The web site of this upmarket haute-Louisiana restaurant—part of a growing upmarket concept group that also includes Ceiba, DC Coast, and TenPenh—describes the restaurant's casually elegant design as inspired by "drunken Romans." Actually, it's a shame that the inspirational Romans weren't a bit more plastered, because Acadiana could use some Mardi-Gras-style energy (or just a few rounds of Bourbon) to liven it up.

Don't get us wrong—the food isn't bad. Addictive warm buttermilk biscuits start things off right. Chicken-and-andouille-sausage gumbo is pleasant and hearty, and "classic turtle soup," that culinary gimmick to end all gimmicks, is worth trying. It's smooth and well seasoned, but if you like it, don't assume it's because of the (relatively flavorless) turtle meat. It's probably more that you like its reinforced stock, its "traditional garnishes" including spinach and hard-boiled egg, and the shot of dry sherry that's ceremoniously dumped in. Ever heard of soup from a stone? (At our last visit, the sherry was brought out awkwardly far in advance, leading us to wonder if the house was just in a good mood and sending out some shots. We almost downed it.)

Sautéed veal medallions are heavy and one-dimensional, with an overrich, overbearing wild-mushroom gravy, although we do like the jalapeño cheese grits beneath. This is the sort of dish of which it's quite difficult to eat more than a few bites.

Brunch is a fun way to go here. "Eggs Acadiana" are a nod to the restaurant's supposed roots, with crab cakes and Louisiana crawfish, but it's another case of heavy and buttery without enough counterbalancing acid or heat. Raisin-bread pudding works well enough—it's sweet without being overwhelming. Beignets have a thick, unusually dense doughiness that's cut somewhat when a slightly bitter coffee crème anglaise seeps in.

We just wish Acadiana had a bit more of a feel for the energy and playfulness of Louisiana. The décor is more drab than drunken, and the food—though technically well-executed—could use a bit less butter and more soul. –RG

# ACKC Cocoa Bar

Spunky, eclectic, fun, and flashy—but short on the sweets, where it counts

**4.8** Food   **7.0** Feel

## Sweet drinks, Baked goods

Café   **$10** Price

www.thecocoagallery.com

Mon–Wed 10am–9pm; Thu
10am–10pm; Fri 10am–11pm;
Sat 9am–11pm; Sun 9am–9pm
Hours vary by location

**Bar** None
**Credit cards** Visa, MC, AmEx
**Reservations** Not accepted
Date-friendly, delivery, kid-friendly,
outdoor dining, veg-friendly, Wi-Fi

**Logan Circle**
1529 14th St. NW
(202) 387-2626

**Alexandria, VA**
2003 Mount Vernon Ave.
(703) 635-7917

Entering ACKC Cocoa Bar is like walking into someone's inner fantasy in the form of a retail store. For the record, this someone really likes chocolate, orchids, greeting cards, dessert-themed gifts, and the color red. Despite the seeming incoherence, the store is fun. If ACKC Cocoa Bar were the product of someone's imagination, that someone would be a sassy broad who used to sing for the troops and now warbles in an art-gallery-cum-chocolate-store amidst strings of musty plastic flowers, a gaudy chandelier, and lots of color. She's pretty cool in a retro kind of way.

Drinks at ACKC are named after different leading ladies with elements that reflect their personalities. Hot chocolate is made with hot shavings in steamed milk and infused with other flavors via a strainer. The effect is inconsistent depending on the drink. "Liz," for instance, is lavender-infused, semi-sweet chocolate. The floral note is so light, however, that all that's left is a very slight bitterness and none of the aroma you would expect. Furthermore, for a cocoa made with shredded chocolate, the base is thin and watery, containing none of the deepness and richness that we seek. Whipped cream is so meek that it quickly disappears under the chocolate.

The fiery "Lucy" performs better. Though it's still thin, an infusion of chili peppers in the piping hot cocoa leaves your mouth with the same burn that you'd get from a good bowl of hot-and-sour soup—a prickly heat that slides down your throat and collects above the stomach. This is a drink you need to sip carefully. To balance out the heat, you may consider one of the sandwiches or pastries made by a local baker. Be warned: though they are passable, they often contain flaws like dryness and less-than-freshness.

A visit to ACKC is like a trip to your batty Aunt Mildred's. You will ooh and aah over her newest collection of furniture and art and have a good cackle over a warm drink and an ordinary sweet. And although you'll leave with a generally positive impression, you won't be quite sure when—or if—you'll go back. –JC

# Aditi Indian Cuisine

Not-so-exciting Indian food in strange Georgetown digs—we don't get it

**4.9** *Food*  **3.2** *Feel*

## Indian

Casual restaurant  **$35** *Price*

www.aditibistro.com

Mon–Thu 11:30am–2:30pm,
5:30pm–10pm
Fri–Sun 11:30am–10pm

**Bar** Beer, wine
**Credit cards** Visa, MC, AmEx
**Reservations** Not accepted
Delivery, kid-friendly, veg-friendly,
Wi-Fi

**Georgetown**
3299 M St. NW
(202) 625-6825

**Vienna, VA**
405 Maple Ave. E.
(703) 938-0100

This big Georgetown Indian restaurant, on a well-travelled block of M Street, must stay in business by getting a lot of walk-ins and tourists from its location. We doubt it could be the food, which is below-average, dumbed-down Indian, although there's a nice focus on vegetarian.

The rooms, both upstairs and downstairs, are strange and often empty, with a white spiral staircase and tacky mirrors. You feel as though you're wandering the deserted ruins of a 1980s rap star's Malibu pad. In every possible way, the place is inferior to its vegetarian spin-off, Amma, which is down the street.

It's not the worst Indian food we've ever had; tandoori chicken is fairly moist, and lamb vindaloo's not bad. Chicken tikka masala, that Brit-Indian standby, is spicier than average; the meat is tender and thick, and the gravy is rich and creamy. Anything with chickpeas is a good vegetarian choice, as is the okra, when available: the latter is chock full of tomatoes that have been stewed down almost to a paste.

But saag (spinach) dishes are watery and underseasoned, with the spinach showing little character and black pepper as the only discernible flavor. Many of the basic curries, vindaloos, and so forth suffer from that problem, too; instead of the rich spice mix that Indian curries can be, there's just a one-dimensional heat (or, in some cases, a zero-dimensional lack thereof). Samosas are soggy, and naan bread gets extremely chewy as it cools; this is a problem at many Indian restaurants, but it seems to happen quicker here.

Then there's Aditi Bistro, in Vienna, Virginia, which is wrap-heavy, a sort of attempt at Indian-American burritos. Contributing editor Tyler Cowen has quipped: "imagine trying to do Chipotle with Indian food." –FC

# Adour

This master chef throws his hat into the DC ring—
when he's not hanging out in the Eiffel Tower

**9.1** Food  **9.1** Feel

## French

Upmarket restaurant

**$125**
Price

www.adour-washingtondc.com

Mon 7am–11am, 11:30am–
2pm; Tue–Fri 7am–11am,
11:30am–10pm; Sat 7am–
noon, 5:30pm–10pm; Sun
7am–noon

**Bar** Beer, wine, liquor
**Credit cards** Visa, MC, AmEx
**Reservations** Accepted
Date-friendly, good wines, Wi-Fi

**Downtown**
923 16th St. NW
(202) 509-8000

There is perhaps no chef in the world whose reputation is as carefully cultivated—or as easily ridiculed—as Alain Ducasse's. Although his entry into the US market, at New York's Essex House, actually lasted seven years before going under, the consensus is that he was pretty much run out of town by the city's sophisticated skeptics.

At least you can't call Ducasse a quitter. He's determined to figure out the Americans yet, so he's reinvented himself yet again by opening two Adours, in swanky St. Regis hotels in New York and DC. Thankfully, prices are well below Essex House levels, and after some initial bumps in the road, the food is currently delivering as promised. The atmosphere is as slick, moneyed, and unselfconsciously trendy as you'd expect, with wine walls glowing in the posh darkness and irritating continuous bench seating for the less valued guests.

That's not to say that the maverick chef is actually hanging out in DC, because he's got another new project going too. It seems that two St. Regis hotels weren't touristy enough for the guy, so he's also opened a restaurant in...drumroll please...the Eiffel Tower. That's right—there, Ducasse has opened Le Jules Verne, which is actually *inside* the tower, where for a mere 200 euros ($263), you can rub elbows with some of the world's most gullible and/or price-insensitive diners and gaze out over the City of Lights.

So if you thought that $26 was a lot for the starter of pressed chicken and foie gras with black truffle condiment and leek vinaigrette—a lovely indulgence with unexpected textural diversity—consider that it could be pricier. Seared foie gras has been excellent, too, as has light, zippy cucumber-marinated yellowtail with radish and green-apple mustard, and creamy sunchoke soup cleverly matched with bacon foam. Magnificently indulgent ricotta gnocchi are like the comfort food of the upper class, with sautéed lettuce, crispy prosciutto, and earthy mushrooms. Adour is also turning out the city's most consistently brilliant preparations of lobster, often paired with some version of reduced shellfish stock.

There have been service issues—pomposity, and worse still, incessant efforts to squeeze more money out of customers: pushing bottled water, upselling wine. A bit of trivia to keep in mind: this is not quite a carbon copy of the New York Adour. On one visit, the waitstaff admitted to us that the DC menu was "less interesting," with "less focus on organ meats and such," because the palates of DC diners were "less adventurous." The white-coats are coming! The white-coats are coming! Revolt, good District citizens, revolt! –RG

# Afghan Grill

A delightfully authentic Woodley Park deviation
from the DC ethnic routine

**7.8** Food
**7.0** Feel

## Afghan

Casual restaurant

**$40** Price

www.afghangrill.com

Daily 11am–11pm

**Bar** Beer, wine, liquor
**Credit cards** Visa, MC, AmEx
**Reservations** Accepted
Outdoor dining, veg-friendly

**Cleveland Park**
2309 Calvert St. NW
(202) 234-5095

Elegance is emphasized at this second-level nook in Cleveland Park. Once you've cleared the dingy nail salon below, the subdued riches of Afghan Grill await: the restaurant's tables are well dressed in white cloth, and splashes of silver ornaments light the space. The walls hold several excellent daily-life photographs of Afghanistan, printed largely and in precise colors. Behind the small wooden bar is an attractively shelved collection of wines, and the extensive menu further reflects a collected attention to detail.

Nonetheless, the joint can feel a bit cramped, whether you're pressed against the wall at a small table or bumping elbows and chairbacks in the larger tables in the center of the restaurant. A single waitress aspires to serve all tables; on a busy Friday night, this endeavor may strike you as naïve at best, maddening at worst (depending on your level of hunger). Occasionally, a kitchen assistant will come to her rescue and bus a few trays, but more often than not, every interaction will begin with her apologies for the wait. Not terribly elegant.

Luckily, the food is well worth the wait. First to arrive will be the poofy grilled bread, light and doughy, served with a fresh green herb-oil-and-vinegar dipping sauce. Headlining a generally superb group of appetizers is bulanee; it's flat pastry filled with mashed leek and potato, beautifully browned and well paired with yogurt and mint. Also worth a taste are the mantoo dumplings (which can also be ordered as a main course) and the sambosy goshti, which look like miniature versions of Indian samosa, and are similarly spiced: this Afghan version is filled with ground beef, chick peas, and green peas.

Not to be missed, as an appetizer or main, is the kadu buranee, an exceptionally bright pumpkin dish simmered with oil and garlic and served with a light yogurt sauce. Also good is the sabzi chalao, an earthy plate of lamb and spinach, served with a simple rice pilaf. –CK

# Afterwords Café

Literature, food, and delicious desserts, late into the evening—is this a lost Renaissance?

**8.0** Food **9.7** Feel

## American

Café **$35** Price

www.kramers.com

Sun–Thu 7:30am–1am
Fri–Sat 24 hours

**Bar** Beer, wine, liquor
**Credit cards** Visa, MC, AmEx
**Reservations** Accepted
Date-friendly, kid-friendly, live music, outdoor dining, veg-friendly

**Dupont**
1517 Connecticut Ave. NW
(202) 387-1400

The Afterwords Café, which is part of Kramerbooks, one of the city's most beloved independent booksellers, is an absolute DC original—yesterday, today, and hopefully forevermore. Kramerbooks is certainly a wonderful retreat in and of itself, serious but also social. It's only logical that such a place would install a complementary café to allow its patrons to graze titles over coffee, wine, and appetizers. Still, many Washingtonians bypass the literature and local authors and head straight to brunch—or take advantage of the late hours to stop at the end of the night for dessert and cocktails. This is an establishment with endurance.

The clientele at Afterwords includes a healthy mix of coffee-hugging solo readers, friendly duos catching up over brunch, and groups of four or five sharing beer and steamed mussels. Most of the café (except the bar scene) is housed in a sky-lighted annex to Kramer's; the greenhouse effect makes the place cozy in winter, and air-conditioning keeps it cool in the summer. It's an ideal place to meet friends for beer and wine accompanied by a plate of the well-loved, sky-high nachitos. They're just what you'd expect: tri-colored chips, good-quality shredded cheese, chili, salsa, and sour cream—in short, more than enough toppings to completely smother the chips.

The notion of pairing food and books is indeed a fine one, and Afterwords goes far beyond nachitos and the traditional coffee-plus-pastries of chain bookstores—you might say it's politically-influenced New American (and up-to-date, too; in 2008, there was already a sandwich named for Obama in the early primary season). The café's most popular meal, by far, is brunch. Many of the egg offerings are quite rightly lauded. The "Nouvelle Leo," for example, is a scramble of "café-cured Atlantic salmon" coupled with scallions and sweet peppers and topped with a dollop of caviar. The selection of Benedict dishes is no less creative, and the eggs, whether scrambled or poached, are prepared with a light touch, even if the toast is plain and bagels seem to be of the frozen-and-toasted variety.

By night, many come just to partake of the "Death By Chocolate," a flourless cake that has a deservedly serious following. Delicious though it may be, it's not just the cake they're following. It's the commitment to the idea that in a world of chains, an independent, literary way of life is still possible. –CK

# Agraria

Rustic, clean, simple, and American are the buzzwords here

## New American

Upmarket restaurant

www.agrariarestaurant.com

Tue–Fri 11:30am–10pm
Sat–Sun 11:30am–11:30pm

**Bar** Beer, wine, liquor
**Credit cards** Visa, MC, AmEx
**Reservations** Accepted
Date-friendly, outdoor dining,
Wi-Fi

**Georgetown**
3000 K St. NW
(202) 298-0003

Lurking in a cave under the hulking edifice of the Georgetown waterfront, Agraria is something of a mystery. It's pretty dark inside, and dining rooms of various sizes open upon each other like so many caverns. Some are absolutely exquisite—like the single round table surrounded by hundreds of bottles of backlit wine. Throughout the restaurant, country accents of wood paneling and rough-hewn stone are dressed up by plate glass, rich textiles, and twinkling candlelight. The result is classy, sedate, and clean.

One of the big downfalls of Agraria is that its menu is too generically American and pricey for the average diner to just stop in. Yet more experienced diners will notice that the restaurant follows a philosophy of seasonal, sustainable dining and support for collective farming; in fact, it was created by such a collective, the North Dakota Farmers' Union. The food reflects the philosophy; preparation is simple, flavors are clean, and ingredients are fresh. It tastes virtuous and good.

Melon salad is a light and rich combination of summer flavors; thin shaved cantaloupe and honeydew are amped up by spicy toasted hazelnuts and house-cured duck prosciutto. The overall effect of the dish is more sweet than it is savory, but it's a delicate starter made even more complex and enchanting by lavender and vanilla vinaigrette.

Main courses are also carefully executed. Steaks are generously cut, correctly cooked to temperature, and served with toppings so clean they never take your attention from the meat. Vegetables taste, thankfully, like vegetables, delivering on the promise of artisanally sourced produce that is too often just a form of puffery in the restaurant rat race.

A dish of plump sea scallops is a beautiful rendition of fisherman's victuals, just seared on the ends and basking in rich, creamy chowder with half potatoes and asparagus. Rough bread is re-imagined as two fans of crouton arching over the plate. It is an ideal balance of opposites: rustic but upscale, filling but not overwhelming, rich yet fresh and light. Some desserts at Agraria don't quite hit the mark—chocolate mousse is overpowered by soggy phyllo—but flops are generally rare. –JC

# Akosombo

Delicious African food that does your body good

| 7.8 | 7.0 |
|------|------|
| Food | Feel |

**Ghanian**  Casual restaurant  **$15**
_Price_

Mon–Sat 11am–8pm

**Bar** None
**Credit cards** None
**Reservations** Not accepted

**Mt. Vernon Square**
613 K St. NW
(202) 408-1133

While Ghana Café bursts at the seams with pretty Adamsmorgansters and Senate interns, the Ghanaian cab drivers have retreated to Akosombo, a grimy cafeteria near the Convention Center. You can expect to eat out of a Styrofoam take-out dish at a rickety table, in the company of irritable voices, a ringing phone, and a television blaring the latest reality show, but you can also expect to eat very well.

For six dollars, you'll get both sides of a take-out dish filled with any combination of meats, fish, beans, and stews, plus fried plantains and rice. The food is served cafeteria-style out of metal receptacles replenished throughout the day, and you almost have to beg the server to slow down as she heaps scoop after scoop of stews with a metal spoon into your dish.

Begin with the peanut soup, a thick, creamy, hazardous blend of beef trimmings, fish, blended nuts, and nut oil, and more than a fair share of hot chile oil. The hazard of the soup lies in the small fish bones bobbing on the surface and hidden in the murky peanut depths; unless you have a gullet of steel, we recommend deploying a slurping action to stop bones before they pass your lips and pass mercilessly down your throat. Luckily, the spicy soup is worth the risk.

The same advice holds for the whole fish dish; in this case, the cooks have removed the heads and prepared just about every other part of a basic white fish with spicy oil and garnished the dish with thin-sliced carrots. The flesh is soft but not overcooked, and make sure to eat the skin, which seems to have retained the grand majority of chile.

One of Akosombo's most successful stews is made with large cubes of beef in a light but very spicy red sauce. The spinach stew has hints of the sweeter spices of Indian cuisine, and the plantains are of the smaller, sweeter variety and burnt crisp on the outside. Akosombo's sole misstep is the chicken stew: the pieces of bird are mostly bone, and the flesh is overcooked and tough.

When you're full, simply fold up your Styrofoam dish to carry home the leftovers; the flavors will blend together further for a treat the next day. –CK

# Al Crostino

Some of the city's best homemade pasta in an
unlikely wine-bar package

**9.0** *Food*  **8.0** *Feel*

## Italian

Upmarket restaurant  **$55** *Price*

www.alcrostino.com

Daily 5pm–9pm

**Bar** Beer, wine, liquor
**Credit cards** Visa, MC, AmEx
**Reservations** Accepted
Date-friendly, veg-friendly

**U Street**
1324 U St. NW
(202) 797-0523

From outside—and even when you first step in—Al Crostino seems like
nothing but a sleek little neighborhood wine bar. And its prices hardly
hint at the notion that this is one of the city's best Italian restaurants.
Protein mains—a brilliantly juicy, well-peppered, arugula-dressed tagliata
di manzo (ribeye), for instance—are priced scarcely above the *appetizers*
at some of the city's more pretentious restaurants.

The space is small and cozy, which is part of why it can be so difficult to
land a seat here—even on a weeknight—unless you reserve (although
sitting at the bar is often an option). As for the wine-bar bit, well, yes, the
Italian wine selection is well chosen and well priced, worthy of the title.

Al Crostino's homemade pastas are hardly groundbreaking in concept,
but they're uniformly excellent. Mezze lune (half-moon-shaped ravioli),
however they're prepared, make for one of the best stuffed-pasta plates
in the city, while gnocchi in Gorgonzola sauce—whether spinach or
ricotta—are powerfully soft and rich. House-made pappardelle have
shown up with a tender lamb ragú whose tomato is sweet and well
integrated.

Unlike at some of the other top Italian contenders in town, however,
the pastas don't overshadow the meat and fish mains, like that delicious
tagliata; a well-pounded pollo alla Milanese (breaded, fried chicken
breast); or a whole branzino that's lovingly roasted and served, as it
should be, with simple herbs, lemon, and olive oil.

The weakest dish we've had has been a beef carpaccio with arugula,
Parmigiano-Reggiano, olive oil, and lemon; the meat has come over-cured
by the lemon, and thus not as tender as it should be.

We also wish that the menu changed more often, and that the noise
level were lower. And beware: as at sister restaurant Tiramisú, prices for
the specials of the day can sometimes be priced out of control—and you
might not find out about this until the check arrives. But such problems
are easily overcome: make a reservation, go on a weeknight, and ask for
the prices of specials.

Al Crostino is not just a wine bar. It is one of our favorite Italian tables
in the city. –RG

# Al Tiramisú

Authentic Italian brilliance can rise from the most unpredictable places

| 8.8 | 9.0 |
|-----|-----|
| Food | Feel |

## Italian

Upmarket restaurant

**$55**
Price

www.altiramisu.com

Mon–Fri noon–2:30pm,
5:30pm–10:30pm
Sat 5:30pm–10:30pm
Sun 5pm–9:30pm

**Bar** Beer, wine, liquor
**Credit cards** Visa, MC, AmEx
**Reservations** Accepted
Date-friendly, good wines,
veg-friendly

**Dupont**
2014 P St. NW
(202) 467-4466

Are you kidding? This restaurant's name is so tacky that, for any Italophile—or, for that matter, for anyone who approaches these types of places with a critical eye—it starts the evening with a strike against it. The narrow rooms and cozy, warmly lit tables are well conceived, equally well suited to a date or business dinner. But then comes strike two: when you sit down, the staff speaks to you in a tone of voice that evokes a patronizing Italian waiter at a tourist-menu restaurant just off St. Mark's Square. Al Tiramisú's food *couldn't* be good—could it?

You'd better believe it. While the menu is hardly creative, the kitchen executes with consistent fidelity to the provenance of its recipes; clearly, it's run by people who know what these dishes are supposed to taste like. If you can tolerate blatant Italophile-speak for a sentence, it's as if you can *taste* the fact that the place is run by real, live Italians.

Outside the confines of the printed menu, daily specials like a delicious orata (a species of white, delicate Mediterranean bass also known as "dorado" or "dourade") or pasta with sardines and tomato (an underappreciated Sicilian dish) are often among the best choices here. Off the menu but on demand, they'll also hook you up with an assortment of small-portioned starters, which, at one recent visit, featured creamy mozzarella di bufala with a sweet cherry tomato; an unusually flavorful marinated Portobello mushroom with goat cheese, the sort of preparation of which we're usually quite scared; swordfish a bit over-cured by its citrus, but still enjoyable; and sensational whole squid, lightly breaded and then grilled.

If there were a lowlight, it's a slightly dry boneless-skinless-chicken-breast main—a dish that's essentially doomed from the start—yet even this turns out better than most, marinated, aggressively seasoned, and well paired with authentically Italian oven-roasted potato medallions, which compensate for the inauthenticity of the protein. The downside is that the prices here can really creep up on you, but the authenticity and atmosphere justify them. Now if they only changed the name of the place, they'd be unstoppable. –RG

# Alberto's Stone Oven Pizza

**5.3** Food  **4.1** Feel

As with soup, you need more than stone for good
pizza—but few care at 4am

## Pizza

Counter service

**$5** Price

www.albertospizzeria.com

Mon–Wed 11am–midnight
Thu–Sat 11am–5am
Sun 11am–2am

**Bar** None
**Credit cards** Visa, MC, AmEx
Delivery, veg-friendly

**Dupont**
2010 P St. NW
(202) 986-2121

**Adams Morgan**
2438 18th St. NW
(202) 332-2234

The real talent of Alberto's might not be pizza-making, but rather self-
promotion; in our estimation, this basement's joint success seems to owe
largely to the fact that the place advertises its pizza as "stone-fired,"
creating the specter of a competitive advantage—at least in the foggy
minds of post-bar revelers at 2:30am—where, qualitatively, there really is
none. Generally speaking, Alberto's pizza is barely passable.

In keeping with the Adams Morgan/Dupont late-night trend, what
Alberto's calls a slice is actually one quarter of a very large pie, which can
be acquired for a fairly steep $3.85 (cheese) or $4.95 (any of four topping
combinations on offer daily). Both thin and thick crusts are homemade
and light, with a touch of whole wheat flour (a completely whole wheat
or garlic crust can also be ordered), but the dough is more or less
tasteless. Alberto's red sauce is a bit thin; sweet and tart flavors are nicely
balanced, but the sauce is underseasoned, and while a mixture of soft
(mozzarella) and dry (parmesan) cheeses sounds like a good idea, there's
too much cheese and too little flavor.

The one virtue of Alberto's pie is the light-handed application of
toppings, making slices more manageable and less heavy than they might
be otherwise. Alberto's offers a deliriously long list of toppings (only a few
are truly weird: chopped walnuts, jalapeños, shiitake mushrooms), which
are generally wholesome and well applied. Artichoke hearts are soft,
tomatoes small and fresh. The little green clubs that pass for spinach,
however, tend to dry out atop the thin crust.

If you're looking for atmosphere, you won't find it here. This place is
mostly take-out (the Dupont location, a block from the fountain, makes it
a classic pre-picnic or post-bar stop), but indoor seating at the thin
counter is limited, and it can be hard to count on utensils. Even waiting
around for a take-out pie can call up claustrophobia; it's best, especially at
busy times, to call ahead.

One caveat: Alberto's is among the few Washington pizzerias offering
Chicago-style pizza, and it's one of the only places we've found that does
it well. Deep-dish pizza is much mushier than the thin-crust version, and
the sauce and cheese much deeper; given how many better places there
are in town for thin-crust, the Chicago-style slices turn out to be Alberto's
most redeeming raisons d'être. Otherwise, stone-oven pizza is all hype.
Like soup from a stone. –FC

# Alero

East Coast Tex-Mex at its finest—for what that's worth

| 6.5 | 8.2 |
|-----|-----|
| Food | Feel |

## Mexican

Casual restaurant

**$40**
Price

www.alerorestaurant.com

Sun–Thu 11:30am–11:30pm
Fri–Sat 11:30am–midnight
Hours vary by location

**Bar** Beer, wine, liquor
**Credit cards** Visa, MC, AmEx
**Reservations** Not accepted
Outdoor dining

**U Street**
1301 U St. NW
(202) 462-0834

**Dupont**
1724 Connecticut Ave. NW
(202) 234-9885

**Cleveland Park**
3500 Connecticut Ave. NW
(202) 966-6876

There's a myth out there that Tex-Mex is just an inferior version of real Mexican cuisine. Let's put it to rest here and now. Tex-Mex is a viable genre in its own right, diverging from the traditional with (let's be honest) copious amounts of melted cheese, flour tortillas, blandly addictive brown gravy, and the like. And when it's done right, it's damn good. But East Coast Tex-Mex so often hopelessly misses the mark that it's hard to be nice about it. Nonetheless, if you try hard enough, you can find some bright spots.

And in the case of Alero, there are a few. They poke through from underneath a thick layer of chile con queso (and, alas, queso skin)—or "Cheese Dip," as it's Yankeeified here. (In Texas, queso is as commonplace a term—and appetizer—as guacamole.) Chiles en nogada are surprisingly elegant, their filling of picadillo, dried apples, and raisins carefully balancing savory with sweet. The walnut sauce in which they're bathed, our waiter once gravely counseled us, is served at room temperature, the idea being that the hot pepper melts the sauce. (Apparently, some patrons have attempted to jump ship and send the whole thing back, thinking the dish was flawed.) Enchiladas, a seemingly more foolproof order, don't quite have it going on, especially when it comes to their fillings. Chicken is dry and underseasoned, while spinach is watery and underseasoned.

DC's three Aleros have quite distinctive personalities. The Dupont location often feels sad and empty, although it packs 'em in on weekends. Cleveland Park is the location to hit up in good weather, with a lovely raised patio overlooking Connecticut that's great for passing away the afternoon with a pitcher of sorts. The best atmosphere, though, is at the U Street location, which is a warm, buzzing, upscale departure—with a sort of yuppie-Santa-Fe feel—although its menu is virtually identical to the others'. All three also have a decent tequila list that goes beyond Spring Break in Cancún, and even includes mezcal, that deliciously smoky elixir from the hills of Oaxaca. House margaritas get the job done without being too sweet or puckeringly limey.

But let us stop now, lest we get ahead of ourselves. Until the Texas diaspora gets a little bigger, we'll just have to wait for Tex-Mex that's actually *good* to work its way north. That, and to keep our eyes out for Continental Airlines specials down to the Lone Star State. –AH

# Al's Pizza

A pizza joint that's pretty far away, but not exactly far out

**6.4** | **5.0**
Food | Feel

## Pizza

Counter service | **$20**
| Price

Daily 10am–10pm

**Bar** None
**Credit cards** Visa, MC
Veg-friendly

**Purcellville, VA**
761 E. Main St.
(540) 338-5700

Al's is shamelessly promoted by everyone from residents of this little area of Purcellville, Virginia, to the elite DC food media. Although the pizzeria is close to many hearts, we'd advise against venturing out to these parts from further afield simply for a pie. Al's is a neighborhood joint for a reason: it serves the neighborhood well, and it owes much of its local following to friendliness and convenience rather than to the global superiority of its pies. The place makes a decent New-York-style pie, but it's a bit thicker than is traditional, and the sauce and cheese don't quite make it far enough to the edges from the center of the pie.

Many Al's aficionados will rave about its crust, but we find that it looks better than it tastes. Al's sauce is a classic, thin-spread red, and its cheese selection doesn't venture into the gorgonzola-and-feta universe you might find at pizzerias in the northwest. The toppings list is standard, although Al's is more liberal with its veggies than are many New York-style joints.

In about the only attempt at atmosphere, the walls are lined with competing posters: one aerial shot of pilgrims at Mecca, one line-up of the DC United soccer team, a yellowing news clip, and a paper menu taped up to the window. Orders are placed through a wide window, through which you can see the whole pizza-making operation. You can, if you're so inclined, sit at the stools facing out from Al's big picture window—a symbol, perhaps, of the extent of its symbiotic relationship with the neighborhood.

Still, we caution you to look past the hype; Al's is only worth the trip down here if you're already on one. –CK

# Amici Miei

**6.6** **6.0**
Food Feel

Surprisingly authentic Italian tucked away in a strip mall in Maryland

## Italian

Casual restaurant

**$50**
Price

www.amicimieiristorante.com

Mon–Thu 11:30am–2:30pm, 5pm–9pm; Fri–Sat 11:30am–2:30pm, 5pm–10pm; Sun 5pm–9pm

**Bar** Beer, wine, liquor
**Credit cards** Visa, MC, AmEx
**Reservations** Accepted
Kid-friendly, outdoor dining, veg-friendly

**Potomac, MD**
1093 Seven Locks Rd.
(301) 545-0966

The strip-mall environs and bland interior of this neighborhood Italian restaurant might lead you to expect bottled red sauce and parmesan cheese out of a green can, but Amici Miei's owners are honest-to-goodness Italians who generally let the food speak for itself. A signature dish is the grilled fish, served head-on and bone-in, with simple vegetable accompaniments and a wedge of lemon—the perfect antidote to the traditionally heavy, cheesy, breaded chicken-parmesan-style Italian-American. Nobody, after all, in Italy lives very far from the coast, and a whole grilled fish with oil and lemon might just be Italy's national dish.

The atmosphere here is chatty and family-friendly, as befits the suburban location, but still elegant enough to feel like a restaurant rather than a theme park. Muted tones of sage and beige dominate the dining room, whose walls feature those almost-clichéd black-and-white photos of Sophia Loren and the like, matted in white and framed in gold.

Most of the successes here are modest. Homemade agnolotti, gnocchi, and ravioli are admirable, though they sometimes come overcooked. Generally minimalist pizzas are hit or miss, sometimes scoring with a crisp, slightly charred crust, and other times plagued by sogginess. Kids will enjoy choosing their own dessert from a rolling trolley. The wine list is unsurprising and Italian-focused, with an average markup. The food is not particularly authentic beyond the grilled fish and homemade pasta; this place is not competing with top-end Italian.

In the end, the authenticity of this friendly Italian spot goes deeper than any perfectly calibrated reproductions of rustic or refined native dishes. The service is warm even if it's often amateurish. The cooking is familiar without being trite, well executed without dressing itself up any more than necessary. And that, perhaps, is what's most truly Italian about Amici Miei: the emphasis on family, friendship, and fresh food prepared simply and ideal for sharing. –CD

# Amma Vegetarian Kitchen

**7.6** Food    **6.0** Feel

Meatless South Indian that you don't have to be a vegetarian to love

## Indian

Casual restaurant    **$20** Price

Mon–Fri 11:30am–2:30pm, 5:30pm–10pm; Sat 11:30am–3:30pm, 5:30pm–10:30pm; Sun noon–3:30pm, 5:30pm–10pm
Hours vary by location

**Bar** Beer, wine
**Credit cards** Visa, MC
**Reservations** Accepted
Delivery, kid-friendly, veg-friendly

**Georgetown**
3291 M St. NW
(202) 625-6625

**Vienna, VA**
344 Maple Ave. E.
(703) 938-5328

Hidden away up the stairs from a frou-frou Georgetown candy shop is a southern Indian gem that serves up a colorful eye- and palate-candy of curries and dosai. The carnivorous may be wary and should be forewarned: Amma's offers nary a touch of meat, flesh, or fish. But it may not be what you'd expect, either, if your conception of vegetarian restaurants entails dry pita bread and undersalted hummus. Nope, this restaurant is a coup not just for vegetarians, but for all of us. You won't find lackluster tofu at Amma's: only good, fresh vegetables; careful sauces and deeply reduced stews; good bread; and a collection of intelligently applied seasonings and herbs.

Many of Amma's offerings, in fact, can only be described as intense. If you're so inclined, we'd recommend beginning with the restaurant's salty lassi, which packs a serious punch. Served in a small glass, the drink shrieks with cold and puckeringly sour yogurt, and manages to toe the salt line without crossing it.

Intensity of flavor also marks a number of Amma's sauces and curries. The aloo chole preparation gives life to chickpeas and potatoes—vegetables that can turn bland and starchy in lesser hands—with a curry that's full of cardamom, cinnamon, cumin, and pepper (there's even a whole cinnamon stick left in the bowl for show). Brown lentil sambar is creamy and full, tailor-made for moisturizing dry vada (a rice flour doughnut), and pickled peppers can add as much bite as you'd wish.

Amma's earns high marks on the starch front, as well. Although the dosai are grandiose, the uttappam deserves an honest try as well. The pancake-like creation is left soft and doughy, with the outside buttered and brought to a crisp.

An added perk is the restaurant's quiet perch above the bustle of M Street; the medium-sized dining room is pleasantly populated and never loud. While Georgetown's many overpriced restaurants sit below, smugly preying on tourists, Amma's patrons sit above, reveling in their own brand of more deservedly smug vegetarian bliss. –CK

# Amsterdam Falafel Shop

**5.4** Food  **5.3** Feel

Do-it-yourself falafel sandwiches whose broad appeal spans oceans

## Middle Eastern

Counter service

**$10** Price

www.falafelshop.com

Sun–Mon 11am–midnight
Tue–Wed 11am–2:30am
Thu 11am–3am
Fri–Sat 11am–4am

**Bar** None
**Credit cards** None
Outdoor dining, veg-friendly, Wi-Fi

**Adams Morgan**
2425 18th St. NW
(202) 234-1969

The Amsterdam Falafel Shop is a neighborhood institution whose owners are attempting to transform it into a national one. The inspiration, however, is global: the Adams Morgan shop takes its lead from the style of inexpensive holes-in-walls that Middle Eastern immigrants have opened across Europe. These "döner kebap" shops have become the representative fast food of Amsterdam and a quick-dining staple in many other European cities, too.

It's no secret that Amsterdam's owners have an eye on opening more shops based on this concept, perhaps as franchises outside of DC. The writing is already on the wall—literally. The concept is simple: you are given a pita with three or four small falafel balls. You fill the remaining open space inside the pita with any number of salads, vegetables, sauces, and spices from a salad bar of options. You can also order drinks and frites—which are offered with a different, more limited set of toppings options—but not much else.

The blackboard-style menu is clean and concise, and posters near the salad bar lay out the house rules: no utensils; all salad items must fit inside your pita; no refills, except to add more tahini. There are even a couple of "tips" (e.g. if you want to fit more in your sandwich, try mashing up your falafel; to minimize mess, add wet ingredients like sauces before the vegetables).

One particularly colorful poster offers a legend to the salad bar. It aims to help you distinguish the hummus from the baba ganoush (smoky, the best thing in that bar), and to inform you just how spicy the spicy peppers are. On the whole, the toppings are varied but uninteresting: most of the salads taste, well, clean. The spiced tomato sauce is well worth a try. When available, roasted cauliflower and sautéed eggplant are also worth seeking out.

Beyond clean salad, there's other evidence that the shop is engaged in standardizing itself to suit the average American palate and disposition: for the healthy crowd, Amsterdam offers whole-wheat bread. Most tellingly, the heart of the operation—the falafel—is not as well spiced as it could be. And soon, if all goes as planned, that not-well-spiced falafel will be within walking distance of you, too, wherever you are. –CK

# Annan-Gol

Grill your own succulent pork bellies

**8.9** Food

**7.6** Feel

**Korean**

Casual restaurant

**$20** Price

Daily 11am–midnight

**Bar** Beer, wine
**Credit cards** None
**Reservations** Not accepted
Date-friendly, kid-friendly

**Annandale, VA**
4215 Annandale Center Dr.
(703) 914-4600

It looks like nothing from the outside, but this is officially the Center for BBQ Pork Addicts Anonymous. It's as dark and mysterious as any secret meeting place; the windows are covered, sparing diners from the blaring reality of the ugly parking lot outside. Walls are green, and sticky with the habits of the wild-eyed pig fiends within.

There are six—six!—versions of pork bellies to throw on your table grill: marinated, spicy, sang…there's beef, too, but the pork is the star here. It all comes with green onions and salty soybean paste, to be scooped up with lettuce leaves. Your intestines will welcome the roughage.

Fat rules here. It drips across the table grill, its smell wafts up through the smoke hoods that sit over each table. Ceiling fans collect it like cotton candy batons and send aromas of grilling meat and onions and garlic around the room. Don't wear anything you wouldn't wear to a smoky club. And no white.

Other dishes are competent. Chewy noodles are fun, texturally, and spicy with a little acetic tang to them. If you dig chewing, the octopus is a good bet.

Did we mention the pork? As you lay tender and fatty bits on the grill, there's an unabashed primal pleasure in every pop and sizzle, in the charred edges, and in watching the color go from bloody rose to palest pink. It's just plain fun. No wonder it's such a popular joint.

Brillat-Savarin said, "Tell me what kind of food you eat, and I will tell you what kind of man you are." Well, we've been called much worse. –FC

# Annie's Paramount

Experience the sobering effects of late night steak and eggs

| 6.9 | 8.1 |
|------|------|
| Food | Feel |

## American, Steakhouse

Casual restaurant

**$35**
Price

Mon–Wed 10am–11:30pm; Thu 10am–1:30am; Fri–Sat 24 hours; Sun 10am–1:30am

**Bar** Beer, wine, liquor
**Credit cards** Visa, MC, AmEx
**Reservations** Accepted

**Dupont**
1609 17th St. NW
(202) 232-0395

"Let's grab brunch at that steakhouse around the corner."

Not something you hear often. But then again, eating at this steakhouse-in-a-diner isn't an experience you're going to find just anywhere. The clientele is almost exclusively gay men, which isn't surprising, given Annie's location in the heart of DC's vibrant—and sizeable—gay community. Brunch is a party, as it should be, with tables knocking back Bloody Marys first and foremost and then putting something greasy into their stomachs to soak it all up.

As fun as Annie's may be now, it was even more fun back in the day. Prices have slowly been creeping upwards, and hints of formality are working their way into the service. (Plates are no longer delivered in that gruff, almost diner-esque style.) Annie's food, too, is caught somewhere between straight-up steakhouse and pub grub. You can get a decent steak here, but you can also get jalapeño poppers—try ordering those at The Palm. We must profess to liking the more downmarket items. Thickly battered fried shrimp are addictive. A burger is straightforwardly good (although overcooked sliders are less impressive). Fries, too, disappear quickly. An egg sandwich with bacon and cheese also comes with lettuce and tomato—a move rarely seen, but one that works.

Not everyone is upset about Annie's makeover. The black-and-white interior, while still straightforwardly dinerish, is now, by commercial restaurant-catalog standards, upmarket too. It's sleek and clean, and lighting isn't too bright. But that late-night vibe (after the bars close, Annie's takes on a life of her own—it's packed and it's fun) is a little different now; there's something incongruous about a sobering meal in a setting that's not dumpy.

On to the real heart of the matter: how is the steak? Eh, it's not bad. They'll cook it to temperature (three cheers for not overcooking meats!), and ultimately that's what matters most. It's hardly Prime dry-aged beef, but given the reasonable prices, how could it be? In any case, you're way more likely to find us at Annie's for brunch, with a plate of eggs and a Bloody Mary. Or in the wee hours, with a plate of eggs and a Bloody Mary. –AH

# Ardeo

Stylish surroundings and thoughtful preparations
will keep your attention

## New American

Upmarket restaurant

**$65**
Price

www.ardeorestaurant.com

Mon–Thu 5:30pm–10:30pm
Fri–Sat 5:30pm–11pm
Sun 11am–2:30pm, 5pm–10pm

**Bar** Beer, wine, liquor
**Credit cards** Visa, MC, AmEx
**Reservations** Accepted
Date-friendly, good wines, outdoor
dining, veg-friendly

**Cleveland Park**
3311 Connecticut Ave. NW
(202) 244-6750

The slim storefront that conceals Ardeo opens up to a remarkably efficient dining space, with softly lit tables set up in a front area to the left; a dim, backlit bar to the right; and two more levels above. It doesn't feel at all cramped, thanks to light-colored walls and tables that aren't packed together. The restaurant displays its own art collection on the walls, giving a gallery-like feel that's elegant without being stuffy. (We wish we could say the same for the attentive but soulless service.)

The cooking is simpler and more honest than the chic, polished setting might suggest. Many of the initial flavors are elemental, as in big, plump mussels that come in a broth that's an interesting combination of fennel, thyme, and cider vinegar. Octopus (from the section of the menu that's marked, rather stylishly, as "medium plates") comes with its promised char blending delicately with the briny taste of the sea creatures, plus some depth added by warm olive vinaigrette.

Bigger plates tend to feature proteins, which are generally well prepared, but sometimes oversalted. (At least this gives us something different to complain about; Cleveland Park and Woodley Park restaurants are more frequently guilty of underseasoning.) We've also been disappointed with a cloyingly sweet Korobuta pork loin coated in kumquat marmalade whose sourness was overwhelmed by the gummy sugar.

The popular Sunday brunch here is mainly savory. Several dishes from the dinner menu (including the aforementioned veal meatloaf) survive the night, and are augmented by mid-morning favorites like eggs Benedict (served here with crab and Serrano ham) and pumpkin challah French toast. But our favorite time to hit up Ardeo is on a warm late summer evening, when you can spend hours on the airy roof deck—or at one of the front tables by the tall front windows, which open completely to merge the restaurant into the sidewalk and street scene beyond. in the breeze, when there is one.

The affordable, diverse wine list is commendable for being both affordable and diverse, with many bottles in the under-$40 range. It's shared with Bardeo, the informal wine-bar area of the restaurant. Speaking of Bardeo, if you feel like something more casual or inexpensive, you should definitely consider dining over there instead. Although the kitchen is shared by the two, we often find that we actually prefer Bardeo's menu—sometimes, less elaborate and ambitious can mean better. –CD

# Armand's

We know we're not in Chicago, but you can still do better in the District

**5.7** Food  **5.5** Feel

## Pizza

Casual restaurant

**$25** Price

www.armandspizza.com

Sun–Thu 11:30am–10pm
Fri–Sat 11:30am–11pm
Hours vary by location

**Bar** Beer, wine, liquor
**Credit cards** Visa, MC, AmEx
**Reservations** Accepted
Delivery, kid-friendly, outdoor
dining, veg-friendly, Wi-Fi

**Capitol Hill**
226 Massachusetts Ave. NE
(202) 547-6600

**Arlington, VA**
2151 Arlington Blvd.
(703) 526-9800

**Georgetown**
4231 Wisconsin Ave. NW
(202) 363-5500

**Additional locations**
and more features at
www.fearlesscritic.com

People in Washington love Armand's. As the Chicago-style pizza chain will not hesitate to mention, it's been voted "Best Pizza in DC" in one magazine for 17 years running. We know that the idea of representation can be a touchy issue in this town, but one can't help wonder what kind of Rep DC would elect if residents crown such a bad pizza "Best."

We'll try to be non-partisan. Armand's isn't terrible. In fact, it's a pretty good bet if what you're interested in is a classic Chicago-style deep dish to fill you up on a cold day. But with so many interesting and tasty pizza shops in the area, it's baffling that Armand's would be popular with anyone but the most undiscerning of eaters.

More importantly, if you tried shipping an Armand's pie to a colleague in Chicago, it would be laughed back to Washington before it even cleared customs at O'Hare. The crust is too bready, the cheese is rubbery, and the sauce is practically non-existent. Although some of the combination pizzas sound interesting, toppings tend to be imbalanced. If we really wanted chicken fajitas, we wouldn't order the Chicken Fajita pizza, we'd just go to a Mexican place. Ditto for the Bacon Cheeseburger: we'll trust burger guys over pizza guys with this one. On the Greek pizza with onions, olives, grilled feta, and spinach, Armand's skimps on almost every topping except sliced black olives. You have to strain to make out (or for that matter, to taste) an onion or mushroom amidst the dollhouse tire-dump of olive rings.

Each Armand's also offers a decent salad bar, common pizza accoutrements such as beer, wings, and garlic bread, a flat-screen TV blaring The Game, and 20-ounce servings of fountain soda with free refills. But unless you can stomach enough refills to drink back the money you spend on mediocre pizza, we'd recommend you find somewhere else to eat. –CK

# Aroma

Really unexciting Indian that needs to work on the most basic of basics

4.7 Food | 7.0 Feel

## Indian

Casual restaurant

$25 Price

www.aromarestaurant.com

Mon–Thu 11:30am–2:30pm,
5:30pm–10pm
Fri–Sat 11:30am–2:30pm,
5:30pm–10:30pm
Hours vary by location

**Bar** Beer, wine, liquor
**Credit cards** Visa, MC, AmEx
**Reservations** Accepted
Outdoor dining, veg-friendly

**Farragut**
1919 Eye St. NW
(202) 833-4700

**Arlington, VA**
4052 S. 28th St.
(703) 575-8800

Aroma is yet another mediocre Indian restaurant that gets business by dint of location. The grimy (and often empty) interior might lead you to believe it's an undiscovered gem—though we must say that the décor has been moving slowly towards the fancy side of things. Nonetheless, a good find this is not. The restaurant is a standard place to get a plate of a-bit-too-oily curry and warm fluffy naan: nothing more, nothing less.

A weekday buffet—of course there's a weekday buffet!—gives you the best opportunity to hit upon something tasty. We wish you the best of luck. While you won't find anything out of the ordinary here, even the classics are unfortunately a bit bungled up.

Aroma's tandoori dishes come dry: instead of succulent meat, you have its spiced-up remains. Even drier vegetable dishes (such as the okra) can come out as parched as the Phoenix desert; the kitchen will dig up some kind of soy-heavy "dipping sauce" if you ask for some moisture.

The restaurant's naan is just what you'd expect at an Americanized Indian joint: fluffy but uncharismatic. Conveniently, it's just what you need to soak up somewhat drippy curries: the matter paneer's peas spread like a green avalanche to all sides of the plate.

In light of the wet curry and dry tandoor situations, a fictional management consultant might advise Aroma to "more efficiently allocate its moisture assets." We consult you to just stay away. –CK

# Asia Nine

This Pan-Asian failure is more lounge than
restaurant—use it that way

4.8 Food
2.0 Feel

## Pan-Asian

Casual restaurant  **$35** Price

www.asianine.com

Mon–Wed 11am–11pm
Thu–Fri 11am–midnight
Sat–Sun noon–midnight

**Bar** Beer, wine, liquor
**Credit cards** Visa, MC, AmEx
**Reservations** Accepted
Outdoor dining, veg-friendly

**Penn Quarter**
915 E St. NW
(202) 629-4355

Asia Nine has a flashy website and a downtown Penn Quarter location,
but the restaurant unit of the operation can't deliver the promised glitz.
For the "lounge" feeling, head upstairs to the second-floor VIP room,
where loud music pulses on weekend nights. For the restaurant portion of
the program, you'll be seated in the cavernous ground-floor dining room,
which can often be practically empty. Asia Nine is clearly not designed
with diners in mind; the floor is a hard slate tile better for dancing (and
easy clean-up) than for allowing conversation; the ceilings are high; and
the bars (one for alcohol, one for sushi) are long. The furnishings,
however, seem a flimsy afterthought, and the menu is so over-inclusively
pan-Asian you get the sense that no one tried very hard to edit or refine
it.

Pork gyoza are agreeable, with a meaty but slightly underseasoned
filling. Sushi rolls are barely acceptable, not the freshest. Lemongrass
curry—as with most main dishes on the menu (curries, noodle dishes, and
fried rice), available with your choice of chicken, beef, or shrimp—is
inoffensive enough, though the sauce is somewhat watery and the
broccoli an undercooked afterthought planted on top. Many of Asia
Nine's standard Americanized dishes fall victim to the plague of the genre:
a pervasive over-sweetness that touches the curries, soups, and dipping
sauces. A notable exception is the larb gai, a ground chicken salad in a
sour-and-tangy citrus and chili dressing, served with sharp red onion and
scallion.

The best dish on the menu might be the mango sticky rice, where the
sweetness is actually an asset. Ripe, in-season mangoes are generously
laid atop a mound of pleasantly salty rice and crunchy toasted mung
beans. But a list of cocktails in candy colors, with names like the "E-Z
Kiss" and "Sun of a Peach," tend back toward the unpleasantly sweet
category.

Even for passable, broadly pan-Asian dishes, there are better restaurant
bets. Asia Nine probably bills itself as a "bar & lounge" for good reason;
its cavernous space, dramatic bars, and overly inclusive menu aren't
signals of a dining-centric experience. Maybe you're better off sticking to
the E-Z Kiss and the dance floor. –CD

# Asian Spice

Some things just can't be left behind—like bad service at a hole in the wall

**5.1** Food

**6.0** Feel

## Chinese, Pan-Asian

Casual restaurant

**$40** Price

Sun–Thu 11:30am–10:30pm
Fri–Sat 11:30am–midnight

**Bar** Beer, wine, liquor
**Credit cards** Visa, MC, AmEx
**Reservations** Accepted
Delivery, outdoor dining

**Chinatown**
717 H St. NW
(202) 589-0900

Asian Spice is the new kid on the block in Chinatown. Next to the dilapidated store fronts and holes in the wall, Asian Spice is the belle of the ball. Its outdoor patio, chic lighting, and mysterious name establish it as a new kind of Chinese restaurant—one that can charge high prices because of its fancy cocktails and aerodynamic dinnerware. Unfortunately, despite high hopes born of a facelift and a tummy tuck, this proves to be nothing more than just another average Asian restaurant.

Though the place has tried to distance itself from its Chinatown peers, chronic service issues abound—it's as if the staff is willfully inconsiderate. Frozen drinks come with straws too thin to sip through, and all dishes come to the table at once in a veritable horde of clinking china. It wouldn't be such an issue if the tables were bigger, but alas, you may find yourself seeking refuge (and real estate) from nearby diners. Fruit flies and smelly napkins add to the carnage.

Experienced diners know that Chinatown food is often worth the inconvenience. This rule holds true about half the time at Asian Spice, where the menu gallops across Asia and beyond. Sushi is fresher and more competently made than other similarly priced restaurants. It's not the best around, but it's not dangerous either. Bulgogi—a hard find in the city—is tender and sweet; thin slices of beef are appropriately crinkly and very juicy. Kimchi is pleasantly stinky but still mild enough for the masses.

The menu also includes less traditional fare. Crab dip is translated (quite literally) into Asian "chips and dip," in which crab stick is grilled until smoky, pulled apart, and tossed with tangy Asian barbecue sauce and sriracha. The chips are soggy from sitting in the dip and there aren't nearly enough to go around, but at the end of the day the dish is fresh and original.

Asian Spice has some identity issues to work out: is it the chic restaurant that its image suggests, or is it really just another neighborhood joint in a new outfit? Either way, a decision must be made, because at the moment, the prices are too high for what you get, and the service is too poor for the décor. –JC

# Astor Mediterranean

**6.3** **7.0**
Food   Feel

Family-friendly falafel and Egyptian pizza from a friendly family

## Middle Eastern, Greek

Casual restaurant   **$20**
Price

www.astormediterranean.com

Mon–Sat 11am–10:30pm
Sun 11am–9:30pm

**Bar** None
**Credit cards** Visa, MC, AmEx
**Reservations** Not accepted
Kid-friendly, outdoor dining,
veg-friendly

**Adams Morgan**
1829 Columbia Rd. NW
(202) 745-7495

**Arlington, VA**
2300 N. Pershing Dr.
(703) 465-2306

Smashed between high-end restaurants, dollar shops, and the mishmash of people that is Adams Morgan, Astor Mediterranean is a pleasing blend of all of its neighbors. The little storefront is neon-bright, a spot of harsh but homey light on a dim street. A lone chalkboard sign loiters casually by the door, advertising the Egyptian pizza in a friendly, neighborly manner. Marvelous whiffs of spicing and baking and frying beckon unsuspecting pedestrians toward the light. (The Arlington branch is somewhat less evocative.)

The inside of Astor Mediterranean is cheap but clean. Red walls are lined with family pictures of promisingly fat babies, and coolers buzz along with the rest of the noise. There is a general low roar of familial noise. In fact, with the refrigerator cases with big bowls of pre-made food and the snap and sizzle of fryers and grills behind the counter, Astor Mediterranean feels more like a family-run greasy spoon than anything else.

Like the décor, the food at Astor is charming but unspectacular. Those whose hearts are swayed by big portions of homey-looking food will be pleased. Egyptian pizza is garlicky and strong with such formidable toppings that you must race against the clock to finish the pie before the overwhelmed dough gets soggy. A huge mezze platter includes acidic, chunky baba ghanoush that is quite good, tangy stewed eggplant, and paprika-smoky hummus. One of the winners at Astor is the falafel, which is singularly crisp, with plump, herby breading that is coarse and light and thoroughly delicious—it's almost like eating a rice cracker.

Meats from various kabob versions are less exciting. Chicken is citrusy and nicely flavored, but finicky. It reminds you that chicken is not the best meat for kabob. The more traditional ground lamb tends to have a very strong "lamby" flavor, which we like. But dry, chewy beef kebabs have been overcooked. And some misguided wise guy decided to use puff pastry instead of phyllo in the spanikopita, leading to a very wrong entity that is all butter and no olive oil.

Still, at Astor, very nice people will feed you very unpretentious Middle Eastern food, and that in itself is worth a visit. As you sip on sweet and strong hibiscus water and nibble at your heaping plate of food, you'll feel yourself melting into the neighborhood. It's a good feeling. –FC

# Asylum

Vegan and vegetarian bar food take center stage at a musical grunge

**5.9** Food

**6.1** Feel

## American

Bar

**$25** Price

www.asylumdc.com

Mon–Fri 5pm–1am
Sat–Sun 11am–4pm, 5pm–1am

**Bar** Beer, wine, liquor
**Credit cards** Visa, MC, AmEx
**Reservations** Not accepted
Live music, veg-friendly

**Dupont**
2471 18th St. NW
(202) 319-9353

What's the worst part about being a vegetarian?

That's a seemingly endless question for carnivores. But think about this: when the carnivores are at a bar and snacking on buffalo wings and chili cheese fries and beefy nachos, what are the vegetarians eating? The celery that's served with the wings, plain fries, or naked nachos? That's not cool.

But at 18th Street's Asylum, vegetarians are allowed to enjoy decadent bar goodies too. Fried vegan wings boast a crisp exterior, a faux-chicken interior, vegan sour cream, hot sauce, and a wooden stick that acts as the bone in the wing. Satisfyingly smoky vegan chili, loaded with beans and corn, is chewy and hot and hearty and topped with a layer of vegan cheddar cheese; you won't miss the meat here, especially when it's loaded on top of waffle-cut fries or nachos. Mozzarella sticks go beyond the traditional packaged breaded batons; here, the cheese is wrapped in an egg-roll skin, fried, and served with hot, fruity apricot-mustard chutney which beats Ragù tomato sauce any day. Non-vegetarians will also be satisfied when chicken and beef poke their heads out in the form of sandwiches, tacos, and wraps. And to top it all off, the prices couldn't be better—it's difficult to find an item on the menu that tops $10.

Asylum is a cross between a biker bar, a bohemian coffee shop, and a haunted house that plays rock. Mellow light, red leather booths, and wooden tables make for a sort of mysterious, almost demonic ambiance that is at once intriguing and welcoming. The basement is home to a pool table, and live music attracts large, diverse crowds. And if you show up on the right night, you might get to witness the city's only vegan Jell-O wrestling matches. How's that for an asylum? –SDC

# Austin Grill

An embarrassment to the food of the Lone Star state

## Mexican

Casual restaurant

www.austingrill.com

Sat 9am–midnight
Hours vary by location

**Bar** Beer, wine, liquor
**Credit cards** Visa, MC, AmEx
**Reservations** Not accepted
Kid-friendly, outdoor dining

**Penn Quarter**
750 E St. NW
(202) 393-3776

**Alexandria Old Town**
801 King St.
(703) 684-8969

**Silver Spring, MD**
919 Ellsworth Dr.
(240) 247-8969

**Additional locations**
and more features at
www.fearlesscritic.com

Austin, Texas is most certainly a special place. It's the gateway to the Texas Hill Country, to the miles and miles of gently rolling hills that are covered in a layer of beautiful green foliage come springtime. It's the self-proclaimed "live music capital of the world," playing host to two major annual music festivals—Austin City Limits in the fall and South by Southwest in the spring. It's home to the massive University of Texas, and to their mighty Longhorns.

It's also home to some of Texas's best native cuisine. Barbecue is second to none here (well, save for some of the small towns outside of the city). Delicious Tex-Mex is inescapable—everywhere you turn there are decadent cheese enchiladas, fajitas, and, of course, margaritas and Mexican martinis. Oh, and breakfast tacos. Bacon, egg, cheese, and a dash of hot sauce—all wrapped up in a tortilla—is heavenly.

So what is going on with Austin Grill? They've got some cleverly named dishes that will amuse former Austinites: Bevo's salad, Lake Travis nachos. But said expats would be even more amused if the food were palatable. Chile con queso—an app not taken lightly in Texas—is a failure here. It tastes too much like ballpark nacho cheese—and not in the Velveeta way, as it should; the crucial chile is nowhere to be found, nor does its advertised Shiner Bock beer seem to impart any flavor. Complimentary salsa is in the gazpacho school of thought (blended to an equalized smoothness), and it's not bad, but it could use some more kick.

Enchiladas, in total contravention of Austin style, come with sour cream on the side, but the plate as a whole is poorly integrated; beans are dry, rice is flavorless, and vegetables are disconcertingly cold. Margaritas, thankfully, are quite good—we favor the LBJ and the Presidente—but Mexican martinis are nonexistent. Blasphemy!

Over-the-top Texas paraphernalia can't fool us. This food can't hold a candle to even a mediocre Austin institution. Check out the *Fearless Critic Austin Restaurant Guide* to read up on all the places that can. –AH

# Axum

Nothing beats good injera—especially not bland pasta

| 7.1 | 6.6 |
|-----|-----|
| Food | Feel |

## Ethiopian

Casual restaurant

**$25**
Price

Sun–Thu 10am–2am
Fri–Sat 10am–3am

**Bar** Beer, wine, liquor
**Credit cards** Visa, MC, AmEx
**Reservations** Not accepted
Live music, veg-friendly

**Shaw**
1934 9th St. NW
(202) 387-0765

With so many Ethiopian restaurants on this block, it can be hard (but fun) work picking a favorite. It's easier if you're a bee, in which case Axum's shiny red exterior will draw you. Axum is not quite in the same culinary league as the much-more-heralded nearby Etete; it's not as modernized and pretty, either (and thus not as full of curious novices not yet brave enough to venture elsewhere). But in many ways it's more legit. In fact, Axum's legitimacy seems underscored by the population of Ethiopian diners here, as well as the spare décor.

There's an unusual focus on Italian-influenced pasta dishes here—e.g. fried chicken cutlet with spaghetti and red sauce—if you like that sort of thing. Don't forget that Eritrea wasn't the only East African country occupied by Italy—Mussolini, crashed the party in Ethiopia, too, from 1936 to 1941. So this is the food of the oppressor. Do Indian restaurants serve bangers and mash? Kippers? Okay, we're crawling back under our rock now. Our real point is that the Italian red-sauce fare is completely forgettable here, even if it's popular with some of the local Ethiopian community.

There are some nice touches, like the ubiquitous egg in doro wat having a delicate, salty exterior. The stew itself tastes almost fruity, like spicy tamarind, a notch more complex than we've seen elsewhere. A queso-fresco-like cheese is crumbled on top of some dishes, which we usually don't see, and adds a cool little sour note. Stewed green beans, carrots, and potatoes are sweet but uninteresting. Collard greens are good, but when aren't they?

Most of our problems have been with texture. The kitfo (Ethiopian steak tartare) is occasionally a bit tough, and we've found the lamb in a yellow curry dish sinewy. Alicha has good flavor, but the beef has sometimes come overcooked. If you like Etete but don't feel like dealing with the wait, or are ready for something a little more street, Axum's a good play. –FC

# Bacchus of Lebanon

**6.8** **6.0**
*Food* *Feel*

Bold Mediterranean and Middle Eastern flavors can't save messy dishes and inauthentic décor

## Middle Eastern

Upmarket restaurant

**$60**
*Price*

www.bacchusoflebanon.com

Sat–Mon 5:30pm–10pm
Tue–Fri noon–2pm, 5:30pm–10pm

**Bar** Beer, wine, liquor
**Credit cards** Visa, MC, AmEx
**Reservations** Accepted
Live music, outdoor dining, veg-friendly, Wi-Fi

**Bethesda, MD**
7945 Norfolk Ave.
(301) 657-1722

When someone says "Lebanese restaurant," what comes to mind? An abundance of fake coliseum-style pillars? We didn't think so. Nonetheless, whitewashed Roman columns, both outdoors and inside, dominate Bacchus's décor, detracting from the few choice chairs, ornaments, and tables made of intricately laid wood and the attractively Eastern light fixtures. It's best, though, to avoid the stuffy dining room and opt instead for one of the umbrella-shaded outdoor tables where you'll join couples and groups of friends (mostly of the graying but young-at-heart variety) as they tuck into mezze.

Although the menu boasts nearly two dozen main courses, it seems as though most patrons choose to share a wide variety of warm and cold appetizers instead. We endorse this plan of attack, especially if you are less familiar with this cuisine. The food is hit-or-miss, beginning with the dry pita and dull za'atar olive oil dip. Kibbe bel hamod—a cracked wheat, ground meat, onion, and pine-nut fritter slathered in a tangy pomegranate sauce—boasts an array of bold flavors and varying textures. It's a shame that the dish is so messy, becoming a muddled heap after only a few bites.

The same goes for the fattet makdous, where fried bread surrounds fried eggplant topped with ground beef, yogurt garlic sauce, pine nuts, and pomegranate sauce; this heaping portion is too big and greasy. Overpowering garlic mars the typical bamye bel zeit (okra in a coriander tomato sauce)—and it's come to the table seemingly straight from the refrigerator. The excessive sliminess helps the okra go down, although we could do without the brain freeze.

The wine list is nothing special, with only four Lebanese bottles on the entire list, and it seems to follow the trend here: a lack of attention to detail makes for a mediocre meal that, in spite of the authentic recipe names, lacks the sort of hospitality and finesse that we associate with Lebanese food. –SDC

# Bagels & Baguettes

A decidedly un-"Lobbyist" joint whose bagels are preeminent in town

**6.7** *Food* **7.0** *Feel*

## Sandwiches, Baked goods

Café **$10** *Price*

www.bagelsandbaguettes.net

Mon–Fri 7am–4pm
Sat–Sun 8am–3pm

**Bar** None
**Credit cards** None
Outdoor dining, veg-friendly

**Capitol Hill**
236 Massachusetts Ave.
NE
(202) 544-1141

Hill life getting pricey? If you can't afford the noontime steakhouses and so-called "grilles" of the lunching lobbyists, Bagels and Baguettes might come in handy. This deli-cum-bakery is the stomping grounds of the Capitol underclass: the pages and LAs and other assistants who grace the halls of Congress with youthful energy, if not wealth. As if in collaboration, the deli accepts cash only, not plastic. On the weekends, the hole-in-the-wall bagelry (which features an ample outdoor deck) transforms into a popular brunch spot for neighborhood residents.

This café makes a very good bagel. The product is knobby and sour, with a substantial crust and a rich, chewy inside. These are some of the strangest-looking beasts around: many are flattened out or asymmetrical, further hints that yeast is used sparingly, and boiling is *de rigueur*. The bagels come in all of the traditional flavors and a few traditional "specials" like sun-dried tomato.

The staff is skilled at making the best of these often-oblong sandwich boards: the bagels are sliced evenly and spread thickly with your combination of choice. Fresh, thick lox is applied with a generous hand, but it's probably the only topping here that belongs uniquely on a bagel. The remaining options are clear (and rather uncreative) translations from the sandwich world, with appearances by turkey breast, chicken salad, and so on. A single concession is made to the deli's Capitol Hill location: the classic Reuben is reincarnated as the "Lobbyist" at Bagels and Baguettes—if there's a pun or joke, it's lost on us, but seven bucks will buy you a bagel with corned beef, sauerkraut, Swiss, and Russian dressing.

Lest we forget the second half of its title, we'll merely mention that the bagels, and not the uninteresting baguettes, make this place worth visiting. The café also offers a few types of pastries and smallish cookies, but aside from the powdered-sugar-doused almond croissant, none are noteworthy. Stick to the bagels—at least until you work your way up. –CK

# Banana Café & Piano Bar

**5.6** Food  **7.0** Feel

A fun, funky tropical dive with live piano music and lots of quirkiness—but not enough flavor

## Cuban, Latin American

Café  **$30** Price

www.bananacafedc.com

Daily 10am–11pm

**Bar** Beer, wine, liquor
**Credit cards** Visa, MC, AmEx
Live music, outdoor dining

**Capitol Hill**
500 8th St. SE
(202) 543-5906

The Banana Café is a quirky place, with a sombrero-wearing plantain for a mascot, a locally famous (within a radius of four blocks) piano bar, and a menu that offers a modest list of selections from Tex-Mex, Cuban, and South American cuisines. If the food comes from a country that puts lime in their alcoholic drinks, then that food apparently qualifies for Banana's menu.

In spite of the café's wide geographical ambition, however, the cuisine is notably non-quirky, and it never oversteps its bounds. Many of Banana's basics are rendered well, if without much spirit. The black beans that accompany the Cuban dishes are full-flavored and cooked just short of bursting, and refried beans are expansive, if unexciting. In any case, there's no mixing of legumes across cuisines, and "To Each His Bean" may be Banana's prevailing philosophy.

For texture and taste, the stuffed yuca is a good place to begin. The dish is more casserole than stuffed vegetable, as the edges of the yuca become difficult to disambiguate from stuffing, and the shape of the thing winds up resembling the emptied contents of an upside-down bowl. Thick masa, sweet corn, peppers, and plenty of soft cheese hold the dish together; the yuca maintains a roasted flavor without tasting smoky.

Banana's meats are much more ordinary. The ground beef in the Cuban picadillo, for example, is too fine, and its juices are nearly flavorless. There are raisins and olives here and there, but if the fried egg on top of the picadillo lends richness, the whole thing suffers from not having been cooked long enough to allow flavors to meld.

We wish we could praise one of the few things that unites Banana's disperse cuisines: the restaurant's limey drinks. Unfortunately, margaritas are extremely weak, and taste as if they've been made with some kind of mix rather than fresh citrus. And much of Banana's food is as thin as its margaritas, perhaps because, with its hemisphere-spanning menu, the restaurant has spread itself so. –CK

# Bangkok 54

Bangkok by way of Studio 54? Amidst some nonsense, the food is solid

| 7.2 | 7.9 |
|-----|-----|
| Food | Feel |

## Thai

Casual restaurant

**$35**
Price

www.bangkok54restaurant.com

Sun–Thu 11am–10pm
Fri–Sat 11am–11pm

**Bar** Beer, wine, liquor
**Credit cards** Visa, MC, AmEx
**Reservations** Accepted
Delivery, live music

**Arlington, VA**
2919 Columbia Pike
(703) 521-4070

The best way to enter the Bangkok 54 restaurant is through the affiliated grocery store on Columbia Pike. Wind your way through the narrow aisles of rice noodles, canned coconut milk, Thai DVDs, okra, and lychees, and a certain dizziness may begin to set in. If it does, don't worry: simply walk out the back door of the grocery store and you'll hit the entrance to the restaurant.

Either way, you'd better be prepared for the change of pace. If the grocery store is one of the closest things you'll find to Southeast Asia in DC, then the restaurant is pure Vegas. Waiters rush to and fro with acrobatic agility. A huge, open, bustling kitchen presents itself as you enter, with chefs wildly chopping vegetables and adding garnishes. The dining area is noisy and dim, with flashy ornaments and dark tables. In the center of each table is a vase with a dozen sets of cherry-red chopsticks. Cocktails are served in twisted glasses, and many look as though they were produced in nuclear factories, so bright are their lime-green and magenta hues. The "54 Mai Tai" even arrives with a burning lemon rind.

Luckily, Bangkok's food is far less frou-frou. While a few of the appetizers benefit from a Vegas-style detail—the excellent fresh rolls, for example, are tweaked with a slice of avocado in addition to the usual mint and Thai basil—most of the food is blissfully free of frills and frumps. A crispy whole fish is complemented but not overwhelmed by a chili-filled glaze and delicate slices of vegetables and green mango, while the restaurant's green curry is a subtle and basil-filled take on a dish that's typically appropriated for the worse by Thai-American impostors. A crispy, succulent pork belly, served a variety of ways, has a loyal following, as do the restaurant's crispy squid. Bangkok 54's spicy roast duck, however, is fried too dry to permit the enjoyment of an entire plate; if you must order it, ask for a dipping sauce.

When it comes to dessert, the restaurant shines anew with homemade ice creams, which are garnished with tiny fruits carefully crafted from red bean paste. Unfortunately, a Vegas-level roar can make enjoying such delicacies rather trying in busier hours. Plan a civilized early weekday dinner, and as the crowd heats up, slip quietly out the way you came, leaving the masses to gamble with their flaming fruit. –CK

# Bangkok Joe's

This dumpling bar and café prepares stylized Thai
street food that's not so street

**5.5** Food **6.5** Feel

## Pan-Asian

Casual restaurant

**$45** Price

www.bangkokjoes.com

Mon–Thu 11:30am–10:30pm
Fri 11:30am–11:30pm
Sat noon–11:30pm
Sun noon–10:30pm

**Bar** Beer, wine, liquor
**Credit cards** Visa, MC, AmEx
**Reservations** Accepted
Outdoor dining, veg-friendly

**Georgetown**
3000 K St. NW
(202) 333-4422

It seems that every Thai restaurant in DC is required to bear a punny
name. Bangkok Joe's is no exception. Located on the Georgetown
waterfront in what used to be a bank building, the self styled "dumpling
bar and café" serves up "Thai street food" in its alley-narrow space. The
dark, wood-paneled dining area is a tad confusing in an art-deco-meets-
Dalí kind of way. Dripping, metal accents are not particularly Asian, and
waitstaff wear black t-shirts with loose-wide pants in a mix of East and
West.

The dishes at Bangkok Joe's are satisfactory, but not particularly
authentic or special. Happy hour specials feature "street-style" finger
foods. Meatballs are scented with white pepper and trussed up on a stick,
with meat so finely ground that it's unclear what, or where, it came from.
Disappointingly bland satay is dense and overcooked but without the
deep char that you would associate with true street food. Drinks tend
toward the frozen and sweet. A particular favorite is the ginger iced tea, a
pungent take on the Arnold Palmer that tastes strongly of ginger and
lemon. It is sour and intense rather than refreshing.

A vast array of dumplings incorporates both traditional and non-
traditional ingredients. On the more traditional end, minced chicken
comes off bitter and harsh against a fluffy, sweet bun. On the fancier
side, dishes like the "Peking Duck Roll" dress up normally scrap-food
dishes with fatty, chewy duck meat. Green onions in a log of fried
wonton wrappers are barely cooked. Exotic fillings like butternut squash
and sweet potatoes are pan-fried in thicker wrappers. They are poorly
seared on the outside, charred but not crunchy.

Even if we respect Bangkok Joe's menu—generally speaking—on an
ideological note, there is something off-putting about seeing a handful of
dumplings carefully presented on a fancy plate. True street food is
plentiful and careless, cooked fast over hot flames, trailing wafting
streams of smoke. The only smoke here is being blown by the menu's
claims of authenticity. –JC

# Bardeo

A sparkling neighborhood spot for uncomplicated small plates, fresh cocktails, and okay wine

**7.8** Food  **8.2** Feel

## New American

Wine bar  **$35** Price

www.bardeo.com

Mon–Thu 5pm–11pm
Fri–Sat 5pm–midnight
Sun 5pm–10:30pm

**Bar** Beer, wine, liquor
**Credit cards** Visa, MC, AmEx
**Reservations** Not accepted
Date-friendly, good wines, outdoor dining, veg-friendly, Wi-Fi

**Cleveland Park**
3309 Connecticut Ave.
NW
(202) 244-6750

The Uptown movie theater almost demands a smart but easy, casual but stylish, spot for a snack and a cocktail in Cleveland Park before the film starts. Bardeo, the sibling of the more elaborate, expensive Ardeo (with which it shares a space), strikes the right balance. This low-key bar has deep red walls and substantial burgundy booths, offset by natural wood seats at the cool gray countertop. The lighting is dim in a hip, loungey kind of way, but just bright enough to allow you to read the menu. The noise level is chatty, yet subdued enough to allow a conversation.

The menu gives a sensible spin on the familiar drinks-and-small-plates format, rarely straying too far in the direction of froof. Seasonal cocktails, like a tangy mango-chipotle-and-tequila summer cooler, incorporate fresh ingredients without being gimmicky. But this self-proclaimed wine bar also offers a short, relatively uninteresting selection of glasses, half-glasses, and "flights." The friendly, knowledgeable bartenders are generally happy to suggest something new that won't break the bank. As is so often the case, bottles, several in the $30 range, are usually a better deal than drinking by the glass.

The dinner plates are equally thoughtful: an order of the house polenta and potato fries is a fun complement to a glass of wine in an irreverent way. Seared tuna isn't revolutionary, but it's executed ably, and priced at around $11; it's just right for a light meal. Pillow-soft gnocchi are a marvel in a salty, peppery salad with a lemony vinaigrette.

On one visit, the perky bartender seemed almost comically assiduous, lavishing us with thanks—but we found we didn't mind. This little wine bar is eager to please, yes, but not offensively so—quite the opposite, with its careful food and wine choices, flattering lighting, and intimate setting. The funny thing is that what it's trying to be—a "wine bar & café"—is, for us, only secondary to what it really is: one of Cleveland Park's more reliable dinner tables. You might come for a pre-movie snack, and find yourself drawn to stay for a cheese plate and another glass of wine. And then another. Who needs a movie, anyway? –CD

# Bastille

French food at the far end of Old Town

**6.9** *Food*  **8.2** *Feel*

## French

Upmarket restaurant  **$55** *Price*

www.bastillerestaurant.com

Tue–Thu 11:30am–2pm, 6pm–9pm; Fri 11:30am–2pm, 6pm–10pm; Sat noon–2:30pm, 6pm–10pm; Sun 11:30am–2:30pm, 5pm–8pm

**Bar** Beer, wine
**Credit cards** Visa, MC, AmEx
**Reservations** Accepted
Outdoor dining

**Alexandria Old Town**
1201 N. Royal St.
(703) 519-3776

From afar, Bastille seems like a place for a country French meal, as if its quaint interior were concealing an old woman hunched over a pot of soup that she had carefully been reducing all day. We imagine oozing croque madames and steaming pots-au-feu coming out of the kitchen. Older men in sweaters smoking Gauloises and talking politics out in the garden. Carafes of cheap, but good, Burgundy sitting on each table, glasses of choice being stemless—and not in the trendy Riedel sense.

But perhaps we need to engage in daydreaming that's a bit more sympathetic to time and place. The real version of Bastille sits on the marginal outer fray of Old Town—it might even be a stretch to still call it that neighborhood—a few blocks from the water. There is a patio, and it's nice enough, especially on a late summer evening. But the French men of our daydreams are nowhere to be found. Instead, the clientele is largely domestic; women in flowing dresses chat about their grandchildren, how their NGO is doing, and how *lovely* everything is. Their conversation is rather frequently put on hold by the roar of a plane overhead taking off from or in its final descent to Reagan National Airport. (The noise is, in fact, quite a problem; we once moved our meal inside to get away from it.)

And the food isn't the hyper-traditional French that you might expect. Like a misguided teenager applying makeup for the first time, it's been dressed up, but not made better. A grilled branzino (Mediterranean sea bass) filet (not whole! what a shame!) is totally overwhelmed by its balsamic-tomato-caper-vinaigrette; the fish should be left to speak for itself, not shouted over. And such is the problem with many dishes here; their balance and execution don't quite live up to Bastille's carefully cultivated reputation. More successful is a beet salad with a "Bleu des Causses Pannacotta" (a sort of blue-cheese flan) whose flavors are a good match for one another. For dessert, tarte tatin is a good bet, but it doesn't go with the suggested Moscato pairing. Rather, there are a few late-harvest wines on the list that cry out to be paired with the pastry.

The wine list is organized by region (whew) but with some varietal explanation along the way, i.e. "Bourgogne: Chardonnay." The focus is clearly on France, but there are a few cameos by some big ol' California wines, too. Now what would our Old World grandmother in the kitchen think of *that*? –AH

# Beacon Bar & Grill

**5.2** Food  **5.0** Feel

An unremarkable restaurant, an unremarkable bar

## New American

Casual restaurant   **$45** Price

www.beaconbarandgrill.com

Daily 6:30am–11pm

**Bar** Beer, wine, liquor
**Credit cards** Visa, MC, AmEx
**Reservations** Accepted
Outdoor dining, Wi-Fi

**Dupont**
1615 Rhode Island Ave. NW
(202) 872-1126

On a stretch of Rhode Island Avenue just southeast of Dupont Circle lies Beacon Bar & Grill, an inelegant bar masquerading as a restaurant. With $5.25 house martinis (all day, every day, in flavors ranging from classic to peach), happy hour specials of mini cheeseburgers and buffalo wings, and a brunch renowned for its bottomless mimosas and Bloody Marys, Beacon is carefully calibrated to draw a daily crowd. Judged as a restaurant, however, Beacon falls short.

Among other sports-bar touches, the acoustics are loud and clattery; the aggressive air conditioning introduces an arctic chill; and flat-screen TVs dot the walls (including one in the ladies' room). An enormous lamb steak, pounded thin and topped with a heterogeneous sprinkling of feta, grape tomatoes, and olives—a Balkans dish, perhaps?—is accompanied by sweet-potato fries. Guacamole and salsa are common condiments on everything from a crab quesadilla (with little evidence of any actual crab) to the sweet-and-spicy ancho-glazed salmon (dry and overcooked—this one needs the guacamole). However, crowd-pleasing sides like cheesy polenta and french fries are always available.

The dessert menu features an array of serious assaults on the sweet tooth. A dense chocolate torta studded liberally with hazelnuts and topped with ice cream satisfies a chocolate craving, while a dulce de leche cheesecake is super-sweet and jarringly grainy in texture. Both desserts come liberally decorated with piles of whipped cream, berries, chocolate and raspberry sauces.

But if Beacon Bar & Grill really aspires to nothing more than glorified bar-hood, the drinks menu has some surprising shortcomings. In addition to the aforementioned house martinis, the drinks menu features a range of seven- and eight-dollar cocktails that prodigiously overuse the '-tini' suffix. Only a few wines are available by the bottle, generally in only one exemplar of each varietal, many in the $35-and-up range. While we can't recommend Beacon as a dining destination, if you're the kind of person that goes in for $5.25 "house martinis," the happy-hour bar food specials certainly won't ruin the mood. –CD

# Bean Counter

Sandwiches seem a lot better when you're
enjoying yourself this much

**6.7** **7.0**
*Food* *Feel*

## Baked goods

Café **$15**
*Price*

Daily 7am–5:30pm

**Bar** None
**Credit cards** Visa, MC
Outdoor dining, veg-friendly, Wi-Fi

**Georgetown**
1665 Wisconsin Ave. NW
(202) 625-1665

Like the café's name, the Bean Counter's sandwich menu is a financial
tour de farce, with titles such as "Gold Standard" (chicken with pesto),
"Blue Chip" (roast beef and Brie), "Mass Merger" (roasted turkey and
cranberry sauce), and "Non-Profit" (tomato, Brie, and greens; no meat).
The odd man out of the capitalist game, it seems—although perhaps less
so with Raúl's new regime—is the Cuban (roasted pork, ham, melted
Swiss cheese, sweet and slightly spicy pickles), which also happens to be
the café's most well-advertised special. And deservedly so: the pork
juices—so often missing in lesser incarnations of this sandwich—soften up
a crusty Cuban roll, and the combination of melted cheese, sweet ham,
and crunchy pickles is heavenly.

A surprising sleeper is the "Emerging Market" (a pressed panino with
fresh mozzarella, pesto, tomatoes, and onions). Although the bread (top
quality whole wheat, but still pre-sliced) is a bit disappointing, it is
transformed by the grill, and although we normally avoid pesto at
sandwich joints, the homemade version here is popping with basil. The
fresh mozzarella, melted just enough, lends a greasy cohesion to the
sandwich.

Don't count on the Bean Counter's pastries: they're disappointing
saran-wrapped creations from another bakery, consisting of floury cookies
and oily muffins. The espresso drinks, however, are well made, and if
you're here for breakfast it would be a shame to pass up what is perhaps
Wisconsin Avenue's most indulgent creation: the Thomas' english muffin,
peanut butter, and Nutella sandwich. It can only be described as follows:
two piles of goop—one light brown and one dark—intermingle on the
warm surface of the muffin, until they finally melt and begin to drip from
the sides. There's a sink upstairs.

The Bean Counter is small, its menu options aren't particularly creative,
the espresso drinks are good but not supreme, the pastries are imports,
and the wireless internet doesn't always work. But there's something
about this little place: it's clean and it's homey, and a fat slice of sunlight
comes in through the west-facing glass panels on winter afternoons.
Someone has put on a CD of soft Turkish music, and there's the smell of
good bread grilling. Like the sandwiches, which take nothing-special
ingredients and transform them, the Bean Counter is somehow more than
the sum of its beans. –CK

# Belga Café

A cozy hideaway out of whose kitchen comes some
good Belgian cuisine

| | |
|---|---|
| **7.0** | **8.8** |
| Food | Feel |

## Belgian

Casual restaurant

**$30**
Price

www.belgacafe.com

Mon–Thu 11:30am–3pm,
5:30pm–10pm; Fri 11:30am–
11pm; Sat 10am–11pm; Sun
10am–9:30pm

**Bar** Beer, wine, liquor
**Credit cards** Visa, MC, AmEx
**Reservations** Accepted
Date-friendly, outdoor dining

**Capitol Hill**
514 8th St. SE
(202) 544-0100

The Belga Café does justice to a cuisine known popularly for just four items: beer, frites, mussels, and chocolate. Although the first three of those have kept many a bar from sinking into ESPN oblivion, and there are a bunch of Belgian moules-frites shops springing up in New York these days, there are only a few US restaurants in which Belgian cuisine has been fully realized.

Belga is one of those few. Although the glimmer of Napa Valley stylings and the glint of New York chefs have made Belga's takes on traditional Belgian recipes lighter, more colorful, and a touch more whimsical, it's hard to complain: the resulting combinations are both unexpected and tasty. We appreciate, too, the casual atmosphere and happy, laid-back servers, who don't take themselves too seriously.

The restaurant's décor is of two minds. Outdoors, a casual mood prevails, with sidewalk tables covered in cheery yellow cloths, umbrellas, and a pot of fresh herbs on each table. On either side of the door to the restaurant is a pot of tiny jalapeños, filled with stop-sign-red peppers. Inside, however, is a world apart: brown leather chairs, glass and fine wood, steel lighting fixtures. A long bar extends along one wall, so that waiting patrons need not wait without a pint. Belga's beer selection is indeed impressive, but the wine list offers solid competition: the former is housed in a descriptive booklet complete with tasting notes. A few wines are available by the glass, too.

Mussels can be ordered one of six ways, in various baths of butter and beer. The Rodenbach creation comes lathered in the ale, with a sauce of asparagus and bacon; the curry version is very good, too, soaking in a slightly spicy coconut broth with ginger, red peppers, and lemongrass. Although Belga's frites—diminutive and tasteless, speckled with fresh herbs—don't do justice to the legendary appellation, the main dishes are prepared with a creative touch: gerookte zalm wafel, for example, places lush smoked salmon and roasted tomatoes between a few sheets of puff pastry, and flattens the creation in the waffle iron. It's accompanied with a chive-y cream cheese with roe, greens, and a pinch of Japanese-style seaweed salad: euro fusion, perhaps, but not in the negative sense of the F-word.

Our major qualm? Small portion size is not a feature of any Belgian cuisine we know, and Belga's food is expensive for what you get. We know the euro's strong these days, but is the exchange rate really *that* bad? –CK

# Ben's Chili Bowl

A DC favorite that's changing with the times—even if the chili is immortal

**8.1** Food | **9.2** Feel

## American

Counter service | **$15** Price

www.benschilibowl.com

Mon–Thu 6am–2am
Fri–Sat 6am–4am
Sun 11am–8pm

**Bar** None
**Credit cards** None
**Reservations** Accepted
Kid-friendly, veg-friendly, Wi-Fi

**U Street**
1213 U St.
(202) 667-0909

**Nationals Park**
1500 S. Capitol St. SE

Ben's Chili Bowl is not just a landmark eatery—it's a landmark in its own right. With the immense changes that have overcome the U Street neighborhood lately, replacing jazz musicians and Bill Cosby with preppy twentysomethings in Polo shirts, we wonder if the cooks have changed their tune. The restaurant has made some slight alterations, including the recent opening up of the next-door bar and restaurant called (believe it or not) Next Door, and, more darkly, the opening of an outpost at Nationals Stadium.

They certainly don't seem to have changed their recipes, though, and Ben's no-nonsense offerings (at no-nonsense prices) curry what might be called a cult following, which now includes (and has now been multiplied by) Barack Obama. Still, now that the restaurant has gotten uncomfortably crowded—especially on weekend nights—and has lost any semblance of atmosphere or hints of personal attention, there's not a whole lot to distinguish Ben's beyond the cheap and plentiful nature of its offerings. The chili-cheese half-smoke, the canonical order, is delightful, but you could make most of what's on the menu at home: the chili is red-kidney-bean heavy, although its intense flavor indicates sufficient stewing. The half-smokes are standard but nicely charred on the grill, and the French fries are a bit wet (okay, you probably don't have a deep fryer at home, but that doesn't mean you can't deep fry). Ben's also serves breakfast (alas, only at breakfast hours), with sides of grits or apples and sticky maple syrup.

Maybe the best thing about Ben's is that it's *not* home, that it's Ben's, that there are a hundred dogs roasting and fifty burgers grilling and order upon order of french fries frying. Come in at midnight, and you don't know if the folks behind you are wrapping up their evening or just getting it started. And could you really pour chili all over your burger at home? And even if you could, *would* you? Would you pour chili over everything in sight, be it a hot dog, a plate of chips, or a sub?

Well, maybe you would, but it still probably wouldn't be as enjoyable as it is at Ben's, with its plastic booths and beaten-down spinning barstools and its cafeteria mentality. The Bowl may have become a strange facsimile of its old self as the neighborhood's changed, but it continues to feed that same hunger—most acute at 2am—which is only sated by an "Original Chili Half-Smoke." –CK

# Bertucci's

One of the few chains that we've long loved to love—but can't they ditch those pastas?

**5.7** | **6.4**
Food | Feel

## Italian, Pizza

Casual restaurant

**$35**
Price

www.bertuccis.com

Sun–Thu 11am–10pm
Fri–Sat 11am–11pm

**Bar** Beer, wine, liquor
**Credit cards** Visa, MC, AmEx
**Reservations** Accepted
Delivery, kid-friendly, veg-friendly,
Wi-Fi

**Dupont**
1218-1220 Connecticut Ave.
NW
(202) 463-7733

**Foggy Bottom**
2000 Pennsylvania Ave. NW
(202) 296-2600

**Arlington, VA**
2700-2800 Clarendon Blvd.
(703) 528-9177

**Additional locations**
and more features at
www.fearlesscritic.com

It's nice when one of the McFamilyRestaurant chains turns out to serve reasonably good food in a reasonably pleasant atmosphere. For a long time Bertucci's did so—and made Olive Garden look really, really bad in the process—both aesthetically (Bertucci's doesn't try as hard to be fake Italian, and thus comes off less awkward, although we can't get with the new logo, whose pizza-slice apostrophe looks accidentally un-curly) and taste-wise (they make good use of that oven and don't overcook pasta as much). Even if it's a family "casual dining" chain at its heart, it's a unique New England version of one (the chain calls the Boston area home), and an exposed kitchen gives the place a surprisingly upscale flair.

If you can look past the mass-produced aesthetic of the menus, they also show spikes of sophistication. Three-cheese focaccia, on the menu for years, is a crispy starter that comes with a winning sauce of smoky tomatoes. Among mains, we strongly favor the pizza (traditional, not deep-dish). There's a real brick oven here, and it can turn out some enjoyable pies. Crusts are pleasingly crispy, cheese is well handled, and ingredients taste fresh. Meat eaters will find the Sporkie, with mild ricotta and sweet sausage, easy to love. The segmented Ultimate Bertucci also fares well; one quarter of the disc boasts fragrant rosemary ham. For those less carnivorous, the Lestina deep-dish pizza, with sun-dried tomatoes, mushrooms, and roasted garlic, can be nice, especially when it's not overwhelmed with a carpet of chewy sage leaves.

Lunch begins with a free salad; you can get one for $2 with dinner. Here, though, you get what you pay for: a curious mix of iceberg lettuce and bell peppers, shredded American cheese, and a gloopy supermarket-style vinaigrette. Then there are the famous Bertucci's dinner rolls (they're served at lunch as well)—warm, bagel-dense doughballs that have built up a cult following, perhaps in large part because they arrive hot enough to melt butter, a quality that has undeniable appeal. We don't like many of the huge-portioned pasta dishes, especially the ones with shrimp, lobster, or any sort of chicken. The trend there is that they either perish in a sea of cream or are bland and dry. Worse yet is the expanded menu of "dinners," which are abominations like "balsamic chicken" (which comes with broccoli and mashed potatoes) or (yikes) breadcrumb-crusted tilapia on a bed of spinach. Here they're trying to compete with Olive Garden. Don't buy it. Locals in the know stick to the pizza, and so should you. –RG

# Bethesda Bagels

**7.7** **6.0**
Food   Feel

Some of the best bagels in the area—even a New
Yorker will be impressed

## Sandwiches, Baked goods

Counter service   **$10**
Price

www.bethesdabagels.com

| | | |
|---|---|---|
| Mon–Sat 6:30am–5pm | **Bar** None | **Bethesda, MD** |
| Sun 7am–3pm | **Credit cards** Visa, MC, AmEx | 4819 Bethesda Ave. |
| | Delivery, veg-friendly | (301) 652-8990 |

Even if you have trouble adhering to the doctrine that real bagels do not
exist outside the confines of New York City, it requires no exceptional
insight to note that DC is not really a bagel town. Most often, the choice
you'll encounter is one of Starbucks versus Au Bon Pain, which is to say,
no choice at all, bagel-wise (the former is compact and stale, the latter is
sprawling and dry; both are bad). If you're lucky enough to live or work
near Bethesda Bagels, however, the difficulty of decision-making will
present itself only once you've entered the store.

For the aforementioned lucky eaters, the burden of good options will
be evident immediately: should you elect the lox or salami? (The first is
thicker than most, the second thinner than most.) Should your beef be
roast or corned? (We prefer the former, but only slightly.) Do you order
roasted red pepper or raisin walnut cream cheese, or do you stick to the
straight-and-narrow plain? (Depends on your bent.) Not to mention the
need to decide between over a dozen types of bagels. These options may
not seem insurmountable to those who've grown up with a good deli
nearby (or, for that matter, to those who have learned decision-making
skills from an impatient deli owner), but if your domain of debate has
been confined to the Starbucks-ABP showdown, the bounty of choice
may indeed overwhelm.

We'll offer a typical (but reassuring) stock phrase: there's no such thing
as a bad choice, so long as your choice includes at least one bagel. These
bagels are compact, chewy, and slightly tangy. They are baked on fine
cornmeal, some of which remains on the bagel bottom for a nutty texture
and taste. The bagels become dry, tubular rocks after just two days, but
with some foresight (advanced slicing) are wonderful toasted, with melted
butter or cold cream cheese.

Forgive us if we sound like dogmatic and evangelical New Yorkers still
fretting the departure of that "little shop on the Lower East Side," when
we pronounce: just go here. It's hard to find a better bagel. At least in
DC. –CK

# The Big Hunt

It's happy hour, the food is bad, the beer's great, and the place is creepy, freaky, and grand

**5.8** Food

**8.8** Feel

## American

Bar

**$20** Price

www.thebighunt.net

Mon–Thu 4pm–2am
Fri 4pm–3am
Sat 5pm–3am
Sun 5pm–2am

**Bar** Beer, wine, liquor
**Credit cards** Visa, MC, AmEx
**Reservations** Accepted
Date-friendly, outdoor dining, Wi-Fi

**Dupont**
1345 Connecticut Ave. NW
(202) 785-2333

What would you get if some circus carneys decided to open a creative-safari-themed bar? Probably something close to the Big Hunt. A red-and-yellow-striped awning shields the door in full circus-tent glory, and tattooed, oddly hirsute bouncers and mustachioed waiters almost feel like they've been cast for their roles. They're delightfully fitting next to the walls sprouting a mouthful of stalactite teeth, a collection of shrunken heads, and tribal masks.

It doesn't stop there.

Like a carnival funhouse, the interior of the restaurant seems to go on forever. Doors open onto new rooms with new creepy artifacts (a giant dinosaur!), activities (pool tables!), and bars (more beer!). Our favorite—in the rare times that it's not overcrowded—is the outdoor patio, which is reached through the second-floor bar in back, and is almost always lively, no matter the season.

Perhaps most disturbing and awesome is its arcane and seemingly logic-less music selection. At any given time you can be treated to an onslaught of boy-band crooning or R. Kelly's *Trapped in the Closet* in its entirety.

The drink selection reflects the damn-what-you-think attitude of the place. A significant draft menu includes Stone Arrogant Bastard Ale, hoppy and uncompromising enough to finish your night; Stone Ruination IPA, another wallop of American-micro-brewed-beery-ness that's heavy, bitter, and citrusy; and Bell's Two Hearted Ale, drier, milder, floral and stealthily alcoholic. You'll notice sooner or later that the beer at Big Hunt is stronger than most. If you're not careful, you'll find yourself believing that the walls are trying to eat you.

With all that drinking, you're bound to be hungry for fried goodness. But more often you'll have to settle for just "fried." Options vary: some are delightful, and some are better after your second or third. On one end are the addictive Cajun fries. They are a bit spicy, extra salty, and super crisp—better than you could have hoped for. On the other end is the lotta-layer dip—a morass of ingredients drowning in a chili swamp. Odd bits (pieces of lukewarm leafy lettuce) seem to have been thrown in just to add a layer. Fitting for a carney-safari bar, the burgers are a safe bet. Even more fitting for a carney-safari bar, they seem always to be out of veggie burgers.

What better place to get drunk than one that so openly raspberries the stodginess of DC? Make sure you visit the dino. –JC

# Bistro Bis

Worthy of its buzz, this airy, sophisticated spot
lightens up the French classics

| 8.9 | 7.8 |
|-----|-----|
| Food | Feel |

## French

Upmarket restaurant

**$70**
Price

www.bistrobis.com

Daily 7am–10am, 11:30am–
2:30pm, 5:30pm–10:30pm

**Bar** Beer, wine, liquor
**Credit cards** Visa, MC, AmEx
**Reservations** Accepted
Date-friendly, good wines, outdoor
dining, Wi-Fi

**Capitol Hill**
15 E St. NW
(202) 661-2700

With its high ceilings, pleasant atmosphere, and a constant lively
soundtrack of tinkling flatware and excited conversation, Bistro Bis has
captured the crème de Washington. The food is well-executed, the service
is attentive and easygoing, and comes across as neither stuffy nor boring.
It's no surprise that so many of the Hill's heavy hitters dig this place,
which is located just a hop from the Senate side of the Capitol.

It's hardly the Michelin-star mythos where the maître d' will fall upon
his sword should your flambé extinguish en route to your table, but the
French classics are all accounted for, judiciously updated (that is to say,
hardly) and beautifully presented. Pâté de campagne comes studded with
gems of cornichons, pistachios, and fatty, gelatinous pockets. It is a
veritable fugue of texture and flavor. Onion soup is wonderfully fragrant
with a restraint that gives it depth but not heaviness, the broth beefy and
clouded with billowy gruyère. Trout is cooked with crisped skin and
glistening with oil. Though filleted, it is every bit as flavorful as it would be
whole. At times, it can endure a medieval oversalting, but mistakes like
this are an exception rather than a rule.

Bistro's sweets exercise a similar, refreshing restraint. Where French
desserts can easily become a sloppy nightmare of butter and sugar, here
they are treated with deference and a deft hand. Crème brûlée offers a
more complex flavor than the usual globs of burnt vanilla cream. The
custard is deep and just sweet enough to allow you to finish the entire
thing without destroying your pancreas. "Tarte au Citron" pairs a
miraculously dense and compact layer of crust with a puckery curd and
peaks of toasty, airy meringue. It is a textural masterpiece, and evidence
of the kitchen's commitment to excellence.

The wine list is gorgeous; a high-dollar tour of France's best regions,
with a few under-$50 bottles sprinkled throughout. Some bottles are
even a steal (we won't say which because we hope it's still there when we
go, but it rhymes with Man Doll.) There are many restaurants in DC that
aren't worth the hype. Bistro Bis deserves every bit of its loyal clientele.
Even the biggies. –JC

# Bistro Français

Isn't it nice to get a French meal in the wee hours of the night? Good food would be even nicer...

**5.9** *Food*  **8.8** *Feel*

## French

Casual restaurant

**$40** *Price*

www.bistrofrancaisdc.com

Sun–Thu 11am–3am
Fri–Sat 11am–4am

**Bar** Beer, wine, liquor
**Credit cards** Visa, MC, AmEx
**Reservations** Accepted
Date-friendly

**Georgetown**
3128 M St. NW
(202) 338-3830

At first glance, Bistro Français resembles many other Georgetown restaurants. Floor-to-ceiling windows display an inadvertent ad campaign of well-dressed and happy diners, and it exudes an aura of easy refinement. In a sea of peers serving food that's expensive and terrible, Bistro Français offers sometimes enjoyable meals at very reasonable prices. Factor in its late-late night full menu, and it is clear why when other restaurants are empty the Bistro is still alive with candlelight and clinking glasses.

The interior of Bistro Français is pleasant but generic, consisting of wood paneling, brass fixtures, and art deco accents typical of the faux-French school. Unlike those at many of its G-town counterparts, the menu here is nicely balanced and sets a standard for what customers can expect—thankfully, not everything is served with frites. Food tends toward the rustic and, at its best (as in a decent duck confit) is a fine interplay between light and rich. Asparagus soup makes a normally heavy base light and clean. Sparing use of cream and a hint of ginger in the crouton turn a weighty vegetable into a refreshing summer dish.

Main courses vary wildly. Fish mains sometimes fall flat, overcooked and tasteless, although we've enjoyed a tender, flaky (if uncreative) baked trout topped with mushrooms and shrimp. The breading lends a pleasant weight to the trout and adds textural complexity to the dish. A generous amount of lemon butter is almost too rich, but still manages to be sharp enough to lend some much needed acidity and ease the stomach. Crab-and-leek soufflé tastes simple, fresh, and sweet, dissolving in your mouth in steamy, eggy clouds. A glass of free house wine is an unusual and welcome element to your set-price meal (at press time, about $25), but it's of really poor quality, exuding cheapness, even if it's easy to drink quickly.

One significant complaint about Bistro Français is the dessert. Pastries are beautiful but poorly executed. The dough in an apple tart is chewy rather than flaky, and thick layers of syrupy jam hold meek fruit slices hostage.

Still, if it's really late, a trip to the Bistro is a good decision. In the wee hours, you'll be a proud member of the in-crowd looking out at the street from your window seat: glamorous, celebratory, and most importantly, well-fed. –JC

# Bistro Italiano

Decent red-sauce Italian-American that's tucked
away and hard to find

| 6.9 | 8.2 |
|------|------|
| Food | Feel |

## Italian

Casual restaurant

**$25**
Price

Mon–Fri 11am–2pm, 5pm–
10pm
Sat 5pm–10pm

**Bar** Beer, wine
**Credit cards** Visa, MC
**Reservations** Accepted
Date-friendly, delivery

**Penn Quarter**
320 D St. NE
(202) 546-4522

All 300 or so square feet of Bistro Italiano are tucked into a diminutive
townhouse on a one-way street northeast of the Capitol, and nearly every
feature of the bistro seems designed to discourage patronage. Overgrown
trees hide a small box housing the yellowed menu, while a recessed entry
and frequent (2pm-5pm daily and all day Sunday) closings foment
uncertainty about whether the place is open for business at all. As a
result, the restaurant may be one of the most easily missed in DC. But
with a satisfied cadre of regulars to keep the dining room brimming most
weeknights, the Bistro is in no need of marketing.

Inside, a pair of young and slightly awkward waiters weave between
the dozen or so small tables. The Bistro's walls, meanwhile, display a set
of paintings (seascape, country picnic, pastoral farmland) typically reserved
for chain motels and dental offices. In a strange counterpoint to the décor
(to make things worse, the tables are covered in dainty cloth, and there
are a few requisite garlands of dried garlic), the dimmed lighting is
decidedly upscale-Italian-American-romantic, rather than downtown-cozy.

Most importantly, the red-sauce fare is pretty satisfying. Bistro Italiano
serves carafes of table wine, and they're generally pretty cheap. The wine,
which is nothing special, pairs well with the honest Italian-American food
that is made special by its simplicity. The bistro's red sauce is light, tangy
and neither salty nor sweet; the taste of roma tomatoes dominates but
allows the pasta to retain a slight taste as well as a texture.

Mussels are mostly left to be, prepared with white wine and a hint of
garlic and butter, and served with lemon wedges. Their briny flavor is not
masked in sauce or butter, but comes cleanly to the fore. You can also
order frivolities like garlic bread, potato skins, or chicken fingers, but if
you must stray from pasta dishes, the bistro's pizza is more worthwhile
than those pub-food staples. Although the pizza's crust is a little too
crunchy, the meat toppings, especially the well-spiced sausage bits on the
"Bistro Italiano" pie, are top-notch.

If you're lucky enough to find the bistro, it's unlikely you'll leave
hungry, or—at these prices—out more than 25 bucks or so. –CK

# Bistrot du Coin

Quirky and fun, yet still reliable

**8.3** *Food*  **9.3** *Feel*

## French

Casual restaurant  **$50** *Price*

www.bistrotducoin.com

Sun–Wed 11am–11pm
Thu–Sat 11am–1am

**Bar** Beer, wine, liquor
**Credit cards** Visa, MC, AmEx
**Reservations** Accepted
Date-friendly, good wines

**Dupont**
1738 Connecticut Ave.
NW
(202) 234-6969

At every turn in this roaringly lively space, you'll see its mascot: a jowly, portly, apron-clad chef, chest hair proudly displayed, hands on hips, nose in air. The little man, who also sports a beret and clogs, might just be an ideal representative of the Bistrot: comically French, pointedly mismatched, and full of whimsy.

The décor matches our miniature chef friend. The walls are lined with posters, photos, signs, and perhaps some out-of-season Christmas paraphernalia. Yellow lighting, paper linens, and disco balls…are you dining in your batty uncle's attic? As the tables are jammed close together, it's impossible not to be jostled. On a single visit, we've made contact with two men in berets, three men with very nice canes, and four priests. Waiters have their hands full navigating: plates teeter and threaten to bash into diners' heads before landing on tables too small to host them. It's a total pain—and it's endlessly fun.

As for what's on those plates, a good bit of it is delightful, especially the brasserie classics. French onion soup bubbles over a cast iron bowl; it's oily but rich, with cheese that oozes into tiny filaments that end up everywhere. Mussels have been even better; moules normandes, for instance, feature leeks, potatoes, bacon, and a cream sauce that begs to be scooped out with mussel shells and then sopped up with bread until the bowl is dry. Postage-stamp ravioli are translucent green and erupt in herby-creamy goodness. Steaks are properly cooked to temperature. French fries are consistently some of the best in the city. And an underappreciated element of the Bistrot is its carefully chosen, low-markup wine list, whose reasonably priced midrange Burgundies should be the envy of many a more pretentious joint.

Certainly there are some corners cut here, though, especially with salads. Raw artichokes and asparagus taste canned or jarred. A tartiflette is far too rich and badly needs something to cut through the grease. The "French style" banana split and profiteroles look better than they taste. Even so, we don't understand why Bistrot du Coin has so many harsh critics in town. Surly service aside, this is one of the most reliable tables in the Dupont Circle area—and they serve dinner later than almost anyone around.

Around nine, previously unnoticed strobe lights flash and Whitney Houston's "I Wanna Dance with Somebody" inexplicably comes on. The gregarious owner, a few glasses of wine into the night, starts wandering the room with mike in hand, interviewing random customers like a daytime talk-show host. No one is phased. Dessert gets ordered, and more wine. Odd uncle indeed. Enchanté! –FC

# BlackSalt

It's fun, but a fish restaurant in the back of a fish store should be even better

| 7.9 | 8.2 |
|-----|-----|
| Food | Feel |

## Seafood

Upmarket restaurant

**$45**
*Price*

www.blacksaltrestaurant.com

Mon–Thu 11:30am–2:30pm; Fri 11:30am–2:30pm, 5:30pm–11pm; Sat 11:30am–2:30pm, 5pm–11pm; Sun 11am–2pm, 5pm–9pm

**Bar** Beer, wine, liquor
**Credit cards** Visa, MC, AmEx
**Reservations** Accepted

**Palisades**
4883 MacArthur Blvd.
(202) 342-9101

If there were a single best possible sign that you're in a good seafood restaurant—better than being in view of a fishing port, better than a queue running out the door, better than anything else, really—it would be that the place also operates as a fishmonger.

In the case of BlackSalt, on a somewhat lonely stretch of road in Palisades (near Makoto and Kotobuki—quite the fish neighborhood, this), you actually have to walk through the (sustainable) fish store to get to the restaurant in back. The fish that's for sale (at quite high prices) is resting on ice, and if you see anything you like—yellow tilefish, soft-shell crabs, rockfish, or skate wing, for instance—it doesn't matter if it's on the restaurant's menu; they'll cook it up. Think of it as an enoteca for fish.

The space in back is well divided and congenial, and although the service can be aloof, we appreciate the old-mannish seriousness of the waitstaff. They might not make you feel better about yourself, but they make you feel better about the prospects for your fish.

Given all the buildup and excitement that comes from the fishmonger area in front, we must admit that BlackSalt is a slight letdown. We'll begin with the good news: oysters on the half shell are excellent, even the cheapies from the Chesapeake. We've had terrific baby octopus, tenderly braised and served simply with garlic, parsley, and olive oil. The kitchen also has a way with the deep fryer, and we've enjoyed extremely tender fried calamari with chipotle remoulade; fried clams with "Madras aioli" (translation for Belgophiles: curry mayo); and a fried tilapia sandwich, an unusually good treatment of this bottom-of-the-barrel fish.

Wood grills are gaining more and more favor these days, especially for cooking fish, and it's for good reason: a wood-burning fire has a unique ability to endow certain fishes with smoke and char that can often function as a beautiful counterpoint to their delicate flesh. At BlackSalt, however, things are sometimes left in there for a bit too long, resulting in a slightly overcooked rainbow trout, for instance, or sardines that lose their punchy full flavor. Certain other preps are too complicated, like a skate wing that's overwhelmed by crab bisque, asparagus, and apple-chive relish. Keep it simple. Another chronic problem is underseasoning; we were delighted to find shad roe, during the season, but when cooked, it suffered from a total lack of salt.

Although we like BlackSalt—and we especially like shopping for fish there—these flaws are perhaps less easy to forgive in this kind of exalted fish environment. –RG

# Black's Bar & Kitchen

**7.9** Food  **8.0** Feel

A fresh standout among neighborhood look-alikes with well-executed fare and well-chosen wines

## New American, Seafood

Upmarket restaurant  **$75** Price

www.blacksbarandkitchen.com

Mon–Thu 11:30am–2:30pm, 5:30pm–10pm; Fri 11:30am–2:30pm, 5:30pm–11pm; Sat 5:30pm–11pm; Sun 11am–3pm, 5:30pm–9:30pm

**Bar** Beer, wine, liquor
**Credit cards** Visa, MC, AmEx
**Reservations** Accepted
Date-friendly, good wines, live music, outdoor dining, veg-friendly, Wi-Fi

**Bethesda, MD**
7750 Woodmont Ave.
(301) 652-5525

Even in restaurant-dense downtown Bethesda, Black's sets itself apart with modestly impeccable execution in the kitchen, creatively conceived cocktails, and a wine list that rewards curiosity. They're clearly proud of the wines: a glass wall of a cellar divides the clean, spacious restaurant into a light, bright bar area—where the full dinner menu is served—and a dimmer, more intimate dining area with one long wall papered with a gorgeous photo-mural of trees in silhouette. From kitchen to restaurant to bar, it's all simple and solid, elegant but un-stuffy—an object lesson in the ways that a restaurant can stand up against the city's trendy onslaught of froof.

This menu is calibrated to delight without being pretentious or heavy-handed. Seek out seasonal dishes, featured daily specials, and fresh fish. On an early summer visit, fresh fava beans and pancetta starred in a deceptively simple dish. Not to be missed in any season are cod brandade fritters, bite-sized spheres that maximize the ratio of crispy exterior to creamy interior; they come in a pool of intensely flavored rosemary and lemon sauce spiked with black pepper. Our favorite main is Black's seared-scallop dinner, which comes in a creamy thyme-scented sauce dotted with tender crayfish, garlicky mashed potatoes, and spinach. A careful saffron-and-fennel-brothed bouillabaisse features tender squid and mussels, flaky fish, and just-firm prawns; the dish is diminished, though, by underperforming toasted croutons, which arrived cold at one visit—they couldn't be salvaged, even by a spicy, garlicky slather of rouille.

For dessert, choose key-lime cheesecake (accompanied by a snowflake-shaped crispy cinnamon churro), or opt for one of the "small bites"—half-priced plates that will satisfy a sweet craving without overloading you after a rich dinner. Passion fruit panna cotta, served in a shot glass, comes with three tiny, buttery but fairly unremarkable cookies.

As for that wine list they're so proud of, they've got license. Divided into sections according to region which are then subdivided into whites and reds, the list—as with so much else at Black's—is clearly the product of care and attention. It's a bit California-Chard heavy, but there are also reasonably priced bottles from lesser-known New World regions like South Africa, and thankfully, plenty from the Old World (Italy, Spain, and France) with a specific commitment to lesser-known producers. For wine as for food, it's a welcome reminder of our need to fight the fashion-industry model of the modern restaurant, and to reward, instead, a more plodding commitment to good taste. –CD

# BLT Steak

One of the better of DC's steakhouses, but the prices are still on up there

**8.7** Food    **8.4** Feel

## Steakhouse

Upmarket restaurant    **$95** Price

www.bltsteak.com

Mon–Fri 11:30am–2:30pm,
5:30pm–11:30pm
Sat 5:30pm–11:30pm

**Bar** Beer, wine, liquor
**Credit cards** Visa, MC, AmEx
**Reservations** Accepted
Outdoor dining, Wi-Fi

**Farragut**
1625 Eye St. NW
(202) 689-8999

The Fearless Critics have no general objection to the expensive-steakhouse genre, but in our opinion, DC's steakhouses, as a group, are among the most overpriced and disappointing representatives of the city's restaurant repertoire.

This one is actually better than most—but it's even more expensive than most, too, which means the unconscionable value proposition remains constant. We do love the interior design, which ditches the traditional leather-dark-wood-and-humidor look of the business-account steakhouse for something more trendy and more fun, with the loud buzz of a lounge-that-turns-nightclub, along with a few Vegas-celebrity-chef-outpost touches like an ever-changing wall-mounted menu and a glass wall of wine, which is quickly becoming the first-decade-of-the-21st-century's version of the restaurant industry's 1990s penchant for abstract expressionist wall art.

That wall, which also highlights the spectacular markups of the wine list, might feature iceberg hearts with blue cheese and thousand island, a perfectly fine version, with welcome bacon and an extremely unwelcome $14 price tag. A seafood sampler features sweet, enjoyable Jonah crab claws (most of the work is done for you); good raw oysters, which come with a welcome mignonette; and somewhat less good massive shrimp (overcooked) and clams (too briny).

The steaks, which come out in miniature cast-iron skillets, are advertised as either "USDA Prime or Certified Black Angus," without any specification of which is which. We're always amused by the "Black Angus" designation, which is just a marketing ploy—a patented breed, not a marbling guarantee—but whatever the grade of the $79 Porterhouse for two, it's delicious, meeting—or even exceeding—its lofty-price-based expectations. Especially delicious are the bites with melted herb butter. The sauces (well-reduced red wine sauce and rich peppercorn sauce, for instance) are totally unnecessary.

Notwithstanding BLT's well-loved creamed spinach, however, there is a serious problem with vegetable sides here; they're occasionally too tough to chew, as in a preparation of ramps.

And then there are the moments when the prices rise from high to insulting: a 12-ounce strip of Japanese Kobe beef, for example—according to our calculations—would run more than $300. For that price, we think it should come with Client #9 service under the table. –RG

# Blue Duck Tavern

Fresh ingredients and seasonal menus, but more
buzz than bite at warm neo-American glam-fest

| 7.8 | 9.3 |
|-----|-----|
| Food | Feel |

## New American

Upmarket restaurant

**$80**
Price

www.blueducktavern.com

Daily 6:30am–10:30am,
11:30am–2:30pm, 5:30pm–
10:30pm

**Bar** Beer, wine, liquor
**Credit cards** Visa, MC, AmEx
**Reservations** Accepted
Date-friendly, good wines, outdoor
dining, veg-friendly, Wi-Fi

**West End**
1201 24th St. NW
(202) 419-6755

The Tavern looks anything but; gleaming floor-to-ceiling windows and
shimmeringly beautiful people are on display for both sidewalk
pedestrians and fellow diners. Central to the "story" of the Park Hyatt
Hotel's restaurant is a nominal commitment to classic American style,
embodied here in attractively weathered wooden furniture, warm golden
lighting, and green apples—which, on the occasion of our last visit, were
mounded into an attractive centerpiece decorating the shelf separating
the entryway from the open kitchen area where a cook busily scooped
vanilla ice cream onto individual deep-dish apple pies. Unfortunately, we
grew all too familiar with that heap of apples in the time we stood
waiting to be noticed by the host—and, to boot, the pie wasn't even that
great.

That same kind of vaguely aloof attitude permeates not only the self-
possessed but somewhat detached service, but also—unfortunately—the
food. Blue Duck trumpets its commitment to local purveyors and top-
quality locally-sourced ingredients, but we found ourselves surprised to
learn that the mass-gourmet producer D'Artagnan, of all brands, can be
considered a local artisan.

The idea here is "family-style" dining, which is a great way not to have
to commit to just two or three dishes. The menu is wide-ranging but
mostly familiar: updated versions of classics like macaroni and cheese,
Brussels sprouts, French fries, and roast chicken share menu space with
cholesteriffic superstars like bone marrow and pig's trotter. Sadly, the
wine list is too California-centric—mostly Napa.

That bone marrow comes dramatically presented in beef bones cut
lengthwise to reveal slabs of the inner good stuff. The house-made
bratwurst is Blue Duck's take on choucroute garnie—and a pretty good
take at that, the sauerkraut pungent with hints of juniper and tomato. At
our last visit, we felt let down by the pig's trotter, an outwardly crispy but
inwardly gelatinous sort of fritter, with little real pork taste. Goulash is
generously spiced with paprika and onions, but its spot-on seasoning was
wasted on overcooked veal cheeks that could have been any sort of
cafeteria mystery meat. While the lighting is flattering, the furniture
handcrafted, and the menu locally sourced, the Blue Duck Tavern
ultimately comes off as more focused on the story it's trying to sell than
on the food. The kitchen would do well to use its regional artisanal
ingredients to serve us a delicious meal instead of just reminding us how
great it should be. Show, don't tell. –CD

# Bobby Van's Steakhouse

**8.5** Food  **8.2** Feel

The porterhouse and creamed spinach are some of the city's best—but beware the rest

## Steakhouse

Upmarket restaurant  **$95** Price

www.bobbyvans.com

Mon–Fri 11:30am–10pm
Sat 5pm–10pm
Sun 5pm–9pm

**Bar** Beer, wine, liquor
**Credit cards** Visa, MC, AmEx
**Reservations** Accepted
Outdoor dining, Wi-Fi

**Downtown**
1201 New York Ave. NW
(202) 589-1504

**Downtown**
809 15th St. NW
(202) 589-0060

The porterhouse for two at Bobby Van's is one of the best pieces of meat in the city. The meat is dry-aged for six weeks—longer than most—and charred beautifully on the outside in the way that you don't have at home, unless you happen to have a 100,000-BTU, 1500-degree radiant broiler in your kitchen. Don't look for bistro-style quadrillage (grill marks) here; this is New York steakhouse cooking, and the whole crust of the meat is like one big grill mark. Scrape off a bit of meat between the bone and the inside edge of the sirloin (larger) side of the porterhouse, and swallow the dreamily fatty essence of the particular American corn-fed steak experience. But if you're not ordering for two, you're missing out. Sirloins and ribeyes—though dry-aged as well—are completely inferior to the porterhouse, and they've come under-charred on the outside.

Unless you're ordering filet mignon (which you shouldn't), be warned that this kitchen actually undershoots cooking times. Rare can mean barely seared. For ribeye and bone-in sirloin, this is insufficient; a Van's medium-rare (which is like rare-plus elsewhere) brings out significantly more complexity in the meat by allowing some of its fat to melt.

An appetizer described only as "jumbo pepper shrimp broiled with white wine" is, surprisingly, a crowd-pleaser par excellence, with copious doses of salt, butter, and lemon, and the unusually sweet, enormous shrimp are cooked not a second too long. Rich, complex, oniony creamed spinach is probably the best in the city, and some of the best anywhere. Lumpy mashed potatoes are just okay, though.

The wine list is an embarrassment. At our last visit, all seven wines by the glass were New World. That's right—you can't drink even one French, Italian, or Spanish wine with your steak unless you plan on ordering a bottle. Better would be to stick with martinis from the legendary old-school bartenders. They're Van's real drinks program.

The branch of Bobby Van's that opened in 2000, two blocks from the White House, is the third outpost of a minichain that began in Bridgehampton, Long Island, in 1969. There are now seven, but none of them are more than a couple of blocks from the traditional channels of money and power: midtown Manhattan, lower Manhattan, and DC. We like the laid-back bar area at the 15th Street branch. It has sidewalk seating, and even inside, it's a less hands-on and less pretentious experience than the steakhouse. On the other hand, for some, maybe pretentious is the whole point. For us, it's the porterhouse. –RG

# Bob's Noodle 66

**8.6** Food   **6.8** Feel

If Rockville is the new Chinatown, this could be its
City Hall

## Taiwanese, Chinese

Casual restaurant   **$15** Price

Daily 11am–10pm

**Bar** Beer, wine
**Credit cards** None
**Reservations** Not accepted
Kid-friendly, veg-friendly

**Rockville, MD**
305 N. Washington St.
(301) 315-6668

With DC's "Chinatown" mostly reduced to a decorative gate and a few
mediocre $4.95-lunch-joints sprinkled among chain restaurants sporting
bilingual Chinese-English signage (just in case the disappointed
Midwestern tourists who show up here speak only Chinese), seekers of
authentic Chinese food must follow the actual Chinese population. And
these days, Chinese people live in the suburbs. That's why Bob's Noodle
66 is located in a nondescript strip mall north of Rockville's main drag,
and it's also why this inelegant, homey restaurant is packed with real
Taiwanese and Chinese people—they live here, and this is the food they
want to eat.

Pig's blood, duck tongues, kidneys, and tripe are among the more
interesting ingredients, but top-notch noodle soups and seafood dishes
are also hallmarks of Taiwanese cuisine. A hybrid pancake of eggs and
sweet-potato flour, studded with oysters and topped with a sweet and
spicy sauce, makes an unusual but satisfying appetizer. From among the
dizzying array of noodle soups, try the traditional Taiwanese version,
which features a rich chicken broth, slivers of pork, and spinach, with your
choice of round or flat rice noodles, rice cake, or udon. The chef's
specialties often feature seafood, like the addictive crispy stir-fried shrimp,
served head-on and in the shell with deep-fried basil leaves and a salt-
and-pepper sauce with scallions.

At a home-style place like this, the tired décor is beside the point. Seat
cushions covered with vinyl and industrial ceramic dishes are stock
accessories at any budget-friendly Chinese restaurant. A few stunning
calligraphy and watercolor paintings on the walls are easy to miss, but
worth a look. Service is friendly and efficient, even if you only speak
English; hot tea, small bowls for sharing soup, and ice water are
forthcoming. Don't be afraid to ask your neighbors what they're eating;
frequently, two or three generations of a single Taiwanese family will be
sharing the best dishes in the house, and they won't hesitate to help you
out.

Better yet, ask Bob himself for advice; he's always happy to translate,
and makes an affable tour guide to the foreign soil of suburbia. –CD

# Bombay Bistro

Blandly furnished suburban Indian with some
great, veg-friendly Southern flavors

**7.4** | **5.5**
Food | Feel

## Indian

Casual restaurant

**$25**
Price

www.bombaybistro.com

Mon–Thu 11:30am–2:30pm,
5pm–10pm; Fri 11:30am–
2:30pm, 5pm–10:30pm; Sat
noon–3pm, 5pm–10:30pm; Sun
noon–3pm, 5pm–10pm

**Bar** Beer, wine
**Credit cards** Visa, MC, AmEx
**Reservations** Not accepted
Kid-friendly, veg-friendly

**Rockville, MD**
98 W. Montgomery Ave.
(301) 762-8798

**Fairfax, VA**
3570 Chain Bridge Rd.
(703) 359-5810

The must-have item at Bombay Bistro is the masala dosa, a south Indian crêpe-like pancake whose fermented-lentil-and-rice-flour batter gives a pleasantly sour taste, with a crisp exterior and a tender interior wrapped around a potato filling. Seemingly a couple of feet in diameter, Bombay's dosa extends past the edges of the plate, and the accompanying coconut chutney serves as a fragrant and cooling condiment. Aloo gobhi, lamb rogan josh, and biryanis are thoughtfully spiced without being too creamy or suffering from the sameness that can make one suspect that an Indian restaurant uses a single base for all of its stews. Order a thali—either vegetarian or not—to get a selection of three dishes, served with lentils, puri, and raita.

The bread basket is notable for its diversity and its consistent quality. Papadam are crisp and spiced with warming black pepper and cumin; deep-fried puri arrive puffed and golden brown, and we rip into them before they get a chance to deflate on their own; you should do the same. Breads are good, but saag paneer can be regrettably flavorless, the cubes of fresh cheese cooked to a tough and almost rubbery consistency. A better choice to accompany those breads is the traditional dal makhani, whose complexity proves that the kitchen takes few shortcuts; the lentils are tender, the sauce slightly soupy but not watery, and the dish mildly but pleasantly spiced with garlic, ginger, and the like. The best drink is the lassi, which you can order sweet, salty, or mango-flavored. A small selection of beer and wine is also available but generally forgettable.

The décor is neither modern nor particularly elegant, but the service is warm; accordingly, the clientele consists mainly of families with children and local residents of these suburban areas. The open kitchen extends along one side of the restaurant; patrons have a view over the counter of the tandoor oven and the cooktops. Guests are seated at utilitarian booths and tables with laminate tops. A back wall is decorated with a mosaic of shards from mirrors and jeweled bangles, but the espresso machine and water pitchers stand in plain sight directly in front of it. The space can feel somewhat cramped, especially at peak hours. None of this is worth driving from the District to Maryland for, but if you're in the neighborhood, it outperforms expectations. –CD

# Bombay Club

Get over the outdated colonialist décor, and enjoy
the updated Indian fare

**8.1** Food
**6.8** Feel

## Indian

Upmarket restaurant

**$45**
Price

www.bombayclubdc.com

Mon–Thu 11:30am–2:30pm,
5:30pm–10:30pm; Fri
11:30am–2:30pm, 5:30pm–
11pm; Sat 6pm–11pm; Sun
5:30pm–9pm

**Bar** Beer, wine, liquor
**Credit cards** Visa, MC, AmEx
**Reservations** Accepted
Live music, outdoor dining,
veg-friendly, Wi-Fi

**Farragut**
815 Connecticut Ave. NW
(202) 659-3727

At first glance, Bombay Club looks like the stuffy lobby of an overly priced
colonial hotel in Miami Beach. A room replete with sea-foam-green chairs,
peach walls, and live music in the evenings (only a piano, thankfully) isn't
quite where you'd expect to get a good Indian meal. Our advice, weather
permitting, is to try to sit on the patio instead, where you can forget the
white piano and the country club décor and focus on the food.

Sometimes it seems as though every naan you find in US Indian
restaurants is the same. Bombay Club, though, pays attention to the
quality of its naan, which has a thin, crisp bottom and a doughy but light
center.

But this sort of attention to detail extends beyond the bread. Indian
food begs to be shared, and Bombay Club makes it quite easy. On our last
visit, the kitchen took the time to split the dishes for us, a detail that
makes for a more refined and elegant sharing experience.

It's important to visit Bombay Club without a preconceived menu in
mind—they tend to offer a wide variety of lesser-known dishes that are
worth a try, especially seafood dishes. The tandoori scallops, for
example—marinated in yogurt, mustard seed, and chili—are smoky, hot,
and tender. The more mundane chicken tikka displays an unusually bold
layering of garlic, cilantro, mint, and basil. Vegetarian dishes, which can
be ordered in large or small portions, abound.

Lasooni palak is a smooth, light, not-too-garlicky spinach dish. The
roster of interesting preparations continues: spicy duck kebab, calamari
peri peri, tandoori trout. For dessert, try the sticky toffee pudding with
chocolate-cardamom ice cream, an exotic take on a British classic. It'll help
distract your attention from the sticky toffee décor. –SDC

# Bombay Curry Company

**7.2** Food | **6.9** Feel

A little bit of authenticity and a little bit of inauthenticity—all pretty good

## Indian

Casual restaurant | **$20** Price

www.bombaycurrycompany.com

Sun–Thu 11:30am–2:30pm,
5:30pm–9:30pm
Fri–Sat 11:30am–2:30pm,
5:30pm–10pm

**Bar** Beer, wine
**Credit cards** Visa, MC, AmEx
**Reservations** Accepted
Delivery, kid-friendly, veg-friendly

**Alexandria, VA**
3110 Mount Vernon Ave.
(703) 836-6363

Although many of its greatest mysteries were resolved soon after the advent of satellite technology, the field of geography continues to astound and puzzle. How, for example, can four separate sandwich chains (Potbelly, Schlotzsky's, Quiznos, Subway) thrive on half as many blocks in Van Ness? Why are all of the decent Mexican restaurants prohibitively far from metro stops? And perhaps most intriguing of all: why is one of DC's best Indian places tucked away into a tiny strip mall in Salvadoran-heavy Del Ray?

To call Bombay Curry Company's storefront unassuming would be an egregious understatement. Its gray-on-black-lettering is identical to that of next-door Cosmic Nails and the neighboring Pho King (yes, funny name), and the entire complex faces an uninspiring parking lot. But Bombay is, surprisingly, more upscale than its exterior suggests. Along with placemats, silverware, and a (serviceable if limited) wine list, you can expect a menu and prices in line with middle-line competitors: $10 for an average main.

For these prices, Bombay sits a few cuts above its rivals. First of all, the restaurant offers a number of dishes, such as the Kadai dishes, that you'd be hard-pressed to find at another Indian establishment in DC. More importantly, the food is excellent. Bombay's creations tend to be spicy rather than creamy, and to juxtapose interesting flavors. The samosas, for example, are stuffed with cumin-heavy curried potato, and paired with a tamarind chutney and light yogurt sauce. The Dal Wali Murgee chicken is an inspired curry of lentils, tomatoes, chilies, and small chunks of meat.

One of the highlights of Bombay's menu used to be the tandoori sandwiches. Although this lunch item—essentially a very large slab of tandoor-cooked beef or chicken wrapped inside a very large slab of naan, with sauces and vegetables—may be an affront to authenticity, it is also downright delicious. For some reason, the sandwiches have disappeared from the menu, but they can still be ordered off-menu at lunch.

Bombay may be tricky to find, but a short study of local geography will be richly rewarded by your meal—trust us. –CK

# Bombay Restaurant

**5.6** Food    **4.1** Feel

Strip-mall, surly-service, subpar-kitchen proof that
all the critics can be wrong

## Indian

Casual restaurant    **$30** Price

www.bombayindianrestaurant.com

Sun–Thu 11:30am–3pm, 5pm–
9pm
Fri–Sat 11:30am–3pm, 5pm–
10pm

**Bar** Beer, wine
**Credit cards** Visa, MC, AmEx
**Reservations** Accepted
Kid-friendly, veg-friendly

**Silver Spring, MD**
11229 New Hamphire Ave.
(301) 593-7222

It's a familiar story: it's an unknown neighborhood restaurant until one
newspaper writes about it. Other newspapers follow suit. Magazines jump
on the bandwagon. Online and print survey scores begin to parrot the
party line. Eventually, the front window of the generic-strip-mall
restaurant is plastered with so many awards from critics, newspapers,
magazines, and books that you can barely see through the glass to the
almost absurdly spartan room within, whose yellow wall paint seems to
be the only attempt at décor.

Before all the hype, Bombay Restaurant wouldn't have been such a
letdown: it's an average Indian restaurant packaged exactly as such. But
given all the misinformation out there, we are compelled to set the record
straight: there is nothing special about this Indian food. The highlights are
expertly fried, well-textured samosas; deeply seasoned vegetarian dishes
like eggplant and okra; and goat dishes (there's curry on the menu, and
biryani occasionally appears on the good-value lunch buffet line) with
good flavor, if lacking the fatty richness of the animal at its best.

Otherwise, the menu is generally rote—and rife with disappointments.
Aloo saag (spinach with potatoes) and yellow dal (lentil stew), unlike some
of their vegetarian counterparts, are both unusually flavor-poor; we
expect some richness from the former and better seasoning in the latter.
Curry gravies are decent, but the underlying meats sometimes aren't.
Tandoori chicken is dry. Lettuce salad is useless. Chewy naan is some of
the worst in the city, a chore to eat. Among desserts, kheer (rice pudding)
is mild and milky, more like the Latin American version, without the
aggressive cardamom flavor that can sometimes dominate the dish. But
it's far from enough to rescue this restaurant to recommendability.

To complicate matters further, the service is unusually poor, especially
when compared with the attentive Indian-restaurant norm. Water glasses
are refilled only sporadically, and servers assent to orders with a mere
grunt. At one visit, we were actually kicked out of our table after lingering
over a meal an extra half-hour or so, even though the restaurant was
open for another hour—and only half full. If this bad attitude has been a
side effect of the restaurant's newfound fame, then the unwarranted
publicity seems to have taken a mediocre restaurant and made it even
worse. –RG

# Bookbinder's Old Town

**6.7** **7.3**
Food Feel

All the accoutrements of a high-class steakhouse—
but the steaks and service don't live up

## Steakhouse, American

Upmarket restaurant **$80**
Price

www.bookbindersoldtown.com

| | | |
|---|---|---|
| Mon–Thu 11:30am–10pm | **Bar** Beer, wine, liquor | **Alexandria Old Town** |
| Fri 11:30am–11pm | **Credit cards** Visa, MC, AmEx | 109 S. Saint Asaph St. |
| Sat 5pm–11pm | **Reservations** Accepted | (703) 684-7008 |
| Sun 11am–9pm | Outdoor dining | |

The traditional American steak-and-chop-house props are all present and accounted for: long wooden bar, nautical prints on the wall, antique light fixtures glowing amber. These charming, if staid, details are most prominent in the front section of Bookbinder's, where a bar, a few high-top tables, and a row of booths seem unified by dark wood and clean lines.

But there is an element of luck to being seated at this Alexandria outpost of the prominent Philadelphia restaurant. In the atrium, brick walls and sage-green carpeting give the impression that the decorator has left his work unfinished. As an added misfortune, the atrium seems almost wholly disconnected from the action of the restaurant; while the glass ceiling affords a sense of airy spaciousness, the emptiness of the room and the inattentiveness of the service underscore the physical barrier separating this room from the cozier front of the house.

Unsurprisingly given that it's a mainstream minichain, the menu consists of familiar steak-and-seafood classics. Not so successful is the cold seafood sampler, which on our visit included some meager lobster meat, several decent oysters, and ice-cold shrimp cocktail. When will America learn that ice-cold shrimp cocktail is a doomed recipe? It continues to boggle our minds that otherwise respectable steakhouses continue to embarrass themselves by serving these pasty, thawed-out, flavor-free creatures.

Steaks are generously sized and cooked properly to temperature, but the New York strip seems surprisingly flat in flavor. Familiar side dishes of mashed red potatoes and creamed spinach are executed competently, but on one visit, steamed asparagus arrived limp and the accompanying hollandaise failed to display its subtle kick of acidity and depth. For dessert, an over-sweetened key lime pie feels store-bought-and-pre-cut (even if it's not), and ice cream is advertised as Häagen-Dazs. The wine list features a fairly well-edited, if mostly standard, selection with a focus on California and familiar French, Spanish, and Italian offerings—although a few token bottles of "Mid-Atlantic" wines from Virginia are a nod to the restaurant's new location.

The real surprise at Bookbinder's—though perhaps it shouldn't be so surprising in the steakhouse category—is the pricing. With single steaks starting at $30 and rising, sides at six dollars, and sauces adding another two bucks each, building a complete dinner plate becomes a fairly expensive proposition. At these prices for straightforward classics and basic accompaniments, Bookbinder's should excel; but neither the food nor the atmosphere are polished enough to deliver. –CD

# Boulevard Woodgrill

**5.3** | **4.0**
*Food* | *Feel*

This could do itself a world of service by keeping things simple

## New American

Casual restaurant

**$45**
*Price*

www.boulevardwoodgrill.com

Mon–Thu 11:30am–10:30pm
Fri 11:30am–11:30pm
Sat 10:30am–11:30pm
Sun 9:30am–9:30pm

**Bar** Beer, wine, liquor
**Credit cards** Visa, MC, AmEx
**Reservations** Accepted
Kid-friendly, outdoor dining

**Arlington, VA**
2901 Wilson Blvd.
(703) 875-9663

Boulevard Woodgrill is like a kid at a party who's desperately trying to be cool. True to the kid's efforts, there are moments of brilliance. The outfit is respectable—note Boulevard's pretty deck full of pretty flowers and pretty diners. The place also talks a big game: the menu is laced with delicious sounding dishes, overflowing with adjectives and ingredients. Descriptions project upmarket flair with words like "woodgrilled," "encrusted," and "duckling."

However, like the un-cool kid it really is, Boulevard Woodgrill can't help but show its true colors. The sense of class that it tries to project is defeated in the details. Despite the handsome space and nice wood booths, the feel of the grill is ruined by some unfortunate accessories. Fake flowers and red track lighting call the aesthetic into question, and a soundtrack of adult top-40s evokes the bland and generic. Though it may try to be something more special, it's just another mediocre, suburban restaurant.

The grill's menu seals its fate. Most of the time, the recipes are just trying too hard. Take, for example, Kingston Jerk Wings, which are "dusted with Carribean jerk" and served with "sweet guava and scotch-bonnet pepper" sauce. The wings are dry enough to be gritty from their jerk "dusting," and though the sauce is sweet, it's sweet in the worst way—like fruit jam. Even the scotch-bonnet version, which you'd expect to be intensely hot, is only discernible through a nose-hair-stirring tickle.

A luxurious-sounding "roasted duckling salad" is worse. The duck (whether or not it's a -ling) is overcooked and chewy, and doesn't seem to belong on the dish. In fact, the dish is crammed full of so many ingredients that it's difficult to eat. Fried onions share a bed of arugula with candied pecans, orange segments, hearts of palm, dried cranberries, and citrus vinaigrette. It seems that in its eagerness to add adjectives and ingredients, Boulevard Woodgrill has forgotten that there should be some semblance of order to a dish and that often, less really is more.

Instead of trying so hard to be something you're not, sometimes it's better to admit who you really are and roll with it. In the end, everyone might actually like you more that way. –JC

# Bourbon

You'll leave this place happy and whistlin' dixie

| **8.1** | **9.0** |
|---------|---------|
| Food | Feel |

## American

Bar **$35**

*Price*

www.bourbondc.com

Mon–Thu 5pm–2am; Fri 5pm–
3am; Sat 11:30am–3am; Sun
11:30am–2am
Hours vary by location

**Bar** Beer, wine, liquor
**Credit cards** Visa, MC, AmEx
**Reservations** Not accepted
Date-friendly, outdoor dining

**Adams Morgan**
2321 18th St. NW
(202) 332-0800

**Glover Park**
2348 Wisconsin Ave. NW
(202) 625-7770

In DC, you are officially south of the Mason-Dixon Line. As such, you should learn to love the things that symbolize the South: seersucker, sweet tea, grits, and that most heavenly of beverages, Bourbon. Made with at least 51% corn mash, aged in charred oak barrels, and federally regulated, this drink truly is a Southern institution.

The eponymously named bar reflects the whiskey's recent run of popularity. This isn't a place where Billy Bob ferments corn in bathtubs out back. Indeed, it is quite the opposite: tasteful, comfortable, and unassumingly classy. Simple wood paneling and exposed brick line the dining area, and deep leather seats and low tables turn a third-floor loft into a place quiet enough for conversation. If you avoid times when drunken mobs wander indiscriminately in and out of bars, it won't feel like you're in Adams Morgan.

The food at Bourbon consists of proficient bar room classics. Burgers are big and juicy, with a high meat-to-bun ratio. The version made with ground ostrich is lean, firm, and more like beef than chicken. Bourbon baked beans are sweet and smoky; waffle fries topped in Old Bay are crisp and golden, their ridgy surfaces gleaming with tangy spice. Grilled cheese is a formidable opponent to the fries, formed of thickly sliced, eggy bread that delivers both crunch and chew. Most exciting may be the mounds of loose, crumbly tater tots that burst open in your mouth with a poof of steam in a way they never did in your cafeteria lunch room. They look even better when you're drunk.

And then, of course, there's the Bourbon. Oh, the Bourbon. The bar's list is the size of the average restaurant's wine selection, and it includes good beers and other whiskeys to boot. Waiters, in fact, claim that it's a comprehensive list of every single Bourbon you can find in DC. Favorites include the surprisingly sweet and fruity Four Roses Single Barrel, and the smoky and deep Buffalo Trace. All are poured with a liberal hand, and prices are phenomenally reasonable.

When that sweet, amber liquid turns into a warm glow heating your belly, and you are buoyed by the promise of the next basket of tots, it's easy to understand what it means to sing the song of the South. –JC

# Bourbon Steak

Butter and oak don't make it better—is this the steakhouse equivalent of California Chardonnay?

**7.3** Food   **8.6** Feel

## New American

Upmarket restaurant   **$115** Price

www.michaelmina.net

Mon–Wed 11:30am–2:30pm, 5:30pm–10pm; Thu–Fri 11:30am–2:30pm, 5:30pm–10:30pm; Sat 5:30pm–10:30pm; Sun 5:30pm–10pm

**Bar** Beer, wine, liquor
**Credit cards** Visa, MC, AmEx
**Reservations** Accepted
Outdoor dining

**Georgetown**
2800 Pennsylvania Ave. NW
(202) 944-2026

How did it take so long for Georgetown's Four Seasons Hotel to realize that its "fine-dining" restaurant (oh, how we loathe that term—yet it describes Seasons perfectly) was done? That elite hotel guests sought something beyond roast-beef carving and omelette stations on Sundays?

To fix matters, they brought in Michael Mina, a flashy celebrity chef who brought a new gimmick to the table: slow-poaching steaks in clarified butter and then grilling them over wood. Mina, who originally made his name at Aqua, a San Francisco seafood restaurant, is now well known in San Francisco and Vegas, where he runs a high-flying restaurant group with his partner Andre Agassi. In fact, Mina has by now opened so many casino restaurants that he's been inducted into the American Gaming Association Hall of Fame.

Call us party poopers, but we don't happen to think that chain restaurants bearing the names of absentee celebrity chefs are necessarily much more than chain restaurants. And we don't believe Vegas to be quite the culinary wonderland that some think it is.

Bourbon Steak, which also has branches in Miami, Scottsdale, and Detroit, is no exception to this rule. It's stupendously overpriced and quite spotty, beginning with nothing-special starters like ahi tuna tartare (tasteless, in spite of the ancho chili, pear, mint, and "toasted sesame oil"). A lamb-loin salad takes 16 words to set forth on the menu ("Elysian Fields Lamb Loin, Niçoise-Merguez, Chickpea Fritters, Arrowleaf Spinach, Green Olive Tapenade, Walnut Muhammara, Grilled Pita"), but it could be better described with just three: heavy, chewy, confused.

The seafood and fish mains—maybe the Aqua pedigree is relevant after all—have generally been good, and duck-fat fries are undeniably delicious. But the best thing we've sampled here has been a pasta dish: ricotta cavatelli, cooked to an ideal al dente, interestingly paired with crispy fried oysters and subtle mushrooms.

The problem is, every steak we've had here has been overcooked to medium or beyond. And these cuts are unbelievably pricey: $46 for a 14-ounce ribeye, $145 for a kobe steak. We don't know whether the overcooking is a symptom of poor execution, or just an inevitable result of the Mina butter-poaching method (we have had butter- and olive-oil-poached steaks elsewhere that weren't overcooked). Either way, a Prime steak that is barely pink in the center loses a lot of its flavor—which can't all be substituted back merely by the obvious, overbearing oakiness that comes from the grill. Call us crazy, but we actually prefer the flavor of Prime beef to the flavors of butter and wood. –RG

# Brasserie Beck

A well-themed Belgian beer bar that follows
through with execution in the kitchen

| 8.4 | 9.1 |
|-----|-----|
| Food | Feel |

## Belgian

Upmarket restaurant

**$55**
Price

www.beckdc.com

Mon–Thu 11:30am–11pm
Fri 11:30am–11:30pm
Sat 5pm–11:30pm
Sun 11:30am–9pm

**Bar** Beer, wine, liquor
**Credit cards** Visa, MC, AmEx
**Reservations** Accepted
Date-friendly, outdoor dining,
Wi-Fi

**Downtown**
1101 K St. NW
(202) 408-1717

With its cavernous ceilings, dark wood, plate-glass paneling, and collection of large clocks (all are set to a different city), Brasserie Beck has the feel of a very fine rail-station café. Cobalt blue tiling, a huge open kitchen hung with copper pots, and the bustle of very clean cooks form the centerpiece of the dining area. The design of the space—all bold colors and simple lines—echoes the chef's attitude. Even the hefty silverware is no-nonsense: these are serious utensils for serious food. Portions are large, flavors are heavy, sauces are strong, and nobody is apologizing.

The moment you sit down, your waiter will swoop down with a basket of steaming bread that instantly melts the huge pats of butter you'll slather on (it is a Belgian restaurant, after all). You might start with an order of wonderfully crispy herbed fries; they're generously salted and presented with a trio of mayonnaises, including a tangy-spicy curry, sweet-sharp tomato, and traditional garlic. Shallot-and-onion soup, made with five kinds of onions (including scallions), tastes sharper than its French cousin—and deeper, too, with its pleasantly bitter aftertaste. It goes superbly with a glass of Belgian beer, which is picked from an encyclopedic list and shepherded by the beer specialist on staff. The brews alone are worth many return trips.

Among mains, roasted rabbit loin comes with a Kriek (raspberry beer) sauce that is so deeply reduced as to be viscous, and too bitter when eaten with just the root vegetables. It is, however, a fine bedfellow for the compact, tender rabbit meat, which is packed onto the bone. We're overwhelmed—almost grossed out—by the richness of the highly touted choucroute in puff pastry; we'd prefer the more modest, better-balanced real thing. The sausage is rich enough not to need pastry.

Pear tarte tatin is a dense, thin disk of salty pastry coated with poached pears and served with mascarpone ice cream. Welcome salt from the pastry enhances the smoky-sweet flavor from the dark caramel sauce; both are lightened by a bright citrus note in the ice cream. Like the other dishes at Brasserie Beck, its presentation is simple, rich, and straightforward.

Brasserie Beck's unpretentious kitchen is refreshingly honest. We applaud the chef's conviction to food that is comforting, generous, and free of unnecessary frills—and, above all, for feeding us so amply and well. –JC

# Brasserie Monte Carlo

**4.9** Food **7.3** Feel

Like a trip to the beach, with all its fun and pitfalls

## French

Casual restaurant

**$45** Price

www.brasseriemontecarlo.com

Mon–Thu 5pm–9:30pm; Fri 5pm–10:30pm; Sat 11:30am–2:30pm, 5pm–10:30pm; Sun 11:30am–2:30pm, 5pm–9:30pm

**Bar** Beer, wine, liquor
**Credit cards** Visa, MC, AmEx
**Reservations** Accepted
Date-friendly, kid-friendly, live music, outdoor dining, veg-friendly

**Bethesda, MD**
7929 Norfolk Ave.
(301) 656-9225

You'll want to like Brasserie Monte Carlo, which lounges proudly on the corner of a busy intersection in Bethesda. Its happy blue awning, dotted with hanging flowerpots, makes the place feel welcoming and quaint—like a brief vacation to somewhere beachy and French. The interior perpetuates the myth. A wall-length mural shows beachgoers strolling along the sea, and bright blues and yellows on the crockery bring a cheerful feel to your meal. Edith Piaf croons over the speakers. In summer, an outdoor patio opens and periodically hosts live harp or guitar.

However, like a beach vacation, it can go awry rather quickly. Indeed, eating at Brasserie Monte Carlo is like going to the beach on the off-season when no one is there and the tourist industry has gone sloppy. For one thing, the Brasserie is usually empty—stunningly empty; empty in such a way that the few staff members huddle in the corner and awkwardly lurk around the few diners. It also smells bad—faintly—in the way buildings that have been unoccupied for too long smell. It's just enough to catch your attention and make you question its cleanliness.

Sadly, though you may expect the food from such a charming, to-hell-with-it-all place to taste delicious, it doesn't. In fact, it's hugely disappointing. Meals start off on the wrong foot with flavorless, mundane rolls and blocks of rock-hard butter that you'll have to carve out of the ramekins. While descriptions of dishes seem simple, they come to the table in wildly different forms from what you'd expect.

Poached eggs are hard and overcooked, floating in what resembles warm gazpacho (a dish available only in the summer) but tastes too bland. What are advertised as "roasted potatoes" come to the table as wedges of barely cooked spuds. These fundamental mistakes make the kitchen seem like an uppity home cook trying too hard to be fancy. Bacon-wrapped quail should be luxuriant and rich. Instead, it's puny. The three tiny breasts are cooked until the meat is tough and stringy. The bacon is dry and so resilient that it's hard to cut through. Mushroom jus is rich and dark, but bitter and over-salted. Undercooked carrots complete the disappointment.

A small saving grace is the apple tart. It's sweet and buttery (albeit with puff pastry that tastes store-bought) and so hot that the ice cream melts instantly. It's not the best tart in the world, but it's not a disaster. But don't be tempted by the Brasserie's charm. There are plenty of other places that can deliver upon the promise. –JC

# Bread & Chocolate

We don't need to tell you what to order—it's all in the name

**7.2** **5.8**
Food Feel

## French

Café **$15**
Price

www.breadandchocolate.net

Mon–Thu 7am–7pm
Fri–Sat 7am–8pm
Sun 8am–6pm
Hours vary by location

**Bar** Beer, wine
**Credit cards** Visa, MC, AmEx
Outdoor dining, veg-friendly, Wi-Fi

**West End**
2301 M St. NW
(202) 833-8360

**Chevy Chase, MD**
5542 Connecticut Ave. NW
(202) 966-7413

**Alexandria Old Town**
611 King St.
(703) 548-0992

Here's a brunch spot that's true to its name: this café near Eastern Market whips up a creamy, transporting chocolate made with Dutch cocoa and served in an enormous white cup, and it pairs well with any of the rich homemade breads available (sliced, in a brunch basket, or by the loaf) for dunking.

Bread and Chocolate's ethnic origins, however, are difficult to discern: while the name conjures up the Netherlands, the restaurant also serves several Norwegian smoked-salmon numbers, a "house special" German muesli, pfannkuchen (what one waitress described as "flat pancakes"). You can order your omelette Western-style or you can have it Mediterranean, and the tarts in the display case are pretty enough to have been made in a Parisian patisserie.

In the end, all questions of heritage are moot: it's good food no matter where it's from. The breakfast bagel is chewy and sour, and is served with fresh tomato, capers, too-cold cream cheese, and a small mountain of the thickest, richest lox around. The muesli is peppered with whole walnuts, mixed berries and melon, and sweetened yogurt, although a single serving won't quite suffice for brunch.

Egg dishes are not the café's forte: all are accompanied by a pitiful scoop of cubed roasted potatoes that err on the side of dryness, and some omelettes are rendered with too much oil and not enough salt. The Mediterranean omelette is a delightful exception, filled with a salty tapenade of olives, feta, and roasted red peppers.

If you're coming for a meal other than breakfast or brunch, you have some options. There are a few tartines, and some panini, too; we especially like a version with roast beef, blue cheese, and horseradish. Greece makes an appearance in the form of moussaka and pastitsio.

Bread and Chocolate has achieved a happy medium between dumpy and posh. The restaurant feels a bit tidier (and less rambunctious) than the most "down-home" of brunch spots, yet the place isn't as upscale, haughty, or expensive as the majority of places that do themselves up for a Washington "Sunday Brunch." The windows are big, the crowd is refreshing (some families, some couples, a few single joggers with newspapers and mimosas), and the chocolate is transporting. The service is attentive, but far from invasive. Best of all, there's no false advertising—only excellent chocolate. –CK

# Bread Line

A well-oiled sandwich machine

**8.1** Food

**5.0** Feel

## Sandwiches

Café **$15** Price

www.thebreadlinedc.blogspot.com

Mon–Fri 7:30am–3:30pm

**Bar** None
**Credit cards** Visa, MC, AmEx
Delivery, outdoor dining,
veg-friendly, Wi-Fi

**Farragut**
1715 Pennsylvania Ave.
(202) 822-8900

Behold the factory line in all its glory! There is the foreman, brow furrowed, shouting at his crew. Next to him each worker, again and again, repeats his task, fabricating a small piece that will eventually combine to make the whole. The bread is sliced, the greens are washed, the mayonnaise is spread, the cheese added, the sandwich folded together.

Bread Line is a much-sanitized scene from Upton Sinclair. Instead of a Chicago slaughterhouse, however, we have a do-goody bakery that also happens to make some of the best bread in Washington. The line of corporate and World Bank-type lunchers wrapping through the store and out onto the Pennsylvania Avenue sidewalk seems something out of farce (or Soviet Russia): the length of the line is almost enough to make an interloper turn around and march right down to the Così next door, compromising quality for the freedom from crowds.

But unlike the Soviet ration lines, Bread Line's lunch queue moves quickly. The order takers are adept at turning down substitution requests, and referring still-wavering diners to the menu out front. Cashiers ring in orders in record time, and begin to sigh audibly at wallets buried too deeply inside bags; every second counts.

Bread Line's resulting sandwiches are delicious; they offer proof that good food can be made without art (no one is thinking about your individual sandwich as he slaps tomatoes on a hundred of them). The basis for such quality is, of course, the bread, all of which is baked in-house. Bread Line's famous baguette is sour and dense, with a crunchy exterior and a consistency that requires a strong jaw to pull free a bite. The sliced whole wheat is held together more loosely, and features a small enough sprinkling of barley and oats to give the bread flavor without weighing it down.

The sandwich combinations are thoughtful with respect to taste and texture: the baguette pairs well with salami, cheese, red peppers, and arugula, while the wheat gives a fine mix of textures with dill-and-caper cream cheese, thin-sliced lox, chunks of cucumber, and a heaving handful of spicy watercress. Not every combo will be earth-shattering, and $9 for a ham sandwich might seem a bit steep, but when you consider the great bread, fresh veggies and the distance to the nearest excellent banh mi, it seems worth it. –CK

# Brickskeller

A fun laid-back dive bar with a beer list that reads like a thesis

**4.0** Food  **9.3** Feel

## American

Bar  **$15** Price

www.lovethebeer.com

Mon–Tue 5pm–2am; Wed–Thu 11:30am–2am; Fri 11:30am–3am; Sat 6pm–3am; Sun 6pm–2am

**Bar** Beer, wine, liquor
**Credit cards** Visa, MC, AmEx
**Reservations** Accepted
Date-friendly

**Dupont**
1523 22nd St. NW
(202) 293-1885

It's in fashion to be a beer nerd these days. Just about everyone has a book on home brewing lying around somewhere in their house. For the sedentary, there are beer-of-the-month clubs, where you can try something new every month without even leaving the house.

But for those of us who like to get out a bit, there's Brickskeller. This split-level space—we drastically prefer the subterranean area to its upstairs counterpart—is part of the bigger Brickskeller Inn. (Hey, at least you know there's an easy plan B if you engage in too much imbibing to make it home.) Downstairs you'll find a fun beer-hall atmosphere. The absence of outside light keeps it nice, dim, and comfortable. Darts and pool tables are there if you get antsy. The beer list is staggering. More than 1,000 bottled beers, from Russia's Baltika to Ethiopia's Harar, are here. How, you ask, are they possibly keeping all those bottles fresh?

The short answer: they're not. Sometimes a request for one of the more obscure beers cannot be met because they don't have it. Other times they do, but the beer has lost its unique flavor profile after being in the bottle too long—which, in most cases, is just a couple of months. The trademark of this spoilage is a honeyish aroma and sweet taste. So before you get too excited about having a Suprema and reeling in nostalgia as you reminisce about that vacation in El Salvador, think about when that beer was probably last ordered.

As for the food, we recommend that you think long and hard about anything before you order it. Nearly everything we've had here has been a disaster. Particularly bad was a rendition of buffalo cheese sticks; they arrived too cool—the cheese wasn't even melted—and their sauce had no resemblance whatsoever to that delicious vinegary substance we like on our wings. Potato skins are made with laughably low-quality ingredients: chunky sour cream, dried-out hunks of bacon, and ballpark-style cheese. Burgers are decent—on a good day.

But come here for the brews (remember, get the ones with high turnover), comfy digs, and drinking games, and you'll be one happy guest of the inn. –FC

# The Brown Bag

5.1 **Food**  5.9 **Feel**

Do-it-yourself breakfast-and-lunch fare that would benefit greatly from a real chef

## Sandwiches

Counter service · **$15** *Price*

www.brownbagonline.com

Mon–Fri 7:30am–3:30pm

**Bar** None
**Credit cards** Visa, MC, AmEx
Outdoor dining

**Downtown**
1099 14th St. NW
(202) 408-0777

**Logan Circle**
1099 14th St. NW
(202) 408-0777

**Foggy Bottom**
818 18th St. NW
(202) 293-0092

**Additional locations**
and more features at
www.fearlesscritic.com

You may be aware, if you've studied high school chemistry, that atoms can combine in any number of ways to form more complex molecules. Brown Bag, a big-windowed breakfast-and-lunch spot just off of Farragut Square and in the shadow of the World Bank, no doubt reveres this principle. The café presents to its lunch patrons a slew of edible building blocks, a haphazard pan-global tapestry stretching from Italy to Thailand out of which each can build his own salad, omelette, sandwich, or pasta dish.

Unfortunately, not all molecules taste good, and this culinary cosmology is apocalyptic. A chef is not an ingredient salesman. He is supposed to design and refine his recipes through trial and error, thus justifying his margins vis-à-vis supermarkets.

A Brown Bag pasta consists of exactly one base (pasta pre-cooked in a large vat), one sauce (generally oily and separated), and up to two free "toss-ins" (or more than two at extra cost), thrown into a to-go dish. Here, the customer-knows-best philosophy is taken to such a perverted extreme that it seems to dismiss as old-fashioned the ideas of culinary training or talent. In this new world order, the notion that amatriciana sauce is designed to be paired with bucatini or penne because of the way the sauce's texture adheres to the ridges—or the principle that ravioli are designed for the simplest of preparations, so that the pasta pillow's filling, instead of the sauce, can be left to drive the flavor profile—are dismissed as customer-unfriendly. "Toss in" the ingredients of your choice; toss out the culinary arts—the idea that the chef is, or can be, an artist.

Brown Bag's sandwiches are slightly more successful; choose-your-own breads include wonderfully sour ciabatta and a good baguette, and they're overstuffed with quality meat. But these are small consolations. The idea that do-it-yourself restaurants like Brown Bag don't just open, but actually succeed, is as damaging to our future (teaching our children that the restaurant kitchen is just a robot-staffed dartboard) as it is to our past (teaching them that half a millennium of culinary history is worthless). Restaurateurs who open places like this shouldn't just be avoided—they should be jailed. –FC

# Buca di Beppo

**2.7** Food  **6.0** Feel

How has the idea of Southern Italian food gotten so twisted?

## Italian

Casual restaurant

**$30** Price

www.bucadibeppo.com

Mon–Thu 11am–10pm
Fri–Sat 11am–11pm
Sun 11am–9pm

**Bar** Beer, wine, liquor
**Credit cards** Visa, MC, AmEx
**Reservations** Accepted
Kid-friendly

**Dupont**
1825 Connecticut Ave.
NW
(202) 232-8466

This chain Italian-American restaurant with its tentacles everywhere seems to embody everything that is soulless and wrong with the restaurant business: mass production of family-style food, prioritizing volume over quality, without doing justice to any culinary tradition—not even to the Italian-American one.

Mass-reproduced posters, faux-old-world memorabilia, and everything else fake Italian is flaunted at this cluttered mess of a restaurant that pretends to highlight the cuisine of Italy's south. Buca di Beppo will have your southern Italian grandmother rolling over in her grave to think that her descendants might be experiencing this as somehow Italian. She'd also be appalled by the behavior of the kids–with all the running, jumping, and screaming, Buca di Beppo can look like a daycare center where the supervisor forgot to show up. Hardly a date spot, this.

The menu is like a roll call of so-called "Italian" dishes that were actually invented in America: chicken parmigiana, fettuccine alfredo, stuffed shells, and so on. We call this cuisine "Italian-American 1.0." Granted, Little-Italy apologists might argue that Italian-American 1.0 is an authentic cuisine in its own right. But what would they say about Buca's attempt to look creative, too, by throwing together ill-executed dishes that cluelessly amalgamate trendy ingredients, like apple-and-gorgonzola salad? We're not sure if that's Italian-American 2.0, but it sure is gross.

The large portions at Buca are meant to be served family-style; this is one of the chain's gimmicks, a nod to gluttonous American eating habits. But even a glutton wouldn't want this much bad food. Lasagne tastes reheated, its tomato sauce strangely minerally, lingering in the back of your mouth for the duration of the meal. Gnocchi are too dense, and spaghetti comes spectacularly overcooked, although fist-sized meatballs are actually tasty and surprisingly flavorful. Chicken parmigiana (also available in individual portions) is the dark-horse winner here. It's everything you want it to be: flavorful, cheesy, and delicious. For once, poultry comes through!

If you must swallow your pride and eat this food in these portions, our advice is to starve yourself for at least two days beforehand. As Cervantes once said, hunger is the best sauce. –FC

# Buck's Fishing & Camping

**8.4** Food

**9.2** Feel

Some upscale takes on American fare in a
restaurant that brings in the great outdoors

## Southern, New American

Upmarket restaurant

**$60** Price

| | | |
|---|---|---|
| Tue, Wed, Thu, Sun 5pm–9:30pm | **Bar** Beer, wine, liquor | **Upper NW** |
| | **Credit cards** Visa, MC, AmEx | 5031 Connecticut Ave. |
| | **Reservations** Not accepted | NW |
| | Date-friendly, kid-friendly | (202) 364-0777 |

Do you ever just want to get away from it all? The suits, the lobbying, the power lunches, the gin martinis? (Okay, maybe not the martinis.) Do you ever just want to scurry out of the city in search of a moon-lit night, a campfire, and a star-filled sky? Wishful thinking, we know. Plus, who wants to deal with the mosquitoes and the whole tent business?

For a taste of rustic paradise, one need only go as far as Upper Northwest DC. The inviting, lamp-lit Buck's Fishing and Camping is filled with wooden tables and chairs, Depression-era trinkets, hunting-themed throw pillows, a hanging canoe, and a canopied ceiling. It's cute, but also mawkishly sentimental in a way that seems cruel when the bill arrives.

And while on an ordinary camping trip you would expect to eat canned baked beans and hot dogs on a stick and get sticky with s'mores, here you get the luxury of real food that's pretty good. A word of caution: we should warn you that the brief menu is almost solely composed of meat and seafood; substitutions are not accommodated and later in the night, some items tend to run out. Having said that…

Slightly upscale American picnic fare and steakhouse denizens abound on the menu (which never changes). Dishes waffle on a scale of execution that rarely reaches astounding, nor scrapes abject failure. The classic iceberg wedge salad is as it should be: crunchy and refreshing with a tangy blue cheese dressing and plenty of thick-cut, applewood-smoked bacon. You might ask for a bit more dressing, as the center of the wedge doesn't get nearly enough loving (and iceberg isn't the world's most interesting flavor). Wood-grilled shrimp served with sausage and cheese grits are homey and comforting, heavily seasoned and filling. And for dessert, nothing beats the Texas-style chocolate sheet cake. It's moist, decadent, and generous.

In short, we love this concept. In a modern American restaurant world in which every concept starts to seem trite and theming is passé, Buck's boldly busts out of both boxes and does its own fun, lovely thing. Service has been remarkably inconsistent: often slow and even rude, sometimes friendly and helpful. To have the best experience here, use the same guidelines as when you're camping. Arrive early, let go of your expectations, and just take in your surroundings. –SDC

# Burma

Burmese food for the uninitiated—but it's not the best the country has to offer

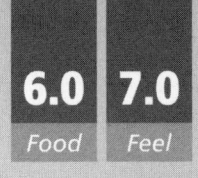

**6.0** Food    **7.0** Feel

**Burmese**

Casual restaurant

**$25** Price

Mon–Fri 11am–3pm, 6pm–10pm
Sat–Sun 6pm–10pm

**Bar** Beer, wine, liquor
**Credit cards** Visa, MC, AmEx
**Reservations** Accepted
Veg-friendly, Wi-Fi

**Chinatown**
740 6th St. NW
(202) 638-1280

It's possible that you've never eaten at a Burmese restaurant before. That wouldn't be surprising, given the uneven proliferation of immigrants: more arrive from certain countries; some foodstuffs are more quickly shipped, tempered, and tweaked for the American palate; and the American palate adapts to accept and even enjoy other flavors.

But Myanmar, whose military regime is shrouded in legendary secrecy and shunned by the US government, can point to a particularly severe case of culinary separatism. Most Americans have never set foot in a Burmese restaurant, and if you fall into that majority, we'd caution against making this restaurant your first.

Although some critics have raved about Burma Restaurant, which is housed in Chinatown on the second story up a set of dusty linoleum stairs, it's difficult to affirm any of this acclaim beyond the objective statement that Burma offers a nice change of pace from its Chinese noodle-shop neighbors. And we're not even certain about that: the few uniquely Burmese flavors that come through in the cooking are weak, and the dishes don't end up with a much different taste from what's achieved by the noodle-makers next door.

The thing is, there are at least two other Burmese restaurants in the DC area that go much further than this. Shrimp paste, for instance, should play a central role, but here it's conspicuously absent. Unfortunately, the deeply, darkly developed flavors of Burmese stews at their best are also absent from these preparations: spices are underutilized, the soups are watery, and meatiness doesn't shine through the meat dishes.

We had high hopes for a soup that promised potatoes and vegetables steeped in a rich tamarind broth. To our dismay, the broth was extremely weak; conjuring any tamarind required a considerable stretch of the imagination. The vegetable mixture turned out to be composed of about 80% cabbage, with a few pieces of carrot and eggplant (the thin, pale Japanese variety) thrown in for color.

"Mandalay Noodles," meanwhile, are dominated by the pasta itself, with a topping of chicken for good looks. The flavors in this dish are more rewarding, as is the crunchy texture of shrimp bits and bean sprouts cooked to a crisp in chili oil. But this is hardly sufficient to redeem a restaurant that still needs to develop its menu, and its cooking, before it can represent its enigmatic country's cuisine well. –CK

# Burrito Brothers

Brotherly love all wrapped up in a tortilla

| 5.9 | 5.7 |
|-----|-----|
| Food | Feel |

## Mexican

Counter service

**$20**
Price

www.burritobrotherscapitolhill.com

Mon–Fri 10:30am–9pm
Sat 10:30am–8pm
Sun 10:30am–7pm
Hours vary by location

**Bar** None
**Credit cards** Visa, MC, AmEx

**Foggy Bottom**
1825 Eye St. NW
(202) 887-8266

**Capitol Hill**
205 Pennsylvania Ave. SE
(202) 543-6835

It's hard to expect much from a place called Burrito Brothers, and if you've lived any length of time in DC and have any appetite for Mexican food, you've probably learned to set your expectations low regardless. But Burrito Brothers packs a small surprise. While it still falls short of spectacular, the restaurant offers decent Cal-Mex fare at reasonable prices.

Burrito Brothers has two outposts—one on Pennsylvania Avenue and one on Eye Street—both of which are, without a doubt, unspectacular. If you order at the Pennsylvania location, skip the squished bar stools and take your taco to the tables outside the Library of Congress. Be warned: the Brothers' tacos are messy, and take-out orders are enclosed in aluminum foil rather than in Styrofoam cases, which means your meal is liable to explode upon opening. Take plenty of napkins.

Much of Burrito Brothers' food can end up tasting plain: the beans and tortillas aren't fried enough, and the salsa lacks sufficient bite. They've got their starting points in order: well-prepared meat and fresh ingredients. Too bad they don't treat them any better.

The restaurant offers burritos, tacos, quesadillas, and "platters," with an array of sizing options that makes Starbucks' scheme look simplistic. The restaurant's tacos are sized in accordance with the Americanized Mexican standard—that is, a fair helping of meat on a six-inch corn tortilla—but the quesadillas tend to run small by American measures. Burritos are offered in three sizes: regular, super (includes cheese), and the "little brother," which clocks in at about half the volume of the regular, and does not bear a maximum age requirement.

The meat here isn't half bad (the carne asada is chewy and dark) and the portions are generous. Although the guacamole isn't anything special, the restaurant uses fresh avocado, slices of which are also available in the tortilla soup upon request.

But you'll probably be too full from your gargantuan burrito, anyway.
–CK

# Busboys & Poets

A unique, melting-pot coffeeshop-bookstore-performance space with decent food

| 7.5 | 9.7 |
|---|---|
| Food | Feel |

## American

Casual restaurant

**$25**
Price

www.busboysandpoets.com

Mon–Thu 9am–midnight
Fri–Sat 9am–2am
Sun 9am–midnight
Hours vary by location

**Bar** Beer, wine, liquor
**Credit cards** Visa, MC, AmEx
**Reservations** Not accepted
Date-friendly, live music,
veg-friendly, Wi-Fi

**Mt. Vernon Square**
1025 5th St. NW
(202) 789-2227

**U Street**
2021 14th St. NW
(202) 387-7638

**Arlington, VA**
4251 S. Campbell Ave.
(703) 379-9756

It's the rare establishment that can successfully fuse the check-out-how-hot-I-am nightlife vibe with the don't-bother-me-I'm-working-at-my-laptop coffeeshop vibe. But it is truly incredible that such an establishment could, in a city that segregates itself all too often, also attract a steady crowd that is as diverse as the District itself, from age to race to sexual preference.

It seems that almost everyone winds up at Busboys and Poets—named for Langston Hughes, who was a busboy at a DC hotel before his career took off—sooner or later. Some come simply to chill with a drink or to study, others for its poetry and open-mic events, and still others for its political bookstore. And some just come to have a bite and soak up the distinct U Street feel. Tables and a stand-up lounge area play host to a lively mix of plugged-in laptop users and gussied-up alcohol users; the one trait they all seem to share is that they dress pretty well. So do the servers, who are cool cats indeed.

Although the food has never been the real reason to come here, it isn't bad. There's an array of mostly vegetarian pizzas, sandwiches, burgers, salads, and homey main courses like meatloaf, lasagne, and beans and rice. Smooth, light yellow gazpacho with a dollop of guacamole is a simple but flavorful way to start an afternoon or evening meal. Pizza has a satisfyingly crispy crust and comes with your choice of '90s-chic sauce (sundried tomato and garlic, garlic and olive oil, or pesto), plus an assortment of topping combinations—our favorite, though, is the simple but fresh tomato and cheese. We like the seared-tuna sandwich, an eminently satisfying lunch.

If sandwiches are more your thing, the Portobello panino, grilled until toasty, oozes garlicky pesto and mozzarella cheese and is stuffed with roasted red peppers, spinach, and juicy mushroom slices. All sandwiches are served with a choice of thick-cut steak fries, fruit salad (pineapple and berries on one visit), or kettle chips. None of this is spectacular, but most of it is pleasant enough and varied enough to be enjoyed while reading, chatting, or hearing a spoken-word piece at this bright, eclectic establishment that has become perhaps the single most canonical embodiment of the new U Street. –FC

# Byblos

Mediterranean food that's more friendly than tasty

**5.6** Food **6.0** Feel

## Greek, Middle Eastern

Casual restaurant **$25** Price

www.byblosdc.com

Mon–Sat 11am–9pm
Sun noon–7pm

**Bar** None
**Credit cards** Visa, MC, AmEx
**Reservations** Not accepted
Delivery, outdoor dining,
veg-friendly

**Cleveland Park**
3414 Connecticut Ave. NW
(202) 364-6549

If you adhere to the notion that anything tastes better when wrapped in a pita, you'll find meet company at the Byblos Deli. In fact, there's little beyond flatbread to unite the multi-cultural menu that includes falafel, dolmade, hummus, shawarma, and spanikopita. The friendly Cleveland Park eatery is actually run by West Africans, but serves up food from what you might call the "pita crescent," with an emphasis on Greek and Lebanese fare.

Diners can choose from a long list of platters and sandwiches. The former come with pita bread and range from tabbouleh to baba ghanoush to a roasted half chicken. Sandwiches are served burrito-style (rather than as half-moons), and come loaded with vegetables and enough hummus or tzatziki to soak a layer or two of bread. The meat in the kafta kabab is rich and spicy, making it one of the top choices at Byblos. The gyros are also decent, but the greasy dolmade overwhelm the grape-leaf sandwich.

Byblos also offers ham sandwiches, cheeseburgers, salads, and fries. A tasty but undistinguished piece of baklava might round off a hit-or-miss meal. The deli doesn't serve alcohol, but the sodas are cheap, and with efficient service and outdoor tables facing Connecticut Avenue, Byblos is an ideal spot to while away an afternoon with a newspaper. Come to think of it, it might be better to skip the food altogether. This place has a lot more atmosphere than Fresh Med across the street, but for better food, you'd be wise to cross Connecticut. –CK

# C.F. Folks

Join the throng of lunchtime revelers for daily specials and the city's best crab cakes

| 8.1 | 7.9 |
|---|---|
| Food | Feel |

## American

Casual restaurant

**$20**
Price

www.cffolksrestaurant.com

Mon–Fri 11:30am–2:15pm

**Bar** None
**Credit cards** Visa, MC, AmEx
**Reservations** Not accepted
Kid-friendly, outdoor dining

**Dupont**
1225 19th St. NW
(202) 293-0162

C. F. Folks is the kind of restaurant you could walk past every day without stopping in. With its chalkboard specials and tiny storefront, it looks like it should be ignored. Yet if you observe more carefully, you'll realize that when it's open, this lunch-only joint is crammed full; it's so busy that waitresses buzz back and forth between tables and the kitchen at a jog. The décor is haphazard, peculiar, and endearing. Behind the long counter, racks of old cookbooks share space with old postcards, a stereo system, odd knick knacks (including Presidential Barbie), and a boisterous staff. Orders are barked from afar and cooks declaim their opinion on everything. It is loud, scrappy, and delicious.

We like the Reuben, but in general, sandwiches are nothing extraordinary. The best food at Folks is the rotating menu of daily specials (Monday: Louisiana, Tuesday: Tex-Mex, Wednesday: Italian & Indian, and so on). At many places, the specials are something you avoid because you can't imagine that it could deliver—especially with the pan-world menu. Yet at Folks, savvy diners order plate after plate, gleefully scarfing it all down.

Food is delicious the way home-cooked meals are delicious—simple, hearty, and filled with...well, love. You'll be served half a cow with hanger steak salad, flesh loose and tender and charred from the grill atop a bed of arugula. You'll be surprised by the quality of the blue cheese. Crowned with crisp apples and toasted walnuts, it is a basic dish, but wonderfully executed. Bolognese is homey and thick, several meats cooked down to a thick ragù and dashed haphazardly on a nest of pasta. Eating it is like being a child at a table in front of your favorite dinner. People in DC and Maryland are always looking for or claiming to have the best crab cake in town, but C.F. Folks actually has it (or has something very close to it).

Folks' dessert specials also change by the day and feature honest, clean food. Blocks of dense shortbread scented with vanilla and lemon are crumbly and buttery, baked until crisp on the edges. Surrounded by fresh berries and a thick fruit purée and topped by a big dollop of ice cream, it all tastes wholesome, fresh, and sweet: like 4th of July in the Heartlands.
–FC

# Café Asia

**5.0** Food    **4.0** Feel

A Pan-Asian joint that's by no means ideal, but it can certainly satisfy shameful cravings

## Pan-Asian

Casual restaurant    **$30** Price

www.cafeasia.com

Mon–Thu 11:30am–11pm
Fri–Sat 11:30am–midnight
Sun noon–11pm

**Bar** Beer, wine, liquor
**Credit cards** Visa, MC, AmEx
**Reservations** Accepted
Delivery, veg-friendly

**Farragut**
1720 Eye St. NW
(202) 659-0756

**Arlington, VA**
1550 Wilson Blvd.
(703) 469-1953

If you work in downtown DC, chances are you have had several run-ins with Café Asia. As an option that's legitimate enough to justify a lunch with colleagues, it's also seedy enough to satisfy covert cravings for Asian food of dubious authenticity. Décor at the café is alternately clubby and chic. The location on Eye Street favors industrial tones, plasticky furniture, and a DJ booth, while the Arlington location is a virtual pine forest à la Ikea. Service is functional; you can expect waitstaff to forego chattiness or solicitude for efficiency.

Don't be mistaken: Café Asia is exactly as its name implies. It does not adhere to any specific region, and it bravely toes the line between authentic and blatantly Americanized. In fact, in accomplishing neither, it creates its own special genre and expertly satisfies a very specific craving. Take for example, beef satay, which is topped with fried onions and peanut sauce. Like most meats cooked over an intense and irregular flame, it is hunter-gatherer delicious for the first five minutes, pretty good for the next five, and then rapidly declines into tough and chewy. Equally chewy drunken noodles are topped with gravely textured minced chicken and slivered vegetables, and happily Chinglish in their ubiquitous brown sauce.

Some dishes do offer some good with the bad. Fat-capped tom yum soup emits a creeping tiny stink, round and pungent and reminiscent of streetcarts all over Asia. Sadly, the smell isn't matched by the taste—the soup's vegetables are barely cooked. Chirashi (sashimi atop a rice bowl) is sized for the American belly, but fish is sometimes haphazardly cut and sinewy. Drinks are middling Asian versions of Western cocktails (more exciting during happy hour than with dinner), and desserts are strung together with pre-purchased items.

Café Asia is certainly not a dining destination, but that's kind of the point. The next time you get an itch for the Asian equivalent of chain pizza, have no shame. Say it loud and proud: on that day, at that hour, this is exactly what you wanted. –JC

# Café Atlántico

Fusion that extends well beyond the reaches of the
Atlantic Ocean

## 7.8 | 7.8
Food | Feel

## Nuevo Latino

Upmarket restaurant

## $75
Price

www.cafeatlantico.com

Tue–Thu 11:30am–2:30pm,
5pm–10pm; Fri–Sat 11:30am–
2:30pm, 5pm–11pm; Sun
11:30am–2:30pm, 5pm–10pm

**Bar** Beer, wine, liquor
**Credit cards** Visa, MC, AmEx
**Reservations** Accepted
Good wines, outdoor dining

**Penn Quarter**
405 8th St. NW
(202) 393-0812

Welcome to the fusion funhouse. Sexy Café Atlántico is the most far-reaching outpost of guru Jose Andres' fiefdom: any nation with Atlantic beaches is fair game for influence. Although South America is most heavily emphasized, Andean countries are not excluded despite their lack of Atlantic Ocean frontage, and the eastern Atlantic—Mediterranean Europe—lends mostly spiritual influence. Dominican mofongo is only as far away as an Argentine parrilla (about 25 minutes, unless it's a very busy night), and salmon from northern waters is paired with quinoa from the southern mountains. To borrow words from a squarely non-Atlantic land, "Oy vey!"

There are moments of brilliance—tasting-menu specials sometimes evoke the exclusive Minibar, one of DC's top dining experiences, which sits in tantalizing reach of the upstairs dining room. In a sense, this just makes Café Atlántico more frustrating, because you sense what it could be: a whole sea urchin, spines and all, is roasted and dressed with miso, pineapple, and crisped quinoa; the bottom scoops, where the urchin's orange gonads were gently melted by suffused heat, are sublime. "Bacon and eggs" are created with pork belly, a carefully poached egg, well seasoned beans, and pork rinds—a profoundly reimagined brunch dish. Potato mousse is light and buttery, brightened by black pearls of American caviar.

But too often it seems that the main thing that's been picked up along the Atlantic's route is a container of adjectives. We don't know which is worse, the pretentious English ("Dominican conch fritters with a liquid center, jicama-avocado raviolis and passion-fruit oil") or the opaque Spanish ("Fritura de Lambi como la hacen en Santo Domingo") description of this appetizer. Eleven dollars for a soggy miniscule portion of gussied street food wouldn't fly in Santo Domingo, nor would "ravioli" that taste exactly like Atlántico's guacamole–which is patronizingly prepared (and underseasoned) tableside. That's $13 for the ritual sacrifice of an avocado or two.

Dinner mains include a decent striped bass spoiled by an olive-heavy Veracruz-style preparation, and a feijoada that's inexplicably deconstructed, with meat and dressings in separate piles, and adorned with a dry pork chop.

Best might be to stick to a couple apps and one of Atlántico's rightly lauded cocktails (perhaps the not-too-sweet and just-too-spicy passion fruit, ginger, and jalapeño martini, or a flawless margarita) in the trendy two-floor space or the pleasant sidewalk seating. And to end it with that.
–FC

# Café Berlin

**7.2** | **8.0**
Food | Feel

The Germany of American stereotypes, in various forms that can please anyone

## German

Café | **$35**
Price

www.cafeberlindc.com

Mon–Thu 11:30am–10pm
Fri–Sat 11:30am–11pm
Sun 4pm–10pm

**Bar** Beer, wine, liquor
**Credit cards** Visa, MC, AmEx
Date-friendly, outdoor dining

**Capitol Hill**
322 Massachusetts Ave. NE
(202) 543-7656

Although 21st-Century Berlin may be best known for its edgy arts scene, its cutting-edge café culture, and döner kebap, Café Berlin transports us to the Germany of our stereotypes and imaginations. Big plates of homemade sausages? Check. Starchy sides? Yup. Sour cabbage? Of course. Cold beer? Check, and in large quantities.

And they've got the feel down too—which isn't a surprising, given that the owners are German. Requisite lace curtains lull you into Europhilia, and the rest of the décor—slightly dull and dated—sends you reeling, too.

If you're here to fulfill those stereotypes (or for the opportunity to over-pronounce German words), the obvious place to begin is with the Deutsche Wurstplatte. The plate comes with two very large sausages—Bratwurst and Weisswurst (a white sausage that's eaten for breakfast in Munich)—as well as sauerkraut and buttered-up potatoes (no skins).

If you're here to test the cultural extensions of the former empire, you might opt for the excellent, paprika-redolent ungarisches gulasch; try not to budge if the waitress attempts to steer you toward a more traditional dish. If you're here for old time's sake, the homey-tasting Wiener schnitzel is a good choice, made modern by a creative cut of lemon.

If you're here by mistake, on the other hand, the "Low-Fat Entrée" may be for you. The selection rotates; at one point it was a grilled flounder "topped with stewed fresh tomatoes served with parsley potatoes and house salad with low-fat ranch dressing." There is little a food critic can add when a recipe is so facially disastrous. Sometimes the text speaks for itself. If you're here to partake of Schadenfreude (and, again, for the opportunity to over-pronounce German words), convince your dining companion to order the above.

No matter why you're here, and to complete the tableau, you must order the Black Forest Cake. –CK

# Café Bonaparte

Seeking la vie en rose through crêpes and mirrors

## French

Café **$45**
Price

www.cafebonaparte.com

Mon–Thu 10am–11pm
Fri–Sat 10am–1am
Sun 9am–10pm

**Bar** Beer, wine, liquor
**Credit cards** Visa, MC, AmEx
Date-friendly, outdoor dining,
veg-friendly

**Georgetown**
1522 Wisconsin Ave. NW
(202) 333-8830

There are many things about Café Bonaparte that resemble its namesake. Like the emperor, it is marooned in its own little Elba, in this case far up Wisconsin Avenue. And like Napoleon, it's also comically short in stature yet boldly gilded, European style. Brilliant reds, yellows, and greens are paired with exposed brick, and the silver-embossed ceiling glints off a mirror of comedically narcissistic proportions. A tiny outside dining area sports two lone tables under a picturesque awning. Waiters at Bonaparte are very French—they're stylish, beautiful, and a bit aloof.

Though the menu includes French classics like steak frites, escargot, and an excellent French onion soup, the word "crêpe" emblazoned across the awning emphasizes the restaurant's specialty. The savory crêpes menu reads like a primer on French colonial history; ingredients go from the traditional to the exotic.

Sadly, what sound like wonderful combinations often fall short of expectations. For example, the "Verona," filled with a tantalizing combination of sausage, caramelized onions, and green peppers, tastes predominantly sour. The sausage comes off too oily, and the smoky fontina that ties it all together is unevenly sprinkled over the burrito-like roll. The crêpe is thin and eggy, good but not the focus of the dish. The "Lisbon," filled with not-so-smoked salmon, tastes predominantly of dill. Its filling is compressed from cooking, but even more so from being excessively finely diced, leaving a texture that bores the mouth.

Sweet versions are much better, primarily because they keep their sweetness in check. "Crêpe St. Germain" is a hulking wonder, bursting at the seams. Its strawberry filling is hot and cooked through, but neither syrupy nor stewed. The dish is so hot that barely-sugared whipped cream dissolves into oozy foam. The "Cigar Chocolat" is filled with an air-light chocolate mousse, loose and downy and pleasantly mild; its hazelnut gelato is nuttier than it is sweet and flavorfully anchors the lightness of the mousse.

As its cozy, sparkling interior will confirm, Café Bonaparte is awake and alert to what seduces Americans about the French. Thus even the sprightly cocktails follow pop-French themes, with names like "Le Rendez-Vous" and "Amelie," and wines from the glass come from a capable, decently priced list. Better than both are the strong espresso and coffee blends brewed at the bar. Their aroma conjures a bewitching Parisian haze, and even non-smokers will be tempted to light up a stylish slim and bask in the glory of it all. –JC

# Café Citron

A hot Latin club and happy-hour locale that serves
mean drinks and lame food

| 3.5 | 8.5 |
|---|---|
| Food | Feel |

## Nuevo Latino

Casual restaurant

**$35**

*Price*

www.cafecitrondc.com

Mon–Thu 4pm–midnight
Fri–Sat 4pm–1am

**Bar** Beer, wine, liquor
**Credit cards** Visa, MC, AmEx
**Reservations** Accepted
Live music, veg-friendly

**Dupont**
1343 Connecticut Ave. NW
(202) 530-8844

Café Citron is a hotspot, a place where the good-looking (and sometimes the not-so-good-looking) go to down mojitos, dance to live salsa, and eat fried plantains, usually in that order. The multilevel-but-still-cozy place is dimly lit with all sorts of light fixtures (sometimes color-changing…) and candles in huge vases; antique mirrors line the back of the bar giving depth to the narrow space.

The combination of the blasting Latin music, the array of bartenders muddling limes and mint and sugar, and the ubiquitous DC politicos trying their pickup lines on anything that moves makes for a bar scene that feels like a cross between a hot Miami nightclub and the Republican National Convention. Luckily, though, the music is so loud that you can almost ignore your fellow eaters and drinkers.

Speaking of drinking, this place produces wonderfully strong—maybe the strongest in town—mojitos and caipirinhas (by the glass or by the pitcher) which are individually and expertly made by the bartenders using large plexiglass muddlers—a show in and of itself. By the end of the night, and sometimes earlier, shots of tequila and bottles of Dos Equis replace the handcrafted drinks.

The overly long menu of vaguely Latin-themed food at Café Citron should be consumed on a need-only basis. To put it nicely, it goes better with strong drinks and a bit of a buzz than with sobriety and a discerning palate. Fried zucchini and yellow squash are surprisingly good and addictive, but items like quesadillas, fried plantains, and fajitas are well below average—fried foods are soggy, meats are tough—but satisfy the craving for greasy Latin food. The island shrimp cocktail—seven large shrimp rolled in salsa and served in that same salsa with tortilla chips and a few chunks of avocado—is boring and lazy. But it's not nearly as bad as the horrifically fishy, chewy ceviche, perhaps the worst we've ever tasted. And we've tasted a lot of ceviche.

Then again, nobody really goes to Café Citron for the food. They go for the samba and the salsa, the mojitos, and the caipirinhas, and everything that results therefrom. –SDC

# Café Divan

A cozy, charming Turkish restaurant with more
highs than lows—and good feelings, too

**7.4** | **8.6**
Food | Feel

## Turkish

Casual restaurant

**$35**
Price

www.cafedivan.com

Sun–Thu 11am–10:30pm
Fri–Sat 11am–11pm

**Bar** Beer, wine, liquor
**Credit cards** Visa, MC, AmEx
**Reservations** Accepted
Kid-friendly, veg-friendly, Wi-Fi

**Glover Park**
1834 Wisconsin Ave. NW
(202) 338-1747

Walk into Café Divan and you're bound to be charmed. This small, awkwardly shaped Turkish restaurant in upper Georgetown sort of embraces you as you fill its small space. Large windows look out onto Wisconsin Avenue, and choice banquettes fill every nook and cranny. Old and young couples, families, and groups of friends show up for the pretty good Turkish food.

A meal here begins, quite delightfully, with addictive, freshly baked, still-warm bread that you can dip into extra-virgin olive oil. It's a reminder that the custom of dipping bread into olive oil is (insofar as it's derived from any foreign cuisine at all) probably more Southern Mediterranean than it is Italian. If you're as much of a sucker for sampler platters as we are, get the mixed meze platter for one or two, which allows you to sample the dolmade (uninspired), hummus (pleasantly tangy), feta (briny and fresh), lentil kofte (tart and chewy), and sigara borek (oozing with feta cheese and parsley).

After that, the standout dish is the yogurtlu kebab. Thin slices of beef tenderloin, crisp and caramelized, are slathered in yogurt and tomato sauce and served over homemade pita bread, the perfect sponge for all the drippy goodness. Rotisserie lamb, a Thursday night exclusive, is also a real treat: a whole lamb is cooked for hours over charcoal until it's practically falling apart; then it's deboned and served with homemade yogurt and rice pilaf. The lamb is mildly spiced but truly wonderful—even if its boiled vegetables merely serve as unattractive scenery on the plate. Some other dishes, such as the koy chicken, need a bit of a kick. Fried eggplant with yogurt sauce tends to be greasy and underseasoned.

Desserts, whether Turkish or not (peach melba? chocolate mousse?), aren't great. Finish your meal instead with strong, sweet Turkish coffee. And don't be shy; linger at Café Divan for a while. It's not every day that you get a cozy window seat with a view. –SDC

# Café du Parc

Expertly prepared classic French dishes in an enchanting setting

**8.6** Food  **9.3** Feel

## French

Upmarket restaurant **$60** Price

www.cafeduparc.com

| | | |
|---|---|---|
| Mon–Fri 7:30am–10:30am, noon–2pm, 6pm–10pm Sat–Sun 7am–11am, noon–2:30pm, 6pm–10:30pm | **Bar** Beer, wine, liquor **Credit cards** Visa, MC, AmEx **Reservations** Accepted Date-friendly, good wines, outdoor dining, Wi-Fi | **Downtown** 1401 Pennsylvania Ave. NW (202) 942-7000 |

If you stroll for long enough along Pennsylvania Avenue, you will eventually find yourself at the imposing Willard InterContinental Hotel overlooking Pershing Park. And at the foot of this imposing hotel you'll see the über-French Café du Parc, where you'll long to enjoy a meal at the alfresco tables shaded by bright blue umbrellas. But you might resist sitting at one of these tempting tables for fear that the food will be mediocre and overpriced and the service worse still. But resist your prejudicial intuitions and give it a shot. Go ahead; take a seat and order. You will be more than just pleasantly surprised.

As clichéd as it sounds, this bistro feels like Paris. The kitchen even turns out dainty pastries in between meals. The French waitstaff can be a bit pedantic but also helpful and knowledgeable. Small, round tables fill the patio.

Perhaps in part due to the influence of an Alsatian chef that was brought in to reinvent the Willard's whole culinary concept, this food is authentically French, too. Bright greens in the "salade du parc" are topped with bacon, comté cheese, buttery croutons, and a delicate poached egg. This larger, more modern version of frisée et làrdons is a satisfying lunch meal that works beautifully as a dinner appetizer. A heaping bowl of succulent steamed mussels lounging in a shallot, parsley, garlic, white wine bath come with a basket of frites that beg to be dipped in this glorious pool.

But perhaps the best dish we had here (and one of the best dishes in DC, period) is the 24-hour sous-vide pork, which has a decadent layer of fat and an audibly crisp salt-crusted exterior. Sitting in a shallow pool of thyme and garlic jus, it is a gorgeous specimen, the ideal combination of meltingly tender meat and salty crackly skin. This is black-tie comfort food, served with your choice of impeccable side dish (potato purée, noodles in butter, green lentils, or cauliflower gratin). For dessert, we encourage you to indulge in the oversized French macaroon, which is filled with whipped cream and berries and served with a rich berry sorbet—a phenomenal, über-French end to an über-French meal.

When it comes to wine, take advantage of the knowledgeable sommelier, who focuses on lesser-known boutique wineries of France. Preconceived notions be damned. –SDC

# Café Luna

Simple food that needs to grow up a bit

| 4.3 | 6.5 |
|-----|-----|
| Food | Feel |

## American, Italian

Casual restaurant

**$35**
*Price*

www.skewers-cafeluna.com

Daily 10am–10pm

**Bar** Beer, wine, liquor
**Credit cards** Visa, MC, AmEx
**Reservations** Not accepted
Delivery, live music, outdoor
dining, veg-friendly, Wi-Fi

**Dupont**
1633 P St. NW
(202) 387-4005

Café Luna is unpretentious, unassuming, and quite frankly un-delicious. It tugs at the heartstrings to pan a place that's as cozy, as friendly, and serves food as cute as does Luna, so we'll offer this disclaimer: if you're after coziness, friendliness, and cute food, go here. If you're looking for flavor, don't bother.

Café Luna serves dishes a bit like what your college sweetheart might have cooked a couple of months after graduation, in the kitchen of his first apartment. His general recipe probably went something like this: 1. Cook pasta. 2. Warm pre-made sauce. 3. Sauté chopped veggies. 4. Mix together; grate mild cheese on top. The preparation may be endearing, even touching, but the experience might inspire you to give him a cookbook and a couple of months—and bolt.

Your manners and the charm of the basement dining room, which features low lights and a kitchen you can look straight into, might keep you seated at Café Luna, even if the flight instinct hits when you're handed the menu: a cutesy cartoon heart denotes "healthy" and a yin-and-yang means a dish is vegetarian. Cuisine options veer dangerously from Italianesque to Chinese-like, careening past gazpacho and plunging into Greek salad. Vegetables are referred to as "veggies."

The pasta dishes taste like little more than ordinary red sauce on noodles. The pesto is made with too much cream, and only hints at basil. The bruschetta is just as simple: toasted sourdough topped with chopped tomatoes and oil; Luna can hardly be bothered to add basil, olives, or other accoutrements. If nothing else, the fried calamari offer a greasy counterpoint to the combinations of otherwise bland vegetables doused in olive oil.

Luna also lets you "build your own" pizza, pasta dish, or omelette: you choose the base or type of pasta (angel hair, penne, etc.), then choose toppings. So there's no intellectual capital, no authoritative creativity, no skillful execution…just where is what the consultants might call the "value add?" If you want a home-cooked meal, why not cook it at home—or better yet—why not ring a college sweetheart? By now, chances are good he's learned a few more kitchen tricks than Luna. –CK

# Café Milano

**6.1** Food  **6.5** Feel

Overpriced Italian dishes at a touristy Georgetown restaurant. What else is new?

## Italian

Upmarket restaurant

**$75** Price

www.cafemilano.net

Mon–Tue 11:30am–midnight
Wed–Sat 11:30am–1am
Sun 11:30am–11pm

**Bar** Beer, wine, liquor
**Credit cards** Visa, MC, AmEx
**Reservations** Accepted
Outdoor dining, veg-friendly

**Georgetown**
3251 Prospect St. NW
(202) 333-6183

The general consensus about Café Milano is that it is expensive. Not pricey—expensive. We aren't the types to complain when a superb, memorable meal is priced accordingly; but when it seems as though you're paying more to be seen than to eat, we begin to get annoyed.

Packed with expense accounts, tourists seeking out the upscale Georgetown scene, and overly primped women, this wannabe hotspot needs to loosen its red-and-blue tie a bit. If you do go, insist on an outdoor table, which will at least provide for some entertaining people-watching and will allow you to avoid some of the dining-room stuffiness.

Most ingredients (prosciutto, tomato and mozzarella, for instance) are of high quality. But sometimes, the menu totally trips up: a salad of steamed vegetables, tuna tartare and a lemon basil mustard sauce is bewildering not only for the ill-fated pairing of flavors, but also because this small dish costs $15. Pizzas are just fine, but at four slices for $17, you come to expect great.

Delicate homemade pastas are clearly the specialty. Orecchiette with rabe, pork sausage, and pecorino is a dish you see everywhere, but it's a good way to go here. Classic Italian desserts are fine. But when it comes to wines, expect to pay upwards of $12 by the glass and upwards of $50 by the bottle.

In the end, there's little excuse for this level of execution for these prices. Even touristy Georgetown is capable of much better. –SDC

# Café Olé

**6.5** Food  **7.8** Feel

An un-fussy, inexpensive, just plain fun spot for outdoor cocktails and small plates

## Middle Eastern, American

Casual restaurant

**$30** Price

www.cafeoledc.com

Sun–Thu 11am–9pm
Fri–Sat 11am–10pm

**Bar** Beer, wine, liquor
**Credit cards** Visa, MC, AmEx
**Reservations** Not accepted
Date-friendly, kid-friendly, outdoor dining, veg-friendly

**Upper NW**
4000 Wisconsin Ave. NW
(202) 244-1330

Happy hour at Café Olé has the casual, effortless feeling of a cocktail party thrown by your best friend. The vibe is relaxed, the service is honest and friendly, the drinks are large and plentiful, and the food is creative without being overdone. We wish we could throw parties like this.

This Tenleytown favorite, unlike some so-called "Mediterranean" places that are really just Middle Eastern, actually tries to dabble in every Mediterranean cuisine in existence, with varying results. The prices, at least, are affordable enough to merit a celebration of their own. Each small meze plate is just $6 to $8, and the portions are generous enough to accommodate sharing. Order two plates per person and no one will go home hungry. The cold sampler platter offers both traditional and black-bean hummus, a lemony baba ghanoush studded with pieces of eggplant rather than puréed, and a chunky house tapenade that's (happily) mostly harissa, preserved lemon, and pine nuts. The substantial pita chips are a great vehicle.

Our favorite of the meze is the Lebanese-style lamb shawarma—savory, spicy, juicy morsels of meat served over lettuce and tomato with lots of garlicky yogurt and pita. "Spanish Gold" is a forgettable riff on paella that's based on orzo instead of rice; while the sausage and seafood are tasty, creamy tomato aioli mutes the flavor. Sicilian tuna kebabs come out overcooked, which the savory depth of the unmistakably Mediterranean flavors of tomato and olive can't rescue.

Happy hour means generous drink specials like $10 sangría pitchers, but even afterwards, there are plenty of $5 glasses of wine and a narrow selection of domestic and imported beers to get you through the night. This neighborhood café has no delusions or pretensions, sticking instead to drinkable, affordable beverages. The short wine list offers little more than mainstream selections, but refreshingly, at press time, no bottle was over $30. The beer list is likewise limited to eight or ten selections, most under $5. Cocktails, whether classic gin fizz or gimmicky "Blue Blue Martini," run an equally reasonable $7.

At these prices, and in this unpretentious, laid-back atmosphere, it's hard to get too upset that the desserts are trucked in from Patisserie Poupon down the street. Finish your meal with an Illy espresso, and enjoy the fact that you won't have to clean up after this party. –CD

# Café Pizzaiolo

Great beer and wine, solid pizza—it's a good-luck charm

| 7.3 | 7.0 |
|:---:|:---:|
| Food | Feel |

## Pizza, Sandwiches

Casual restaurant

| $35 |
|:---:|
| Price |

www.cafepizzaiolo.com

Mon–Thu 10:30am–9:30pm
Fri–Sat 10:30am–10pm
Sun noon–9pm
Hours vary by location

**Bar** Beer, wine
**Credit cards** Visa, MC, AmEx
**Reservations** Not accepted
Delivery, good wines, kid-friendly,
veg-friendly, Wi-Fi

**Arlington, VA**
507 23rd St. S.
(703) 894-2250

**Alexandria, VA**
3112 Mt. Vernon Ave.
(703) 837-0666

The Arlington branch of Café Pizzaiolo sits on one of the accursed spots in the world of commerce: a storefront that, like a bachelor with roving eyes, cannot seem to keep the same occupant for more than a season or two. In distant memory, the 23rd Street joint was a sheet-music-and-saxophone vendor; more recently, a coffeeshop.

If anyone has half a chance at achieving longevity in spite of the odds, it's Pizzaiolo. We can't comment on its ability to overcome the curse of a bad corner (although the rest of 23rd Street seems to be booming), but as far as food is concerned, the café has a lot going for it.

For starters, Pizzaiolo's beer and wine selection is exemplary. We've found a few rare picks—including the Hemingway-inspired Two Hearted Ale—from Bell's Brewery in Michigan, along with a small but thoughtful range of other bottles, sold individually to drink in the café, or by the six-pack to go. For wine drinkers, Pizzaiolo might double as a wine purveyor. Although its selection is inclined toward simpler wines, and you can't expect as much input from the staff as you would in a store, there is a range of good reds, each accompanied by a short tasting note. Pizzaiolo even offers a discount on six or 12 bottles purchased at a time.

The café is a lovely spot to while away an evening or afternoon, whether with beer and wine, coffee, pizza, dessert, or some combination of the above. The single room is airy and well-lit, and there is a rotating showcase of (above-average) works from local artists. In one corner is a messy stack of board games and newspapers—a lone spot of disorder in an otherwise spotless establishment.

We're not quite sure what Pizzaiolo means by "Stone Hearth NY and Neapolitan Style Pizza," but the result is tasty: the crust is thin and white, with a touch of sourdough, the red sauce is applied with a feathered touch. The Neapolitan features rounds of fresh mozzarella, with the option to add slowly-caramelized red onions or any variety of fresh meats and vegetables.

Perhaps South Eads and 23rd has finally found its mate. –CK

# Café Saint-Ex

A drawn-up and whimsical restaurant that's more fun than tasty

**6.2** Food   **9.4** Feel

## French, American

Casual restaurant   **$40** Price

www.saint-ex.com

Mon 5pm–1:30am
Tue–Thu 11am–1:30am
Fri–Sat 11am–2:30am
Sun 11am–1:30am

**Bar** Beer, wine, liquor
**Credit cards** Visa, MC, AmEx
**Reservations** Not accepted
Date-friendly, kid-friendly, outdoor dining

**U Street**
1847 18th St. NW
(202) 265-7839

Named for the aviator and writer Antoine Saint-Éxupery, who once flew for the Aéropostale and wrote *The Little Prince*, Café Saint-Ex is a restaurant with a profound sense of identity. For those grownups who are no longer interested in anything but figures, here are a few flowery details: in a little corner house, flanked by an outdoor deck and vigilant host stand, the place always seems to bustle with activity. Whether it's kings, tipplers, businessmen, lamplighters, geographers, or just people who gather in its basement to dance, Saint-Ex is a lively little planet of its own.

The décor reflects its personality. Wooden pilot propellers and other aviation parts festoon the walls, and stickers from around the world pepper the walls of the basement like a trunk. On the menu, Southern dishes mingle with Belgian beers and eco-friendly options. A perpetual favorite includes the hulking fried-green-tomato BLT, a masterpiece of delicious elements brought together by virtue of surrounding bread. The bacon is thick and chunky and more meaty than crisp. The tomatoes add softness and warmth (literally) to the sandwich. The bread is a bit thick for the sandwich, but perhaps the bacon demands this.

A meaty pork tenderloin is topped with tangy, crunchy marmalade that brings fruity zing to the chop. A unique dessert of brown-sugar oat sandwiches brings class and an adult palate to the ice-cream sandwich. Oat tuilles are dipped in rich caramel and filled with lemon ice cream. They are creamy, sweet, and small enough to enjoy without feeling sick.

A note of warning: The cooking at Saint-Ex is not always superb, and some dishes read better than they taste. You'd expect mussels with chilies, cilantro, and lime to be zesty and light, but instead, the broth brings out the bitterness in the flesh. Sweet-potato fries are not that grand, either—they can come out soft instead of crisp. You must endure the presence of two or three caterpillars if you wish to become acquainted with the butterflies—so these things can be borne.

All men are stars, and for different men, Café Saint-Ex will represent different things. However, for many, it will be a place of solace, warmth, and fun. –JC

# Café Tu-O-Tu

A tasty little café that's worn at the edges in all the right ways

**7.7** Food  **8.6** Feel

## Turkish, Sandwiches

Counter service

**$15** Price

www.cafetuotu.com

Mon–Fri 9am–7pm
Sat 10am–7pm
Sun 10am–6pm

**Bar** None
**Credit cards** Visa, MC, AmEx
Date-friendly, delivery, kid-friendly,
outdoor dining, veg-friendly, Wi-Fi

**Georgetown**
2816 Pennsylvania Ave. NW
(202) 298-7777

Café Tu-O-Tu's website plays a breezy soundtrack of João Gilberto tunes. It may seem a little odd for a restaurant with a Turkish twist, but the soundtrack encapsulates both the food and the feel of this odd little café on the edge of Georgetown. Located in a cozy house, Tu-O-Tu is a place where most people wouldn't mind living. The stereo playing cheerful world music skips affectionately, and crockery looks well-worn and well-loved. Particularly wonderful is the backyard patio, fitted with cushioned benches and flower beds, and atinkle with wind chimes. It has a lazy, familiar feel—books, magazines, and laptops lie around haphazardly and the hum of the generator next door is oddly soothing.

Tu-O-Tu's menu centers on salads, wraps, and sandwiches. Ingredients are fresh and combinations are satisfyingly substantial. For example, a wrap is crammed full of smooth smoked salmon, creamy herb spread, sprouts, and tomato chunks. The quantities are well composed—the mark of a good sandwich—with crunchy sprouts adding a little bite to the rich salmon and juicy tomato. The spread is thick and well distributed, moistening each bite and taking the edge off the fish.

Particularly satisfying are the small dishes, labeled "appetizers," including baked eggplant stuffed with onions, garlic, and parsley, roasted until tender, and served cold. Mixed vegetables are soft and tender, with pools of olive oil waiting to be soaked up by hunks of bread. The "Dip It" pairs finger-scorchingly hot pita slices with three spreads, each better than the next: sweet, smoky red pepper and garlic in cheese; a classic pesto as good as any fresh version; and a bold, punchy sun-dried tomato paste. Each is so good that you'll want to buy it in a jar to use in your own dishes.

Sandwiches go well with the strong coffee Tu-O-Tu brews, including a grainy-sandy Turkish version, or with some of the rarer imported beverages like Turkish soda and yogurt drinks. Desserts are limited to ordinary cookies and brownies, and baklava that is disappointingly slick.

For anyone looking for a hidden place to relax and pass an afternoon, Café Tu-O-Tu offers a welcome, homey retreat. You're almost tempted to pack a bag and move in for good. –CK

# Cakelove and Love Café

Lovely cakes sold at sky-high prices

**7.0** Food

**6.7** Feel

## Baked goods, Sandwiches

Café **$10** Price

www.cakelove.com

Mon–Fri 8:30am–7pm
Sat 10am–5pm
Hours vary by location

**Bar** None
**Credit cards** Visa, MC, AmEx
Delivery, kid-friendly, veg-friendly

**U Street**
1506 U St. NW
(202) 588-7100

**Arlington, VA**
4150 Campbell Ave.
(703) 933-0099

**Silver Spring, MD**
935 Ellsworth Dr.
(301) 565-2253

**Tysons Corner, VA**
1961 Chain Bridge Rd.
(703) 442-4880

In a town where how much you care can often be benchmarked by how much money you give, a bakery like Cakelove—which charges unheard-of prices for cakes, yet somehow gets people to fork it over—is hardly unusual. If the warm, fuzzy history of the business can sound cloying, the cakes and other creations, fortunately, are anything but.

Cakelove is the love child of an ex-lawyer and Ivy League grad (again, hardly an anomaly in DC) who decided that litigation wasn't nearly as interesting as baking delicious cakes (quite a bit more of an anomaly). Cakelove produces massive pink-and-white creations which look as if they've been plucked from an Alice in Wonderland scene (perhaps the Mad Hatter's tea party), complete with decadent frosting, oversized adornments, and life-defying proportions.

Layer cakes are the most popular format for the store's creations, although wedding cakes and cupcake trees are a close second and third. The formula is generally the same for each: a light (buttery but not dense, slightly sweet and never dry) cake, coupled with rich, creamy frosting that bursts with sugar and other clear, focused flavors (such as coffee or vanilla buttercream). Cupcakes come with a generous smothering of the same frosting (the pink variety tastes something like raspberries without being too fruity, and a lot like fresh cream) atop the same cake. Unfortunately, Cakelove's cupcakes are not immune from the classic cupcake scourge of dry bottoms. (We still don't get America's cupcake obsession.) The store's excellent cookies are made with extra brown sugar and butter, and large chocolate chips.

Across the street at the Love Café, you can order cookies and cupcakes, dressed with a frosting of your choice, along with middling sandwiches and lunch items, appropriately decadent hot chocolate, and a good selection of teas. The café itself is somewhat sterile, however, and the service isn't particularly friendly.

The major downside is financial, not fluffy. Sure, the cakes will sate both taste buds and guilt (the owner donates a part of proceeds to help young entrepreneurs). But these prices are *high*; on the bright side, thought, at least they're cheaper than litigation. –CK

# California Tortilla

A caricatured version of California except the part about good burritos

| 2.8 | 3.0 |
|-----|-----|
| Food | Feel |

## Mexican

Counter service  **$10**
*Price*

www.californiatortilla.com

Mon–Thu 11am–10pm
Fri–Sat 11am–11pm
Sun 11am–9pm
Hours vary by location

**Bar** Beer
**Credit cards** Visa, MC
Kid-friendly

**Chinatown**
728 7th St. NW
(202) 638-2233

**Cleveland Park**
3501 Connecticut Ave. NW
(202) 244-2447

**Arlington, VA**
2057 Wilson Blvd.
(703) 243-4151

**Additional locations**
and more features at
www.fearlesscritic.com

Entering the downtown outpost of California Tortilla, with its luridly bold colors, black and white checks, and stark neon lighting, feels eerily similar to walking onto the set of Saved by the Bell—specifically, the Max, that preferred hangout of Zach, Kelly, Slater, and Screech.

This place is just as hard to stomach, but the two or three kinds of beer they serve will help. The menu includes all of the expected fast-food Mexican basics, as well as ill-advised "specialty burritos" that incorporate gringo ingredients like wing sauce, ranch dressing, and "tangy vinaigrette." America's fusion craze has officially gone too far. A Thai chicken burrito (aside from sounding grotesque) combines spicy peanut sauce with salsa and lettuce. Its bad, cheap flavor reminds you why you don't see this in more places.

Queso, a Tex-Mex rather than Cal-Mex invention, is Velveeta-esque: gooey and thick, with a penchant for forming a rubbery skin as it cools. Fajitas are gloppy on Styrofoam plates, the beef so overcooked that it's chewy, and slathered in something like…barbecue sauce? Vegetables are mushy and black beans are sludgy; both get precipitously worse as they cool.

The best thing about your meal will be obliterating it with some of the available hot sauces that range from the standard to the bizarre. If you are at all curious, you may find yourself trying to get through all of them. Particularly interesting are some sweet hot sauces like "Apple Sass" and "Mango Meltdown" (from the Maui Pepper Company) and "Toad Sweat's Key Lime Dessert Hot Sauce." The former are interesting enough to make you consider eating more of your burrito; the latter, despite tasting a bit like cough syrup, is arrestingly tingly.

There are many better options even for mediocre, chain Mexican food in DC. If you feel a particular need to sample dozens of hot sauces, it might be worth a visit, but that's the only reason we'd advise going. –JC

# Camille's Sidewalk Café

Fast-food goes nouvelle-Californian—we
recommend that you stick to the smoothies

| 4.5 | 6.0 |
|---|---|
| Food | Feel |

## Sandwiches, Baked goods

Café **$25**
Price

www.camillescafe.com

Mon–Fri 7am–8pm
Sat–Sun 10am–7pm

**Bar** None
**Credit cards** Visa, MC, AmEx
Delivery, outdoor dining,
veg-friendly, Wi-Fi

**Penn Quarter**
650 F St. NW
(202) 639-9727

**Downtown**
1420 New York Ave. NW
(202) 737-9727

Camille's fits in well in the middle of workaday Washington: it's healthy, quick, and an unabashed child of the chain-restaurant world. Although the classic ornaments of a massive chain still dominate Camille's Verizon Center shop (the menu is standardized across locations, the napkins and cups are branded with the Camille's logo, and requests for ingredient substitutions are met with hesitation), the menu and atmosphere cling to the delusion that Camille's is above all that.

But it's not. Camille's was started as a small café in the plains states, has since expanded to 35 U.S. states; and is eyeing various locations in Latin America. The food is American chic, with a few Wolfgang-Puck-and-progeny touches such as flatbread pizza and panini. All of the ingredients are fresh, and the pairings between meats, vegetables, and cheeses are made with an eye on current fads. The "Bangkok Thai" wrap, for example, is stuffed with an only slightly unpredictable mix of chicken, provolone (?!), water chestnuts, spouts, carrots, and crunchy bits of noodle. It's a disappointingly flat attempt at Asian fusion.

But the panini are Camille's *most* disappointing option. The sandwiches are generally pre-made (so you can't ask for extra tomatoes, or for the mayonnaise to be held), and toasted when you place your order. The habanero turkey is overstuffed (which is a nice, filling touch, even if it deviates from the European-style panini) with middling meat; and cheese, which emerges in a drippy, orange ooze, is only one or two notches up from pre-sliced American. Camille's also aims to improve upon its fast-food roots by offering a handful of dry tricolor corn chips and a pot of (very ordinary) homemade salsa in lieu of fries or chips.

Camille's smoothies, on the other hand, are fresh and delicious. The drinks are gently sweetened with honey rather than syrup or ice cream. The banana-berry flavor, especially, is well-proportioned and refreshing, making it a better choice than what can be found at strictly-smoothie franchises. But for sandwiches, why not go somewhere local? The bread will be better, the cheese less industrial, and the corporate logos less overbearing. –CK

# Cantina Marina

It's five o'clock somewhere...

**7.2** Food **8.0** Feel

## Southern

Casual restaurant **$35** Price

www.cantinamarina.com

Tue–Sun noon–10pm

**Bar** Beer, wine, liquor
**Credit cards** Visa, MC, AmEx
**Reservations** Not accepted
Date-friendly, kid-friendly, outdoor
dining, Wi-Fi

**Southwest DC**
600 Water St. SW
(202) 554-8396

Most of the restaurants on the Southwest waterfront are pretty dubious. It's hard to imagine they do enough business to be anything other than a money-laundering front. Cantina Marina is a ray of (neon) light in this sketchy gloom. Once you find the place (travel down a path from Water Street), it looks exactly like the name suggests: a fun waterside bar with draft beers in plastic cups and Jimmy Buffett playing on the speakers. Listening to the Potomac waters slap the concrete deck of this lime-green-and-turquoise cantina is about as close to Margaritaville as DC gets.

Aside from the spring-break vibe (we should mention it's closed during the winter) of fake palm trees and parrots, there's an eclectic mix of ages and financial statures. Game nights are pretty riotous here.

The generally Gulf-oriented food is much better than you'd expect: gumbo, catfish, po' boys, and so on. Baja-California-style tacos are served open-faced on corn tortillas and topped with fried shrimp (gloriously light), a tangy cabbage slaw, and a dollop of sour cream. Crab balls come small, loose, and hot from the fryer, and are a fun cross between croquettes and crab cakes. The cornmeal is thick enough to keep the crabmeat together without being too much filler, and a duo of tangy garlic mayo and lemony olive oil makes a nice accompaniment. If fried seafood isn't your bag, there's the ubiquitous lineup of linguine with white clam sauce, New York strip steak, and chicken-fried steak, all of which are decent, though not exactly life-changing.

Dessert is totally unrelated to this oddball cuisine, except that it, too, takes nothing seriously. In other words: Snickers pie with a huge bowl of ice cream. It's chunky with peanuts, slick with caramel, rich with chocolate. You'll want to eat it until you're sick, as you did when you were a kid. Oh, nostalgia!

If the lofty menus and high expectations of your adulthood ever get you down, come have a margarita and watch the sun move over the water. Bring your flip flops; leave your expectations. –JC

# Capital Grille

Dry-aged steaks derailed by unnecessary jus at
Darden Restaurants' latest acquisition

**6.5** *Food*  **7.0** *Feel*

## Steakhouse, American

Upmarket restaurant

**$85** *Price*

www.thecapitalgrille.com

Mon–Thu 11:30am–3pm, 5pm–
10pm; Fri–Sat 11:30am–3pm,
5pm–11pm; Sun 5pm–10pm
Hours vary by location

**Bar** Beer, wine, liquor
**Credit cards** Visa, MC, AmEx
**Reservations** Accepted

**Penn Quarter**
601 Pennsylvania Ave. NW
(202) 737-6200

**Tysons Corner, VA**
1861 International Dr.
(703) 448-3900

The pride of RARE Hospitality International, Inc. (which was acquired by Darden Restaurants, parent of the Olive Garden and Red Lobster chains), is often mistakenly assumed to be a DC original (it actually started in Providence, RI). Its 34 locations pulled in more than $8.1 million in revenues per chain branch in 2008, according to its annual report.

You'd assume a giant metal bald eagle, regally perched between kitchen and dining room, to be tongue-in-cheek at most restaurants. Likewise for a room full of somber Americana, like pious John-Singer-Sargent-like portraits of dead white men, and sweeping manifest-destiny landscapes. Not here. Maybe there's something about listing on the NASDAQ that renders the restaurant business a touch less wacky. Here's a taste of the annual report: "A 4.4 percent decrease in same-restaurant guest counts [was] partially offset by a 3.3 percent increase in average guest check." This particular American culinary Dream—Darden's 2008 revenues were$6.63 billion—seems about as humorless as the expression on the eagle's face.

Lighting is appropriately dim, service appropriately fawning, and seating appropriately posh, but culinary fireworks don't often result when a restaurant group is run by businesspeople, not chefs. Rather, the focus is on producing nothing out of the ordinary. Amongst starters, fried calamari aren't bad, getting a welcome kick from hot cherry peppers. That's where the fun ends, though. The cold shellfish platter is a pricey disappointment, and lobster and crab cakes are bland. In a sad concession to small-town tastes, they hard-boil the egg in the steak tartare instead of using the proper raw egg. Prosciutto-wrapped mozzarella is flavorless, and lobster bisque is creamy but not very complex or interesting. We can only wonder which member of the Board was behind the fatal mistake of drowning dry-aged ribeyes and sirloins with Capital's "jus," an aggressive, cheap-tasting glaze that distinctly evokes cafeteria roast beef. Broiled, dry-aged steaks, including Capital's, deserve deferential treatment: they should be served with nothing but salt, pepper, and perhaps butter.

Darden stock might make a good addition to your portfolio, but at dinnertime, your corporate credit card would be better used elsewhere. –RG

# Capitol City Brewery

**6.6** Food  **7.0** Feel

A beer lover's delight, and the food even hits some of the right notes

## American

Casual restaurant

**$35** Price

www.capcitybrew.com

Sun–Thu 11am–11pm
Fri–Sat 11am–midnight
Hours vary by location

**Bar** Beer, wine, liquor
**Credit cards** Visa, MC, AmEx
**Reservations** Accepted

**Downtown**
1100 New York Ave. NW
(202) 628-2222

**Capitol Hill**
2 Massachusetts Ave. NE
(202) 842-2337

**Arlington, VA**
4001 Campbell Ave.
(703) 578-3888

A good beer, like a good attitude, goes a long way, and Capitol City is lucky enough to have both. Together, they allow you to forgive the place its bumbling blonde waitresses, the super-sizing of the "local brewery" concept, and the fact that the wide-screen TVs are always tuned to C-SPAN. Then again, this is DC.

The three Washington locations all have open floor plans, excellent lighting, a genuine if bouncy staff, and tables big enough to accommodate your beer, food, and elbows. This is no dive bar. The downtown branch has high ceilings and copper vats behind the bar; on summer nights, a keg is tapped outside, pints are $3 until the brew runs out, and the spacious patio makes a fine drinking outpost.

Not to mention, you'll be drinking some of the finest micro brewed ales and lagers in the city. Capitol City has a half-dozen standard brews and rotates in other choices seasonally, and you can always count on a selection of at least ten beers in a number of styles. The Prohibition Porter is a perennial favorite, as is the superlatively hoppy Imperial IPA.

But perhaps you came for a meal. Capitol City's food is above average in the realm of upscale beer gardens, but don't expect your crab-cake sandwich to form the basis for lasting memories. The brewery goes beyond the classic burger-and-wood-oven-pizza spread, with such offerings as "Bayou Jambalaya" and "South of Philly Steak and Cheese." Despite the ubiquitous geographical tags, there is no pretense of authenticity. Capitol City knows its "Hofbrau Bratwurst Sandwich" is squarely American, and the extensive description (each item of the menu is panned in full sentences) includes the proud disclaimer that the sausage comes on a hoagie roll with a pickle spear. But no matter: the meat (and roll) is damn good.

The salads, especially the perfectly-proportioned Cobb, are better than most, and the Texas Chili Nachos are magnificent, with beef, cheese, and guacamole cascading down a mountain of tricolor chips. An often overlooked value is Capitol City's selection of sides: for $2, you can't afford *not* to order the enormous plate of sweet-potato fries—especially as an accompaniment to beer, which is the main reason to frequent Capitol City, after all. –CK

# Carlyle

A caricature of American dining that makes safe anything but sound

**6.9** *Food*  **7.0** *Feel*

## New American

Casual restaurant

**$40** *Price*

www.greatamericanrestaurants.com

Mon 11am–10:30pm; Tue–Thu 11am–11pm; Fri 11am–midnight; Sat 10am–midnight; Sun 9:30am–10:30pm

**Bar** Beer, wine, liquor
**Credit cards** Visa, MC, AmEx
**Reservations** Accepted
Kid-friendly, outdoor dining

**Arlington, VA**
4000 Campbell Ave.
(703) 931-0777

Carlyle is the Cadillac of suburban family dining. It's got manor-sized dining rooms in prime real estate, giant booths backed by large sturdy mirrors, sassy Art Deco posters framed and hung about, and, well, it's got a similarly aristocratic name.

Indeed, in all of its glossy grandeur, Carlyle could very well be a caricature of American dining. From the unfocused melting pot of its menu (Tex-Mex egg rolls?), to its shock-and-awe assault on the palate, the Carlyle has all the elements of a well-produced commercial: impersonal, glossy, plastic, and aggressive.

The food here is about as subtle as a punch in the face, but it's quite consistent for a chain. This is especially true at brunch, when you're less concerned with subtlety and more on having fun and getting your fix. And by "fix," we mean an amazing chocolate waffle that will win over even the savory-brunch-only crowd. The service is great—another brunch boon—and it's more than worth a trip on a Sunday afternoon.

But at night, things are less clear. Lobster bisque is a tangy, smooth sea of dependable, consistent, and wholly boring flavor. It is so un-fishy and un-briny that its saltiness is more evocative of canned tomato soup than anything from the sea. Shrimp and grits are an unmitigated disaster: the shrimp is overcooked and doused in Velveeta-thick sauce; add to this a hog's worth of pancetta seeping in the rapidly-congealing goo in which sad little kernels of corn beg for rescue.

Grit cakes are marvelously textured—crisp melting into fluffy—but who would bother when they're so salty that each bite requires half a glass of water? Cheers to the Carlyle for baking their own bread (next door at their Best Buns bakery), but even with this, the place can't escape a non-specific identity, the inescapable fact of being the offspring of a restaurant group.

Dessert is a supreme emblem of trite overindulgence—a passion for anything that can give you diabetes and a heart attack in one fell swoop, regardless of its flavor. The furiously praised bread pudding is a mess. All cloying sweetness and no flavor, all mush and no chew; even the ice cream is freezer-burned.

But in general, Carlyle, like the Cadillac, might have once been impressive—a dependable status symbol. Now, it's more of a Sunday driver. —JC

# Cashion's Eat Place

**7.9** Food  **9.4** Feel

A hip, chef-driven Adams Morgan standby for trusty food and cozy fun

## New American

Upmarket restaurant

**$60** Price

www.cashionseatplace.com

Tue 5:30pm–10pm
Wed–Sat 5:30pm–11pm
Sun 11:30am–2:30pm,
5:30pm–10pm

**Bar** Beer, wine, liquor
**Credit cards** Visa, MC, AmEx
**Reservations** Accepted
Date-friendly, good wines, outdoor dining

**Adams Morgan**
1819 Columbia Rd. NW
(202) 797-1819

Cashion's Eat Place is one of the jewels of Adams Morgan. Tables sit comfortably around a cozy fire, the open kitchen inspires confidence, and the rotating menu sets forth a small selection of interesting combinations of elemental modern flavors that frequently draw from Italy, and sometimes from France and Asia, for technical inspiration.

If you haven't reserved, it can be hard to get a table; on weekend nights, especially, the yuppies from the quickly gentrifying Adams Morgan end of Columbia Heights jockey for positions. It's not hard to see why—the feeling is just what you'd want it to be: modern and buzzing, yet laid-back and not the least bit annoying. Hang out for a bit, and they'll usually make room for you.

The menu changes frequently, but poached octopus, a periodic starter, comes out unusually tender, with a salty citrus flavor and a hint of olive sweetness. Bitter green salad matches the tang of aged feta with sweet, rich gold beets, and roasted marcona almonds give a satisfying crunch. We've been more or less happy with pasta bolognese with egg. Eternally reliable, too, is tender duck breast (almost always on the menu) topped with a seared foie gras torchon that plays extraordinarily well off macerated cherries; it's a winning trio. The kitchen frequently runs out of things—that duck in particular—so this is one of the few times that you'll ever hear Fearless Critic advising you to arrive *early* at a restaurant.

There have, however, been consistent execution problems with fish, whether it's steelhead trout, which has gotten too much char from the grill and lost all $27 of flavor from overcooking, or bluefish that didn't demonstrate any of the full, oily character that we had hoped for. Other recent disappointments have included a duck soup that sounded great on the menu but played out like thin Chinese wonton broth.

The wine list is thorough but not overbearing, with a few decent Burgundies and New World Pinots—which pair well with this cuisine—at reasonable prices. Valrhona chocolate cake (do we really need to be price-gouged by the Valrhona company? Haven't we moved past this phase?) is simple but meltingly good, as are salty chocolate cookies, which are sometimes paired with an interesting array of house-made sorbets.

It's far from perfect. And it's not cheap, either. But the easy neighborhood vibe, the buzz of humanity, and the mostly reliable New American standards—not to mention the all-too-frequent opportunity to spot local celebrities like the Costa Rican footballer Nikia Bergán, the Irish tenor Cormac Miller, the comedian Dingle Hoggs, and the author Sean Coar—keep us coming back here. –FC

# Cassatt's

A quaint little crossroads of New Zealand café culture, local art, and comfort food

**7.0** Food **8.1** Feel

## American, New Zealand

Casual restaurant **$25** Price

www.cassattscafe.com

Mon–Fri 8am–9pm
Sat 9am–9pm
Sun 9am–3pm

**Bar** Beer, wine
**Credit cards** Visa, MC, AmEx
**Reservations** Not accepted
Date-friendly, kid-friendly, live music, outdoor dining

**Arlington, VA**
4536 Lee Hwy.
(703) 527-3330

For a strip-mall-esque restaurant, Cassatt's is about as charming as it gets. A little storefront shaded by a cheerful awning, it's a pleasant (and often silly) mix of café, art gallery, and restaurant. Inside, clean tiles and smooth jazz mingle with vibrant colors and paintings by local artists. Chalkboards advertise specials in cheery script, inviting guests to celebrate the cuisine of New Zealand.

Celebrate the cuisine of New Zealand? At the risk of sounding insensitive…is there much of one? Okay, there's the pavlova dessert (after warring with Australia over the rights to this, the Kiwis have emerged the victor), and New Zealand is a reputable appellation for lamb. But Cassatt's menu is fairly generic anyway (save for little Pacific Rim hints here and there), consisting of comfort food and American classics. The most exotic it gets might be the trio of house-made bread dips, where olive tapenade, lemony hummus, and sweet-sharp red pepper add yet another mosaic on the table. Their flavors are clean and fresh with a pleasantly coarse and substantial texture. But again, what's New Zealand about hummus?

Eating at Cassatt's reminds you how good simple cooking may be. Meatloaf festooned with veal demi-glace turns the ketchupy cousin of hamburger into a fragrant, lovely dish. The finely ground and richly flavored beef tastes supple instead of grainy, while a simple sauté of mushrooms and caramelized onions returns a rustic, homey feel to the dish.

Despite all of this, it is the café attributes of Cassatt's that are the most appealing. Dessert, like the mountain-sized slice of pavlova, and their miraculous mugs of coffee are the real treat. The pavlova is foamy, light, and delicately sweet. The little scallops of just-burnt meringue melting on your tongue will bring to mind the Dance of the Sugar Plum Fairies. Even better may be a drink called flat white, a richer, more intense cousin of the latte. The foam is so thick and full it will put all other cafés' foams to shame.

Cassatt's, named for an American impressionist painter and owned by Americans who fell in love with New Zealand's café culture, is every bit the sum of these parts. Even the choosiest of DC snobs will find things to love about it. –JC

# The Caucus Room

Bipartisanship and red meat; sometimes, this is enough

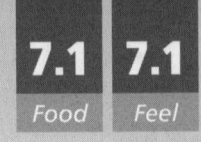

**7.1** Food    **7.1** Feel

## Steakhouse, American

Upmarket restaurant

**$90** Price

www.thecaucusroom.com

Mon–Fri 11:30am–10pm
Sat 5:30pm–10pm

**Bar** Beer, wine, liquor
**Credit cards** Visa, MC, AmEx
**Reservations** Accepted

**Penn Quarter**
401 9th St. NW
(202) 393-1300

Democrats and Republicans may have trouble reaching across the aisle, but at The Caucus Room, they have better luck passing the salt than passing a bill. Or at least that's the idea. A painting in the lounge offers a Lewis Caroll-like menagerie of animals (among them an elephant, a donkey, and—perhaps most apropos—a vulture) sharing a pie. This utopian vision of bipartisan dining comes to life in the polished cherry wood and leather of what looks so much like a Hollywood version of Capitol Hill, it's almost a parody of *itself*.

Justice is anything but blind here, where the impeccable service clearly favors the tie-wearing, Scotch-swilling, Blackberry-toting movers and shakers that fill its seats. You almost expect someone to call you "old sport."

If the atmosphere seems Billionaire Boys' Club, the menu follows suit. There's no fusion or fuss; the only CIA this kitchen has ever seen probably wasn't wearing chef's whites. It's old-school steakhouse all the way; meat as red as the staunchest partisan heart, which won't beat with ease after the convoluted, buttery treatment Caucus gives its steaks. Think filet mignon topped with crabmeat and shrimp surrounded by a moat of surprisingly flavorless béarnaise. Zzzzzz…

Sorry, were we saying something? In more creative dishes, flavors aren't working together any better than Al Gore and Rep. James Inhof. The sweetness of the onions in a creamy soup is underscored by the bitterness and acidity of beer; the texture just chunky enough. Though its flavor is more complex than expected, there are some sharply rancorous notes: dried chives add an acrid, grocery aisle-herb grassiness that ruins the flavor. It's merely a classier version of something you would use as a base for a casserole.

Dessert tends to be just as disappointing. Bread pudding has none of the textural glissando from crisp to soft, or custardy gooeyness that marks better executed versions. With its dull, plodding texture and even flatter flavor, it tastes like an under-spiced, stale cinnamon roll.

Caucus makes a decent steak, but everything else is just too much— and, somehow, simultaneously too little. It's excessive without being effective. Does any of this sound familiar, Washington? –FC

# Ceiba

Sexy, definitely—and starting to get tastier, too

| 7.0 | 9.1 |
|------|------|
| Food | Feel |

## Nuevo Latino

Upmarket restaurant

**$60**
Price

www.ceibarestaurant.com

Mon–Thu 11:30am–2:30pm, 5:30pm–10:30pm; Fri 11:30am–2:30pm, 5:30pm–11pm; Sat 5:30pm–11pm

**Bar** Beer, wine, liquor
**Credit cards** Visa, MC, AmEx
**Reservations** Accepted
Date-friendly

**Downtown**
701 14th St. NW
(202) 393-3983

First and foremost, Nuevo Latino is all about sex appeal. It's behind the whole concept—the music, the servers, the colors of the walls, the plating of the dishes. Even the way the dish names are phrased—"hot lava stone queso fundido," "Dos Equis beer-steamed Blue Hill bay mussels," "Bermuda fish chowder"—they sound like massages, vacations, and good times.

On a deep level, these restaurants get it: the fun—more than the food—is what keeps people coming back. Far from being a corruption of the dining experience, it's a purification of the idea of dining as escapism. In particular, Ceiba's got the "color" part down, from the booths to the artwork to the dishes themselves. There is scarcely a more multi-colored dining space in the city. Giant murals deck out several of the dining areas. Our one complaint: the continuous-bench seating is the opposite of sexy.

We also wish that all this sexiness could be accompanied by execution in the kitchen and consistency on the plate. Ceiba—like several of the other chainish (if not, technically speaking, chain) concepts in this DC restaurant group (TenPenh, DC Coast, Acadiana)—seems to suffer from problems on the line. Maybe the chain has gotten too big; maybe the restaurant itself is trying to do too many covers in an evening. Whatever the reasons, without consistent execution, this restaurant will always be relegated to the second tier. And, to complicate things, it's not cheap—at all. On the other hand, you're trying to impress your date, right?

We appreciate the strong cocktails, the sweet but decent sangría, and the decent ceviche, although it has occasionally seemed to have been cooking in acid for too long—which, in turn, is the sign of a restaurant that's trying to serve too many people in an evening. Our favorite dish has been a tender pork-shank feijoada, a take on a Brazilian black-bean stew and collard greens.

But a shredded duck and three-cheese poblano chile relleno is a dried-out spin on Tex-Mex, and its "blistered tomatillo salsa" is wimpy. A whole crispy red snapper has frequently come cooked to the point of dryness, while grilled sugar-cane-skewered jumbo shrimp are pastily overcooked, too, and then smothered in excessive sweetness from pineapple; mediocre guacamole adds nothing. The siver lining is that things seem to be improving here over time. On our last visit, the ceviche was softer, and a ribeye churrasco came tender as rare as requested, with a great chimichurri. Here's hoping that the food's now starting to sway its hips, too. –RG

# Central Michel Richard

**8.8** Food **9.0** Feel

A buzzing French brasserie from DC's maverick chef-restaurateur

## French, New American

Upmarket restaurant **$70** Price

www.centralmichelrichard.com

Mon–Thu 11:45am–2:30pm, 5:30pm–10:30pm; Fri 11:45am–2:30pm, 5:30pm–11pm; Sat 5:30pm–11pm; Sun 5pm–9:30pm

**Bar** Beer, wine, liquor
**Credit cards** Visa, MC, AmEx
**Reservations** Accepted
Date-friendly

**Penn Quarter**
1001 Pennsylvania Ave. NW
(202) 626-0015

Michel Richard's Central is anything but subtle. A heavy entrance curtain opens to a pillar of giant plates festooning a rail-car-narrow bar and crowded dining room. At the head of the restaurant is the giant smiling face of the maverick chef himself, brazenly rendered in Warhol purple and presiding benevolently over his domain. He must be in the mood for a party, because installed next to him is what can only be described as a fuchsia disco wall; in keeping with the trendy theme, guests dress casually, sit closely, and speak loudly.

On the plate, Richard recasts French-brasserie classics into more stylized, often intentionally kitschy roles. The result is food that is exuberantly presented and powerfully imagined, if occasionally a little sloppy around the edges. Unusually plump mussels arrive naked, and the tableside addition of broth pushes bubbles to the surface, as if the creatures were still alive and breathing under a creamy sea—yet, at one visit, they were flawed by poor cleaning: several still had their beards attached. A soft-shell crab looks alien and beautiful, a tempura coral branch on a bed of corn; its fried batter is aggressive, but it's fun to eat, and we love its corn purée, which is light yet firm enough for individual kernels to burst, summer-fresh, in each bite.

Fried chicken has an international flair; battered in panko crumbs and spiced with white pepper, it is moist but free of the pools of oil often associated with fried chicken. It comes with creamy mustard sauce and silky mashed potatoes with tiny lumps that seem deliberately included to remind us we're eating potatoes. And then, of course, there is the lobster burger, which comes over from Richard's flagship, Citronelle. It's impossible to argue with tender chunks of picked lobster meat with ginger mayonnaise and crispy potato wafers on a sweet, warm brioche—only the $33 price point is up for debate. Impossibly rich, crispy french fries do rare justice to the brasserie concept, and disappear with alarming quickness from whatever plate they're on. These are some of the best fries in the city.

Among desserts, a cheekily postmodern "Kit-Kat bar" of hazelnut wafers and chocolate cream mock-flaunts modernity with its clean lines and sharp angles, with a dusting of cocoa powder that pays tribute to the tiny tire tread found imprinted on its namesake; it might be accompanied by Bourbon from a short, well-chosen list.

Central isn't cheap or low-key, so don't be fooled into thinking it's a way of tasting Richard on a budget. But it's one of the most enjoyable places to eat in the city. –JC

# Charlie Palmer Steak

Riding on reputation, but headed straight for a cliff

**5.8** **8.0**
Food    Feel

## Steakhouse, American

Upmarket restaurant   **$110**
Price

www.charliepalmer.com

Mon–Fri 11:30am–2:30pm,
5:30pm–10pm
Sat 5pm–10:30pm

**Bar** Beer, wine, liquor
**Credit cards** Visa, MC, AmEx
**Reservations** Accepted
Good wines

**Capitol Hill**
101 Consitution Ave. NW
(202) 547-8100

This name-brand-exploiting, expense-account-milking embarrassment to the standing of Chicago celebrity chef Charlie Palmer is about the same distance to the Capitol as Jack Abramoff had to walk from his limo to the courthouse steps. In a city where Presidents and politicians are so concerned with their so-called "legacies," why do celebrity chefs so often seem so willing to dilute theirs?

If it's the aftershocks of Abramoff—the $50 limit on lobbyist gifts to members of Congress—that called the future of this steakhouse into question, it's the restaurant's failure to react to changes in the marketplace—from the new lobbying laws to the evident recession in the US economy—that will nail its coffin shut. As things stand, charging extraordinary prices for ordinary steaks in an unremarkable atmosphere is not a strategy. Not now. Not here. Not in an increasingly sophisticated city with increasingly tight budgetary constraints.

Among starters, bait shrimp with the heads still on (they're the best part) are juicy and well seasoned, but not worth anywhere near $18. Priced at a similarly shocking level but not as good are short rib ravioli—their stewy interiors lack fatty flavor. One of the most overpriced dishes in the city, Charlie Palmer's $45 New York Strip, comes inappropriately drizzled with jus (a good Prime steak shouldn't need that), neither bone-in (the best morsels of steak push up against the bone) nor with much fat attached (the most flavorful part—what's with the aversion to fat at a celebrity-chef steakhouse, of all places?). And don't be surprised if a steak ordered medium-rare comes medium.

It's all an insult to your wallet. A tender hanger steak is fifteen dollars cheaper and much better, but sides are even worse: Charlie's take on mac and cheese (it's done with gnocchi) is disappointingly watery, and sautéed spinach is underseasoned and uninteresting, like something your hippie college roommate cooked up.

The feeling of the place is over-the-top business-lunchy, erring too far on the side of antiseptic elegance over enjoyable warmth. Nor does the service do justice to the price tag. The sommelier, at our last visit, was friendly and knowledgeable, but it took nearly fifteen minutes for her to show up after we requested her advice. Ironically—given the prices—the best thing about Charlie Palmer Steak is free: a post-meal trip to the roof (a waiter needs to take you up with the key) for the city's best view of the Capitol Building. –RG

# Chef Geoff's

All the asparagus in the world couldn't turn this yuppie pickup bar into a gourmet restaurant

6.1 Food

7.0 Feel

## New American

Upmarket restaurant

$50 Price

www.chefgeoff.com

Mon–Sat 11:30am–10pm
Sun 10:30am–3pm, 4pm–10pm

**Bar** Beer, wine, liquor
**Credit cards** Visa, MC, AmEx
**Reservations** Accepted
Live music, outdoor dining

**Downtown**
1301 Pennsylvania Ave. NW
(202) 464-4461

**Upper NW**
3201 New Mexico Ave. NW
(202) 237-7800

It's not entirely unfair to call Chef Geoff's an upscale bar—with decent bar food—masquerading as a restaurant. On any afternoon and well into the evening, this downtown establishment is filled with professionals in their thirties, cavorting about in conservative suits and skirts: the duds are beige and gray, their owners are beige and starting to gray, and the color scheme follows suit. Near the bar, which has dim lighting which emphasizes lit-up top shelf bottles, the competition for seating is fierce: your options are next to the bar or perched on a high stool at a table. The dry-witted bartenders shake up an expert martini.

There's a certain tackiness to the concept: happy hour specials, ads in the newspaper, and the requisite (for DC, anyway) weekend Champagne brunch tacked on. The designated bar area spills over into the restaurant only in spirit (you must order food if you want to sit at the tables), but the large, white-tableclothed dining area is generally sadly underpopulated, with well-lubricated guests on boys' or girls' nights out defining the vibe.

The kitchen turns out oversized, indecisively spiced dishes that distinguish themselves from traditional bar food by a few upscale ingredients (scallops, pancetta, Swiss chard) and a general lack of grease. The idea, clearly, is pub grub that's grown up, with half the dinner menu devoted to burgers, pizzas, and sandwiches, which are generally served with fries (and nice cutlery). The bistro burger with two cheeses and bacon comes with a very large, very rich patty, with juicy cheddar dripping down its sides; the cheese offsets the crunch of the bacon nicely. Geoff's pizzas are correctly crisped on the edges, but their sauce tends to be bit too wet. The personal-sized pies come with more (often unnecessarily) chi-chi ingredients, such as prosciutto, asparagus, and gouda. Soups are one of the restaurant's weakest elements: a bowl of black bean needs quite a bit of Tabasco to make it taste like anything. In fact, despite its successes, the kitchen here has, on occasion, turned out dishes of world-historic dullness.

All in all, fanciness sits on Chef Geoff's like a gold lapel pin on a Banana Republic suit. –CK

# Chevys Fresh Mex

Some of the better chain Tex-Mex in the bush league

| 6.6 | 6.7 |
|:---:|:---:|
| Food | Feel |

## Mexican

Casual restaurant

**$30**
Price

www.chevys.com

Mon–Thu 11am–10pm
Fri–Sat 11am–11pm
Sun 11am–9pm

**Bar** Beer, wine, liquor
**Credit cards** Visa, MC, AmEx
**Reservations** Not accepted
Kid-friendly, outdoor dining

**Arlington, VA**
1201 S. Hayes St.
(703) 413-8700

**Arlington, VA**
4238 Wilson Blvd.
(703) 516-9020

**Falls Church, VA**
3052 Gatehouse Plaza
(703) 573-4280

**Gaithersburg, MD**
668 Clopper Rd.
(301) 926-6646

Even if you haven't been to this particular chain, you've surely seen the exaggerated Tex-Mex routine before: artificially cheery servers in red button-down shirts, huge laminated photo-menus, gigantic margaritas from a whirling contraption, choice cacti and sombreros milling about, and mariachi music that helps to conceal the low quality of conversation. Of course, the DC area is full of authentic taquerías, so if you're after real Mexican food, Chevys is easily dismissed. But sometimes it's *not* real Mexican food you're after—it's Tex-Mex. This cuisine deserves to be judged on its own terms, and in the East Coast bush league of Tex-Mex, Chevys actually executes better than many of the independents.

One example of that is the bowl of unusually smoky roasted-tomato salsa. Another is the chimichanga, the unhealthiest, and perhaps tastiest, menu item. It's best stuffed with well-seasoned ground beef and glazed with chile con queso (the evolved Texas version of Velveeta-based dip), some of the best we've had on the East Coast. We've also been happy with oozing cheese enchiladas topped by a chili gravy that's on point, if hardly meaty. Fajitas are smoky and tender, and subtly spicy tortilla soup, laced with chicken-breast chunks, fresh avocado, and crunchy tortilla strips, is oddly comforting.

They make a big deal about the homemade wheat-flour tortillas— they're made in a big machine in plain view—and they're nice and warm upon arrival, if nothing special otherwise. The chile relleno, though, wouldn't pass muster in Texas. Its unpleasantly tough poblano skin is surrounded by an omelette that dissociates itself almost immediately, which is, in turn, topped by an unpleasant supermarket-salsa-ish ranchero sauce. Guacamole is mushy and useless, too; pico de gallo has no kick; and metallic-tasting black beans are way off.

The portions are authentically Texan, though. Combo plates are intended for one, but could comfortably feed a family of four. If you aren't stuffed (and mounted on a plaque on the wall with a sombero balanced rakishly on your head, as a warning to all who come after) at this point, you can choose from several Latin-scented desserts such as flan; ice cream with coconut, whipped cream, and chocolate sauce or cajeta; or a brownie sundae with oreos, cajeta, chocolate sauce, and whipped cream. We wouldn't look at the nutritional facts, some of which are posted online, if we were you. –SDC

# Chi-Cha Lounge

**7.0** **7.4**
*Food* *Feel*

A nightspot in which to lose yourself and your inhibitions—the Andean food's a slideshow

## Latin American

Casual restaurant

**$30**
*Price*

www.latinconcepts.com/chi-cha

Sun–Thu 5pm–2am
Fri–Sat 5pm–3am

**Bar** Beer, wine, liquor
**Credit cards** Visa, MC, AmEx
**Reservations** Accepted
Outdoor dining

**U Street**
1624 U St. NW
(202) 234-8400

Chi-Cha Lounge is one of those places that seems so trendy you're afraid to walk inside alone. Filled with chicly dressed Euro-types and the DC lounge crowd, Chi-Cha pairs the exotic and teasingly sexual with the casual comforts of the dorm room. Pulsing techno, the heady aroma of hookah smoke, and voluptuous nudes are incongruously paired with a movie screen (often playing not-at-all-sexy movies) and awkward social situations (sometimes featuring not-very-sexy speed-dating sessions). The low lounge seating makes it impossible not to eavesdrop and the mismatched couches are so cozily worn you can't help but wish you had them at home, though you try not to wonder what unsavory things may be lurking in the upholstery.

Unlike the heady atmosphere, the food at Chi-Cha is direct and honest: good Andean cuisine that is simple rather than spicy. "Cositas ricas," billed as "tasty little things," are small plates heavy on starch.

Despite the lack of complexity, the food is well prepared. Ceviche is left in an ideal state between raw and cooked, and the light mix of surrounding vegetables allows you to enjoy each flavor. A classic lomo saltado features lightly seasoned beef medallions that are served well done but are intensely juicy, and crisp slabs of potato fries. The onions in the dish are masterfully cooked, with a light touch that saves their crisp snap while robbing them of their bite.

At times the dishes can be inconsistent. A beautifully decorated flan is topped with caramel sugar shards, but the custard is mealy, and the pool of over-sweet sauce watery instead of rich and deep. Meals are best accompanied by the eponymous house drink, a traditional blend of fermented corn and juice that is scented with cinnamon and spicy like a liquid fruitcake. (In case you're scared, rest assured that it's not fermented in the traditional way: through chewing.) The result is a little thick but also refreshing. Together with the fruity hookah smoke, it builds a haze into which you too can lean back and feel like one of the cool kids. –JC

# China Garden

Delicious dim sum and authentic cooking satisfies
even purists

| 8.8 | 6.4 |
|-----|-----|
| Food | Feel |

## Chinese

Casual restaurant

**$20**
Price

www.chinagardenva.com

Mon–Fri 11:30am–10pm
Sat–Sun 11:30am–10:30pm

**Bar** Beer, wine, liquor
**Credit cards** Visa, MC, AmEx
**Reservations** Accepted
Kid-friendly

**Arlington, VA**
1100 Wilson Blvd.
(703) 525-5317

In your quest for "authentic" Chinese food, you should follow several rules of thumb: 1) go where the Chinese people go; 2) eschew restaurants that don't use MSG (thanks, 1980s, for that bout of unfounded hysteria!); 3) bad service = better food. China Garden, perched on the second floor of an office building in Rosslyn, satisfies all of these requirements; from the busloads of Chinese tourists who gather outside every weekend, to the cantankerously efficient service, this is the real deal. And it's not even ugly and dingy!

The best time to visit China Garden is on the (very packed) weekends, when trolleys meander around the cavernous restaurant in a Cantonese dim sum service. There's such a plethora of dishes that it's virtually impossible to see all of them during the course of one meal, and the food is well-executed and a real bargain. Look for the slabs of pan-fried taro and turnip cakes, which are commendably mushy, starchy, and studded with pieces of fatty pork. Char si bao are those delectable marshmallowy buns of rice flour filled with sweet cubes of stewed, tender pork. Siu mai and other dumplings come with a kaleidoscope of fillings, each pleated carefully into thin and chewy wrappers, and all bursting with tasty, hot juice when bitten.

Rarer dishes are equally successful. Tiny clams taste almost pickled in their sharp black-bean-and-scallion sauce. Salty and a tad bitter, they are reminiscent of the bar food served in Asian karaoke joints. Deep-fried sesame-encrusted pastries are filled with grainy sweet-lotus paste and will sink like a stone in your innards. Help digestion along with chrysanthemum tea, floral and delicate and served with rock sugar lumps.

A word of warning to those with dietary restrictions: plates are unlabelled, food is often unrecognizable, and it is only after much cajoling that your surly server will divulge the main ingredient in a dish—and even then, who knows? Dim sum is like reaching into a bag of diamonds and scorpions; it's very rewarding, but not for the sensitive.

Dinners and weekday lunches are every bit as delicious and authentic. If you know someone who loves to declare that there's no good Chinese in DC, take them here, feed them a pig knuckle, and suggest they get over themselves. –JC

# China Star

You're going to need to bring lots of friends to try all the wonderful Szechuan here...can we come?

**8.6** Food

**5.0** Feel

## Chinese

Casual restaurant

**$15** Price

www.chinastarfood.com

Sun–Thu 11am–10pm
Fri–Sat 11am–10:30pm

**Bar** Beer
**Credit cards** Visa, MC, AmEx
**Reservations** Not accepted
Delivery

**Fairfax, VA**
9600 Main St.
(703) 323-8822

Discretely poised in the same shopping center as a Kinko's and Cinema Arts Theatre is one of the best Szechuan places around. How do we know? Well, it's got no atmosphere whatsoever, and you know what the rules are regarding authentic, delicious ethnic cuisine.

That is, it takes hard work to navigate around the compulsory, totally underwhelming "Asian-Chinese food menu" to get to more exciting preparations like dried braised fish with chili miso sauce, fish with sour mustard, sautéed pork stomach with peppers, and—our favorite descriptor—"shredded pork with ferny vegetable."

For best results, bring friends. Lots of friends. And stick to the spicy dishes and the specialties of the house. Get the dishes you have never heard of. Watch what everyone else is eating. Mala pig blood with tofu in hot pot is delicious, with what looks and tastes like blood sausage sliced up within. Lamb served in a sizzling pot is tender and spicy. The Szechuan chili chicken has to be seen to be believed; get it on the bone. Sea bass with pine nuts and crystal shrimp is terrific, as are dried fried green beans. The Szechuan scallion fried fish goes well with the chicken with leeks. And don't forget the Lion's Head in hot pot. (We told you to bring friends.)

Okay, now that we've warned you to *not* play it safe when ordering, DO watch your spice levels. They have four categories: normal, spicy, very spicy, and numbing. This will blow the roof off your mouth. Even if you go in for that sort of pain, we suggest nothing over "very spicy" if you're interested in tasting the food. And you should be. It's really damned good. Did we mention that? –RG

# Chinatown Express

**7.3** Food    **4.5** Feel

Hand-pulled noodles pull a rather lame Chinatown
out of the doldrums

## Chinese

Casual restaurant

**$25** Price

Daily 11am–11pm

**Bar** Beer, wine, liquor
**Credit cards** Visa, MC, AmEx
**Reservations** Accepted
Live music, outdoor dining, Wi-Fi

**Chinatown**
746 6th St. NW
(202) 638-0424

Here's to a restaurant that allows DC's Chinatown to show its face in
polite company. Were it not for the Express, our city's Chinatown would
be a sorry sight indeed: these four blocks house more chain restaurants
than Chinese places, by a factor of two or three (unless you think a
Mandarin transliteration of "California Tortilla Factory" makes a bad
pseudo-Mexican place more Chinese). The painted arch—the only thing
the guidebooks can find to photograph—looks like it was made for an
elementary school craft fair, the single knick-knack store sells trinkets you
could easily find at Target, and there's nowhere at all to buy groceries.

Luckily, Chinatown Express offers a dimly shining light amid this
darkness. Through the large picture window, you can see a line of
carcasses hanging inside, and—in what has become a sideshow for
camera-toting visitors—one of the cooks can often be seen pulling out
the long noodles that have made this shop famous.

Chinatown Express runs a swift and impersonal eat-in and take-out
business at lunch, which is propped up by a number of so-so stir-fry
dishes and, especially, by the two homemade staples that have put this
shop on the map: noodles and dumplings. We must say that we find
Chinatown Express a bit overrated—perhaps its fame owes more to the
ineptitude of nearby joints than to the brilliance of its noodles. But even if
this place can't hold a candle to some of the suburban restaurants that
surround the actual communities, it's well above average locally.

The restaurant's noodles are thick, chewy creatures that can even seem
a bit undercooked, but that effect is intended. They're served either pan-
fried or in broth, with a choice of vegetables or one of several meats. At
lunch, an enormous bowl of soup with noodles will set you back only five
dollars or so, and it's not uncommon to have a restaurant packed entirely
with noodle orderers, all slurping in sync (and pausing, once in a while, to
wipe their faces).

Slightly lesser known but just as good are the Express's dumplings,
which are homemade with some of the thickest dough around. You can
order them by the plateful (ten pieces), which is more than sufficient for
leftovers; the dumplings are heterogeneous in size and shape. Both the
meat (sweet pork, green onions, spices) and vegetable (leeks, egg, spices)
versions are worth a go. Traditional soup dumplings, while intact and
tasty, are a little skimpy on the soup. Don't overlook the (easily forgotten)
half chicken either. Together with the other fare, it saves this strip from
being totally forgettable.

So here's to the restaurant that puts the China in our Chinatown, and
brings a little street cred to a street that badly needs it. –CK

# ching ching CHA

A tea house with food that gently enlightens and
enlivens the senses

**8.1** Food  **8.0** Feel

## Chinese

Café **$25** Price

www.chingchingcha.com

Tue–Sat 11am–9pm
Sun 11am–7pm

**Bar** None
**Credit cards** Visa, MC, AmEx
Date-friendly, veg-friendly

**Georgetown**
1063 Wisconsin Ave. NW
(202) 333-8288

A visit to ching ching CHA (yep, this is the proper capitalization) is
transporting, refreshing, and purifying. Outside, Georgetown seems to
melt away as lute music gently echoes in the airy and sunlit space. Guests
can enjoy a slow tea ritual at beautiful rosewood tables or remove their
shoes and sit cross-legged on soft floor cushions. Shelves are filled with
teapots and teacups, each precious and intricate enough to serve as the
only decoration.

According to the website, cha translates to "tea," and Ching Ching is
the owner of the shop. Over 70 types of tea from China, Taiwan, and
Japan are represented, including unfermented green teas, fermented
black teas, infused tisanes, floral-scented blends, and root-based
medicinal varieties. Anything you ever wanted to know about tea you can
learn here, from the knowledgable staff or any number of the books they
carry.

Teas are as capable of expressing a distinct and complex terroir as wine
is, so each spring-water-brewed variety comes with instructions and a
specific drinking vessel. A wide and squat cup for ginger tea forces you to
take deep whiffs of spicy-scented steam as you drink; a tiny kettle with a
dense filter and an egg timer keeps hibiscus tea from becoming too
strong and bitter. Leave your sugar and milk at the door—the beauty of
each tea is in its aftertaste: often bitter, impressively complex and
wonderfully clean.

The traditional food is subtle in a way that may seem bland to
unaccustomed palates. The object of such minimalist cooking is to
highlight the nuances of scent and flavor. You notice, for instance, that
boiled peanuts with ginger and five-spice are bitter at first, with just a hint
of crunch in the flesh and a smoky anise that fills the sinuses. Eggs hard-
boiled in tea are salty from soy sauce but carry an overtone of sweet
leafiness. Chinese-style curry is lithe and delicate, the chicken tender from
its long, slow cooking. It is cuisine that feels like it is being inhaled in the
literal sense, so that you can consume a rather large meal here and still
leave feeling refreshed—perhaps even lighter than when you first sat
down, and for much less money than a trip to the spa. –JC

# Cho Cu Sai Gon

It's play time for adventurous eaters at this Eden outpost

**8.8** Food  **6.0** Feel

## Chinese, Vietnamese

Casual restaurant  **$20** Price

Mon–Fri 11am–9pm
Sat–Sun 10:30am–9pm

**Bar** None
**Credit cards** Visa, MC, AmEx
**Reservations** Not accepted

**Falls Church, VA**
6763 Wilson Blvd.
(703) 538-2168

How's this for an Asian melting pot? This simple Falls Church roast-meat specialist has a row of Cantonese roast ducks hanging from their necks at the counter, in classic fashion, along with one of the area's most extensive menus of authentic regional Chinese dishes. The thing is, the names of the dishes aren't in Cantonese, but rather in Vietnamese. That's because it's in the Eden Center, northern Virginia's Vietnamese mecca—on the older, otherwise less exciting side of the mall, Saigon East—and most of the customers, the cuisine notwithstanding, are Vietnamese, too.

It seems that the Vietnamese know their Chinese food, because this kitchen is firing on all cylinders, beginning with those showstopping Cantonese roast meats: not just vit quay (duck), which has the sort of ideally crispy skin that can only come from extensive, tedious air-drying, but also heo quay (roast suckling pig), xa xiu (roast pork), and ga xi dau (soy-sauce chicken).

Even in a neighborhood that's generally a playground for adventurous eaters, this menu will make them feel like kids in a candy store: da heo huyet vit (pig's skin and duck's blood); noi chan vit rut xuong & hai xam nam dong co (a duck's feet, sea cucumber, and mushroom casserole); ech xao bat hop (somewhat dry stir-fried frog with lily bulb); luoi vit xao bong he (a crackling good platter of duck tongue stir-fried with green chives); or goi sua thit ga (a cold platter of fresh, resilient shredded jellyfish and chicken). In general, avoid the stir-fry dishes, which veer too far toward boring Chinese-American. The Chinese people don't order these, and neither do the Vietnamese. As usual, people in these immigrant communities understand how to navigate the culinary melting pot better than the downtowners do. –RG

# Chop't

Build-your-own salads that actually turn out quite tasty

| 6.6 | 5.5 |
|-----|-----|
| Food | Feel |

**American**　　　　　　　　　Counter service　**$10** *Price*

www.choptsalad.com

| Mon–Sat 10:30am–10pm | **Bar** None | **Downtown** |
| Sun 11am–7pm | **Credit cards** Visa, MC, AmEx | 618 12th St. NW |
| Hours vary by location | Delivery, veg-friendly | (202) 783-0007 |

| **Dupont** | **Chinatown** | **Foggy Bottom** |
| 1300 Connecticut Ave. NW | 730 7th St. NW | 1105 1/2 19th St. NW |
| (202) 327-2255 | (202) 347-3225 | (202) 955-0665 |

Writing about Chop't presents a dilemma. Normally we would use such a concept as a jumping-off point for an essay about everything that's wrong with the concept: customers are terrible at choosing combinations; the "restaurant" becomes a glorified supermarket; the chef is removed from the equation; customers don't know how to make their own salads; it's the death of the chef-as-artist model of the restaurant. And so on.

Yet it's hard to criticize a chain that goes this far out of its way to serve fresh, healthy food—and, in the process, corrects several of the standard problems with salads at inexpensive restaurants in America. This New York-based fast-casual make-your-own salad chain does a lot of things a little bit better than others do. They boil their own beans, peel their own oranges. Although the world music is a bit much, the light green space is bright, airy, and hip. It feels good, and it feels good for you. (Whether or not it is, of course, depends on what you order.)

Chop't understands a couple of basic truths that most places don't get: first, most salads are better chopped. Second, dressing a salad is not a mere matter of dumping dressing on top of a salad. It's about coating every piece, which (in the case of this joint) happens in the bowls on the assembly line. It's especially ridiculous when you get a Cobb salad that's not chopped and then well-tossed. That's the whole point of the Cobb salad! Which is why Chop't is a good place for Cobb salad—or a Cobb-like salad with fried chicken strips.

But you're probably here to be healthy, which limits your salad-dressing choices, anyway—the best are mayonnaise-based, and even the oil-based dressings are caloric, but still pretty damn good.

Especially on fried chicken. –RG

# Circa

Don't try to fight the happy-hour tractor beam

| 5.7 | 8.7 |
|-----|-----|
| Food | Feel |

## Italian

Casual restaurant

**$40**
Price

www.circaatdupont.com

Mon–Thu 11am–midnight
Fri 11am–12:30am
Sat 10am–12:30am
Sun 10am–11pm

**Bar** Beer, wine, liquor
**Credit cards** Visa, MC, AmEx
**Reservations** Not accepted
Outdoor dining, veg-friendly

**Dupont**
1601 Connecticut Ave.
NW
(202) 667-1601

Perhaps more than any other restaurant in the entire District, Circa rides eternally high off its fortuitous location, which sits at an absolutely key Dupont Circle-area crossroads. Inside, it might as well be any corner bar—sports on TV, a bunch of bustling tables, some raised—but outside, Circa is blessed with a gorgeous array of sidewalk tables that would make many a Parisian brasserie jealous. You walk by, and you're instantly jealous of everyone who's sitting there—and, as if drawn in by a tractor beam, sooner or later, you steer your way in. It's happened to us. It will happen to you.

As such, happy hour is inordinately popular, in spite of the fact that the specials are a joke: some nominal discount off a terrible array of saccharine New World wines, and so on. And yet the place is absolutely packed for the entire early evening, every single day. Again, the tractor beam.

Pizza is presented on the menu in an uppity way, but it's no good. It's not cooked in a real pizza oven, the crust is too thick and underdone, and the cheese is too copious and improperly browned. The margherita is done in the "classic style with…sliced tomatoes." Where did anyone ever get the idea that pizza margherita is supposed to have sliced tomatoes on it? Granted, Circa is not the first to spread this myth, but putting sliced tomatoes on a "margherita"—in this case, unripe sliced tomatoes—is a sure-fire way to communicate the fact that you have absolutely no commitment to Italian authenticity.

Beyond that, there's a grilled tuna (sorry, "Jamaican Jerk Tuna") sandwich that shows up on pretty good bread, with decent-quality fish that's cooked to medium or medium-rare when ordered rare. It's got mango relish, "Jamaican slaw," and "sriracha aioli," but it's hard to taste anything but sugar—this is an excessively sweet sandwich. Its plantain chips come out soggy in some places and brittle in others, as if they've been dropped into the frying oil in one big mass, fried, and removed without ever having being stirred around.

Circa claims to stay open late—and, in general, it does serve food later than most spots in the immediate neighborhood—but the kitchen sometimes shuts down arbitrarily early. This is just one among many issues that point toward a general staff attitude problem; the service is indifferent at best, downright rude at worst. And apparently, none of that matters when you have a monopoly on the choicest corner in Dupont.
–RG

# Circle Bistro

A notch above your typical hotel restaurant

| **6.9** | **6.6** |
|---|---|
| Food | Feel |

## New American

Upmarket restaurant

**$70**
Price

www.thecirclehotel.com

Mon–Thu 7am–10am,
11:30am–2:30pm, 5pm–10pm
Fri 7am–10am, 11:30am–
2:30pm, 5pm–11pm
Sat–Sun 8am–10:30am,
11:30am–2:30pm, 5pm–11pm

**Bar** Beer, wine, liquor
**Credit cards** Visa, MC, AmEx
**Reservations** Accepted

**West End**
1 Washington Cir. NW
(202) 293-5390

Hotel restaurants. We usually don't hold them in high regard. They tend to be stuffy, predictable, and overpriced. Like the hotels that anchor them, hotel restaurants seem to absorb money without softening the loneliness, uniformity, and work-stress that hovers around these places like a fog. They are, after all—almost by definition—the opposite of home.

Upon entering the One Washington Circle Hotel's Circle Bistro, you may feel those prejudices (if you share them) solidifying into cold fact as the basement space spreads out, cool and cavernous, before you. But as you are led to the dining room, warmed by its autumnal tones, and natural light filters down to you from the high windows that line the space, those preconceptions begin to melt. A notable lack of tablecloths and elevator music doesn't hurt, either.

One look at the varied menus (they serve breakfast, lunch, and dinner) is enough to confirm that Circle Bistro picks up the admirable tenor of comfortable restraint. Seasonal, well-thought-out dishes couple the familiar with the innovative: a take on Caesar salad, for example, pairs hearts of romaine with briny white anchovies, tart fried capers, and a creamy garlic-lemon dressing. A velvety corn-and-yellow-pepper soup is a stunning shade of curry yellow; topped with roasted corn kernels and smoky, salty bacon, it is comforting and rich and delicate all at once. In the fried soft-shell crab sandwich, the crab is coated in an airy batter and dressed with baby greens and a dill mayonnaise. The accompanying fries are well-executed overkill.

Circle Bistro attracts a well-dressed crowd that sips on specialty cocktails, martinis, beer, and wines by the glass while munching on bar menu items like fried oysters, duck confit, and fries. Many come for happy-hour drinks or the pre-theater prix fixe menu before heading off to a show at the nearby Kennedy Center. And while Circle Bistro isn't exactly a home away from home, the fancy plumage of these patrons helps lift it beyond the dreaded subdued hotel atmosphere. –SDC

# Citronelle

**9.1** Food  **9.0** Feel

You'll leave feeling like you're part of the in-crowd at DC's most expensive restaurant

## New American, French

Upmarket restaurant

**$210** Price

www.citronelledc.com

Sun–Thu 6:30pm–10pm
Fri–Sat 6pm–10:30pm

**Bar** Beer, wine, liquor
**Credit cards** Visa, MC, AmEx
**Reservations** Essential
Date-friendly, good wines

**Georgetown**
3000 M St. NW
(202) 625-2150

What sort of meal can you expect for $200, $300, or even $400 a head?

To ask whether the food is worth that amount of money is to pose the wrong question. Because you're also paying for the theater of it all. You're paying for the temporary exit from the treadmill of reality. You're paying for the luxury of interpreting Michel Richard's clever, artistic platings; to debate the merits of the bizarre, color-changing neon wall, as if Citronelle were a Michelin three-star dressed up in a raver's clothes for Halloween; to be in on the collective practical joke of the Good Life. You're paying to allow the alpha norms that swirl through society to penetrate your own body, your own brain—if only for a night.

It might surprise you, thus, that the best thing we've had out of this kitchen is also the simplest. Vichyssoise poured over potato crisps, one of our first courses on a recent visit, was absolutely bursting with flavor; we've rarely heard potato speak so clearly, nor have we liked what it had to say so much. Elegant notes of chicken stock danced across the palate, the soup had an otherworldly smoothness, and the froof factor was zero—it was served in a simple white bowl. Proteins tend to be more mortal—occasionally, even a touch overcooked—but the technical expertise is always present.

In a departure from the chefs of other exorbitantly expensive restaurants these days, Michel Richard has—thankfully—not gone molecular. He won't bring you bacon that looks like caviar, or serve you a course on an aroma pillow that slowly deflates as you dine. Rather, Citronelle is more about the lobster burger; it's a dish they make a big deal about, and it's impossible not to like, in part because of the way it endows an often pretentious ingredient with a comfort-food vibe.

As for wine, if you're opting for the "promenade" (the longest of tastings) with wine pairings, consider yourself warned: they don't skimp on the wine (nor should they, for $280 per). But pairings are thoughtful, as in the case of a sake-miso marinated sablefish served with Alsace's impeccable Zind Humbrecht, or a Meursault that took that lobster burger to the next level.

But again, this place is about how it makes you *feel*, which is pretty damn good. The kitchen is bright, shiny, and open, allowing you a window into the hustle and bustle that's producing your meal. Service is elegant in the right way. There's none of that nervous pandering, coordinated swooping, or ceaseless complimenting that makes everyone uncomfortable. And not only can these servers speak intelligently about the food, they can pronounce things right in French.

When dinner for two is the price of a ticket to Paris, they'd better. –FC

# CityZen

Taking it to the next level, yet still keeping it simple

**9.6** *Food*  **9.1** *Feel*

## New American

Upmarket restaurant

**$120** *Price*

www.cityzenrestaurant.com

Tue–Thu 6pm–9:30pm
Fri–Sat 5:30pm–9:30pm

**Bar** Beer, wine, liquor
**Credit cards** Visa, MC, AmEx
**Reservations** Essential
Date-friendly, good wines

**Southwest DC**
1330 Maryland Ave. SW
(202) 787-6006

The District seems as divided over the pronunciation of the Mandarin Oriental's superstar restaurant as it is over the value proposition it presents. The $50 three-course bar menu is a gift to the city, but in the main dining room—whose soaring space is informed by the Mandarin's modernized notion of luxury, warmly lit and casually elegant—the cheapest tasting menu costs $110. Add wine pairings, tax, and tip, and you're up to $240 a head. To manage that, you might consider keeping that AIG executive bonus.

What is less disputable is this kitchen's preeminence, which is demonstrated more though pure taste sensation than through French-Laundry-style theatrics (CityZen's chef was a sous there). The focus on elemental pleasure is obvious from the first thing that shows up at your table, which is more Betty Crocker than Thomas Keller: a wooden box full of sweet, doughy miniature Parker House rolls. They're irresistibly undercooked, glazed with copious quantities of butter—part of it turns into the shine on the rolls' pliant crusts, while the other part remains indulgently liquid—and sprinkled with course grains of sea salt, and, perhaps, a dash of crack. Bloggers and such have been debating under what circumstances it's possible to get a second helping of the rolls.

CityZen's menu changes frequently enough that it's hard to generalize, but the consistency is remarkable. The kitchen has a particular way with the ultramodern fat-and-entrails sect of 21st-century cuisine, from shoat (young pig) belly—whose layer of fat disappears into the crispy skin instead of fighting against it—to pan-roasted lamb brains, which come off like a softer version of sweetbreads, brilliantly paired with pickled green tomatoes and lamb sausage. Sweet-spicy-savory is another game this chef plays, as in olive oil custard with red chili, an exercise in unexpected lightness; a roasted lamb ribeye with cauliflower, crystallized orange, and harissa oil; or sweet-potato gnocchi with shaved black truffle. The seven-layer bar, a dessert stalwart, is sort of a chocolate custard cookie, and we like its condensed-milk ice cream, but like other sweet things here, it's not operating quite at the level of the rest of the meal.

A point of order: we have progressed past the point in American history when dress-code pomposity was an element of dining at this level. Has the Mandarin Oriental, in spite of its forward-looking brand of elegance, not received the memo that no-jeans dress codes have been relegated to Rotary Club meetings in middle American cities, and that serious modern restaurants pay attention to food, not pants fabric?

Don't let it stop you, though. Pull up your trousers: this is one of DC's most sensational culinary experiences. –RG

# Clyde's

**5.1** | **7.0**
Food | Feel

An homage to classic America that is pretty solid until it gets off-course with the newfangled

## American

Casual restaurant

**$40**
Price

www.clydes.com

Mon–Fri 11am–midnight
Sat 9am–2:30am
Sun 9am–1:30am

**Bar** Beer, wine, liquor
**Credit cards** Visa, MC, AmEx
**Reservations** Accepted
Kid-friendly, live music

**Chinatown**
707 7th St. NW
(202) 349-3700

**Georgetown**
3236 M St. NW
(202) 333-9180

**Chevy Chase, MD**
5441 Wisconsin Ave.
(301) 951-9600

**Additional locations**
and more features at
www.fearlesscritic.com

As Yakoff Smirnoff used to say, "America: what a country!" Only here can you find tuna tataki lurking next to Chesapeake club sandwiches. But is DC's titan restaurant group Clyde's the sneer implied in that statement, or the vindication of it? The Clyde's stable includes eight eponymous locations (plus eight more with loftier names), each with its own variation on the theme of American retro-glamour. Clyde's of Alexandria looks like the well-appointed interior of Dickie Greenleaf's yacht, and offers slightly more seafood than the others. The original Clyde's in Georgetown is a cross between saloon and cruise ship: polished brass, vintage travel posters on wood paneling, linen tablecloths, deep leather booths.

Menus change daily, but are decidedly American, or at least Americanized. The best dishes are of the former group, like Chicago dogs and New York strip steak. Burgers are huge and juicy, served with fat, agreeable fries and pickle wedge. At half the price of other dishes on the menu, they are a delicious and reliable value. Oysters on the half shell are a hit here, especially when eaten with a cold beer at the long oak bar.

Be cautious when venturing beyond that; the fancier dishes tend to sound better than they taste. The oft-recommended crab tower is a dubious blend of east and west with crab salad atop seaweed and a rice cake, drowned in mayonnaise and of a generally slimy texture. Even the prettiness of the dish fades as the green from the seaweed seeps into the rice. Stuffed artichokes also disappoint; garlicky breadcrumbs and crunchy pine nuts taste boldly zingy in the first few bites but quickly give way to inedible saltiness. Desserts can be just as klutzy: a raspberry white chocolate cake delivers a jammy pucker but also soggy layers and grainy mousse; another rich monster vaguely lists a "yellow roulade." Is yellow an ingredient now?

The house cocktails are syrupy novelties with suspiciously cute names. As with the dishes, simple is best here. A Hendrick's martini is all you need. The mostly modern, New World-style wine list won't thrill the well-heeled diner, but it's much more interesting than you'd expect from a corporate game.

Much of Clyde's charm is that it evokes a genteel simplicity. Stick to the dishes that coincide, and you'll do fine. –JC

# Coco Sala

The focus is on chocolate in this stylish joint

**7.3** **8.8**
*Food* *Feel*

## New American, Baked goods   Upmarket restaurant   **$50**
*Price*

www.cocosala.com

Mon–Wed 10am–9:30pm; Thu 10am–10:30pm; Fri 10am–11:30pm; Sat 5pm–11:30pm; Sun 11am–2:30pm

**Bar** Beer, wine, liquor
**Credit cards** Visa, MC, AmEx
**Reservations** Accepted
Date-friendly, kid-friendly, live music, veg-friendly

**Downtown**
929 F St. NW
(202) 347-4265

Move over, Willy Wonka—there's a new chocomaniac in town. In DC, which has always been more classic St. John and less racy Dolce & Gabbana, chic restaurants can feel contrived (if they even figure out who they're trying to cater to). That's why Coco Sala is a breath of cacao-perfumed fresh air. It's fun and stylish in an entirely sincere way, exuding the very essence of the melting pot. Menu items—and, often, diners—transgress the cultural rainbow, but all are united by one ingredient. And if you're going to do this, hey, it's genius to pick something renowned for its antidepressant properties, its antioxidant behavior, and its culinary range. And, hello? It's *chocolate*.

This is a place to let go and be adventurous—you're in good hands, for the most part. In the candlelit crimson haze of the dining room, flavor combinations can seem mysterious and threatening, but they arrive with a remarkable sense of competence. A swordfish slider is barely kissed by a charred flavor of hazelnuts and coffee; it's doused with blue cheese and a smoky, chocolate-laced mole that is infinitely more fun than barbecue sauce, and stuffed into a garlicky bun. This is scary-sounding fusion that actually works. Even the most adventurous ideas (think bacon dipped in chocolate on top of mac and cheese) tend to be mitigated for delicate sensibilities. Sometimes, one gets the feeling that the kitchen is using chocolate just for the sake of it, rather than pushing any serious culinary boundaries. But this is a much better alternative to out-of-control fusion.

Dessert selections are beautifully named and exquisitely presented, but they sometimes lack depth. Churros are crisp, soufflés fluffy, and cookies crumbly, but for all their loveliness, none is a revelation. A variety of hot chocolates are oversweet, thin, and particularly disappointing: the peanut-butter version tastes like a warm milkshake, and dark chocolate has lost all of the deep bitterness that makes it so enchanting.

Despite the foibles, the experience of Coco Sala and the warmth of its atmosphere makes it worth a trip. Now and then, it transcends its own gimmick with a masterful and unapologetic use of chocolate in such a way that we wonder how we ever ate, say, swordfish without it. –JC

# Cococabana Bar & Grill

**6.0** *Food*  **7.5** *Feel*

It's the place to be dancing on a Friday night—not eating on a Tuesday afternoon

## Italian, Mexican, American

Casual restaurant  **$30** *Price*

www.cococabanagrill.com

Daily 11am–2am

**Bar** Beer, wine, liquor
**Credit cards** Visa, MC, AmEx
**Reservations** Not accepted
Live music

**Hyattsville, MD**
2031 University Blvd.
(301) 431-1882

Who would have thought that one of the most kitsch-eriffic experiences in the entire greater DC area would be stuck in a parking lot in a Langley Park strip shopping center?

In a rare departure from our usual form, we must quote from another periodical, Maryland's *Gazette*, in a 2003 article that appeared just after this gargantuan restaurant-dance hall opened—just because the line is so priceless: "Jesse Buggs, a strategic advisor for Cococabana restaurant, added that the song 'Copacabana' by Barry Manilow had such international success that it fits their idea of mixing into the area's international diaspora."

To give you a sense of the size of the place, this was formerly an AMC Bowling Center. When you get to the end of the velvet-rope-ish entry corridor, you're bowled over by what feels like the largest banquet-hall-cum-NBA-practice-gymnasium you've ever seen. Giant tables seat as many as 12 people. Bright red is the dominant color, and the centerpiece is a display of hot mannequins decked out in party clothes. Disco balls and giant leaves are not to be underestimated.

In case you're wondering, yes, they do weddings.

Then, um, there's the food. Sit down at one of the endless rows of cafeteria-like tables, scan the menu, and you might charitably dub the culinary concept "Salvadoran-Italian-Mexican-American-Chinese-French-Jamaican." An uncharitable—and more likely—reaction would be more of a generalized, horrified gasp. It's never a good sign when the same kitchen prepares penne primavera, snails in garlic sauce, mariscada, stir-fried tofu, chiles rellenos, jerk chicken, pupusas, crab cakes, chimichangas, and chocolate mousse. Whatever you do, stay away from the "vegetarian specialties" portion of the menu. Surprisingly, the pasta-and-meat dishes aren't that bad. But in case you haven't figured out by now, that's hardly the point.

The point is that, unless you're plugged into the Maryland Latin-dance community and are used to this sort of scene, it's one of the most hilariously foreign experiences that you can have in your own country. Mondays are tango nights—and, sometimes, tango classes, too. Live bands visit periodically. Fridays and Saturdays are "DJ nights," when one of the areas of Cococabana turns into a fairly rowdy nightclub. You've got to be ready to make a night of it, and keep your wits about you—fights are not unheard of. On weekends, the nightclub has a cover charge, too. On the flip side, if you come just for the club, a free buffet might just roll out at some point in the wee hours.

But again, that's hardly the point. –RG

# Com Tam Saigon

Come for the com tam specialties

**8.7** **6.2**
*Food* *Feel*

## Vietnamese

Casual restaurant

**$10**
*Price*

www.edencenter.com

Daily 9:30am–7:30pm

**Bar** None
**Credit cards** None
**Reservations** Not accepted

**Falls Church, VA**
6795 Wilson Blvd.
(703) 533-8440

A classic Eden Center find, this tiny 30-year-old corner joint—completely within the mall—is distinguished, if you want to call it that, by bluish walls, knickknacks, and about six little tables full of local Vietnamese people, who are lorded over by a weird, cheesy wild horse poster and the obligatory television. Nothing else stands out, and the most notable thing about the space, really, is its smallness.

But small can also mean serious, and this kitchen—perhaps more than any other in the DC area—is really, really serious about com tam, a typical peasant dish that begins with what's alternatively described by Vietnamese food aficionados as "broken rice" or "crushed rice." (Traditionally, it would be leftover fragments that had broken off a quantity of whole rice.) The result is a texture somewhere between traditional steamed rice and cous cous.

That's just the base of the dish. There are five potential toppings for the com tam, of which the best is a combination of grilled pork ribs, shredded pork skin, and eggs. Roasted quail is an interesting alternative, but the version with a pork chop, tofu, and Chinese sausage is less exciting. All of the com tam dishes are served with various greens and accoutrements, plus—of course—nuoc cham (fish sauce) to add salt and umami.

Although almost everyone here comes for the com tam, it doesn't end there; they also do a good banh xeo (Vietnamese omelet) and respectable bun (noodle) preparations, including a nice mi thap cam (combination) and a competent version of bun mam (in a salty fish stock with shrimp, fish, and lemongrass). Throw in the helpful English-language menu and the unusually polite staff, and you've got an experience that is, even by itself, worth the trip from the District to Eden. –RG

# Comet Ping Pong

Hipsters flock to this hangout more for the fun
than the flavor

**6.9** **5.0**
Food Feel

## Pizza

Casual restaurant

**$35**
Price

www.cometpingpong.com

Mon–Thu 5pm–9:30pm
Fri 5pm–10:30pm
Sat 11:30am–10:30pm
Sun 11:30am–9pm

**Bar** Beer, wine, liquor
**Credit cards** Visa, MC, AmEx
**Reservations** Not accepted
Live music, outdoor dining,
veg-friendly

**Upper NW**
5037 Connecticut Ave.
NW
(202) 364-0404

Comet Ping Pong bounced into town in late 2006, boasting a "New
Haven" influence and promising to take the neophyte pizza-eaters of
Washington by storm. Located next to Buck's Fishing and Camping, and
operated by the same folks, Comet, like Buck's, planned to take a generic
foodstuff (pizza), add a catchy tag (in this case, "New Haven"), and an
additional gimmick (here, three ping pong tables), and wait for the
hipsters and (fast-)foodies to descend.

Well, the idea worked. Comet Ping Pong is a busy place despite its
somewhat out-of-the-way location north of Van Ness (the restaurant does
benefit, however, from spillover from the Politics and Prose bookstore).
And it is a sight to see: on any given night, the pizzeria's dimly-lit hall is
populated by beautiful girls in 1980s-style black jeans and beautiful boys
in vintage cowboy shirts, with a large enough smattering of folk from the
neighborhood to make the place look credible as a culinary destination.
The décor, however, is clearly aimed at the hipsters: you'll eat your meal
from atop a worn-down ping pong table while seated in a "vintage"
wooden booth, and apparently Comet is a little too hip to own up to its
bathrooms: their cunningly hidden doors blend into the wall without a
mark (really, not the best game plan, when you have increasingly
inebriated young people on your hands). On another wall, unsmiling black
and white portraits, faces turned from the camera, in various sizes, form a
depressing montage.

Comet's pizzas, by contrast, are all one size: extra-small. Count on at
least one pizza per person. And at thirteen to seventeen bucks a piece,
this pie comes at a premium. Compare it to the pies of Comet's supposed
progenitors, and you might begin to feel like you're being robbed at
gunpoint: at the famous New Haven places (Pepe's and Sally's), a pizza
four times the size of Comet's goes for about fifteen dollars. But we don't
really recommend the comparison—Comet would fare too badly. While
we like the simplicity of Comet's yuppie-topping structure (there are only
six "combo" options, all wisely matched, such as asparagus, potato, and
fontina), the pizzas aren't great: the crust is flavorless and the cheese too
rubbery. These doughy creations really don't deserve to wipe up the oil
that drips from Sally's savory, charred, and delicate masterpieces.

Like the pies, Comet's $5 salads are diminutive creations, consisting of
about three leaves of red lettuce tossed with oil in a bowl: no toppings,
no nuthin'. At least the ping pong is fun—and unlike Comet's other
miniaturized amusements, it's free. –CK

# Commissary

Like a community mess hall—great friends, bad food

**4.0** Food    **9.1** Feel

## American

Casual restaurant    **$30** Price

www.commissarydc.com

Mon–Thu 8am–11pm
Fri 8am–midnight
Sat 9am–midnight
Sun 9am–11pm

**Bar** Beer, wine, liquor
**Credit cards** Visa, MC, AmEx
**Reservations** Accepted
Delivery, kid-friendly, outdoor dining, veg-friendly, Wi-Fi

**Logan Circle**
1443 P St. NW
(202) 299-0018

Like an art-and-gathering space for Logan Circle hippies, Commissary is the restaurant we would have opened as 17-year-old restaurateurs. There, *of course*, has to be beer. And all the biggies are here on Commissary's short menu: Sam Adams, Yuengling (remember, a teen is too young to know that this Pennsylvania brew is nothing special), Brooklyn Lager. A blueberry lager for the girls who don't like beer. Allagash to show how hip we are. And Dogfish Head 60 Minute IPA—just so that we can show that our beer knowledge knows no limits as we expound upon the beer's hoppiness (and alcohol).

And we can't forget the cocktails—"Pear-ian Berry" (vodka, pear juice, sour mix, blueberries, and Triple Sec), "Hurricane Joe" (rum, fruit juices, grenadine, and lime), and a watermelon margarita (you can figure that one out on your own)—all of which seem to have been born at a party thrown for no better reason than that the fact that someone's parents were out of town. The wine list looks about like what you'd get back when you gave someone who's "of age" some cash and told them to buy you something nice, but also to stretch it as far as possible.

The food at Commissary? A chicken salad is just about average for chicken salad. Its accompanying pita is squishy, hot, and satisfying, but lacking the tasty char that we look for. Eggs come, thankfully, not too dry, but rather underseasoned. Not so in the case of fries—they are just as mushy as they are flavorful (which is to say, very). Other mains are nothing out of the ordinary: grilled veggies with hummus. Chicken kebabs. It's all painfully reminiscent of a post-prom meal...

But you're not here for the food. You're here for the scene—both interpersonal and aesthetic. There's *definitely* a heavy Americana influence. (Totally not how we would have decorated as teens...the whole look is way too wholesome for an appropriately rebellious youngster.) And it all works, when you consider that Commissary is striving to be a neighborhood hangout. And they're getting there—note the number of lone diners, Sunday Times in hand, on a weekend.

But even if the place feels a little immature, sometimes the distinctly un-jaded perspective of a promising young teen is all you need. –AH

# Commonwealth

A gastro-pub with some British fare, some British beers, and some friendly faces

| 8.0 | 9.0 |
|-----|-----|
| Food | Feel |

## British

Casual restaurant

**$40**
Price

www.commonwealthgastropub.com

Sun–Thu 11am–10pm
Fri–Sat 11am–11pm

**Bar** Beer, wine, liquor
**Credit cards** Visa, MC, AmEx
**Reservations** Accepted
Date-friendly, outdoor dining,
Wi-Fi

**Columbia Heights**
1400 Irving St. NW
(202) 265-1400

One would think that a native speaker of English would be able to navigate a British menu with the utmost ease. If it's second nature to American foodies that oeufs are eggs, pescado is fish, gai is chicken, contorni are vegetables, and pivo is beer, then we should easily recognize rollmops, frog in a puff, bubble and squeak, and Welsh rarebit. Easy. Right?

We do like Commonwealth's Welsh rarebit (too often hilariously misspelled as "Welsh rabbit," which would be a different thing entirely). A nicely fluffy piece of toast is topped with lots of cheese and a Worcestershire-heavy sauce, which adds a nicely zippy element to what could otherwise sit like a rock in your stomach. Scotch eggs (boiled, wrapped in sausage, then deep-fried) are just as good as their recipe makes them sound. Tikka masala, once famously named the national dish of Britain, makes an obligatory appearance on the menu.

But what Commonwealth really excels at is charcuterie and innards. Standouts on the butcher plate (three or five items of your choosing) include an appropriately piquant garlic sausage or murderously rich head cheese (made in-house). If offal is more your thing, go for the stuffed trotters or deviled sweetbreads.

The beer selection here, while not exhaustive, has a good showing of UK brews. (During the late-night happy hour you can get $2 PBR in a can, if your tastes lean toward domestic...and cheap...and watery.)

Servers are warm, knowledgeable, and, above all else, enthusiastic. And frankly, it's hard not to feel good in Commonwealth's cozy and welcoming digs—even if you are on the clock. Warm woods and low lighting encourage you to cozy up and tuck in to what's in front of you, be it food, drink, or a date. The outside world seems to melt away with each sip of beer—unless, that is, you're sitting on Commonwealth's decidedly-less-than-romantic patio overlooking concrete and a commercial center. No matter how nice the weather, this patio can be a little hard to love.

But let's face it: you're here for the beer and the gastro-pub fare. And to brush up on your English. –AH

# Coppi's Organic

**8.0** Food **9.0** Feel

Authentic Italian in a subterranean hideaway: one of the icons of the new U Street

## Italian, Pizza

Upmarket restaurant

**$50**
Price

www.coppisorganic.com

Mon–Thu 6pm–11pm
Fri–Sat 5pm–midnight
Sun 5pm–10pm

**Bar** Beer, wine, liquor
**Credit cards** Visa, MC, AmEx
**Reservations** Accepted
Date-friendly, good wines,
veg-friendly

**U Street**
1414 U St. NW
(202) 319-7773

Coppi's is one in a row of U Street nooks whose atmosphere can change dramatically depending on your mood. The small space, with a carved bar and wood-fired oven in the back, can feel wonderfully intimate in the winter, or cramped in the summertime. When it's nice outside, the dark wood and dimly lit, richly scented interior can be a little overwhelming.

But the restaurant's décor is captivating. Coppi's (whose name derives from a legendary Italian bicyclist) is clearly run by a set of nationalist packrats: every inch of two walls is lined with paraphernalia from the Italian National Cycling team. Photos stack upon photos, punctuated by a few blue-and-white jerseys. The effect is certainly striking, but something about the package seems excessively vain. Take the wood-burning oven: its prime location behind the bar seems to benefit the customers more than the cooks, who must scuttle out of their way to reach it. Is it equipment or mere embellishment?

Your waitstaff is likely to be a team of three or four strapping young Italians, who switch positions as the meal progresses: one might bring your drinks, the next your appetizers, and the third your pizza. By the end of the meal, you almost feel as if Coppi himself should emerge, triumphantly, from the rear of the drafting line to bring you your check.

Just to reiterate, having real, live Italians—not third-generation Italian-Americans—cooking and serving your Italian meal is a very good thing. And while not all is perfect at Coppi's, the authenticity goes a long way, beginning with the well-chosen Italian wine selection. (Even if we, like the Italians, prefer our pizza with a beer.)

Appetizers include good charcuterie, but Coppi's is really known for its pizzas, which are cooked in a fairly authentic wood-burning brick oven. Their hallmark is exceedingly thin crusts. If 2 Amys is going for a thicker Neapolitan theme, Coppi's seems to be mimicking Italy's north, where cracker-thin crusts are more the norm. We like them, even if the crust goes so far in the thin direction at times that it approaches the texture of a saltine cracker. The Saraceno is topped with excellent spiced lamb, mint, and boldly smoked mozzarella.

Even if salads are disappointing and the organic shtick only goes far, a well-textured, authentic pizza in a fun, warm atmosphere make for one of our favorite ways to spend an easy night. The confluence of these things is a surprising rarity around here. –CK

# Corduroy

A deliciously modern kitchen that's firing on all cylinders—if only the place were more fun

| 8.8 | 6.8 |
|-----|-----|
| Food | Feel |

**New American**      Upmarket restaurant

**$70**
Price

www.corduroydc.com

Mon–Sat 5:30pm–10:30pm

**Bar** Beer, wine, liquor
**Credit cards** Visa, MC, AmEx
**Reservations** Accepted
Good wines

**Mt. Vernon Square**
1122 9th St. NW
(202) 589-0699

The old location of Corduroy, inauspicious though its surroundings might have been (the second floor of a Sheraton Four Points—could it get any worse?), had a certain quirky it's-surprising-how-good-this-place-is charm. But the restaurant had clearly outgrown its kid clothes.

The choice to move to Shaw, rather than one of the city's more traditionally trendy neighborhoods, was admirable. And we wanted nothing more than to rave about the new location of this ambitious New American concept. In culinary theme and business model, it's just the kind of place we love to love: it's small, it's unpretentious, it's chef-driven, and the kitchen is serious and modern in the very best sense of the word.

Yet there's something impersonal—even stuffy—about the feeling in Corduroy's new home, which is in a renovated townhouse. There's been such a big deal made these days about noise levels in DC dining rooms that it seems like this one has overreacted by almost imposing quiet time on its guests. We're in the school of thought that a restaurant should feel warm, intimate, easy, and—yes—fun, even at the temples to fine dining. But this mirrored dining room feels cold and hushed, the seating layout impersonal and awkward, the mirrors unforgiving. It's not a space we look forward to inhabiting.

A soup of rouge vif d'temps (red pumpkin) is poured over diced bacon to create a savory-and-only-slightly-sweet combo for the ages—and a reminder of how overlooked soup is these days. Sea urchin endows homemade pasta with a sweet, sexy, ineffable lightness. Duck-leg-and-duck-egg salad is a comfortable but haute homage to the French bistro.

Mains benefit from the kitchen's clever hand with side starches and vegetables: Le Puy green lentils play beautifully off tender, juicy lamb loin; a crispy striped bass absorbs the earthiness of black trumpet mushrooms; and sushi rice lifts seared tuna—so often a pan-Asian banality—to dizzying heights. It begs the question: why, in the fusion frenzy of the 1990s, didn't this far more appropriate starch partner for tuna become the standard instead of heavy wasabi mashed potatoes?

You've got to come ready to spend at Corduroy—and ready to focus more on the company than the environment. But on the plate, all is forgiven. –RG

# Cork

There's lots more to like than dislike at this hyper-cool wine bar

**7.5** Food

**9.1** Feel

## New American

Wine bar

**$40** Price

www.corkdc.com

Tue, Wed, Sun 5:30pm–midnight
Thu–Sat 5:30pm–1am

**Bar** Beer, wine, liquor
**Credit cards** Visa, MC, AmEx
**Reservations** Not accepted
Date-friendly, good wines, outdoor dining, veg-friendly

**Logan Circle**
1720 14th St. NW
(202) 265-2675

An evening at Cork is a bit like being in limbo. It's not a bar (they only serve wine), and it's not a restaurant (they only serve small plates). But being in limbo, Cork limbo, isn't as bad as Dante might suggest. While spending eternity surrounded by dark wood and exposed brick could get a bit dull, spending a few hours here makes for a lovely evening. Just don't get too stuck in: while the front of the restaurant is open and inviting, the warm and cozy back area begins to feel oppressive and claustrophobic within the first ten minutes.

Most wine bars, in an attempt to compensate for the fact that all they serve is wine, offer too many choices—many of them undoubtedly mediocre and expensive. In focusing on a few select countries and maintaining a controlled selection of wines by the glass and the bottle, Cork manages to eliminate bewilderment, confusion, and general anxiety. And if that isn't enough, servers are generally knowledgeable and ready to steer you in a good direction.

The advantage of small plates (divided into hot and cold) is that if something isn't great, you aren't stuck with a huge amount of it. And you can pawn it off on your companions. The disadvantage is that if a plate is really great, there's only a little bit of it. We suggest that you strategically grab said plate, pull it towards you, and say, "You wouldn't like it. I'll just finish it and get it out of the way." This works most effectively to your advantage in the case of the grilled bread (topped with a layer of creamy goat cheese and oil-cured tomatoes) and the decadent exotic mushroom duxelle. Other dishes, though well thought out, fare less well. The beautifully presented smoked trout tastes too much like herring and is paired with elements (orange segments and lightly dressed mache) that don't stand up to it.

The kicker is that we find ourselves at Cork quite a lot, really. And actions speak louder than words. Just be aware that the restaurant, like some other heavenly destinations, doesn't accept reservations (exceptions are made for pre-theater meals before 6:30), and that you'll generally find a crush of people who are just as eager to get served as you are. We recommend calling ahead half an hour before you want to eat, and putting your name on the waiting list. Otherwise, you might find yourself stuck in a more painful kind of limbo. –SDC

# Cosmopolitan Bakery

**8.1** Food
**5.0** Feel

It's Bosnian food (and plenty of it!)—isn't that enough of a reason to give it a try?

## Balkan

Café **$25** Price

www.balkangrill.us

Mon–Sat 10am–8pm
Sun 10am–5pm

**Bar** None
**Credit cards** Visa, MC, AmEx
Delivery

**Alexandria, VA**
5902 N. Kings Hwy.
(703) 329-3303

It's lucky that the Cosmopolitan—a Bosnian joint that's more deli than café, although there's a lot of baking too—brews a strong cup of coffee. Otherwise, the outsized portions of meat and bread could turn even the fittest, most capacious youth into a comatose beast.

The Cosmopolitan is really a small kitchen that adjoins a small market selling Balkan specialties, which adjoins a third, still smaller, room with a narrow bar and five stools. One of the two owners usually mans the register while the other presides in kitchen; by mid-morning, the fluffy, slightly sour loaves of Bosnian bread have already been baked for the day's sandwiches.

As in many of the Balkan cuisines, the secret staple of Bosnia is bread. It's cheap, portable, and, when prepared correctly, absolutely heavenly. The Cosmopolitan's has a crisp, golden-brown crust and an airy interior, and the loaves are well sized for holding a steaming hunk of meat or chicken. The former comes most compellingly in the shape of cevapcici: spicy dark sausages made with beef and grilled to a grandly textured finale, and served in a portion whose size would daunt even the most dedicated of eaters. If you opt for the chicken, be forewarned: this isn't a meal for the faint of heart, either. Half a bird is grilled in flavorful oil, covered with grilled onions, and immediately smacked into a loaf of bread. Both sandwiches are served with a heap of sour yogurt and, upon request, a generous dabble of mild red pepper sauce (the irresistible Balkan staple, Ajvar).

Also good are the burek—phyllo dough pastries filled with either potatoes and onions, slightly sweet beef, or fresh farmer's cheese; we recommend the understated potato version, especially if you intend the burek to serve as a prelude to a meatier dish. Cosmopolitan also makes a decent soup and a few desserts: the baklava, like its savory counterparts, is enormous.

Step through the doorway to the Euro Foods market for candies, sodas, and condiments from the Balkans, or simply ask for another round—to go—at the Cosmopolitan: in addition to sandwich-sized and larger loaves, you can buy Bosnian burgers by the dozen. Be sure to get some coffee, too. –CK

# Costa Verde

Where the grass really is greener

**8.5** Food
**4.3** Feel

## Peruvian

Casual restaurant

**$30** Price

Mon–Fri 11am–9pm
Sat 10am–10pm
Sun 9:30am–9pm

**Bar** Beer, wine, liquor
**Credit cards** Visa, MC, AmEx
**Reservations** Not accepted
Delivery, kid-friendly, Wi-Fi

**Arlington, VA**
946 N. Jackson St.
(703) 522-6976

Despite an abundance of Latin fusion and melting-pot restaurants in DC, it's difficult to find a pure example of any one Latin cuisine anywhere Northwest. But if you venture into the Commonwealth, you can find some fine places. Take Costa Verde. A ways from the Clarendon Metro, past a few empty lots and next door to a Jiffy Lube, it's the kind of restaurant that may make you grumble, at first glance: "I followed the Fearless Critic's advice and came way the hell out here for *this*?"

Costa Verde resembles a cross between an English manor and seedy bar somehow transplanted into a strip mall; in other words, it feels both out of place and depressingly familiar. Once you step inside, however, little details will begin to hint at its quality. You'll notice the customers that look like regulars, comfortable and happy despite the lack of niceties and stray house flies.

Flavors are wonderfully candid: you actually get to taste what you ordered. For example, the beef in the lomo saltado, sautéed to a medium well, is tender and loose, juicy and sweet from a rich marinade and rounded out by fresh herbs. Thick French fries, tomatoes, and red onions are all thrown into the mix and cooked together in Peruvian stir fry. There is a profound beefiness to the dish, as juice from the meat infuses everything else around it. The pescado saltado (stir-fried fish) version is good, too; both remind you of the Chinese influence in Peru.

A rarer find is a whole trout, lightly breaded, flash fried, and served with everything still attached. The breading is salty and the flesh is juicy and rich, good enough to more than justify its glassy-eyed appearance. Adventurous diners should munch on the fins, crisp like fishy potato chips. Pickled red onions add a fine note of acidity. You'll wonder why it's so hard to find places that will serve fish like this.

But best of all has been an absolutely mind-blowing seco de res (braised short rib) stew, redolent of cilantro and herbs, which achieves an ethereal softness. Drinks at Costa Verde are limited but do include an authentically prepared pisco sour that's frothy with beaten egg white—think of a delicious alcoholic Sprite. Desserts are small and rich. The crema volteada sandwiches thick, dark caramel between crumbly shortbread rounds. It's just enough to satisfy your sweet craving at the end of a hearty meal. Though Costa Verde is dismally remote for most of us, it is well worth a trip. Look past its crumbly exterior and painfully slow service. Sometimes, far away, the grass *is* greener, and the meat juicier. –JC

# Couscous Café

Speedy and generic lunches, but tasty desserts

**5.7** Food **7.4** Feel

## Moroccan, Middle Eastern

Counter service

**$10** Price

www.couscouscatering.com

Mon–Fri 8am–8pm

**Bar** None
**Credit cards** Visa, MC, AmEx
**Reservations** Accepted
Delivery, kid-friendly, outdoor
dining, veg-friendly, Wi-Fi

**Dupont**
1990 M St. NW
(202) 689-1233

In an area liberally speckled with lunch spots offering a range of affordable options, Couscous Café stands out as a homier, more genuine restaurant than most. Though it keeps typical workday hours—closing at 8pm and for the whole weekend—and occupies a nondescript storefront, the Algerian owner has worked to bring a taste of home to the undistinguished location. The interior walls are painted in shades of muted gold and burnished orange that bring a pleasant light into the room, which has the surprisingly hushed feel of a coffee house. Where other lunch destinations in this corner of the District can feel hectic and crowded, Couscous Café seems unhurried and relaxed.

A corner of the space displays North African and Middle Eastern foods like Algerian harissa and Moroccan mint tea; glass-fronted cases on either side of the cash register show off homemade salads and desserts. The star in the latter category, and the single best reason to visit Couscous Café, is the baklava, which is honey-sweet and satisfyingly flaky, but has a real pistachio flavor that rescues the pastry from being too cloying. Another sweet worth trying is a semolina-based, bar-like cookie that's baked in trays and then cut into rectangles, each piece studded with an almond and flavored with honey-and-rose-water syrup.

While desserts balance sweetness with textural and flavor contrasts, the dishes on the lunch menu don't succeed as well. The chicken bastilla is filled with spiced roast chicken and wrapped in crispy layers of phyllo dough, but the overpowering tastes here are cinnamon and the flurry of powdered sugar on top. On one visit, the chicken tagine featured dry nuggets of all-white-meat chicken; we skipped them, instead sopping up the saffron- and cinnamon-scented sauce with the green olives, bits of preserved lemon, and rice that accompanied the meat.

With lunch mains averaging around $8, it's hard to recommend the place for lunch. But you can stick to the sweets and the North-African-style mint tea and enjoy the refreshingly tranquil surroundings at this little oasis. —CD

# Crème

Down-home comfort food gets streetwise and chic

**8.0** Food  **8.9** Feel

## Southern

Casual restaurant

**$45** Price

www.cremedc.com

Mon–Thu 6pm–10:30pm; Fri 6pm–11:30pm; Sat 11am–3pm, 6pm–11:30pm; Sun 10am–3:30pm, 6pm–10:30pm

**Bar** Beer, wine, liquor
**Credit cards** Visa, MC, AmEx
**Reservations** Accepted
Date-friendly, kid-friendly, live music

**U Street**
1322 U St. NW
(202) 234-1884

In the up-and-coming neighborhood of U Street, Crème (pronounced "crem," not "cream") is a refreshing return to the down-home classics, but restyled for a hip crowd. One doesn't generally associate comfort food with sleek artsiness, nice flatware, or upscale service. But in the absence of a Southern grandmother's house, this place might just be the most pleasant atmosphere for it.

This theme of contrasts starts with the space, which juxtaposes soft pastels with stark black, concrete flooring with aerodynamic light fixtures. It's sparse but intimate. Seating is close, with a long bar, low banquettes, and higher tables all jumbled together and navigated by waiters clad in black. By night, live jazz transforms the cozy quarter into a romantic hotspot.

The menu, too, takes this idea of accessible comfort food and adds sophisticated twists: shrimp and grits, meat and potatoes, pork and beans. The latter comes as a braised, tender shank with caramelized onions speckling a bed of lima beans. At the popular brunch, wild mushrooms are substituted for ham in an eggs Benedict, creating an earthier version that is pleasantly light. Chicken and waffles are terrific, too, the batter thin and crisp. It feels strange to get your hands so gleefully sticky and greasy in this pretty little space, but it's also liberating.

There are only a few missteps here: grits have come appropriately thick, but lacking that deep corniness that keeps them from mimicking Cream of Wheat. Nevertheless, their shrimp are sweet and cooked to temperature.

The beverage program is a glaring oversight. Both iced coffee and iced tea are flaccid—it's clear they were brewed hot and poured into a glass full of ice instead of brewed and stored chilled. The wine list is all grocery-store plonk (served in tumblers, but you wouldn't want to smell Clos du Bois anyway), and the cocktails are sweet and vacuous—totally unworthy of the excellent food here.

Service is warm and hospitable, the recipes passed down through generations and reinvented with care; all this in a space that forswears the troubles of the world outside. Now if they would just change this silly name. –JC

# Crisp & Juicy

A no-frills Latin purveyor of memorable rotisserie chicken that lives up to its name

**7.7** Food

**4.0** Feel

## Latin American

Counter service

**$10** Price

www.crispjuicy.com

Daily 11am–9:30pm
Hours vary by location

**Bar** None
**Credit cards** Visa, MC
Kid-friendly, outdoor dining

**Arlington, VA**
4540 Lee Hwy.
(703) 243-4222

**Silver Spring, MD**
1314 E. West Hwy.
(301) 563-6666

**Falls Church, VA**
913 W. Broad St.
(703) 241-9091

**Additional locations**
and more features at
www.fearlesscritic.com

It's not often that we get effusively excited about chicken. As a matter of fact, it's most frequently the menu item that we ignore at restaurants. But that's impossible at this Latin American joint, a favorite among bargain-hunting foodies in the know, where the star of the menu is this underdog. Available whole, halved, or quartered, these are some of the best birds in DC. Marinated, rubbed, seasoned, probably even massaged, pampered, and coddled, this rotisserie chicken is just as the restaurant name says it is: crisp on the outside and juicy on the inside. The skin is crackly, salty, and heavily seasoned with an array of herbs and spices while the meat is moist and tender.

Once you begin digging into this bird, it's almost impossible to stop. Although you'll probably start with a fork and knife, we won't judge you if you switch over to your fingers, the best tools to extract the juiciest bits—which tend to be the dark meat, rather than the light. The whole shebang is accompanied by fried yuca and sweet, supple fried plantains. The fries aren't that great, and neither is the dry, mealy yuca. It becomes much better, however, after a dunk in its sauce, which is a creamy, spicy concoction the color of French dressing.

There are also menu items beyond rotisserie chicken, but we recommend avoiding them and sticking with the foolproof chicken platter, but even here anything beyond the chicken is a mild disaster. House salad is a useless mix of shredded lettuce and carrot, underripe tomato, and a supermarket-quality gummy vinaigrette. The dinner roll is standard-cafeteria-issue. Peruvian Inca Kola holds up well, however.

Eating at Crisp & Juicy is informal and low-key, where plastic chairs and disposable plates help create a no-frills vibe, more or less like a fast-food restaurant. We've had some lonely visits, though; it seems that taking out seems to be the well-respected norm, although it's hard to imagine exercising the self-control necessary to avoid devouring the chicken on the ride home. –SDC

# Cubano's

A lively Silver Spring destination where the flavors run wild

**6.2** Food  **7.7** Feel

## Cuban

Casual restaurant  **$35** Price

Mon–Fri 11:30am–10pm
Sat–Sun noon–10pm

**Bar** Beer, wine, liquor
**Credit cards** Visa, MC, AmEx
**Reservations** Accepted
Date-friendly, kid-friendly, live
music, outdoor dining

**Silver Spring, MD**
1201 Fidler Ln.
(301) 563-4020

Starting with the arrival of the Discovery Channel building and continuing now with the development springing up around the AFI Silver Theatre, Silver Spring is being reinvented as a suburban DC destination. Just off the newly-beaten path is the family-owned Cubano's, a nice alternative to the chains popping up in the area. Relatively authentic Cuban food is served in a surprisingly polished atmosphere; walls painted in vivid shades of red, yellow, and green spotlight unframed oil paintings of tropical scenes. Spanish-language music plays audibly but not too loudly; dark wood chairs set off the white tablecloths covered in crisp, clean paper.

The bread basket contains toasted slices of soft baguette spread with garlic butter, and there's more garlic and parsley coating our favored appetizer of long, crispy plantain chips (mariquitas). Yet more garlic flavors the vibrant red dipping sauce for crisp baton-shaped croquetas de jamón. Strange, then, that several of Cubano's main dishes seem to lack seasoning. Ropa vieja, cooked to a tender tangle of shredded beef, is served in a pleasant tomato-based sauce without much depth of flavor. Picadillo (ground beef) likewise benefits from a dash of hot sauce from the Goya bottle. Traditional black beans and rice (moros y cristianos) are the exception to the underseasoned rule; they're the perfect accompaniment to the hearty beef, chicken, and pork stews that form the backbone of the menu. For dessert, the creamy flan in a deep golden caramel sauce is a treat.

The bar near the front of the restaurant offers everything from house mojitos and sangría to the full range of rail drinks. Sangría is potent, but features no better than canned fruit; the mojitos are good but not great, although they have a loyal following. A full complement of staff are friendly and solicitous—when they remember to pay attention to you. This neighborhood restaurant isn't perfect, but it's a breath of fresh air in an area where increasing commercialization has brought national chains to the newly developed shopping plazas. A few drinks in, when the bright walls begin to swing a little to the beat of the flamenco dancers (live on Wednesday nights), even Silver Spring can begin to look a little colorful.
–CD

# Cucina Vivace

Italian done well and done right

| 7.2 | 7.0 |
|---|---|
| Food | Feel |

## Italian

Upmarket restaurant **$55**
Price

www.cucinavivace.com

Tue–Thu 5pm–10pm
Fri–Sat 5pm–11pm
Sun 5pm–9pm

**Bar** Beer, wine, liquor
**Credit cards** Visa, MC, AmEx
**Reservations** Accepted
Outdoor dining, Wi-Fi

**Arlington, VA**
509 23rd St. S.
(703) 979-7676

At its best, honest, simple Italian food can rise to great heights. At its best, Cucina Vivace's does so, bringing just enough wit and whim to down-to-earth ingredients, and pairing the food with heartfelt service, a casual but knowledgeable approach to wine, and not a hint of pretense on the menu or on the plate. Some inconsistency and a lack of certain sophistication keep the place down a bit, but it's still a neighborhood find.

The restaurant is located in a shotgun-style building: seating in front, small wine bar toward the back, and kitchen in the far rear. The two rows of simple dark wood tables are nothing fancy, and a comfortable bench runs the length of one of the walls.

Often, Vivace is empty enough to be serviced by a sole waitress; we hope and trust that as this place becomes better discovered, the staff numbers will creep up. The out-of-the-way location is not without its benefits, of course: Vivace can maintain a neighborhood feel and not succumb to the business lunches and happy hours that plague other fine restaurants downtown.

In authentic Italian format, Vivace's menu is divided into appetizers, salads, primi, and secondi; some primi can also be ordered in larger sizes to serve as secondi. Pastas are freshly made, but the restaurant also excels at seafood. Feathery scallops retain a briny taste, which works well with the oil in which they're grilled; they're paired with a lightly grilled polenta, which in turn hides a heady parsnip mash. The restaurant's savory fish balls are also superb, made with delicate spices and a touch of ground onion and served in a tart tomato sauce that tempers the fish. Delicious, too, are unassuming sides of grilled eggplant and fennel salad.

The problem is that Vivace's menu is often so "simple" and "honest" that it verges on boring. For instance, on a recent menu the only four pastas were a ricotta-stuffed raviolo in tomato sauce; tagliatelle with oil and garlic; spaghettini in tomato and hot pepper; or gnocchi in cream sauce and pancetta. We also can't endorse the failure to use whole fish for secondi, but rather fillets. That contradicts the message of simplicity and good ingredients.

But we heartily salute the broad, well-developed, well-priced Italian wine list. This really is a neighborhood gem. –FC

# The Dairy Godmother

Delicious frozen treats in a cozy neighborhood
kind of place

## Ice cream                                    Counter service

www.thedairygodmother.com

| | | |
|---|---|---|
| Wed, Thu, Sun noon–9pm | **Bar** None | **Alexandria, VA** |
| Fri–Sat noon–10pm | **Credit cards** Visa, MC | 2310 Mount Vernon Ave. |
| | Kid-friendly, outdoor dining, | (703) 683-7767 |
| | veg-friendly | |

Do you have fond childhood memories of eating frozen custard on the
Atlantic City boardwalk? Or of a Midwestern grandmother who served up
the treat by the pint? Well, even if you don't (and far be it from us to
judge the wisdom of bringing a child to Atlantic City, even for the alleged
frozen custard), you can experience the delicacy in all its glory at The Dairy
Godmother, a frozen custard (not ice cream!) shop in the Del Ray
neighborhood of Alexandria.

Just as Custard puts to shame its thinner cousin Cream, the frozen
version of the former renders ice cream reminiscent of chilled water. The
Dairy Godmother, a Wisconsin-style custard shop formerly known as The
Dreamery, keeps it simple with only three flavors on any given day: vanilla,
chocolate, and the current special. Don't want to miss the tiramisù
version? The shop prints up a calendar (now available online as well)
revealing its "flavor forecast" for the month, with varieties ranging from
butter pecan to raspberry to thin mint cookie to Mozambique.

In addition to scoops and cones, The Dairy Godmother bakes and sells
cookies (ginger, chocolate chip, sugar), which are also sold sandwiched
around a hunk of custard for an exquisite treat. There is also a fair
selection of homemade sorbets, with piquing flavors such as Lemon
Ginger, Santa Rosa Plum, and Red Zinger Tea. And in dog-friendly Del
Ray, the Godmother would be remiss not to stock a set of canine treats,
apt to make any custard-loving dog owner cringe: "made primarily from
spent barley malt." Why not buy the pooch custard instead? –FC

# Darlington House

**5.6** **8.5**
Food Feel

A style-over-substance restaurant whose main selling point is its sidewalk tables

## New American

Upmarket restaurant

**$65**
Price

www.darlingtonhousedc.com

Mon–Thu 11:30am–3pm,
5:30pm–10:30pm
Fri–Sat 11:30am–3pm,
5:30pm–11:30pm
Sun 11am–3pm, 5pm–10pm

**Bar** Beer, wine, liquor
**Credit cards** Visa, MC, AmEx
**Reservations** Accepted
Outdoor dining

**Dupont**
1610 20th St. NW
(202) 332-3722

The Darlington House seems to derive quite a bit of popularity from its Dupont-area location. It also lures people in with its airy awning aesthetic, which is particularly enticing at brunch; and with its five-course, $48 prix-fixe dinner (including two wines), for which you have to sign up in advance online. The main restaurant, upstairs, is modern but not minimalist, colored with ivories, beiges, and browns. On most nights, it's got a fun, energetic din but retains a certain intimacy, too. Service is friendly, but sometimes bumbling.

Highlights of the upmarket-American-crossed-with-Italian menu are a well balanced arugula salad with thick parmesan shavings, lemon oil, and not-too-sweet pears. We've also enjoyed a very tender glazed pork chop, although its polenta was weak and grainy. Halibut in cider sauce has come undersalted but soft and pleasant, with beautifully fried shallots (like onion rings with more flavor and more crunch). We've been less impressed with a cloying butternut squash soup, whose amaretto cookies take its sweetness beyond even dessert levels. Worst of all, though, have been pastas, or, more specifically, pasta sauces—like the underreduced, totally tasteless sausage-and-cherry-tomato ragú that topped (appropriately al dente) cavatelli. Best among desserts has been an unusually light, mousse-like pumpkin cheesecake with caramel sauce and homemade whipped cream of excellent consistency.

Given how long they tend to leave bottles open that they're pouring by the glass, this restaurant is either (a) not very serious about wine or (b) too serious about saving money. That stingy attitude also seems to inform the happy hour "drink specials" at the downstairs "cantina" ($4 Peroni? Wowee!), which shares a kitchen (and, upon request, a menu) with the upstairs restaurant.

The sampler of six bar snacks offered at the cantina might include properly textured but bland mozzarella; underwhelming heirloom tomatoes; an average slider with a sweet bun and good cheddar; sweet, crispy candied pistachios; or figs with goat cheese and a useless spot of balsamic vinegar. Avoid, at all costs, the melon in a strange, oily sweet sesame-oil concoction; and the chorizo empanaditas, whose tough skin and tough filling give them that fresh-from-the-freezer feel. If the upstairs Darlington were better, this would be the sort of place one might describe as "a lower-priced opportunity to try the Darlington's cooking." Not really. The only real selling point are the sidewalk seats. But there are always free public benches around, too. –RG

# Daruma Japanese Market

A homey little place whose goods fill the homes of
DC's Japanese-Americans

## Japanese, Groceries

Counter service

www.darumajapanmarket.com

Daily 11:30am–6pm

**Bar** Beer
**Credit cards** Visa, MC, AmEx
Veg-friendly

**Bethesda, MD**
6931 Arlington Rd.
(301) 654-8832

You'll have to jockey with Bethesda soccer moms in BMW SUVs for
parking—you'll find some next to the CVS and the dry cleaners—but
you'll probably have unassuming Daruma Japan Market to yourself. At
first glance it's just another ethnic market—small, slightly dingy,
fluorescent lighting. You can amuse yourself browsing the shelves of
Japanese groceries; there are some good frozen products in the freezer
case, and a wide selection of soy sauces, rice vinegars, and sake. If the
vegetables look a little wan, it's probably because there's little turnover,
but there are plenty of condiments, candies, and other treats to spark
your curiosity, such as an impressive collection of Pocky—those little
dipped breadsticks with the sinfully-addictive snap (including dark-
chocolate "Men's Pocky"—we kid you not). There is also a Japanese video
rental service (we're talking VHS here), further confirming that Daruma
caters to the real deal.

The hidden secret within this already well-hidden shop is the home-style
Japanese food, available for eat-in or take-out. During the day, you'll find
fresh sushi in the large refrigerated case. The quality and pricing are good,
but not great. Until 6pm, however, you can also order a variety of hot
dishes. The friendly Japanese staff will help you choose from among the
meals pictured on the laminated menu taped to the counter.

Gyudon, a stir-fry of paper-thin slices of beef with tendon served over
sticky rice, is a surprisingly sweet dish balanced only partially by the slivers
of bright-red pickled ginger on top. Standard bowls of decent ramen
noodle soup and curry rice are also available. While perhaps less familiar
to Americans who picture mostly sushi and empty wallets when they think
of Japanese food, these simple dishes are prime comfort food for
Japanese natives. Daruma doesn't really reach past the limits of its
relatively modest blueprint, nor does it try to. This food aims more at hot
then haute.

The setting isn't elegant; with just a few café tables that look almost
abandoned near the front of the restaurant, this isn't a place to linger. But
this little shop is a winning reminder that even in Japan, most of the time
cooking means a mom or a dad trying to get something filling onto the
table for their kids when they get home from school. –CD

# DC Café

It's nothing too fancy, but there are some surprising sleepers on the menu

**6.3** **4.8**
Food   Feel

## Middle Eastern

Counter service   **$25**
Price

Daily 11:30am–3am

**Bar** Beer
**Credit cards** Visa, MC, AmEx
Outdoor dining, veg-friendly

**Dupont**
2035 P St. NW
(202) 887-5819

DC Café certainly isn't out to impress. Despite its prime location on the corner of P and 21st, the eatery faces swift competition from its myriad Dupont neighbors, and it's hardly conscientious in attracting clients. The main room is poorly lit (in a non-romantic fashion) and grimy, and the display cases are too scratched to do justice to the offerings in their hold. There are rarely more than a couple of customers eating in; most are there for take-out.

In the summer months, the café is redeemed by a fenced-in outdoor patio; eating outside tends to make the food from inside more palatable. Which is fortunate, because despite the gritty interior of the café, it would be easily to overlook the fact that much of the food is actually quite all right, even though the quality fluctuates wildly between dishes. Similarly, the menu seems put together with little forethought. The café touts its Lebanese roots, even though many of the menu offerings are Greek or Turkish in origin. And Asian-style teas are stocked alongside Turkish jellies and juices for sale on the extremely dusty dry-goods shelf.

The vegetable mains are among DC Café's most impressive. The okra is stewed with tomatoes, oil, and a muted allotment of spices in the Turkish style. Large chunks of eggplant, with skin attached and all bitterness removed, are coated in fragrant olive oil and need little else. All main courses—meat or vegetable—are served with a rather ordinary hummus, tzatziki that's creamy if a tad sour, parsley-heavy taboulleh, and a blend of white and wild rice with a slight dryness that works well with the mushy mains.

The falafel, however, doesn't taste much more interesting than that from a boxed mix, and it's worth steering clear of all of the vegetables that accompany falafel and gyro meat: the lettuce is shredded iceberg and the tomatoes are old and dry. Although many of the prepared pies and dishes look like they've borne a lengthy tenure in the display case, they sometimes shine: a chicken pie encloses slightly sweet shredded meat inside a light and bready casing. –CK

# DC Coast

Rich—very rich—fish dishes served in an Art Deco space with oceanic accents

| 7.3 | 8.4 |
|-----|-----|
| Food | Feel |

## Seafood, New American

Upmarket restaurant

**$75**
Price

www.dccoast.com

Mon–Thu 11:30am–10:30pm
Fri 11:30am–11pm
Sat 5:30pm–11pm
Sun 5:30pm–9:30pm

**Bar** Beer, wine, liquor
**Credit cards** Visa, MC, AmEx
**Reservations** Accepted

**Downtown**
1401 K St. NW
(202) 216-5988

Dining at DC Coast is like being invited to an expensive wedding reception in an elegant hotel ballroom. A dramatic, soaring space and decorous, slightly detached service seem tailored to a grand celebration. It's hard to mistake the emphasis on seafood here when an enormous bronze mermaid statue greets you at the door. The aquatically Art Deco dining room, accented with honey-colored wood, sea-green, gold, and mirrors, plays host to expense account power-diners and eager first dates.

The food here—which emulates the cuisine of the mid-Atlantic, Gulf, and Pacific coasts—certainly exceeds the standards of typical banquet catering, but it doesn't quite hit the high notes. The "tower" of crab, combining a crab cake with its deep-fried soft-shell cousin in a puddle of corn succotash, is more rich than flavorful. The celebrated (though only occasionally available) "Chinese-smoked" lobster isn't smoked in the traditional sense, but cut into sizeable shell-on pieces and stir-fried with soy sauce in a super-hot wok. Once pried out of the shell, each morsel of lobster is tender and savory, though the accompanying bed of deep-fried spinach can taste too charred. Fish is rarely overcooked or mishandled, but preps tend to be overrich and often don't integrate interesting flavor combinations. Pork chops are tender, brightened by cherry chutney, and served on a bed of mashed sweet potato (does anyone not like sweet potato?).

The wine list is diverse in region (though the domestics are heavy with overblown, overpriced mass-producers, Old World cult wines are a good bargain here), and includes just as many bottles in the $80-$125 range (and up) as in the $30-$65. A succinct selection of half bottles and glasses are also available, but at significant mark-ups.

Huge portions of indulgent, creamy dishes won't fail to satisfy, but the prices might not feel earned. As at many K Street restaurants, a three-course meal with wine here can run you about $80, which starts to feel excessive when the meal is merely *good*. When it first opened, DC Coast created a lot of buzz among diners, but since then, the city has outgrown the original excitement factor. Nevertheless, the first dates, anniversaries, power lunches, and client dinners continue to happen here; at more than a decade and still going, this popular oceanic dinosaur won't be changing it up anytime soon. –CD

# Dduk Sarang

**8.7** Food  **6.8** Feel

They got the Korean porridge and oxbone soup to soothe your savage beast

## Korean

Casual restaurant

**$15** Price

Daily 9am–9pm

**Bar** None
**Credit cards** Visa, MC
**Reservations** Not accepted

**Annandale, VA**
4231 Markham St.
(703) 916-0006

Porridge! It's not the bland, vaguely buttery mush they served at early-20th century British orphanages anymore. It's a filling, tasty meal rather like a soupier risotto. It's also the ideal medium for just about any substance on the planet. Shoe and crawfish? Probably. Buick and rattlesnake? Why not!

Luckily, the combinations here are more digestible (and even tastier) than automobile. The headliner—bar none—is seolleongtang, translated roughly as "beef bone and tripe soup," and more prominent in the restaurant's storefront signage (at least in English) than its real name. Marrowy and deep, this is one of the best seolleongtangs around—and one of the best hangover cures, like milky white Jesus Juice. In fact, hangover sufferers fall into one of three camps: the menudo camp, the pho camp and the seolleongtang camp. It is best not to argue with them about which camp they are in, because the next time they are hungover they will throw up in your car in retribution. Ask us how we know.

Tuna with assorted vegetables gives off this slight funky taste that you find yourself missing as soon as you swallow it. There are other things, aside from porridge, like dumplings, which are very good and squirt a little flavorful juice in your mouth at first bite. Who doesn't love that?

For such a traditional menu, the atmosphere at Dduk (also spelled Dduck, which brings to mind a pantless, hostile cartoon) is strangely modern. Wood-paneled walls host traditional artifacts and a strange, football-shaped metallic lighting track gives off a warm, soft glow. You'll, of course, be given lots of banchan to nibble on. Kimchi is a touch mild here, but fish cakes are addictive. Fermented eggplant is alluring, in that it's-kind-of-sick-but-I-can't-stop sort of way. On the way out, don't forget the dduk, tasty little rice cakes they sell at the front. They come in all sorts of flavors and have a fun, chewy texture, not at all like our crunchy Westernized diet snacks. You can use them to make amends with your menudo- and pho-eating friends. –FC

# Dean & Deluca

One of America's foremost specialty groceries—
and a sidewalk-café hotspot, too

## Groceries

Market

www.deandeluca.com

Daily 8am–8pm

**Bar** Beer, wine
**Credit cards** Visa, MC, AmEx
Good wines, kid-friendly, outdoor
dining, veg-friendly

**Georgetown**
3276 M St. NW
(202) 342-2500

Nestled comfortably on the main drag of Georgetown in a handsome red brick warehouse, the DC branch of Dean & Deluca is filled with foodie delights. A wine cellar lives next to a chocolate counter, and fine meats (both fresh and cured), cheeses, fancy pantry items, and exotic produce all cohabitate with a bakery and plates of prepared food. The store is immaculate. Like their groceries, Dean & Deluca's prepared foods are shiny, well presented, and expensive.

If you choose prepared foods, you can bring your picnic of pristine takeout containers to the lively, shady, expansive outside café, where well-groomed, well-off shoppers dine on baked goods and sip lattes with equally well-groomed dogs in tow. It's a beautiful place just to sit with a coffee on a nice day, too—no food necessary.

Among prepared foods, we favor the baked goods. A hunk of cornbread is sweet and crumbly, studded with whole kernels, and moist enough to assure a liberal use of butter—a requirement for good cornbread. Best of all are the gelati from the café's cart. Chai-flavored gelato is creamy and spicy, just as rich as Dean & Deluca's liquid version, while a strawberry-lavender version of the Italian ice cream is a tour of flavors, starting with the aromatic bitterness of lavender, moving into the full sweetness of strawberry, and finishing on a hint of citrus. At $3.50 for a not-so-small small, it's a remarkable value.

We love the pâtés and charcuterie. Wines are New-World-centric, carefully chosen, and elite; the wine manager is operating on the level of a top restaurant sommelier. If you're one of the people for whom food-and-wine shopping is not just a household need, but more of a sport, you might wind up spending an inordinate amount of time here. –FC

# Deli City

It ain't the prettiest place, but get the corned beef sandwich—trust us

**7.6** Food    **5.0** Feel

## Southern, Sandwiches

Counter service    **$15** Price

Mon–Fri 6am–5pm

**Bar** None
**Credit cards** None
Kid-friendly

**Northeast DC**
2200 Bladensburg Rd. NE
(202) 526-1800

Deli City is one of those DC microcosms that brings together people from all sorts of ethnic and socioeconomic backgrounds. Although the owner and his mother are of Eastern European descent, the rest of the counter staff and cooks are more of the Southern persuasion. And the menu reflects this: corned-beef sandwiches and pork chops share the same stage. The staff at Deli City—from the sweet, chatty register lady to the women in colorful nurses' scrubs who take your order at the counter—are helpful and low-key. In essence, because the place is so small, they treat you like family.

Although many people take their orders to go, it's worth sitting down for a while and enjoying the unique ambiance at this joint. Taxi drivers, construction workers, and old friends enjoy a leisurely lunch at faux-wood cafeteria tables studded with fresh carnations. And although the well-lit dining room is a bit rough around the edges (the deli used to be a gas station), the magnificent sandwiches make up for it.

Corned beef on rye, maybe with a little bit of deli mustard, is definitely the way to go. Salty, moist, and tender, the meat completely falls apart in your mouth—it's impeccable. Also recommended is the turkey reuben, made with thinly sliced turkey, tart sauerkraut, and a smear of Russian dressing. These sandwiches' platform—griddled rye bread—tastes like all the good stuff that has been cooked on that griddle before it. The fatty pastrami, also a highlight, boasts a peppery crust and tastes exactly as it should.

DC has an incredible mix of people, cultures, and cuisines. Deli City represents that blend in a unique way, bringing together people that truly appreciate discussing church politics over a great corned beef sandwich, washed down with a glass of sweet tea. –SDC

# Dickey's Frozen Custard

You're never too old for ice cream

## Sandwiches, Ice cream

Counter service

Mon–Fri 7am–5pm

**Bar** None
**Credit cards** Visa, MC, AmEx
Delivery, kid-friendly, veg-friendly

**Farragut**
1710 Eye St. NW
(202) 861-0669

**Arlington, VA**
1235 Jefferson Davis Hwy.
(703) 416-2700

If you have ever spent a full summer in DC, you have probably developed a deep sympathy for everyone that is condemned to stroll the streets in a suit. Given that, it's no surprise that you may stand witness to one of the most whimsical sights in Farragut—that of the grown businessperson ravenously licking an ice cream cone.

There are many ice cream options in DC; from full-fledged, old-fashioned ice cream stores to "real" frozen yogurt, you can find a full range of textures. Though many seem to melt together, one stands out from its peers: the frozen custard at Dickey's.

Dickey's Frozen Custard is a pretty standard lunch joint. Sandwiches and pitas satisfy working-lunchers and an array of potato chips, coffee dispensers, and bottled drink coolers fill up the small storefront. During busy hours, Dickey's becomes a veritable sandwich conveyor belt, with lines out the door fulfilled as efficiently as any well-oiled factory.

The sandwiches at Dickey's are fresh, good, and pretty plain-vanilla. A well-grilled veggie pita is stuffed full of crunchy sprouts, cucumbers, tomatoes, sweet dressing, and warm, creamy hummus. The "Italiano" is decidedly white-bread: mid-quality deli meats like capicola and mortadella are doused with oil and vinegar, then smashed between dry, bleached ciabatta slices and toasted with provolone until it is a melty, gooey mess. Very little about it is Italian.

The best part about Dickey's is undoubtedly its eponymous sweet treat. Frozen custard is offered simply as chocolate, vanilla, or a swirl, and can be topped with a variety of fresh fruit, chopped nuts (try the home-candied walnuts!), or mashed cookie bits. However, after tasting this thick, velvety custard, you may decide it doesn't need any additional fuss. The texture is a cross between soft serve and ice cream, and nowhere near frozen yogurt. The flavor is mildly (not artificially) sweet, the overall effect luxuriant.

Ice cream aficionados would be well served to pay Dickey's a visit. After all, you're never too old or too well-dressed to enjoy a cone, especially in the summer. –JC

# Diner

Bad food and good conversation all night—an Adams Morgan icon, now and forever

**4.1** **8.3**
Food  Feel

## American

Casual restaurant

**$25**
Price

www.trystdc.com/diner/

24 hours

**Bar** Beer, wine, liquor
**Credit cards** Visa, MC, AmEx
**Reservations** Not accepted
Veg-friendly

**Adams Morgan**
2453 18th St. NW
(202) 232-8800

This all-night eatery-coffeeshop-community center-pickup scene-impromptu youth hostel has become an absolute icon of the young (some would say rowdy) Adams Morgan nightlife—a symbol of the new 18th Street. This is the sort of place that everyone ends up at sooner or later, like it or not. And just about everybody has experienced Diner's indifferent service, its white-walled aesthetic, and—at certain times of certain nights—its insufferably long queues.

That said, most people that have sampled Diner's late-night fare have been either totally drunk or bleary-eyed and starving (or all of the above) at the time, and have cared little for the drawbacks. But it is our duty to serve as food critics, sacrificing our bodies for the good of our readers—and, in this case, even staying sober for the good of our readers.

So, drumroll please…is the food actually good?

Nah. The food's terrible. Big surprise. It's beside the point, but salads are under-dressed, burgers are gray and overcooked, and (we wince as we recall it) a veggie burger falls apart into what feels like a pile of black-bean mush. Even the coffee's weak—but maybe that's just an attempt to honor the diner genre and keep it real.

But if it's 3am, you're stumbling around Adams Morgan (or, for that matter, you've got to pull an all-nighter for a morning deadline), and you want to sit down and get served a plate of scrambled eggs, Diner's got a monopoly. There's no arguing with that, and for that, we're glad it's there. —FC

# Dino

Good Italian food in a cozy setting makes Dino an affordable sure thing

## Italian

Upmarket restaurant

**$50**
Price

www.dino-dc.com

Mon–Thu 6pm–9:30pm
Fri 6pm–10:30pm
Sat 5:30pm–10:30pm
Sun 5:30pm–9:30pm

**Bar** Beer, wine, liquor
**Credit cards** Visa, MC, AmEx
**Reservations** Accepted
Good wines, outdoor dining

**Cleveland Park**
3435 Connecticut Ave. NW
(202) 686-2966

Dino, Cleveland Park's rustic Italian restaurant, is that vital ace up the sleeve when you're in need of a good, no-frills meal that consistently hits the mark.

The gregarious owner greets patrons as they enter his two-story dining room, whose burnt yellow and orange walls boast an array of contemporary Italian art from his own private collection. Wine aficionados will find a kindred spirit here; he's crafted a tome of great Italian producers, and he serves his wines at the proper temperatures—something we rarely (if ever) see. If his adorable and enthusiastic descriptions don't help you, the knowledgeable wait staff will. Check for frequent specials on wine and on Thursdays there's no corking fee (a gracious move for someone with such a gorgeous list).

The menu changes often as fresh ingredients come in, which elevates this restaurant far above most of its ilk. The hot and cold antipasti present some of the kitchen's best work. Three plump pork and veal meatballs seasoned with garlic and fresh herbs pair ideally with a chunky sauce of ripe tomatoes. Cured-meat and cheese enthusiasts will appreciate Dino's stellar selection of Italian imports, including a subtle but creamy buffalo mozzarella that's flown to the States twice a week from Puglia. This and a slice of warm crusty bread, with air-bubble "cubby holes" that capture heaps of tangy olive and roasted red pepper tapenade, allow diners to truly appreciate the pleasures of simple country cooking.

It's easy to fill up on small plates, but the homemade pastas and mains also deserve high marks. Now and then you might run into less meritorious dishes, like a fusilli with a white wine ragù of ground duck, pork, and veal that, when compared to his other work, is somewhat disappointing. But this is rare.

Excellent homemade gelati and a decent tiramisù make the requisite Italian dessert menu appearances, but another highlight includes a surprisingly fluffy Nutella-and-mascarpone mousse playfully served in a chocolate shell resembling an espresso cup. Whether this "Cappuccino di Nutella" or an actual coffee serves as the meal's finale, there's little need to squirm once the check arrives. Dino, after all, isn't about the splurge—instead, each step of the meal focuses on the strong execution of simple, affordable flavors that combine to make the place a sure thing. –WS

# DISH + drinks

The restaurant formerly known as Dish has added some drinks

**7.4** | **8.0**
Food | Feel

## New American

Upmarket restaurant

**$55**
Price

www.theriverinn.com

Mon–Fri 9am–9pm
Sat 8am–11am, 5pm–9pm
Sun 8am–11am

**Bar** Beer, wine, liquor
**Credit cards** Visa, MC, AmEx
**Reservations** Accepted
Wi-Fi

**Foggy Bottom**
924 25th St. NW
(202) 338-8707

The restaurant at the River Inn formerly known as Dish has been renamed something far more pretentious: "DISH + drinks." Why? Were people unclear about the presence of beverages before? Mostly, this seems like a good excuse to give the space a facelift, adding a couple of higher community tables and boldly striped bamboo flooring. Like the boutique hotel that houses it, DISH + drinks is charmingly diminutive. It takes roughly ten tables to fill the space, and a miniature bar seats no more than a handful of people. Sedate grays and blacks give the room a certain sophistication that finds levity in portraits of Wegman's mopey Weimeraners.

Come during quieter times, and you'll feel like part of an exclusive, secret club. At busier times, such as the pre-theater rush, the noise level gets quite high (and is not helped by a flatscreen TV over the bar). Multi-tasking servers are personable and knowledgeable. The regionally diverse wine list is aptly suited to this cuisine, and nearly every bottle is also available by the glass. A caveat, though: ask when your wine was opened—long glass lists increase your chances of getting a raisiny specimen. There are also several Chimays among the beers and some pretty pricey cocktails. 5-7pm happy hours every day but Sunday, though, reduce prices.

It is surprising that a restaurant this small can execute a rather large menu so well. An elegant dish of tempura-fried softshell crab is the ideal balance between light and filling. The batter on the crab is denser than typical tempura batter, but also less oily, allowing the flavor of the meat to come through. Succotash, which includes edamame, bacon, potatoes, and roasted corn, is a kaleidoscope of textures with an unexpectedly hearty flavor. It demonstrates that you can borrow elements from other cultures without railroading the original concept of the dish.

Many of the desserts here attempt to defy gravity with their complex constructions, incorporating several flavors as well as textures. Frozen white chocolate mousse is layered with bananas, phyllo, dark caramel, and hint of pistachio. The effect is luxuriant and multi-layered—an adult, nuanced version of a banana split.

While there are some gaffes (tequila-cured salmon is served in a taco bowl with a mouth-slicing shell), the menu at DISH + drinks far outperforms that of many other hotels, making this not just an incidental spot, but rather a destination. –JC

# District Chophouse

Beer, beef, and big bellies

**7.1** Food  **7.5** Feel

## Steakhouse, American

Casual restaurant

**$45** Price

www.chophouse.com

Sun–Mon 11am–10pm
Tue–Sat 11am–11pm

**Bar** Beer, wine, liquor
**Credit cards** Visa, MC, AmEx
**Reservations** Accepted
Kid-friendly, Wi-Fi

**Penn Quarter**
509 7th St. NW
(202) 347-3434

Located in what used to be an old bank building, District Chophouse and Brewery is the classiest kind of chain. Between the deep leather booths, towering ceilings, and private dining room (in what used to be the bank's vault), it's nice enough to escape most negative associations of restaurant clones. At the chophouse, big families chomp peacefully alongside big men in suits; everything—from the scale of the building to the patrons and the plates from which they sup—is large and loud and predictably American.

The menu at District Chophouse is exactly what you'd expect: fried appetizers, sharable pizzas, and lots of meat. The most exotic flavor on the entire thing may be a shiitake mushroom or two and some miso butter. Ingredients and descriptions pay homage to the cowboy beef-eaters that make America proud, and portions celebrate the excess that other nations mock.

The Chophouse's food isn't bad, but it's nothing special. Fried goodies taste, well, fried, and taste the same as well done onion rings, calamari, and chicken tenders anywhere. Pizzas sound better than they taste. One version combines steak and mild cheese with overpowering amounts of rosemary that add a dusty flavor that doesn't make sense with the rest of the ingredients. The overabundance of cheese turns the flatbread soggy very quickly.

Steakhouse classics perform somewhat better. A cartoonishly hefty 24-ounce porterhouse is served with a generous pat of Bourbon steak butter and salty, fluffy mash. They are not afraid to serve things rare. The culinary highlight at the District Chophouse is a cast-iron skilletfull of cornbread. Honestly, what could be better than a cast-iron skilletfull of cornbread? It has the deep flavor and rough texture of toasted corn; it's sticky like cake and you can glaze it with sweet whipped honey butter that isn't gritty like many of its peers.

The best reason of all, though, to go to the District Chophouse is their original beer—more specifically the Bourbon Stout: a cask ale made from oatmeal stout aged in bourbon barrels for six weeks. The result is a caramel-gold wonder of alchemy, a love child of whiskey and stout—mellow and smooth, with a port-like thickness, bitter like coffee, but spiked with licorice and mellowed with a touch of vanilla.

This is the place to celebrate the good ol' US of A. As we go to press, you can even raise a glass of "Barack Bock" to toast the new prez. And the District Chophouse really is American in terms of its priorities; it is neither high art nor lowfat, but it sure as hell cares about its beer. –JC

# Dolcezza

With a touch of Italy, and a touch of Argentina,
this little spot sells our chosen frozen

## Ice cream, Baked goods

Counter service

www.dolcezzagelato.com

Sun–Thu 1pm–7pm
Fri–Sat 1pm–8pm

**Bar** None
**Credit cards** Visa, MC, AmEx
Date-friendly, delivery, live music,
veg-friendly, Wi-Fi

**Georgetown**
1560 Wisconsin Ave. NW
(202) 333-4646

**Bethesda, MD**
7111 Bethesda Ln.
(301) 215-9226

The history books are full of unsavory cases of stolen intellectual property, but one of the world's most savory examples of imitations (on a national scale) is Argentina's delicious appropriation of Italian gelato. Although gelato means "ice cream" in Italian, it is no ordinary version, being thicker and made with less dairy. To Italy's recipe, the Argentines have added flavors like dulce de leche and accoutrements like alfajores (small, rich cookies). If, in fact, you ever find yourself in Buenos Aires, we recommend you find a Freddo (a popular chain) and stay there.

There is, of course, a broad range of quality in gelato, with the lowest end tasting much like sugary bulk ice cream and the highest quality gelaterias employing exceedingly fresh ingredients, so that the taste of mulberry or tiramisù or banana is powerful and clean. Luckily, Dolcezza, our very own Argentine gelateria, which occupies a small space between Georgetown and Glover Park, is of the latter persuasion.

Take, for example, the hazelnut flavor. Dolcezza has restored to its former glory what had become one of the most exploited nuts of our modern age of affluence (think Starbucks lattes). Instead of being an afterthought to coffee or chocolate, the hazelnut here takes center stage: in a not-too-sweet blend the almost bitter nuttiness comes through. Similarly, Dolcezza's pistachio does justice to the nut: rather than inserting the tasteless chunks that fill many "pistachio" ice creams, the smooth gelato packs in the full, unsalted flavor of the fruit.

Dolcezza does, admittedly, take a few stabs in the dark. What, for example, is an Australian wattle seed, one of the shop's staples? The best answer from behind the counter, which arrives in Spanish, is "It's a seed, from Australia…" Well, okay. In the end, it doesn't much matter, since whatever taste the wattle may carry is overwhelmed by the tiny flakes of chocolate and vanilla woven in.

Nuts and seeds aside, it's the fruit flavors that really sing at Dolcezza. The blood orange is sweet, full, and just as sour as the fruit itself. The humble strawberry, critcally injured by overly creamed and artificially flavored versions, springs back to brimming life in Dolcezza's sunny rendition.

Dolcezza's one downside? Your Yankee Peso won't get you far here: a small scoop will set you back four dollars. –CK

# Don Pollo

This chicken is throwing a party for your taste buds

**8.0** Food    **4.5** Feel

## Latin American

Counter service

**$15** Price

Sun–Thu 11am–10pm
Fri–Sat 11am–11pm

**Bar** None
**Credit cards** Visa, MC, AmEx
Outdoor dining

**Hyattsville, MD**
2065 University Blvd.
(301) 434-5001

Within the Beltway and beyond, holes-in-the-wall serving pollo a la brasa (chicken spit-roasted over charcoal) to a largely Latino clientele are legion. It can be exceedingly hard to distinguish between them, to sort them out. Trust us, this wasn't an easy task for the Fearless Critic team; even aside from the dominant chains (Pollo Rico, Crisp & Juicy, and such), there are parts of the Maryland and Virginia suburbs—and Hyattsville is one of them—where it seems there's another independently owned chicken joint around every bend in the road, along every single strip center, in every single jumble of commerce.

In a decidedly modest genre, Don Pollo is at the most modest end of the spectrum. It's got just a few tables, and—aside from the atmospheric effect of the lively local crowd, the regulars joking and shouting in Spanish—arguably less atmosphere than your average fast-food restaurant. Yet the place is popular enough that there's scarcely a time of day when you won't have to wait in line for your deliciously juicy plate of expertly cooked fowl and Latin American accoutrements. But when you do get to the front of the line, expect friendly, patient service, which is part of why the line seems to move so slowly

It's also among the cheapest of the pollo-a-la-brasa joints. A quarter chicken (dark meat—you must order dark meat) plus two sides runs less than $5. Don't expect any surprises with the sides, but yuca fries are an excellent choice, as are sweet fried bananas. Skip the salads—they're really not worth it—but do get rice and beans and, if you're in a Mexican mood, an order of tortillas. There's also pollo guisado (chicken stew), which comes with rice, beans, and tortillas, and it's deep, rich, and excellent.

Don't expect anything more than that. But come for the "fiesta para 4"—one whole chicken and four sides—and, stay in or take out (there's even a drive-thru); we promise a gustatory party. –RG

# Dukem

Good Ethiopian fare with plenty of space for you to eat it all up—and admire the staff

| 7.8 | 6.3 |
|-----|-----|
| Food | Feel |

## Ethiopian

Casual restaurant

**$25**
Price

www.dukemrestaurant.com

Sun–Thu 11am–2pm
Fri–Sat 11am–3pm

**Bar** Beer, wine, liquor
**Credit cards** Visa, MC, AmEx
**Reservations** Accepted
Live music, outdoor dining,
veg-friendly

**Shaw**
1114 U St. NW
(202) 667-8735

Dukem is perhaps the best-known and most lauded of restaurants in U Street's microcosmic Ethiopia, and while we actually prefer Etété down the road, the restaurant has certainly earned its popularity. An isolated handful of dishes have more acutely piqued our attention at other places along the strip and farther afield; but sometimes one is looking for all-round contentment rather than memorable standouts, and Dukem is an excellent, classic option for Ethiopian food that will consistently satisfy you.

And luckily, Dukem is one of the only places in the neighborhood equipped to accommodate the large crowds that tend to descend on the restaurant in merry masses. The dining room feels downright spacious compared to the tight real estate of many nearby Ethiopian restaurants (we're all in favor of the shared dining that Ethiopian presentation encourages, but would rather not share our neighbor's seat). Here, the dark, wooden tables give the place a generous, established atmosphere. The restaurant also has a small patio with outdoor seating (although the view of U Street is less than picturesque), some ready-made and quickly-prepared options for take-out, a full bar, and live entertainment nearly every night.

Dukem's kitfo—spiced raw beef—is some of the spiciest in town; this is no mere tartare. Both the "Regular Tibs" and "Special Tibs" benefit from an extra dose of rosemary, and throughout, the dishes are creamy and well-integrated. Dukem's competition tends to be fiercer on the vegetarian side, however. While the two types of lentils are rich and full of butter, Dukem's greens fall a bit short—they're barely flavored and taste quite raw, and its salad is little more than chunks of dry beefsteak tomatoes and a few leaves of lettuce.

While the service is relatively rapid, total time from sitting down to eating can be prolonged by the restaurant's verbose menu, which offers countless combinations and permutations of the same dozen dishes. Fortunately, you can relieve the tedium with surreptitious glances at Dukem's stunning Ethiopian wait staff, in their beautiful traditional dresses.

That eye candy pairs nicely with the Ethiopian wines on offer. In addition to the traditional honey wine and several national beers, Dukem sells three of the country's reds and one white. The names can sound unappealing—Axumite sounds like a mineral. We recommend the Gouder—it'll complement your food, and embolden you to compliment your server. –CK

# Dupont Italian Kitchen

**3.6** Food  **8.0** Feel

Italian-American all the way, baby

## Italian

Casual restaurant  **$40** Price

www.dupontitaliankitchen.net

Mon–Thu 11am–11pm
Fri 11am–1am
Sat 10:30am–1am
Sun 10:30am–11pm

**Bar** Beer, wine, liquor
**Credit cards** Visa, MC, AmEx
**Reservations** Accepted
Delivery, outdoor dining,
veg-friendly

**Dupont**
1637 17th St. NW
(202) 328-3222

This place is textbook Italian-American—the food that the middle America of the last generation thought was the real, exotic, deal. For instance: fettuccine alfredo, that creamy creation that, on a good day, is an indulgent and fulfilling comfort food, but on a bad day can be put-you-to-sleep bland; gnocchi, those little guys whose pronunciation is so often butchered by a well-meaning American; or spaghetti marinara, a creation whose American incarnation has nothing to do with the *mare* from which its name comes. These were the treasures supposedly brought across the Atlantic. Once exotic, they are now as accessible as can be, thanks to the efforts of individuals such as Chef Boyardee. So if Joe the Plumber can whip up his own manicotti with cheese, one should expect any restaurant worth its salt to offer an improvement on his version.

Dupont Italian Kitchen (or DIK, as it's commonly abbreviated) woos its diners by starting them off with bread studded with garlic—a sly move, but one that backfires, as the quality of the bread itself is not so great. Moving along, you'll see that there's nothing extraordinary on the menu; the only things that diverge from standard-issue Italian-American (and that's not necessarily a good thing) are hummus with rosemary pita and French onion soup. The breading on eggplant parmigiana is slightly soggy, and the whole thing could use a generous dose of salt. It comes perched atop a mound of red-sauce spaghetti that, aside from being a meal for two on its own, is overcooked, watery, and utterly devoid of flavor. (Pastas here stand out as a weakness among weaknesses—a dish of cheese-stuffed ravioli has come out criminally overcooked, seeping water from its crevices.)

But ultimately it's what's going on outside of and on top of the restaurant that's the real draw. Tables that line the sidewalk offer prime people-watching real estate in the very heart of DC's gay nightlife (and daylife)—it's a great place to be on a beautiful spring afternoon. The kitchen also keeps relatively late hours (for this neighborhood at least) staying open until 11pm on weekdays. And many are drawn to DIK bar (tee hee), just upstairs from the restaurant. Karaoke, drag queens, and a happening bar scene—what more could a patron want?

Decent food, perhaps. –AH

# Eamonn's

You'll have to be diverted to Shannon to find fish and chips as good as these

**8.7** *Food* **8.0** *Feel*

## Seafood, Irish

Casual restaurant

**$20** *Price*

www.eamonnsdublinchipper.com

Mon–Wed 11:30am–10pm; Thu 11:30am–11pm; Fri 11:30am–midnight; Sat noon–midnight; Sun noon–9pm

**Bar** Beer, wine, liquor
**Credit cards** Visa, MC, AmEx
**Reservations** Not accepted
Kid-friendly, outdoor dining

**Alexandria Old Town**
728 King St.
(703) 299-8384

What a great concept! Old Town's King Street, which is too often a mixture of tourist traps and fusion-furious showcase restaurants, really needed this: a simple, honest eatery that's both laid-back and food-obsessed. No wonder—it's from the same chef who brought us the noble Restaurant Eve. It's an elegant Irish pub—with such an attention to thematic detail that it feels like Disney's Epcot—with a playfully snarky attitude.

The menu is unbelievably simple: fish and chips, basically. Really spectacular fish and chips.

What's great about the fish and chips is that they're made with market fish, changing daily. When was the last time you saw that in this particular preparation? A thin but tender fry-up of ray, like skate, is the tenderest fish here, but we're still suckers for the cod. While the fish flesh inside is meltingly beautiful in your mouth, the batter is perfectly crispy—what a texture matchup!

Prawns are less exciting, if only because they're less unique. Hand-cut fries are thick and a bit soggy—not our favorite style—but they're good for what they are. The slaw is also well executed, and the imported mushy peas first-rate. Douse everything in lots of malt vinegar and house-made sauces for chips, including a delicious curry just like we've seen in Belgium. Plus there's Guinness on draft. We unabashedly love this place. Even those of us who've had earth-shattering fish and chips in Norway and New Zealand and Newfoundland heartily recommend it.

After dinner, you can head to the PX Lounge next door (yes, it's named after Pedro Ximénez, the grape behind some of Spain's sweetest, most viscous sherries); PX is a speakeasy that's right up there with New York's Milk & Honey and PDT, with terrifically artisanal cocktails, all served in a very cool and exclusive atmosphere that manages to avoid being annoying. Up there, you'll surely toast your satisfying, inexpensive dinner with Eamonn's cheeky motto: Thanks be to cod. –RG

# Earl's Sandwiches

**7.5** Food  **6.0** Feel

Good sandwiches made better by exemplary meats

## Sandwiches

Counter service  **$15** Price

www.earlsinarlington.com

Mon–Sat 10:30am–8pm
Sun 10am–4pm

**Bar** None
**Credit cards** Visa, MC, AmEx
Outdoor dining

**Arlington, VA**
2605 Wilson Blvd.
(703) 248-0150

It's not Earl's sandwiches we're so enthusiastic about, but rather Earl's meat. Far be it from us to propose a name change (and in any case, Earl's Meat doesn't sound like an establishment that's open for lunch, or for that matter, to ladies), but we will say this: at Earl's, what counts is what's on the inside.

Take the "Roasted Earl." A heap of roasted pork, sliced thin as can be, is stuffed inside a rather ordinary sesame roll, along with a serving of roasted green peppers. If it doesn't sound delicious, trust us, it is, largely because the meat is top-notch. If only more than the standard dab of garlic mayonnaise were added to integrate the different elements, this sandwich would be a true standout. Or more than a dab of something. The imitation wood table and metal counters at Earl's are littered with a dozen condiment bottles each, and a helping of smoky-chipotle-Tabasco sauce is able to do the Roasted Earl some justice. But the condiment should have really gone on behind the counter, with lead time to soak into the meat and bun.

Earl is much more thoughtful with his turkey offerings; even if many sandwich choices resemble something you'd eat the day after Thanksgiving, the taste is leagues beyond the mushy leftovers typical of a Friday After luncheon. The Pearl, for example, smothers some of the juiciest turkey we've tasted (and this from a bird that's known to be dry) with homemade gravy and cranberry relish. Other turkey sandwiches are made with cranberry mayonnaise, and the meat is always fresh, juicy, and plentiful.

The restaurant also offers a selection of soups and all-beef chili, as well as decent "hand-cut" French fries, which are well executed (crispy and oily, not limp with grease). But Earl's would benefit from a lesson in Sauces (or condiments writ large: a turkey-on-wheat was smothered with far too much generic yellow mustard) in order to more elegantly transform its Meats into Sandwiches. –CK

# Eastern Market

Your eyes will rapidly outgrow your stomach at
this treacherously tempting market

## Groceries

Market

Tue–Sat 7am–6pm
Sun 9am–4pm

**Bar** None
**Credit cards** Visa, MC, AmEx
**Reservations** Not accepted
Kid-friendly

**Capitol Hill**
306 7th St. SE
(202) 543-7470

"A trip to the market" can mean many different things to different
people. To those at South Hall in Eastern Market, it means an opportunity
to buy your food in a purer, more personal form. If you're willing to make
the trek, you will be rewarded with hard-to-find wares and great prices.
You'll also have the opportunity to make friends with the merchants who
will pleasantly tip you off to what is the freshest.

In butchers' stalls where huge cuts are laid out, old-school, on trays,
you can find some of rarer meats (ducks, goat, rabbit, bison) that are a
headache to find elsewhere. Butchers make their own sausage in endless
varieties like chicken and apple (sweet and mild) and chicken, habanero,
and tequila (daringly spicy and acidic). Their stuffing has a hearty, smooth
texture and the casing pops gleefully in your mouth when you bite in.

The pork products are a meat lover's dream. The best bacon in DC is at
Eastern Market: peppered, smoked, skin on, thick and thin. It barely
shrinks when cooked because it hasn't been pumped full of water, and
gives off clear fat you will be tempted to reuse. Pancetta, jamón serrano,
and other cured meats are fresh and cheap. Cracklings and organs are
sold by the bucket and signs advertise that "if it's on a pig we sell it." On
the off-chance you decide to make head cheese, you'll know where to
start.

Bowers Fancy Dairy Products is a jewel for dairy lovers. Whether you're
curious about local goat cheese in various stages (the lightly-aged crottin
is sharp, full, and slightly sour) or blue cheeses from around the world
(Spanish cabrales is stinkily delicious) or odder combinations (try the
mottled jade blocks of sage in mild cheddar) the staff at bowers is
knowledgeable and generous, slicing huge samples for you to taste. Fresh
butter is sold by the block and awesomely cheap. It smells milky and
sweet and holds excellently in pastries. Slather it on sour and chewy
loaves from the baker next door.

Several items at South Hall are overpriced. Produce looks beautiful but
costs more than it would at Whole Foods (go outside in the summer and
buy them from farmers' stalls) and handsome fresh pasta is appetizing but
on the expensive end. Eastern Market is a joy for those who are serious
about where they buy their food. Ingredients this good will make a great
cook out of anyone. –JC

# Eat First

A common Chinatown motto: Eat first, ask later

**5.3** Food  **3.0** Feel

## Chinese

Casual restaurant

**$20** Price

Mon–Thu noon–1am; Fri–Sat
11am–2am; Sun 11am–1am

**Bar** Beer, wine
**Credit cards** Visa, MC, AmEx
**Reservations** Accepted
Delivery

**Chinatown**
609 H St. NW
(202) 289-1703

With all due respect, Eat First is a dump. Formica tables are sticky and scratched, the condiments on them look like they fermented sometime in the '70s. The carpet is tattered and permanently dotted with clods of gum, and several anemic ducks garroted in the kitchen window are more depressing than appetizing. The bar in the back has been taken over by old receipts and office supplies even older than the condiments. But as most gastronauts know, the greater potential for food poisoning, the greater chance for culinary glory.

Eat First clearly diversifies its menu to attract the full breadth of clientele; signs advertising $3.95 lunches comingle with a mosaic of handwritten specials. The vaguely-named choices will be something of a mystery to those for whom Chinese is not a primary language. Because of this, eating here is like a culinary Choose Your Own Adventure. You order, scrutinize, sniff, taste, and then decide if you want to continue on or try another page. Hey, a rewarding life involves some risk.

Shrimp with walnuts features that rare and baffling of substances, Chinese white sauce (made with a base of condensed milk). It is a surprisingly complex dish, with multiple textures (fluffy batter, springy shrimp, soft-sticky sauce) and flavors (walnuts add a woodsy depth). Noodle soup with fish balls smells worse than it tastes, the thin noodles delightfully springy. Equally hearty and warming is the eggplant stewed in a clay pot, with a thick broth brightened by ginger and suffused with murky garlic.

Some items are less approachable, like a rich sauce of pork and hot peppers punctuated by pungent little clams with a handful of tiny dried shrimp thrown on top. The texture of damp cardboard is not for everybody.

Eat First is not the most brilliant Chinese food you'll ever find, but it is an interesting, fine place to experiment. Be adventurous, try new things, and get excited about the mystery of your food. If you hit a wrong door, you can always go back and try again, and at these prices, it's a cheap education. –JC

# El Chalán

Knock out Peruvian food that will leave you sated, whoever you are

**7.1** Food  **7.3** Feel

## Peruvian

Casual restaurant    **$45** Price

Mon–Fri 11am–3pm, 5:30pm–10pm
Sat 1pm–10pm
Sun 1pm–8pm

**Bar** Beer, wine, liquor
**Credit cards** Visa, MC, AmEx
**Reservations** Accepted

**Farragut**
1924 Eye St. NW
(202) 293-2765

El Chalán is an honest restaurant with honest food. This Farragut feedery offers interesting Peruvian dishes, in filling portions, with a pinch of creativity—but free of bells, charms, and whistles. The wine list is solid, the waiters are helpful but unobtrusive, and the prices are reasonable. You can expect to get more than what you've paid for.

Before considering the menu, however, order a pisco sour. This El Chalán specialty is an honest-to-God standout. The drink arrives in a short flute with a good-sized dollop of raw-egg-white froth and a sprinkle of nutmeg. Its diminutive size is perhaps the single deceptive element at El Chalán: the restaurant makes one small but potent pisco, with a full zesty flavor and very little sugar.

Cooking aromas disperse quickly in the small, cute, half-underground space, and if your blood is quick, you'll turn quickly to the main offerings, which are varied but not overwhelming: the menu includes four soups, a dozen salads and appetizers, and three or four dishes each of seafood, chicken, beef, and goat. Good ways to start are anticuchos de corazón (marinated beef hearts) or ceviche. And order starters at will, without fear of future portion size: the main courses have lost little volume in their journey north from the plates of Andean cowboys to a more pallid DC crowd (although half of El Chalán's tables, reassuringly, are generally occupied by Spanish speakers).

El Chalán's highlights include a suite of seafood dishes, such as a boldly spiced parihuela: a seafood soup with made with five types of fish and shellfish enveloped in a chile- and cilantro-infused broth. Also try the ají de gallina a la arequipeña (chicken in a spiced peanut sauce) and the excellent cabrito norteño (goat stew with a side of mushed white beans). All dishes are accompanied by a tangy cucumber-chile relish and helping of rich, sweet bread so plentiful it can only be called—well—honest. –CK

# El Charrito Caminante

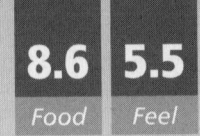

**8.6** Food  **5.5** Feel

Some of the best tacos in the greater DC area are coming out of this little hole-in-the-wall

## Mexican, Salvadoran

Counter service **$15** Price

Wed–Mon 10am–10pm

**Bar** None
**Credit cards** None
Kid-friendly

**Arlington, VA**
2710 Washington Blvd.
(703) 351-1177

Don't go to El Charrito Caminante expecting huge, overstuffed burritos with all sorts of random accoutrements. Don't go expecting fried tortilla shells brimming with ground "beef," bottled salsa, and guac. Go expecting tasty, cheap, and authentic tacos and pupusas, and you'll be satisfied.

The joint is totally tucked away, a hidden Arlington gem. In the window, amateur pictures of the featured dishes serve as a forecast of things to come. The counter is lined with five or so stools for the lucky few who get to spread their meals out and enjoy them fresh from the griddle. But most people take their orders to go.

Smells from the open kitchen waft toward the counter as the various cooks fill pupusas, heat tortillas, fry plantains, and assemble tacos. The crowd varies from lingering chatterboxes who share their life stories with the owner to businessmen picking up lunch orders to authentic-taco aficionados who swoop in from all corners of greater DC to get some of the best in the area.

It's hard to pick favorites here; everything we have sampled has been quite delicious. On the Salvadoran side of things, cheese-and-loroco pupusas are creamy, fragrant, and cheap. Mexican-wise, authentic corn-tortilla tacos are filled with chicken, shredded beef, chorizo, lengua (tongue), or goat (the local favorite), and topped with a cilantro, onion, and radish salad that provides a refreshing contrast to the well-seasoned meat. A squirt of lime and not-too-hot salsa verde seals the deal. Given that they're $2 each, you have little excuse not to sample a few. Tasty, too, are fried plantains, which sit in a pool of too much grease and are served with refried beans and thinned-out sour cream. $3 gets a huge container, but we recommend that you pace yourself while trying to eat them alongside tacos and pupusas. A huge cup of fresh but very sweet tamarind juice is one of the few drink options that will help cool you down after a satisfying meal. –FC

# El Dorado

Not really golden, but worth of a bronze

| 7.9 | 6.5 |
|-----|-----|
| Food | Feel |

## Salvadoran, Latin American

Counter service

**$10**
Price

Daily 7:30am–10pm
Hours vary by location

**Bar** None
**Credit cards** Visa, MC
Kid-friendly

**Hyattsville, MD**
2200 University Blvd. E.
(301) 445-1274

El Dorado is the big, bustling lunch stop-bakery of your Central American dreams. The friendly neighborhood spot draws a healthy mix of local Latinos and Salvadorans (plus a few Caucasian stragglers). There's an unusual lightness and happiness to the space, like a community gathering place, that makes it a lot nicer than the local competition. You'll see whole local families coming in for lunch, and others just coming in to buy meats or baked goods.

At the Salvadoran/pan-Latin steam-table buffet, you'll find stews and soups, including a smooth, rich version of lengua guisada (stewed tongue), and tender pollo guisado (chicken stew). Chops (e.g. costilla de cerdo, pork chops) and fish fillets tend to be overcooked. We prefer the liquid-based dishes like soups and stews, which are excellent. The menu boasts pan-Latin dishes such as sopa de res (beef)/mondongo (tripe)/pollo (chicken), perhaps with the addition of chicharrones (pork rinds).

There are also distinctly Salvadoran dishes like properly prepared pupusas (say that five times fast), plato típico (with rice, beans, plantains, eggs, and tamales), pescado rojo frito, big sausages, and chicken tamales.

El Dorado, that mythical city of gold that drove men to murder and ruin. For those of us seeking excellent Central American fare, that lust can only drive us to bad decisions. And El Dorado actually exists. Isn't that a better scenario? –FC

# El Khartoum

Treat yourself to some Sudanese grub

**7.5** Food
**4.3** Feel

## Sudanese

Counter service

**$20** Price

Daily 9am–3am

**Bar** None
**Credit cards** Visa, MC
Delivery

**Shaw**
1782 Florida Ave. NW
(202) 986-5031

At first glance, this just looks like another dumpy African-Middle Eastern joint, albeit one in an advantageous location on the well trafficked intersection of 18th and Florida; it's on the edge of Adams Morgan but reachable from Dupont. And, indeed, the interior of El Khartoum is as dumpy as the exterior. There are just a few tables in the humble space, and none for more than four people. The atmosphere is zero; even the office ceilings are falling apart at the seams.

But El Khartoum is much, much more than that—and not just because of the owner's unusual friendliness. It almost feels like it *tries* not to be— at least to the outside world—caught up in serving the usual Middle Eastern-Greek-American suspects that are often, inexplicably, dubbed "Mediterranean." That's not to say that El Khartoum's versions of these dishes are bad; there's quite good pita; decent versions of gyro, shawarma, shish tawook (marinated chicken); and a not-so-decent version of…drumroll please…pizza. But this tiny kitchen—really more of a galley—is capable of far greater things than that.

Order the Sudanese dishes from the interesting buffet—eggplant, foul, lamb, and so on—and you'll be in for a surprise Adams Morgan treat. Best of all—and, at press time, just $4.50 at lunch—is a dish of stewed fava beans, which are decked out with jalapeños, tomatoes, pickled beets, feta, pickled onions, and various sauces. (It's also available topped with smashed falafel.) This is hearty, delicious Sudanese peasant food at its best—and it's not on the menu. The best thing on the menu is not on the menu (par for the course, you might say, for DC ethnic food). Another unusual Sudanese treat, available only sometimes, is gourrassa, a soft, circular wheat flatbread (in the family of Ethiopian injera) topped with (ideally) stewed lamb or spinach and okra.

Now we're talkin'. –RG

# El Pollo Rico

A no-frills atmosphere and brusque service, but good, cheap rotisserie chicken and bold sauces

**8.5** **4.0**
Food / Feel

## Latin American

Counter service **$10**
Price

www.ilovethischicken.com

Daily 11am–10pm

**Bar** None
**Credit cards** None
Delivery, kid-friendly

**Arlington, VA**
932 N. Kenmore St.
(703) 522-3220

**Wheaton, MD**
2517 University Blvd.
(301) 942-4419

Tucked into a no-nonsense building along nondescript strip malls in Arlington and Wheaton, this cavernous, clattering space is generally filled with families and groups of friends chattering in a mix of Spanish and English. It's industrial, to be sure, but in a good way: the main attraction consists of hundreds of chickens packed tightly onto spits, where they rotate in a massive oven and baste in their own juices. The service is abrupt; make sure you have your order decided by the time you get to the counter, and be ready to pay cash only.

Fortunately, the choices are limited. Order your whole, half, or quarter chicken (dark meat in the last instance), with steak fries on the side, but skip the mayonnaisey, watery cole slaw. To drink, traditionalists choose the neon-yellow Inca Kola or bright-orange Champagne Soda. Grab a tall stack of paper napkins from the counter, carry your tray to a sticky table, check your chair for grease or soda spots, and sit down to enjoy a meal that's surprisingly satisfying.

The chicken itself is juicy and true to its own flavor, although its skin is crunchy in spots and flabby in others. The fries, while clearly not homemade, are crisp and golden, and a convenient vehicle for mopping up the flavorful chicken juices. The accompanying sauces—a mayonnaise spiced with yellow chilies and a fiery green-chile chutney spiked with lime and cilantro—are formidable condiments for chicken and potato alike.

El Pollo Rico does brisk business at the dinner hour, so be prepared to battle for a parking space in the cramped lot. While this restaurant won't win any beauty contests, the atmosphere is jolly and noisy; the high-ceilinged, cement-walled room fills with a boisterous communal spirit. But the chicken—not the place where you sit to eat—is the real destination. In a place where five dollars cash (there's an ATM near the front) buys you a quarter-chicken meal dripping with authentic flavor, little else matters. Come hungry, eat (or take out), and go back for seconds. –CD

# El Tamarindo

**5.9** Food   **6.2** Feel

A decent Salvadoran spot that could do without the international additions and the price hikes

## Mexican, Salvadoran

Casual restaurant   **$40** Price

www.eltamarindodc.com

Mon–Thu 8am–2am
Fri 8am–midnight
Sat 24 hours
Sun midnight–2am

**Bar** Beer, wine, liquor
**Credit cards** Visa, MC, AmEx
**Reservations** Accepted
Wi-Fi

**Adams Morgan**
1785 Florida Ave. NW
(202) 328-3660

Sticker shock is the first thing likely to hit you at this sit-down Salva-Mexi-dorian restaurant; the prices are extraordinarily high for a place this casual, perhaps because of the choice location on the Dupont end of Adams Morgan. The value proposition is even harder to accept at lunchtime, when there are no lunch specials: $12 for a plate of enchiladas or $15 for fish soup at noon on a weekday is tough to swallow anywhere, never mind in a homey, kitschily downmarket Mexican-Salvadoran hybrid.

Along those homey lines, large oil paintings line the walls, and big chairs and solid wooden tables dot the otherwise bland space, which heats up on weekend evenings when people start ordering the sharp margaritas or Mexican beers. At other times, it's not unusual to see a wide range of ages at the restaurant, which sets it apart from many of its neighbors that cater principally to a younger crowd.

The dressed-down staff is friendly, if disorganized (a waitress brings water and chips; a second appears a minute later to ask if we've been served), and there's no hint of pretense in the entire place. There's no "concept" or "creative takes" here, whether with Mexican or with Salvadoran. Pupusas are correctly executed, if hardly sublime; our favorite way to have them is revueltas (stuffed with chicharrones, beans, and cheese). We also salute the availability of loroco (an herby Salvadoran green) as a filling. Salvadoran tamales are even better, moist and delicious; sweet, ripe plantains hit the spot; and a simple bowl of red refried beans, whipped into smooth sensuality, epitomizes what this restaurant does best: real Salvadoran food.

Unfortunately, that's not what makes up the vast majority of dishes on the weighty tome of a menu, The many attempts at Tex-Mex—enchilada plates and such—fall flat on their faces like dominoes, one worse than the next, and the more authentic preparations, like an inedibly dry whole fried fish, fare scarcely better. And what is the useless salad of droopy lettuce and unripe tomatoes doing on almost every plate?

The restaurant's dessert list is ordinary, too, and the flan is par for the course. If you're still hungry, try the interesting (if heavy) sweet plantain empanada. It's yet another reminder that Salvadoran is what El Tamarindo does best. And that filled pockets (tamales, empanadas, pupusas) are what El Salvador does best. We only wish El Tamarindo would follow that lead, wrap those extra menu pages around that wilted lettuce and enchilada nonsense, and throw the whole package out the window. –FC

# Eli's

Try as it might, it ain't Katz's, and Dupont Circle ain't East Houston Street

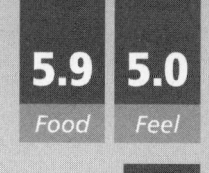

**5.9** Food   **5.0** Feel

## Sandwiches, American

Casual restaurant

**$20** Price

www.elisdc.com

Sun–Thu 11am–9pm
Fri 11am–2:30pm

**Bar** Beer, wine
**Credit cards** Visa, MC, AmEx
**Reservations** Not accepted
Delivery

**Dupont**
1253 20th St. NW
(202) 785-4314

Without its own equivalent of a Lower East Side, DC must make do with a very humble clutch of kosher eateries around Dupont Circle. Among these, Eli's has the market cornered, but perhaps not due to the merits of the food.

There's this curious half-hearted attempt at a bistro; tables are clothed in white linen, which are then topped by the more authentic cruddy plastic ketchup and mustard bottles. A red brick pattern has been painted on some of the walls, also adorned with WASPy Victorian gas lamps. Despite trying to have it both ways, the interior comes across appropriately drab (chopped liver is the preferred cuisine of misery, after all). At lunch, most diners are in suits and kippot, and the discussion tends toward politics (rather than finance—the preferred lingo of the Lower East): phrases like "the Assistant Secretary and his wife" are dropped both in sotto voce and aloud, depending on the intended effect.

The menu is a co-mingling of standard deli fare and some cursory dullards like chicken tenders and salads. The latter of these are abundant and topped with the low-hanging fruit of American cuisine (blackened tuna, greasy ribeye, more chicken tenders). The overstuffed sandwiches, made with high quality cuts of meat and good inserts like sautéed mushrooms, are decent, but they taste like what you'd get at a healthy bakery rather than a Lower East Side deli.

For pure pastrami and nothing else, the straight-up deli sandwiches are piled pretty high with meat that can be dry, leathery, and a bit underwhelming (it reminds us of Annie Hall: *The food here is terrible...I know! And such small portions!*); the cole slaw is hyper-mayonnaised, but the pickles are crisp and juicy. Funny enough, the biggest treat at Eli's is the availability of kosher hamburgers, and these are really quite good by any burger standard.

Perhaps because Eli's knows it has kosher DC somewhat over a barrel, the prices here are abusive—a sandwich and soda will run you about $15 before tip, and it certainly won't be that transcendent experience that a warm, dripping pastrami on rye can be. It's more convenient than beloved; some competition would help. –CK

# Ella's Pizza

They've got the equation down for decent pies

| 6.9 | 7.5 |
|-----|-----|
| Food | Feel |

## Pizza

Casual restaurant

**$40**
Price

www.ellaspizza.com

Mon–Wed 11am–9pm
Thu 11am–10pm
Fri–Sat 11am–11pm
Sun 4pm–9pm

**Bar** Beer, wine, liquor
**Credit cards** Visa, MC, AmEx
**Reservations** Accepted
Kid-friendly, outdoor dining,
veg-friendly

**Chinatown**
901 F St. NW
(202) 638-3434

The formula for an upscale DC pizza restaurant seems simple: one wood-burning oven (or at least rumors of an oven), basic pizza dough rolled out thin, a few signature exotic-sounding toppings (proffered sparingly), pretty people, plenty of wine, and outrageous prices. Throw in some pomegranate cocktails and boutique beers, and you've got yourself a business.

A few of these establishments are redeemed by the fact that they actually serve a decent pizza, in addition to throwing a good party and facilitating bragging about how the beer you drank was micro-brewed in a state with a population half the size of Washington's. Ella's, on the other hand, remains unredeemed, although the place does throw a good party.

The latter is evidenced by the fact that during happy hour the place is invariably packed—so much so that it can be difficult to find a place to stand, much less to get a table. The former (lack of redemption) is evidenced, perhaps, by the fact that pizza is given away for free during happy hour, making Ella's a good deal for a cheap dinner, provided you can grab the pizza before other patrons as it rolls out of the oven. The restaurant does make a mean sangría (plenty of fruit, not too sweet), which is probably part of what draws the crowds in the first place.

Ella's deserves commendations for a balanced pie: the crust is rolled very thin, the toppings are well-matched (the soppressata combines sausage, fennel, and parmesan, for example; the "Pucillo" sports prosciutto, arugula, and smoked mozzarella). But the pie suffers from a boring sauce and a crust that is too dry; the crust is so thin and spiceless that it almost disappears without the stop-gap addition of red pepper flakes and grated parmesan.

After a few pitchers of sangría, fans of Ella's may comment that the restaurant has got its pizza-making down to an art; we prefer to call it science. After all, the concept is nothing if not formulaic. –CK

# Equinox

A focus on local and sustainable ingredients sets a
standard worth following

| 7.6 | 8.5 |
|------|------|
| Food | Feel |

## New American

Upmarket restaurant

**$75**
Price

www.equinoxrestaurant.com

Mon–Fri 11:30am–2pm,
5:30pm–10pm
Sat 5:30pm–10:30pm
Sun 5pm–9pm

**Bar** Beer, wine, liquor
**Credit cards** Visa, MC, AmEx
**Reservations** Accepted
Date-friendly, delivery, good
wines, outdoor dining, Wi-Fi

**Penn Quarter**
818 Connecticut Ave. NW
(202) 331-8118

Though treaded by upscale heels (two of which belong to Michelle
Obama, who celebrated her birthday here), Equinox stays true to its noble
aim: to carefully prepare foods made (mostly) from local ingredients.
What's more, Equinox is not presumptuous; prices are relatively
reasonable, at least well worth the sensory nirvana a night here entails.

Nor is Equinox stuffy, by any means. It's classy and spacious, with a wall
of windows that let the outside world in. While ties are appreciated,
they're certainly not required, and servers easily fluctuate between heady
wine connoisseurship and light-hearted banter.

The kitchen is not especially ambitious or daring—that's not the point.
It is guided instead by classic flavor combinations, a feat of balance, and
the knowledge that most of a chef's work is done at the farmer's market.
Heirloom tomato soup pairs the season's best with simple parmesan
crisps; the contrast of sweet acidity and nutty cheese is transcendent.
Another soup unites the earthy sweetness of autumn kabocha squash and
roasted pumpkin seeds with their soul mate: pancetta. Pointedly, a
swordfish puttanesca (loosely, whore's pasta) is anything but whored up,
its requisite tomatoes and Niçoise olives made novel only by upgrading
from tuna. One suspects that other restaurants sharing Equinox's limelight
would tart it up as some Asian fusion fiasco like miso-marinated salmon
"puttanesca"...with chipotle aioli. And though it may sound whimsical, a
foie gras "Fig Newton" is code for a natural pairing of dried fruit, buttery
bread, and lightly seared liver.

The only extravagances arrive on dessert plates. A few puritans, such as
a pear tartlet with cream, battle against hyper-indulgences such as the
triple chocolate mousse terrine with praline ice cream and gooey
chocolate sauce. Not much beats an exquisite sorbet here.

While one of the better wine lists in town, it stoops somewhat as a
mere Who's Who of Wine Spectator winners: certainly grand, but
curiously lacking many of the small grower-producers and artisans that
are in keeping with the kitchen's philosophy. It reads a bit like crashing
cymbals over the top of the Beatles' "Day in the Life."

The restaurant's not perfect, and it's not groundbreaking—perhaps it's
even feeling a bit dusty—but in a District with too many restaurants bent
more on overcharging for flashy adjectives, we could all use a return to
the deliciously sensible and sustainable. –FC

# Etete

This high-flying little Ethiopian place deserves top marks

| 8.8 | 6.4 |
|-----|-----|
| Food | Feel |

## Ethiopian

Casual restaurant

**$30**
Price

www.eteterestaurant.com

Daily 11am–1am

**Bar** Beer, wine, liquor
**Credit cards** Visa, MC, AmEx
**Reservations** Accepted
Live music, outdoor dining,
veg-friendly, Wi-Fi

**Shaw**
1942 9th St. NW
(202) 232-7600

Etete has made the most of its narrow space in a shotgun rowhouse between U Street and Shaw. Polished wood tables line each side of a skinny aisle, which a waitress paces with extreme poise—as if on an airplane—to deliver huge round platters of injera and steaming meats to each of the eight or so tables. The bay window offers prime seating with an elevated platform, wrap-around bench, and woven-basket table. You'll have to place your drink on the windowsill, but no matter.

And the squeeze is worthwhile: Etete offers one of the best Ethiopian meals in town. In fact, the tight space lends itself to service that is warm and never clumsy: the waitress remembers and greets even infrequent customers, and leads them almost intuitively to the table they occupied on their last visit. The drink service is very rapid, and Etete has a wine list that, if short, is thoughtfully composed and features reasonably priced bottles. The food, luckily, does not lag too far behind the drinks.

The quality of Etete's injera distinguishes the restaurant from its neighborhood competitors: the bread is soft, stretchy, and a bit lemony, and is probably the tangiest we've tasted on this strip of Ethiopian restaurants. And when the injera is paired with the spicy meats, the resulting combination is remarkable. One of Etete's specialties is the derek tibs: spicy beef cooked with tomatoes in a rich sauce that takes like fresh creamed butter.

Etete is also one of the better places for vegetarians, with a number of main-course-sized non-meat options, as well as a full "Fastening Plate" which includes a selection of the vegetable dishes, with or without fish. Gomen is a combination of softened vegetables in large chunks—green beans, potatoes, and carrots—which are cooked in a ginger-tomato sauce. The lentil dishes are also excellent, with plenty of red pepper and an integrated taste and texture to match.

If you're in search of late night dining or drinking, Etete is open until 2am, although the kitchen closes at 1. Be safe and order those tibs early. Then sit back, relax, and enjoy the night. –CK

# Etrusco

This promising Italian mainstay can't quite keep its promises

**6.2** *Food*  **7.9** *Feel*

## Italian

Upmarket restaurant  **$60** *Price*

Mon–Sat 6pm–9:30pm

**Bar** Beer, wine, liquor
**Credit cards** Visa, MC, AmEx
**Reservations** Accepted
Date-friendly, outdoor dining

**Dupont**
1606 20th St. NW
(202) 667-0047

On a gorgeous evening, when autumn had just begun to creep quietly into the District, we wondered why there were no tables on the attractive outdoor patio at Etrusco (though outdoor seating is available at times). It was just one way in which this potential gem failed to take full advantage of its natural assets. We were seated instead in the dimly lit intimate dining room, half church vault, half covered wagon, that is one of the restaurant's grace notes. Etrusco embraces the low-key, and, encouraged by the lack of pretense in the staff, the menu, the space, and the patrons, we had hoped that this longstanding Italian spot would be the sort of neighborhood refuge whose short, just-printed paper menu would sing to us night after night. Somehow, however, Etrusco's various pleasant strains never quite harmonize.

We give the kitchen high marks for the pared-down simplicity of its menu. Skewered fresh grilled squid are bright and just barely cooked and beautifully done. We appreciate their smoky charred flavor, enhanced by a squeeze of lemon juice, but the squid seem uncomfortable on their bed of hard kidney beans, which have an oddly soapy aftertaste. Bucatini all'amatriciana fit more easily into this cozy upscale trattoria. The spicy bacon-laced sauce gets into the pasta and begs to be slurped up; a rather largely diced onion adds to the rustic feel of the generous heap. Unfortunately, a much-lauded swordfish main is anything but cozy—it's hard to imagine the dish springing from the same culinary imagination. A skimpy bland steak is served with a few cold grilled zucchini sticks that are only somewhat atoned for by chunks of silken, lightly garlicky eggplant. We could have done with more of the eggplant and less (fine, none) of the zucchini.

Etrusco's menu likely benefits from the restaurant's prime location only steps from the Dupont Circle farmer's market, and we laud the fresh intentions of its chef. A place with so much potential, Etrusco would benefit from focusing on what it already does right—simple preparation of local ingredients. But we're still waiting for that neighborhood siren that sings just the right melody to entice us inside on a cool Autumn night. –SDC

# Restaurant Eve (Bistro)

**8.4** Food | **8.0** Feel

A return to eating local and natural foods made with care and innovation

## New American

Upmarket restaurant

**$60** Price

www.restauranteve.com

Mon–Fri 11:30am–2:30pm, 5:30pm–10pm
Sat 5:30pm–10pm

**Bar** Beer, wine, liquor
**Credit cards** Visa, MC, AmEx
**Reservations** Accepted
Date-friendly, good wines

**Alexandria Old Town**
110 S. Pitt St.
(703) 706-0450

There are three ways to do Restaurant Eve. One is the Chef's Tasting Room (reviewed separately), an intimate 34-seater where five- and nine-course prix-fixe menus allow diners to sample the daily bounty from the local farmer's markets, assembled in exquisite (and exquisitely expensive) sensory blasts. Our favorite way of dining here (we'll get to the third later) is in the more accessible, casual Bistro. The menu still changes daily (for the most part), and still employs many local and organic ingredients, often right out of the restaurant's own garden.

One big winner on this side is the house-made charcuterie. An ever-changing assortment of sausages, pâtés, and terrines comes accompanied by whole-grain mustard and cornichons, best enjoyed with the house-made bread, which is crusty outside and light in texture. Mussels, in a fragrant broth rich with spicy pimentos and smoky bacon, are a delight. Pork belly has been heaven, succulent and not too fatty.

The Bistro usually hits it out of the park, but sometimes not. Fish dishes have often been overcooked, and an artichoke barigoule has come underseasoned. The few execution hiccups are dwarfed by an overall vision and attention to detail, though, from the hospitable hostesses to the Irish butter on the table.

The dessert menu sets a playful tone with choices such as "Birthday cake…just because," and the selection of ice creams and sorbets is wonderful. Molten chocolate cake has come suspiciously chilled (is this an energy-saving move?).

Eve's acclaimed wine list, which is available in the Bistro as well, cuts a broad swath through New and Old World, but is tightly focused and includes more exciting domestics and sparklings than we've been seeing. The cocktail list is an innovative nod to the classics; tonics, bitters, and vermouth are made in-house, further evidence of this restaurant's commitment to excellence.

As part of Eve's responsibility to the world's resources, there's no bottled water, and the kitchen composts about half of its waste. Sometimes this level of commitment begs patience and acclimation: the very green move of tinting the skylights in the Bistro casts a sort of murkiness on diners that even fireplace flames and candles don't quite correct.

If you're still gun-shy, sample the lunch menu (served weekdays only) in the Lounge—the "Lickety-Split" format allows you to choose any two items from a list of fantastic cocktails and wine, salads, sandwiches, light mains, and desserts—for just $13.50. Eve is more fun at night, but this is certainly the cheapest of all options. –FC

# Restaurant Eve

They execute ideally on the date-night ambitions—
and usually on the high-flying food, too

**8.8** Food **9.6** Feel

## New American

Upmarket restaurant **$150** Price

www.restauranteve.com

Mon–Fri 11:30am–2:30pm,
5:30pm–9:30pm
Sat 5:30pm–10pm

**Bar** Beer, wine, liquor
**Credit cards** Visa, MC, AmEx
**Reservations** Essential
Date-friendly, good wines

**Alexandria Old Town**
110 S. Pitt St.
(703) 706-0450

"I'd say about 80 percent," said the waiter with an almost imperceptible smirk in response to one customer's query as to how many of Restaurant Eve's patrons are celebrating a special occasion on any given night. These sorts of special-purpose restaurants can be hard to write about, because what people seek from their experience—an elaborate arc of a meal, servers that seem in effortless cahoots with their intention to impress their dates, the subtle presentation of a candle with a dessert course, and a ribbon-tied bag of goodies with the check—are so different from the sorts of things a food critic looks for.

The most expensive restaurant in Old Town—the mandatory prix fixe starts above $100—does some of each. There are local ingredients, a good range of interesting wines, and recipes that are refreshingly reined in despite their ambition (there's foie gras and caviar, but they won't try to put them on the same plate). Tables are well spaced, lighting is warm, waitstaff is knowledgable.

When the combinations of seasonal ingredients work, they can be dazzling. Often what is simplest is best, like a rich duck consommé—an amuse at one visit—with a little round flan in its center that played like a cream of broccoli soup in a more solid form; an asparagus "panna cotta," flanked by local morel mushrooms, less gelatinous than expected, but wonderfully light and earthy, like the taste of springtime; or braised pork belly and creamy sweetbreads set atop bright green fava beans, a study of three different forms of crisped softness. What's called a boudin blanc feels more like a crispy pudding, studded with bacon and chanterelles, and it's delicious. Homemade pastas are expertly assembled and cooked to a careful resilience; tortelloni might come with house-made ricotta—one of the ingredients of the moment in US urban food circles—along with aromatic Parmigiano-Reggiano and unnecessary, but very fresh, leaves of swiss chard.

The chard is representative of a recurring, if hardly fatal, problem here: high-concept mismatches that can diminish slightly from the impeccable freshness and provenance of the kitchen's ingredients. To wit, we've had tempura-battered soft-shell crab that clashed with its so-called "liquid gold" broth, whose chicken stock and pearl onions cried out for a less delicate protein, and a dense, bready syrup cake that distracted attention from the sharp, simple strengths of the Wisconsin cheddar in a cheese course. Desserts have been consistently disappointing; worst has been a very dry black forest roulade whose black pepper ice cream lacked any pepper character. Sweet things are big with the special occasion set, so that problem is less excusable here than it might be elsewhere. –RG

# Evening Star Café

**6.6** **7.4**
Food    Feel

Oversalted and overpriced food makes for a
forgettable night in the suburbs

## New American

Upmarket restaurant

**$55**
Price

www.eveningstarcafe.net

Mon 5:30pm–10pm; Tue–Thu
11:30am–2:30pm, 5:30pm–
10pm; Fri–Sat 11:30am–
2:30pm, 5:30pm–11pm; Sun
10am–3pm

**Bar** Beer, wine, liquor
**Credit cards** Visa, MC, AmEx
**Reservations** Accepted
Live music, outdoor dining, Wi-Fi

**Alexandria, VA**
2000 Mount Vernon Ave.
(703) 549-5051

Thirtysomething couples with a third grader in one hand and Fido's leash
in the other typify Alexandria's Del Rey neighborhood. Though many
eating and shopping destinations embrace the kid-friendly factor, a few
grown-up reprieves still exist. With its bright yellow walls, fire-truck-red
tables and royal blue dining room chairs, Evening Star Café looks at first
like a box of crayons gone wild, but the effect becomes muted once you
settle into an oversized wooden booth dimly lit by bronze wall sconces.
The inviting yet sophisticated scene is altogether fitting for a distinctly
adult establishment in an otherwise family-oriented neighborhood.

When it comes to appetizers, Evening Star offers a fairly dated selection
of finger foods. Crisp "flash-fried" squid comes with a honey-chipotle
dipping sauce that adds kick but stops short of masking the fresh seafood
taste, while a garlicky basil purée provides a savory embellishment to
tender duck spring rolls, which have come a bit greasy. Creamy baked
brie (who's still serving this early-'90s fad dish?) oozes from beneath a
thin crushed-almond crust and, when scooped onto a slice of tart green
apple, warrants a moment of pause as a warm gooey nuttiness glides
down the gullet.

Mains are a bit more sophisticated, integrating some interesting
updated versions of Southern classics—pumpkin and andouille sausage
hash, tasso ham and blue cheese grits, crispy spaetzle—but it rarely sings.
Moist chunks of chicken fall neatly off the bone, but thyme cannot save
an oversalted gravy that's best scraped aside. A small round of grilled beef
tenderloin topped with fried onion rings, one of Evening Star's signature
dishes, comes medium-rare but lacks a beefy distinction, overpowered
instead by an aggressive pool of maroon Bordelaise sauce and garlic
mashed potatoes.

All this would bother us less were it not for the top-end pricing. While
the atmosphere suggests an upscale neighborhood standby, the prices
make for an expensive night out for food that merely suffices. Eight
dollars for a slice of dry layer cake imported from Buzz Bakery hardly
seems worth it. It's redeemed, in part, by the access to the 1,000-bottle
wine cellar at Planet Wine next door. –WS

# Evolve

**6.5** **7.0**
Food     Feel

This sophisticated, vibey spot is a surprising refuge of warmth, despite its underwhelming kitchen

## New American

Upmarket restaurant     **$40**
Price

www.evolve1817.com

Sun–Thu 5pm–11pm
Fri–Sat 5pm–12:30am

**Bar** Beer, wine, liquor
**Credit cards** Visa, MC
**Reservations** Accepted
Live music, outdoor dining

**Adams Morgan**
1817 Columbia Rd. NW
(202) 518-3865

Evolve shines in the drunken mecca of an Adams Morgan night like a beacon of cleanliness and class. Yet it seems to somehow avoid the cold and aggressive vibe of a "restaurant group," instead owned by four friends that give a sort of homegrown tint to its all-white furniture and "Blue Steel" face-making. Service is warm and enthusiastic, and the food is clearly made with love.

If it feels like you're simply hanging out at a very stylish friend's house (but with drinks you have to pay for), the food drives this point home. Humble executions and sloppy presentations stand out like a Sears outfit in this otherwise glossy joint. Like the menu at your average post-college dinner party, nothing is outright terrible, nor does it sing. Take bacon-wrapped shrimp, which is a literal translation of cooked shrimp, applewood-smoked bacon (which is becoming a boring decoy for lazy kitchens who won't make their own), and a bath of barbecue sauce that tastes more Heinz than the purported "Asian." Pepper-crusted Black Angus (another vapid marketing ploy) is just as drab: it's a hunk of meat crusted in pepper, grilled, sliced, and served with horseradish sauce that tastes fresh…out of the jar. Spiced fries are hand-cut with the standard chiffonade of fresh herbs. Hey, it drives us nuts when diners ludicrously claim "I could just make this at home," but in this case, they might be right.

The beverage program is aggressively average: a nonspecific list of wine varietals, sans producer names or vintages, is unceremoniously offered alongside a frat-house bar selection of mixers. Where Evolve does impress is in all things sweet. A cranberry-oatmeal-cookie sandwich pairs a dry but chewy cookie with tart lemon sorbet. The transition from grainy, doughy oats to leathery cranberry to smooth sorbet is fantastic, twinkling with acidity. Impromptu hot chocolate is thick and creamy; the chocolate is dense, and more bitter than sweet. It's not on the menu, but we recommend it on cold nights.

That's one bonus of such a friendly vibe: if there's something you crave that they don't offer, the staff is eager to accommodate you. Evolve is capable of wonderful moments—it is a restaurant where you feel sincerely taken care of, where the food that is put in front of you really matters to someone. On a madhouse Saturday night in Adams Morgan—or anywhere—that's rare. Better food and drinks aren't. –FC

# Faccia Luna

The Pizza Pie grows up and buys a house in the suburbs

**7.1** **6.6**
*Food* *Feel*

## Italian, Pizza

Casual restaurant

**$40**
*Price*

www.faccialuna.com

Mon–Thu 11am–11pm
Fri–Sat 11am–midnight
Sun noon–11pm
Hours vary by location

**Bar** Beer, wine, liquor
**Credit cards** Visa, MC, AmEx
**Reservations** Not accepted
Outdoor dining, veg-friendly

**Arlington, VA**
2909 Wilson Blvd.
(703) 276-3099

**Alexandria Old Town**
823 S. Washington St.
(703) 838-5998

The District of Columbia proper can claim a number of excellent pizzerias; further out in the suburbs, good pies are fewer and farther between—but they're by no means impossible to find.

Faccia Luna is one of Northern Virginia's most upscale pizzerias, and it pulls off this role nicely. With two locations—one in nouvelle-chic Clarendon and the other in Old Town Alexandria—the restaurant is convenient for pizza lovers south of the district border (the mini-chain also operates two locations in Scranton and State College, PA). The original Faccia Luna was actually opened by two Penn State fraternity brothers in Washington's Northwest quadrant. That store is no longer open, but its southern siblings remain.

As befits a restaurant started by frat boys, Faccia's beer selection rocks, but it's much more serious and grown-up than what we associate with the fraternity lifestyle. The warming week-old keg of Miller Light has been replaced by a selection of microbrews and waiters who have no problem describing a lager's body and aroma; instead of flea-ridden couches there are cherry wood tables and stools, black and white photographs, and sleek steel light fixtures.

The pizza, especially, is miles removed from the halls of Alpha Sigma Phi. The Arlington location, at least, fires theirs in a wood oven. Instead of a crust bready enough to mop up a Friday night's worth of beer, Faccia's is only slightly thicker than a classic New York pizza's, but still thin enough to crisp ever so slightly. The sauce tastes of pure Roma tomatoes, a far cry from the sticky sweet red sauce on a 3am Papa John's pie. Although the white pies can get a touch dry, ingredients such as fresh artichoke hearts, spicy nuggets of sausage, pungent goat cheese, and creamy gorgonzola make for some much more sophisticated eating.

A number of pastas are also available, but they're not nearly as good as the pizza, which, like all good suburbanites, aims for the middle: sorta fancy, sorta not, sorta thin, sorta thick, (unfortunately, sorta expensive): fortunately, Faccia strikes pretty close to the bull's eye. –CK

# Fadó

Everything that we love about Irish pubs—and better food than usual

**6.8** Food  **8.0** Feel

## Irish

Bar  **$27** Price

www.fadoirishpub.com

Mon–Thu 11:15am–10pm
Fri 11:15am–11pm
Sat 6:30am–11pm
Sun 6:30am–10:30pm

**Bar** Beer, wine, liquor
**Credit cards** Visa, MC, AmEx
**Reservations** Accepted
Live music

**Chinatown**
808 7th St. NW
(202) 789-0066

Why is it that you can find an Irish pub in practically every city in the world? These days, in America, it's starting to feel like you can even find a Fadó in every city. This chain, with locations from Seattle to St. Louis, clearly has a firm grasp on what it is that makes Irish pubs such nice places in which to spend an evening.

The food easily lives up to its Irish-pub-fare pretensions. It's overpriced, but we've been consistently happy with it. We especially like the fish and chips, with their delicate batter. Chicken pot pie, too, is a warm winner, with a delicate crust and none of the gelatinous goo that so often sinks the dish. The Irish breakfast is a good order, with baked beans, sunny eggs that are usually nicely runny, sausage that is appropriately bready yet still well seasoned, a couple of rashers of Irish bacon, fried tomatoes, and some sweet brown bread to mop up leftovers. Corned beef is slow-cooked on the premises, and don't miss the delightful brown-bread ice cream for dessert.

Sure, there are the requisite annoying affectations of most things "Irish" on this side of the pond: the Guinness paraphernalia, shamrocks, green plaid. Musicians perform the obligatory U2 songs. Somewhat inexplicably, the cozy interior is dotted with pillars that look like tree trunks.

But there is a lot about the pub that feels genuine. It regularly shows live footie without a cover. The room is comfortable, and there is a warm patina to all surfaces, especially the low, wood ceilings.

Service is welcoming and chatty, with a wicked Irish warmth well expressed on the menu:

May you have food and raiment.
A soft pillow for your head.
May you be forty years in heaven,
Before the devil knows you're dead. –RM

# Farrah Olivia

A thoughtful and playful experience with innovative food

| 8.0 | 8.9 |
|:---:|:---:|
| Food | Feel |

## New American

Upmarket restaurant

**$65**
Price

www.farraholiviarestaurant.com

Mon–Fri 5:30pm–10pm

**Bar** Beer, wine, liquor
**Credit cards** Visa, MC, AmEx
**Reservations** Accepted
Date-friendly, outdoor dining

**Alexandria Old Town**
600 Franklin St.
(703) 778-2233

When asked to describe Farrah Olivia, two words immediately come to mind: thoughtful and beautiful. The dining room is both amusing and welcoming, with dark brown chairs, playful but subdued animal-and-plant wallpaper, hanging glimmering fixtures, and a plethora of natural light. The kitchen plays with colorful Afro-Franco-American flavors, and pulls off impeccable artistic presentation, with an attention to detail that's careful without being stuffy

The chef draws upon his Ivory Coast upbringing, synthesizing those recipes with French, Middle Eastern, and American flavors. Orange-scented salmon, for example, is paired with a fermented yuca couscous that's incredibly innovative—slightly sour, crunchy, comforting—and a "shrimp essence" that's unfortunately imperceptible. Manhattan-style chowder is delicate, smooth, and smoky.

At times, Farrah Olivia's dishes can actually seem too thoughtful. "Shocked escolar" with soy pearls, pickled pears, and wasabi is visually dramatic, tiny, and precise, but it takes a delicate hand and a lot of patience to enjoy this dish. Because there are so many elements arranged separately on the plate, one has to construct every bite, combining each of the elements to create a purposeful mouthful.

And once that bite is constructed, the flavors and textures are so subtle that it turns into a game of "Guess That Spice." Dessert, on the other hand, keeps it simple, delivering on both creativity and taste. Take, for instance, an "Apple Pizza" with Calvados ice cream (yum!), toffee sauce, and fig jam. Now there's creativity we can get behind. –SDC

# Faryab

Afghan food that could stand to be a lot better

**6.3** Food **4.0** Feel

## Afghan

Casual restaurant

**$25** Price

Tue, Wed, Thu, Sun 5pm–10pm
Fri–Sat 5pm–11pm

**Bar** Beer, wine
**Credit cards** Visa, MC, AmEx
**Reservations** Accepted
Kid-friendly, veg-friendly

**Bethesda, MD**
4917 Cordell Ave.
(301) 951-3484

In many ways, Faryab is just a generic ethnic restaurant: on the outside, a nondescript storefront is easy to miss on a restaurant row packed with more glamorous neighbors; on the inside, a few Afghan textiles decorate the stark white walls, and purely functional furniture stands a little drably upon the plain tiled floor. Even the Afghan cuisine isn't as exotic as you might think; those familiar with Middle Eastern, Indian, and Eastern European foods won't be taken aback by the dumplings, rich vegetable stews, flatbreads, and frequent appearances of yogurt and ground meat.

But plain though it is, this small restaurant is familial and upbeat, with several tables sporting strollers parked nearby, and a lively rapport building between the staff (especially the gregarious manager) and regular customers.

The food is comforting rather than revelatory, the spices subdued and the textures mostly soft, which is a pity, because Afghan food can sometimes wow with the best of 'em. Dumpling starters are available steamed or fried, stuffed with either undercooked scallions or the more popular meat-and-mashed-potato filling that recalls good old-fashioned American comfort food. The bread basket is piled with puffy, dimpled squares of a rather dull snow-white bread. One of the things we love about Afghan food is its seductive blending of savory and sweet, but here a celebrated pumpkin dish called chalow kadu is overpoweringly sugary, despite its supposedly "spiced" yogurt sauce.

Service is earnest and soft-spoken, and the regular crowd has clearly found more than enough to enjoy on the concise list of dishes that wanders only tentatively beyond the most familiar boundaries. The wine list, clearly an afterthought, caters to tired parents who may want to sneak a glass or two before heading home. Faryab offers up two important lessons in restaurant appeal: one—that restaurant patrons are far-sighted; a spot that achieves the feel of a neighborhood hangout can easily overcome any failings that come into focus from a distance. And, two, that foodies are always willing to give the benefit of the doubt to an enterprise that isn't just another burger bar, pizza joint, or curry house.

In the end, however, Faryab reminds us of the old truth about small packages: sometimes, they just hide something small. –CD

# 15 Ria

**5.9** **5.2**
Food  Feel

Mediocre food in a dull space makes for
unpleasant upmarket meals

## New American

Upmarket restaurant

**$60**
Price

www.15ria.com

| | | |
|---|---|---|
| Mon–Fri 6:30am–11am, | **Bar** Beer, wine, liquor | **Logan Circle** |
| 11:30am–2pm, 5:30pm–9pm | **Credit cards** Visa, MC, AmEx | 1515 Rhode Island Ave. NW |
| Sat 7am–1pm, 5:30pm–9:30pm | **Reservations** Accepted | (202) 742-0015 |
| Sun 7am–2pm, 5:30pm–9pm | Outdoor dining, Wi-Fi | |

It's fine to eat great expensive food or great cheap food or even mediocre cheap food. It's not fine to eat mediocre expensive food. It just makes you feel cheated. And unfortunately, 15 Ria is one of the many spots in DC that falls into this disappointing category. Located inside the Doubletree Washington Hotel, this has the unmistakable feel of a hotel restaurant: dim lighting, a lack of windows in the back room where you might be seated, rushed service, and stuffy chairs and tables that weakly attempt to seem luxurious.

Although the menu tries to be innovative and seasonal, it doesn't achieve either of these goals. Braised beef short rib, tender but coated in a too-sweet sauce, is served over a bed of stiff grits, shallots, and spinach. This heavy dish is most certainly not appropriate for spring and summer in hot hot DC. Correctly-seared-but-salty sea scallops served over crisp-but-too-greasy crab cakes rest atop creamed spinach and lobster sauce, which tastes a lot like cream and very little like lobster, and the sauce surrounding pan-seared salmon tastes suspiciously similar. The salmon was nicely cooked, but the squash and zucchini that came with it were blah.

Cocktails are decidedly new school—pear-infused Bourbon, cucumber cosmopolitans—and it's hard to see the appeal of a froofy cocktail in a sleek and trendy bar. But when it comes to both wine and dessert at 15 Ria, nothing stands out. Wines are fine but not exciting, and while the desserts are also seasonal, they generally feature the same lineup of the usual suspects at this type of restaurant: crème brûlée, pineapple upside-down cake, molten chocolate cake, sorbet, and so on. Regardless, after such a mediocre meal, who's in the mood for dessert anyway? –SDC

# Filomena

An oddly creepy, oddly loveable, oddly mediocre
Italian restaurant

**5.8** **7.5**

*Food* *Feel*

## Italian

Casual restaurant **$50**

*Price*

www.filomena.com

Daily 11:30am–11:30pm

**Bar** Beer, wine, liquor
**Credit cards** Visa, MC, AmEx
**Reservations** Accepted
Date-friendly, kid-friendly, Wi-Fi

**Georgetown**
1063 Wisconsin Ave. NW
(202) 338-8800

Filomena looks like what you would get if Miss Havisham were middle-class and Italian, and decided to turn the preserved crumbs of her wedding banquet into a restaurant. The grotto of a dining room is preceded by a steep flight of stairs and guarded by, of all things, a real Italian grandma, hand rolling pasta like some benign, matronly Keebler elf. Inside, a decades-old kitchen fights with fake garden fronds, statuary, odd knick-knacks, and art of dubious taste. It looks vaguely like home—if your home popped up in the vision of a slightly unstable, and not particularly promising, soothsayer.

Perhaps it's the promise of a home-cooked meal or the hangover-soothing darkness, but Filomena is beloved by both students and tourists alike. High traffic times include the Sunday brunch buffet, when the restaurant tempts the hungry with all-you-can eat pizza, pasta, salad, and dessert.

Incidentally, no price or quantity can mitigate the mediocrity of the food. Real Italian grandmas hand-rolling pasta or not, the food served at the buffet is neither authentic nor good. Unflattering red heat lamps dry out the puffy, bloated pizzas, and salad offerings are comparable to what you'd find at a Ruby Tuesdays. Pastas include mushy little tubes floating in a blasé rose sauce littered with chunks of poorly cleaned, overcooked seafood. The solicitous and sweet wait staff tempers the quality of the food, but not by much.

Ordering off Filomena's full menu is a much safer choice. This is where the handmade pasta is actually used. While the pasta itself is good (a bit soft as hand-rolled dough is wont to be), filled varieties are particularly tasty. Mushroom ravioli taste deep and earthy with accompanying sauce that is good but overabundant in a more American fashion. Desserts are sweeter than expected, thickly jammed and iced. They make you want to hum the Godfather theme song.

Whatever the quality of the food, the patrons of Filomena clearly love it very much. Diners know the waiters, and the place often tops the list of readers' favorites. But whether they would choose it for their wedding banquet is another question. –JC

# Finn & Porter

A bumbling chophouse chain that can't execute anywhere near its attempted level

## American

Upmarket restaurant

**$75**
Price

www.finnandporter.com

Daily 5pm–11pm
Hours vary by location

**Bar** Beer, wine, liquor
**Credit cards** Visa, MC, AmEx
**Reservations** Accepted
Wi-Fi

**Downtown**
900 10th St. NW
(202) 719-1600

**Alexandria, VA**
5000 Seminary Rd.
(703) 379-2346

Watching an upscale restaurant mini-chain try to break out of its upscale hotel maxi-chain environs is like watching a Texas politician trying to rally the masses in broken Spanish: while on some level you have to admire the effort, it's sometimes hard not to wince at the bumbling execution.

The kitchen, like everything else here, has ambition but exercises it without grace. Once, an amuse-bouche of mushroom consommé was overwhelmed by parsley. The sushi bar hawks some truly exotic—and truly expensive—pieces of fish, but they fall flat. O-toro, for example, the fattiest of the fatty tuna, tips the monetary scales at $15 for two pieces, but was disappointingly stringy at a recent visit. Even worse was fishy chu-toro, a less fatty stomach cut, but one that still should be meltingly tender. Finn & Porter further cheapens the deal by offering such silly rolls as "Texas Cowboy," with asparagus, paprika, and filet mignon.

Amongst the main courses, crab cakes, though meaty, are humdrum and not really the focus here; their corn relish and mustard sauce are a bit out of place. A New York strip is stodgy. A dessert of pumpkin cheesecake with chocolate sauce is better, and quite decadent.

While the Finn & Porter in the District is not actually in a hotel, it's still got that prefab feel. High ceilings, gauzy curtains, dark wood, and low (but funky) lighting work collectively in an attempt to make you feel like one of the cool kids (with a fat wallet in tow). The outpost in Alexandria, not surprisingly, has a very similar feel. And this one *is* in a hotel—the Hilton.

At up to $100 a head, this restaurant has us scratching ours. –RG

# Firefly

Down the Hobbit hole

| 7.9 | 9.3 |
|-----|-----|
| Food | Feel |

## New American

Upmarket restaurant

**$60**
*Price*

www.firefly-dc.com

Mon–Thu 7am–10am,
11:30am–2:30pm, 5:30pm–
10pm; Fri 7am–10am,
11:30am–2:30pm, 5:30pm–
10:30pm; Sat 8am–10am,
5:30pm–10:30pm; Sun 9am–
2pm, 5:30pm–10pm

**Bar** Beer, wine, liquor
**Credit cards** Visa, MC, AmEx
**Reservations** Accepted
Date-friendly, Wi-Fi

**Dupont**
1310 New Hampshire Ave. NW
(202) 861-1310

If fashionable Hobbits decided to become restaurateurs, the product would probably look like Firefly. From the lantern-hung tree at a place of prominence in the middle of the dining room, to the low ceilings, bucolic stonework, burnished copper, and bark accents, the feel is warm and inviting—even magical. And in true Hobbit style, the space is small. Your hostess might have to pull the table out to get you seated.

The food at Firefly is fresh and earthy. The chef uses local suppliers and organic food in seasonal dishes. The menu, although refreshingly short and focused, cites numerous local farms and producers. The cooking style is simple; Bortnick relies more upon imaginative combinations of ingredients than fancy techniques. Glistening chicken-fried oysters re-sprout gnarled shells of batter and leak briny, piping-hot juice into your mouth. They're overly greasy, but you'll probably finish them all.

A seared yellowfin tuna BLT is a fine balance of disparate flavors. Multigrain bread lends an oatey spice, while a thick tuna steak is fine-grained and well balanced by chunks of bacon hidden in avocado. Parmesan and truffle combine to scent fries with intimations of earth. Strawberry shortcake—a seasonal dish—adds surprising notes of fresh rosemary in the dough; the dusty, sharp note of the herb plays off a cool, woodsy bite of Bourbon in the cream.

Firefly's service is exquisite. Attentive waiters know their food, and are unafraid to make suggestions; several staff members are likely to stop by and check on your meal. Given the thematic vibe, small details like copper buckets for your bread and bell jars poked with holes containing the check seem not quite over the top. Our one complaint is that the cocktails don't boast the fine balance of the food. The "Topaz," for instance, tastes overwhelmingly of tequila, and the kumquats in the "Sunrise" give it a bitter, rindy taste.

Otherwise, a meal here is like an evening in the home of a dear and solicitous friend. If this is what a Hobbit hole is like, we wouldn't mind staying for a while. –FC

# Firehook

Delicious treats and surprisingly good sandwiches, slowly taking over

## 7.2 Food
## 7.0 Feel

## Baked goods

Counter service

## $10 Price

www.firehook.com

Mon–Fri 6:30am–6pm
Sat–Sun 8am–8pm
Hours vary by location

**Bar** None
**Credit cards** Visa, MC, AmEx
Veg-friendly

**Cleveland Park**
3411 Connecticut Ave. NW
(202) 362-2253

**Downtown**
555 13th St. NW
(202) 393-0952

**Alexandria Old Town**
105 S. Union St.
(703) 519-8021

**Additional locations**
and more features at
www.fearlesscritic.com

Firehook is known to stock the kind of cookies you're liable to have cravings for. Luckily, the bakery-cum-sandwich shops have proliferated in the district and northern Virginia, with 11 locations open today, including two in the lobbies of museums. Which means that another helping of those chocolate-chip marvels is never too far from reach.

Many hurried businesspeople know that, in addition to breakfast and afternoon sweets, Firehook makes a mean lunch sandwich. But unbeknownst to many, one or two locations also offer the occasional "weekend omelette station," at which you can order your eggs with any number of vegetable and meat toppings. This perk might end up being more sensational than sating, if it weren't for the generous portion of fresh Firehook bread that accompanies every order. Whether you choose the slightly tangy sourdough or the nutty whole wheat, it's difficult to go wrong.

Which brings us to the sandwiches. Normally, we're inclined to prefer a toppings-to-bread ratio that is greater than one, if only because in a world rife with questionable delis and rolls drier than Arizona, more meat (even if it's mediocre) always seems a better value. Not so at Firehook. In fact, we raised nary a whimper when our turkey-and-sun-dried tomato foccacia clocked in around one-to-five for toppings-to-bread. The enormous slab of chewy focaccia, with the tangiest, crispest crust in DC, is something you can, to put it mildly, really dig into.

Our advice on the soups is generally to skip them, if only to leave room for a dessert or two. The oatmeal or chocolate chip cookies are sure bets, as are any of the muffins or cupcakes. Firehook's scones are less reliable: they sometimes fall on the dry side, and rarely have enough dried fruit or chocolate chips to make the dough worthwhile.

While the food is consistent across bakeries, the atmosphere can vary. The Cleveland Park spot boasts an outdoor garden with trellised flowers and a fountain; Metro Center's is merely a hole-in-the-wall-with-muffins. Alas, most Firehooks close early, but you can count on a few local grocery stores to stock their goods and sate those late-night cravings. –CK

# Five Guys

Meat haikus

**7.4** *Food*  **6.0** *Feel*

## American

Counter service  **$10** *Price*

www.fiveguys.com

Daily 11am–10pm
Hours vary by location

**Bar** None
**Credit cards** Visa, MC
Kid-friendly

**Chinatown**
808 H St. NW
(202) 393-2900

**Capitol Hill**
13th St. NW and F St. NW
(202) 393-2135

**Downtown**
13th and F St. NW
(202) 393-2135

**Additional locations**
and more features at
www.fearlesscritic.com

To commune with flesh.
To feel it fall like pleasure
from your lips. Five Guys

strips your hunger raw.
Hedonistic animal
possessed. Get some now.

Five Guys gets you in
your gut. Feeds your empty with
hope and calories.

The whole room is bare.
Ordering is like high school.
It doesn't matter.

Get yours like we get
ours: Two plump patties, cheese, stuffed
between seeded buns.

The secret is the
better bread. Buttery sweet.
Changing everything.

Like a meat grilled cheese
Candies drip. And forbidden flesh
(bacon) taut and crisp.

You can never get
enough. You will never get
enough. Die happy.  (*Guest review by Lil' G*)

# Fleming's

A middling corporate steakhouse with only a few deviations from the standard menu

**6.9** | **7.5**
*Food* | *Feel*

## Steakhouse

Upmarket restaurant

**$90**
*Price*

www.flemingssteakhouse.com

Mon–Thu 5pm–10pm
Fri–Sat 5pm–11pm
Sun 5pm–9pm

**Bar** Beer, wine, liquor
**Credit cards** Visa, MC, AmEx
**Reservations** Accepted
Wi-Fi

**Tysons Corner, VA**
1960-A Chain Bridge Rd.
(703) 442-8384

Eh. What can we say about Fleming's? It's your average corporate-expense-account chain steakhouse that has managed to sprawl across most of the US—and quite quickly, we might add. The original branch was opened only in 1998. And the power of this name recognition cannot be underestimated. Traveling executives come to know and trust it, ordering the same thing every time, every location, knowing there won't be any deal-spoiling surprises. People who just eat there because they like it do the same—"My husband always gets the ribeye, and I get the filet mignon." And this, ultimately, is what chains really provide us with: consistency nationwide. Service varies, but when you get the trusted "Fleming's Potatoes" or Chili's "Awesome Blossom," you know exactly what you're going to get.

The sad thing is that this is still an incredibly successful business model in the American restaurant scene, even for restaurants as high-end as Fleming's. Surely a large part of it is all the visiting businesspeople; but we need restaurants for ourselves, too. We need human chefs behind our food. The Fleming's web site, for instance, reads like a corporate document. The visitor is wooed by numbers and commitments to this and that. If you're looking for a job, rest assured; Fleming's understands the importance of balancing work with play.

Teasing aside, the space, at least, is well-executed: they have good booths, large and comfortable, and there's a nice bar area. A few sides here are out of the steakhouse norm: chipotle cheddar macaroni and cheese, potatoes with jalapeños and cheddar cheese. They make for the sort of steak dinner we would have imagined as kids, unabashedly hitting all the pleasure points in one meal.

But it's the steak that defines the place. Fleming's are decent, but they're wet-aged, not dry aged. Boo hoo. The chain also claims to undersell other steakhouses, and it's true by a few dollars, but after a nice bottle of wine—which you wind up ordering at a place like this—what's the difference between $88 and $94? And anyway, if it's not on your dime, what does it matter? –FC

# Florida Avenue Grill

Dangerously tasty southern breakfasts that'll finish
you off before you've started

**7.2** **8.6**
Food Feel

## Southern

Casual restaurant **$15**
Price

Tue–Thu 8am–9pm
Fri–Sat 8am–4am
Sun 8am–4:30pm

**Bar** None
**Credit cards** Visa, MC, AmEx
**Reservations** Not accepted
Kid-friendly, Wi-Fi

**U Street**
1100 Florida Ave. NW
(202) 265-1586

Tucked neatly on the corner of 11th and Florida, the ramshackle little
building known as the Florida Avenue Grill proudly advertises its "world
famous" status. Crowds of diners wait outside the tiny space to join in the
tradition of patrons like Janet Reno and Ludacris. Inside, a hive of activity
buzzes constantly—whether it be the waitresses sprinting from table to
table (and occasionally taking their hand at the grill) or the diners
squeezing past each other to get at their tables. The Grill is loud, hectic,
and alive.

This is pure, down-home Southern cooking that pulls no punches—it's
heavy. Whether it be pork chops or biscuits and gravy or pancakes the
size of a tablemat, the result will be a full belly and an endangered heart.

Though your dishes may not be upmarket, they are good. Pancakes are
maximally fluffy, lighter and airier than their peers. Slabs of bacon are
pulled out of giant metal troughs and flattened under irons. The Grill uses
good bacon—the finished product remains plump and thick and barely
shrinks at all. These are breakfast staples done at their best.

Southerners will not be let down: biscuits are soft and moist, and best
garnished by "butter spread" (52% vegetable oil!) that adds movie-
theater popcorn zing. For traditionalists and adventurers, gooey,
unidentifiably chunky, gray-brown gravy is a tantalizing alternative. Be
forewarned—the gravy is all fat and no salt, and tends to congeal into
rubber-skinned sculptural elements if left alone too long.

Some things at the Grill are a bit particular, though. Fried apples are
distinctively spiced with licorice flavors but unbearably sweet. Grits are
wonderfully sticky-gooey, but end up at your table undressed and a bit
boring. And, with all the activity, it's not exactly clear whether the
flatware you're eating off of is really clean. One other caution: even
though the menu mentions that egg beaters and turkey bacon are
available, don't count on it. The Florida Avenue Grill is all about feeding
people until they have no option but to concede the rest of their day in
favor of napping. The next time you're craving a breakfast to end all
breakfasts (whether it's morning or 4am), go to the Florida Avenue Grill.
You'll love it—and you may never eat breakfast again. –JC

# Fogo de Chão

**6.7** Food    **7.0** Feel

Stuff yourself full of meat—as long as you haven't already stuffed yourself too full with salad

## Brazilian, Steakhouse

Upmarket restaurant    **$80** Price

www.fogodechao.com

Mon–Thu 11am–2pm, 5pm–10pm; Fri 11am–2pm, 5pm–10:30pm; Sat 4:30pm–10:30pm; Sun 4pm–9pm

**Bar** Beer, wine, liquor
**Credit cards** Visa, MC, AmEx
**Reservations** Accepted
Kid-friendly

**Downtown**
1101 Pennsylvania Ave. NW
(202) 347-4668

One of the most eternally popular and exalted meat chains in America, Fogo de Chão probably owes less to its kitchen or its ingredients than to its Brazilian concept, which scales the heights of themed gimmickry. Turn your table's token onto its green face, and the meat-shavers (dressed humiliatingly as gauchos), who roam the restaurant with enormous skewers and long knives, will keep stopping by to shave hunks of deliciously fatty ribeye and "house special" sirloin, along with dozens of other lesser cuts of meat, onto your plate. Turn the token red, and the barrage will subside.

Fogo has hit upon the same crowd-pleasing formula as Benihana, combining interactive cuisine and faux-exotic theming with utterly familiar, kid-friendly tastes. There are other versions of the Brazilian steakhouse in town, but this is probably the highest-revenue practitioner of the art. The genius of the sprawling salad bar, and of the irresistible little hot cheese buns that show up first at your table, is that you spend the first part of your meal filling up on high-margin items like starches, salads, and beans. If you actually measure the amount of (lower-margin) meat you wind up eating, the $45 or so you're paying for "all you can eat" (not including drinks or dessert) starts to look like less and less of a good deal.

Our advice is to save virtually all of your appetite for the meat, because the salad bar is a minefield. The few highlights include intensely smoked salmon of the cooked-through variety, which comes with pleasant dressing; decent giant asparagus; and equally enormous hearts of palm, which are always a welcome delivery system for salt, acid, and bright textural punch. But potato salad is underseasoned and mealy; artichoke hearts, meanwhile, are enormously overmarinated and oversized, dominated by the classic taste of jar juice. Many meats are problematic too—bacon-wrapped chicken is terribly dry, filet mignon is cooked to oblivion, and so on. In the end, we'd take one competently prepared steak, and perhaps a simple salad and side, over the many different manifestations of mediocrity that adorn this overrated, spectacularly profitable chain. –RG

# Founding Farmers

Let's do this thing!

**8.2** Food | **9.2** Feel

## American

Upmarket restaurant **$50** Price

www.wearefoundingfarmers.com

Mon–Wed 8am–10pm; Thu 8am–11pm; Fri 8am–midnight; Sat noon–midnight; Sun 10am–9pm

**Bar** Beer, wine, liquor
**Credit cards** Visa, MC, AmEx
**Reservations** Accepted
Date-friendly, kid-friendly, veg-friendly

**Farragut**
1924 Pennsylvania Ave. NW
(202) 822-8783

Founding Farmers is the populist answer to the DC steakhouse. Owned by a cooperative of farmers and proudly located in a LEEDs-certified space, it ushers in an era of eco-conscious dining. The airy, well-appointed interior looks like it could be serving any fare, but the pastoral accents, like rows of giant jars that proudly display the vibrant hues of pickled vegetables, drive home the ethic. It feels warm and lively, effervescent with activity and honest pride, from the constant thrum of diners to the small army of cooks prepping and assembling dishes in the open kitchen window.

We don't know if it's just the high of knowing you are doing a good thing and doing it well—or maybe it's the popcorn machine in view—but there's definitely a merriness at hand. Simple, popular American fare is given a magic touch. Many basic elements of dishes are house-made, like thick rashers of bacon, deep brown and kissed with sweetness; dense and hearty bread; and handmade pastas that produce thick pillows of perfectly al-dente ravioli, bursting with earthy butternut squash in the fall. Deviled eggs are a sinful treat, with creamy, melty insides that would shame any drab church picnic's. A cheese platter gleefully shouts, "We Want the Funk, Give up the Funk!" No, really. It's named this because the cows who produce its milk spend all day in a warm barn listening to jazz. After all, it's been proven that happy, mellow animals do produce better cheese. (Hey, wouldn't you?) A grilled-cheese sandwich layers gruyère and cheddar in the homemade bread which, when paired with a bowl of fresh tomato soup, is as nostalgic and comforting as your inner child wants, but much more complex and grown up than you remember.

Eating food raised responsibly and prepared carefully and with simplicity and skill is immensely satisfying. Founding Farmers honors the multitudes that have a hand in shaping your meal; the many brows and many hands that have grown and coaxed and shaped. Dining here is participation, an act of recognition, joy, and ultimately, of thanks. It's unfortunate that this is rare in America, but it is. –JC

# Fresh Med

The interior lacks pizzazz, and the food could use a bit of kick, too

**8.1** Food  **5.5** Feel

## Middle Eastern

Counter service  **$20** Price

Sun–Mon 11am–9pm
Tue–Sat 11am–10pm

**Bar** None
**Credit cards** Visa, MC, AmEx
Delivery, veg-friendly

**Cleveland Park**
3313 Connecticut Ave.
NW
(202) 244-3995

Fresh Med puts up such a modest front—a bare store on busy Connecticut Avenue, unadorned cafeteria-style tables, and employees in hideous "Fresh Med" polo shirts—that you'd be forgiven for thinking you'd just walked out of Washington and into a new Lebanese franchise in Akron, Ohio. But Fresh Med is neither a chain (it's a lone operator), nor Lebanese (it's run by Turks); moreover, it serves up some of the best Middle Eastern fare in the District.

There's nothing special on the menu here beyond the usual pan-Middle-Eastern classics: falafel, shawarma, gyros, and kabobs. But the typical fare is done well: the meat is infused with spice; the falafel patties are well textured without being dry; and the thick pita almost tastes homemade. The shop also offers side salads: hummus, taboulleh, and baba ganoush, and inches its way west with dolmade and spanikopita. The creamy lentil soup is a real treat. All of the offerings are, give or take a few hundred miles, "Med." And although the shop doesn't take on a cloying attitude about its "Freshness," the food is indeed just that.

Fresh Med also has a wall stocked with Turkish imports ranging from sour cherry juice to crackers and spices to boxes of Turkish Delight. The eastern Mediterranean takes pride in its sweets, and Fresh Med doesn't fail to deliver on this count. The small pieces of baklava are doused in enough oil and rosewater to damp the flakiness of the filo dough, with a generous dose of walnut filling. Fresh Med does offer tea, but, unhappily, it's made with a bag.

Served until 4pm, the inexpensive lunch special (a few bucks for a sandwich, drink, and side) is a filling proposition, and Fresh Med even offers delivery. Chances are good that your own dining room beats the nothing-fancy atmosphere and buzzing halogens of the eating area: if you want a spicier soup, expect to use Tabasco, and you'll mop up that last bit of tahini from your paper plate with a plastic utensil. –CK

# The Front Page

Cheap happy hour and crowded bar scene, but
most definitely not a serious place to eat

**3.8** Food | **6.8** Feel

## American

Casual restaurant | **$35** Price

www.frontpagerestaurant.com

Mon–Thu 11:30am–11pm
Fri 11:30am–midnight
Sat 11am–midnight
Sun 10am–11pm

**Bar** Beer, wine, liquor
**Credit cards** Visa, MC, AmEx
**Reservations** Accepted
Kid-friendly, outdoor dining, Wi-Fi

**Dupont**
1333 New Hampshire Ave.
NW
(202) 296-6500

This just in! 3 tacos for $1, plus $2 Coronas will pack a joint that normally
doesn't deserve it! This is exactly the kind of deal calibrated to fit hordes
of DC summer interns who, by necessity, are walking Yellow Pages of the
cheapest food and drink on any given night.

The atmosphere is shabby-elegant; white brick walls are accented with
wood trim and chairs, and a selection of framed newspaper front pages
fills the spaces between a couple of flat-screen TVs. It gets awfully noisy
when the overworked young crowds file in, looking for a cheap good
time. You could escape outside, but to rickety tables and chairs balancing
precariously over subway grates.

On any occasion other than happy hour, we can firmly recommend
against dining at The Front Page, which is really trying to be a nightclub
more than anything else. The decidedly all-American menu includes grilled
chicken salad, cheeseburgers, and other bar standards, but nothing is
worthwhile. Buffalo wings come slicked in a moderately spicy (though
flavorless) sauce that stains your fingers orange, alongside a watery "blue
cheese" dressing (with no detectable blue cheese) and a few desiccated
celery sticks. Crab cakes contain a good amount of lump crabmeat, but
the seasoning is lacking. Baby back ribs, advertised as a house specialty,
are slathered in super-sweet barbecue sauce; while appropriately fatty and
falling off the bone, the meat is bland. Sides of cole slaw and potato salad
emphasize mayonnaise above all. Desserts—again, standards like
cheesecake, carrot cake, and an ice cream sundae—appear pre-sliced and
individually chilled.

The higher end of the menu reads like a decaying old hotel banquet:
seared salmon, bowtie pastas with heavy cream sauces, stuffed chicken,
and such, all of which are served with "rice and vegetable of the
evening." This, for $18 a pop? Even Olive Garden has more self-
awareness than this.

The wine list emphasizes mass-produced domestic bottles with familiar
names (can we get off the overpriced, overblown Silver Oak already?) and
few surprises. Here's the real news: white linen and an extra "e" on the
end of "grille" don't change the fact that The Front Page is predominantly
a bar. –FC

# Full Kee

Still the emperors of Chinatown, and don't they know it

**7.8** Food | **6.5** Feel

## Chinese

Casual restaurant | **$25** Price

www.fullkeedc.com

Daily 11am–2am

**Bar** Beer, wine
**Credit cards** Visa, MC
**Reservations** Accepted
Kid-friendly

**Chinatown**
509 H St. NW
(202) 371-2233

**Falls Church, VA**
5380 Columbia Pike
(703) 575-8232

Full Kee might not be the best restaurant in Chinatown, but it's the reigning champion of public opinion. And as the reigning champion, it wears its big, shiny belt with obvious pride. The interior is bright and mostly clean. '80s-department-store fluorescent lighting bounces off the bold yellow walls.

The most enchanting thing about this place is the mini kitchen at the front of the restaurant. With its shiny metal fixtures piled full of cheap rice bowls, hanging ducks, and big steaming pots, it's as if a street trolley from the streets of Asia has been magically transported into Full Kee. It is nostalgic and whimsical and captivatingly homey.

Indeed, it's this feeling of hominess that makes Full Kee so successful. Whether it's the mismatched serving dishes or dollar-a-dozen acrylic dinnerware, it's mom-and-pop in the best kind of way. So is the food. Dishes here may not be the loudest or jazziest, but they're sincere and good—more family food than restaurant food.

Bricks of fried tofu luxuriate in mild sauce with Chinese broccoli and shiitake mushrooms. Their spongy texture soaks up the juice around it and squirts back when you bite in. It is not an exciting dish—in fact, it's roughly the equivalent of a green bean casserole—but it is filling and comforting.

One noodle soup combines sweet, smoky strips of duck meat (and skin) and tender chicken with slivers of shiitake and bamboo. The giant bowl is heaped mountain-full of rice noodles that float and braid and bunch like strands of hair. The broth is stained dark from bitter greens. It is simply flavored yet deep and rich, dotted with suds of duck fat that slide down slurped noodles. Think of it as a fancier, Eastern version of chicken noodle. Even more authentic are the pulverized fish balls, which have that texture somewhere between chewy and spongy that is uniquely Chinese. Like the roar in a conch-shell, they remind you vaguely of the sea.

Full Kee is not without its foibles. The many Americanized dishes are still pretty bad. And as at many good Chinese joints, the wait staff aren't so keen on waiting: a conspicuous clout of impatience will hang over your table until you order, and then again, within half an hour, until you pay. Still, on the bright side, service is remarkably quick and efficient. And if you get into the spirit of things, you'll warm right up to the general bustling old-hand competence of the whole enterprise. –JC

# Fusion Grill

Oh dear, not again: fusion food—fad to fossil in
four seconds

**4.8** *Food*  **7.0** *Feel*

## Pan-Asian

Upmarket restaurant

**$55** *Price*

www.fusiongrilldc.com

Mon–Sat 11:30am–10:30pm
Sun noon–10pm

**Bar** Beer, wine, liquor
**Credit cards** Visa, MC, AmEx
**Reservations** Accepted
Delivery, live music, outdoor
dining, Wi-Fi

**Capitol Hill**
515 8th St. SE
(202) 546-3874

Fusion Grill at least does this: it tells you it's going to be boring and
overpriced, right in the name. Listen, if you have a hackneyed culinary
concept, you ought to downplay it, gloss it over as much as possible, and
then find a way to make your food surprise and delight the jaded among
us who are over the fusion thing. Fusion Grill does exactly the opposite;
clearly, they have no clue.

It's like when you go to the Dollar General and find some weird, cheap
version of something that used to be big years ago, like wine glasses with
flowers painted on them. Not long ago, this location was a modest
Chinese place called Szechuan House, which hustled Chinese-American
take-out standards for 22 years to the residents of Barracks Row. In 2006,
the owners slapped on some dark paint, dimmed the lighting, and put out
cloth napkins and minimalist arrangements of food on square plates; thus
was a cheap, mediocre restaurant replaced by one that is mediocre and
expensive.

Fusion Grill's food is not just generic but also poorly executed: it's like
peanuts and lemongrass are piled on in hopes of making something bad
more palatable. Appetizer dumplings are rather slippery and
unsubstantial, while oversalted salmon is accompanied by a bright but
boring assortment of peppers and other vegetables, the whole thing
doused, again, in lemongrass. And what's with these pan-Asian
restaurants assuming they have to drown everything in sugar to win over
American palates? Haven't we outgrown the ketchupy brown sugar sauce
omnipresent with every dish, from "Thai" curry to "miso" glaze?

Predictably, there's a menu of syrupy cocktails which tend to end in "-
tini," and the wine list's jammy clobberers are an even worse match for
the (normally) subtle spices of Asian cuisine. Even the website looks like it
has no idea what it's doing.

It's all so rote, messy, and overpriced that it makes us nostalgic for the
days when we could walk in and order the $5 lo mein…"unfused,
please." —CK

# Gamasot

**8.9** Food  **7.2** Feel

Hung over? You have lots of good, nourishing
soups to choose from here (ugh, choices)

## Korean

Casual restaurant  **$15** Price

www.gamasotrestaurant.com

Daily 9am–11pm

**Bar** Beer, wine
**Credit cards** Visa, MC, AmEx
**Reservations** Not accepted
Date-friendly

**Springfield, VA**
6965 Hechinger Dr.
(703) 256-0780

The name Gamasot refers to the cast-iron cauldrons in which the restaurant's claim to fame, seolleongtang, is brewed all day long. Every time we type that word, we screw it up, accidentally delete the sentence above it as well, hit Ctrl-Z, and start all over again. We repeat this pattern for about half an hour and our productivity is going down in ways that this economic climate will not support, so instead of typing seolleongtang (which everyone will complain has four different spellings and we're not using their favorite one anyway), we're going to call it oxbone soup. 'Cause that's what it is.

Traditionally, this soup is made from the bones of all four legs of the beast. Your first thought is: that's a mighty big seolleongtang! (Dammit.) It takes all day to extract the marrowy richness from the bones, and the soup, which is milky white (like the cow in "Jack and the Beanstalk"), is left bare of seasoning, which we like, so you can add as much or as little salt as your palate desires.

The version here comes with thin slices of beef and skinny noodles. Ask for tripe to add complexity, although its evocative barnyard aspect isn't for everyone. It is, however, for anyone with a hangover. It totally beats Saltines and 7-Up. But wait! There's also haejahnkook, which literally translates to "hangover soup." A similar conceit, but spicier and even more flavorful, if your tum-tum can handle such a thing.

Banchan (free small starter plates) are generous; the different kinds of kimchi are cut by hand at your table. Soondae (blood sausage) has also made an alluring and smoky appearance here. Dumplings are very good, and the early hours make for some great breakfast alternatives when dim sum, huevos rancheros, and pancakes get dull.

The décor at Gamasot is surprisingly more modern than that of its rivals. Cherry wood floors and accents give it a little elegance, and frosted glass windows help obscure the strip-mall world you're in. Some low cushions and tables are optional for a more traditional Korean feeling, but if you've come to nurse your hangover, snuggling up on those—with the quiet Korean television in the background—may lull you to sleep in your soup. –FC

# Georgia Brown's

A classy, upscale homage to the South whose brunch does regional justice

| 8.0 | 8.9 |
|---|---|
| Food | Feel |

**Southern**      Upmarket restaurant

**$55**
Price

www.gbrowns.com

Mon–Thu 11:30am–10pm; Fri 11:30am–11pm; Sat 5pm–11pm; Sun 10am–2:30pm, 5:30pm–10pm

**Bar** Beer, wine, liquor
**Credit cards** Visa, MC, AmEx
**Reservations** Accepted
Date-friendly, kid-friendly, live music, outdoor dining

Downtown
950 15th St. NW
(202) 393-4499

Sunday brunch at Georgia Brown's is a veritable institution in DC. Reservations and fasting are prerequisite. Billed as three acts, brunch manages to incorporate two buffets *and* a prepared main, for about $35 per person (plus drinks).

Just walking into the elegant restaurant puts you at ease. Swathed in warm peach (natch) with a rolling, bronze ceiling, the space feels almost womblike. A live jazz band alternates between standards and bossa nova, and a jovial crowd sips strong drinks.

With all the build-up, jaded diners might expect to be disappointed by the food, yet it manages to meet and even exceed expectations. Most of the items in this hedonistic cornucopia are well prepared: grits are some of the best in the city—thick, coarse, and cheesy; biscuits are buttery and flaky and begging to be doused in thick gravy. At the carving station, generous cuts of meat are at their Thanksgiving best: roast beef is delicately pink at the center, vivid with black peppercorns; turkey is clean and moist; ham is deliciously salty with a hint of smoke. And that's just the first act.

Between the first and third binges, you'll be encouraged to take home a main course. Even reheated, the Carolina shrimp and grits are decent, brinier and more complex than competing versions (due to the use of clam broth). Dessert is an exercise in overindulgence, whether you prefer dipping various bits of fruit and cake into a chocolate fountain or nibbling on about a dozen different kinds of pie.

The most impressive thing about Georgia Brown's isn't even the food, but rather its mastery in creating a dining experience that bursts with warmth and hospitality—one where you don't mind dawdling for another half-hour and having another cup of coffee. Soul-food purists might find GB's a little too fancy-schmancy to be authentic. After all, the best soul food in the South is slopped onto plastic plates by people who don't go in for linen and fine service. But if you want it both ways, GB's is a fine compromise. –JC

# Good Stuff Eatery

Burgers done up all fancy-like—without big, fancy prices

| 7.0 | 7.9 |
|---|---|
| Food | Feel |

## American

Counter service

**$15**
Price

www.goodstuffeatery.com

Mon–Sat 11:30am–11pm

**Bar** Beer
**Credit cards** Visa, MC, AmEx
Date-friendly, kid-friendly, outdoor dining, veg-friendly

**Capitol Hill**
303 Pennsylvania Ave. SE
(202) 543-8222

It is unclear why semi-celebrity chef Spike of "Top Chef" fame chose to come to DC to open a burger place, but he did. How he managed to capture the spirit of the funkier side of Capitol Hill so well is even more unclear. Good Stuff Eatery serves burgers in a near-spastic barn-party atmosphere. The interior is whimsical; it's a modernized Heartland, with beautiful exposed beams, barn doors, and nifty cow and cow-bell art pieces. There is a lively joviality about the space. The hustle and bustle of diners seems almost choreographed to the party music blaring over the speakers, and both customers and staff tend towards young and cheerful.

The menu is also self-consciously updated and fun: permutations of burgers are piled high with exotic toppings and wrapped into waxy paper. The Blazin' Barn, a testament to Spike's love for Vietnamese food, features a slaw of pickled daikon and carrots, mint, cilantro, basil, and Sriracha-spiked mayonnaise. The gingery zip and chili heat manage to tickle the palate, even through the fattiness of the meat (that said, we won't go replacing our livery báhn mì anytime soon). "The Spike's Sunnywide" sounds tempting (cheese, bacon, fried egg, barbecue), but it's a sloppy, greasy mess. There is so much oily runoff that it is hard to finish. Oh, but so possible.

Though the fries can be a bit brown and soggy, they are still worth the alchemical experiment you can perform with four different kinds of flavored mayo (including a sweet-spicy Sriracha, and bold and classic Old Bay). Of course, you have to wash it all down with a milkshake, which is made rich, creamy, and intensely dairy-flavored.

Good Stuff doesn't purport to be a great dining institution, but it is refreshing and exciting (best of all, it's really cheap—some people try to charge $10 for burgers like this). Besides, for a city that has a tendency to take itself too seriously, it's a good place to go for a spot of fun, and to try out the influence of different cultures on a good old American classic. —JC

# Gooldaegee (Honey Pig)

A fun place with delicious meat, any hour of the night

**8.8** *Food*  **9.1** *Feel*

## Korean

Casual restaurant

**$20** *Price*

www.kt411.com/bbq

24 hours

**Bar** Beer, wine
**Credit cards** Visa, MC, AmEx
**Reservations** Not accepted
Date-friendly, kid-friendly

**Annandale, VA**
7220 Columbia Pike
(703) 256-5229

The name translates as "Honey Pig," and that should give you a good idea of how much fun you're going to have here. This is easily the most enjoyable place to eat Korean barbecue in the DC area, and it's also one of the best.

Picture an entire room full of rows of smoke hoods, under which people are occupied with one thing only: having a grand old time. The dark, expansive, low-ceilinged room sizzles all night long with frying meat and hearty laughter. Aromas of pork fat, sweet spice, and pickled vegetables power through the room. There's smoke everywhere, but it's safely channeled into the hoods.

Step inside the door, and you'll be beckoned in by a sweet, if slightly surly, staff, as if you're in a semi-illegal secret club. "Lots of international people come here," she told us at our last visit, as if we were vacationers in Seoul looking for a place with an English-language menu. "American people." In fact, Annandale isn't far off from that setting, given the proliferation of spectacular food at spots where non-Asians will get weird looks if they try to order from the real menu.

That won't happen here. Honey Pig seems to have a particular penchant for marketing and advertising. They'll foist glossy business cards and brochures on you—in English, at that. There's a sort of totem pole of colorful advertising outside, and flashy, photo-happy neon décor within. But don't take any of this loud self-promotion to imply that the food is anything less than authentic; the raw meats that they'll whisk out to your table—ready for you to throw on the grill—are right on the money: spicy barbecued beef ribs. Barbecued tripe. Pork belly with red pepper paste, a fatty treat that you'll have real trouble locating inside the District.

And—get this—Honey Pig is open 24 hours. Catering to Americans? Not really. They're catering to anyone and everyone, from anywhere and everywhere, who enjoys a memorable meal of meat—anytime and every time. –RG

# Gordon Biersch

A few biersch in, and you'll hardly notice that the food's lame

| 4.9 | 6.6 |
|-----|-----|
| Food | Feel |

## American

Casual restaurant

**$35**
Price

www.gordonbiersch.com

Mon–Thu 11am–midnight
Fri–Sat 11am–1am
Sun 11am–11pm
Hours vary by location

**Bar** Beer, wine, liquor
**Credit cards** Visa, MC, AmEx
**Reservations** Accepted
Outdoor dining, veg-friendly, Wi-Fi

**Penn Quarter**
900 F St. NW
(202) 783-5454

**Tysons Corner, VA**
7861 Chain Bridge Rd.
(703) 388-5454

**Rockville, MD**
200 E. Middle Ln.
(301) 340-7159

**Additional locations**
and more features at
www.fearlesscritic.com

The chain brewery format is by now a familiar one. Like its peers, Gordon Biersch isn't trying to impress you with great food—it's trying to get you drunk. No surprise, then, that the menu emphasizes bar food, with no clear unity of provenance, but enough grease to fuel you through another round of the decent house beers.

A representative item is the chef's sampler of specialty starters: "Southwest Egg Rolls" stuffed with cheese, black beans, and chicken; shrimp and chicken pot-stickers served with a sweet "Asian" barbecue sauce; and chili-ginger-glazed chicken wings. The key ingredients here are chicken (cheap), grease, and sticky-sweet sauces (thirst-inducing).

Pizzas, steaks, and fish and chips are all available, naturally, and most are passable. Indeed, the menu covers far-ranging territory from seafood pastas to Reuben sandwiches, without a hint of irony. If it's something you might crave while you're drunk, you can get it here.

As for the beer, the five "signature handcrafted" brews are eminently drinkable and unmistakably American. Even Märtzen, the darkest of the bunch, is merely reddish and no more than a pleasant, mild lager. Seasonal brews change quarterly and add a welcome hint of variety to the standard lineup of light, golden beers. A modest selection of ordinary wines, mostly from California and nearly all under $50, is available by the glass or bottle.

Classic American desserts round out the menu, and in a popular gimmick, $2 mini desserts like chocolate peanut butter pie or strawberry cheesecake are served in glorified shot glasses.

The cavernous, echoing space, propped up by towering marble columns, fosters a cacophonous, cheerful, meat-market atmosphere that's popular among DC happy-hour revelers. Gordon Biersch isn't out to break the mold or win your heart with fine cooking, but you can get drunk quickly, easily, and cheaply on the uncomplicated house brews, and eat just enough of the mediocre bar food to get you through the night. –CD

# Granja de Oro

Don't sell yourself short and only get the chicken

**8.7** Food | **4.7** Feel

## Latin American

Counter service | **$20** Price

Sun–Thu 11am–10pm
Fri–Sat 11am–11pm

**Bar** None
**Credit cards** Visa, MC, AmEx
Kid-friendly, outdoor dining

**Adams Morgan**
1832 Columbia Rd.
(202) 232-8888

Most of the DC area's great places for pollo a la brasa (chicken spit-roasted over charcoal) are in the Maryland and DC suburbs. Granja de Oro is no exception—it's in Falls Church—but it's also in the District, on the border of Adams Morgan and Columbia Heights, making it a whole lot easier for District residents to enjoy top-notch Peruvian mixed grill.

One thing that distinguishes Granja de Oro is its commitment to go beyond the roast-chicken-with-yuca standards and delve into some serious Peruvian-style charcoal-grilled meats, including rich innards and organ meats like anticucho de corazón (skewered beef hearts), pancita (tripe), and hígado (calf's liver, which comes pan-fried—a la plancha—rather than charcoal-grilled). In fact, they do a better job of these things than any of the Adams Morgan upmarket Peruvian restaurants. Perhaps shockingly given the storefront, which is clearly all about chicken, even the seafood—well, the ceviche anyway (weekends only)—is good and fresh. Less impressive are the standard Peruvian-Chinese fusion dishes (e.g. tallarín saltado—stir-fried noodles), and you should safely avoid the gyros, steak-and-cheese, and house salad. But you don't need us to tell you that.

The best way to go is to get the "Parrillada Mixta Granja de Oro," a mixed grill that easily feeds two people for about $15. The parrillada includes the canonical chicken plus marvelously tender pork chops, challengingly gamy beef skewers, and good chorizo—all of it well seasoned and herbed with oregano and such. The platter comes with okay fries and a delicious salsa, redolent of smoky hot pepper (ask for extra!), that takes things to the next level.

The Falls Church branch has live music on some nights, but otherwise, the interior of each is pretty standard—it's hard to say "substandard" when you're talking about a genre where "fancy" means dishware and silverware instead of plastic—but it's made up in friendliness from the staff. Spanish is a better language of commerce than English here, but they'll do their best even for non-*hispanohablantes*. Whatever your language of choice, expect to wait in line—especially at prime time—before placing your order at the counter. If you're eating in, they'll bring your tray out to your table when it's ready (which is generally about four minutes later). Now *that's* upscale. For pollo a la brasa, anyway. –RG

# Granville Moore's Brickyard

**6.0** | **7.7**
Food | Feel

Fries and beer are movin' on up, with prices to match

## Belgian

Casual restaurant **$40**
Price

www.granvillemoores.com

Sun–Thu 5pm–midnight
Fri–Sat 5pm–3am

**Bar** Beer, wine, liquor
**Credit cards** Visa, MC, AmEx
**Reservations** Not accepted
Date-friendly, delivery, outdoor dining

**Northeast DC**
1238 H St. NE
(202) 399-2546

The uppest-and-comingest place on up-and-coming H street, Granville Moore's manages to be comely without appearing uppity. It's unclear whether the model for this townhouse watering-hole-cum-bistro is borrowed from the Brussels pub scene, a New England apothecary, or a Western dive bar; in any case, it's a bit dim and raggedy, but never too noisy. The bartenders are appropriately ironic, with black tanks, hair awry, and tight ripped jeans; although Dr. Moore's stocks a full bar and short wine list, you're better off choosing from the extensive menu of Belgian brews. Sit at the bar, and you're practically guaranteed a fun conversation. To complement that chat and your pint, you might order some of Granville's excellent frites (they're crisp and sprinkled with big salt and fresh parsley, and served with a dijonnaise or other choice of sauce).

If only the rest of the food here matched the frites. Mussels—already the proletariat of the sea—are pushed further into mediocrity by Granville's soupy sauces, and the bread for dipping is a starchy "baguette" akin to what you'd buy in the Paris, Texas supermart. The cutesy sandwiches are made on better bread, and pressed with plenty of olive oil and fresh meats for a delicious result; unfortunately, at $12 for a European-sized sandwich, one can't help thinking that someone used Euros to calculate prices.

The sides follow suit with an array of too-small dishes at too-high prices. Although the asparagus are delectable, the soups can vary (one summer night's gazpacho was quite good)…and again, if you are a dipper you'll be disappointed by the bread.

Like Brussels itself, this pub has a divided heart and uncertain cuisine, much of it overpriced, but at least it keeps its patrons happy with good beer and fried tubers. Hey, we District residents will drink to that. –CK

# Grapeseed

An American bistro and wine bar that does both
well—and badly, too

**5.9** Food | **7.6** Feel

## New American

Wine bar | **$75** Price

www.grapeseedbistro.com

Mon–Thu 5pm–10pm
Fri–Sat 5pm–11pm
Sun 5pm–9pm

**Bar** Beer, wine, liquor
**Credit cards** Visa, MC, AmEx
**Reservations** Accepted
Good wines, veg-friendly

**Bethesda, MD**
4865 Cordell Ave.
(301) 986-9592

Behold, the chef-driven wine bar, a chance to exercise your palate with a variety of portion sizes and recommended pairings. But with so many restaurants trying to capitalize on America's growing obsession with wine, the line between Genius and Gimmicky is easily crossed. Let's see how Grapeseed measures up, shall we?

Gimmicky: A splashy suburban housewife-friendly logo and website overwrought with exclamation points!!!

Genius: Warm, cozy digs that open up in summer to airy spaciousness.

Gimmicky: Everyone loves Top Chef, but the open kitchen just adds to the noisy din of the hardwood dining room. Two private rooms encased in glass make uncomfortably sterile people-quariums.

Genius: The menu changes seasonally, and is divided into "beginnings" (small plates), "middles" (salads and soups) and "ends" (main courses). Stick to the beginnings for a greater variety; they're more focused.

Gimmicky: Execution and balance issues, especially on the larger dishes. Some components have been inedibly salty; others, bland and underwhelming.

Genius: Some suggested pairings. Smoked trout joined by diced pear, salmon roe, and crème fraîche made a creamy, light spread for crostini and was framed by the bright acidity of both a balsamic reduction and the recommended Riesling. Fried clams that retained their brininess under a crisp coating were complemented by a lightly maritime Muscadet.

Gimmicky: Flights. No serious wine program offers them. Unless they're selling four of each flight a day, you'll likely end up with wine that's been open too long.

Genius: Exposure to some lesser-known varietals.

Gimmicky: Though sizeable, the wine list is all over the map. Domestics reign here, which is odd, given that they are notoriously less food-friendly than the abundance of interesting, lower-priced Old Worlds out there. Grapeseed does carry many of these, but by choosing the most expensive producers, they cannot offer these selections by the glass, so no one is going to try them. The Alsatian selections are among the strongest, with Champagnes looking like they were phoned in. Sauvignon Blancs are a mess: no Zealands or Loires by the glass?

With a wine program that at least tries and food that ranges from okay to really good, it's hard to get worked up either way about Grapeseed. And for this price, shouldn't you get a little worked up? –FC

# Great Wall Szechuan

**8.5** **5.0**
Food  Feel

Hole-in-the-wall Szechuan with some holes in the menu, but a jackpot, too

## Chinese

Casual restaurant

**$25**
Price

Sun–Thu 11am–10pm
Fri–Sat 11am–10:30pm

**Bar** None
**Credit cards** Visa, MC
**Reservations** Not accepted

**Logan Circle**
1527 14th St. NW
(202) 797-8888

Despite a name that screams crappy campus take-out, Great Wall has all the trappings of the ordinary concealing the extraordinary: waiters who don't speak English, glaring bright lights and a dusty cafeteria floor, rickety tables, strange sodas, and a slightly sketchy location. Plus, the place is open late.

Which is not to say that the restaurant is without its endearing quirks: in addition to family-style tables with lazy susans (and oh, how we love lazy susans!), Great Wall has perhaps the most interesting assortment of plates and cutlery you'll see in Washington: the collection includes an eclectic mix of plastic plates with children's themes and Chinese village pictures, complemented by plastic serving spoons with yellow-pink swirls on the handle.

Like at many Chinese finds, the menu has a Jekyll-and-Hyde quality to it: the Ma La Szechuan dishes are sensational, and the rest of the menu is mediocre. Ma La is the classic Szechuan combination of chili oil, Chinese peppercorns, and other herbs, which can leave your tongue pleasantly numb, your mouth quivering, your eyes streaming, and you begging for more. Great Wall does as well with this cuisine as any restaurant in the District. The best dishes take advantage of all the pungent flavors Szechuan cooking has to offer: try the Ma La dumplings or the chewy, rich double-cooked pork. The Ma Po tofu with ground pork is an incredible combination of blazing heat and cool, smooth tofu. Szechuan green beans are a reliable staple as well. Eggplant is well prepared, if a bit oily. Only the Ma La chicken is a disappointment, due to ordinary noodles and rubbery meat.

One caveat: when ordering, you'll have to look your server in the eye and really convince him or her that you really mean it when you say "spicy"—otherwise, they'll bring out a version toned down to suit Western eaters. If you're lucky, and you play your cards right, you might just leave mumbling, because that's all your shocked, numbed lips will be up to: Ta ya Gra Wa, Ma La wa yum! –CK

# Greek Deli

Simple, no-fuss Greek: get there early for the specials

**7.1** **6.0**
Food    Feel

## Greek, Sandwiches

Counter service    **$15**
Price

www.greekdelidc.com

Mon–Fri 7am–4pm

**Bar** None
**Credit cards** Visa, MC, AmEx
Kid-friendly, outdoor dining,
veg-friendly

**Farragut**
1120 19th St. NW
(202) 296-2111

The lunchtime line out the door of Greek Deli says it all. Tucked into a storefront on 19th Street, this carryout-only joint is a single long room barely wide enough for two people to stand shoulder-to-shoulder; the line snakes forward along the right side to the cashier in front of the kitchen, and then people step to the left to await their white Styrofoam containers of authentic Greek food.

The pace is swift, so make up your mind before you reach the front of the line. The specials tend to run out quickly, but you won't go wrong with most of the choices, like spanakopita, here a surprisingly light dish, with layers of flaky pastry encasing a tender, creamy spinach and cheese filling that can be cut even with a plastic fork.

Hot baked dishes, such as mousaka or pastitsio, are accompanied by plain orzo, salad (mainly ho-hum iceberg lettuce), and the vegetable of the day (such as creamy white beans and green beans stewed with tomato and oregano), all dished out by owner Kostas himself. Also available are acceptable gyros, juicy but with minimal lamb flavor under garlicky tzatziki, as well as other sandwiches on lightly toasted, soft pita. Greek salads come in lunch-sized portions, topped with your choice of protein (lamb, grilled chicken, falafel that is perfectly crispy on the outside and gooey on the inside, etc). Grab a slice of Kostas's homemade bread, a simple, dense, white loaf with a mild flavor that's perfect for mopping up extra juices and sauces.

The baklava is almost too crunchy and sweet, but since you're only here for lunch anyway, you can do without dessert. The real draws here are the approachable Greek classics, prepared by a native who cares about the quality of his food. While on the pricey side for a lunch place, you are paying for something rare in DC—convenient, authentic Greek made with gruff love. And the chance to annoy your cubicle neighbors with pungent odors. –CD

# Green Papaya

This average Vietnamese restaurant hits the sweet tooth harder than the sweet spot

**5.5** Food
**4.5** Feel

## Vietnamese

Upmarket restaurant

**$35** Price

Mon 11:30am–2:30pm, 5pm–9:30pm; Tue–Fri 11:30am–2:30pm, 5pm–10pm; Sat 12:30pm–10pm; Sun 5pm–9:30pm

**Bar** Beer, wine, liquor
**Credit cards** Visa, MC, AmEx
**Reservations** Accepted
Live music, outdoor dining

**Bethesda, MD**
4922 Elm St.
(301) 654-8241

Ooh, that salty, sour, spicy, sweet spot—that spot that only the crisp, fresh ingredients in Vietnamese food can satisfy. At Green Papaya, the emphasis lands squarely on the sweet, and while the cooking is skilled, as a holistic experience, the restaurant is as likely to miss as to hit its mark.

A relatively substantial drinks menu signals Green Papaya's intention to be taken seriously, but it's hard for us to fully comply. The wine list features a majority of California wines in the $35-to-$70 range, and the cocktail selection leans heavily on too-sweet fruity rum drinks. They offer a suitably representative introduction to the meal.

For starters, the atmosphere at Green Papaya is incongruous. The space is decorated with a vaguely absurd collection of sculptures, prints, and bric-a-brac. Some of it is definitely Chinese in origin, but the soundtrack on our last visit consisted of Italian opera. While certainly not unpleasant, the restaurant's interior feels a little cluttered and outdated, with pieces of tile chipping off the enormous water feature behind the bar.

Nonetheless, some of the menu items are refreshingly unfamiliar. Our favorite starter, bo la nho, consists of mildly-spiced ground beef wrapped in vine leaves and then charbroiled to a smoky, crispy exterior, served with fish sauce for dipping. The ubiquitous fish sauce also accompanies a less successful goi tom ngo sen, a flat-tasting julienne of lotus, carrot, and green papaya topped with meager slivers of cooked shrimp.

For a memorable main course, choose bo luc lac—"shaking beef," a dish whose name refers to the motion of the cubes of meat as they are tossed in a searing-hot wok. Bite-sized pieces of beef are cooked just to medium (better yet, ask for them rare) and tossed with potato cubes and cherry tomatoes in a savory lemon and black pepper sauce. The menu features an entire category of "caramelized" meat dishes, as well as sections devoted to more familiar players like pho and rice vermicelli. In this last category, the pork version has good flavor from pungent lemongrass and the smokiness of the grill, but has arrived lukewarm.

That's how we feel about this place. –FC

# Grill from Ipanema

**5.1** **6.2**
Food Feel

Get this grill drunk, and you may have some fun with her

## Brazilian

Casual restaurant **$45**
Price

www.thegrillfromipanema.com

Mon–Fri 4:30pm–11pm
Sat noon–11:30pm
Sun noon–10pm

**Bar** Beer, wine, liquor
**Credit cards** Visa, MC, AmEx
**Reservations** Accepted
Live music, outdoor dining

**Adams Morgan**
1858 Columbia Rd. NW
(202) 986-0757

It's got a funny name but the Grill serves food that is overpriced and under-flavored. Not that this observation would occur to a clientele that is generally one or two signature caipirinhas on the wrong side of sensible to notice flavor.

Though this Adams Morgan spot has prices that would settle comfortably into the plush menu of a first-class eatery, the Grill's atmosphere and kitchen creations make it appear more a happy-hour hotspot than a place in which food is taken particularly seriously. The restaurant takes its inspiration—of course—from the cuisine of Brazil, but it differs somewhat from the traditional Americanized Brazilian steakhouse in corporate downtowns: Ipanema has a plentiful selection of chicken and seafood mains (and a handful of vegetarian salads), as well as the typical meat offerings.

The thing that saves the Grill (and the thing that appears to have made it) is that caipirinha and its many avatars. The restaurant makes a decent one, with plenty of quartered limes and fine sugar. If the drink is a little on the sweet side, the misstep is forgiven by the generous use of lime juice and cachaça: there's very little ice or water in these drinks. The Grill also offers a less interesting caipiroska (made with vodka), a couple of fruit-filled batidas, and a plain old shot of cachaça.

The Grill's seafood is mostly fresh, but nothing special. Fish can arrive rather parched, so be sure to specify your doneness preference. You also have an choice of two types of clay-pot stews that can be made with any assortment of fish and shellfish, including white fish, shrimp, scallops, squid, mussels, and clams. One of the better options, the moqueca a capixaba, is a tomato-based stew made with cilantro and a few slices of bell pepper—the acidity of the vegetables goes especially well with mussels or shrimp.

Both staff and diners tend to be tall, tan, young, and—on the whole—lovely, at least as far as looks go. In terms of manners, though, the prevailing mindset falls somewhat short of that mark; the atmosphere can be noisy and the overheard conversation boastful. Add to this the overpriced fare, and the Grill from Ipanema is a sad song indeed. –CK

# Grillfish

Dining with Indiana Jones

**6.3** Food   **7.0** Feel

## Seafood

Upmarket restaurant

**$45** Price

www.grillfishdc.com

| | | |
|---|---|---|
| Mon–Thu noon–10pm | **Bar** Beer, wine, liquor | **West End** |
| Fri noon–11pm | **Credit cards** Visa, MC, AmEx | 1220 New Hampshire Ave. |
| Sat 5pm–11pm | **Reservations** Accepted | NW |
| Sun 5pm–10pm | Outdoor dining | (202) 331-7310 |

Well after our first encounter, we are still confused by Grillfish. Its name would suggest a low-key seafood joint, and from the outside, that's exactly how it looks; a small patio is surrounded by potted flowers and chalkboards listing drink specials. Inside, the first thing you'll notice is a huge mural with naked figures writhing in moody sepias and grays. The bar is broken by a giant hunk of archaeological detritus and oddly festooned with tiki accents and large jars of dubious content. The dark velvet curtains, faux-stone walls, and flickering wrought iron chandeliers are oddly reminiscent of the Temple of Doom—this time filled with groups of older gentlemen in their work clothes. It's gloomy, but also strangely comforting.

Staff tend to be surprisingly chipper given their surroundings. A short but competent drinks list features (predictably) cocktails with a tropical twist and (more refreshingly) fish-friendly beers. Appetizers are as addictive as potato chips: a subtly battered ginger calamari, for instance, that's coated in a punchy-tangy sauce and topped with a sprinkle of raw scallions, although its wilty cabbage bed adds an unnecessarily slimy texture to an otherwise great dish. Fried buffalo shrimp arrive in a pool of Cheeto-orange sauce that's strongly redolent of blue cheese. You'll dip your bread in it when the shrimp is gone, and then shamelessly lick your fingers.

Sadly, the weakness of the menu is the namesake of the restaurant: grilled fish. A mixed-grill main combines salmon, shrimp, mahi mahi, scallops, and swordfish. All come well cooked with fine textures, but also disturbingly unseasoned and flavorless. The two sauces are overpowering: one is so full of cumin that it's hard to think of anything else, while the other is candy sweet and oil-slick greasy. We tend not to use either.

Chocolate cake, however, is a wonder of baking texture. The cake arrives warm and manages to stay moist yet light and fluffy; the "black Russian" sauce adds a playful nip of alcohol. In the end, you'll enjoy your stay with Indiana Jones: a funky décor, a friendly staff, and addictive snack food. But you might want to skip dinner. –JC

# Guajillo

Decent upscale Mexican—but when will we get *great* upscale Mexican?

**7.6** Food  **7.5** Feel

## Mexican

Casual restaurant **$35** Price

www.waheeyo.com

Mon–Thu 11am–2pm, 5pm–10pm; Fri 11am–2pm, 5pm–11pm; Sat 5pm–11pm; Sun noon–10pm

**Bar** Beer, wine, liquor
**Credit cards** Visa, MC, AmEx
**Reservations** Accepted
Outdoor dining

**Arlington, VA**
1727 Wilson Blvd.
(703) 807-0840

Guajillo is accessible. We don't simply mean the restaurant is near a metro station (although it is—you can walk to Guajillo from the Rosslyn station), or that it boasts the convenience of a parking lot and a friendly set of waiters with smart recommendations. It's that Guajillo makes no bones about its appeal to non-Mexicans; in fact, the restaurant has a pretty English-language website advertising its "family-friendliness" and listing its menu options. More revealing is the website's domain name: waheeyo.com—a phonetic pronunciation of the restaurant name—with further tips offered on the homepage as a quick guide for gringos with a lumbering command of Spanish.

This earnestness is part of why we like Guajillo. The other part is that the food, while similarly translated, is good. Guajillo will not appeal to those seeking the most authentic Mexican meal, or an exclusive culinary scoop. The restaurant's location is no big secret, there's no mystery chile that spikes the sauces, and the place is sufficiently mainstream for waiters to place a big basket of tortilla chips on your table when you sit down, but the dishes are coherent and regionally inspired—not just Tex-Mex. The meats are excellent, the ingredients are honest, and the sauces pack more than a little punch.

One of our favorite dishes is Guajillo's tamal, a small, creamy number made with a darker, almost nutty-tasting masa and steamed to the point of cohesion but not dryness: this is one of the moistest tamales we've tasted in DC. The meat inside is plentiful, and the corn-to-meat ratio is excellent. Because there is little else inside the tamales, however, the dish benefits from the addition of Guajillo's house salsa, which is a well-blended mixture of stewed tomatoes, onions, tomatillos, and additional spice. We also salute the availability of tacos de borrego (lamb) which are stewed with—what else—guajillo peppers; and of decent carnitas.

Other offerings, such as enchiladas, sometimes err on the side of dryness, and we wish the tortillas were a bit fresher. If you're familiar with top-notch Mexican, you may miss the lard in the beans and other signatures of the real deal. But Guajillo's meats make up for any shortcomings in its starches: the pulled beef is smoky, rich, and tender. All this in a nicely appointed dining room with large oils in the style of Diego Rivera. Like the food, the art isn't concerned about authenticity, but it's darn good. –CK

# Hai Duong

**9.0** **6.8**
Food  Feel

You haven't lived until you've tried the fragrant
doi (Vietnamese innard terrine) here

## Vietnamese

Casual restaurant  **$15**
Price

www.edencenter.com

Daily 8:30am–9pm

**Bar** Beer
**Credit cards** Visa, MC
**Reservations** Accepted
Outdoor dining

**Falls Church, VA**
6796 Wilson Blvd.
(703) 538-5289

Even among rows of refreshingly authentic Vietnamese storefronts in the
Eden Center's Saigon West, Hai Duong is a standout. Like many of its
neighbors, the space has no exterior windows or natural light; rather, the
front door simply opens onto a corridor of the mall. The décor is pretty
cookie-cutter: tables of assorted materials (faux-marble, light wood
veneer); cheap chairs; white walls; cheesy Asian music videos on a flat-
screen TV; neon signs in primary colors; and, of course, the classic totally
random wall art, cheaply framed and haphazardly hung. Still, the bright,
yellowish lighting lends a cheery air to the space, an artificial-sunlight-like
effect, and when the place is crowded (as it often is at lunchtime), it has
some real atmosphere—definitely a feat for the Eden Center.

In any case, the kitchen is where the magic happens. The menu's poorly
translated, but it's hard to go wrong. The various versions of pho ("bible
tripe," soft tendon, fatty brisket, and so on) are popular, and they're quite
good—as are the bahn xeo (Vietnamese crêpes)—but why not appreciate
the more unique offerings? How about bo tai chanh (beef
"underdone"—i.e. rare—with lime), bun bo hue (wider-than-usual rice
noodles in a spicy soup of beef and pork feet), or cha ca thang long (a
deeply spiced fish filet)? Sweet, crispy quail is excellent, too.

You can skip the cold salads, whose peanut-and-fried-onion crunch is
too often brought down by overcooked, flavorless proteins (shrimp, thin
pork slices, and such), although one version—goi sua tom thit—is partially
rescued by resilient jellyfish strips, and any can be brightened by the
extremely hot homemade chili sauce and savory fish sauce.

Best of all, though, is chao long, a rice porridge whose menu
description, "combination pork liver and intestines," leaves out some of
its key elements: rich pork hearts, cubes of congealed pork blood, and
magnificent slices of doi, a fragrant terrine of pork innards, lemongrass,
and black pepper that's wrapped in pork skin and steamed. The soup
comes with a plate of fried doughnuts that, by themselves, are fish out of
water—chewy and boring—but when dropped into the broth like
croutons, turn into something really wonderful, absorbing prodigious
quantities of broth while still maintaining their doughy fattiness. Ginger,
fried onion, and fried garlic add even more complexity to a broth whose
sweet finish seems to last forever.

Prices, as ever in Eden, are below reasonable. It's yet another reminder
of the often-inverse correlation between price and taste in the nation's
capital. –RG

# Hank's Oyster Bar

Oysters and seafood as perfect as pearls

**9.1** *Food*  **9.1** *Feel*

## Seafood

Upmarket restaurant

**$45** *Price*

www.hanksdc.com

Mon–Wed 5:30pm–10pm
Thu–Fri 5:30pm–11pm
Sat 11am–3pm, 5:30pm–11pm
Sun 11am–3pm, 5:30pm–10pm
Hours vary by location

**Bar** Beer, wine, liquor
**Credit cards** Visa, MC, AmEx
**Reservations** Not accepted
Date-friendly, kid-friendly, outdoor
dining

**Dupont**
1624 Q St. NW
(202) 462-4265

**Alexandria Old Town**
1026 King St.
(703) 739-4265

At first, Hank's Oyster Bar might look like another small, casually upmarket bistro with a hip vibe and unassuming sidewalk tables on a lovely street corner. It's got a chilled-out local crowd, hanging out under high ceilings, slurping oysters, digging on lobster, and generally just having a good time. All of this downplays the fact that Hank's might just be DC's best seafood restaurant.

That's a combative statement, for sure, but at a minimum, it's certainly the best spot in the District to sample oysters on the half shell, whether from this coast or others. The staff is well-versed in oyster geography, and will encourage you to develop your own ostreaphilia: do you prefer briny, creamy, or sweet? Small, large, or medium bodies? An answer, however equivocal, of "briny and large," for example, might land you a selection from a cutely named bay in Massachusetts, depending on the day's catch. An ever-changing blackboard lists a diverse range of appellations. (Conversely, we wish Hank's would get up the guts to refuse cocktail sauce; to purists, this is a bit like putting Splenda in your Burgundy. Stick with mignonette.)

Oysters here are just the beginning. Ceviche is extraordinarily fresh, its fish cooked gently by citrus, preserving a velvety rareness while absorbing treble notes of lime and cilantro. A broth of extraordinary depth and subtle creaminess highlights a superb bowl of mussels, easily the best in the city. A crab cake, simple and very light on the breading, is one of the best in a crowded field, too. Humble sablefish (this is by no means a shellfish-only spot) is treated like royalty, and fried oysters—whether on their own or in an eminently satisfying po' boy—are expertly textured, retaining their little pop of briny heaven under crispy batter. A lobster roll is another winner, fleshy and sweet, the best in town. The excellent-value wine list is full of exactly the crisp, Old World whites you'd want to drink with this menu, like Muscadet and Grüner Veltliner.

Even the non-seafood dishes are worth seeking out—nightly meat specials like molasses-braised short ribs, and sides such as macaroni and cheese with just the right texture and slight bite of blue cheese. Unsurprisingly, Hank's can get crowded on weekend nights, but its reasonable prices, ever-changing market menu, and casual, local feeling make it kind of like a perfect oyster, hitting all the right notes. –CK

# Harar Mesob

**7.1** Food

**6.0** Feel

Solid Ethiopian welcomed with open arms (and white flags) in the suburbs

## Ethiopian

Casual restaurant

**$25** Price

www.harar-mesob.com

Daily 11am–11pm

**Bar** Beer, wine, liquor
**Credit cards** Visa, MC, AmEx
**Reservations** Accepted
Delivery, outdoor dining,
veg-friendly

**Arlington, VA**
423 23rd St. S.
(703) 553-5500

The simultaneous opening of two restaurants on opposite sides of the street does not usually cause consternation for anyone but the respective owners. But when a particular pair of restaurants—one Ethiopian and one Eritrean—cut their ribbons across the street from one another on South 23rd Street in Arlington, you can imagine that a few hairs grayed on the heads of members of the neighborhood association. Cuisine rivalries often mirror soccer rivalries, which often mirror (or augment) geopolitical upsets. If Eritrea and Ethiopia's relationship is marred on the political front, God only knows what devastation is possible when the fight turns to food. (While the two cuisines share many elements, Eritrea's is more influenced by Italy, its former occupier.)

Several weeks later, however, it was clear that there would be no tomatoes flying across 23rd Street; that the only local war would be for the hearts and wallets of diners. Another source of relief was the fact that these two restaurants filled a gap in south-of-the-District-border cuisine: while excellent Ethiopian food is readily available in Washington, the options in Northern Virginia are harder to find.

Harar Mesob is on the Ethiopian side of the street, sitting behind a big, wooden porch. Inside, the dark wood and tapestries lend elegance to dinner, and larger tables encircle an inner sanctum of mesob, or traditional Ethiopian seating of woven tables and stools. Because of its centrality and fishbowl feeling, the diner who elects to sit in this area must be intent on an authentic experience; the big chairs along the perimeter are much more comfortable.

Although the execution is not of the caliber of Ethiopian so readily available in DC, a few dishes stand out. The chicken doro wat, for example, is an exceedingly rich and spicy red paste, served with two hard-boiled eggs rather than the typical one. The green bean salad offers colorful touches from several other vegetables. The injera bread, however—critical to the success of an Ethiopian meal—is somewhat drier than some found elsewhere.

With the Eritrean place (it's called Enjera) so close in proximity, though, you can size up the two restaurants yourself. Just keep your opinions on the down-low. –CK

# Hard Times Café

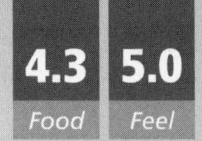

**4.3** Food | **5.0** Feel

A gimmicky franchise that celebrates America: land
of cheese and meat and cheese. And meat.

## American

Casual restaurant | **$20** Price

www.hardtimes.com

Mon–Fri 11am–11pm
Sat–Sun 10:30am–11pm
Hours vary by location

**Bar** Beer, wine, liquor
**Credit cards** Visa, MC, AmEx
**Reservations** Not accepted
Kid-friendly, outdoor dining

**Nationals Park**
1500 S. Capital St. SE

**Arlington, VA**
3028 Wilson Blvd.
(703) 528-2233

**Alexandria Old Town**
1404 King St.
(703) 837-0050

**Additional locations**
and more features at
www.fearlesscritic.com

Hard Times Café advertises "world famous chili and other American
favorites" like wings, burgers, and barbecue ribs with such hokey theatrics
that you hear a Hollywoodish cowboy voice-over in your head as you read
the menu. The décor is of that kitschy, corporate-conceived ilk: out-of-
date knick-knacks and vintage country music posters hang next to Bud
and Miller ad campaigns. (And you can hardly swing a lasso anywhere in
the tri-state area without hitting one of these.)

Chili comes in four varieties. The quality varies with the type. "Original
Texas Chili" looks glum, with meat that's so finely chopped that the
texture is dry and uniform, and with no vegetables to provide any textural
counterpoint. Don't Texans love chilies? Where are those?

Another Texas take, "Terlingua Red," is a better option. A tomato base
renders the chili softer and more liquid, and the spices used in this version
make for a sweeter stew. Even the vibrant red color is more visually
pleasing. If you throw in some jalapeños and onions (both finely diced) for
crunch, it gets even better.

All chili is served with cornbread (standard issue, on the dry side), but
you can purchase it with several "others": over spaghetti, in a bowl with
corn bread, in a tortilla, or (most arrestingly) over a bowl of Fritos. You
may be tempted to try some of crazy combinations. You would do best to
stay away from the "Chili Mac," in which a scoop of chili is
unceremoniously dumped on a plate of gummy spaghetti. It seems like an
homage to Cincinnati, where chili is served over spaghetti, too, but there,
it's like a bolognese, and it actually works. Here, you're looking at
something that resembles your worst middle school cafeteria experience.

Other offerings at Hard Times are just as discouraging. Wings, also in
four flavors, don't quite manage to convey as much flavor as their name
suggests. Even burgers look hastily made. On the other hand, you can get
pretty full for only $10, so maybe a trip to Hard Times is only rewarding
when you've fallen on them. –JC

# Harmony Café

**3.7** **5.0**

*Food* *Feel*

Over-sauced Chinese-American food that at least gives vegetarians plenty to chew on

## Chinese

Casual restaurant

**$15**

*Price*

Daily 11:30am–11pm

**Bar** Beer, wine, liquor
**Credit cards** Visa, MC, AmEx
**Reservations** Accepted
Veg-friendly

**Georgetown**
3287 ½ M St. NW
(202) 338-3881

Harmony Café is inconspicuous, to say the least, hidden away in a basement off the main Georgetown drag. One of the few indicators that it's there is a small green sign. Like Alice's journey down the rabbit hole, it gets a bit weirder. The landing is deserted, except for an empty fish tank and some fake flowers. A lone pedestal houses a patched-up menu as if it were a sacred relic. The décor downstairs is not like that at other Chinese restaurants—with its carved wooden spires and hanging bunches of grapes, it seems more South Asian than anything else.

The menu at Harmony is alarmingly vast. Pages upon pages of items unfold in seemingly endless permutations, some amended with handwritten sticky-labels. A particular amenity is the vegetarian option for every dish. Billed as vege-pork, vege-beef, and vege-chicken, the soy-based "meat" brings to mind Buddhist restaurants. You may very well find yourself wondering how one restaurant can produce all of this food, and how anything made of plants could in any way resemble each of these meats.

The answer to both is sauce—here, the sugary brown sauce that is ubiquitous in bad Chinese-American dishes. This phenomenon is heavy-handed enough to obscure all other elements of a dish, including fake meat and whatever else may be inside. A dish of minced chicken is so drenched in the stuff that it floods its lettuce wrap and makes a mess. Though the filling contains a fine balance of crisp vegetables and diced chicken, you can barely taste it. All of the interplay between the various textures and flavors are literally drowned out.

"Eight Treasure Eggplant" may have eight treasured ingredients, but they're lost in another goopy sauce. It is barely spiced and so salty that you'll need more rice. Spongy fried tofu, known for its absorptive powers, must be wrung out before eaten. Dishes without the sauce are even worse. Minced-chicken sweet corn soup is too thick, and the flavor is bland and vaguely salty instead of sweet.

Despite its shortcomings, Harmony Café remains a much-loved spot among the locals. Is it because of the lack of availability of good veggie options in the neighborhood? Or because we don't know any better, most of us only having had exposure to the globby flavor wheel of bad, Americanized Chinese?

It's a mystery befitting lair-like Harmony Café. –JC

# Harris Teeter

It's hard to beat the Teet: collectible produce and comestible sandwiches abound

## Groceries

Market

www.harristeeter.com

Daily 7am–11pm

**Bar** Beer, wine, liquor
**Credit cards** Visa, MC, AmEx
Good wines, veg-friendly

**Adams Morgan**
1631 Kalorama Rd. NW
(202) 986-1415

**Capitol Hill**
1350 Potomac Ave. SE
(202) 543-1040

**Arlington, VA**
900 Army Navy Dr.
(703) 413-7112

**Additional locations**
and more features at
www.fearlesscritic.com

This nickname-inspiring mega-grocery store is known by many tags, all of which are quickly making inroads to the mouths and hearts of Washington area residents. "Harry T's," despite prices that creep well above the average, offers food that is exceedingly fresh and well presented. Rows of gem-like peaches, plums, and apricots fill the shelves during the summer, and in fall the number of different squashes rivals that found at top farmer's markets. The organic and international food aisles are well-stocked, and the wine and beer selections are top quality; the only headache comes from navigating the Teet's many aisles to find that last item on your list.

In addition to its overall fitness, in biological terms the supermarket might also be called an "indicator species:" its presence denotes that a neighborhood's gentrification trajectory has passed the critical point, and the influx of wealth is inevitable. Some of the savviest real estate mavens must sit on Teeter's board: when the supermarket comes in, you can be sure that a once-questionable neighborhood now houses, well, the kind of people who can afford to shop at Harris Teeter.

But don't be fooled by the store's high produce prices if you're considering a lunchtime (or even dinner) stop. Sure, the organic cassava might send you to the cleaners, but for less than three bucks, one of Washington's biggest subs—customized with any range of toppings—is yours to take away (Harris Teeter, needless to say, wants for a good seating area). Have a little extra cash? The on-site sushi chefs have whipped up many better-than-supermarket lunches in their day: six dollars will buy you a large serving of salmon roll; fancier combinations can push up the price a bit. And desserts are not to be missed: a four dollar crème brûlée, for example, is rich and creamy, with a crisped sweet top.

But the real draw of the supermarket is its sandwiches, made with fresh deli meats, top-quality cheeses, and crispy vegetables, although the bread, unfortunately, is a bit too puffy. Each weekday has a "special," which goes for only three bucks: you may be stuck with Tuna on Thursday, but Tuesdays are super: that's the day you can get any sandwich half off. –CK

# Harry's Tap Room

**6.7** Food  **5.5** Feel

American classics made with mostly local, organic ingredients, served in classy, timeless digs

## American

Casual restaurant  **$50** Price

www.harrystaproom.com

Mon–Fri 11am–10pm
Sat–Sun 10am–10pm
Hours vary by location

**Bar** Beer, wine, liquor
**Credit cards** Visa, MC, AmEx
**Reservations** Accepted
Kid-friendly, outdoor dining

**Arlington, VA**
2800 Clarendon Blvd.
(703) 778-7788

**Arlington, VA**
1100 S. Hayes St.
(703) 416-7070

**Dulles International Airport**
1 Saarinen Circle
(703) 572-4699

On the website, Harry's story begins: "We came to a startling revelation. People don't need more of the same kind of restaurants they already have—mass-fast-and-cheap or fancy-and-over-priced. They need a place with that elusive combination—terrific food at a reasonable price in a relaxed atmosphere." We agree with the first half of this statement, but the second part sort of aims kind of low for a "startling revelation;" DC already has an abundance of affordable, tasty food in casual atmospheres. What we need more of are restaurants committed to using local, organic ingredients, and meat from naturally- and humanely-raised animals. Harry's is on the right track here.

It doesn't hurt, either, that Harry's looks as though it's out of a Pottery Barn catalog. Dark wood furnishings are sturdy and broad, the chairs cushioned with leather. It's stylish, but not trendy enough to alienate anyone preferring a neutral atmosphere for, say, business lunches. Nor is it stuffy.

Seasonal ingredients are arranged in full panoply of combinations, mostly American (or Americanized). PEI mussels are a must-have here, as are steaks—and prices are generous compared to like places (except where ahi tuna is concerned, but then this shouldn't even be offered). Sometimes, though, what arrives is hard to handle. A grouper sandwich is plated as a slab of (nicely) poached fish layered with mashed avocado on a roll, and half an entire mango lost on the side. Throw in the mango-lime chutney on a separate dish, and you won't know where to begin. In some cases, ingredients even come as a not-so-pleasant surprise. Chicken salad comes with an unmentioned tarragon (good) but also a distinctly cinnamon taste that is interesting at first, then quickly off-putting.

For a restaurant with the word "tap" in its name, the beer selection is somewhat lame. Though there are more than 30 varieties, all at decent prices, most are standard and not that hard to find. The rarer beers tend toward crowd-pleasing instead of interesting. Wines follow suit. You can manage to be "all-American" and still showcase some microbrewers and small grower-producer wines that are better and more balanced that the big names we could find at the nicer grocery stores. Wouldn't that be more in keeping with the noble ideals of the kitchen?

Most importantly, Harry's needs to work out some execution kinks, but what they're doing is totally worth the trouble. –JC

# Heritage India

Enjoyable Indian food all dressed up for a night out

**7.2** **7.1**
Food    Feel

## Indian

Casual restaurant    **$40**
Price

www.heritageindiausa.com

Daily 11:30am–2:30pm,
4:30pm–10:30pm

**Bar** Beer, wine, liquor
**Credit cards** Visa, MC, AmEx
**Reservations** Accepted
Delivery, kid-friendly, veg-friendly,
Wi-Fi

**Dupont**
1337 Connecticut Ave. NW
(202) 331-1114

**Glover Park**
2400 Wisconsin Ave. NW
(202) 333-3120

Heritage India stands out among DC's higher-end Indian food destinations. The swanky décor encourages special occasions and romantic encounters, and the long bar attracts a dedicated group of happy-hour regulars. The interior of Heritage India is luxurious in a way that is a bit uncomfortable in daylight. Textured accents like carved doors and windows combine with murals, foliage, and gilt objects to form a landscape that is luxuriant but also a bit cheesy.

The cooking at Heritage is not consistently authentically Indian; in fact, some of the best dishes are the informal, embellished small bites that combine both old and new. Papri chat, a traditional Bombay street dish, is tangy with tamarind, heated by ginger, and cooled with cilantro and yogurt. It tastes sweet and acidic, with dough that's loose but not flaky; the entire dish is expanded by the heavier textures of potatoes and onions. Golgappas use the same flavors but intensify them. The tamarind water poured into dough puffs is sharp, pungent, and delightfully smoky from black salt. Other great dishes include naan studded with ground, spiced lamb—mild and rich—that's brought up further by a smoky masala blend.

Not all plates are created equal. Fish amritsari is bland and quickly soggy. Rockfish has a great meaty texture, but it's not enough to excuse its lack of flavor. A dish called "Mango Tango" is a mishmash of tandoori chicken, mango slices, lettuce, and asparagus. The chicken is so strongly flavored that it hides any chicken-ness, and its heat unappealingly wilts the lettuce bed. Mango slices and ginger strips are incongruous with the other flavors, reminding us, perhaps, that the tango requires a fluid compatibility that this dish just doesn't display.

But many other dishes dance beautifully, and you're likely to leave Heritage India feeling thoroughly satisfied with your meal. That is, unless the annoying little à la carte charges—a little extra here for rice, or there for bread—ruin your rhythm. –JC

# Hong Kong Palace

General Tso surrenders to Szechuan peppercorns

**8.9** Food  **5.5** Feel

## Chinese

Casual restaurant

**$15** Price

www.hkpalace.webs.com

Sun–Thu 11am–10pm
Fri–Sat 11am–11pm

**Bar** Beer
**Credit cards** Visa, MC
**Reservations** Accepted
Delivery, outdoor dining

**Falls Church, VA**
6387 Seven Corners Center
(703) 532-0940

In the space formerly known as Saigon Palace, with Home Depot and Barnes and Noble as mall-mates, Hong Kong Palace is the premier Szechuan place around. It used to be all about Cantonese, but the menu has changed…and the result is vastly improved over anything it did before. Szechuan is much more spice-intensive than other Chinese regional cuisines. The almost 100% Chinese clientele here is encouraging, as is the seizure-inducing website that is barely in broken English.

As this place is totally authentic and excellent, we could just drop you off and say "order whatever," but as we acknowledge that the menu looks a little intimidating—even to those who have stepped outside of General Tso's greasy clutches—we'll try to give you some guidance.

We highly recommend the most popular dish from the region, ma po tofu, sizzling hot in its bean-and-chili oil with minced meat. If you've never tried those acerbic Szechuan peppercorns before, you will *never* forget the taste. Lamb with cumin is excellent, dan dan noodles are very good, and—as of right now, at least—not bastardized with peanut paste like some more Americanized versions. Beef with bamboo shoot is a great, approachable dish for the squeamish, as are Chengdu dumplings. But hands down the most addictive thing here is a hot pot of fish and chilies.

Even if you've never extended yourself past sesame chicken and those other gooey, bland takeout losers, you should come here and experiment. Dive right into those specials, and you won't be sorry. But do prepare for some mouth-numbing spices. On the spice scale, Szechuan is capable of pain only elsewhere seen in Thai food, and numbness that's not seen anywhere else. If you're not ready for that, just ask for it mild, and try to work yourself up to higher heat, where the flavors are enhanced.

For less than $20, in other words, you can become a happier, wiser individual. –RG

# Hook

The once-proud, ever-trendy sustainable-fish showcase that changed Georgetown

| 8.3 | 8.8 |
|-----|-----|
| Food | Feel |

## Seafood

Upmarket restaurant

**$80**
Price

www.hookdc.com

Tue 11:30am–2:30pm, 5pm–10pm; Wed–Fri 11:30am–2:30pm, 5pm–11pm; Sat 11am–11pm; Sun 11am–10pm

**Bar** Beer, wine, liquor
**Credit cards** Visa, MC, AmEx
**Reservations** Accepted
Date-friendly, good wines, live music, Wi-Fi

**Georgetown**
3241 M St. NW
(202) 625-4488

When Hook burst onto the Georgetown scene in 2006, this was the most exciting new place to hit the neighborhood in years—and, indeed, one of the most groundbreaking arrivals in the whole city. Geor Sustainable fish—often sashimi-quality, often raw, and invariably cut with the sure knife skills of a line cook who might as well have been a sushi chef—was served in what was certainly the sexiest dining room (or, rather, set of dining rooms) on M Street, which seemed almost taken aback by this level of youthful exuberance. Raw sea bass had a bounciness rarely seen outside a top sushi restaurant; the fish danced around on top of playful, fruity notes of delicate oils and pickled vegetables. Arctic char, only gently touched by the fire, scaled new heights here.

The magic wasn't just in the food, though. Hook's gently arched ceilings, elaborate retro lighting fixtures, and warm glow of the dining room, and the long, bar-stool-lined counter table in the bar area did a great deal to reverse Georgetown's reputation for stuffiness. Yes, it was—it still is—trendy, perhaps too tailored to the shop-and-be-seen crowd. But it was also magnificent.

We rarely discuss chefs by name. But in this case, the well-publicized departure of heartthrob-environmental-guru chef Barton Seaver—or, rather, his transition into a role as "consultant" rather than "chef"—seems to have had a material impact on the state of the restaurant.

We don't want to jump to conclusions of causation, but we'll say that our visits since Seaver's departure haven't compared with our visits before. Although we still occasionally dine well at Hook, we no longer consider the restaurant quite worth the money. The kitchen still has a way with raw oysters and delicately full-flavored bluefish, and we still love the place for the variation in its sustainable fish specials. But we've had disgustingly skunky sea urchin, and a new-style sashimi preparation of koni kampachi that was one of the fishiest examples of raw jack fish we've ever tasted.

Service is better on less touristy weekday evenings; on weekends, expect to wait even with a reso. At a recent visit, when we were brought the wrong starter, our apologetic waiter requested that keep and enjoy it while we waited for the correct order to come out. Seems obvious, right? Wrong. Most DC restaurants will take it back in that situation, forcing the wronged table to endure yet another wrong—the awkwardness of some having food, others not. But this staff knows better.

Still, we want the old kitchen back. –RG

# Houston's

**8.0** Food  **8.6** Feel

You can find great burgers at this chain—which, by the way, is not native to Texas

## American

Upmarket restaurant

**$55** Price

www.hillstone.com

Sun–Thu 10:45am–10pm
Fri–Sat 10:45am–11pm

**Bar** Beer, wine, liquor
**Credit cards** Visa, MC, AmEx

**Rockville, MD**
12256 Rockville Pike
(301) 468-3535

You might assume this ultrapopular restaurant to be Texas original—most of its considerable cult following already assumes that to be so. In reality, though, the warm, well-loved, upmarket-yet-moderately-priced chain actually started in 1977 in Nashville, Tennessee (although for some reason, the LA-based Hillstone Restaurant Group, the chain's current owner, seems mighty protective of that fact).

Its success since then (Houston's branches now grace most big American cities) has been legendary, owing largely—but by no means solely—to the delicious grilled burger, the icon that Houston's cult following tends to worship most. It comes in several configurations of accoutrements (a California version, for instance, includes avocado, jack cheese, and arugula), but all of them taste of a good smokehouse grill, rather than the dirty griddle you might find in lesser kitchens. Get it medium-rare, and it will really come that way. Don't miss some of the best fries in the city, either—they're crispy, salty, and exemplary.

You should probably start with an inspired version of spinach dip, whose followers are legion. Filet mignon is unusually flavorful and beefy, although we wish a fattier cut were available. Still, this is top-steakhouse quality in a less pretentious atmosphere, at a price that undersells the big names by a bit. The menu continues with almost caricatured straightforwardness, with reliable meats, from chops to ribs.

The outlandishly energetic, almost disturbingly attentive waitstaff has a feel-good attitude; we mean it in the best sense when we say that they're like cheery TGI Friday's employees trained at a higher level of sophistication. The restaurant's inoffensive decorative theme integrates some elements that seem almost faux-Navajo; shiny, curvy red banquettes are a bit too brightly lit but certainly comfortable. All of it works well for families or groups, less well for romantic dates.

Houston's can get crowded and busy on the weekends, so expect a wait; but this is a volume restaurant, so it won't take forever. They bring 'em in and push 'em out with a smile and a complimentary mint. Wait it out at the bar and enjoy a good cocktail—or, if you simply can't take the wait, order at the bar and eat there. It's not a culinary temple, but for a chain, it does an unusually good job of pleasing a lot of different palates with uncanny reliability. –FC

# Hudson

A lounge with an ambitious beverage program; if
only the restaurant would follow suit

**5.8** **8.0**
*Food*   *Feel*

## New American

Upmarket restaurant

**$65**
*Price*

www.hudson-dc.com

| | | |
|---|---|---|
| Mon–Thu 8am–midnight | **Bar** Beer, wine, liquor | **West End** |
| Fri 8am–1am | **Credit cards** Visa, MC, AmEx | 2030 M St. NW |
| Sat 5pm–1am | **Reservations** Accepted | (202) 872-8700 |
| Sun 10am–10pm | Date-friendly, live music, outdoor dining, Wi-Fi | |

If the menu at Hudson looks familiar, it's probably because you've seen it all before: derivative "contemporary comfort food" items such as seared scallops, iceberg wedge salad, brick-oven pizzas, upscale fried chicken, and gourmet mac and cheese. At best, the food is serviceable: scallops have a golden-brown exterior yielding to a tender interior, and the accompanying applewood-smoked bacon and mushrooms add a welcome savory dimension. Deviled eggs are tasty and just the right consistency (and thanks to many family get-togethers, we know how easy it is to mess up a deviled egg). But execution problems have plagued the kitchen. Pizzas have a chewy crust. Steak on a salad has come chewy, too.

More importantly, aren't we tired of all this? It's not as though the ingredients are local and organic; there's no fun with classic European cuisine (but thankfully, no hyper-zealous fusions, either). What is Hudson's bringing to the table that we don't already have in abundance? Okay, pretty good matzoh-ball soup that tastes light and healthy, but what else?

The real answer is served up in the sleek and stunning lounge, where a striped carpet and beige suede chairs bathe in the pale pink light emanating from behind the bar. A curving banquette cordons this space off from the dining room. It's a stylish setting for a girls' night out with Hudson's ambitious beverage program, which is the real reason to come here. A seasonally changing cocktail list employs infusions, mixers, and garnishes that are made in-house—everything from dried strawberry slices to tonic water. One drink combines lemon-infused vodka with a touch of rye and mint in a summery, sweet tartness. A diverse and relatively well-chosen wine list is acceptable, and at times even transcends its competition.

While the participation in the cocktail renaissance is applause-worthy, we *cannot* understand the beer selection: $7 Corona? Pabst Blue Ribbon in a can for $5? Is this a joke? Offer one free with every meal, if you want to be ironic. We'll just stick to the cocktails—especially at happy hour, when $25 pitchers of Hudson's signature white sangría-margarita hybrid go even farther to make the food better, at least in our foggy memories.
—CD

# Hunan Dynasty

This overrated Capitol Hill lunch spot explains Americans' lack of faith in government

**4.7** Food    **6.0** Feel

## Chinese

Casual restaurant    **$25** Price

www.hunandynastydc.com

Mon–Fri 11am–10:30pm
Sat–Sun 11:30am–10:30pm

**Bar** Beer, wine, liquor
**Credit cards** Visa, MC, AmEx
**Reservations** Accepted
Delivery

**Capitol Hill**
215 Pennsylvania Ave. SE
(202) 546-6161

Although Hunan, being a province and not a clan, never took well to dynasty, plenty of restaurants have since taken to calling themselves Hunan Dynasty (though the popularity of the name on Google is slightly exaggerated by the existence of "Hunan Dynasty," the gay short flick released in 2001). The top Hunan Dynasty restaurant, again per Google, is located in Washington DC, on Capitol Hill and not two blocks from that great domed monument to America's own special breed of dynasty, the Houses of Congress, in which in which our elected elite work hard to ensure that citizens have both the opportunity to eat mediocre Chinese food, and the freedom, if they wish, to avoid it. Besides, even legislators need lunch.

Freedom notwithstanding, it is arguable that the former dynasty (Hunan) plays a small but significant role in fueling the latter (American) one. A New Yorker article once outed some leading Hunan loyalists (Schumer likes the kung pao chicken; Kucinich prefers tofu), and Hillary beams repeatedly at patrons from the framed prints along the stairwell to the second floor.

Inside, Hunan's décor is shiny and ostentatious. The roomy dining area is lavishly adorned—a five-foot-long illuminated photo of a Chinese river scene sprawls over one wall. The chairs have very high backs and very thick padding (a note of modesty comes only at the end, when your leftovers are wrapped up in the white to-go cartons that unite Chinese restaurants high and low).

But for the frills and prices, however, you might as well be at one of the nothing-special carry-out joints, at least to judge from Hunan's food. Main dishes are presented lovingly, but the flavor is lacking. Spring rolls are soggy and disappointing, and the rice and noodle dishes are bland. Amongst the few winners are a smoky hot and sour soup (a favorite of many Senators, it's said) and a surprisingly buttery oolong red tea. But if our fearless leaders really believe that the Hunan Pork, sautéed with broccoli, has a sauce that's "hot and spicy"—as the menu claims—then it's really not hard to see why our nation's image has suffered abroad.
–CK

# I Ricchi

What could possibly explain this restaurant's continued existence?

| 3.7 | 6.5 |
|------|------|
| Food | Feel |

## Italian

Upmarket restaurant

**$80**
Price

www.iricchi.net

Mon–Fri 11:30am–1:45pm,
5:30pm–9:30pm
Sat 5:30pm–9:30pm

**Bar** Beer, wine, liquor
**Credit cards** Visa, MC, AmEx
**Reservations** Accepted
Veg-friendly

**Dupont**
1220 19th St. NW
(202) 835-0459

This was once an Italian restaurant. Nowadays, it seems like more of a scam operation that somehow manages to prey on unsuspecting passersby.

It's not clear whether the customers are mostly walk-ins—perhaps wooed by the warm lighting, the tacky sky-blue walls, the faux-Renaissance murals and pottery, the plant-happy décor—or whether they've mistakenly booked dinner here based on some decades-old recommendation from a travel guide.

Whatever the reasons, I Ricchi somehow manages to stay in business. The Italian-themed wine list isn't so bad—the markups are reasonable. But they'll gouge you on the little things like water and coffee.

Don't get us started on the service. The staff is condescending, clueless, can't serve wine properly, get things wrong, don't apologize…this isn't a one-time occurrence; it's a well-documented pattern. It boggles the mind to imagine how the management can justify what's going on on the floor.

Or in the kitchen. They advertise themselves as "Authentic Tuscan and Regional Italian Cuisine," and to their credit, the menu does in fact stay more or less true to Tuscan and Italian standards without lapsing into red-sauce Italian-American or pan-world cuisine. It's nice to see dishes like ribollita (a Tuscan bread-and-vegetable soup) on the menu.

They're not good, though. This food is overpriced, pretentious, ill-executed, and that's pretty much the deal. Pasta dishes are the least of evils on this menu, but they come uniformly overcooked. The meats are dry. Osso buco is like a paperweight. Polenta is mealy. Vegetables are underseasoned. Desserts are amateurish.

We could go on, but a simple sentence should sum it up: we haven't the foggiest idea what keeps this restaurant in business. –FC

# Il Mulino

Roses, red sauce, and extra cheese

| 5.3 | 7.7 |
|-----|-----|
| Food | Feel |

## Italian

Upmarket restaurant

**$80**
Price

www.ilmulino.com

Mon–Thu 11:30am–2:30pm,
5pm–10:30pm; Fri 11:30am–
2:30pm, 5pm–11:30pm; Sat
5pm–11:30pm; Sun 5pm–
10:30pm

**Bar** Beer, wine, liquor
**Credit cards** Visa, MC, AmEx
**Reservations** Accepted
Outdoor dining

**Downtown**
1110 Vermont Ave. NW
(202) 293-1001

Since the days when Il Mulino was just a famous Italian restaurant in New York, it has been known for its exaggerated Lady-and-the-Trampish atmosphere. As tends to happen sometimes when money starts rolling in and new branches start rolling out, the exaggeration has only grown over time. If one of the current outposts of rose-strewn, wrought-iron-chandeliered Italhambras were just outfitted with a few vibrating beds and ceiling mirrors, the management could potentially dispense with the ill-fated restaurant idea entirely and just turn it into a full-on hourly-rate hotel for the Frances Mayes fan club.

The locations of some of Il Mulino's newer outposts—Atlantic City, Vegas, Disney World, and Long Island—should give you a hint of just what sort of lady, and just what sort of tramp, this chain is currently pursuing. (We have yet to hear if they've signed leases for space in Lake Charles, Niagara Falls, Biloxi, or Gatlinburg.)

There was a time when Il Mulino—the one in New York, anyway—was actually pretty good. It was Italian-American in the right way, unapologetic about serving a veal chop the size of a VHS boxed set of all three Godfather movies and drowning it in red sauce, ham, and melted cheese whose squared-off shape wouldn't be out of place on Tex-Mex enchiladas—which, like the veal chop, can be delicious when done right.

But the kitchen has more to apologize about these days, beginning with the series of unexpected—and, once tasted, unwanted—gifts that start off a meal: bread that's been sitting around too long; tough, improperly sliced cured meats; underseasoned, stale-tasting bruschetta; or fried zucchini rounds that sog sadly in giant pools of over-garlicked oil. The only thing they don't manage to screw up is hunks hacked off a Parmigiano-Reggiano wheel. When mains come, whole cloves of garlic seem to stow away almost everywhere; but when you're dealing with uniformly overcooked meats and fishes, this isn't necessarily a bad thing.

On the off-chance that you are, in fact, sleazy enough to try to woo a date here, you're best off sticking with the pleasantly eggy homemade pastas, which tend to come reasonably al dente. Bolognese—made from beef, veal, and pork—performs reasonably well.

There are a few other things you'll have to keep in mind if you're hoping to get lucky: First, make sure your date gets an "accidental" glance at the wine over-prices. Second, try to speak with an affected Italian accent. (Ask your waiter for tips.) And finally, even if your Lady is panting and drooling by this point, make sure you don't leave before she gets her complimentary glass of strawberry-infused grappa. –RG

# Indique

Sadly, it's a little too much for show at this popular Indian spot

| 6.2 | 8.0 |
|-----|-----|
| Food | Feel |

## Indian

Upmarket restaurant

**$40**
Price

www.indique.com

Sun–Thu noon–3pm, 5:30pm–10:30pm
Fri–Sat noon–3pm, 5:30pm–11pm

**Bar** Beer, wine, liquor
**Credit cards** Visa, MC, AmEx
**Reservations** Accepted
Date-friendly, outdoor dining, veg-friendly, Wi-Fi

**Cleveland Park**
3512 Connecticut Ave. NW
(202) 244-6600

Indique excels at first impressions. The wide bay windows and sleek but subdued interior are inviting, a sumptuous smell pervades the entryway, and the two dining rooms are well appointed and comfortable. After you're seated by a gracious host, who offers cylindrical pillows for lumbar support, the waitress brings a hand-carved boat with the classic trio of appetizer sauces in silver dishes. Even the restaurant's website has been perfected, with a flashy opening pane and link to photos of U.S. Senators smiling over steaming plates of curry.

If only the subsequent impressions lived up to that first one. Although the waiters and hosts carry the opening act through latter courses with aplomb, and the presentation continues to amaze, the food itself is gastronomically equivocal. It's easy to be guided by your sense of sight, instead of listening to its more important brothers: smell and taste.

Mains are served in white ceramic bowls constructed with an Escher-esque twist, and accompanied by a flawlessly molded brick of steamed white rice. One cherry tomato sits gracefully atop a dashing leaf of lettuce, and the tripartite sauce-boat sails with you through the meal. But what is the point of a garnish without much flavor to back it up? These curries are saucy without sassiness; they lack the thickness or spice to complement the meats. The product is a dish in which the tomato or coconut base provides greater backbone than does the cream or ghee. Without due creaminess, the meat and other elements are not fully integrated.

The Tamil fish curry is an exception, because in this case the prevailing lightness turns out to be an asset. The dish is made with a subtle sauce that complements the delicate texture of the fish, and the tamarind is flavorful without overwhelming the light curry sauce or perfectly tender pieces of fish. The small black lentil accompaniment is another delight from unexpected quarters: the creamy little bowl of dal can be used to thicken otherwise sickly curries.

In keeping with the kitchen's theme, naan should be ordered for show and not for taste. The oblong-shaped loaf makes your dinner table look lovely and complete. If only the flatbread were less dry, and sturdy enough to mop up curry. So much for first impressions. –CK

# The Inn at Little Washington

**8.0** | **9.8**
Food | Feel

A lovely, spectacularly expensive restaurant
pretending to have a world-class kitchen

## New American

Upmarket restaurant

**$250**
Price

www.theinnatlittlewashington.com

Wed–Mon 6pm–8:30pm

**Bar** Beer, wine, liquor
**Credit cards** Visa, MC, AmEx
**Reservations** Essential
Date-friendly, good wines, outdoor
dining

**Washington, VA**
309 Middle St.
(540) 675-3800

Even in a world of fluffy credentialling organizations, the Relais & Châteaux experience tends to be specific and consistent. A drink before dinner—in the evocative garden, perhaps, or the warm, cozy library—is an aristocratic expectation. Servers strike a fine balance: unpretentious yet encyclopedic, personal yet not too folksy. A series of rooms is illuminated by a genteel gauze of orange light, appeasing the geezers with sufficient quantities of blown glass and patterned wallpapers without coming off like shiny Rococo ballrooms. The room smells of candles and fresh flowers. A meal here—an hour's drive from DC—is a full evening's entertainment. It is expensive. It is civilized. It is life-affirming.

Relais & Châteaux has a problem on its hands, though, when one of its restaurants doesn't seem to have noticed that romance-novel nouns (it's a "fantasia," not a salad; a "marriage," not a pairing) were long ago relegated to the first-class cabins of domestic airlines, or that people now expect serious, cutting-edge execution from $500 meals.

The Inn at Little Washington does seem to have a way with tuna. An impeccable tartare (here it's a "mélange"), well set against a strong yuzu sorbet, isn't overwhelmed by mango and avocado, while a cooked version (here it's "pepper-crusted tuna pretending to be a filet mignon") might come wisely topped with an expertly seared lobe of duck foie gras. Rigatoni, aged Gouda, country ham, and faint black truffle are comforting flavors and textures in "macaroni and cheese"; spinach raviolini exude the very essence of the vegetable.

Too often, though, the kitchen fails to fulfill the promise of its overambitious menu. "Pan-seared New England cod" comes chewy and overcooked, unenhanced by its wimpy pork crust. Cold foie gras torchon—a simple test of a kitchen's exuberance—is cooked to excessive softness, a far cry from the firm, buttery mi-cuit sort that makes your eyes roll back into your head. Heirloom tomatoes come with buttery mozzarella but inexcusably little sweetness. Crab cakes are standard; lobster is undistinguished; lamb carpaccio is tender but underflavored; an over-roasted, uninteresting roast veal loin, dubbed "veal parmesan reincarnated," makes us wistful for the Italian-American original.

The Inn's wine list is elaborate, well constructed, and conceals a few rare treats in the far reaches of the cellar (a simple but intact 1982 Volnay-Taillepieds for $50), and the sommelier knows her stuff. Still, it's almost impossible to get out of the Inn for less than $200 a head—even on lower-priced weekdays. Get the tasting menu with wine pairings, and it's more like $400 per person. Now *there's* a financial crisis. –RG

# Irene's Pupusas

The pupusas are served with a side of melodrama at this popular Central American mini-chain

## Salvadoran

Casual restaurant

Daily 10am–2am

**Bar** Beer, wine, liquor
**Credit cards** Visa, MC, AmEx
**Reservations** Not accepted
Kid-friendly, live music

**Hyattsville, MD**
2218 University Blvd. E.
(301) 431-1550

**Silver Spring, MD**
11300 Georgia Ave.
(301) 933-2118

**Silver Spring, MD**
2408 University Blvd. W
(301) 933-4800

Going to Irene's Pupusas feels almost like going to a sports bar, except that the wings are replaced with pupusas, the football on the big screens is replaced with Spanish talk shows, and hail marys with the latest intrigue between the beautiful but poor María and her supercilious aristocratic lover. However, there are still plenty of signs advertising different kinds of beer, leather booths, tables with good viewing access, and friendly Central American waitresses. We should note that speaking Spanish (or recruiting a Spanish speaker to be your friend for the day) is helpful. The crowd varies depending on the time of day. The weekday lunch crowd mostly does take out, although a handful of locals always populate a few of the tables. In the evening, families sit in the booths while bachelors crowd around the bar, and weekends feel like a Honduran family reunion.

The stars of the show here are the cheap, handmade pupusas. These greaseless masa patties are filled with various combinations of cheese, loroco, chicken, pork, and/or beans, and griddled until golden. Our favorite, as usual, is the revuelta: salty cheese, creamy beans, and porky chicharrones ooze out of the hot pupusa. Enjoy them topped with red or green salsa and tart curtido (pickled slaw). Although many eat these as an appetizer or snack, making a complete meal out of a few of them isn't uncommon.

Another standout dish at Irene's is the greaseless, golden plantains with refried beans and cool, thin Salvadoran sour cream. Among more substantial dishes, try the baliadas, which brim with beans, beef, and avocado; or the spicy lomo saltado with caramelized onions. With huge portions at cheap prices, you won't go hungry. Wash everything down with a cold beer or a glass of horchata and linger for a bit to catch the end of the latest fiasco on *El Gordo y La Flaca*. You may find yourself growing so fond of this place that you'll be trending more towards the former than the latter. –SDC

# The Islander Caribbean

**5.7** Food  |  **6.5** Feel

The food at this Caribbean joint tends to start with a bang and end with a whimper

## Caribbean

Casual restaurant

**$25** Price

www.islandercaribbeanrestaurant.com

Tue–Thu 3:30pm–10pm
Fri–Sat 3:30pm–11:30pm
Sun 3:30pm–11pm

**Bar** Beer, wine, liquor
**Credit cards** Visa, MC
**Reservations** Accepted
Live music, outdoor dining

**U Street**
1201 U St. NW
(202) 234-4955

Expect to eat copiously here. The Islander does not skimp on portions; even the "side dish"-sized rations of the main offerings are extremely generous—nearly half a chicken, or over a pound of meat. The interior of the Islander does not exactly conjure the open-air dining rooms and ocean-side cafes of the Caribbean (it's more "Royal Carribbean"), but the attempt is endearing. The restaurant features potted palms and a few posters of beach scenes, but if you happen to be seated by the window overlooking U Street traffic, a glance outside may ruin the mood. The tables feature cheap, pale-colored coverings, and the chairs can be rickety.

The flavors, like the décor, also fail to be wholly transporting. Although meats and seafoods are well-prepared, there seems to be something lumbering and heavy about the recipes: each dish hits you with one punch, without subtlety or attention to complementing one element with another. Pineapple shrimp, for example, is completely bathed in sweet fruit juices, and served with additional chunks of pineapple and a few garnishing vegetables. The shrimp itself tends to be a little oily, and the juice of the pineapple is only interesting for so long: after a short while, the dish begins to taste saccharine. Likewise, "Calypso Chicken" is roasted in a blackened crust, but the flavor is only skin deep: half an inch in, the juices and spices have not penetrated, and the meat tastes completely unaffiliated with Caribbean cooking.

Each main dish comes with a choice of plain rice or rice and peas (i.e. beans): the first is unremarkable, the second is mushy and good, though not interesting enough to enliven the meats. Some of the vegetable offerings, however, will redeem the lagging mains; try, for example, the simmering curried chickpeas. The vegetable of the day that accompanies main courses—broccoli, at one visit—is often disappointing. Ours was steamed and limp, a northerner who strayed too close to the equator. After fighting your way through one of the Islander's vast portions, you'll know how it feels.

The Islander's service is nothing to write home about, and the staff will get itchy if you sit too long even if the room is empty. This ain't exactly mini umbrellas on the beach, folks. Unless you're looking for a change of pace (literally, as the service can be slow), you'd do better to stick to the mainland. –CK

# The Italian Store

It's packed, and it's packed for a reason

## Pizza, Sandwiches, Groceries     Counter service

www.italianstore.com

Mon–Fri 10am–9pm
Sat 10am–8pm
Sun 11am–6pm

**Bar** Wine
**Credit cards** Visa, MC, AmEx
Good wines, kid-friendly, outdoor
dining, veg-friendly

**Arlington, VA**
3123 Lee Hwy.
(703) 528-6266

At Arlington's Italian Store, things are not as chaotic as they seem. On a late weekend morning, you'll be surrounded by a crowd of hungry locals gripping paper numbers as proof of their entry time. Knots of customers clog the aisles of this Italian imported-foods grocery, but everyone is civil, and the sandwich-makers are remarkably efficient at taking orders and making subs before sending people on their way. Good to know: you can skip the line (and the number-taking) if you just want to carry out a slice of their much-lauded pizza.

That pizza is perfectly serviceable, but if a friend gushes on and on about how it's the best in the DC area, find yourself another pizza guru. Man, pizza-ravers: we could write a book…(we practically have). The Italian Store's pie is more or less of the New York persuasion: i.e. greasy, with a thin, relatively floppy crust (here slipping dangerously towards soggy), copious gooey cheese, and a wide selection of toppings.

We think you're better off choosing a hefty sub from among the list of various Italian-deli-meat-and-cheese combinations (vegetarian versions are also available). These subs have a vast and loyal following, and they've earned it, bringing a little Jersey 'tude into your northern Virginia day. Choose a hard or soft roll, but if you plan on enjoying the "special dressing," definitely go with the chewy kind (soft ones just fall apart). And don't forget the pickled peppers. Our only complaint is that if you want tomato, you have to know to ask for it (and pay 25 cents extra).

The atmosphere at this carry-out shop isn't much to speak of, with the focus on speed and convenience (although let's not kid ourselves: you could easily wait a good twenty minutes for your sub). But something about the jolly tangle of friends, lovers, and families, office lackeys with massive orders and yummy mummies, strollers stuffed any which way into a corner, local regulars, and DC punters, conjures a charming familial vibe. While you wait for your number to be called, browse the crowded shelves of imported Italian coffees, cookies, pastas, and tinned goods. In the front, there's a surprisingly broad selection of affordable Italian table wines. Freezer cases along the back wall display frozen and fresh pastas, mains, and desserts—including the much-lauded Berger cookies. (Indigenous to Maryland, these cakelike cookies with a thick layer of fudgy icing are like black-and-whites, forget all that white nonsense).

It's always nice when a specialty grocery declines to be pompous or dainty. Hell, in a pinch, you can even pick up a *gallon* jar of Nutella here. Respect. –CD

# J. Paul's

A fratty bar and restaurant that dishes out
mediocre American classics, chain-restaurant style

| 4.3 | 4.0 |
|-----|-----|
| Food | Feel |

**American**

Casual restaurant

**$45**
Price

www.j-pauls.com

Mon–Thu 11am–11:30pm
Fri–Sat 10:30am–1am
Sun 10:30am–4pm

**Bar** Beer, wine, liquor
**Credit cards** Visa, MC, AmEx
**Reservations** Accepted

**Georgetown**
3218 M St. NW
(202) 333-3450

J. Paul's mixes several worlds. On one hand, the exposed-brick, proudly displayed raw bar, and M street location suggest upscale American watering hole. On the other, giant fake plants, general mustiness, and an improbable cigarette vending machine imply something else. It's more mature than "frat-house," but not by much. Depending on the time of day, you may dine alongside visiting parents and giddy tourists or find yourself among not-so-young adults reliving their rowdier years.

In general, the food at J. Paul's sounds more exciting than it tastes. Baskets of soft pretzels replace bread, but are often soggy and completely encrusted with salt. Oysters with fresh horseradish are smooth and mild but sometimes stubbornly attached to their shells. Drinks and service are middling: a full bar serves standard drinks and wait-staff is competent and efficient, but not particularly considerate. More than anything, J. Paul's will strike you as an upscale version of any national chain, where fried, slathered, and processed are the norm, and the kitchen strives to create the largest portion known to man.

Surf-'n'-turf sliders are just as heavy on calories as flavor. The mini beef and crab cake burgers are loosely packed, allowing the stringy texture of the crab and juiciness of the beef to strike a great balance with the amount of bun (a perennially difficult slider calculus). The presence of both swiss and cheddar, and the use of sweet instead of sour pickles, makes these burgers so good they don't need any of the three sauces provided. In fact, you might find that even ketchup ruins the fine balance. Desserts, however, are a buzzkill.

If you're considering a place to drink, J. Paul's provides ample sources of people watching and a lovely antidote to the thirst-munchies. If you're looking for a decent dinner, you might want to keep looking. –JC

# Jackson 20

A modern American tavern that would satisfy
Jackson's own Kitchen Cabinet

**7.4** Food  **8.1** Feel

## New American

Upmarket restaurant  **$65** Price

www.jackson20.com

Mon–Thu 7am–10:30am,
11am–2:30pm, 5pm–10:30pm;
Fri 7am–10:30am, 11am–
2:30pm, 5pm–11pm; Sat 8am–
2:30pm, 5pm–11pm; Sun 8am–
2:30pm, 5pm–9:30pm

**Bar** Beer, wine, liquor
**Credit cards** Visa, MC, AmEx
**Reservations** Accepted
Outdoor dining

**Alexandria Old Town**
480 King St.
(703) 842-2790

The maître d' at Jackson 20 is a pig. No, really. A bronze one, to be exact.
Traditionally a tavern symbol of hospitality and, well, good eatin', this
preliminary porker welcomes you to a modern take on the taverns of yore,
with reclaimed walnut and gunmetal-gray stone lending just the kind of
sternness our floppy-haired Old Hickory would appreciate. Perhaps
because of the open kitchen and floor plan, a lively buzz seems to
pervade the place even when it's half-empty.

Many of the regional, traditional dishes are wood-fired but can be hit or
miss. Cornmeal-crusted oysters are crispy and juicy, but barely detectable
under batter, though the spicy tomato remoulade is a wonderfully kicky
accompaniment that would go great with just about anything. Grilled
romaine hearts, served with crispy capers and Caesar dressing, are just
barely wilted and charred—a welcome adjustment to a boring standby.
And how can you dine at a Southern restaurant and not get fried
chicken? Here, it is moist and juicy and served alongside smoky braised
kale. But hold the crab sauce! Poured over the chicken, its fishy tang is
too jarring a contrast to this otherwise delicate and subtly seasoned dish
(but it works beautifully on fried green tomatoes). The slow-braised short
rib, on the other hand, is decadently sweet and spicy, and it's nestled on a
cloud of buttery mashed potatoes; our only complaint is that there isn't
enough of it. For dessert, the peanut butter-chocolate bar is a must.
We've seen many a table devour it with reckless abandon.

The theme of 20 carries over to the wine list, where you can find the
somewhat gimmicky "20 bottles for $20." But for that price, you can
expect the grocery-store plonk. The rest of the list is pretty thin, but
there's a decent little sherry selection you should check out...or, better
yet, go with the flow and order a Tennessee Whiskey.

The trendy atmosphere can be trying. Noise reverberates off the brick
walls and hardwood floors when the restaurant is crowded. Service is
friendly, and quite relaxed (appetizers might arrive before cocktails).
There, at least, it's doing the tavern thing rather well.

It's fitting, this devotion to the $20 bill. Jackson 20 is not precious and
excellent enough to be a C-note, but not as commonplace and cut-rate as
a single. No, we'd say 20 is right on the money. –SDC

# Jaleo

Tapas that have a wide range from boring to oh-so-exciting

| 7.3 | 8.3 |
|-----|-----|
| Food | Feel |

**Spanish**                     Upmarket restaurant     **$50**
                                                        Price

www.jaleo.com

Sun–Mon 11:30am–10pm
Tue–Thu 11:30am–11:30pm
Fri–Sat 11:30am–midnight
Hours vary by location

**Bar** Beer, wine, liquor
**Credit cards** Visa, MC, AmEx
**Reservations** Accepted
Outdoor dining

**Penn Quarter**
480 7th St. NW
(202) 628-7949

**Arlington, VA**
2250 Crystal Dr.
(703) 413-8181

**Bethesda, MD**
7271 Woodmont Ave.
(301) 913-0003

Jaleo is the cornerstone of maverick chef José Andrés's fiefdom. The Spanish restaurant trio is the only of Andrés's concepts with multiple locations (Penn Quarter, Bethesda, and Crystal City), the only one to serve tapas-sized portions of food from a genuine tapas-serving country, and (perhaps because of its high ceilings and ample square-footage) the one that tends to cater to the most diverse mix of food-seekers, fun-seekers, and expense-account-spenders, most of them with the same combination of aloof resignation and bustling pride at how much fun this whole "little plates" thing is.

There's no question that Jaleo's layout is beautiful. All locations feature a red-and-orange baseline palette: a boldness tempered by the magnificent dining area with curving bars and benches, chair-backs with thin interwoven strips of wood, hanging glass lights, tall mirrors, and tables tiled with aquamarine mosaics. The effect is a sort of "nowhere in Spain" atmosphere that could only be made in America, although the efficient waiters, tall water glasses, and elegant table settings are surely more reminiscent of Barcelonean business than Sevillian sloth.

Despite its trueness to concept relative to Andrés's Zaytinya and Café Atlántico, Jaleo lacks culinary precision. While the menu showcases combinations that excite the palate and once in a while blow the mind, and the presentation of dishes is artistic and elegant, only about half of the dishes stun the senses.

Conejo en salmorejo is one of those dishes: the rabbit is cooked with fresh herbs that complement the gamy meat, set atop a smooth and buttery mash of potatoes, and topped with a smoky black olive. Atún fresco is just barely seared; cut the steak lengthwise, and fresh, rare tuna meat stares out at you, intelligently paired with well-done roasted peppers. And the asado, filled with dried fruit, onion confit, and pine nuts, is magnificent. Cured hams and stuffed peppers have been reliable, too.

The only thing that's been actually *bad* has been a plate of inedibly skanky raw oysters. But Jaleo has a minefield of ordinary dishes (cod fritters, mushroom salad) gussied up to sound special. That said, a collection of tapas wouldn't be authentically Spanish if it didn't include the mundane, too. –CK

# Java Green

An all veggie café where it's surprisingly easy being green

**4.9** Food    **5.0** Feel

## Sandwiches, Baked goods

Café   **$20** Price

www.javagreencafe.com

Mon–Tue 9am–8:30pm
Wed–Fri 9am–9pm
Sat 10am–7pm

**Bar** None
**Credit cards** Visa, MC
Outdoor dining, veg-friendly, Wi-Fi

**Farragut**
1020 19th St. NW
(202) 775-8899

If America is in a twelve-step program to free itself from an addiction to bad food, to reverse the damage wrought by the half-century that stretched from war-era rationing to the early, misguided healthy-food movement, then the modern twist on culinary responsibility—the notion of good local ingredients, artisanal producers, localized nostalgia, and good taste all working as one—might be the twelfth step (carrying this message to other addicts, and practicing these principles in all our affairs).

Java Green, a light, airy, lunch-oriented place that's right in the middle of the city's bustle, doesn't seem to have gotten past the first step: admitting that we have a problem. It's unfortunately married to the latter part of that era in which multicultural vegetarian meals rose to prominence—a time when a soy-chicken-avocado-and-cucumber brown-and-wild-rice roll (here, the "California Gimbob") was believed not just to be a healthful combination, but even a palate-awakening one.

The menu is full of pseudo-Korean coinages, and dishes are decorated with fake meats, including the seemingly irreplicable popcorn chicken or the formidable drumstick. Greened Korean foods such as kimchi and bibimbap—here a beef-like tofu that tastes nothing like beef, but is smoky and rich unto itself—are staples in the salads and rice dishes, while the panini are all-American and un-American all at once. The turkey club, unbelievably, is made with two different tofu fabrications that substitute—without replicating—the turkey and bacon. For a few cents extra, the "regular" cheese and breads can be replaced with organic versions.

You'll also find the normal assortment of organic and vegan cookies and cakes: the selection here varies. And although the restaurant does serve decent espresso drinks (fortunately none of them actually green).

It's hard to dislike Java Green, though, when the staff is so lovely and helpful, and take such pride in the food they're serving. They bring it out with a light side of moral worth, as well as a small portion of good conscience. It might ease your palate's woes to know that some of your money is going to charity. Kind of like the day at the college cafeteria when you agreed to fast for a day so that your lunch money would be donated to starving children. –CK

# Java House

A cheap and popular neighborhood joe joint with food just good enough to keep you in your seat

**6.6** Food

**9.1** Feel

## Middle Eastern

Counter service

**$10** Price

www.javahousedc.com

Sun–Thu 7am–10:30pm
Fri–Sat 7am–11pm

**Bar** None
**Credit cards** Visa, MC, AmEx
Kid-friendly, outdoor dining,
veg-friendly, Wi-Fi

**Dupont**
1645 Q St. NW
(202) 387-6622

This corner coffee shop is touted by several guidebooks as one of the best places to get your fix in DC. For one thing, they roast their own beans in-house in this huge, gleaming vintage roasting machine—not just roasted in-house, but roasted in your face, so the place always smells amazing. You can choose from bins containing a wide selection of these beans to take home and grind yourself. The espresso shots taste rich without too much bitterness, and have a nice crema on the top. Foam is usually just the right consistency, and chai is made rich and thick with whole milk.

Though small, this often-crowded spot has plenty of seats; outside you'll find more electrical outlets than inside. Table service can be slow, so order at the counter and bring it to your table for best results.

A pastry case is always full of fresh-baked batches of cookies, pies, cakes, and tarts, as well as croissants and bagels in the morning. The latter two make for a good breakfast with ham, cheese, and egg stuffed inside. At lunch, you have your pick of several sandwiches and salads, as well as a daily soup, and these are pretty good for coffeeshop fare.

Sandwiches are just good enough, but hummus is delicious here, as are most of the Middle Eastern snacks. Steer clear of the gazpacho, which can come a bit flavorless and oily. But ordering the food here is really just an excuse for hanging out all day in really pleasant digs, with great smells and free WiFi, without passing out from low blood sugar. At a minimum, $2 buys you a coffee-scented seat on a prime Q Street patio, while the suckers at nearby Starbucks branches stand around in overcrowded, slightly dingy environs waiting for tables. –FC

# Jimmy T's

It is what it is: a greasy spoon, in all its glory

**7.2** | **7.5**
Food | Feel

## American

Casual restaurant

**$25**
Price

www.jimmytsplace.com

Wed–Fri 6:30am–3pm
Sat–Sun 8am–3pm

**Bar** None
**Credit cards** None
**Reservations** Not accepted

**Capitol Hill**
501 E. Capitol St. SE
(202) 546-3646

In a town with a dearth of diners, we're lucky to have Jimmy T's: a greasy spoon par excellence. The walls are grease-stained, the cups are coffee-stained, and the main attraction is a long counter across which the two friendly owners can turn from their toasters and pans to chat with customers. There are a few tables and booths as well, and a duo of surly waitresses to seat, staff, and bus them. The plates are made of off-white plastic, the silverware is cheap, and the mugs look as though they've been collected from Salvation Army stores in Nashville or Missoula.

This is a book you can judge by its cover: Jimmy T's décor (and the smell inside) dispels any doubt about the type of food the eatery serves. Like many greasy spoons, Jimmy T's feels compelled to fill three pages of a menu with elaborations on a theme that could easily be expressed in a sentence: countless combinations of eggs, sausage, and bacon fried in grease and accompanied by toasted, buttered bread, and/or potatoes. Plus juice and coffee.

The execution of eggs and such is flawless. Pancakes don't figure highly on the menu here, but Jimmy's is blessed with a pair of round Belgian waffle makers, from which emerge a series of popular combos: half waffle with sausage and two eggs, half waffle with bacon and scrabbled eggs, whole waffle with banana and eggs on the side, and so forth. The fake maple syrup (which is served in plastic ketchup-style dispensers) does wonders to integrate the sweet crisped dough with the more savory eggs and meat.

Greasy spoons rarely garner kudos for creativity, and Jimmy's is as staid as the rest. The most daring dish might be the spinach, mushroom, and cheddar or feta omelette with homefries, although patrons are free to add or select from a (rather limited) list of omelette add-ins at will. The potatoes are sliced round rather than cubed, but they're not quite crisp enough to offer the proper counterpoint to eggs. Jimmy's toast is, well, toasted sliced bread (white or wheat), and the jam comes in little packets with removable tops.

Jimmy's is an excellent, if predictable, diner, and a surprising retreat from the frills of the weekday Hill. –CK

# Johnny Rockets

**5.6** **6.5**
*Food* *Feel*

1950s nostalgia, fully themed, packaged, and ready for the greasy grill

## American

Casual restaurant

**$25**
*Price*

www.johnnyrockets.com

Sun–Thu 10:30am–10pm
Fri–Sat 10am–1am
Hours vary by location

**Bar** None
**Credit cards** Visa, MC, AmEx
**Reservations** Not accepted
Kid-friendly

**Dupont**
1718 Connecticut Ave. NW
(202) 332-8883

**Foggy Bottom**
2000 Pennsylvania Ave. NW
(202) 822-1260

**Georgetown**
3131 M St. NW
(202) 333-7994

**Capitol Hill**
50 Massachusetts Ave. NE
(202) 289-6969

What began in 1986 as a Southern California outpost of greasy burgers, cheese fries, and malts has grown into a veritable empire: you can find Johnny Rockets in 29 states, purchase a line of souvenirs and apparel, or visit one of the 25 new locations opening each year. Yet with its mid-'80s inauguration having fallen three decades after the era it seeks to emulate, the chain has some explaining to do. "Johnny Rockets was founded on the belief that everyone deserves a place where they can escape today's complicated world and experience the food, fun, and friendliness reminiscent of feel-good Americana," boasts the corporate website.

We'll leave it to the cultural anthropologists and corporate marketing executives to debate the relative complexity of the 1950s and 2000s. Suffice it to say that the faux diner's appropriated world of Coca-Cola kitsch, rowdy customers, and paper-hat-topped waiters doesn't seem entirely complication-free. The Pentagon City mall location's floor plan leaves nary an inch of elbow room between you and the shopping-bag-laden family from Ohio, and if you dare the Dupont Rockets on a weekend night, your banana split is bound to be cut short by an over-eager busser. Repeated cries for mustard go unanswered, the music is loud, and the bright lights on linoleum are blinding. And Johnny's burgers are laden with grease.

Nonetheless, the Johnny Rockets experience can be fun, and the food is not that bad. Burgers take on the happy patina of the griddle, although the buns are a bit limp. The chili is filling; breakfast toast is thick yet crisp; and the cheese on the cheese fries tastes real. The #12 version comes with a spicy if soupy red sauce (it may not be salsa, but it's better than ketchup). And although the milkshake flavorings aren't homemade, the product is predictably good and sweet. But don't expect 1950s prices. In this complicated town of often-overpriced eats, Johnny Rockets' 5-cent jukeboxes may be the only good deal left. –CK

# Johnny's Half Shell

The old boys still know how to live

**7.8** | **8.5**
Food | Feel

## Seafood

Upmarket restaurant | **$65**
| Price

www.johnnyshalfshell.net

Mon–Fri 7:30am–9:30am,
11:30am–10pm
Sat 5pm–10pm

**Bar** Beer, wine, liquor
**Credit cards** Visa, MC, AmEx
**Reservations** Accepted
Date-friendly, kid-friendly, live
music, outdoor dining

**Capitol Hill**
400 N Capitol St. NW
(202) 737-0400

Johnny's Half Shell is deep in Hill Country; it's the kind of bar at which bowties are worn without irony, oversized cigar butts tower in ashtrays, and patrons look like Ivy-League graduates, circa 1962 (think clean parts and eager smiles). Despite its somewhat stodgy clientele, Johnny's is a lot less stuffy than you'd expect. Orange walls are hung with whimsical ornaments, and on many nights, you can find a jazz combo cheerfully proffering Southern-tinged melodies in the dining room.

The staff at Johnny's is wonderfully unpretentious but still manages to run a tight ship. Drinks, though on the pricey side, are sized for maximum happiness—translate gimlet into "mug of gin" and you'll get the idea. Cocktails are expertly mixed, and because Hill folk enjoy their booze, you can be assured of a buzzing bar and a packed house. Sitting in Johnny's will make even the shyest person feel sparkly and social.

The menu looks like that of the typical seafood restaurant you'll find in the District: mostly American flavors with Southern accents and a distinct bias toward the Chesapeake. However, unlike many seafood restaurants in the District, dishes remain refreshingly down to earth (or sea). Johnny's generous happy hour menu lets you try a bit of everything.

Standouts include barbecued shrimp and asiago cheese grits that are a strong contender for the best grits in DC. Lightly seasoned shrimp, butterflied to maximize grill char, frolic in a sea of thick, cheesy-chunky goodness; a generous slick of electric orange sauce adds flavor and smoke. Mini Asian tuna sandwiches are served with an effervescent slaw that tickles your tongue and brightens the fish. Gravlax (cured salmon) is softer and richer than other varieties, with a consistency that's a lot like smoked salmon, but with a fresher flavor and more vibrant texture. Even Johnny's wings are good; they strike the ideal balance between meatiness, skin, and sauce without dripping pools of oil onto your napkin.

Dessert is a good encapsulation of the Johnny's experience. Though the plates aren't as pretty as at most other places, their contents are charmingly sincere. Fluffy chocolate angel food cake rests in a pool of caramel sauce that tastes like essence of fall. At the end of the day, don't be fooled by the bowties or politics-speak. Even for those without a Hill office, Johnny's is pretty great. –JC

# Julia's Empanadas

**7.1** **2.0**
*Food* *Feel*

Tasty little pan-world packets that are even tastier in the wee hours

## Latin American

Counter service **$5**
*Price*

www.juliasempanadas.com

Mon–Wed 10am–midnight; Thu
10am–2am; Fri–Sat 10am–
4am; Sun 10am–8pm
Hours vary by location

**Bar** Beer, wine, liquor
**Credit cards** None
Veg-friendly

**Dupont**
1221 Connecticut Ave.
NW
(202) 861-8828

**Adams Morgan**
2452 18th St. NW
(202) 387-4100

**Columbia Heights**
3239 14th St. NW
(202) 328-0008

Julia herself is Chilean, but her empanadas claim a broader birthright. In addition to Chile, her recipes purport to include Argentine, Spanish, Bolivian, and even Jamaican-style concoctions and ingredients. (Jamaican beef patties, like Indian samosas and British pasties, are basically empanadas.) Although the expatriate array of Julia's savory packets have more in common with one another (in terms of size, spicing, taste) than with their compatriots back home, they also share the common feature of tasting very good.

The classic Chilean empanada is made with ground beef, hard-boiled egg, onion, olives, and raisins (Argentines sometimes claim that the Chilean version of their national dish is onion-heavy and light on beef—boosting as proof the much larger Argentine beef industry—but we'll spare Julia's these sibling rivalries). The stuffing is made with large pieces of olive and egg, rather than in a more integrated fashion, allowing each bite to taste a little different. The beef is delightfully spiced.

All of Julia's empanadas are baked rather than fried. Shapes differ, however; they range from triangular to oval-shaped. The dough is generally the same for all of the savory choices: a smooth white-flour wrapping baked to a golden crisp. The sweet empanadas, though, are made with a flakier crust.

With eight appealing options, it can be hard to decide what to order. The empanadas are larger than most seen in South America, and a single one almost constitutes a meal. The salteñas, named after Salta, a northern Argentine city near the border with Bolivia, are made with chicken rather than beef (we're not sure why—beef is as popular in Salta as it is anywhere else in Argentina), as well as potatoes, green peas, egg, and olives. These tend to be a little less spicy than their Chilean or Jamaican beef counterparts, but Julia's happily provides a squirt of hot green tomatillo sauce to those who ask.

Also available are chorizo, jalapeño-turkey, and a vegetarian choice that changes weekly (on a recent visit, the latter was stuffed with a spicy lentil, cabbage, and green bean mixture), but we favor the meaty ones. Julia's has three tiny locations—true holes-in-walls with little atmosphere. Happily, two of them are open until 4am on weekends—a scheduling choice that seems to make disputes over the empanada's origin all but inevitable. –FC

# Jumbo Slice

They're jumbo, all right, and best enjoyed—
perhaps only enjoyed—by the inebriated

**3.5** **1.2**
Food    Feel

## Pizza

Counter service    **$5**
Price

| | | |
|---|---|---|
| 24 hours | **Bar** None | **Adams Morgan** |
| | **Credit cards** Visa, MC, AmEx | 2341 18th St. NW |
| | Veg-friendly, Wi-Fi | (202) 234-9700 |

If there were a muse of fraternal drunkenness, it would be Jumbo Slice. The eatery has almost single-handedly fueled scores of second (or third) winds of weekend revelry, intervening just when flagging spirits and empty pitchers seemed to portend the end of a night. One wonders what such spirits did before there was Jumbo Slice (although of course, Adams Morgan was a very different place before there was Jumbo Slice).

Many are aware that pizza, in general, is an ideal sponge to soak beer from tired stomachs and temper impending hangovers. As such, this restaurant's name is on the tip of nearly every drunken tongue along the Adams Morgan strip, and among a certain crowd it's not uncommon to hear the phrase, offered over the course of recollecting the events of the previous night: "Was that before or after we went to Jumbo Slice?"

The shop's pizza is nothing if not utilitarian. The pies are enormous—nearly two feet across—but thin, and very, very greasy: perfect for mucking up beer juices from the stomach, while made with enough cheese to provide protein for the night. And the pizza is not overly bready: it won't weigh you down.

It's practically unheard of to order an entire Jumbo Slice pizza; instead, you buy a slice at a time. And a slice can easily be shared by two or three, by tearing off pieces in strips, although you may prefer your own (one slice makes a meal, more or less). The preferred mode of eating a Jumbo Slice is to fold the triangle together once or even multiple times (a feat allowed by the monstrous surface area to thickness ratio), and to consume the slice as you might a burrito or other wrapped food: from one rolled end to the other.

In the end, the pizza is pretty bad: it's too greasy, the sauce is flavorless, the crust is helpless to withstand a soaking from the grease. But Jumbo Slice (and its duo of knockoffs along the same strip) has a calling and fulfills it well; in the end, we'd be sad to see it go. –CK

# Jyoti

Above-average Indian that is geographically challenged

**7.1** Food

**7.0** Feel

## Indian

Casual restaurant

**$25** Price

www.jyotirestaurantdc.com

Sun–Thu noon–10:30pm
Fri–Sat noon–midnight

**Bar** Beer, wine, liquor
**Credit cards** Visa, MC, AmEx
**Reservations** Accepted
Delivery, outdoor dining,
veg-friendly

**Adams Morgan**
2433 18th St. NW
(202) 518-5892

This restaurant sits right in the middle of a mostly nightlife-oriented strip of Adams Morgan, so it's no surprise that it attracts a lot more attention at night than it does during the day. What is a bit of a surprise, though, is that the food is better than expected for mainstream Indian. Jyoti's masala gravy, for instance, has an unusual buttermilky flavor, as if something beyond the usual cream is used to thicken it; spicing is mild, but the extra dairy kick gives the concoction more complexity than usual. We like the aloo gobi, a potato-and-cauliflower curry that could be heavy—with potato and those irresistible cheese cubes; it's good, light, and not too creamy. Spinach dishes are merely average, but paneer, wherever it shows up, is spongy and as delightful as usual. Chickpeas are a touch overcooked in chana masala, but naan is unusually good; it's thin, not too doughy, and clearly homemade.

Jyoti is a pretty place: shiny hardwood floors, exposed brick, and warm orange walls go beyond cookie-cutter Indian décor. Although the walls bear the usual weavings with the customary sparkles and an illustration of an elephant reception, there are also some original paintings. There are, perhaps, too many tables crowded in the middle of the main room, but upstairs in back is a cozier space. In the middle of everything is a sculpture of the Hindu elephant god, with flowing orange and turquoise robes covering the elephant; this centerpiece sort of brings all the other weavings to life. The Indian pop-ballad soundtrack is a fun touch.

Jyoti's $7.95 lunch special, too, is a slight cut above the norm. Instead of the buffet, they do something classier: basically, a thali, with five metal bowls of curries and vegetable dishes, rice, and naan. But even this doesn't bring many people in. Adams Morgan is just not a lunch neighborhood. Our heart goes out to restaurants like Jyoti, which practically have to beg to get lunchtime customers—and then must compete against a formidable crowd of neighbors at night for customers who aren't always choosing based on whose kitchen is superior. On every level, Jyoti is a bit better than it has to be, and it deserves to thrive, even in this difficult territory. –RG

# Kabob Bazaar

This humble Persian eatery serves up the real deal

**8.0** *Food*  **5.0** *Feel*

## Middle Eastern

Casual restaurant  **$20** *Price*

www.kabobbazaar.com

Mon–Thu 11am–10pm
Fri–Sat 11am–11pm
Sun noon–10pm

**Bar** Beer, wine
**Credit cards** Visa, MC
**Reservations** Accepted
Kid-friendly, live music, outdoor
dining, veg-friendly

**Arlington, VA**
3133 Wilson Blvd.
(703) 522-8999

For a treat in Clarendon, duck into this unassuming restaurant. The décor is gussied-up cafeteria, with cheap tables covered in nice cloth, a few artistic touches, and a long bar whose tenders will look after you as long as you like. The waitstaff's tone is appropriately relaxed and uninvasive, and whether you sit and the bar or at a table, you're mostly left alone to enjoy the kitchen's delights.

While there are a few strange elements of the menu (we'd like a word with whatever consultant advised the Bazaar to add a "low-carb menu," which consists of kabobs atop lettuce…), if you avoid the obvious blunders, it's hard to go wrong. Kabobs are only supporting players in a deep and diverse menu. The Ash-e-Reshteh soup offers a lovely combination of textures and tastes: buried at the bottom are snaking Persian noodles, and above which you'll find spinach and plenty of warm spices. The whole concoction is topped by thick yogurt, fried onions for crunch, and fresh mint. And those familiar with Persian fare will be pleased to find an appetizer of tahdig on the menu—the crunchy rice crust from the bottom of the pot makes a lovely accompaniment to stew.

For the main course, the Bazaar offers a number of kabob combinations—manna for the indecisive. The truly hungry might opt for the Super Soltani, which includes one each of chicken, lamb, and beef kabobs—and be warned, the portions are large. Chicken, which is served off the bone, is a slight weak point here, but all of the mains are helped by one of the tastiest green sauces this side of the Atlantic, as well as with a plate of greens to add to your dish at will. Wash it all down, if you dare, with a glass of doogh, the classic Persian fizzy yoghurt beverage. The sour drink pairs nicely with all that is so sweet about the Kabob Bazaar. –CK

# Kabob Palace

Follow the masses to some good grilled meats

**8.6** Food

**5.0** Feel

## Middle Eastern, Afghan

Counter service

**$20** Price

www.kabobpalace.net

Daily 11am–midnight

**Bar** None
**Credit cards** Visa, MC, AmEx
Outdoor dining

**Arlington, VA**
2315 S. Eads St.
(703) 486-3535

It's old hat that the best dining advice is often "follow that cab (driver)!" And one is apt to forgive a taxista all of his traffic misdeeds once he's tipped you off to the Kabob Palace, a true gem of a restaurant near South 23rd Street in Crystal City.

These days the secret is out, though, and several DC food critics have popularized this Afghan hole-in-the-wall in recent years. In fact, Kabob Palace is not one place but two: the original line-order-and-take-out dump crowded with cabbies, and the adjacent "family restaurant" which has only slightly better service and a menu that is no less delicious. Both restaurants have plastered their walls with effusive reviews from local and international media; the rest of the décor is incomprehensible at best: why the Gyros posters and cheap oil paintings of Greek seascapes? Why the ads for Vitamin Water?

And why, while we're at it, the bowl of iceberg lettuce and ranch that accompanies every main course at the family place? Luckily, if you can overlook the fact that the complimentary end-of-meal tea is served in styrofoam, iceberg is the Palace's single failure. Everything else we've tried has been exemplary, and liable to incite kubideh cravings at all hours.

If kabob is all you're after (or if you're at the take-out place, where the options are fewer), the lamb is perfectly tender and coated in sweet spices; the combination platter will allow you to sample the kubideh as well. All mains arrive with rice and a mushed, greasy, but ever-delicious chickpea side, or with spinach. And once you've stuffed yourself past sanity, there's almost always a cab outside. The cab drivers know, after all. —CK

# Kanlaya

Chinatown's flashy, neon beacon of American Thai
is overshadowed by nearby Chinese

**6.0** *Food*    **7.0** *Feel*

## Thai, Chinese

Casual restaurant

**$30** *Price*

www.kanlayathaicuisine.com

Sun–Thu 11:30am–10pm
Fri–Sat 11:30am–10:30pm

**Bar** Beer, wine, liquor
**Credit cards** Visa, MC
**Reservations** Accepted
Delivery, kid-friendly, outdoor
dining, veg-friendly

**Chinatown**
740 6th St. NW
(202) 393-0088

In a tangle of cheap and unreliable Chinatown restaurants, Kanlaya Thai—with its splashy neon sign that screams "flaming cocktails within!"—is a breath of fresh air. At least visually. The dining room isn't just clean, it's downright pretty, with cherry wood furnishings, deep red accents, linen and…a flatscreen TV? The lively atmosphere is serviced by a friendly and helpful wait staff that won't hesitate to recommend (or steer diners away from) menu items.

Despite the name, "Kanlaya Thai Cuisine" actually offers both Thai and Chinese fare. Why? Whenever this spirit of "divide and conquer" is present in an Asian restaurant, it usually means it won't do either very well. Nevertheless, (mostly) younger crowds flock here for serviceable, recognizable standards. The requisite tom kha soup balances sweet, salty, sour and spicy; its only downside is the nuisance of untrimmed shards of lemongrass. Veggie dumplings have a shiitake earthiness that works with their smoky, sweet-soy-based sauce. Panang shrimp curry has a coconut milk sweetness, but some chili and fresh Thai basil prevent it—though barely—from being cloying. But where are the real Thai spices and flavors? The fiery chili, the kaffir lime leaf, the balancing sourness?

Among Chinese dishes, crunchy, juicy, and pleasingly bitter kana fai daeng (stir-fried Chinese broccoli) is dressed with a chili-and-bean sauce that is hot, salty, and fragrant. Tofu nueng gets its assertive flavor from a delicate black bean sauce and an abundance of fresh ginger, and is light without being bland (the downfall of many tofu and vegetable dishes). Desserts in Asian restaurants are rarely worth the trouble, but when mangoes are in season, the usual mango and coconut-laced sticky rice is lovely.

But back to these flaming cocktails. Yes, they actually exist. But the floater on top is the only alcohol you'll find here. Overall, the cocktails here are syrupy and weak. Fire will only distract drinkers for so long.

Even though Kanlaya is the prettiest girl on the block and even does a decent job, you'll likely find better Chinese in one of those "cheap and filthy" places around it. As for authentic Thai, well, at least that's not nearby, either. –SDC

# Kanpai

We'll toast to the lunch specials

**5.9** **5.0**
*Food* *Feel*

## Japanese

Casual restaurant

**$30**
*Price*

www.kanpai-sushi.com

Mon–Fri 11:30am–10:30pm
Sat 12:30pm–10:30pm

**Bar** Beer, wine, liquor
**Credit cards** Visa, MC, AmEx
**Reservations** Accepted
Kid-friendly, outdoor dining

**Arlington, VA**
1401 Wilson Blvd.
(703) 527-0110

The exhortation "kanpai" literally translates to "empty your glass," a Japanese version of "down in one" or "cheers!"

There are things to celebrate at this out of this way restaurant, but not enough to warrant such a hearty exclamation. A few blocks north of the Rosslyn metro stop, and recessed from the side of the road, Kanpai is the unobtrusive sort of place you could walk past every day and never notice. Amidst a jumble of office buildings and sandwich joints, the red lanterns bedecking the place look a little out of place, although they are meant to add a festive touch. Yet the dull concrete hides a few thrills: if you can, make the trip to Kanpai on Thursdays, when a farmer's market sets up shop right by the restaurant's outdoor deck. In the summer, the abutting yard is the site of outdoor concerts.

The restaurant has a quiet but devoted following, especially during weekday lunches. You, too, might happily toast the lunch specials. For under $10, you can sample from a wide range of Americanized Japanese dishes. The pork cutlet in the katsu-don is pounded until tender, delicately breaded with flaky panko crumbs, and fried a deep golden brown; it is served with a deep, plummy sauce. Vivid yellow pickled daikon tastes as tangy and bright as the color suggests. But the quality of the food can fluctuate. Teriyaki, for example—beyond being a sweet-tooth recipe that's doomed from the start—has a tendency to appear tough and dried out. This points to a larger problem here: too much sugary Japanese-American slop, not enough subtlety.

Vegetables in tempura are thickly cut, sometimes so much so that the inside is still undercooked, but the tall prawns and smushy yams are still mostly fun. Sushi and sashimi at Kanpai aren't great, but at least the maki are traditional and humble, more delicate than the monster rolls that have proliferated in American-Japanese cuisine.

Service at Kanpai seems designed for hurried work lunches. Food appears in rapid-fire fits and spurts, and niceties are often neglected in favor of efficiency. Servers are not particularly chatty or well versed in making recommendations, but if you sidle up to the sushi bar, and give the chefs a sweet smile, they'll be pretty straight with you about what's hot and what's not.

Given the dinner prices and the location, there are far better sushi options in town. But lunches, anyway, offer an affordable relief to the workday doldrums, and hey, we'll drink to that! –JC

# Kaz Sushi Bistro

**8.4** | **7.8**
*Food* | *Feel*

A hip spot that vastly exceeds downtown sushi
expectations—as long as you keep it simple

## Japanese

Upmarket restaurant

**$55**
*Price*

www.kazsushibistro.com

Mon–Fri 11:30am–2pm, 6pm–
10pm
Sat 6pm–10pm

**Bar** Beer, wine
**Credit cards** Visa, MC, AmEx
**Reservations** Accepted

**Downtown**
1915 Eye St. NW
(202) 530-5500

For excellent sushi in a fine but unstilted atmosphere, we offer you Kaz.
The restaurant does have some premeditated flair and creative quirks, but
they tend to be endearing rather than annoying. While Kaz's more daring
dishes are hit-or-miss, traditional sushi offerings are extremely fresh, and
food is presented with a simultaneous eye for detail and tongue-in-cheek
salute to style.

Those who find pedigrees reassuring will be delighted to learn that
head chef Kazuhiro Okochi "Kaz" is certified in the art of preparing fugu.
On occasion, the restaurant offers invitation-only tastings of the blowfish
(its flesh, if cut incorrectly, can be fatally poisonous), and such lore, as well
as Kaz's full biography (he was previously an artist, pastry chef, and ice
carver), is dangled in front of diners as they peruse the menu. The
restaurant is organized into a main seating area and a smaller, sharply
angled room a half-story up. Kaz is graced with the requisite tropical fish
aquarium, slinky tables and chairs, zigzagged lighting, and minimalist
place settings. Although the furniture is trendy and the average age of
diners is on the younger side (thirtysomethings dominate), the
atmosphere is quiet and elegant.

Many of Kaz's menu offerings seem like trendy propositions (tuna with
roasted almond, kalamata olive, or black truffle, for example, or plum-
wine-infused-foie gras), but flavors are well-matched rather than
spuriously combined, and the final execution is elegant. Rolls are cut into
pieces of different heights and adorned with curly springs of baby
watercress or thinner-than-matchstick carrots.

In season, the soft-shell crab special must be tried: the pieces of meat
are cut large, and the creaminess is allowed to show through without
much adornment from the kitchen. And Kaz excels at traditional,
unornamented nigiri (sushi pieces) too: the yellowtail, again, is served in
large pieces, and the flavor is cutting and clear. We have almost never had
a piece of fish here that tasted anything less than bouncily fresh, and that
is a rare thing indeed.

The restaurant also serves bento boxes at lunch and noodle dishes for
dinner, but we'd recommend sticking to the pure sushi. And flavor-
mongers, beware: the wasabi at Kaz is just as cutting and tasty as the fish,
but it's very hot. –CK

# Kemble Park Tavern

**7.1** | **8.6**
*Food* | *Feel*

A comfortable place where the food will make you
smile, but won't challenge you

## New American

Upmarket restaurant

**$60**
*Price*

www.kembleparktavern.com

Mon–Thu 4pm–11pm
Fri 4pm–midnight
Sat 9:30am–3pm, 4pm–11pm
Sun 9:30am–3pm, 4pm–9pm

**Bar** Beer, wine, liquor
**Credit cards** Visa, MC, AmEx
**Reservations** Accepted
Date-friendly, kid-friendly, outdoor
dining

**Palisades**
5125 MacArthur Blvd.
(202) 966-5125

Kemble Park Tavern bills itself as "a place where one can catch up with
old friends, the weary may rest, and all can dine and drink in a place
that's the next best thing to home." And unlike some of DC's many
taverns, Kemble Park is clean, elegant, and marvelously hospitable. It's
filled with deep browns and rusty reds, carved wood, and quietly glowing
glass—a place that feels safe and warm. Deep leather couches with
pristine pillows surround white-clothed tables, at which groups of all
shapes and sizes convene in comfortable, easy-going merriment.

The menu here is reasonably priced, but it's obviously more upmarket
than a traditional tavern's would be. Yet elements of the old dust-tracked,
ale-stained rooms are also present: large hunks of meat are prevalent, and
portions and presentation are undeniably masculine. The food is
somewhere between fancy and rustic, comforting but nothing exemplary.
A braised lamb shank, pocketed with fat and caveman-large, rises like a
colossal, gnarled tree branch out of a hill of grits. The lamb has a
refreshing gaminess that some restaurants might mistakenly try to
obscure. Each bite reveals something different: smooth fat slides into
chewy meat, flecks of char, and moments of gristle, all companioned by
creamy grits and chin-streaking jus. While the dish is texturally fascinating
(some would say barbaric), it's also monotoned, with few spices to break
up the muttony barnyard flavor. Spinach gnocchi are plump and fluffy,
basted with truffle cream, and not to be missed. These are not the light,
airy kind of gnocchi. They are the kind that you can chew in wads of
starchy goodness until the cows come home. It's not for everyone, but we
can't deny it's sort of fun.

Cocktails are made with fresh-squeezed juices, and dessert is a
highlight—a boon to those who prefer sweets with some restraint.
Chocolate pot de crème, charmingly served in a mason jar, is more bitter
than sweet, deep in flavor but light in texture.

Servers are warm and hospitable, just as promised. Though calling this
place a "tavern" is a little like calling The Watergate an "inn," it is indeed
a place of comfortable and affordable replenishing. –JC

# Kenny's BBQ

Neighborhood and wallet-friendly, but hardly heavenly 'cue

**6.1** Food

**5.4** Feel

## Barbecue

Counter service

**$20** Price

Mon–Thu 11am–9:30pm
Fri–Sat 11am–10pm

**Bar** None
**Credit cards** Visa, MC, AmEx
Outdoor dining

**Capitol Hill**
732 Maryland Ave. NE
(202) 547-4553

On hot days, the smell from Kenny's can carry down the block and even, sometimes, around the corner. Washington humidity may not be worthless after all: the heavy air can help the smell of cooking pork and baking cornbread anneal and spread. Unike some other summer smells, Kenny's is one you don't mind descending from above.

This isn't barbecue sent from heaven; make no mistake. But it's not bad. Kenny's is an unpretentious neighborhood place in the Northeast devoted entirely to barbecue and its accoutrements. A large painted sign outside advertises Kenny's picnic packages, a sort of slowed-down catering gig. Basically, if you come in with six or more people you can order, for $8.50 per person, a predetermined but made-on-the-spot package with a variety of barbecued meats, plus cornbread and vegetable sides. If you optimize based on volume-to-cost-ratios, this is not a deal to pass up.

If you like to optimize taste, however, you'd do well to look more carefully at some of Kenny's sides, rather than leaving the choice to chance. The potatoes, for example, look as though they've been aged a few days too many behind the dirty display case, and the collard greens seem to drown in a bath of their own juices (tasting the greens confirms the sight: they're under-salted and limp, watery not buttery).

At seven or eight bucks a pop, Kenny's sandwiches tend toward the expensive side in the barbecue world (although a fish sandwich rings in at five). Here, again, the volume may be large enough to merit the price: a pulled pork sandwich spills out of a very large bun; to call it "overstuffed" would be an understatement.

Kenny's meat is generally good, but the sauce isn't potent enough to do it any justice. The place serves the kind of mild barbecue sauce you could easily fix at home, without the smokiness or fire it needs. Even when you specify "hot," the meat is prepared with barely any bite.

Within a radius of—well, about as far as the smell carries—Kenny's is a serviceable place for the neighborhood-bound. There are a set of very nice outdoor tables. But be prepared for some disappointment: this barbecue, alas, smells better than it tastes. –CK

# Kinkead's

Competent but overpriced fish amidst pomp and somewhat undeserved fame

**7.3** Food  |  **7.5** Feel

## Seafood

Upmarket restaurant  **$75** Price

www.kinkead.com

Mon–Fri 11:30am–2:30pm,
5:30pm–10:30pm
Sat–Sun 5:30pm–10:30pm

**Bar** Beer, wine, liquor
**Credit cards** Visa, MC, AmEx
**Reservations** Accepted
Live music, outdoor dining

**Foggy Bottom**
2000 Pennsylvania Ave. NW
(202) 296-7700

This restaurant is preceded by its reputation. It helps to have a reputation when your entrance is at the end of a long, genteel awning on the street side, and through a shopping mall on another. Or is it vice versa? Do you need the reputation (e.g. Commander's Palace) to earn the awning?

Kinkead's really does seem to have that sort of status, more or less, in DC: travel guide write-ups, reader awards. It's amazing how many of the warmly lit, slightly overdressed tables that sprawl across several rooms on two floors—the upper with a bustling open kitchen—tend to be full. Foreigners flock to the place, giving it a certain air of intrigue. You might see a suave, questionably married Danish diplomat entertaining a beautiful, questionably married Chinese woman who's in town for business. Or you might be seated, as we once were, beside a silent British-American family whose 18-or-so-year-old daughter carved raisins out of her bread slice with surgical precision while her squat father displayed equally impressive speed and efficiency: by the time he would begin chewing one bite of his grilled red snapper "Tampico," he'd already positioned the next.

As for the snapper, it comes out whole but overcooked, with a bright, not-too-sweet pineapple pico de gallo and a dry shrimp tamale. There's a pleasant achiote rub, too, but its chile character doesn't filter through the fish's skin, which, at our last visit, scales rendered inedible.

We certainly appreciate Kinkead's ever-changing menu, the carefully fried soft-shell crabs, and a certain depth of respect for noble Atlantic blue-collar fish traditions that's displayed in dishes like crispy clams with tartar sauce, cleverly updated with fried lemons. Simple salads succeed too, like a summer plate of sweet heirloom tomatoes, basil oil, and very creamy Laura Chenel chèvre (America's seminal goat cheese "log," introduced by Alice Waters at Chez Panisse in 1980). And freshness shines through raw oysters—whoever orders these clearly prefers the sweet and creamy style, as do we—and exemplary cherrystone and littleneck clams.

But there are too many problems here to justify the cost. Pasty, overcooked shrimp bring down the shellfish platters. Fish mains (beyond just the snapper) often come overcooked unless otherwise requested. Dinner rolls come tough, bread chewily half-toasted. And, surprisingly for such an expensive restaurant, Kinkead's often fails to execute on service details: waiters are aloof, bathrooms aren't spotless. Maybe the restaurant's a little too big, or a little too old. But these days, Kinkead's can't hold its own with the top fish houses in town. –RG

# Komi

DC's best restaurant is vaguely Greek, vaguely molecular, and entirely amazing

**9.7** Food
**8.3** Feel

## New American, Greek

Upmarket restaurant

**$140** Price

www.komirestaurant.com

Tue–Sat 5:30pm–9:45pm

**Bar** Beer, wine
**Credit cards** Visa, MC, AmEx
**Reservations** Essential
Date-friendly, good wines

**Dupont**
1509 17th St. NW
(202) 332-9200

In its precocious half-decade of life, Washington DC's best restaurant has evolved from the pure, ingredient-driven love child of an obsessive local chef to a nationally known gastronomic destination.

Few can afford to make dinner here a regular affair: the prix-fixe runs $90 to $125 without wine, and for the privilege of spending this much, you must book weeks ahead. Yet the price is fair; there are restaurants in the city where you can spend twice this much on an experience that's not in the same league.

The meal itself is the night's worth of entertainment—and romance, too; it all happens in a sparse but candlelit dining room, set in an old brownstone. Even overzealous bloggers are forced to be more romantic than usual: photographing the food is prohibited.

The meal begins with "mezzethakia." This is Komi lingo for a progression of small tastes, most of which occupy a space somewhere between minimalist and molecular. A recent visit yielded two tiny quenelles of hanger steak tartare and black truffle ice cream—a nod, perhaps, to the French Laundry school of modern American Europhilia. Sea-urchin vinaigrette and frozen shiso-leaf sorbet brought remarkable depth to a tartare of salmon, one of the most overused fish varieties today. Diver-scallop sashimi was served in two preparations, one with black truffle and the other suspended in gelée and finished with sea urchin, seamlessly blending the most rarefied tastes of the earth and the sea.

When the kitchen drifts away from pure ingredients and introduces more pretentious, technique-driven dishes—foie gras cream puffs, cheese animal crackers, goat cheese marshmallow s'mores—flavors can fall flat.

But few kitchens in America have as deft a handle on pasta as Komi's. House-made spaghetti with sea urchin cream, fresh spring ramps, crab, fiery but judicious habanero, and Catalina uni is as complex and interesting a starch as has been served in DC all year.

The meats match the intensity of the pastas. In an age when many chefs gently bathe their meats in sous-vide pouches or olive oil, this one instead turns to the fire, creating textural studies like katsikaki (slow-roasted goat shoulder), matched with pickled cabbage, smoky eggplant purée, and other condiments. Some parts of the shoulder's interior are tender, others supple and moist from the slowly melted collagen; the exterior is like a crisp, goat-flavored cracker.

Komi is competing on a national stage. With time, we're confident that the culinary focus and experience here will only improve. Being there to witness the journey is one of the best parts of living in DC. –FC

# Kotobuki

**8.3** Food **7.0** Feel

Cheap sushi that manages to not taste cheap? Who struck this devil's deal?

## Japanese

Casual restaurant **$25** Price

www.kotobukiusa.com

Tue–Thu noon–2:30pm, 5pm–
9:30pm; Fri–Sat noon–2:30pm,
5pm–10:30pm; Sun 5pm–
9:30pm

**Bar** Beer, wine, liquor
**Credit cards** Visa, MC
**Reservations** Not accepted

**Palisades**
4822 MacArthur Blvd. NW
(202) 625-9080

There's a certain genius to putting a lower-end sushi restaurant on top of a trendier, more highly acclaimed one. Think of the floods of people who may not be so picky as to endure the weeks-ahead reservation routine—or, worse still, the attempt at a walk-in—for Makoto, and who are drawn like moths to the lights of Kotobuki overhead. This thumbnail of a sushi restaurant often sees a line of people winding down the stairwell, perhaps to see which restaurant calls their name first. But look closer and you'll find a strong contingency of fierce Kotobuki supporters, Makoto notwithstanding.

Kotobuki is like the poor man's Makoto, with a more authentic (read: somewhat stark and utilitarian) feel to it. Lighting is much too bright to suggest that this place cares about ambiance. On the other hand, there is one particularly adorable feature: the constant rotation of Beatles music on the speakers, all Beatles and nothing but the Beatles, at all hours of the day—and not just the most well-known tracks, either. This is clearly the work of an aficionado.

It's almost inconceivable how far your dollar will stretch here: a piece of nigiri will set you back a buck, and almost all rolls are priced under four. Only the enormous Rainbow and Virginia rolls cost any more than $3.50, and these are still under eight dollars each. But is this categorically a good thing? Sushi-grade fish is one area where you get what you pay for. Quality fish from the best markets costs restaurants money, and that's generally why sushi is expensive. So it's suspicious when it comes this cheap.

Regardless, baffled diners agree that the fish tastes surprisingly fresh. (Seriously, is the chef friends with someone over at Tokyo's Tsukiji fish market? Or is he using the downstairs walk-in?) Kotobuki's rolls are simple—no more than two or three ingredients each and no designer names. The yellowtail is fat and buttery, and the eel's natural sweetness comes through with a little light grilling.

The extremely abbreviated sake list has only one cold option, but it happens to be one of the better versions out there. Kotobuki may not be trying for Makoto standards, but cheap sushi that doesn't taste like refrigerator versions? It sure beats the others in its class. –FC

# Kyoto

Big fish in a tiny little pond

| 6.6 | 7.5 |
|:---:|:---:|
| Food | Feel |

## Japanese

Casual restaurant

**$30**
*Price*

Mon–Fri 11:30am–3pm, 5pm–
9:30pm
Sat 4pm–10pm

**Bar** None
**Credit cards** Visa, MC
**Reservations** Accepted

**Capitol Hill**
201 Massachusetts Ave. NE
(202) 546-2597

This tiny sushi restaurant just north of the capitol packs in a staggering array of menu options: if you actually decided to read the menu before ordering, you (and everyone behind you in line) could easily be there all day. Not only are there more than two dozen special rolls in addition to all of the "ordinary" combinations and plain nigiri, but Kyoto also boasts a long list of appetizers and tempura specialties from which to choose. If that weren't enough to satisfy the choosiest chooser, he might check the teriyaki, yaki soba, and donburi (rice bowl) specials, each of which is served with a side of vegetables and/or a staid lettuce salad.

Lest we forget, there's also an eight-item series of sushi and sashimi specials—essentially pre-arranged sets of rolls and nigiri. And if this summary alone has left you winded, you might simply try the "Kyoto $7 Maniac Lunch Special"—advertised in big letters above the cashier—which changes daily but usually involves teriyaki, and includes a number of sides, and a 20-ounce soda.

Walking into Kyoto feels something like walking into a doll house. The restaurant is located up a set of iron stairs in the front room of a Capitol Hill rowhouse. A few high tables are nested into a miniature back room, while in front the sushi bar is too close to the opposite wall to allow for any stools. Instead, there are three small tables so close to the bar that the chef may as well throw his creations over the counter to his hungry patrons. A single waitress scurries about to dispense with this potential informality.

Luckily, the atmosphere at Kyoto is merry. The sushi is good, although it won't knock your socks off. Most rolls are large, and the proportions seem even more out of sync given the size of the place: a single Rainbow roll, for example, is coated with big slabs of tuna, salmon, and mackerel, and is almost enough to be a meal in itself (it's also topped with a smattering of roe: a nice touch). Kyoto's tempura is delicate, and the deep-fried salmon is unusually good. In keeping with the miniaturized atmosphere, prices shrink as the sun goes down: Kyoto flaunts a 99¢ sushi happy hour. Now that's a happy hour indeed. –CK

# La Baguette

DC's lonely, laboring lunchers, rejoice: this
sandwich joint's for you

| 8.0 | 6.0 |
|-----|-----|
| Food | Feel |

## French, Sandwiches

Counter service

**$15**
Price

Mon–Fri 7am–4:30pm

**Bar** None
**Credit cards** Visa, MC
Delivery, kid-friendly, outdoor
dining, veg-friendly

**Dupont**
2001 M St. NW
(202) 293-3265

People in DC are always looking for the perfect, easy lunch. It is the modest dream of a working town: a decent, affordable sandwich that you can grab in that crucial half-hour lunch break. The working lunch is a familiar piece of American atomization—a woman sits alone, her cell phone on the table in front of her, a sandwich in her hand, a blank look on her face, and a cup of coffee growing cold beside her. Few cities embrace the lonely, busy work-a-day lunch with the gusto that DC does.

Unfortunately, the city does not offer many hug-worthy lunch establishments. But La Baguette de Paris in Dupont Circle comes close, delivering some of the best sandwiches in town at great prices. The pretty little shop, simple but always clean, has a few outdoor tables to complement its small interior. The sidewalk-café effect adds a touch of the Old World to an essentially New-World concept: made-to-order sandwiches that come in combo meals. But the majority of the clientele grabs its sandwiches, baked goods, salads, and soups to go. If you're lucky enough to not work during the week, a La Baguette sandwich, rounded out with a drink and chips or something baked, can turn into a wonderful picnic meal. The staff here is friendly, helpful, and attentive to requests (hold the onion, extra avocado, and so on).

Given that the menu features more than 30 sandwiches on your choice of bread (French, croissant, bagel, pita, rye, whole wheat, or seven-grain—we recommend French), it's often hard to decide what to get. But given that all the sandwiches are priced under $6, it's almost worth sampling a few. The turkey reuben on rye is wonderfully packed with moist sauerkraut, Swiss cheese, and a smear of Russian dressing, then pressed until warm and melty on the inside and crisp on the outside. The "Primavera," a lighter vegetarian sandwich is surprisingly flavorful given its bland-sounding mix of peppers, sprouts, hard-boiled eggs, and mayonnaise, mostly because of the tangy, herby vinaigrette that brings it all together. Other favorites are the beef gyro and the "Supreme" (smoked chicken breast with roasted red peppers).

La Baguette fills DC's emptiness like hot coffee in a paper cup. If only all our working lunches were so pleasing. –SDC

# La Casita

Neighborhood pupusería and market with a mix of authentic and very affordable food

**Salvadoran**

Casual restaurant

**7.9** **7.5**
Food Feel

**$10**
Price

Mon–Thu 10:30am–9pm; Fri–Sat 10:30am–10pm; Sun 10:30am–8pm
Hours vary by location

**Bar** None
**Credit cards** Visa, MC, AmEx
**Reservations** Not accepted
Kid-friendly

**Silver Spring, MD**
8214 Piney Branch Rd.
(301) 588-6656

**Germantown, MD**
18058 Mateny Rd.
(301) 515-8575

This pleasant neighborhood pupusería started out as a Salvadoran market, to which they added some simple tables and chairs. It's bright and lively enough, though there's not much to look at. What attracts the local Hispanic crowd—and the occasional non-Hispanic person, too—are its spectacular, authentic pupusas.

These rounds of masa are top-notch, with homemade curtido that's chopped finer than many, more like a slaw. There are the classic revueltas, with delicious chicharrón—whose crispy porkiness is hard to beat—but it's also nice to see loroco on the menu. The unique tea-leaf flavor stands up to even the spicy slaw.

There are some concessions to American tastes and demands: "vegemixta" (refried red beans, loroco, and cheese) and "marimixta" (crabmeat, shrimp, and cheese). Unusually, the frying oil is vegetable, not lard, but it doesn't take away from how satisfying this stuff is. Lots of things come with cuajada, which is homemade Salvadoran cheese, with a curdy consistency not unlike queso fresco. There are also quite a few egg dishes on the menu, making this a great spot for Latin brunch. Huevos con chorizo with tomato, onion, and pepper are solid, but we're excited about the rarely seen huevos con ejote (eggs with green beans). Many of the egg dishes are actually more Mexican than Salvadoran, but there's nothing wrong with that. We love Mexican breakfast.

You can skip the tacos, though. Enchiladas aren't so hot, either. Desserts are unusually good, like the ayote (sweet squash) en dulce, a preserved fruit similar to Argentine membrillo. Banana empanadas are simple but tasty. Nuegados (fried yuca and cheese dumplings with cane sugar syrup)—wow. There's also a long list of sweet drinks, both heavy (licuados, atul de elote) and light (aguas frescas, horchata).

Oh yeah, and everything is dirt-cheap here, which just warms the heart all that much more. –FC

# La Chaumière

| 7.5 | 9.0 |
|-----|-----|
| Food | Feel |

A French restaurant that delivers sincere charm and sincere, traditional cuisine

## French

Upmarket restaurant

**$60**
*Price*

www.lachaumieredc.com

| | | |
|---|---|---|
| Mon–Fri 11:30am–2:30pm, 5:30pm–10:30pm<br>Sat 5:30pm–10:30pm | **Bar** Beer, wine, liquor<br>**Credit cards** Visa, MC, AmEx<br>**Reservations** Accepted<br>Date-friendly | **Georgetown**<br>2813 M St. NW<br>(202) 338-1784 |

Of the multitude of French restaurants in DC, La Chaumière is a strong contender for being the most, well, *French*. Perhaps it's the menu, with its Rabelaisian classics like calf's brains, liver done every which way, and cassoulet. Or perhaps it's the diminutive awning, which opens into something resembling a rustic French cottage (the meaning of the restaurant's name), with exposed ceiling beams, a stone fireplace, and a cast-iron chandelier dotted with Delft tiles. The effect is decidedly authentic—not to mention romantic.

Dish after dish of carnivorous delight is presented with a brand of grandmotherly elegance that has been lost—for better or for worse—in the modern dining scene. Who uses patterned China anymore? And who covers it with dishes this showy and luxuriant, like a parade of hotel-banquet extravagances, salvaged and restored to their original brilliance? Boudin blanc is a revelation—surprisingly light on the tongue, like a cloud of succulent pork that dissolves into a creamy swallow. Steak frites is one of the best versions in this city. Red wine sauce is salty-smoky-sweet, slick with butter, and gutturally addictive. Salmon en croûte combines buttery puff pastry, fatty salmon, and a lemony cream in a dish that is almost too opulent. While the first bites are magic, when billows of salmon-scented steam erupt from its flaky shell, the dish becomes trying. This is cuisine designed to be consumed with wine—wonderful French wines with a natural minerality that cleans the palate while bringing to light some of the deeper flavors. Happily, this wine list is brimming with them.

If you've ever been sorely disappointed by the abundant (and unpleasant) iterations of profiteroles in this city, get excited: La Chaumière's delivers. The dough is buoyant, flaky, and perfectly crisp—you can actually hear your fork breaking through the many, rapturous layers, and the dark chocolate sauce refrains from being too sweet.

Though prices are safely below power-lunch levels, La Chaumière's lavishness is best reserved for special occasions and celebrations, or burgeoning chefs—this is the very cuisine that hooked Julia Childs, you know. –JC

# La Crêperie

Compulsory, food court-y crêpes that won't go far
beyond fueling shoppers

**5.7** **5.0**
*Food* *Feel*

**French**

Café **$15**
*Price*

Mon–Fri 11:30am–2:30pm,
5pm–10pm; Sat noon–
10:30pm; Sun noon–9pm

**Bar** Beer, wine, liquor
**Credit cards** Visa, MC, AmEx
Live music, outdoor dining,
veg-friendly, Wi-Fi

**Arlington, VA**
1201 S. Joyce St.
(703) 415-0560

In spite of the outdoor café seating and the young waiter with an
appropriate French accent (he's from Morocco), La Crêperie's atmosphere
does not exactly whisk diners away to Paris. Instead, it's a rather generic
storefront that looks out upon a Starbucks and an Irish pub. But we've
seen how attempts to recreate France can be disastrous (La Madeleine?),
so it's hard to exactly *begrudge* a lack of theming.

Many people associate Paris with terrific crêpes, but the ones in the
Capital tend to be made with white flour instead of buckwheat, and are
considered by many French and well-traveled Francophiles to be vastly
inferior to Brittany's version. In that sense, La Crêperie does manage to
emulate Paris. The batter tends toward bland instead of lightly eggy and
the consistency is spongy, becoming soggy when filled with moist
ingredients. The edges meanwhile, are crunchy rather than gently crisped.
The menu is evenly divided between savory and sweet selections (there's
also a short list of simple salads, soups, and espresso drinks).

Fillings can be enjoyable enough, but they're hardly inspiring. A
ratatouille crêpe is filled with a finely cut medley of roasted eggplant,
zucchini, tomatoes, and onions. The peppery flavor of the mix is
complemented with just enough oil, but the tomato sauce can be
overwhelming and bland.

On the other hand, it's hard to ever go wrong with ham and gruyère,
which is appropriately oozy and fatty. Non-crêpe lunches must be
avoided: French onion soup is thin and compulsory; the heap of
nonspecific cheese melted on a toast point doesn't save this Liptonesque
tragedy. Bruschetta (what is this doing here?) is soggy.

Sweet renditions also yield mixed results. While the simple jam, sugar
and butter, or lemon-and-sugar crêpes are excellently rendered, the apple
version is stewy and mushy, with little emphasis on the fruit flavor itself.
Surprisingly, though, it does show restraint with sugar and cinnamon,
saving the thing from becoming something of a Hostess Pie.

The slow, relaxed pace of the café cannot be attributed to an
intentional aesthetic—it's merely unoccupied. While one must never jump
to conclusions about busy restaurants necessarily being better restaurants,
one can safely surmise that a chronically empty one is empty for a reason.
–FC

# La Ferme

**6.0** Food   **8.7** Feel

Inconsistent but honest country-Euro food in an amiable farmhouse setting

## French

Upmarket restaurant   **$60** Price

www.lafermerestaurant.com

Sun–Fri 11:30am–2pm,
5:30pm–9:30pm
Sat 5:30pm–9:30pm

**Bar** Beer, wine, liquor
**Credit cards** Visa, MC, AmEx
**Reservations** Accepted
Date-friendly, live music, outdoor
dining

**Chevy Chase, MD**
7101 Brookville Rd.
(301) 986-5255

This neighborhood restaurant is a two-story hunting-lodge affair, complete with fireplaces and exposed beams, a covered terrace, and French country accents. By day, La Ferme looks like a wholesome brunch spot, while by night it's candlelit and sweetly romantic. Diners are generally older, often regulars, and usually locals. Birthdays, engagements, and family occasions are frequently on display in the open dining room, elevating the mood and saving the restaurant from stuffiness.

While the service can seem fussy—with a dozen different waiters swooping in turns to fill your glass, take your order, bring your food, or clear your plates—the food is generally straightforward and satisfying. The menu reads like Julia Child's 1961 *Mastering the Art of French Cooking*: oyster fricassée, calf's liver sautéed with onions and sherry, and so on. But the kitchen performs confidently in other regions, as well, where a special of pumpkin ravioli (traditionally Northern Italian) sees a gently earthy sweetness, and an accompanying scallop is seared to a golden brown.

A potato-crusted salmon has come with an impeccably seasoned ratatouille, but the potato crust was under-crisped and the fish slightly over-cooked. The famed soufflés, which the waiters will helpfully remind you to order at the outset of your meal, rise to an impressive crown above their generously proportioned ramekins. After all the build-up, however, flavors come off as somewhat muted, and the egg whites not uniformly mixed. These stumbles are far from grievous, yet they keep this restaurant firmly in the category of "reliable standby," and not beyond.

The wine list is refreshing for its range and affordability, encompassing not only France, but also New World regions like California, Argentina, and New Zealand. Some interesting bottles are available for as little as $30, and markups are generally reasonable. In the end, this is a pleasant, sincere restaurant with ample free parking in suburban environs, that generally sticks to what it knows: pan-Euro food that falls slightly (and appealingly) short of downtown pricing. –CD

# La Loma

Never underestimate the redeeming qualities of tequila

| 5.2 | 7.5 |
|------|------|
| Food | Feel |

## Mexican

Casual restaurant

**$30**
Price

Mon–Fri 11am–11pm; Sat 11am–midnight; Sun noon–10pm

**Bar** Beer, wine, liquor
**Credit cards** Visa, MC, AmEx
**Reservations** Accepted
Outdoor dining

**Capitol Hill**
316 Massachusetts Ave. NE
(202) 548-2550

The margarita is a fine invention. This is so not merely because, when properly made, its tang and salty bite offer the perfect coda to a humid Washington afternoon, but also because the drink has helped to redeem from oblivion the legions of Tex-Mex restaurants around the District that serve mediocre food.

Take La Loma. This Capitol Hill eatery would seem to have everything going for it: a mixed crowd of families and younger Hill residents, a location far removed from the trendy margarita bars of Dupont, and a friendly but easy-going set of waiters. La Loma is housed in an old Victorian perfectly situated for Mass Ave. people-watching, and its front patio is one of DC's best spots for a laid-back drink on a summer night. Most importantly, its on-point margarita is always cold and never too sweet.

But alas, the food. While La Loma deserves praise for eschewing pretense, as well as for avoiding gestures toward "updated" or "healthy" Mexican, the kitchen just isn't anything special. Add another tally to your list of well-intentioned but uninteresting Mexican spots that seem to proliferate on the East Coast: the salsa is fresh but under-seasoned and raw-tasting, the beef enchilada comes with too little meat wrapped inside a too-dry tortilla, and the rice is rather plain. A refried mess without much flavor is the only bean option. There are a few exceptions: La Loma's tamales, for example, are made with a spiced masa that's cooked to ideal moistness.

La Loma may not tingle your palate, but it will certainly sate your appetite: the kitchen can't be accused of skimping on portions. Any of the combination plates, which come with rice and beans and can include enchiladas, tamales, fajitas, chiles rellenos, and half a dozen other choices, is almost enough food for two people. The tamales, especially, are enormous.

We'd venture that La Loma's margaritas and its unpretentious atmosphere make a visit worthwhile; the food improves once you've had a few drinks. And if you come just for the food, you might end up needing a drink after all. –CK

# La Madeleine

Cheap "French" fast food that even Marie
Antoinette wouldn't suggest

**5.4** **4.1**
*Food* *Feel*

## French, Sandwiches

Counter service

**$30**
*Price*

www.lamadeleine.com

Mon–Thu 6:30am–10:30pm
Fri–Sat 6:30am–11:30pm
Sun 7am–10pm
Hours vary by location

**Bar** Beer, wine, liquor
**Credit cards** Visa, MC, AmEx
Outdoor dining, veg-friendly

**Georgetown**
3000 M St. NW
(202) 337-6975

**Alexandria Old Town**
500 King St.
(703) 739-2854

**Bethesda, MD**
7607 Old Georgetown Rd.
(301) 215-9142

**Additional locations**
and more features at
www.fearlesscritic.com

This rapidly expanding nationwide chain makes a concerted effort to be the Disney-ride version of a rustic French kitchen. There's vaguely earthen tile, bricked cave walls, and a sort of *Les Miserables* theatrical poverty about it. Instead of fine China, you move down a line with your plastic brown tray, choosing between bland sandwiches, over-dressed salads, and under-seasoned soups (sprinkle shredded cheese into our French Onion? *Sacre bleu!*).

But a cheesy, overstated French theme and hokey convenience aren't the real villains here. It's the food, *stupide*. One sandwich promises an assortment of roasted peppers, portabella, and zucchini. It comes with exactly one mushroom slice, and a terrible, doughy roll that we assume is supposed to be focaccia. Elsewhere, a greasy, soggy croissant is filled with square pieces of processed cheese and deli meat. All sandwiches come with a choice of wilted mixed greens or a halfway-decent Caesar salad (even the one you make from the box they sell in the produce section is halfway decent). Salads can also be ordered as main courses, either solo or in a "trio"—three small servings on a plate—but the other options are bleak, including a Caprese with out-of-season industrial pink tomatoes and a wild rice medley that's evocative of Denny's Early Bird Specials. Quiche is generally heat-lamp warm and tastes like an amateur omelette. La Madeleine advertises its "famous" tomato-basil soup prominently, and sells bottled servings to heat up at home. This is probably the only worthwhile thing here—it's fresh, smoky, and slightly chunky. For dessert, you can have "Strawberries Romanoff"—or make it yourself at home by spraying whipped cream into a brandy glass of cinnamon and tasteless berries.

On the plus side, there's free sliced bread near the water. These sorts of chains generally do better when they serve elemental food that's appealing on a visceral level. Tastelessness is typical neither of fast food nor of France—so why should it suddenly appear when the twain meet?
–FC

# La Prima

Build your own delicious sandwich at this little carry-out—but don't bother with much else

**6.8** Food

**5.0** Feel

## Sandwiches

Counter service

**$20** Price

www.laprimacatering.com

Mon–Fri 7am–4pm

**Bar** None
**Credit cards** Visa, MC, AmEx
Delivery, veg-friendly

**Foggy Bottom**
1001 Pennsylvania Ave. NW
(202) 783-8988

**Tysons Corner, VA**
1751 Pinnacle Dr.
(703) 506-0900

La Prima, which is primarily a catering company, also has a small lunchtime outpost near Foggy Bottom. The take-out spot is housed in an enclosed vestibule along with a few other stores; although there are no tables in the café itself, there's an enclosed public seating area just around the corner, with wrought-iron tables and exposed brick, as well as benches through the little mall.

At La Prima, you begin with a pencil and paper. Each bread, cheese, meat, spread, and vegetable option is listed, and you check off as many boxes as you want. Sandwich-building here is not considered a zero-sum game: if you pick two meats, you get twice as much meat on your sandwich. If you check off all of the vegetables, your lunch becomes a towering stack of fresh produce, but never at the expense of meat or cheese. This is all well and good, but the best part is that the ingredients are much better than usual.

For bread, you can choose between about eight varieties, such as whole wheat or sun-dried tomato. The deli meats include freshly roasted beef and smoked or roasted turkey, and the cheese selection is quite vast. The lettuce is bouncy, and tomatoes are juicy, not mealy. Watch as the sandwich makers read off your check boxes and continue to pile on ingredients, in defiance of all rules of reason and gravity.

You can also order one of several suggested selections, such as the roasted vegetable Mediterranean Hero or the Siena sandwich, which is made with roasted chicken, red bell peppers, and artichoke hearts. Steer clear of the bready pizza and watery soups, though, and avoid the dry, underwhelming pastries at all costs.

La Prima does have a nice selection of juices and potato chips, however. It's all merely in service of the sandwich. –CK

# La Sandía

Suburban Mexican where family-friendly meets upscale

**7.5** Food  **7.4** Feel

## Mexican

Upmarket restaurant

**$50** Price

www.modernmexican.com

Sun–Thu 11am–10pm
Fri–Sat 11am–11pm

**Bar** Beer, wine, liquor
**Credit cards** Visa, MC
**Reservations** Accepted
Kid-friendly

**Tysons Corner, VA**
7852 Tysons Corner Center
(703) 893-2222

One of the only haute regional Mexican restaurants in the DC area, La Sandía calls Tysons Corner Center home. This ensures a captive audience of hungry mallgoers who just want to sit down somewhere because their feet hurt. Then, they want to eat their meal, and continue their shopping. That said, many more would likely visit La Sandía if it didn't mean huffing it out to Tysons Corner, circling endlessly about a parking lot, and trekking through a shopping center. A smattering of tables just outside the restaurant—but still well within the confines of the mall—makes us giggle; does this constitute outdoor dining? As when we're stuck in an airport restaurant, we prefer to burrow in all the way to the back, where it feels nice and cozy, and where lighting is appropriately dim—perhaps even a touch too dim—subsequently encouraging margarita consumption.

Which is fine by us, because the drinks here aren't bad. They, thankfully, avoid a hyper-syrupy fate. (That said, if sugar water's your thing, you really don't have to dig deep to find it; just know that the classics are fairly faithful representations.) Bright, but restrained and geometrically stylish, squares of color run across the wall. Chairs and tables are sleek, with sharp angles. Servers are knowledgeable and friendly, sometimes coming across as if they take their job a bit too seriously—but in an endearing way.

The food is clearly inspired by the upmarket regional-Mex genre spearheaded by Rick Bayless and pals, and it has about the level of sophistication you would expect from a mid-level culinary empire. Sopes feature carnitas atop a black-bean-purée-topped masa cake, which is airily fluffy; shredded cabbage doesn't contribute much to the whole operation, but a few pickled onions add just enough bite. Ceviches throw in a few non-traditional ingredients like tomato, as in the case of the rock shrimp version (shrimp were closer to raw than we expected, but we still would have liked to see it rarer), or poblano-tomatillo in the yellowtail tuna version.

Cheese enchiladas have a nouvelle twist—Gouda. It adds a lovely, smoky dimension to the dish, but when it's combined with two other cheeses and cream, the tomatillo sauce and chile are helpless to cut through that mess of dairy. This dish will remain in your stomach like a rock.

And that certainly makes it hard to continue with your shopping, now doesn't it? –AH

# La Tasca

Stick with the sangría and try to have fun despite the food

| 5.7 | 8.7 |
|-----|-----|
| Food | Feel |

## Spanish

Casual restaurant

**$40**
Price

www.latascausa.com

Mon–Thu 11:30am–midnight
Fri–Sat 11:30am–2am
Sun noon–11pm
Hours vary by location

**Bar** Beer, wine, liquor
**Credit cards** Visa, MC, AmEx
**Reservations** Accepted
Date-friendly, live music

**Chinatown**
722 7th St. NW
(202) 347-9190

**Arlington, VA**
2900 Wilson Blvd.
(703) 812-9120

**Alexandria Old Town**
607 King St.
(703) 299-9810

**Rockville, MD**
141 Gibbs St. Suite 305
(301) 279-7011

If Disney's Epcot theme park had a Spanish restaurant, La Tasca would be it. Faux artifacts hang everywhere; the color is red, and the lighting is warm; and in true Disney fashion, the design theme is executed well enough that you end up having a lot of fun inhabiting the space, even if the food's not up to the task.

Luckily, the appeal of tapas often has less to do with what's on the plate, and more to do with what's going on at the table—or at the bar. In a city as happy-hour-obsessed as DC, tapas can be an ideal excuse for getting so drunk after work—while simultaneously filling up on cheap small plates—that you don't end up needing dinner. As such, during happy hour, you'll see gaggles of girls fresh from the office, early-stage dates converging from their respective workplaces, and entire staffs drowning their layoff worries in sangría. Once you start eating the leftover chunks of wine-soaked fruit, there's only oblivion ahead.

Sangría is the main, if not only, reason to come to La Tasca, but it's a perfectly reasonable one. There are 11 versions on offer, including one made with sherry (very good idea) and one made with Red Bull (very bad idea). Our favorite is "Cadillac Red," which is, the restaurant brags a "step above" their traditional blend because it's made with Sangre de Toro red wine—which costs about $9 a bottle. This begs the question: what are they using in the cheaper version? The answer: it doesn't really matter. Enough fruit and sugar masks the most vile of wines.

At happy hour, a few of the tapas are half-price, and given that there's nothing particularly great here, there's no need to obsess over the choice. Patatas bravas are just fine; better are the fried eggplant chips with Cabrales blue cheese dip. The slices are cut quite thin, and there's not a hint of greasiness to them. Most other plates aren't as successful; there are far better and more sophisticated tapas to be had with Señor Andrés.

The brave can also attempt a full meal here, but we don't recommend it. Paellas are missing the crucial integration of the rice with the juices from the protein; shellfish tends to be overcooked, if garlicky. Most chicken dishes involve only the breast.

Service neither speedy nor accommodating, so our advice is to make your server's job easier by keeping the order simple: sangría. In fact, you can even do the job yourself by ordering at the bar, which will also up your chances of getting checked out by an increasingly tipsy hottie that—who knew?—just happens to work in your building. –AH

# La Tomate

A tourist trap whose Italian menu is just a front for prime-location table rental

| 4.6 | 7.7 |
|-----|-----|
| Food | Feel |

## Italian

Upmarket restaurant

**$45**
Price

www.latomatebistro.com

Mon–Wed 11:30am–10:30pm
Thu 11:30am–11pm
Fri–Sat 11:30am–11:30pm
Sun 11:30am–10pm

**Bar** Beer, wine, liquor
**Credit cards** Visa, MC, AmEx
**Reservations** Accepted
Live music, outdoor dining

**Dupont**
1701 Connecticut Ave.
NW
(202) 667-5505

Riding high on location, location, and location, this is the sort of sorry excuse for an Italian restaurant that gives DC food a bad name by feeding on a steady diet of tourists and outdoor-table hounds willing to lease out their gustatory souls for a couple of hours at an umbrella-shaded sidewalk-side table. La Tomate's name is particularly ironic given the appearance of its signature fruit on a caprese salad totally out of season. Also, why is the restaurant's name in French?

Indifferent service, characterized more by a grunt than a smile, echoes the apparent indifference in the kitchen, which—although you'll often hear Italian spoken in the front of the house—turns out painfully inauthentic specials like stuffed prosciutto cotto (cooked ham), plumped up with spinach and ricotta and drenched in a richly reduced and seasoned but mismatched cream sauce. Prosciutto cotto is a delicate thing, and La Tomate's kitchen toughens it with this brand of coarse re-cooking. In Italy, fish is generally grilled, roasted, or steamed whole, and garnished only with olive oil and lemon, but here, daily fish specials batter fillets into submission with pan-Asian ingredients and sweet, heavy sauces that inhabit the distressing no-man's-fusionland that has come to characterize lowest-common-upmarket-denominator menus like this one.

The rest is just rote: cannelloni, Caesar salad with grilled chicken or shrimp, pasta arrabbiata, blah blah blah. Momentary salvation comes from a properly pounded and nicely fried veal milanese, one of the few dishes on the menu that you might actually find in Italy. But deep-fried dishes need to be salted immediately out of the fryer for the salt to absorb and work its magic, and this one comes with no hint of salt. And what's up with its side of overcooked potatoes and zucchini, which turn the milanese from a light dish (it's often served with fresh cherry tomatoes and arugula in Italy) into a heavy one?

Unsurprisingly, the lovely patio, which wraps around this choice piece of Flatiron-building-style Connecticut Street real estate, is home to a lot of Streetwise-map-brandishing, fanny-pack-wearing customers—not that real live DC residents aren't stymied at times themselves by the baffling grid of state-named streets, although GPS-equipped BlackBerries are steadily working their way into the mix as a discreet replacement for street maps. Ultimately, this restaurant is really just in the business of table rental. –FC

# The Lafayette Room

If this food is fit for a president, it'd be a
pretentious president who's not that into food

**6.8** **6.3**
Food Feel

## New American

Upmarket restaurant

**$85**
Price

www.hayadams.com/lafayette-washington-dc.php

Mon–Fri 6:30am–11am,
11:30am–2pm, 5:30pm–10pm
Sat–Sun 7am–11am, 11:30am–
2pm

**Bar** Beer, wine, liquor
**Credit cards** Visa, MC, AmEx
**Reservations** Accepted
Live music

**Farragut**
800 16th St. NW
(202) 638-6600

The Hay-Adams is an excellent hotel. In fact, the Hay Adams folks will tell
you that themselves: in a statement that would make time travellers Bill
and Ted proud, the website declares that "The Hay-Adams has been
named 'The Most Excellent Hotel' in the United States and Canada." This
fact was not lost on the Obama family, who shacked up there prior to the
inauguration after famously being shut out of the Blair House in favor of
Aussie ex-Prime Minister John Howard.

Given the new First Family's penchant for modern regional cuisine—
Spiaggia, Topolobampo, and such—we hope, for their sakes, that they
didn't wind up having to dine at the Lafayette Room, a reminder that
there's still a serious faction in DC for whom a $15 out-of-season insalata
caprese (actually, it's a slight variation thereon—they call it "Fresh Italian
Buffalo Mozzarella Rusticone," and it's made with arugula, 15-year-old
balsamic vinegar, and underripe tomatoes) is the pinnacle of culinary
prestige.

The best thing we've tried here has been a plate of well seasoned, easy-
to-like grilled gnocchi, which are pleasantly browned. It's also hard to
complain about this kitchen's delicate, extra-lumpish version of crab
cakes—or about their crushed scallion potatoes, which are like an evolved
potato salad—although we will complain about the price point ($31 at
press time). Pan-seared pheasant breast has come out slightly overcooked,
if still juicy enough, with the sort of wintry Eastern European-influenced
side—braised red cabbage, spiced apples, sweet-potato gratin—that
seems to be gaining increasing favor these days on upmarket menus. Like
most of the menu here, it's nothing special.

Desserts outperform mains—one of the best is "truffle cake"—and the
wine list actually has a few decent under-$40 selections if you hunt
around hard enough.

The dated feel of the room—which is essentially an extension of the
(equally dated) lobby area—is just what you'd expect at a fading high-end
hotel. It's got the overdressed tablecloths, but lacks any of the cheeseball
charm that the genre can sometimes achieve. This is the sort of place that
manages to feel lonely even when it's booked to capacity (which is rarely).
The Hay-Adams' merits as a hotel notwithstanding, this is pretty far from
the city's Most Excellent Restaurant. –RG

# Langano

Good Ethiopian for which you won't even have to
leave downtown—downtown Silver Spring, that is

**7.9** | **6.7**
Food | Feel

## Ethiopian

Casual restaurant | **$25**
| Price

www.langanoethiopianrestaurant.com

Sun–Thu 11:30am–1am
Fri–Sat 11:30am–2am

**Bar** Beer, wine, liquor
**Credit cards** Visa, MC, AmEx
**Reservations** Accepted
Delivery, live music, outdoor
dining, veg-friendly

**Silver Spring, MD**
8305 Georgia Ave.
(301) 563-6700

If you live in Silver Spring, you're probably relieved not to have to trek way out to Shaw's Little Ethiopia for your fix. But the news gets even better: Langano is at least as good as (and sometimes even better than) those restaurants. Unlike the 19th-century row houses of Shaw, this downtown storefront is wide, with a front patio and huge windows. The inside is spacious and airy, but it gets a little depressing during their quiet lunches. The strong incense smell also works better at night, when the dark wood tables are filled with Ethiopians and loud live music (call first to verify—some weekends they have it and some they don't).

Portions here are generous, and lunches, in particular, are cheap. A lunch special of $6.95 gets you a combo of lamb and beef or vegetable dishes, which you can just manage to finish if you don't load up on spongy injera. They make their own, and it's terrifically sour and bright—like lemony blini. Don't miss gored gored, tender raw beef cubes with herbed butter and hot chili. It's a chunkier and more unusual version of the classic kitfo (which they also serve). Another great treat, and one that we almost never see around town, is a well-spiced quanta fitfit—dehydrated beef with hot pepper. Don't be afraid of dulet, minced lamb tripe and liver; it brings a unique and complex flavor to the veggie sides that come with it and every other main.

In addition to a forthcoming Ethiopian coffee service, there's a negligible list of wines by the glass, an interesting Ethiopian honey wine, and a full, basic bar. Drinks are pretty cheap. All this *and* outdoor seating? Silver Spring, you lucky dogs! –FC

# Las Placitas

If you're in Capitol Hill, it's hard to do better for
Salvadoran, but go elsewhere for Mex

**7.0** *Food*  **7.8** *Feel*

## Mexican, Salvadoran

Casual restaurant

**$40** *Price*

www.lasplacitas.com

Mon–Thu 11am–3pm, 5pm–
10:30pm
Fri–Sat 11am–11pm
Sun 11am–10pm

**Bar** Beer, wine, liquor
**Credit cards** Visa, MC, AmEx
**Reservations** Accepted
Outdoor dining, veg-friendly

**Capitol Hill**
517 8th St. SE
(202) 543-3700

Some of the Southeast quadrant's best Salvadoran food is served in this
cozy little room, along with passable Mexican (thus the silly sombreros
and piñatas hanging around). But ask anyone punching out of a Capitol
Hill office on a Friday night: it's the margaritas that draw a crowd.

Let's begin, as should any proper meal of this persuasion, with a pitcher
on the rocks. Las Placitas makes a miraculous mix: full of tart lime, plenty
of tequila without too much bite, and a snowdrift of salt crystals on the
rims of the glasses. Even once the ice melts, this drink doesn't taste
diluted.

Much of the non-Salvadoran food at Las Placitas might be called Tex-
Mex-Este, a version of the real thing that *does* get diluted the farther it
gets from the border towns where the margarita is purported to have
been born. The most authentic aspect of the portions are their
presentation: generous and not very pretty. Fajitas are made with thickly
sliced cuts of steak, onions, and peppers, and the guacamole is pleasantly
chunky. Tacos get a gringo treatment with flour tortilla, rather than corn,
and pico de gallo. They taste pretty plain; substandard, when compared
to those found in a few stand-out places in Columbia Heights. Some
other specials flirt with Baja California, the Yucatán, and Monterrey. A
nod to the Southwest comes in the form of chimichangas. Even a Spanish
paella wanders on the set; the kitchen is overflowing with mariscos, so
why not? It's appropriately saffrony, but the seafood is hardly a revelation.

On the Salvadoran side (the menu is literally split), the typical specialties
are offered (plaintain, yuca, chicken, pupusas), most of which are
conveniently congregated in the El Típico plate and its vegetarian
counterpart. The meaty version includes a smattering of very juicy sweet
plantains, some rather dry yuca fries, an ordinary chicharrón-and-cheese-
stuffed pupusa (even ordinary, these are always good), and a so-so
chicken tamal.

To finish an entire main course at Las Placitas is a feat to be
remembered, and perhaps even regretted. The best deal here is to order a
sampling of Salvadoran antojitos, all under six bucks (some way under),
and most very good. –CK

# Lauriol Plaza

This crowded Mexican-American hotspot is the very definition of "overrated"

| 2.2 | 7.8 |
|---|---|
| Food | Feel |

## Mexican

Casual restaurant

**$35**
Price

www.lauriolplaza.com

Mon–Thu 11:30am–11pm
Fri–Sat 11:30am–midnight
Sun 11am–11pm

**Bar** Beer, wine, liquor
**Credit cards** Visa, MC, AmEx
**Reservations** Not accepted
Outdoor dining

**Adams Morgan**
1835 18th St. NW
(202) 387-0035

Lauriol Plaza looms at the southern gateway of the Adams Morgan enclave, and what a bizarre irony that is. In a neighborhood not far from Columbia Heights, the heart of DC's Latino community, *this* is the hot Mexican restaurant? This coldly functional Howard Roark behemoth that looks like it could house whatever cuisine is trendy at the moment? Overflowing past capacity on warm summer nights, and even brimming in the chilly depths of February, Lauriol's lobby resembles a hopping nightclub, or a zoo exhibit of horny coeds. The drink menu online reveals more about the clientele than their own Forever 21 haltertops ever could, simply by following up "Tequila Shots" with a near-ecstatic "!!"

When you've got two disgustingly sweet, soapy tasting margaritas in you from your hour's wait, a hike up three cavernous stories feels like a trudge up Temple of the Moon at Teotihuacan. Blame the throngs of people who insist on showing up, keeping the queue consistently long, all night, nearly every night. Once you get up there, the restaurant's roof deck is one of the best spots in town to enjoy summer breezes and catch a view of 18th Street antics.

But sexy, lively surroundings (and here's a stunner: no immediate competition) is all that Lauriol has going for it. The food, a composite of Tex-Mex, Southwestern, and Cal-Mex, isn't just the worse Mexican in town. It's probably the worst Mexican we've had in the country.

Oh, but in what quantities! You can stuff yourself on any number of combo platters or parrillas (glorious fajitas, served sizzling with accoutrements) full of barely edible meat and seafood. Mains come with oversized helpings of beans that are like big, brown, dry, tasteless clumps of, um, well, use your imagination. As you'd expect, Lauriol's "Burrito Gordo" is enormous, and almost too much for a single diner to consume alone—and it's plagued with the same crackly dryness that seems to pervade everything here. Enchiladas are rolled with crunchy tortilla stumps, their fillings dehydrated and bland.

So why on earth is Lauriol packed night after night? Is it the brain-numbing power of a pitcher of terrible frozen margaritas? Is it that, in a city of monuments, people subconsciously prefer tall, palatial structures?
–FC

# Lavandou

A lovable French bistro that sings a familiar tune, and hits every note

**8.0** Food  **7.9** Feel

## French

Upmarket restaurant  **$65** Price

www.lavandoudc.com

Sat–Mon 5pm–10pm
Tue–Fri 11:30am–10pm

**Bar** Beer, wine, liquor
**Credit cards** Visa, MC, AmEx
**Reservations** Accepted
Date-friendly

**Cleveland Park**
3321 Connecticut Ave.
NW
(202) 966-3002

People spend a lifetime looking for the perfect neighborhood joint—that little French or Italian bistro that they can call their own, the one where the servers know your name, your order, and your birthday; the one where the food is comforting, constant, and unpretentious.

Lavandou does a pretty good job of trying to be that place. Located in family-centric Cleveland Park, it avoids that dreaded DC after-work-crowd feel. The restaurant is typically populated by lovers warming up to their date night, groups of friends catching up, and the occasional odd couple grabbing a bite (including, on our last visit, an older gentleman and his much younger companion discussing how they were going to tell the man's daughter—older than said companion—about their relationship. Good luck with that one…)

The space is classic, with an open window looking out onto the street, wooden tables, and Provençal oranges, yellows, and purples. And although the décor can feel tired and clichéd at times, the atmosphere is mostly low-key and friendly. The service tries to be the same, although you've got to take the bitter with the sweet: the lack of hovering sometimes leads to excessive periods of time without a semblance of waitstaff.

When it comes to food, Lavandou hits the mark time and again. Other restaurants could learn a few things about salad by eating one here. Crisp, fresh baby greens and vibrant tomatoes might come lightly dressed in a sharp, correct vinaigrette. And the poster child of all French bistros—steak frites—proves to be quite wonderful as well. The fries taste homemade, if partly for their inconsistency: while a few wind up slightly soggy, most are fried to a golden crisp. Forego the traditional ketchup and dip them instead into the pool of the meat's rich red-wine-and-shallot sauce. The incredibly tender hanger steak boasts defined grill marks and an ideally red center. Although the generous portion may be difficult to finish, we doubt that your self-control will win this battle. As for dessert, the quintessential crème brûlée is as expected—no surprises here.

And that's the point of Lavandou. It's a nice feeling, at times, to know exactly what you're getting. Familiarity is perhaps the most powerful of all selling points in the restaurant business. –SDC

# Le Bon Café

A little more oh, so-so than ooh la la, but it'll do in a pinch

| 6.2 | 7.0 |
|---|---|
| Food | Feel |

## Baked goods, Sandwiches

Café **$20**
Price

www.splendidfare.com

Mon–Fri 7am–3:30pm
Sat 8am–2:30pm
Sun 8:30am–2:30pm

**Bar** None
**Credit cards** Visa, MC
Outdoor dining, veg-friendly, Wi-Fi

**Capitol Hill**
210 2nd St. SE
(202) 547-7200

Le Bon Café is a darling of the major travel guidebooks and websites, due (we'd surmise) to the fact that the café is the first place upon which a migrant travel writer is likely to stumble after making sure the Capitol and National Mall are still standing and gift-shop doors still open to tourists. Plus, the café and its cutesy décor—the walls are lined with Chat Noir posters and fake blue Parisian street signs, including one that reads "Au Bon Café"—might draw up on our traveler's nostalgia for more cosmopolitan assignments abroad.

Unfortunately, be it nostalgia or be it fatigue, the fawning reviewers have it wrong. Le Bon Café has some merits, but authenticity is not one of them. The café is a serviceable breakfast-and-lunch spot for Congressional staffers and sightseeing out-of-towners with more sense than to settle for the packaged fare at Starbucks, but there's little here beyond the standard amenities of an upscale sandwich shop.

The first reminder that you're not in Paris is the distressingly rapid turnover between when your order is placed and when your food arrives. You barely even have time to stuff your wallet back into your pocket before your lunch tray is slid across the counter. While panini are made on the spot, many sandwiches are created a few minutes in advance.

This turns out to benefit the tomato, mozzarella, and basil (with pesto) sandwich, because the ostentatiously thick layer of pesto has time to sink into the chewy ciabatta, with delectable results. The presence of both pesto and fresh basil is delicious overkill (would there be a better way to go than drowning in basil?), and most of the café's sandwiches feature the herb in one or both of its forms. The tomato, however, tends to be thin and mealy.

Steer clear of Le Bon's soups. A chicken-vegetable undertaking is mostly broth, with a few soppy green beans and chunks of meat lurking in the depths. The homemade granola, on the other hand, is sweet and moist, packed with golden raisins, if a little too much coconut.

If, after all that, you're still hungry, try Le Bon's treats, which are decidedly non-French. We wouldn't dare call them freedom cookies, but one bite of a cinnamony, buttery-thick oatmeal raisin will be enough to make you forget Paris. –CK

# Lebanese Taverna

An empire of carefully styled Middle Eastern
food—coming to a location near you

| 7.5 | 7.6 |
|-----|-----|
| Food | Feel |

## Middle Eastern

Casual restaurant

**$40**
Price

www.lebanesetaverna.com

Mon 11:30am–2:30pm,
5:30pm–10pm; Tue–Thu
11:30am–2:30pm, 5:30pm–
10:30pm; Fri 11:30am–2:30pm,
5:30pm–11pm; Sat noon–3pm,
5:30pm–11pm; Sun noon–9pm

**Bar** Beer, wine, liquor
**Credit cards** Visa, MC, AmEx
**Reservations** Accepted
Live music, outdoor dining,
veg-friendly, Wi-Fi

**Woodley Park**
2641 Connecticut Ave.
NW
(202) 265-8681

**Arlington, VA**
5900 Washington Blvd.
(703) 241-8681

**Bethesda, MD**
7141 Arlington Rd.
(301) 951-8681

**Additional locations**
and more features at
www.fearlesscritic.com

Oh, the mini-chain. It bears the twin burden of convincing patrons that
it's actually not a chain ("we're local!") and of making these same
patrons feel equally at home in each of its locations. Each restaurant, the
chain claims, is true to the brand, but each is unique.

There's nothing wrong with branching out, per se. If a concept takes
off in one neighborhood, why not try it out a few metro stops down the
line? The problem is that so many mini-chains are founded and expanded
on just that: a "concept." All too often, the idea (and creative décor,
lofted ceilings, quirky menu) trumps the cooking itself.

Such is the case with the Lebanese Taverna. It's hard to argue that any
of the chain's four large, airy, and immaculately decorated dining halls
resemble the cozy intimacy of a taverna, which is typically a family-run
establishment without the budget for embroidered pillows or cracked-
glass plates. On the other hand, there is a certain Disneyish charm, like
the Middle East as it would appear in a glossy American travel magazine.
Similarly, the food is vague (and Americanized) Middle Eastern, and
although the staff is for the most part of Lebanese origin, it would be
difficult to make the same case for the cuisine. Dolmade (grape leaves)
share menu space with kibbeh and a "seafood grill." We'd expect to be
hard-pressed to find an "open-faced chicken shwarma pizza," made with
mozzarella and garlic paste, outside of the mini-kingdom of Lebanese
Tavernas.

All of that said, the Tavernas don't make bad food; in fact, most of it is
pretty decent, if overpriced. All sauces and sides, especially hummus, are
perfectly oily. The mini-spinach pies are crunchy pearls of fried filo. The
shawarma is served in thin, subtle strips; for the indecisive, there's a lamb-
and-beef combination plate. And the meals are served with delightful
doughy triangles of bread, ideal for mopping up excess juices.

But the Tavernas don't make particularly interesting food, either. And
for the prices—the so-called "mezza" portions are unnervingly small for
$7-$10, and mains run as high as 20—it's not difficult to do much better.
–CK

# Leopold's Kafe

7.6 **Food**  9.3 **Feel**

Chic little eatery whose overpriced food is less
worthwhile than the sweets and drinks

## Austrian

Casual restaurant

**$40**
*Price*

www.kafeleopolds.com

Sun–Tue 8am–10pm
Wed–Thu 8am–11pm
Fri–Sat 8am–midnight

**Bar** Beer, wine, liquor
**Credit cards** Visa, MC, AmEx
**Reservations** Not accepted
Date-friendly, good wines,
kid-friendly, outdoor dining

**Georgetown**
3318 M St. NW
(202) 965-6005

Just off a Georgetown brick alley is this cute, popular, immaculate
hideaway which hardly bears resemblance to the stereotypical oompah-
meets-Alpine image of Austria, yet manages to duplicate almost exactly
what you might find these days at a chic, urban café in Vienna—or any
other Northern European capital, for that matter. Leopold's shuns
oompah-land theatrics for a slick orange-and-white color scheme, an
abundance of plate glass, and IKEA-like furnishings (even if spelling
"Café" with a "K" is as korny as it gets). Leopold's also, happily, feels
leagues removed from the bustle of M street.

The fare here travels along the Alps, from schnitzel to croque monsieur,
but it definitely hovers around Austria. At first, it seems like a novel and
refreshing place to dine, if for no other reason than we rarely see this
much German on a menu. That said, the prices are obscene.
Miesmuschlen—mussels in a buttery white wine sauce—cost nearly
twenty dollars for a small bowl, and you'll have to order fries separately.
Although schnitzel is a thick, tender cut of veal, properly pounded,
breaded, and fried (if undersalted), it's served with an "Austrian potato
salad" that seems to differ little from the one you'd find at the Greenville,
Iowa Fourth of July community picnic. The huhnersalat is billed as salad
plus chicken, but is really a hefty portion of chicken (though nicely
cooked) surrounded by some field greens.

Desserts and drinks are more interesting, especially the affocato—rich
vanilla ice cream to which you add a shot of hot espresso. Any number of
delectable pastries pair perfectly with the latte and chic ambiance. A list of
candy-store cocktails be damned, the classic martini is strong, chilly, and
quite good. There is also a good Austrian wine list, and some of the
waiters can offer a confident recommendation.

One thing is certain: that courtyard water fountain is great background
music to a beer—real, refreshing, bitter, wonderful Austrian beer, on
tap!—or two. –CK

# Li Ho

Some of Chinatown's best noodles, served in just the right tiny dump

**8.2** **3.0**
Food  Feel

**Chinese**                                    Casual restaurant    **$10**
Price

Daily 11am–1am

**Bar** None
**Credit cards** None
**Reservations** Accepted
Kid-friendly

**Chinatown**
501 H St. NW
(202) 289-2059

Like most excellent, authentic Asian restaurants, Li Ho looks like a hole. Crouched at the caboose of H Street, its storefront is absolutely tiny. On dingy walls, calendar girls from the mid-'90s vie for space with handwritten signs that make no sense. Metal troughs of dubious sterility hold your food; just about everything is stained to some degree. It looks and feels like the more permanent version of a street cart.

The kitchen, too, is magnificently sloppy. Some pots and pans are turned into makeshift steamers, and crates of eggs and sticky bottles of sauce perch above huge cast-iron woks over high flames. It's a kitchen where the chefs use one giant knife and a pair of chopsticks as their only tools. That's all they need.

Pork buns here are magnificent. Five plump, fluffy clouds of white are hot from the steamer and when torn, let out wisps of savory-sweet vapor. The dough's faint sweetness complements the lightly-spiced, tender pork encased inside. They taste like they could have been made in a grandmother's kitchen, and at just five dollars, they may very well be the best deal in the city. Singapore noodles are stir-fried by the bale with slivers of crunchy cabbage. They're glassy without being too oily, and gently-scented with yellow curry. Somehow, they're even better when heaped on vinyl plates from the dollar store. Make sure to order them freshly made, and not from the steam trays where they've been sitting for who-knows-how-long.

Some dishes at Li Ho are not as good as elsewhere. Though dumplings are filled with delightfully tender and flavorful pork and seafood, the skin is so thick it overpowers it. Barbecue spare ribs are all gristle and fat and not enough meat (hey, authenticity isn't always great – sometimes it's born of a poverty of availability, not popular delight). But you can hardly find better noodles in the area.

Definitely finish your meal here with a bubble tea. It's creamy and strongly flavored, with ideal, chewy pearls. It will cap off a superb meal at this brilliant little Chinatown underdog. –JC

# Liberty Tavern

A versatile neighborhood bar and restaurant that far outclasses its local competition

| 8.6 | 8.8 |
|-----|-----|
| Food | Feel |

## American

Casual restaurant

**$40**
Price

www.thelibertytavern.com

Mon 5pm–10pm; Tue–Thu
11:30am–2:30pm, 5pm–10pm;
Fri–Sat 11:30am–2:30pm,
5pm–11pm; Sun 10am–2pm,
5pm–9pm

**Bar** Beer, wine, liquor
**Credit cards** Visa, MC, AmEx
**Reservations** Accepted
Date-friendly, kid-friendly, outdoor
dining, Wi-Fi

**Arlington, VA**
3195 Wilson Blvd.
(703) 465-9360

With windows set far above eye level and a spare, brown-on-brown décor, the intended design effect is immediately understood: the focus here is meant to be strictly on the food. It's a fun, lively neighborhood place that seems equally content to be an after-work bar or a real restaurant. Above the kitchen, a panoramic shot of the kitchen staff adds a sentimental touch to the dining area, a sense that what you eat was made with care.

The menu at Liberty Tavern consists of regional, seasonal dishes, with a concerted effort at using smaller farms and ranches for the best possible taste. Breads are made in-house, as are pastas. But if sourcing the best ingredients is ninety percent of the work, the other ten is in not mucking it up. The capable chefs here display an unusual grasp of balancing textures and flavors within each dish. Pan-fried skate wing is unbelievably tender, with flaky flesh that falls apart with the gentlest nudge of your fork. A sort of beurre blanc is liberally kissed with hazelnuts and wedges of grapefruit, both lending the dish an arresting depth. Summer pizza emerges from a wood-burning oven with its properly crisp dough lightly charred and bubbling. Fresh figs and crisp ham set off tiny fireworks of crunch in your mouth, while sage and creamy Fontina mediate the bitterness of arugula. There have been complaints of oversalting (which seems to be an epidemic as chef's palates—like ours—build immunity to salt over time; anyone hiring tasters?)

The Tavern's crostata is a bold statement of what dessert should be. Its pastry purse cracks open like a pomegranate, revealing steaming, crimson cherry seeds that are rich and so hot that they taste almost savory. Goat-cheese ice cream is stalwartly tangy and smoky, and eating it is an act of poetry, from the lusty display of scarlet filling to the enjambment of savory-sweet. Nothing would pair better with this than a succint Tajlianich White Solero from the dessert wine list.

In an era of flashy restaurant "concepts," industrial meat, and genetically-mutated vegetables, it's refreshing—dare we say, critical—to have those few restaurants that are truly committed to the art of making food that slows you down, makes you close your eyes for a few chews…and *notice*. –JC

# Light House Tofu

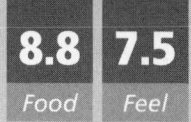

**8.8** | **7.5**
*Food* | *Feel*

The tofu, not the service, is the draw at this cute Korean restaurant

## Korean

Casual restaurant

**$15**
*Price*

Daily 10am–11pm
Hours vary by location

**Bar** None
**Credit cards** Visa, MC
**Reservations** Not accepted
Veg-friendly

**Annandale, VA**
4121 Chatelain Rd.
(703) 333-3436

**Rockville, MD**
12710 Twinbrook Pkwy.
(301) 881-1178

It's an unlikely beacon, this rather industrial-looking building of brick, whose windows are those tiered glass panels that crank outward, threatening to slide out of their worn aluminum sleeves and fall to the pavement below. Yet, there it is, lit up in sun-yellow Korean characters, "Light House Tofu & B.B.Q." Inside, every inch of wall is covered in artful Korean calligraphy. The seating is made from blond wood, giving off a warm, cozy vibe, and clay pots make appearances everywhere, often on tables.

The mostly Asian crowd is lively, and the draw? Tofu. Some of the best in the mid-Atlantic region. It's silky and amazing. Try it in the soon dubu, which everyone who's into Korean food pretty unanimously agrees is the best around. The broth is seafood-based, so if you add only seafood or mushrooms, it's pescatarian. If there is anything wrong with you—emotional, physical, or whatever—the soon dubu here will fix it. Accoutrements abound: there's the raw egg to crack into your stew; banchan dishes of various pickles; and a bowl of rice which, once emptied, is filled with hot water to create a pleasant broth for sipping.

As usual, the portions are generous, bordering on eternal. A nice touch is that your spice levels are entirely up to you—"white" means unspiced, and it goes in degrees to "spicy spicy." A simple "spicy" is great for amplifying flavors without tasting only pain. Seafood always tastes fresh here, unlike at some of the competition, and the pancake makes a great sharing snack. If you need gnarled, glistening meat, get it in the form of barbecue, which is quite good—though maybe not as good as Annan-Gol. But no one's got Light House beat on tofu.

Service ranges from curt to confrontational. But you know what? We love it. It lets us know they aren't trying to pull the wool over anyone's eyes: the food is the real deal. Nothing says lovin' to a food junkie like authentic dishes made fresh to order. Do junkies complain when their dealers don't speak English, offer them a beverage, or smile a lot? They'd better not. That's the fastest way to get shivved. –FC

# Lima

Not-fabulous Cuban fusion in a trying-too-hard-to-be-fabulous setting

**5.0** Food  **6.5** Feel

**Nuevo Latino, Cuban**  Upmarket restaurant  **$55** Price

www.limarestaurant.com

Mon–Thu 5:30pm–2am
Fri–Sat 5:30pm–3am

**Bar** Beer, wine, liquor
**Credit cards** Visa, MC, AmEx
**Reservations** Accepted
Outdoor dining

**Downtown**
1401 K St. NW
(202) 789-2800

Why are so many DC restaurants under the impression that you have to have a totally unique "concept"? That what the city really needs is fresh, new ideas, like fusing all seven continents, dining on a dance floor, or basing an entire menu on a peanut?

Who knows—although we hope not, maybe that's what customers really respond to. Lima is in this vein. The name does not refer to the Peruvian capital, contrary to first impressions; it refers to the Spanish word for "lime" (in some countries, anyway; in others, it's "limón"). As in, everything's painted in lime tones, and just about every dish has lime somewhere in it.

Granted, one could pick a worse ingredient upon which to build a restaurant, but the rest of the concept seems contrived, from the notoriously weak drinks to the giant lime green cushions on exhibit to the street to the red velvet rope holding back…well…nobody. At least there are options at your disposal: you can defer to the ultra-chic basement lounge for bottle service (maybe the biggest crock anyone's ever come up with; why should anyone pay $225 for Captain Morgan Rum?), or to a sleek, lime-toned dining area, where you enjoying your meal while being bathed in colorful lights and suffused in techno beats.

The food, like the concept, feels overzealous and empty. Often, whatever you've ordered arrives somehow morphed into something else. Tuna "ceviche" in soy and sesame is not a ceviche at all—it's a (competent) tartare. The fish is coarsely chopped and still thoroughly translucent, with no acidity to gently cook it. There's a similarly loose interpretation of a churrasco. While the flatiron steak and rice are far from spectacular, it's the chimichurri (or lack thereof) that really disappoints. Instead of fresh herbs in an oil base, it's a pureed and creamy thing. Squid is better, cooked through but still tender, and served in a cream sauce spiked with jalapeño. Empanadas are also a treat, their ground beef the consistency of chili, richly spiced, and encased in a flaky half-moon of pastry. On the other hand, they cost three times more than better versions elsewhere.

The emphasis here is clearly on the lounge, with food as an afterthought. Perhaps the best "concept" here is late-night dining, which happens Fridays and Saturdays until 2:30am. Party people and industry folk still need better options than Taco Bell. –FC

# Little Fountain Café

**5.6** | **9.5**
Food | Feel

A secret, intimate escape from the city streets—if only you could escape from the food

## New American

Upmarket restaurant

**$45**
Price

www.littlefountaincafe.com

Sun–Thu 6pm–10pm
Fri–Sat 6pm–10:30pm

**Bar** Beer, wine, liquor
**Credit cards** Visa, MC
**Reservations** Accepted
Date-friendly, outdoor dining,
veg-friendly

**Adams Morgan**
2339 18th St. NW
(202) 462-8100

One of the most romantic hideaways in Adams Morgan, this subterranean restaurant's got an atmosphere that's really got it going on. You descend into the basement of a cute little townhouse, and you enter a quiet space, in which you can basically stow away from the rest of existence. There's a little fountain, of course—you might want to ask for your money back if there weren't—and there's the priceless value of being underground. If you are looking for somewhere in Adams Morgan to meet your illicit lover, you've found your spot.

You might also want to stow away from this illicit, dated, haphazardly eclectic menu of (in their own words) "Modern International Cuisine," which seems to go further downhill every time we dine here. Or is it just staying the same while the rest of the city grows up?

Either way, not all of it's bad, but it's a minefield. Miniature crab cakes are fine, but steamed mussels underperform; they have a certain skunkiness, and they're underseasoned. Stay away from the vegetable wrap at all costs. And when will restaurants that are pretending to have serious kitchens stop serving boneless, skinless chicken breast on top of Caesar salad? Merely serving this dish sends a loud, clear anti-foodie message to anyone glancing at the menu.

One of our favorite dishes, on the other hand—and this menu changes over geological time, so we imagine it'll still be available for a while—is the marinated pork loin, although we miss the era when the pork was stuffed with shrimp and andouille sausage. These days, the flavors seem to be more muted than ever; now the pork just served with mashed potatoes and green beans. Cioppino is a stew of overcooked shellfish. And could it get any more boring than grilled beef filet with blue cheese butter, matchstick potatoes, and sautéed spinach?

The execution and ingredient quality are just not there to support such a simplistic menu.

Even their website has a food-porn closeup of overcooked meat. That's not so romantic. –FC

# Local 16

A hot proposition that looks good for a one-night stand, but leaves you full of regrets in the morning

**5.5** Food
**8.9** Feel

## American

Upmarket restaurant

**$40** Price

www.localsixteen.com

Sun–Thu 5:30pm–2am
Fri–Sat 5:30pm–3am

**Bar** Beer, wine, liquor
**Credit cards** Visa, MC, AmEx
**Reservations** Accepted
Date-friendly, outdoor dining,
Wi-Fi

**U Street**
1602 U St. NW
(202) 265-2828

No one associates Local 16 with food. It's best known for well-dressed crowds crammed together, cattle-car-like, on Friday and Saturday nights, jostling for a place at the bar and trying to find lost friends with an intensity and devotion akin to Moses parting the seas during the crossing. And it's no surprise. Local 16 looks and feels good. It's what would happen if the Pussy Cat Dolls decided to become interior designers and/or open a bar on U Street. Its red walls, rich textures, baroque fixtures, and dim lighting are positively and titillatingly burlesque.

For those inclined to early-bird specials and happy-hours-turned-dinners, Local 16 is an option. You can actually sit down at a table and enjoy the surroundings without too many interruptions. Like the restaurant, the food at Local 16 is also a tease, but not in a positive way. Menu items tantalize with their odd combinations and lush descriptions and then break your heart when you get to know them better.

The biggest offender in this vein is spinach-and-leek ravioli with mint yogurt and meat sauce. The combination, which evokes Afghan cuisine, is so audacious and new in this setting that it's hard not to order. When it arrives at your table all dressed up, with its gauzy dough bathed in luscious red sauce and draped with white swirls of yogurt, you'll believe, briefly, in love at first sight. When it hits your mouth, all illusions are shattered. The sexy, translucent dough is elastic and chewy, more summer roll than pasta. The meat sauce is capable—but when paired with tangy, acidic mint yogurt, it creates a constricting sensation in your throat. Combined with the can't-be-broken-down ravioli skin and the overcooked leeks, what results is a cloggy, choky feeling. This is love gone sour.

Some of the more mundane items are passable. Shrimp scampi is buttery, garlicky, and acidic. Though the shrimp are a bit overcooked, the dish tastes ripe and big, if only because of all the butter. Baby lamb chops are delightfully fatty and paired with a biting mustard sauce. Though they, too, are overcooked, their flavors are well balanced.

With all of its seductions of style and space, Local 16 is worth an ogle. You may want to stick to drinks, however, and to scoping out potential mates in the endless parade of people. Letting that intrepid spirit spread to your food ordering will probably just spoil the mood. –JC

# Logan Tavern

**3.8** *Food* | **7.7** *Feel*

Make your own Bloody Marys and people-watch—
just stay away from the food

## American

Casual restaurant **$35** *Price*

www.logantavern.com

Mon–Tue noon–10:30pm;
Wed–Thu noon–11pm; Fri
noon–midnight; Sat 11am–
11pm; Sun 11am–10:30pm

**Bar** Beer, wine, liquor
**Credit cards** Visa, MC, AmEx
**Reservations** Accepted
Delivery, outdoor dining

**Logan Circle**
1423 P St. NW
(202) 332-3710

Logan Tavern hardly resembles a tavern in the traditional sense. Yes, it has mostly wooden, distressed furniture, community tables and lanterns in place of wall sconces, but it's also light, airy, and upbeat, and (usually) friendly. It does draw an impressive and lively crowd of locals, perhaps owing to the severe lack of competition in the immediate area. Maybe it's the relaxed vibe. Maybe it's the long happy hour.

Whatever it is, it can't possibly be the food. The lunch and dinner menu reads like a hospital cafeteria line-up: turkey steak? Grilled salmon with rice? These look even worse printed in the restaurant's hokey font. It's an attempt at whimsy and innovation that falls short of the mark. Consider the open-faced Portobello-and-tofu burrito (listed under salads): it's a pile of wet, unseasoned mushroom chunks placed atop a giant flour tortilla, with iceberg lettuce coated in a watery, ill-conceived dressing. Perhaps it's only open-faced because you couldn't possibly wrap this soggy mess.

Pastas have come overcooked and bland, and burgers also come a couple of notches overcooked; only the fries are good. A wasabi-crusted meatloaf (we gave them Baywatch; they gave us wasabi—both have run their course) is sometimes soggy and sometimes dry; on the bright side, that means it's statistically bound to fall somewhere in between. Mashed potatoes taste like they've been hanging out a while.

Brunch is really what this place is best for, especially if you go at off-peak times and commandeer an umbrella-shaded outside table for a slow meal; the P-Street people-watching is superb. Service is pretty anonymous, bordering on neglectful. The usual wardrobe of brunch prevails here—Benedicts, omelettes, and French toast. The vegetables are diced small in omelettes, which can lessen their impact, but the crabmeat generally has a lovely texture.

A pretty solid, affordable wine list far outperforms the beer—isn't this a "tavern"? Where are the draught beers? But this is what Logan is really about: Make Your Own Bloody Mary. This is genius! Why is no one else doing this? An entire page of vodkas, spices, vegetables, and mixers? This might be enough to make even the most blah food a beautiful memory.
–CK

# Luna Grill & Diner

A nice outdoor patio can't make up for veggie-friendly food that isn't that good

**4.2** Food
**4.9** Feel

## American, Italian

Casual restaurant **$30** Price

www.lunagrillanddiner.com

Sun–Thu 8am–11pm
Fri–Sat 8am–midnight
Hours vary by location

**Bar** Beer, wine, liquor
**Credit cards** Visa, MC, AmEx
**Reservations** Not accepted
Delivery, kid-friendly, outdoor
dining, veg-friendly

**Dupont**
1301 Connecticut Ave. NW
(202) 835-2280

**Arlington, VA**
4024 28th St. S.
(703) 379-7173

With both blue-plate and "green-plate" specials—is there anything that's not trying to be "green" these days—Luna is a vegetarian-friendly diner that caters to a Dupont Circle lunch and brunch crowd. Its location, outdoor patio (which can be reached by walking through the kitchen), and reasonable prices—plus the ever-charming kitsch of solar-system murals—make it attractive to the neighborhood's young demographic. (Note that the Luna Grill in Arlington is under different ownership.) The waitstaff is as pleasant and mediocre as the food: they're chatty, attentive, and sometimes clueless.

Sandwiches dominate the extensive menu, but they're not even passable. A club sandwich, served on thicker-than-usual wheat bread, is stacked with sliced smoked turkey, limp bacon, crisp lettuce, and a slice of very unripe tomato (even in late August). Thick Yukon Gold potato fries are crisp on the outside and mashed-potatoey on the inside. If, instead, you make the unwise decision to opt for baked sweet potato, don't be alarmed when huge, oily wedges appear on your plate. That's definitely not the way to go.

But what is? Other typical diner items are similarly average. Watery tuna salad gets crunch from shards of chopped celery. For those seeking adventure, daily specials are always available here. Unfortunately, adventure is not without its risks. On our last visit, a burger wrap with spinach, feta, and what seemed to be canned black olives was up for grabs. The couple at the table next to ours ordered it and couldn't identify the burger meat even after eating half of the wrap. Beef? Pork? Lamb?

Nope. Veggie burger! This would have been a good detail to include on the specials menu. Desserts are outsourced, and the drink menu is appropriately tacky—kamikaze shots, Fat Bastard Shiraz, and "DC Tap Water" (vodka, peach schnapps, black raspberry, blue curaçao, and pineapple juice), to name a few. Cute, amusingly hippie-ish, and pleasantly kitschy though this place may be, its soulless menu and incompetent execution turn the rest into a mere footnote. –SDC

# L'Auberge Chez François

**6.0** *Food*  **9.6** *Feel*

The French country inn of your dreams—as long as your dreams don't include good food

## French

Upmarket restaurant   **$110** *Price*

www.laubergechezfrancois.com

Tue–Fri 11:30am–2pm, 5pm–9pm
Sat 4:30pm–9pm
Sun 1pm–7:30pm

**Bar** Beer, wine, liquor
**Credit cards** Visa, MC, AmEx
**Reservations** Accepted
Date-friendly, good wines, outdoor dining

**Great Falls, VA**
332 Springvale Rd.
(703) 759-3800

As out of an antiquated French honeymoon dream that was dreamt of a half-century ago, a country house appears from nowhere along a dark country road. You step inside, and you're met by a butler, who escorts you to a genteel table in a rambling Tudorish house. It's high-ceilinged and, in a way, formal—yet somehow, perhaps because of the buzz of waiters and cooing romantics, it's also cozy. It's certainly one of the most unique and memorable places to dine within a half-hour's drive from DC.

Unfortunately, the food at Chez François is a rude awakening—especially given the $100-plus wad you'll have to shell out per head. The menu is nominally Alsatian—so is the chef—and apart from a few specials, it doesn't change very often. This should be your first clue that this is not a top kitchen at work. At our last visit, we were pretty excited by a starter of warm asparagus on Virginia country ham with gruyère cheese, capers, and a quail egg, but the dish was utterly undistinguished—the spears were underseasoned, the cheese out of place. If you'd thrown together those ingredients at home, you could have done just as well.

Even more promising in print were veal kidneys, but their brown sauce of Madeira, sherry-wine vinegar, and Dijon mustard was sweet, aggressive, and gummy. Given that choucroute (a version of sauerkraut with various meats) is one of the typical dishes of Alsace, you'd think that "Choucroute Royale Garnie à l'Alsacienne," made with sausages, goose, duck, foie gras, and pork—would be a tour de force. Not so. Most of the meats come tough and overcooked, and although the cabbage has a good bite, there is no synthesis whatsoever. Nor has the preparation of Dover sole, overcooked and overwhelmed by asparagus and tomato, among other things, shown off any of the virtues of that most delicate of white-fleshed fishes. Desserts have been equally disappointing.

What this restaurant is really, really good at—like most highly successful restaurants in the world, save for a few that survive on excellence alone—is coddling its customers into a state of mind that convinces them that they must come back again. This is accomplished through a combination of serving enormous portions, fawning over guests, and connecting with people in whatever way possible. For instance, there's a drawing contest—you fill in the rest of the head of the great chef (or whoever it is), and if your drawing is the funniest (or, judging from past winners, displays the most artistic talent), you can win a free dinner.

It's yet another weapon in this restaurant's formidable public-relations arsenal. Too bad the kitchen doesn't seem to be part of the plan. –RG

# M. E. Swing

An old-time coffee shop where even busy
downtowners stop and smell the coffee

**Baked goods**                                          Café

www.swingscoffee.com

Mon–Fri 7am–6pm          **Bar** None                    **Foggy Bottom**
                         **Credit cards** Visa, MC, AmEx   1702 G St. NW
                         Outdoor dining, veg-friendly, Wi-Fi   (202) 628-7601

We know it's become popular to hate on Starbucks and other cookie-
cutter coffee franchises, but there really is something to the independent
coffeehouse. Coffeehouses are, after all, intricately tied to revolution,
places where the fringes of society met to exchange information. The
coffeehouse has always been a haven for free thought. So it's only natural
that a coffeehouse like Swing's just feels better.

True, the caffeine-deprived can fill up at about eight other spots in a
one-block radius of Swing's 17th and G locale, but the queue that during
the morning rush can stretch out the door attests to the fact that it offers
something beyond the daily caffeine fix. In fact, it embodies one of
Washington's favorite buzzwords: character.

Old photographs and antique coffee grinding equipment from the M.E.
Swing Company's 1916 roasting facility transform the bottom floor of an
otherwise nondescript concrete office building into something of a 20th-
century time portal. Long stainless-steel countertops, mahogany shelves
lined with coffee tins, and old Swing's advertisements all hearken back to
a time when patrons savored a 65-cent cup o' joe over good conversation
and a trusty newspaper. It's easy to imagine rubbing elbows with chain-
smoking White House reporters, clad in tweed suits and felt fedoras,
while seated at one of the dozen or so barstools—although the crowd
today includes a more eclectic mix of Executive Office staffers, World Bank
lawyers and economists, and the occasional DC tourist.

Swing's regular drip coffee is flavorful and strong, and the bold
espresso is stronger still. The wait for hand-blended drinks can be
daunting for those looking to dash to a meeting on time, but an order of
slightly sweet brewed iced coffee from a seemingly bottomless carafe
sends customers on their way within minutes with the perfect remedy for
DC's oppressive summer heat.

Food is more of an afterthought at Swing's. They offer the standard
assortment of breakfast pastries and muffins as well as pre-made
sandwiches and cookies for the afternoon crowd, but the so-so quality
makes clear that people don't come here for the food. It's all about taking
that moment to linger longer while soaking up Swing's old-time nostalgia,
something for which even DC's BlackBerry-obsessed population can make
time while enjoying that initial sip of coffee. –WS

# Madjet

It's not the best, as it claims to be, but don't dismiss it too quickly either

**6.8** Food  **6.2** Feel

## Ethiopian

Casual restaurant  **$23** Price

Daily 11:30am–midnight

**Bar** Beer, wine, liquor
**Credit cards** Visa, MC, AmEx
**Reservations** Accepted
Veg-friendly

**Shaw**
1102 U St. NW
(202) 265-1952

The menu at Madjet boldly declares: "The Best Ethiopian Food in The Nation." Impossible-to-prove claims are only savvy if they come just short of reality, but this U Street restaurant faces extensive (and convincing) competition in its own backyard. Suggestions of preeminence aside, the restaurant is a modest place: the food is good if not stand-out, and the quieter Madjet makes a fine back-up if your usual Ethiopian haunt is jam-packed on a Friday night.

Madjet boasts the standard U Street Ethiopian offerings: beef and lamb dishes such as tibs, gored gored, and the raw beef kitfo prepared in two different manners. There is also a mixed platter of vegetarian sides such as gomen, cabbage, and mashed lentils, the latter of which come three ways and are the best we've tasted in the neighborhood.

On the whole, the meat is somewhat under-spiced, but it's generally prepared well. Madjet's injera—the proverbial backbone and literal serving plate of an Ethiopian meal—is store-bought from a nearby grocer on 7th Street, and thus not as tangy or springy as that of some nearby restaurants.

Madjet offers the traditional sweet honey wine and two Ethiopian reds, as well as an array of beers, soda, and coffee drinks. There is a small bar with mixed drinks and a television tuned to American sports. While it's easy to take issue with Madjet's claim to "Best," the loyal clientele and soft-spoken owners make the menu's assertion seem more a homey invitation than a self-serving or aggressive accolade. –FC

# Mai Thai

A no-surprises, sweet-tooth Thai restaurant with fresh dishes in a warm, modern setting

**5.9** Food

**7.4** Feel

## Thai

Casual restaurant

**$35** Price

www.maithai.us

Mon–Thu 11:15am–10:30pm
Fri–Sat 11:15am–11pm
Sun 11:30am–10:30pm

**Bar** Beer, wine, liquor
**Credit cards** Visa, MC
**Reservations** Accepted
Delivery, kid-friendly, veg-friendly

**Dupont**
1200 19th St. NW
(202) 452-6870

**Alexandria Old Town**
6 King St.
(703) 548-0600

With two Mai Thai branches and two Thaiphoons in the greater DC area, this restaurant group is quickly turning into a Thai-food empire. They seem to have the hip-décor bit, at least, down to a science. The District's Mai Thai is beautiful, with light wood and granite and orange and green hues. Friezes adorn the walls, but very little natural light enters the restaurant, keeping it a bit oppressive during the day. At night, with the bar in action, it feels more like the sort of sleek Asian lounge that's been popping up all over America over the past few years.

Although that Asian-lounge look is often associated with mediocre food, the kitchen at Mai Thai benefits from high turnaround, which keeps ingredients—especially vegetables—fresh. Tom ka gai soup is hardly an authentic Thai version—it's missing the real heat, and slices of chicken breast are not so tender—but its sweetness isn't cloying, and it's brimming with mushrooms, lemongrass, scallions, cilantro, and kaffir lime leaves for a satisfying balance of flavors. We love the green papaya salad, an authentic and wonderfully summery addition to the menu that brings crunch, tang, and some heat (if not enough).

But while some preparations are clean and crisp, others taste muddled or too sweet. Red curry is hot and rich but oversweetened by pineapple chunks. Same story for a vegetable curry of green beans, carrots, red bell peppers, broccoli, and bamboo (the latter two veggies are really Chinese-American elements), which winds up too coconut-syrupy. Pad Thai, though, reins in the sugar, which is where many pad Thais fail; the tiny tofu cubes in the veggie version are tasteless and greasy, but the abundance of julienned vegetables provides flavor, texture, and freshness, making this one of the better versions out there, even if the recipe is fundamentally unbalanced (in Thailand, when the dish is seen—which is rarely—it's spicier, of course, and comes topped with an omelette, adding another much-needed textural dimension). For dessert, sticky rice and mango is as it should be: sweet and chewy with a bit of sourness and a savory element, too.

When will DC's Thai restaurants wake up and realize that the city is ready for real Thai food? –SDC

# Maine Avenue Fish Market

Maritime eye and tongue candy abound—but your
nose might not be happy

## Groceries, Seafood

Market

Daily 7am–9pm

**Bar** None
**Credit cards** Visa, MC, AmEx
Kid-friendly, outdoor dining

**Southwest DC**
1100 Maine Ave. SW
(202) 484-2722

You will smell the Maine Avenue Fish Market before you find it. In fact, you'll most likely get very lost. Perching out over the Potomac along the southwest waterfront is DC's Fisherman's Wharf, though a far homelier and less idyllic version than that association suggests. Grouped around a dilapidated parking lot are a series of wooden stalls, each hawking some combination of prepared and fresh seafood. Similar iterations of prepared food are available from several different vendors and focus on local ingredients: crab, oysters, and shrimp.

This is an entirely different experience than the meticulously prepared and carefully counted seafood you find at a restaurant: everything here is cooked by the vat and consumed by the bucket. Peel-and-eat shrimp are sold from metal troughs. They are barely cleaned, unevenly cooked, and carelessly loaded with salty-spicy Old Bay. $7 will buy enough to make you deliriously ill and wonderfully messy, fingers stained pink from the spice. Deviled crabs are displayed in military formation, balls of doughy crab cake nested in blushing half-shells.

Live crawfish scramble over each other in large tubs feistily trying to break free and hide under slabs of fish. Mountains of blue crabs joust in a mass of wooden crates, fisherman poking and prodding them to show buyers how lively they are. Buy them alive or have them boiled in industrial sized pots. Oysters, clams, and mussels (imported from Boston, but always in stock) run cheap.

Chesapeake Bay oysters are shucked by grizzled old sailors, unceremoniously dumped on a Styrofoam plate in a pool of murky water with dirt still encrusting their shells. Even the bravest may hesitate before using a plastic fork to dig out a piece of lukewarm meat that is much bigger than one swallow. Yet for those that come here again and again, that is precisely the point—you will find yourself returning to celebrate something unique and joyous: cooking that wallows in the ocean's bounteous (if occasionally dubious) juices.

It's no wonder that there is a sense of peace amongst those who dine here. Despite the lack of tables (eat standing or on any flat surface), drinks (soda vending machines in the parking lot), or functioning utensils, this is a place of repose—a place where families stop after church, workers come after their shifts, and fishermen dock to unload their catch at the end of a hard day. So take the trip, get horribly lost, and share a meal of the sea on a packing crate next to a group of strangers. Perhaps one of them will lend you the crab mallet they keep in their pocket. –JC

# The Majestic

**7.7** Food | **9.3** Feel

A cheeky, art-deco, haute-nostalgic Old Town sleekster

## New American

Upmarket restaurant

**$50** Price

www.majesticcafe.com

Mon–Thu 11:30am–2:30pm, 5:30pm–10pm; Fri–Sat 11:30am–2:30pm, 5:30pm–10:30pm; Sun 1pm–9pm

**Bar** Beer, wine, liquor
**Credit cards** Visa, MC, AmEx
**Reservations** Accepted
Date-friendly

**Alexandria Old Town**
911 King St.
(703) 837-9117

This isn't the best restaurant in Old Town, but for us, it's definitely the most fun. You wouldn't know it from the art-deco façade of the Majestic's landmark space, which has housed a restaurant (off and on) for three-quarters of a century.

The folks behind Restaurant Eve took over the place in 2007, and while the haute-nostalgic cuisine isn't exactly showstopping, it's ambitious, at least, and—more significantly—it's offered in one of the most finely crafted interior spaces in which to dine in all of Northern Virginia. The bar feels straight from the 1940s, and the narrow dining room beyond is warmly, dimly lit, with a stylish row of hanging lamps in the middle and an open kitchen beyond. The well-dressed bustle of the young Old Towners helps the fantasy come to life as well.

The most important thing of all is to start out with a serious cocktail, because this is a serious cocktail bar, with all the Prohibition throwbacks that have become so fashionable so quickly in the US in recent years. We've enjoyed the "Scoff Law," with Sazerac rye whiskey, lemon juice, vermouth, and a judicious splash of grenadine that doesn't overwhelm the drink. They crack the ice by hand here, which isn't just for show; it merges well with the sugar to elevate a mint julep to something greater.

Our favorites in the food lineup include a flawless version of fried green tomatoes, whose cornmeal crust attains its ideal level of crispness; the dish comes with a slightly sweet green tomato chutney and a celeriac rémoulade. Whole broiled sardines come in a baking dish with caramelized onions, capers, lemon, garlic, and breadcrumbs; they wind up a bit homier and busier than we would have liked, and the crumbs add unnecessary richness—the sardines might have done better simply grilled or in a basic pickled-onion prep.

Props for serving underrated chicken-liver pâté with toast points, though, and for the throwback plate of calves' liver with bacon and onions. We also appreciate the whole branzino, even if everyone and his mother is serving whole branzino these days; it comes out moist, although, like the sardines, slightly overwhelmed—in this case, by a slightly strange mix of olives and oranges.

Over the top, certainly—but, at least, an understandable homage to the Majestic's storied past—is the Sunday dinner, which converts the kitchen into your grandmother's. Although fried chicken is well executed and it's hard to argue with good collard greens, some of the recipes—baked ham, macaroni salad, pineapple upside-down cake—are broken from the start. But nostalgia goes a long way. –RG

# Makoto

An out-of-the-way but not undiscovered gem of a
Japanese restaurant

**9.4** **8.6**
Food   Feel

## Japanese

Upmarket restaurant   **$80**
Price

Tue–Sat noon–2pm, 6pm–
10pm
Sun 6pm–10pm

**Bar** Beer, wine
**Credit cards** Visa, MC, AmEx
**Reservations** Essential
Date-friendly

**Palisades**
4822 Macarthur Blvd. NW
(202) 298-6866

Believe the hype: like a secret little package that arrives by air mail from
Tokyo, this tiny chef-driven hideaway is making some of the best Japanese
food on the East Coast.

"Quirkily austere" would be one way to describe the bright, simple
environment that lurks behind a humble entrance and anteroom, in which
you are admonished if you don't take off your shoes and don slippers.
Another way, for some people—especially those who are princess-and-
the-peaish—would be "uncomfortable." Just a small handful of four-tops,
plus a row of (preferable) counter seats with a view of the action in the
kitchen and at the sushi bar, make up the entirety of this restaurant.

As such, even in an economic downturn, you've got to reserve weeks
ahead and battle it out with all the Japanese embassy people, the visiting
dignitaries, and of course the food tourists—suffice it to say that the place
has been, um, discovered. Perhaps that's what seems to make the staff
feel justified in condescending to diners that don't follow the dress/shoe-
removal/punctuality protocol exactly.

But the rejection of the customer-is-right philosophy is a good thing
when it comes to dining. Although some DC competitors (e.g. Sushi-Ko)
boast of offering omakase (leave-it-to-the-chef) dining, Makoto is the
closest thing in the area to the more formal, low-table Japanese set-menu
structure known as kaiseki. It's hard to predict what will show up in a
given day's meal, but soft-shell crab is almost always a part of it, and it's
superb, with an unusually coarse rice-cracker-based batter that imparts
more crunch than usual—and, thus, more contrast between the crust and
the silky squish within. Delicious, too, are cold green soba noodles; sweet,
plump eggplant; and an extraordinarily textured sorbet of lemon silky aloe
vera.

We don't quite get the tuna salad canapé or the avocado in miso sauce,
both of which make frequent appearances, and both of which come off
as pedestrian. But the vast majority of small courses are right on the
money, and an extraordinary amount of care is taken with the dashi-
based mushroom broth—in Japan, far from a perfunctory starter, soup is
often one of the centerpieces of a kaiseki meal.

People talk about the fact the Makoto is not really about the raw fish,
but that couldn't be further from the truth. Yes, the sushi and sashimi are
just some among many kaiseki courses, but in the DC area, they are
unsurpassed, from magnificent yellowtail and aji (Spanish mackerel) to
unusually rich ama ebi (sweet shrimp) to sexy, eggy uni (sea urchin).
Spring for the toro supplement; it will make your toes squirm with
delirious pleasure, and luckily, your shoes won't be in the way. –RG

# Malaysia Kopitiam

**7.1** Food  **4.7** Feel

Fairly legit Southeast Asian food just where you'd expect to find it: at a hole in the wall

## Malaysian

Casual restaurant  **$25** Price

www.malaysiakopitiam.com

Mon–Thu 11:30am–10pm
Fri–Sat 11:30am–11pm
Sun noon–10pm

**Bar** Beer, wine, liquor
**Credit cards** Visa, MC, AmEx
**Reservations** Accepted
Veg-friendly

**Dupont**
1827 M St. NW
(202) 833-6232

People are always looking for the quintessential ethnic food experience. Well here it is, right in the heart of Dupont Circle. The run-down décor isn't worth bashing—it's irrelevant. You don't come here for the vinyl booths or the Malaysian knickknacks. You come for the terrific food.

Go with a group of friends, preferably adventurous and open-minded ones. The menu here goes on and on and on, and once you think you're done reading through it, you flip it over…and there's more. It's a good thing that there's a charming picture binder to go along with the menu, each page of which contains a piece of Malaysian advice. For example: "If you have eaten too much hot food, to get rid of the sting in your mouth, turn your plate several times until the sting is gone." Sound advice. Or order a glass of milk.

Malaysian food is a melting pot of Singaporean and Straits cuisine, along with some Indonesian, Indian, and Chinese. Start with roti canai (a delicate pancake fried with indulgent ghee and served alongside a bowl of creamy chicken-and-potato curry). From the Indonesian side there's satay (slightly charred and smoky but still tender, served with an addictive peanut sauce). Then move on to bigger and heartier dishes. Hot, creamy chicken rendang is generously spiced with curry and coconut milk, while mee goreng, with noodles, bean sprouts, shrimp, tomato, and tofu, is spicy and tangy and sweet all at once. The expertly stir-fried kai lan— Chinese broccoli in oyster sauce—is crunchy and juicy, and accompanies the heavier curry dishes quite nicely, although it lacks the authentic spices and flavors of Malaysia. In general, we wish there were more fermented shrimp paste flavors in many of the dishes. One of the very few strikes against this place is a crispy squid salad that's desperately seeking squid.

For dessert, get the ABC shaved ice: red beans, corn, tapioca, peanuts, sugar and milk. It may look like a random assortment of leftovers served over ice, but its variety of textures, temperatures, and flavors make for an exciting and unpredictable ending to an authentic and undoubtedly enjoyable meal here. –SDC

# Mama Ayesha's

## 7.0 · 8.1
Food · Feel

After half a century, we surely respect Mama's cooking, but could you please pass the salt?

## Middle Eastern

Casual restaurant

### $40
Price

www.mamaayeshas.com

Sun–Thu noon–10pm
Fri–Sat noon–11pm

**Bar** Beer, wine, liquor
**Credit cards** Visa, MC, AmEx
**Reservations** Accepted
Delivery, outdoor dining

**Adams Morgan**
1967 Calvert St. NW
(202) 232-5431

The interior of Mama Ayesha's Calvert Café—the little Middle Eastern spot that has survived the hot and cold spells of DC's economic climate in one form or another for almost half a century—is cool in every sense imaginable. Most obviously, the powerfully air-conditioned restaurant provides a welcome refuge from the sweltering summer days of Washington; in the winter, the dark marble-like floors and airy dining hall retain the breeziness of the outdoors, even as the heating cuts its bite. The restaurant centers on a potted tree, with tiles, semi-private booths, brightly colored cloths, and waiters who seem to float through the dining area from the kitchen.

And despite its longtime location in one of the hottest areas in the city—in the middle of the 20-minute-walk corridor from the Woodley Park metro station to the popular bars of 18th Street—Mama Ayesha's keeps its cool in the colloquial sense as well, remaining aloof from the bustle of nearby nightlife. Still, the mural on the outer wall of Mama Ayesha's is enough to draw in more than a few curious (and hungry) diners, as well as loyal oldtimers who remember fondly the days when Mama Ayesha herself, who was once the private cook for the Syrian ambassador, ran the kitchen in the '60s.

With an egalitarian spirit that we much admire, Mama Ayesha's has sought to elevate dishes that are traditionally considered street foods. Much of what is served is beautifully, even immaculately, presented. Stuffed squash, for example, has the rich color of an overripe lemon, and is perfectly skinned and stuffed without scarring. The baked dish is a delight to look upon. But a shish kebab will forever be a shish kebab, however lovingly presented, and it happens that Mama's kebabs suffer from a woeful under-salting. The reason for this oversight may indeed be perverse: street vendors could be inclined to add salt in order to guarantee the raw meat's freshness and the proper reception of the final cooked product (effective salting can easily make up for the failure to add other spices). Mama Ayesha, by dint of a set location and reliable refrigeration, is not beholden to salt. Perhaps the restaurant is a little too cool for its own good.

The ground lamb inside the yellow jewel of a squash, then, tastes rather bland, and the vegetable flesh itself, without spices to bring out its flavor, is almost tasteless. Beauty may be skin-deep, and here, we wouldn't mind ugliness—if only the flavor cut to the core. –CK

# Mandalay

Burmese that doesn't quite do it all just right

**6.5** Food
**4.4** Feel

## Burmese

Casual restaurant

**$25** Price

www.mandalayrestaurantcafe.com

Mon–Thu 11:30am–2:30pm, 5pm–9:30pm; Fri–Sat 11:30am–2:30pm, 5pm–10pm; Sun noon–2:30pm, 5pm–9:30pm

**Bar** Beer, wine, liquor
**Credit cards** Visa, MC
**Reservations** Not accepted

**Silver Spring, MD**
930 Bonifant St.
(301) 585-0500

There aren't many US metro areas in which you can make a statement like "this is not the best Burmese restaurant around." But such is the beauty of greater DC. Mandalay's kitchen doesn't turn out dishes nearly as interesting as the ones coming out of Myanmar in Falls Church, but it's more accessible to the District, and its atmosphere is a bit nicer.

Still, that's not saying much. This is a big space with white walls and poor lighting, populated by a fairly depressing collection of institutional furniture that sits beneath office-building ceilings. Mandalay's staff is a healthy Burmese-Hispanic mix; it's pretty amusing to hear shouts of "ensalada numero siete!" and "la quería picante!" coming from the staff, but such are the delights of melting-pot Maryland.

A salad called baya gyaw thoke is studded with addictive bites of "gram fritters" made from yellow split peas—something like a less spiced falafel—but its charms are diminished by watery throwaway lettuce, underripe tomatoes, and a "Burmese dressing" that's far less exciting than it sounds, tasting merely of fish sauce and lacking acidity.

To add brightness, you should really add a few spoonfuls of balachaung (ngapi) gyaw, which packs a more legitimate punch, integrating dried shrimp, fermented shrimp paste (that's the "ngapi" part), crunchy fried onion and garlic, and chili. Why is this essential Burmese condiment hidden away in a section of the menu entitled "side entrées," with no explanation of how it's supposed to be used? Why should you have to pay an extra $4.95 to get a paltry plate of the stuff to sprinkle on your other dishes? And why doesn't the kitchen use enough ngapi base to begin with—which would better integrate that trademark Burmese fermented-shrimp flavor into your food, rather than forcing you to add it afterward in the form of the balachaung?

Among curries, one of the most challenging flavor profiles belongs to thayetyee hin, which derives a searing salty sourness from strips of pickled green mango. Unfortunately, the meats don't hold up their end of the bargain; tough pork chunks (wetthar), for instance, have the consistency of having been boiled, not simmered. Overcooking the proteins to dry toughness is a systematic problem in Mandalay's kitchen, although chicken is thankfully dark meat. If you choose wisely and avoid the boring Chinese-American-ish dishes that stud the menu (e.g. "sliced beef, broccoli, cauliflower, cabbage, and carrots sautéed with light brown sauce"), you can access a more interesting range of flavors here than you can at most local ethnic restaurants. Better yet, though, would be to wrap around the beltway to Falls Church. –RG

# Mandu

The nibbles are enjoyable enough—just not the spice—at this sweet little Korean sidewalk spot

**6.3** Food  **7.3** Feel

## Korean

Casual restaurant

**$40** Price

www.mandudc.com

Mon–Thu 11:30am–10pm
Fri–Sat 11:30am–11pm
Sun 11:30am–9pm

**Bar** Beer, wine, liquor
**Credit cards** Visa, MC, AmEx
**Reservations** Accepted
Outdoor dining, veg-friendly

**Dupont**
1805 18th St. NW
(202) 588-1540

Mandu—"little dumpling" in Korean—is housed in a cute-as-a-dumpling space just off of Dupont Circle on 18th Street, on the way toward Adams Morgan. The upstairs room feels airy yet intimate, the bright lighting helps preserve the feeling that you're in a Seoul cafeteria rather than a DC hotspot, and the sidewalk tables are as charming as any in the city, ideal spots for Parisian-style people-watching.

Although the cocktails are offensively trendy, Mandu's food menu is as unassuming as the décor. If it feels a little like home cooking, there's a good reason: Mama's in the kitchen. The bowl of bibimbap includes rice, vegetables, and meat, topped with an egg that continues to fry atop the steaming food as the dish arrives—although unfortunately, you have to pay extra for the traditional stone bowl. Clearly, Mandu's management has some background in market segmentation strategy.

The crown jewels of the restaurant's offerings are—not surprisingly, given the name of the place—its dumplings and other appetizers. The modeum jun are precious vegetables and meats fried in a batter that's tempura-like but more nuanced. Also good are the delicate goo jul mari (crêpes); the regular mandu are honest—homemade dough and fresh fillings—but uninteresting.

And unfortunately, in spite of all the homey cuteness, "uninteresting" is a word that describes a lot of what goes on here with the main courses, too. Barbecue dishes lack smokiness or deeply marinated flavor. And where is the heat in the supposedly "spicy" soon doobu (seafood and tofu soup)? Where is the searing sourness of the kimchi? Where is the excitement? Guess Mama's a softy. –CK

# Mar de Plata

This unassuming, old-school Spanish stand-by will charm your whiskers off

**7.4** Food  **8.6** Feel

## Spanish, Seafood

Casual restaurant  **$50** Price

Mon 4pm–11pm
Tue–Sun 11:30am–3pm, 4pm–11pm
Hours vary by location

**Dupont**
1827 Jefferson Pl.
(202) 293-2650

**Bar** Beer, wine, liquor
**Credit cards** Visa, MC, AmEx
**Reservations** Accepted
Date-friendly, Wi-Fi

**Logan Circle**
1410 14th St. NW
(202) 234-2679

Until you're standing inside, Mar de Plata is an enigma. The restaurant's website is oddly reticent, and in the DC restaurant buzz, the name doesn't surface often. It's a shame, because Mar de Plata is a cozy, sweet, family-owned pair of restaurants that are touchingly unpretentious yet professional enough to offer great service and consistent cooking. The interior is the Iberian equivalent of a family trattoria: romantically lit red brick, low ceilings, and close-set tables that reflect the tinkle of candlelight. Very old-school. And very Lady and the Tramp.

While there may not be a canine-loving chef or spaghetti kisses, there is excellent food and the kind of personal service that you get when the waiters are all intimately connected with the place and the food. It's clear that they've tasted everything and feel personal pride that you're here, which goes a long way.

The menu at Mar de Plata includes dressed-up versions of Spanish classics. In paella, grilled shrimp and scallops share a plate with slivered chorizo and rice deeply flavored with fish stock. The chorizo hits your mouth with that wonderful casing pop that delights sausage lovers everywhere. Croquetas seamlessly blend chicken, artichoke, and cheese in a magically smooth and thick texture. Patatas aren't as bravas as you'd like, but effortlessly transition from crunchy to melting in your mouth.

A particular highlight that you'd be hard pressed to find elsewhere is the dish of boquerones—lightly pickled white anchovies in a tangy, spicy vinegar. Mar de Plata's version is thinly slivered and served with a small salad of mixed greens. Get ready: the dense little fillets pack a serious flavor wallop; they are pungently and unapologetically fishy, acidic, salty-briny, and so powerful that their flavor carries you through half the bread-basket and a water refill. This is wonderfully rousing fare.

One odd note is the music—tracks alternate between that distinctive salsa beat and Hindi classics. It's an odd but endearing soundtrack to your meal. If ever you get the urge to kiss over a spool of spaghetti, may we suggest pickled anchovies as an alternative? It may be unorthodox, but the restaurant's version is a definite aphrodisiac. We've fallen in love with Mar de Plata, after all. –JC

# Marcel's

An old-school French restaurant is still the perfect place to be spoiled rotten

| 8.8 | 9.0 |
|------|------|
| Food | Feel |

## French

Upmarket restaurant  **$90** Price

www.marcelsdc.com

Mon–Thu 5:30pm–9:30pm
Fri–Sat 5:30pm–11pm
Sun 5:30pm–9pm

**Bar** Beer, wine, liquor
**Credit cards** Visa, MC, AmEx
**Reservations** Accepted
Date-friendly, good wines, live music, outdoor dining

**West End**
2401 Pennsylvania Ave. NW
(202) 296-1166

From the outside, Marcel's is unassuming. Even the dapper suits on the valets don't quite convey what this restaurant has to offer: an exquisite meal that, on a good night, is one of the finest in the city.

Some aspects of Marcel's are rather pretentious. Somewhere in the restaurant, a piano tinkers away at corny "romantic" songs in a maddeningly florid style—enough dramatic arpeggios and sweeping chords to put you off your dinner, if it weren't such a supremely lovely dinner. The waiter-to-patron ratio is uncomfortably high, and the atmosphere can be stodgy. Rich drapery, antique finishes, and patterned china highlight the air of finery.

But some restaurants earn their pretentions. Waiters know their food and wine, and will actually time your meal so you get on the shuttle in time for your show at the Kennedy Center. At Marcel's, diners pay by the number of courses, and can compose their meal any way they wish. (Yes, you *can* order four desserts.) No matter what you order, you can expect a fine and luxuriously robust meal. A properly-seared sea scallop is presented on a bed of lentils that are so deeply and profoundly flavored with smoky bacon that they almost taste like gravy. Who knew lentils could be so sexy? (Okay, we always kind of suspected something.)

Roast muscovy duck is served skin-on (hallelujah!) and has as much fat and tenderness as the animal is capable of yielding. Citrus sauces are often chosen by default for duck, and too often dominate the flavor mix, but this one is mild enough to merely highlight the flesh. An accompanying bed of spinach is daringly (and wonderfully) garlicky.

Desserts are florid and fanciful, and as visually pleasing as they are delicious. Dark, smoky chocolate sorbet has the feathery texture of frozen ganache, and leaves an aftertaste like that of a fine, smooth espresso. It is placed like a chess piece next to a slice of chocolate torte and orbited by ribbons of tuile and wafer. A bright pool of passion-fruit syrup studded by black teardrop-seeds adds an acid tang to everything it touches.

Certainly this grande dame isn't making the most innovative food in the city, and there aren't many elements of Marcel's that seem to be evolving with the times. On the other hand, these days, a meal focused entirely on the guest, rather than on the chef, is practically avant-garde. You have to be in the mood for Marcel's, but if you are, a little pampering goes a long, long way. –JC

# Mark's Duck House

Decent dim sum, dubious duck

| 6.4 | 5.0 |
|------|------|
| Food | Feel |

## Chinese

Casual restaurant

**$30**
Price

www.marksduckhouse.com

Sun–Thu 10am–11pm
Fri–Sat 10am–midnight

**Bar** Beer, wine
**Credit cards** Visa, MC
**Reservations** Accepted
Kid-friendly, Wi-Fi

**Falls Church, VA**
6184 Arlington Blvd.
(703) 532-2125

Deep in the heart of Falls Church, in a strip mall that is south of depressing, there is a restaurant called Mark's Duck House. Never mind if you've never met an Asian guy named Mark; the duck served at the duck house hangs in true Chinese style, complete with creepy neck-u-bend, and is ripe for the plucking. If you're there on the weekend, you'll see a flood of people streaming through the front door.

The restaurant is appropriately dowdy. A brown shingled exterior leads to a darkish interior that whispers of some fast-food past. By the front door, a glass case prominently displays a dozen garroted fowl and red-roasted ribs. The dining area is packed full of diners clinking dinnerware and voraciously devouring dumplings from little steamers.

Mark's Duck House needs to optimize its dim sum process. Like it or not, the chaos is distracting—carts roll by at such infrequent intervals that it would behoove you to order with your waitress. Sadly, the poor timing takes its toll on the food. Some dishes would be much better if they were only fresher.

Shumai reach the table as if at the end of a rather hard day—though the flavor is good, the dough has dried out. The same affliction has affected steamed pork dumplings. The moist, steamed rice dough has sometimes already begun to crinkle and harden. Fried chili shrimp are inconsistent, occasionally shirking their crucial chili duties.

Some dishes show little flashes of brilliance. Oblong packets of shrimp are briefly pan-fried after steaming so that a light, crispy, crust dances across the surface, and their filling is so loose and sweet it confuses your mouth. Turnip unlike many other versions, are crisp instead of mouth-cloggingly thick. And crispy pork makes an excellent à-la-carte order.

Ironically, one of the most disappointing things about the Duck House is the duck. While some pieces are rich, sweet, and crispy, others are soggy, dripping with oil, stringy, and bland.

As with many such restaurants, in the hands of the expert orderer, a meal at Mark's can be a great success (especially if you arrive early, before the dim sum has given up the ghost). But with plenty of top-notch Chinese in the area, you shouldn't have to trust your luck with a duck.
—JC

# Marrakesh

A seven-course Moroccan experience that's big
enough on drama to excuse kitchen slips

| 6.7 | 9.6 |
|-----|-----|
| Food | Feel |

## Moroccan

Upmarket restaurant

**$50**
Price

www.marrakesh.us

Daily 6pm–11pm

**Bar** Beer, wine, liquor
**Credit cards** None
**Reservations** Accepted
Date-friendly, live music,
veg-friendly

**Mt. Vernon Square**
617 New York Ave. NW
(202) 393-9393

Like many good things, Marrakesh is worth the hassle. Take the cash-only
policy, or the difficulty of actually finding the place, which is in an
unmarked building on a bleak street. The only identifying feature of
Marrakesh is a naked door equipped with a large metal knocker. You will
feel the deliciously secret pleasure of entering a speakeasy when it opens.
The dining area is closed off by heavy carpets. There are no walls and no
windows, just the lush quality of cushions and rugs, mysterious dim
lighting, and pipes, muskets, and metal reliefs on the wall. It feels
pleasantly far removed from the rest of DC. A hand-washing ceremony by
fez-capped waiters prepares diners for a seven-course feast.

The food, eaten with your hands, is often more drama than substance.
Despite the variety, flavors across the seven courses are fairly similar. Most
dishes use the same palate of spices, and many are overcooked. Whole
roast chicken with lemon and olives is lustfully fatty and salty but so soft
it's almost mush. Eggplant hasn't been treated for bitterness and is
stewed with its skin on. Drinks from a very limited list feature a dubiously
sweet house wine. A customer favorite is Bastilla, a puff-pastry chicken
pie dusted with powdered sugar and cinnamon. The mingling of the
sweetness of sugar, nuttiness of almonds and cinnamon, and rich
savoriness of egg and dark meat combine in a uniquely complex flavor.
The flaky pastry, crunchy nuts, and fluffy egg add a textural complexity to
the dish, and the visceral pleasure of breaking through the steaming
dough with your hands turns eating into a singed yet gleeful adventure.

At about halftime, the lights shut off for an admirably tasteful belly
dancer. Guests watch and eat in the dark, unable to decide between two
distractions. Hours after you start, waiters will bring you hot towels and
dessert: baskets of fruit and whole nuts (crackers included), baklava, and
sweet mint tea. The point is that a trip to Marrakesh is much more than
dinner. Though the food makes some mistakes and strange fees may be
tacked onto your bill, there is magic in the sheer extravagance of a meal
that is encouraged to last an entire evening. Even more than that, in a
windowless room on a bleak street, you are transported, if only for a
while, to a faraway place. –JC

# Marrakesh Palace

Not one of the better Marrakeshes in town

| 5.0 | 7.7 |
|---|---|
| Food | Feel |

## Moroccan

Upmarket restaurant

**$45**
Price

www.marrakeshpalace.com

Sun–Thu 11:30am–10:30pm
Fri–Sat 11:30am–11:30pm

**Bar** Beer, wine, liquor
**Credit cards** Visa, MC, AmEx
**Reservations** Accepted
Date-friendly, kid-friendly, outdoor
dining, veg-friendly, Wi-Fi

**Dupont**
2147 P St. NW
(202) 775-1882

Next to the gimmicky and seedy Marrakesh by the convention center, Dupont's Marrakesh Palace is downright tame. Don't be alarmed: the décor comprises hokey cushions and pointedly Moroccan paraphernalia, dim lighting and belly dancing. It's just that Dupont's Marrakesh is cleaned up and updated for that neighborhood's clientele. But along with the abject theatricality, Marrakesh Palace seems to have lost some of its excellence. Indeed, the classic, family-style dishes you see in many Moroccan restaurants are lost, leaving behind expensive food that is prettier, but less tasty, than what you could find elsewhere.

One shocking thing about Marrakesh Palace is how empty it often is. At times, it's so sparse that there are more waiters than diners; at those times, you'll be paid awkward amounts of attention. This might be because the food consistently underwhelms. Bastilla is encased in a thick shell of phyllo dough that's so dense at the bottom that it comes off like a fried wonton skin. Instead of that classic, made-for-sharing sweet-savory pie that can be pulled apart with the hands, it's a tiny, rock-like parcel.

It doesn't get much better as you work your way down the list. Stuffed peppers are texturally interesting but bland—rice and beef are barely seasoned. Slowly cooked eggplant is better, but strongly flavored couscous is substandard: a topping of chickpeas, dried raisins, and currants is much too sweet to reveal any of the tartness or complexity from the fruit. The pattern of one dominant spice overwhelming the dish continues with a chicken tagine that tastes more like salt than anything else. "Beef cigars" are, like taquitos, always pretty good (even when they're not)—but still, they're better elsewhere.

Be forewarned: parties of 4 or more are subjected to a prix-fixe menu whose minimum is $30 per person, but this can actually make ordering much easier on everyone. But a meal here will lead you to understand why the restaurant is so often empty: not all Marrakeshes are created equal. –JC

# Martin's Tavern

The closest thing to an actual tavern in DC might be one of the oldest

**6.4** **9.0**
*Food* *Feel*

## American

Casual restaurant **$35**
*Price*

www.martinstavern.com

Mon–Thu 11am–1:30am
Fri 11am–2:30am
Sat 9am–2:30am
Sun 8am–1:30am

**Bar** Beer, wine, liquor
**Credit cards** Visa, MC, AmEx
**Reservations** Accepted
Date-friendly, kid-friendly, outdoor dining

**Georgetown**
1264 Wisconsin Ave. NW
(202) 333-7370

Oh, if these walls could talk! For more than 70 years, Martin's Tavern has been serving Washington politicos, journalists, and neighborhood joes in its quintessential corner-pub atmosphere. Here, family pictures adorn the walls along the staircase (four generations of Martins have run the joint), plaid curtains keep out the sun, the TV always has the game on, and ample mugs of your standard brews are served to a Georgetown crowd beneath stuffed and mounted pheasants. Slip into a deep booth and you may see an engraved marker denoting that *this*—right where you just dribbled clam chowdah—is the spot where JFK proposed to Jackie.

The food is appropriate pub fare, with some of the modern trends from over the years that have stuck: buffalo burgers, grilled tuna, and so on. In one excellent dish, fat mushroom caps are stuffed with hunks of crabmeat and seasoned with Old Bay. Pieces of sweet, fluffy rye bread stuffed with nuts are a surprising touch. In the "Hot Brown," you get a skillet of toast, sliced turkey, tomato, and bacon drenched with Welsh rarebit sauce. It's lighter than you'd expect: the cheesy covering is mild and complex, made lithe, bitter, and fruity from the added ale. Pot roast, Salisbury steak, and crab cakes are also highly recommended. This isn't the kind of place that lists a daily oyster on the half shell—it's one kind and only one kind here: just Blue Points, the ostrean equivalent to Tiffany (coveted for the sake of being coveted, and just as often counterfeit—though these purport to be the real deal from Long Island's South Bay).

If, after all that cheese and cream sauce, you even *want* dessert, you'll be let down: they're generally overwrought and much too sweet. But what do you want from a place that has Pizza Hut-style stained fiberglass lamps?

Martin's might beg to be judged on different criteria than most restaurants. After all, it's a museum of DC history and it's the American diet; a place stuck in time that cheerfully allows for some change, but not enough to frighten off its ghosts. On some evening around Christmas, tucking into Welsh Rarebit and watching out the window as the snow falls, you can almost feel each of the previous Martins toasting you from that great tavern in the sky. –FC

# Marvelous Market

An overpriced, overhyped specialty grocer with good coffee and pastries

## Groceries, Baked goods

Market

www.marvelousmarket.com

Mon–Sat 7am–9pm
Sun 8am–9pm
Hours vary by location

**Bar** Beer, wine
**Credit cards** Visa, MC, AmEx
Delivery, good wines, outdoor
dining, veg-friendly, Wi-Fi

**Capitol Hill**
303 7th St. SE
(202) 544-7127

**Dupont**
1511 Connecticut Ave. NW
(202) 332-3690

**Downtown**
1800 K St. NW
(202) 828-0944

**Additional locations**
and more features at
www.fearlesscritic.com

This market—with a handful of locations in posh neighborhoods about the city—offers tantalizing eye candy to shoppers and onlookers alike. The Capitol Hill, Downtown, and Dupont locations are all built with large windows and tall shelves that maximize space for novelty granola, fresh juices, and other specialty baubles; the Georgetown location is somewhat more cavernous, but no less finely appointed.

First and foremost, we love the bakery. The chocolate chip cookies are thick, buttery and even a tad salty: they're a spectacular complement to a cold glass of milk or hot tea. Other baked goods follow delicious suit, and a couple of locations offer fantastic fresh fruit pies.

Marvelous Market also sells an array of pre-packaged sandwiches, which remain surprisingly moist. We're big fans of the private-label olive oils, which are sourced by the staff from a frantoio (olive-oil press) in Umbria, then sold in several versions: filtered, unfiltered, or infused with basil, garlic and pepper, porcini mushrooms, white truffle, or rosemary. The market also sources certain recognizable, but carefully chosen, outside brands.

As if all of this weren't enough, they offer a well-pulled espresso, and a seating area in which to sip it—and enjoy a good cake or cookie. All of the locations, except Dupont, feature outdoor café-style seating. Marvelous indeed. –FC

# Marvin

Where the Belgian and the Waffle get it on

**9.1** Food   **9.0** Feel

## Southern, Belgian

Upmarket restaurant   **$45** Price

www.marvindc.com

Mon–Thu 5:30pm–2am
Fri–Sat 5:30pm–3am
Sun 11am–2am

**Bar** Beer, wine, liquor
**Credit cards** Visa, MC, AmEx
**Reservations** Accepted
Date-friendly, live music, outdoor
dining

**U Street**
2007 14th St. NW
(202) 797-7171

At a certain point in his career, after failed marriages, hard drugs, and general chaos, Marvin Gaye found his way to the seaside town of Ostend, Belgium, to rebuild his life and generally detox. This brief period in Gaye's life forms the inspiration for the U Street restaurant and lounge that glows with the unlikely (but somehow immediately right) pairing of Belgian and soul. Old European standbys of dark carved wood, brocades, and gilt mirrors are paired with exposed bulbs, framed records, and a life-sized portrait of the man himself. Far from being contrived or kitschy, the effect is fresh, warm, and surprisingly natural.

Drinks at Marvin (both at the restaurant and upstairs at the lounge) fully reflect the Belgian obsession with beer. Here you'll find a huge selection, with each item on the menu described with loving and almost worshipful prose, and every waiter or bartender is eager to recommend a favorite. Service is friendly and knowledgeable but often slow. On busy nights it may feel like you've been forgotten, and the crush around the bar can be overwhelming, and the noise level deafening.

The menu at Marvin draws equally from Belgium and the American South. Both sides have their moments. Croquettes fall apart in your mouth, loose and bready on the outside, but thick with smooth, mild cheese on the inside. Mussels of all varieties are heaping and satisfying. One version, with bacon and leeks, tastes deep and bitter from its beer-based sauce yet keeps the briny, light flavor from the mussels. Frites are thick and golden, some of the best in the city, served with curry and wasabi-flavored mayonnaises.

Heading South, a huge fried chicken breast, bone in and thickly battered, rests atop a golden (not Belgian) waffle. The meat is salty and remarkably tender, and the juice from the chicken mingles wonderfully with warmed maple syrup and fluffy waffle dough. It's a sensational dish. A bed of collard greens is simply and well prepared. Another soulful prep features shrimp and some of the best cheesy grits we've had, spreading warmth across whatever table orders it. And did we mention one of the city's beefiest, juiciest, downright best burgers? Or the shockingly reasonable prices? How sweet it is.

While in Belgium, Gaye wrote his last great hit, Sexual Healing, and was restored himself. Two years later, Gaye left Belgium and never returned. Yet for those who need a little healing of their own, the memory of his time in Ostend lives on in U Street: and we'll raise a frosty glass to that, any day. –JC

# Matchbox

**7.6** Food   **8.0** Feel

Decent but overhyped pizza and sliders in a
buzzing space—not worth the long wait

## American, Pizza

Casual restaurant   **$35** Price

www.matchboxdc.com

Mon–Thu 11am–10:30pm
Fri–Sat 11am–1am
Sun 11am–10pm

**Bar** Beer, wine, liquor
**Credit cards** Visa, MC, AmEx
**Reservations** Accepted
Outdoor dining, veg-friendly

**Chinatown**
713 H St. NW
(202) 289-4441

Once home to little more than a cadre of sometimes legit, sometimes
crappy, often grungy Chinese restaurants, DC's Chinatown has more
recently been invaded by "destination" ethnic restaurants. Nowadays,
within a two-block radius, you can find variable-quality, invariably self-
promoting takes on Spanish, Greek, Mexican, Thai, Irish, and Burmese
cuisines.

At first, it seems like Matchbox—a casual but inordinately popular
restaurant with a simple American theme of pizzas, burgers, and such—is
the antithesis of these faux-ethnic hypefests. It comes off as something
more honest, more real, a breath of fresh air. The result is that waits on
weekends (and even some weekdays) can exceed an hour. But look closer,
and you'll find that Matchbox might just be the most overhyped kid on
the block.

The pizzas—which are cooked, with great pomp and circumstance, in a
legit-but-misused wood-burning brick oven that's in intentionally obvious
view of the bar—are okay, but they're really a class below those of the
top DC spots (2 Amys, for example). The problem is that the pies are piled
with excessive cheese, which really takes over; the crust seems to melt
away under this oily mess. Moreover, while most of the combinations
(such as the classic veggie or sausage and onion options) are solid, a few
choices are misguided. There's something funny about the prosciutto
white, which pairs kalamata olives and prosciutto with ricotta and
mozzarella. Although the meat is thinly sliced and fresh and the ricotta
has a sweet finish, the two never come together as they should.

Some of Matchbox's non-pizza offerings are considerably better. You
might try the rich burger sliders, which are served in sets of three, six, or
nine as an appetizer for the table. The patties are tasty little meat bites;
they're cooked a bit more than you'd like (ask for them "very rare"), but
they're served in some of the richest, most buttery little brioches we've
tasted. Alongside the burgers is a plate of delicate angel-hair strips of
deep fried onions.

Another excellent choice is the simple salad, which pairs dried cherries,
balsamic vinaigrette, pecorino romano, and parmesan crisps, all atop a big
bed of drop-dead-fresh greens. The salad is a bit preposterous (who came
up with "vintage pizza bistro"?), but it's worth the trouble. We wish we
could say the same for the overall concept—or for the notion of actually
*waiting an hour* to eat here. –FC

# Maté

If you've ever wanted to eat overhyped Latinasian creations on a dance floor...

**5.9** Food    **7.0** Feel

## Pan-Asian

Casual restaurant

**$45** Price

www.latinconcepts.com

Sun–Thu 5pm–1:15am
Fri–Sat 5pm–2:15am

**Bar** Beer, wine, liquor
**Credit cards** Visa, MC, AmEx
**Reservations** Accepted
Live music

**Georgetown**
3101 K St. NW
(202) 333-2006

Well, here we go again. Latinasian fusion sushi red-hot super trendy woo-hoo fun. If the red velvet rope unhooks for you, plop down in some Jetsons-era furniture, shout over the throbbing bass line from an elevated DJ booth/light show to your Spandexed waitress, and order your mango salsa tuna whatever. There's hardly a more befitting name for this than the energy-packed, social-event beverage mate (in Argentina and Uruguay, the mate heartland, people don't spell it with an accent. But whatever.)

One of many siblings in the Latin Concepts family (who doesn't love dining in a "concept" rather than a restaurant?), Maté fuses Asian and Latin cuisine in a loose interpretation of sushi—a pretty natural fit (more natural than other fusions, anyway) that more and more restaurant groups are exploiting. The results here can, at times, be a little more exciting than the ones you find at other like-minded "concepts." The "Tamalito" combines yellowtail, avocado, and plantains in a roll that uses corn masa instead of rice and daikon radish skin instead of nori. The texture of the masa is dense and fine-grained; its distinct flavor against the fish and spicy salsa delivers something entirely unexpected. The downside of using masa is that it's less accommodating than rice; in the (aggressively named) "K-31 Tropical Roll," salmon and mango are too mild to cut through the graininess. Sushi rice is dry and falls apart under pressure from chopsticks.

Aside from some palatable—even interesting—rolls, Maté whores it up with ingredients that go against nature in a way that even creative chefs can't reconcile. A starter of yellowtail with truffle oil is as overbearing as it sounds. The combination makes for an unpleasantly slimy texture, and the earthy flavor of the truffle is too much with the fish. Surf battles with turf, and neither wins!

The drink list is heavy on South American wines and some decent sakes. Cocktails enforce the stereotype that any place that aspires to trendiness must serve a panoply of fruit-flavored –tinis or –jitos. They are sweet and pretty weak—hummingbird nectar designed to attract hot girls who have yet to develop high standards.

In fact, Maté as a whole might make any food lover feel a lot like Steve Carrell in *The 40-Year-Old Virgin* as he tries to find lasting love in a horny, overeager world. This isn't food made with care and passion—it's food with extravagant tailfeathers, fluttering around like some egregious mating display. Are we really going to fall for it again? –FC

# Matuba

It's not good Japanese food, but there's a lot of it—and a conveyor belt to keep the kids busy

**5.5** *Food*  **5.5** *Feel*

## Japanese

Casual restaurant

**$20**
*Price*

www.matuba-sushi.com

Mon–Fri 11:30am–2pm,
5:30pm–10pm
Sat 5pm–10:30pm

**Bar** Beer, wine, liquor
**Credit cards** Visa, MC, AmEx
**Reservations** Accepted
Kid-friendly

**Arlington, VA**
2915 Columbia Pike
(703) 521-2811

Matuba falls squarely into the category of generic, dubious-quality Japanese-American restaurants that dot the DC suburbs. It's well known, though, so we felt it was worth reviewing, if just to break the bad news. The space is tucked into a narrow little storefront, with a dozen tables and a long sushi bar laid out like the cabin of a boat. Standard bamboo decorations and suburban diners add "local color" to the mom-and-pop atmosphere.

The menu at Matuba reads like every other watered-down Japanese menu: sushi combinations, teriyaki and tempura, a few noodle bowls. The food is watered down, too. Tempura is just fluffy enough, while the sushi rolls are not particularly creative but not particularly rank either. Noodles are filling and decently flavored but nothing to write home about. Even the appearance is lackluster. Iceberg lettuce looks like it's on the verge of wilting, and rolls seem weepy, small and sad. Fish benefits from a good dousing with strong wasabi and soy, but on its own, it suffers.

Indeed, eating here feels like a tacit prioritization of quantity over quality. While you may not rave about what ends up on your plate, no one can argue that there isn't a lot of it. Combo meals and extra additions dominate the menu, and for someone who is not particularly choosy about their cuisine but possessed of a mighty appetite, it is an impressive value.

And then there's the conveyor belt—a phenomenon that makes people who don't know any better clap their hands in delight. Who doesn't love a machine? But when you consider that the piece of sushi you just spotted has been going round and round for fifteen minutes, maybe half an hour, or longer, the amusement turns to horror. Sushi is a delicate art, a delicate combination of flavors and temperature and texture, meant to be eaten right away. Giant trays, boats and (worst of all) conveyor belts, do a great disservice to sushi. In certain high-volume Tokyo haunts where every piece of fish is grabbed in minutes, they have their place, but this is a cruel parody.

Ultimately, Matuba is one of those restaurants where America goes to experience its first, benign "Japanese" meal in all its teriyaki sweetness and wasabi-drowned novelty. If it serves as a gateway to finer things, it's hard to complain of its existence, but for those who lust after the precision of fine Japanese cooking, Matuba is not the place to go. –JC

# Max's Best Ice Cream

Retro without the chic, this might be DC's best ice cream

## Ice cream

Counter service

Sun–Thu noon–9pm
Fri–Sat noon–10pm

**Bar** None
**Credit cards** None
Date-friendly, kid-friendly,
veg-friendly

**Glover Park**
2416 Wisconsin Ave. NW
(202) 333-3111

Max's packs big flavor into unassuming plastic cups, which match the unassuming location, décor, and service of this gem of an ice cream shop. You'll often find Max himself behind the counter, waiting impatiently as you try to decide between the hazelnut and the chocolate chip. It's funny how gruffness is so much more palatable when the ice cream is this delicious.

From the outside, the Glover Park creamery looks like a relic of 1950s suburbia—Norman Rockwell on acid. Neon-tube contraptions, including an OPEN sign and a dripping ice cream cone, deck out the picture windows. The plastic spoons come in shades of bright pink and lime, and the cash register is analog. Just when you're expecting the kind of dairy-and-fake-fruit-syrup scoop served even at retro diners, however, Max's throws you for a loop: these are some of the cleanest, freshest tastes in town.

Vanilla, coffee, and other creamy flavors are deliciously rich, and the fruitier flavors possess an uncanny lightness. Blueberry sorbet, for example, is colored by the fruit itself, and tastes as if it's been made with fresh berries rather than the syrupy concentrate that's too often used.

Max's differs from a typical modern ice cream operation in other ways as well. Its selection is meager compared to the near-infinite medley available in many shops. A set of decorated wooden plaques pegged to a wooden board lists the flavors of the day, and the plaques are removed when the supply runs out.

Another thing you're unlikely to see within 100 miles of the eastern seaboard? No matter your age, Max's bubble gum ice cream is a treat. –CK

# Mayur Kabab House

## 7.2 | 6.7
### Food | Feel

A quality Indian-Pakistani purveyor that fills you up on one trip only

## Pakistani, Indian

Casual restaurant

## $20
### Price

www.mayurkababhouse.com

Mon–Wed 11am–10pm
Thu–Sat 11am–midnight

**Bar** None
**Credit cards** Visa, MC, AmEx
**Reservations** Not accepted
Delivery, live music, outdoor
dining, Wi-Fi

**Chinatown**
1108 K St. NW
(202) 637-9770

The Mayur Kabab House offers one of the best Indian lunch buffet deals in town. For around $7, you can feast on an assortment of meat and vegetarian specialties. The going price at the upscale buffets closer to downtown is nearly double that of Mayur Kabab, which sits on a patch of no-man's land just north of Metro Center (it's a not-so-hidden secret). And for an extra buck a pop, you can add a set of supersized samosas stuffed with textured potatoes, whole peas, cumin seed with tang and chile with bite. A sweet but sour tamarind sauce is a fitting companion, and helps soften the fried dough.

Perhaps the lower price here owes to the fact that Kabab House's buffet is governed by an unusually Draconian rule. Here, you can only go through once; no refills allowed. The do-it-yourself aspect of many modern buffets has also been dropped. Instead, one of the cooks scoops enormous portions of rice, meats, curries, and sides into a sectioned Styrofoam plate with the rough precision of an army mess hall manager. There are no written signs to denote the dishes, and the guy doesn't ask you what you want. You take what you get.

Which is fine with us, because, first, all-you-can-eat buffets practically force you into overeating, and second, most of what you get is good. On Mondays, Thursdays, and Fridays, Mayur serves its chicken kabab in enormous quantities; with this dish, exception is made to the "no seconds" rule, and you can stuff yourself silly with the tender, nicely charred meat. It's difficult to say the same for the chicken in some of the curries, which is often overcooked and underwhelming. We like a soup of brown lentils—lightly sweetened—and mung beans. The buffet sometimes features a lemony yellow cauliflower curry full of nicely herbed kofta dumplings. Steer clear of the "vegetarian snack," a breed of Indian nachos made with fried dough, chickpeas, potatoes, and onions, and topped with mint sauce, yogurt, and red paste. The buffet, even without return visits, will do you nicely.

At night, the bargain-seekers are replaced by a small smattering of dinnergoers, but prices remain eminently reasonable, and late weekend hours beckon night owls, too. Our biggest gripe: where's the authentic Pakistani food? The great korma, the haleem? DC is ready for the real deal! –CK

# McCormick & Schmick's

**7.0** Food  **7.5** Feel

Good late-night dining in this chain that gets some things just right

## Seafood

Upmarket restaurant

**$60** Price

www.mccormickandschmicks.com

Daily 11am–10pm
Hours vary by location

**Bar** Beer, wine, liquor
**Credit cards** Visa, MC, AmEx
**Reservations** Accepted
Outdoor dining

**Penn Quarter**
901 F St. NW
(202) 639-9330

**Farragut**
1625 K St. NW
(202) 861-2233

**Arlington, VA**
2010 Crystal Dr.
(703) 413-6400

**Additional locations**
and more features at
www.fearlesscritic.com

Even if you love to hate upscale chain restaurants, it's hard to hate this Pacific Northwesterner. For one thing, they honor their commitment to serve the freshest of fish.

This doesn't necessarily mean that the fish come from waters anywhere near here. But their provenance will be made quite clear to you on the menu. Preparations are generally thoughtful (but beware the stray Asian-style dishes). Your mother makes an unexpected appearance on the plate in the form of bitter asparagus and useless carrot slices, but your childhood ghosts will be exorcised, because she's powerless to make you eat them.

Another good reason not to hate McCormick & Schmick's is the happy-hour deal—and we actually prefer their pubby atmosphere to the more sedate, romantically lit, but generic main dining room. If you're drinking—not just from 3:30-7pm, but also during the Euro-Argentine dinner hours of 9-11pm (but only on certain nights)—they give away giant appetizer plates for two, three, or four bucks: fried calamari (oversalted and slightly rubbery, with subpar sauces), blackened ahi tips, seafood tostadas, and so on. There's a $1.95 cheeseburger. It's one of the cheapest dinners in town. Don't expect service, though—what's attentive in the dining room turns disastrous in the bar.

Yes, the whole thing is a bit contrived. To wit, from the company web site: "The bar at McCormick & Schmick's is ideal for pre-theater, post-museum libations or the perfect location to close a business deal." Would the company like to instruct us on our home mortgage as well?

Still, it's hard to argue with the commitment to seasonal raw oysters, which are right on the money. But then, in an effort to appease the lowest common denominator, the restaurant dilutes its quality by crowding the menu with too many losers: Asian short ribs? Spinach salad with basil Dijon dressing? Blackened chicken linguine with peppers and onions?

Sometimes, chains will be chains. –RG

# Meaza

A letter to our favorite NoVA Ethiopian

**8.6** Food  **8.0** Feel

## Ethiopian

Casual restaurant

**$20** Price

www.meazaethiopiancuisine.com

Daily 10am–2am

**Bar** Beer, wine, liquor
**Credit cards** Visa, MC, AmEx
**Reservations** Accepted
Live music, outdoor dining,
veg-friendly

**Falls Church, VA**
5700 Columbia Pike
(703) 820-2870

Dear Meaza Restaurant,

Excellent Ethiopian that *isn't* in a dump? You spoil us! In fact, you look downright pretty, though that may owe to the slightly uncomfortable absence of lighting in here. Who are you, Blanche DuBois? These are appropriately Southern sensibilities for Virginia, even if it is a little unsettling to eat great Ethiopian on nice furniture with painted walls (and those plaid chairs are decidedly Yankee). We still wish you'd insist on withholding forks from diners who resist the tradition of using your fantastic injera and their own fingers as utensils. Maybe the tablecloths make them nervous.

If this weren't enough, you have a wider variety of dishes, some of which we can't find even over in Shaw. Aren't you the little overachiever! We certainly can't get fish tibs in other places, and your kitfo is first-rate. Of course, your doro wat is a favorite of ours, as is lamb kikil, but that's like saying Meryl Streep is our favorite actress. Greens like collards and cabbage are cooked fresh, so their texture is really great. And for all this, your prices are about the same as anywhere else, and your portion sizes as generous.

It's right thoughtful of you to provide a full bar, though we prefer a simple beer with our alicha wot to a syrupy appletini. That, coupled with a circular two-tiered dining room and a bandstand that plays Friday through Sunday, gives us this '30s club feeling, as if gangsters and molls might be licking lentils off their fingers at the corner table. No wonder you're so crowded on weekends. Since you're being so ambitious and all, could you build a few more parking spaces?

We're also excited about your adjacent café and its free trade Ethiopian coffee, which you roast yourself. And you host poetry readings, film screenings and dances, in addition to a Sunday coffee ceremony? That's pretty cool. And a small food mart? Okay, now you're killing us. We've never felt like such slackers in all our lives. Really, who asked you to be so fabulous anyway? No one likes a show-off. (Can you get us in this weekend?)

Love, –FC

# Mediterranean Bakery

Superb Middle Eastern ingredients to take home—
but try their café first, for inspiration

## Middle Eastern, Groceries

Counter service

Mon–Sat 8am–8pm
Sun 9am–6pm

**Bar** None
**Credit cards** Visa, MC, AmEx
Kid-friendly, veg-friendly

**Alexandria, VA**
352 S. Pickett St.
(703) 751-0030

Mediterranean Bakery is a Middle Eastern food lover's paradise. It's easy to spend an afternoon here roaming the store and sampling the Lebanese delicacies that are cooked and served in the back. The store itself carries cheeses, olives of all colors, various kinds of za'atar, pastries, dried herbs, harissa, candies, rose- and orange-blossom water, grape leaves, yogurt, homemade pita, a dizzying array of olive oils, Indian spices, anchovies, tuna, soap, tobacco…the list goes on and on. Perhaps most enchanting is the fact that the owners and relatives of this family-owned business are always around, cooking, ready to help recommend a product or advise on the use of an ingredient, such that the unfamiliar quickly becomes the familiar.

Aside from the cornucopia of groceries, Mediterranean Bakery has a café in the back that is frequented by a diverse crowd of in-the-know foodies. Our favorite dish here is probably the menoushi, baked pita doused with tangy za'atar and fruity olive oil. Warm and earthy, it is truly wonderful (not to mention addictive). The spinach pizza is another treat: here, the pita is topped with cooked spinach, sumac, lemon juice, onions, olive oil, and cheese. Labne (thick yogurt), hummus, and baba ghanoush are all authentic and homemade accompaniments to the pita bread and the few meat sandwiches.

Everything here is simple, homey, and comforting. Even a chicken-breast sandwich—often such a throwaway—is flavored with olive oil, garlic, and lemon juice. Other Lebanese classics abound, such as lehm bi-ajeen, tangy ground beef atop—you guessed it—pita. But no meal is complete here without a pastry (we recommend the katayef, maamoul, and knafeh) and an impeccable Turkish coffee. –SDC

# Meiwah

A Chinese-American status symbol whose kitchen seems secondary to its clientele

**4.5** *Food*  **8.0** *Feel*

## Chinese, Japanese

Casual restaurant

**$45** *Price*

www.meiwahrestaurant.com

Mon–Thu 11:30am–10:30pm
Fri 11:30am–11pm
Sat noon–11pm
Sun noon–10:30pm

**Bar** Beer, wine, liquor
**Credit cards** Visa, MC, AmEx
**Reservations** Accepted
Delivery, Wi-Fi

**West End**
1200 New Hampshire Ave.
NW
(202) 833-2888

**Chevy Chase, MD**
4457 Willard Ave.
(301) 652-9882

Behold, the grand double-decker temple of Chinese-American food, with giant portions on enormous plates at stratospheric prices.

The lengthy food menu is rivaled only by the longer celebrity guest collage of photographs and names by the restaurant's door. Pity the poor senator from the lonely plains state who has not sampled Meiwah's bounty! Woe to the lobbyist who has failed to treat his charge to lunch! The wall boasts athletes and movie stars, prime ministers and presidents. The restaurant's webpage fills six full pages with photos of famous guests, each posing beside the suited-up and smiling owner.

This trumped-up red-carpet attitude is further punctuated by a hysterical, shrieking drink menu—a cardboard sheet the size of a coffee-table book depicting a dozen radioactively-colored drinks. Photos of Mai Tais and Sex on the Beaches beam in psychedelic pinks and greens and blues, each topped with a mini cocktail umbrella. Luckily, Meiwah has a decent selection of beers.

If only Meiwah paid as much attention to making excellent food as they do to whomever is ordering it. The dishes are just careless heaps of industrial ingredients, the chunks of meat and vegetables cut too thick. The seasonal menu's chicken-and-asparagus stir-fry is overcooked; the bird is so tough that you must tear it apart with your teeth. Enormous shrimp (are these from Woody Allen's *Sleeper*?) come with cashews, doused in a sticky sauce: the result is hardly palatable. The ongoing success of Meiwah supports the theory that most diners will eat anything drenched in sweet, garlicky, salty sauce.

Sushi here is a compulsory afterthought. Cheap nigiri and rolls with cream cheese and mayonnaise fall just short of your garden-variety dive locale. An unspecified "white fish" nigiri doesn't inspire confidence.

Service here is indeed part of the show, accommodating and generous. Food is happily returned to the kitchen for tweaking, and the owner frequently buzzes around the dining room, welcoming even obscure guests. Meiwah partakes of all kinds of superlatives: big, bright, bold. None of these necessarily mean it's great. If you want celebrities, go to the movies; if you're looking for great Chinese-American standards, try your local take-out place. –CK

# Mendocino Grille

New World wines and fancy-sounding dishes at
high prices

| 7.6 | 8.8 |
|-----|-----|
| Food | Feel |

## New American

Wine bar **$60**

Price

www.mendocinodc.com

Sun–Thu 5:30pm–10pm
Fri–Sat 5:30pm–11pm

**Bar** Beer, wine, liquor
**Credit cards** Visa, MC, AmEx
**Reservations** Accepted
Date-friendly, outdoor dining

**Georgetown**
2917 M St. NW
(202) 333-2912

Somehow or other, this cozy, stone-walled cellar in Georgetown seems to have wormed its way onto a lot of people's top-tier upmarket restaurant lists. Although the space is lovely, we're not quite sure how this happened—although we have seen reports of more interesting menus a few years back (apparently featuring whole roasted fish and such). The New American preparations here are clean and competent, but they're often underseasoned, and they're almost always overpriced.

The room is the real attraction; it's a great place to come drink wine, with bottles lining strategic patches of wall and a jovial buzz generally carrying around the whole space, even on weekdays. Unfortunately, the bar tends to keep a few of the wines corked too long—a common wine-bar foul, but one you don't expect at this price point. The wine list is limited to California; it's adventurous within that state, and markups are reasonable. Certainly not the restaurant's fault, but its cross to bear, you might say, is the fact that so many California wines are overpriced. There are some decent values in the Pacific Northwest, particularly in the Columbia and Willamette Valleys, but it would be nice to see even just one accessibly priced wine from an older vintage on the reserve list. Restaurants that are trying to be serious about wine should really consider buying more older bottles at auction—particularly affordable older bottles.

Many come here just for wine and a cheese plate, but the dinner menu is ambitious. Yellowtail carpaccio is fresh and lovely, with some ingredients well matched (sweet cherry tomatoes, aromatic basil), others less well matched (watery cucumber balls, cantaloupe), and some a bit shocking (an intensely sweet dressing). At $14 for four or five bites of fish, there's some sticker shock there. Among recent rotating mains has been a sort of riff on the Portuguese carne de porco à alentejana, a dish of cubed pork, clams, and potatoes. Here, the pork is tough, deeply flavored chorizo; the clams are chewy; the potatoes are good and rich; the broth is bitter; a bed of greens is totally bland; and a fillet of halibut sits proudly on top of it all, moist but practically unseasoned—a competent dish that should be much better at the $28 price point. It's a steep price to pay for stone walls. –RG

# Meskerem

Yesterday's Ethiopian darling has been way outclassed

| 7.5 | 8.5 |
|-----|-----|
| Food | Feel |

## Ethiopian

Casual restaurant

**$25**
Price

www.meskeremonline.com

Mon–Thu 11am–midnight
Fri–Sun 11am–2am

**Bar** Beer, wine, liquor
**Credit cards** Visa, MC, AmEx
**Reservations** Accepted
Date-friendly, kid-friendly,
veg-friendly

**Adams Morgan**
2434 18th St. NW
(202) 462-4100

For a while, Meskerem was the clear favorite of DC's extensive Ethiopian dining scene. This was due, partly, to its prime location on 18th Street in Adams Morgan, well placed for many visitors. The restaurant accommodates three tiers of diners, including a steep loft latticed by woodwork. Low leather poufs decorated with geometric patterns cluster around low wood tables and reed baskets. The interior is graced by bright yellows and sky blues, and musical instruments hang in pairs and trios on the wall. Statuesque waitresses in elegant, floor-length dresses move, nymph-like, between diners.

We have a deep fondness for Meskerem, particularly because of its role in introducing wider DC to Ethiopian food: this is where many DCers wielded their first scrap of injera. But we have to say that the food could generally be much spicier and livelier. While Meskerem's cooking may be honest, it's a bit boring. Flavors are one-dimensional, and even thick sauces can't cover the fact that most of the meat is poorly cooked.

A mixed messob platter allows you to taste everything, sopped up by mounds of yeasty, elastic, spongy-sour bread; it's a nice, user-friendly treat to get an all-in-one option. The injera's sourness adds an extra dimension to the somewhat boring food. It goes particularly well with a dish of mustardy lentils that are a ray of bright flavor in the otherwise dark platter. Beef comes doused in a deep, smoky sauce that is better than the meat itself. Lamb is stewed with carrots and potatoes and cooked until it has completely dried out and lost all tenderness. A hard-boiled egg, which generally anchors a doro wat chicken stew, here marks the bull's eye of the platter. It is a worthy centerpiece; lightly scented by the sauces and cooked until the yolk has taken on a distinct flavor, it is reminiscent of Chinese tea-eggs.

Other highlights on the menu include a mustardy, acidic potato salad that is graced with hints of citrus and crunchy green chilies. It is light and zingy, and unlike its American cousin, you could eat an entire bowl of this stuff without feeling sick. Fried pastries present an Ethiopian take on the spring roll, down to the same crispy, oily texture and fatty filling. A vegetarian version, filled with just-pulpy lentils, is dense and starchy.

Pleasant as the setting is, it is hard to avoid the thought that there are now far better Ethiopian destinations in DC. They may owe a debt of gratitude to Meskerem. But while this once represented the hot new wave of ethnic cuisine in the city, the city has now left it behind. –JC

# Mia's Pizza

Top-notch pizza up in Bethesda

**7.7** Food

**7.4** Feel

## Italian, Pizza

Casual restaurant

**$25** Price

www.miaspizzasbethesda.com

Tue–Thu 11:30am–9:30pm
Fri–Sat 11:30am–10:30pm
Sun 11:30am–9pm

**Bar** Beer, wine
**Credit cards** Visa, MC, AmEx
**Reservations** Not accepted
Kid-friendly, outdoor dining,
veg-friendly, Wi-Fi

**Bethesda, MD**
4926 Cordell Ave.
(301) 718-6427

There's no shortage of pizza egos in DC. And we're not talking about the egos of the proprietors—we're talking about the egos of the patrons. This is a city where one's favorite spot for a pie is a defining characteristic that's worn with pride. You've got your 2 Amys camp (which is where you'll find us), whose followers are rivaled in number by those of the Pizzeria Paradiso persuasion. Then there's a whole class of what we'll call "Jumbo Slicers," but they can't be trusted; they're usually a few too many drinks into the evening.

But tucked away up in Bethesda, on the hip strip that is Cordell Ave., sits Mia's Pizza, which deserves its own following. And clearly it does have one among the locals. Come on a warm summer night, and you'll be hard-pressed to get a seat on the idyllic patio. (The least appealing part of the patio is the noise from the rambunctious crowd across the way at Caddy's, but it's easy enough to tune out.) Inside, the space is fresh and new with bright colors and clean lines. The clientele is a fun, appropriately suburban mix of dates (both young and old), chatty groups of friends, and families with kiddos in tow.

And they're all eating some pretty good pizza. Mia's margherita (our standard test for pies—it's classic, and there's nothing to hide behind) gets our seal of approval. Thankfully, this is one of the few pizza kitchens in town to know that "margherita" doesn't mean "white pizza with fresh tomatoes," but rather a sauced red pie. Mia's tomato sauce is sweet, but not overly so; the cheese is melted, but not stringy or too oozy; and the crust is nicely seared, but still with a bit of puff to it.

The beer selection is decent, and let's face it—beer is pizza's soulmate more than wine will ever be. (Call us snarky Italophiles, but you'll never see Italians having wine with pizza.) We'll even have a Coca-Cola with our pie before wine. How's that for reverse snobbery? –AH

# Mie N Yu

Throwing two cuisines in a blender doesn't always yield such loveable results

**4.8** *Food*  **8.0** *Feel*

## Pan-Asian

Upmarket restaurant

**$55** *Price*

www.mienyu.com

Mon–Thu 5pm–11pm; Fri–Sat
11am–3:45pm, 4pm–midnight;
Sun 11:30am–3:45pm, 4pm–
midnight

**Bar** Beer, wine, liquor
**Credit cards** Visa, MC, AmEx
**Reservations** Accepted
Date-friendly

**Georgetown**
3125 M St. NW
(202) 333-6122

By night, Mie N Yu feels seductive and exotic, with sinuous sitar melodies and pulsing techno beats threading their way through silken cloth hangings and scented wood. Glints of gold echo off statues of fat smiling buddhas, and exquisitely posed bodisattvas on their way to after-hours enlightenment. But by day, Mie N Yu looks defeated—the way a theater set or brothel would look in full daylight—with the colors too harsh. When the sun comes up, what once was polished and glamorous now looks fetishistic and vaguely insulting: it all somehow awakens a vague post-colonial angst.

The food at Mie N Yu is both intriguing and disappointing. Western preparations mix alluringly with Asian accents, but the results are often a bit trite. Take, for example, the "creative sushi" that includes a BLT maki. The rice is overcooked and cruelly mushed together, and the neat package of bacon (a pleasantly thick strip), layers of lettuce and tomato, and a slab of tofu bound by nori obi begs to be taken apart and eaten separately (perhaps ditching the rice in favor of a good wedge of sourdough with some spicy mustard and mayo). None of the flavors are made any better because they're together, and it feels like the food is exotic just to say it is.

Brunch specials (in a wonderful prix-fixe bargain that includes a champagne cocktail) fare somewhat better. Mango pancakes are pretty standard, with only a tiny sprinkling of the fruit, but a rich, sour pomegranate syrup makes up for it. Tempura fried apples, once again, are interesting in concept but mushy and soggy in practice. For those who can stomach it in the early hours, red curry mussels are a wonderful take on a lighter, more subtle spice. They are smoky and salty, with a sweet coconut flavor and a spicy little finish, a lovely combination of light and heavy.

Drinks are generally well executed. A green-tea lassi is thick and scented with cardamom, just a tiny bit salty, and more authentic than you would expect, given the Starbucks-style fusion of its concept. Bloody Marys incorporate beef bouillon with wasabi in a combination that is far manlier than most of its cousins.

Ultimately, Mie N Yu is more expensive than it's worth; Western-Asian romances are old news, and no matter how many ingredients you set up with each other, you cannot guarantee that they'll be happy together in the morning. –JC

# Minibar

Washington, DC's bold entry into the new culinary millennium

**9.5** Food  **8.9** Feel

## New American

Upmarket restaurant  **$160** Price

www.cafeatlantico.com

Tue–Sat 6pm–8:30pm

**Bar** Beer, wine, liquor
**Credit cards** Visa, MC, AmEx
**Reservations** Essential
Date-friendly, good wines

**Penn Quarter**
405 8th St. NW
(202) 393-0812

When, to get a reservation, customers are required to call exactly one month before the date of their seating—sometime between 10:00am and 10:02am—for the privilege of paying, all told, about $200 per head for a meal that's eaten at a counter, the meal had better be really, really good.

So here are the three big questions: (1) Could Minibar, José Andrés's six-seat flagship hidden within Café Atlántico, really be good enough to justify the pomp and perseverance? (2) Isn't Ferrán Adriá's school of so-called "molecular gastronomy"—after which Minibar is modeled—just a dying fad, anyway? (3) Even when we're handed about 30 bite-sized courses in two hours, can we possibly justify paying such prices?

Our answers: (1) yes, it could; (2) yes, but who cares; and (3) yes we can!

What's really impressive here is the sensory experience often outshines the sci-fi pyrotechnics. A lot of the dishes rotate, but some consistent mainstays include the "olive oil bon-bon," a teardrop-shaped, salt-flecked, paper-thin hard candy shell containing a teaspoonful of grassy Spanish olive oil that's meant to be eaten in one bite. "Cotton candy eel" is surrounded in a halo of airy spun-sugar candy and wrapped in nori like a hand roll; it's a sweet-savory match for the ages.

Even when the gimmick overshadows the taste, at least the gimmick is good. In "dragon's breath popcorn," for instance, you're instructed to blow out through your nostrils after popping the dry-ice-bathed kernels, turning your mouth into a smoke machine.

It's that sort of unique culinary moment that makes Minibar not just fun, but actually worth the money. And the setting is better than sitting in a sushi-bar-ish counter might suggest; it's not soft, but it's intimate, with clean lines and glass-fronted cases. Each seat offers a front-row view of the delicately orchestrated ballet of each preparation, cooks swerving around each other, telling you how many bites you're meant to expend on each dish. Even if their attitude is sometimes pretentious (it's not "seaweed," it's "sea greens," you might be reminded) and often distracted, it's something that serving 30 courses in two hours can excuse, and their depth of knowledge and commitment is clear.

The concise, New-World-heavy wine list tends to rocket the check further into the stratosphere, but there are some decent deals hidden within—like a reasonably priced Crémant d'Alsace rosé that, if your 10am timing is exactly right, you might just have the privilege of consuming with some of your 30 memorable courses. –FC

# Mio

This charming venture brings out our possessive side

**7.0** Food | **8.9** Feel

## New American

Upmarket restaurant

**$70** Price

www.miorestaurant.com

| | | |
|---|---|---|
| Mon–Thu 11:30am–2:30pm, 5pm–10pm; Fri 11:30am–2:30pm, 5pm–11pm; Sat 5pm–11pm | **Bar** Beer, wine, liquor<br>**Credit cards** Visa, MC, AmEx<br>**Reservations** Accepted<br>Date-friendly, live music, Wi-Fi | **Downtown**<br>1110 Vermont Ave. NW<br>(202) 955-0075 |

It's always a delight to discover a restaurant. Not to just come across a restaurant but to really find one that fits into your life and your culinary desires. You know that feeling, when you find a place that you immediately develop such a fondness for that you start referring to it in the possessive: "my little trattoria, my corner take-out…." For us, Mio is that kind of place. It is visually beautiful, loaded with dark wood, high ceilings, soft but ample lighting, and a generally chilled-out vibe (emphasized by the lack of tablecloths.)

When the place fills up, it feels trendy and effortlessly cool; when it's less full, it feels homey despite the size of the space. The open blue-tiled kitchen provides an unpretentious feel; the engaging wooden ceiling sculpture helps to break up the room, tying together all of the dark brown elements in the restaurant's seamlessly connected two floors. Our only complaint is that all those hard surfaces can make for a rather loud evening.

The food, like the décor, is thoughtfully coordinated, visually satisfying, and tasteful. Smooth chilled beet soup with creamy goat cheese (a sort of fusion between borscht and the now-classic beet-and-goat-cheese salad) is stunning, sweet and refreshing. An eco-friendly beef Caesar salad, an unlikely duo, really works because the romaine hearts are slightly charred before a light dressing is drizzled over them; the combination of tender grilled beef and smoky, earthy lettuce makes for a clever take on steak salad. It is unfortunate that, on our last visit, the steak was cooked well beyond the requested medium-rare. We've also enjoyed a playful duo of hamachi, and the well-executed Key lime tart.

When it comes to drinks, a well-selected variety of wines by the glass and a well-priced selection of bottles make for a solid and friendly wine list. And the mostly Latin-themed cocktails are irresistible, especially El Embajador (white rum, peach liqueur, house sour, and mango purée) and acai martini (acai purée, cachaça, and guanabana purée.)

All in all, Mio is the kind of place we hesitate to write about, because then we'll have to share it…*Mio*, after all, means "mine" in Spanish. As in "mine, mine, mine!" But we've resolved to stop being selfish and spread the Mio love. You're welcome. –SDC

# Mitsitam Native Foods Café

## 7.9 — Food
## 8.6 — Feel

Is the last exotic frontier our own country's cultural history?

## American

Counter service

### $35 — Price

Daily 10am–5pm

**Bar** Beer, wine
**Credit cards** Visa, MC, AmEx

**Southwest DC**
950 Independence Ave. SW
(202) 633-7038

Come lunchtime, visitors to the National Museum of the American Indian can abandon the sun- and moon-themed rooms (and cheesy kokopelli vendors) for the museum's Mitsitam Native Foods Café. Where DC has a glut of British-influenced American classics in its taverns and tap rooms, Mitsitam (which means "let's eat" in the native tongue of the Delaware and Piscataway people) offers a take on the cuisine that was being enjoyed in this nation before the Mayflower even dropped anchor.

Surely there are culinary academics that will debate the definitions of experiencing authentic native foods. But what's wrong with creative liberties? We don't mind veal terrine with onion confit in lieu of plain maize and beans, even if you won't find any doctoral dissertations to support it.

The space is set up like a (rather silver-plated) cafeteria, with five windows, each of them riffs on the native foods of a different American region: the Great Plains, Northern Woodlands, Mesoamerica, South America, and the Pacific Northwest. The Northern Woodlands station features a maple pudding that's sticky-sweet and hearty, and turtle soup with a gentle, buttery broth. Another successful soup is the Mesoamerican pozole, studded with earthy hominy; you'll find this, too, in modern Mexican cooking, one of the remnants of the more ancient civilizations of the region. We find far more pleasure in these interesting throwbacks than in more common dishes, like guacamole and French fries.

But if this is a small step for broader recognition of Native American cuisine—we'd love to see more of it pop up in restaurants around the country—it's a giant leap for American museum cuisine. Leave it to the Smithsonian to achieve that. –CK

# Mixtec

More Columbia Heights than Adams Morgan—and for that, we like it

**7.3** Food | **4.8** Feel

## Mexican

Casual restaurant | **$25** Price

Sun–Thu 8am–midnight
Fri–Sat 8am–3am

**Bar** Beer, wine, liquor
**Credit cards** Visa, MC, AmEx
**Reservations** Not accepted

**Adams Morgan**
1792 Columbia Rd. NW
(202) 332-1011

Geographically, Mixtec is pretty promising. We assumed, given its location on the border between party-centric Adams Morgan and ethnic food-centric Columbia Heights, that it would be a rockin' good time—either in the traditional sense or gustatorily. Rubbing our hands together in anticipation, we imagined that just beyond its green awning with Aztec-chic fonting might be rows of steamy pollos a la brasa. Or tacos—de lengua, de res, de barbacoa. Or, at a minimum, whiskey shots for $2.

And you'll long for a cheap shot at about five different points in the course of a meal here. The first might be after you sit down but before water glasses are clunked down in front of you—a process that could take up to ten minutes. The next might be after you check out the menu and fear that neither your authenticity hopes nor your party-riffic dreams will be fulfilled.

Because the menu doesn't read like one that's all that authentic. But if you peer into the kitchen in the back, you'll see an old Mexican woman, and once you taste your food, you'll understand that this is clearly home cooking. Execution of rice and beans is spot on, and they're delicious. Chiles rellenos are a good version—appropriately oozy and cheesy, but with an egg batter that's of a certain lightness, and given life by a touch of piquant pepper. It's a simple dish, but oh, how it works. Enchiladas, while not so oozy (this ain't Tex-Mex, after all) are also faithful representations. (Oh, and as for the drinking game? Time to take another shot after you order to tide you through the time that you're going to wait and wait and wait and wait for your food to come out.)

Service, in fact, is Mixtec's weakest point. A bare-bones interior we can easily forgive. But staff might at first seem uninterested in your presence, but they can be won over.

And just as you're riding on that high, you'll run into your second conceit of the night. Look at all the suckers standing in the line for up to an hour to eat at Pasta Mia, and you'll be happy with your decision.

Cheers. –AH

# Moby Dick

A ubiquitous chain serving epic portions of tasty Persian fare without whale-sized prices

**7.0** Food  **5.7** Feel

## Middle Eastern

Casual restaurant  **$25** Price

www.mobysonline.com

Mon–Thu 11am–10pm
Fri 11am–11pm
Sat noon–10pm
Hours vary by location

**Bar** None
**Credit cards** Visa, MC
**Reservations** Not accepted
Veg-friendly

**Dupont**
1300 Connecticut Ave. NW
(202) 833-9788

**Georgetown**
1070 31st St. NW
(202) 333-4400

**Arlington, VA**
3000 Washington Blvd.
(703) 465-1600

**Additional locations**
and more features at
www.fearlesscritic.com

Your guess is as good as ours as to why this Persian kabob place is named after the Herman Melville novel. Perhaps it's for no other reason than the fact that these kabobs, like Melville's tome and its Cetacean subject, are gargantuan.

When we say big, we mean enormous. Like, laughably huge. Not only does a single serving come with what appears to be half of the animal (or in a chicken's case, one and a half), but the offering is served atop either a mountain of rice or a 12-inch slab of fresh-baked flatbread.

Refreshingly, there's no sacrifice of quality for quantity at this chain, which has about 14 locations throughout the metro area. In fact, you can watch most of the operation occurring behind the counter where you pay for your food. The meats are slowly roasted on large skewers, the bread emerges slightly charred, and the cashier sits listlessly before realizing your order is ready and serving it forth. It does seem to be timeliness that is the sacrifice here. There had to be one.

When it does finally come, even after modest cooling, it is delicious: the meat is richly buttered on the outside and tender inside, and the whole affair is accompanied by a cool, herbaceous yogurt sauce, which has a nice kicky tang. The falafel special, if it's available, is worth trying. The (again) oversized balls are loaded not only with chickpeas but also with fava beans, and have an extra pinch of cumin and other spices. The balls are very lightly fried, allowing the full taste of the bean paste to come through. None of this is particularly subtle food, but it's extremely satisfying.

Vegetarians will have plenty of interesting choices, and lunch specials are all in the $7 range, making this a great deal if you save half of your behemoth portion for tomorrow's lunch. Non-alcoholic beverages here include doogh (yogurt soda—it's better than it sounds), both homemade and in fruit-infused bottled form.

As for the name, here's NPR's explanation: "In the shah's time, one of the biggest kebab joints in Tehran, right near the American Embassy, was called Moby Dick, apparently because the owner just really liked the book. So for Iranians, the name Moby Dick is a little in-joke." Well, that makes one part that's little. –CK

# Mogotillo

Salvadoran food, both coastal and inland

**8.2** Food
**7.9** Feel

## Salvadoran, Mexican

Casual restaurant

**$20** Price

Daily 11am–1am

**Bar** Wine
**Credit cards** Visa, MC, AmEx
**Reservations** Not accepted

**Takoma Park, MD**
7637 New Hampshire Ave.
(301) 434-4272

There are plenty of authentic Salvadoran holes-in-the-wall around these parts. But this one, in the dingy-looking Takoma/Langley Crossroads Center, has an unusually fun atmosphere, beginning with the friendly staff and cheery yellow walls. The brown-carpeted space is long and narrow, but it somehow feels like home.

So does the food—if home is El Salvador. Stay away from the Tex-Mex section of the menu (chicken fajitas, crab quesadillas, and such) at all costs, and head straight for the Salvadoran specialties, beginning with sopa de mondongo (a rich tripe soup), or, for the squeamish, the sweeter sopa de gallina (chicken stew). There are delicious Salvadoran enchiladas, which come on a crispy shell piled with meat, vegetables, and egg—more like the Mexican tostada. And there's classic plato típico salvadoreño, with marinated steak, sweet plantains, a tamal, and beans. A fried whole fish is less exciting, fresh enough, but a bit dry.

Oysters on the half shell, ceviche, and sopa de mariscos evoke of the area in El Salvador for which the restaurant is named; it's along the Pan-American Highway, near the coastal city of La Unión. (A kitschy poster with a team photo of the Mogotillo FC soccer side adorns one of the walls.) Add lobster and egg, and they'll call it sopa vuelve a la vida ("come back to life"). Good, too, are the eminently Salvadoran pupusas; you can't find the classic filling of loroco (a green vegetable) and cheese everywhere, but Mogotillo has them. They also have tajadas con carne molida (slices of salty green plantain with ground beef), an authentic treat.

Just remember to keep your wits about you: around every corner of the menu lies another dish with a name like "Nachos Supreme Alex." But you've got navigational skills, right? –RG

# Montmartre

**8.6** Food   **9.2** Feel

A quaint, unpretentious French bistro that delights
American palates while expanding them, too

**French**                    Upmarket restaurant   **$60** Price

Tue–Thu 11:30am–2:30pm,
5:30pm–10pm; Fri–Sat
11:30am–2:30pm, 5:30pm–
10:30pm; Sun 11:30am–
2:30pm, 5:30pm–9pm

**Bar** Beer, wine, liquor
**Credit cards** Visa, MC, AmEx
**Reservations** Accepted
Outdoor dining

**Capitol Hill**
327 7th St. SE
(202) 544-1244

Montmartre is an unassuming delight. Located near Eastern Market, it's
small and set back from the street—the kind of place that can be easily
missed. But it isn't often missed; it's quite crowded, a testament to the
accessible charm of its menu. The place exerts a simple, homey elegance:
walls are painted a Provençal yellow; dark wood furnishings butt up
against each other (it does get cramped); and outdoor seating makes for
great entertainment.

The food is unfussy, rustic French, but with New American efforts
toward balance and presentation. (Note that this is a gentle and natural
influence, and not the concerted effort that foreshadows fusion and
foam.) The treasures of the French bistro are here in such dishes as
mussels in a pastis broth; buttery, garlicky escargot; and duck-leg confit.
Calf's liver is a favorite here, with appropriate balancing accents—on one
visit, notes of blackberry and blue cheese. A chilled cucumber soup is
refreshing, with a touch of cream and a pesto drizzle on top. A few pieces
of fresh mozzarella tease and frustrate with their restraint. Likewise, the
quiche is lighter than many Americans might be used to.

At brunch, most dishes are paired with fancy local greens, and the
presentation is always pretty. Consider the eggs Florentine: instead of a
heaping mess of egg and sauce and English muffin, Montmartre's version
includes two pretty pearls of poached eggs, with rich and runny yolks,
atop a generous bed of sautéed spinach. Instead of toast, there's the
basket of crusty baguette that accompanies every meal. As part of the
ongoing celebration of offal, there's a brilliant array of pâtés and rilletes,
served with cornichons and mustard. Or try a smoked-salmon terrine,
which is dotted with small pieces of mushroom and makes a great
accompaniment to a Bloody Mary (what doesn't?).

The waiters come across as green as the arugula: they can become
harried and careless during rushes. On the other hand, the vibe isn't trying
to be four-star hotel-service French. Montmartre's finishing touch is a
winner: the dessert tray is filled with a delectable assortment of lemon
and berry tarts. Here, the restaurant caters to a weakness shared by both
Americans (who love pie) and French (who love to linger). –CK

# Morrison-Clark Inn

**8.0** Food   **9.2** Feel

Southern living it up (and perhaps dying young?)

## Southern

Upmarket restaurant

**$60** Price

www.morrisonclark.com

Mon–Thu 7am–10am,
11:30am–2pm, 6pm–9:30pm
Fri 7am–10am, 11:30am–2pm,
6pm–10pm
Sat 7am–10am, 6pm–10pm
Sun 7am–10am, 11:30am–2pm

**Bar** Beer, wine, liquor
**Credit cards** Visa, MC, AmEx
**Reservations** Accepted
Date-friendly, kid-friendly, outdoor
dining, Wi-Fi

**Downtown**
1015 L St. NW
(202) 898-1200

The historic Morrison-Clark Inn is a remnant of the genteel South. Just being in the building conjures images of Rhett Butler and Maggie the Cat parading around with cocktails in hand. It is deliciously sumptuous—from the flowers overflowing their beds on the patio to the splendid upholstery, mauve walls, and crystal chandeliers inside. It's no surprise that the Morrison-Clark is steeped in history and wealth. The two Victorian houses which eventually became the Inn were built in the late 19th century by two of DC's elite. After a century as a hostel for military men (graced by leading ladies such as Grace Coolidge, Mamie Eisenhower, and Jackie Kennedy), the inn is now a boutique hotel. Most of its finery is still intact.

Brunch at the Morrison-Clark is as much a lesson in fine Southern living as it is a meal. Dishes are impeccably presented and devilishly opulent. Beignets hot from the fryer are more substantial than doughnuts; they cut a hot, melty trail when dragged through sweet whipped cream. Dense little biscuits, muffins, and scones beg to be slathered in butter as well. Eggs Benedict complete the dairy-fest. They're topped with big, loose crab cakes that are crispy on the outside and laced with lemon. The English muffins are buttered for extra crispness and extra richness. It's enough to turn your stomach, but that's the spirit of the South. When in Rome (Georgia)…you might as well indulge.

In fact, it's hard to find a dish that isn't rich. Even traditionally light dishes are made heavy. Pea soup is gorgeously dressed with whorls of cream and scented with white pepper and curry. It's thicker and richer than most summer soups and made even plusher by shiitake mushrooms and bacon. Similarly, berry shortcake goes from a light summer dish to an act of will. As by this point in the meal, you will have already consumed enough pastry and fat to shorten your life by several years, you may not be able to continue. But it's hard to say no to fluffy mounds of whipped cream and crumbly biscuits studded with crystals of sugar.

You will leave Morrison-Clark with a new respect for Paula Dean's stunning longevity. It's astonishing that a portion of the nation consumes meals like this everyday. They are insane—and insanely lucky. As you roll precariously towards the door, an old southern siren song will echo round those walls: "Y'all come back now, y'hear?" It'll be hard to resist. –JC

# Morton's

The smoothest ship in the steakhouse business

**7.9** *Food*   **7.9** *Feel*

## Steakhouse

Upmarket restaurant   **$100** *Price*

www.mortons.com

Mon–Fri 11:30am–11pm
Sat 5pm–11pm
Sun 5pm–10pm
Hours vary by location

**Bar** Beer, wine, liquor
**Credit cards** Visa, MC, AmEx
**Reservations** Accepted
Outdoor dining

**Downtown**
1050 Connecticut Ave.
NW
(202) 955-5997

**Georgetown**
3251 Prospect St. NW
(202) 342-6258

**Arlington, VA**
1750 Crystal Dr.
(703) 418-1444

**Additional locations**
and more features at
www.fearlesscritic.com

One of the best meals we've ever had at a chain restaurant, anywhere in the world, was at the Morton's in Singapore. To get those Prime cuts of beef there from the American Midwest would have taken Singapore Airlines' new A380 about nineteen hours. The steakhouse décor (corporate luxe, plush booths, dark and elegant, you know the drill) and impeccable service were identical to their counterparts anywhere else. The execution was as good, or better, than it is in Chicago—and Singapore is hardly a city where they're used to broiling steaks at 1800°. That's how smoothly the Morton's machine is running at the moment.

And it's running just as smoothly at District-area branches, which appear to be minting money. One of the trademarks here is the plastic-wrapped beef ritual, wherein your server shows you all the different raw cuts of meat, covered in what looks like Saran wrap, as you're ordering. The idea is to let you choose your Prime weapon, although this steakhouse version of the tableside guacamole routine tends to make at least someone at the table squirm with squeamishness. (There's always someone that loves meat but wants to deny that it ever consisted of living muscle.)

It's pretty hard to go wrong here, except if you consider the effect on your wallet. The only steakhouse chain that beats Morton's is BLT Steak. After that, there's Capital Grille, which is trying, and failing miserably, to make a run for it. Houston's and Outback are more modest. Fogo de Chão, at the end of the day, is a buffet restaurant. Morton's does have one failing: we prefer the funkier flavor of dry-aged beef to the wet-aged version that they settle for. Regardless, three decades after its opening, this remains a genre-defying—or perhaps new-genre-defining—restaurant in the history of the American chain. Certainly Morton's is not the best steakhouse in New York, nor is it the best in the District (we prefer the Prime Rib and Bobby Van's). But even wet-aging, it comes pretty darn close.

And you pay the price. You're best off experiencing all of this with an expense account at your disposal. After all, everyone else in the restaurant seems to be doing so. –RG

# Mr. Chen's Organic Chinese

**4.6** Food   **6.5** Feel

The food's provenance is the best thing it has to offer

## Chinese

Casual restaurant   **$25** Price

www.mrchens.com

Mon–Thu 11am–10:30pm
Fri–Sat 11am–11pm
Sun noon–10pm

**Bar** Beer
**Credit cards** Visa, MC, AmEx
**Reservations** Accepted
Delivery, veg-friendly

**Woodley Park**
2604 Connecticut Ave.
NW
(202) 797-9668

If it weren't for the First Amendment, someone by now would have outlawed the placement of "organic" and "Chinese cuisine" in the same sentence. Or even in adjacent sentences. But we've got our freedom of speech, and what in a more regulated nation would be named "Mr. Chen's" can call itself, in America: "Mr. Chen's Organic Chinese Cuisine."

Remember, organic does not mean vegan or even vegetarian. Nor does the label necessarily imply that the food is good for you, nor that your dumplings will arrive without the shiny veneer of grease to which you are accustomed. The ingredients are fresh, even if the menu choices are staid. Mr. Chen's seems to have been turned organic by some undocumented fluke: in everything but denomination, this is your typical hole-in-the-wall Chinese-American joint with shoddy chairs and a reliable lo mein.

There's really nothing special about Mr. Chen's. Given the near-infinite menu, it's disappointing (if familiar within the genre) to discover that many of the dishes taste quite similar. Mr. Chen's excels at variations on the theme that may be loosely dubbed "stir-fried vegetables and meat of choice, in a very watery soy-peanut bath."

There are some exceptions to the theme, but few successful ones. Four jumbo "Ming" shrimp, for instance, come in a red sauce so cloyingly saccharine that even two servings of rice and ample soy sauce cannot cut its sweetness. The mushrooms are far too mushy, and the bamboo shoots get lost in the bath of sauce that is far more sweet than sour.

In all fairness, the food here is "fresh," "healthy," and, although the claim may be impossible to prove, "organic." Mr Chen's is a clean, well-managed place where the meat is properly cooked and the bathrooms are free of grime. But with excellent Chinese food just a few metro stops away in the suburbs, and decent options on the H-Street strip downtown, why waste your time? If Mr. Chen's organic moniker doesn't already inspire second thoughts, your first dish is certain to do the trick. –CK

# Murali

Getting the job done, one bowl of pasta at a time

| 6.2 | 7.0 |
|-----|-----|
| Food | Feel |

## Italian

Upmarket restaurant

**$50**
Price

www.muraliva.com

Mon–Fri 11:30am–2:30pm,
5:30pm–10:30pm
Sat 11:30am–10:30pm
Sun 11:30am–9pm

**Bar** Beer, wine, liquor
**Credit cards** Visa, MC, AmEx
**Reservations** Accepted
Outdoor dining

**Arlington, VA**
1201 S. Joyce St.
(703) 415-0411

Large portions are de rigueur at Murali, a "business casual" type of restaurant below Bally's Gym near the Pentagon City mall. While no dress code is enforced, and the clientele includes a mix of local shoppers, tourists, and workers from the surrounding office buildings, Murali is clearly the kind of place at which you'd "do lunch": the décor hinges on dark wood, the napkins are cloth, the food is presented attractively, and the service is quick enough to have you in and out in time for your 1pm appointment, even after three courses and a glass of wine. It's your basic uninspired upmarket environment.

Be warned, however, that three courses' worth of Murali's portions may leave you incapacitated for the afternoon: the cuts of meat are plentiful, the cheeses are rich, and the red sauces are hearty. Despite the Venetian canal scenes painted on the outside of the building, the restaurant is agnostic as to its origins within Italy, with gnocchi, risotto, soup with pesto, and Caprese salad all sharing the same menu.

Murali's salads are standard. The Caprese is no less than three separate stacks of tomato slices topped with a generous layer of fresh mozzarella and sprinkled with shredded basil. Sparse dressing prevents the flavors from coming together. The arugula salad is similarly simplistic: greens, parmesan, and walnuts are never integrated by the limited vinaigrette that sits aloofly atop the leaves.

In the main courses, however, the skills of the kitchen staff shine: homemade ravioli are large, fresh, and doughy. Although the pumpkin-filled variety are a rich, buttery standby, Murali frequently features ravioli specials. One recent version was filled with smoky, blended eggplant; the pasta paired well with an herb-filled red sauce that was plentiful enough to nearly drown the pasta.

Mahi-mahi is another exercise in enormity: a sizable steak of fish is done up in white wine and butter, and coupled with a textured blend of chunky tomatoes, potato wedges, capers, and black olives.

Add to this a waitstaff who can describe with pulp-like detail how the dishes are prepared, and the deal looks like it will close: in spite of a few less-than-impressive dishes, Murali is a place that is dressed to impress.
—CK

# Myanmar

**8.2** Food  **5.0** Feel

One of the big players in the area's burgeoning Burmese scene

## Burmese

Casual restaurant

**$30** Price

Tue–Sun 11am–10pm

**Bar** Beer, wine
**Credit cards** Visa, MC
**Reservations** Accepted
Live music

**Falls Church, VA**
7810 Lee Hwy #C
(703) 289-0013

Myanmar is a member of the DC area's small (but hopefully growing) cadre of Burmese restaurants. And given the turmoil that country is facing, it's no surprise that so many asylum-seekers call the DC area home.

This phenomenon has given rise to at least three Burmese restaurants in the DC area. A bit of healthy competition is a good thing. However, it's hard to speak concretely about the authenticity of any of them—because how authentic a meal you get here depends on just how persistent you are.

Here, as elsewhere, be prepared to be steered in the direction of the most boring dishes on the menu. Chicken with rice. Mixed vegetables. They'll tell you to avoid anything with ngapi (the fermented shrimp paste that's actually one of the defining elements of Burmese cuisine). Can these people honestly believe that so many culinary pilgrims would trek out here for another version of Chinese-American take-out? Don't let them keep the good stuff from you. Be strong.

Your pushiness will be met with skepticism. "You must not understand what this is." "You wouldn't like it." (But trust us—you will.)

Squash fritters are innocuous enough. The purée is delicately fried and subtlely addictive. Keep them on the side to munch on. Various salads are all interesting studies in texture; many are made with toasted beans to add a pleasant crunch. A pickled-tea-leaf salad (lahpet thouk) is a special treat, its smoky flavor floral and aromatic, with plenty of sourness there to round it out. And it, too, has an amusing mix of tenderly soft and crunchy elements.

A yellow tofu salad with chickpea has bright kaffir lime leaf and slightly sweet tamarind. But pork with sour greens is a slightly tougher dish to handle; its flavor is puckeringly strong, so much so that any pigginess you might have hoped to find is pretty elusive. Tofu with tomato sauce, mutton curry, and mango salad are all excellent. Order balachaung (hidden away with the sides) to jazz up any and all of your dishes. It's a way of increasing the ngapi quotient in your food.

Now that you've proven that you can handle what their menu's got, make sure to remain a familiar face. That way you can work your way through the menu without having to duke it out each and every time. —AH

# Naan & Beyond

The naan isn't even that good, so only attempt the beyond with trepidation

| 4.4 | 6.0 |
|------|------|
| Food | Feel |

## Indian

Counter service

**$25**
Price

www.naan-and-beyond.com

Mon–Fri 11am–9pm
Sat 11am–5pm

**Bar** None
**Credit cards** Visa, MC, AmEx
Delivery, outdoor dining,
veg-friendly

**Downtown**
1331 Pennsylvania Ave.
NW
(202) 737-0890

**Farragut**
1710 L St. NW
(202) 466-6404

You'd think the founders of a place named "Naan & Beyond" would feel some moral obligation to ensure that the restaurant's namesake tastes good. We expect a supple, slightly browned flatbread with a light doughy flavor. But this two-location chain of quick Indian food fails miserably where it should excel: the limp, dry naan is reminiscent of a thin tortilla, with all the flavor of dried out pita bread. Not surprisingly, the rest of the food follows suit.

The problem with Naan and Beyond is not budgetary. We've seen other Indian mini-chains, such as San Francisco's Naan-N-Curry, succeed in spite of a cheesy name, inexpensive offerings, and unpretentious digs. Naan & Beyond offers much of what its name would imply—line-order meals in a cafeteria-like setting, served on paper plates and indisputably accompanied by a serving of naan—but the restaurant manages to miss the mark on almost every dish.

The chicken curry, for example, consists of too-large cubes of meat bathing in a tub of "curry" sauce that is far too thin—when the server scoops a spoonful to add to your plate, the sauce runs off easily and leaves only a couple of helpless chunks of chicken in the spoon.

Improper viscosity is hard to overlook, but a meek flavor is even harder. The chicken curry seems to be spiced with nothing but paprika and turmeric to lend color, and the most prominent flavor we can pick out in the sauce is that of watered-down butter. Luckily, the meat itself is well-prepared, even if it's not integrated with the curry.

Naan & Beyond also offers "signature" sandwiches, which are again brought down by the restaurant's indelible autograph: bad naan. A piece of the impoverished flatbread is wrapped around tandoor-cooked meat, along with shredded white cabbage and mint sauce or mango chutney. Again, the sauce is too feeble and the bread too dry for the sandwich to truly come together.

The curried chickpeas are hearty and properly spiced, and the biriyani is chock full of vegetables and beef, but these footnotes are too minor to redeem mediocre mains or to restore the downright insulting naan. –CK

# Nage

Fancified American food and a lovely brunch

**7.0** Food    **5.0** Feel

## New American, Seafood

Upmarket restaurant    **$60** Price

www.nagerestaurant.com

Mon–Fri 6:30am–10am,
11:30am–2:30pm, 5pm–10pm
Sat 7am–11am, 5pm–10pm
Sun 7am–11am, 11am–3pm,
5pm–10pm

**Bar** Beer, wine, liquor
**Credit cards** Visa, MC, AmEx
**Reservations** Accepted
Wi-Fi

**Dupont**
1600 Rhode Island Ave. NW
(202) 448-8005

DC brunch culture is a key to the city's weekend happiness. Far more than a meal, it's an institution, an event that continues well after your plates of eggs have been cleared. The time commitment required is well beyond that of lunch, and you shouldn't be surprised if you're still with your fellow brunchers come dinnertime. When tables reach that infamous "Brunch Turning Point," usually two drinks into the meal, a key decision has to be made: either you order one more drink and write off the rest of the afternoon, or you order coffee and move on with your day.

Nage makes that decision pretty easy: order one more drink. Fifteen dollars buys you unlimited "marys and mos" at Sunday brunch, and with a variety to choose from, it's hard not to attempt to try them all. The "Bloody Swine" (horrifying name, yes) is a delicious twist on the traditional Bloody that incorporates…bacon. Chunks float in the drink, imparting it with a smoky, and—let's face it—pork-fatty flavor. Delicious mimosas come in a variety of flavors, too; blood orange is good, as is white peach, which is surprisingly delicate and not overpowered by the bubbly.

"Eggs Chesapeake," with a unique dill hollandaise, do a good job soaking it all up, but the eggs do tend to hang out dangerously on the cooked-too-long end of the spectrum. The "Sunday Morning Kill It Skillet'" is a lethal combination of chorizo, bacon, mac and cheese, fries, and an egg. It's intended to kill a hangover, but it seems just as likely to kill the hangover's host. Just as hard to handle is brioche French toast, with strawberries, ganache, and caramel syrup that goes beyond dessert levels of sweetness.

The heavy-handedness carries over into dinner mains, with a prime rib burger, cinnamon-braised short ribs, and gemelli pasta with duck sausage. Decidedly "rustic," the menu takes American classics and dresses them up, as in the case of a lobster boudin. Pan-roasted frog's-legs are served with tomatoes, capers, olives, and ham—not quite what you see on the average American dinner table.

It's at night that the general aesthetic of Nage works best. What feels sterile at brunch takes on warmth for dinner. And you don't have to worry about that pesky turning point—you can have all the wine you want. But it *will* run you more than $15. –AH

# Nam-Viet

Tasty, steamy Vietnamese comfort—now in DC, too

**7.4** **5.8**
Food Feel

## Vietnamese

Casual restaurant **$30**
Price

www.namviet1.com

Sun–Thu 11am–10pm
Fri–Sat 11am–11pm

**Bar** Beer, wine, liquor
**Credit cards** Visa, MC, AmEx
**Reservations** Accepted

**Cleveland Park**
3419 Connecticut Ave. NW
(202) 237-1015

**Arlington, VA**
1127 N. Hudson St.
(703) 522-7110

Kudos to a spot that's brought good Vietnamese food to the District, without mangling flavors or inflating prices. The Connecticut Avenue shop is one outpost of the two-store chain (the other location is in Arlington), but no spices have fallen overboard in the restaurant's migration across the river. Rather, Nam-Viet is a charming and down-to-earth place to stop for an honest bowl of pho or plate of noodles.

Nam-Viet can be distinguished from its Cleveland Park neighbors (many of which are some kind of "bistro" or "brasserie") by its mustard-yellow sign and the unappealing neon-lit rendering of a bowl of pho in the window. The interior is organized in double-shotgun-style, with an abridged entry and waiting area, and a skinny dining room with three columns of tables mediated by two aisles. If you're sitting at one of the middle tables, your elbows are liable to be bumped by passing patrons. Given that Nam-Viet—even at peak hours—is rarely more than 50 percent full, the owner's motivations for packing in so many tables is mystifying.

But all of this is easily overlooked once the food arrives, and it tends to arrive quickly. The pho is some of the freshest around; although this means a less fatty broth and a more moderated beef flavor, the soup always tastes as if it's been sitting around for just enough time to let the flavors meld, but not grow old. The noodles, as well, taste homemade.

But Nam-Viet is more than just a pho junket. Although some of the other soups entail a mess of soggy vegetables and too-sweet broth, many of the main dishes are quite good. Gently sautéed eggplant is a brilliant purple color, and the vegetable is flavorful and smoky and soft. The shrimp garden rolls, meanwhile, are made with king shrimp, fresh mint, and chewy rice paper; the resulting flavor is refreshing but bold.

Sometimes the steam rising over the rim of a hot bowl and the focused slurp of noodles is all you need to take the edge off a gloomy District evening. –CK

# Napoleon Bistro

**5.5** Food  **7.5** Feel

Bistro fare and a grandiose attitude in over-the-top surroundings

## French

Upmarket restaurant

**$60** Price

www.napoleondc.com

Mon–Thu 5pm–11pm
Fri 5pm–midnight
Sat 10am–midnight
Sun 10am–10pm

**Bar** Beer, wine, liquor
**Credit cards** Visa, MC, AmEx
**Reservations** Accepted
Date-friendly, outdoor dining, veg-friendly, Wi-Fi

**Adams Morgan**
1847 Colombia Rd. NW
(202) 299-9630

What would Napoleon Bonaparte think of this place? We picture him frightened and strangely aroused by the pulsing music, traipsing about comfortably in the dim candlelight, checking himself out in the many reflective surfaces, and feeling right at home among the rich textiles and gilded accents. Sure, it's all the frivolities of the nobility that he rode in on his horse to obliterate, but how quickly and easily he, too, succumbed to the lure of wealth and power. So is it any wonder that Napoleon Bistro somehow feels like a broken promise, something of a cheat?

Concrete and other industrial conceits put the chic back in chicanery (the widespread and fervent embrace of exposed pipes as the epitome of style has saved restaurateurs tens of thousands—genius!), but doesn't it feel a bit insulting to then serve overpriced cocktails in plastic cups? All around, stiletto heels click and clack on a floor that feels unfinished, given the utter lack of rusticity elsewhere, in menu and in overall approach.

The food follows through on this point with a string of monochromatic disappointments that make a mockery of the Emperor's table. Flavors are dull and uninspired, often trumpeting one note ad (literal) nauseum. French onion soup is thin and so supernaturally sweet, you have to wonder: are they using Maui onions in here? It's so saccharine, it's funny (funnier if you aren't the one paying). Crêpes look pretty in the semi-dark, but their flavor evokes unsavory associations. Green curry mussels, a nifty colonial twist, are adequately flavored but cracked and poorly cleaned. Turn the lights down even lower, and no one will notice!

The cocktails here do more harm to Champagne than ever did the Napoleonic Wars. Okay, so it isn't real Champagne, which would be far more egregious a sin given the use of cheap juices and syrupy mixers like Blue Curacao. But Dom Pérignon is also touted here, and rather fittingly: it's overrated and overpriced. In the end, Napoleon turned out to be a tyrant and showboat, failing his country by becoming too greedy, too confident. Have we learned nothing from history? –JC

# Nava Thai

As authentic as they come—for now

**8.4** **7.0**
Food Feel

## Thai

Casual restaurant

**$25**
Price

www.navathai.food.officelive.com

Sun–Thu 11:30am–10pm
Fri–Sat 11:30am–10:30pm

**Bar** None
**Credit cards** Visa, MC
**Reservations** Accepted

**Wheaton, MD**
11301 Fern St.
(240) 430-0495

A foodie consensus seems to have formed that this quirky place in Wheaton is the best Thai restaurant in the DC area. At the moment, they're not wrong. But maybe the best Thai restaurant in the DC area hasn't been discovered yet (by the non-Thais). Nava Thai, which does some authentic Thai food and also dabbles in Chinese, recently moved into a new space that had previously hosted a Greek-Mediterranean restaurant. There, in a melting-pot move for the ages—one of those modern urban moments that makes you proud to be an American—they took the olive-oil bottles that had sat on each table and turned them into fish-sauce dispensers.

Some people have complained that it's not the same since the move. They're right in the sense that the menu has gotten longer, and more dilute. Too many mediocre Chinese-American dishes (steamed dumplings, stir-fried vegetables, deep-fried meats in brown gravies) wrangle their way into this kitchen. There's too much tofu, too, and a lot of this food is still a touch too sweet (sugary chili and tamarind sauces).

But order carefully, and you can eat very well here. We were never as big on the hot-and-sour squid as some (we're not fans of the scored school of squid), but the expertly charred grilled chicken with sticky rice and limey chili sauce is excellent. Pad Thai is good, and we never thought we'd hear ourselves uttering that phrase, at least not in this country, where the noodles are often so sweet that it's a sort of dessert dish. Nava Thai's version of the dish is more smoky, with the noodles nicely wok-kissed. But unless you order it with a mussel omelette (hoi tod), as the Thais generally do, then you've done the equivalent of having a hamburger without the bun.

If ordered spicy, som tam—the green papaya salad that's the icon of Northern Thailand—is an object lesson in the legitimate balance of sweet, sour, hot, and umami flavors of northern Thailand. It's spectacular. Crispy pork and string bean in curry sauce is a hot pleasure, too, redolent of kaffir lime leaf. Floating market soup is in the genre of the wonderful Chinese-influenced noodle-plus-broth dishes that you might find at a Bangkok street market; it's thickened with pig's blood and has thus got some serious depth, and it's appropriately spicy, with bits of pork ball, fried pork skin, and fresh, delicate vegetables.

This is as authentic a Thai restaurant as we've got in the area (or, at least, that we've found in the area). But that doesn't mean we shouldn't keep looking for one that doesn't mix itself up in the business of serving stir-fried baby corn in oyster sauce.

# Negril

Not quite doing justice to some of Jamaica's best

**6.5** Food  **2.8** Feel

## Caribbean

Counter service  **$15** Price

www.negrileats.com

Mon–Sat 11am–9:30pm

**Bar** None
**Credit cards** Visa, MC, AmEx
Kid-friendly, live music, Wi-Fi

**Shaw**
2301 Georgia Ave. NW
(202) 332-3737

**Silver Spring, MD**
965 Thayer Ave.
(301) 585-3000

In Jamaica, there are two things that you can find almost anywhere: jerk chicken and homemade fruit punch. You can find either one along the swarthy streets of Kingston, at the all-inclusive resorts of Montego Bay, at roadside shacks in the crevices of the Blue Mountains. You can find either one at a nocturnal food cart outside a throbbing discotheque, in the dormitories of Portmore and the slums of Spanish Town, and, yes, along the panhandler-infested beaches of Negril, the Jamaican city that has most successfully leveraged the profit potential of the island's skillfully cultivated rasta/reggae/marijuana/take-it-easy-mon image—even while, behind closed doors, locals seem to prefer a quiet game of dominoes to an overpriced bag of schwag.

The primary virtue of jerk chicken in Jamaica is that it's cooked (and not overcooked) over live coals in a grill that billows with smoke; that famous jerk spice rub is really a secondary concern. Unfortunately, while the rub is right at the version purveyed by this Jamaican fast-food minichain, those juicy, smoky signs of the fire aren't there, while the drumsticks tend to be serviceable, thigh meat has generally come out woefully dry. Also absent are the expected moistness of rice and peas (rice and red beans); the savory addictiveness of the beef inside a beef patty; or, seemingly, any seasoning whatsoever on a plate of cabbage.

How about the fruit punch? Well, in Jamaica, it's all balance and complexity, but not at Negril (the restaurant); here, it tastes kind of like syrupy frozen-strawberry purée. Coco bread is sort of comforting, like a warm dinner roll, but the easy highlight is the tender, carefully stewed curried goat, whose yellow gravy carries its curry-powder flavor well. But even that plate is diminished by a useless salad with a sugar-charged version of Russian dressing.

It's all diminished, too, by the thoughtless atmosphere, which is in the McDonald's vein but with plasticky furniture that fails in its most basic mission: to hold food. Tables for two can scarcely fit two meals, and some are falling apart. Still, if do you happen to pass by a Negril branch at lunchtime, it's a serviceable and definitely more interesting alternative to those golden arches (which, by the way—at the Howard University branch at least—are across the street). –RG

# New Big Wong

The beauty is in what's swimming in the tank—not in the tired lunch specials

| 8.8 | 5.0 |
|---|---|
| Food | Feel |

**Chinese**

Casual restaurant

**$25**
Price

Daily 10:30am–5pm

**Bar** None
**Credit cards** Visa, MC, AmEx
**Reservations** Accepted
Delivery

**Chinatown**
506 Eye St. NW
(202) 628-0490

Aside from its chuckle-worthy name, the New Big Wong, from the outside, could be any other highly Westernized Chinese joint in DC's Chinatown. Many others have lesser names, from the forced "Wok 'n' Roll" to the generic "Chinatown Express." And, generally speaking, the others have lesser food, too.

Come in and order the lunch special, and the New Big Wong descends to the lowest level: soggy fried food, chicken diced into miniscule and flavorless pieces, celery and carrots largely replacing vegetables like red peppers and string beans.

Your first hint that the $6.95 lunch might not be what the restaurant is really about is the set of tanks near the doors where you enter, swimming with live bait shrimp (which, when ordered, will be prepared with salt and pepper, with the heads still on), Dungeness crabs (you can get them expertly steamed with ginger and scallion), and sea bass. Your second clue might be the haunting, flowery Chinese tea, which is some of the best in the city.

The problem at the New Big Wong is that almost none of the non-Chinese customers order the real food, some of which is explained on the extensive dinner menu, and some of which isn't on any menu. To those in the know come the spoils: a delicious salad of jellyfish, gently resilient and well spiced. A well-developed soup of oyster, bean curd, seaweed, and egg. Chinese watercress, kissed by a fiery wok (although a bit oily). Fried rice with lobster and dried scallop.

And then there is the best duck dish in Washington DC, hands down. Better than anyone else's. It's roasted in the Cantonese style, its skin dried, beautifully crisped, and lacquered with honey, its melting meat and singed fat bathed in a soy-based sauce of subtle sweetness, gentle acidity, unexpected spice, and profound depth.

The problem with rating such restaurants—and a problem with our numerical rating system as a whole, really—is the difficult question of how much to weigh the terrible Chinese-American lunch menu, which is clearly tailored only to customers without curiosity. There is no excuse for willfully serving bad food, but our imperfect solution is to assume that our readers will order wisely and to weigh the rating heavily toward what the restaurant does best.

New Big Wong is but a dingy basement adorned with Christmas lights, plastic tablecloths, and a few tacky wall hangings in a neighborhood that a lot of foodies have written off. Such is the enigma that is good Chinese food in America, and such is the challenge of finding it, wherever it may hide. —FC

# Neyla

The food of the Fertile Crescent served with the appropriate sex appeal

| 7.4 | 8.0 |
|-----|-----|
| Food | Feel |

## Middle Eastern

Upmarket restaurant

**$70**
Price

www.neyla.com

Sun–Thu 5pm–10:30pm
Fri–Sat 5pm–11:30pm

**Bar** Beer, wine, liquor
**Credit cards** Visa, MC, AmEx
**Reservations** Accepted
Live music, outdoor dining,
veg-friendly

**Georgetown**
3206 N St. NW
(202) 333-6353

Neyla's menu of small, shareable plates accesses a remarkable menagerie of flavors centered around Lebanon, whose culinary history goes back for millennia, but dabbles in several Southern Mediterranean cuisines. You'll sample them in what looks like Warner Brothers' idea of a harem: high, sweeping ceilings; shimmering fabrics and cushions; colorful pendant lamps; dark wood accents…and attentive servers dressed to match.

All of this doesn't come cheap. But first-timers would benefit from the Lebanese mezza, or tasting plates mostly running under $10 each. Fatteh is like Lebanon's five-layer dip: grilled small slices of eggplant, pungent lamb, a creamy yogurt, chick peas, and an oil dressing with a tinge of cilantro. Scoop these up with crispy pita chips. Vegetarians have plenty to choose from, including a surprisingly tasty vegetable kibbeh (softly fried balls of sweet pumpkin, oyster mushrooms, shallots, and walnuts). Four of these guys look positively decorative, drizzled with truffle oil and yogurt, on their long plate. Also excellent is basterma, a Lebanese cured beef that's served with mint, yogurt, and pomegranate seeds. Neyla's bread, a plain, poofy pita, is somewhat disappointing, but at least presented with flair in a wire vase. Country-specific mains (Morocco's is chicken tagine in citrus confit and olives) are pricey.

But then the excitement really begins—it's so rare to find well-made Lebanese desserts like cream pudding with pistachios, banana, and honey; or knafe bil jibneh, whose sweet cheese and baked katafi dough layers make the great effort at pronunciation worthwhile.

This is also a great excuse to sample some truly exciting wines from a region you don't often see on wine lists (it's more an issue of quantity, not quality), or lay low with one of Neyla's two excellent non-alcoholic juices: a sour, mint-infused lemonade, and a watermelon cooler that's refreshing and not too sweet. Neyla's lavish flavors, aromas, and surroundings might just leave you craving your own little block of this coveted region. –FC

# Ngoc Anh

Buffets aren't always a bad thing—especially when they help you navigate faraway flavors

**8.7** Food **7.4** Feel

## Vietnamese

Casual restaurant

**$25** Price

Daily 10am–9pm

**Bar** Beer
**Credit cards** Visa, MC
**Reservations** Not accepted

**Falls Church, VA**
6795 Wilson Blvd.
(703) 327-5712

In the brilliant Vietnamese arsenal that is the Eden Center mall—one of the culinary highlights of the greater DC area—it can be really difficult to choose your weapon. The usual methods of selecting the best (pick the place that's most crowded, or pick the place that has the highest proportion of members of the restaurant's purported ethnicity) don't work here, because at prime times (especially lunch), a good portion of the places are crowded, and they're crowded almost exclusively with Vietnamese people.

The food on offer in this white-walled, Spartan room—which fronts both the mall corridor and the sidewalk outdoors—is excellent, but it has an added advantage, for non-Vietnamese people, over the competition: it's got a buffet.

Don't be scared by this fact. This is not an all-you-can-eat buffet. It's not a pan-Asian buffet. And for the most part, it's not a buffet where things are sitting around getting cold. These are stew dishes and gravies that generally improve over time. And the unique opportunity created by the buffet is that of—instead of trying to navigate a confusing and poorly translated menu—pointing and choosing three or four or even six dishes, depending on your party size; figure on two per person. You pay for each individually; ask for the smallest portions they're willing to dish out so that you can try more things.

The contents of the buffet change daily, but you might get to experience whole stewed or grilled fishes, served with aromatic combinations of herbs and fish sauce; a brilliant minced pork-and-eggplant stew that's meant to be wrapped in a lettuce leaf before eating; or whole shrimp (you eat them that way—head, shell, and all) coated with a palm-sugary glaze that turns them into a sort of shrimp candy.

It is extremely difficult to go wrong at the buffet, but there are also some things that need to be ordered off the menu. Not to be missed, among those, is bo kho, an unbelievably complex broth of braised beef that marries subtle hints of winter-holiday-evocative sweet spice to bright, summery mint and cilantro and plays the crunch of bean sprouts off the soft sweetness of gently stewed carrots.

The disarming charm of the owners—in a mall where some staffs can be somewhat gruff to outsiders—is yet another element of Ngoc Anh's unusual combination of user-friendliness and authenticity. –RG

# Nicaro

It's nice to see Silver Spring diversifying, but this is a pompous way to do it

**7.1** Food

**7.0** Feel

## New American

Upmarket restaurant

**$75** Price

www.nicarorestaurant.com

Sun–Mon 11:30am–2:30pm, 5:30pm–9pm; Tue–Thu 11:30am–2:30pm, 5:30pm–9:30pm; Fri–Sat 11:30am–2:30pm, 5:30pm–10pm

**Bar** Beer, wine, liquor
**Credit cards** Visa, MC, AmEx
**Reservations** Accepted
Live music, outdoor dining

**Rockville, MD**
8229 Georgia Ave.
(301) 588-2867

Downtown Silver Spring is an interesting study in gentrification. While it's still filled with unsung ethnic gems (Roger Miller Restaurant and Thai Market, to name just two), it's also a petri dish of yuppiedom, seeming to breed a new upscale concept every month or two—with varying results.

This is one of the most high-profile efforts to hit the area yet. Just ask the staff: they'll tell you how high-profile they are, how excellent the restaurant is, and so on. We've rarely seen such pompous self-importance from a waitstaff in DC, never mind one in Silver Spring. Or maybe that's the problem; maybe they're not surrounded by enough ambition and competition to realize that self-anointment only goes so far.

The atmosphere gets a lot of praise from some sources. We'll give it a good lighting award, but otherwise, we don't quite get it. Two long, narrow rooms suffer from the annoying continuous-bench seating that creates the very opposite of a good date atmosphere, putting you in a more intimate position with respect to the stranger next to you than to the beautiful boy or girl across from you whose hand you'd ultimately like to hold.

Homemade pasta is what this kitchen does best—by far. Eggy, bright-yellow tagliatelle, which sit atop a well-developed lamb bolognaise, have a beautiful resilience to them. It's such a rare pleasure to eat homemade tagliatelle. There's also a clever take on carbonara, with Parmigiano, green beans, shallots, pancetta, and a touch of nutmeg. Unlike the traditional Italian carbonara, this sauce is driven by cream rather than egg, but the white-coated noodles are inexplicably addictive, like grown-up fettucine-alfredo porn.

But mostly, the kitchen isn't up to the task of executing on the ambition of this menu. Nicaro is not ready to be the restaurant it wants to be—the restaurant its staff wants to boast about. You may serve "the finest seasonal ingredients from local farms & purveyors," but that doesn't mean you prepare them well. Take, for instance, an overseasoned, slightly tough grilled quail with tough winter greens and tougher glazed chestnuts; or a Caesar salad that's pretentious—one or two daintily plated, underdressed romaine heart and one wimpy anchovy—where it's supposed to be elemental.

A decent wine list has acceptable markups, but it's not long enough to be notable. We prefer to stick with the classic, nostalgic cocktails—sidecars and such. In the end, though, all of this is not quite enough. Nicaro needs to modernize—not through more self-promotion or more creative recipes, but rather through greater focus on the line. –RG

# Nirvana

Good-not-great Southern Indian with a wide variety of choices

**6.4** Food  **7.6** Feel

## Indian

Casual restaurant  **$35** Price

www.dcnirvana.com

Mon–Thu 11:30am–3pm, 5pm–9pm; Fri 11:30am–3pm, 5pm–10pm; Sat 5pm–10pm; Sun noon–3pm, 5pm–9pm

**Bar** Beer, wine, liquor
**Credit cards** Visa, MC, AmEx
**Reservations** Accepted
Delivery, kid-friendly, veg-friendly

**Farragut**
1810 K St. NW
(202) 223-5043

Family-owned Nirvana has many different faces. At noon, this downtown Southern Indian vegetarian eatery is a bustling lunchtime stop, with a buffet that features a different vegetarian Indian regional cuisine every day (Mondays are North Indian, Tuesdays Gujarati, Wednesdays South Indian, and so forth). From 4-8pm, Nirvana offers a generously long happy hour in a cramped space (you have to claim one of the dozen or so seats at the bar in order to take advantage of $2 appetizers). By dinnertime, when the K-Street hordes have gone home, the restaurant becomes a calm, lovely environment in which to try some of the dishes less seen at more Americanized Indian restaurants.

The staff is warm and avuncular (we have yet to see a waiter who looks under 40) and excels at unobtrusive efficiency, only offering guidance on the menu when it's asked for. If the environment is a little benign, or even boring, the food tends to follow suit. One great standout here is the well-textured dosa, a rolled rice-flour pancake, most of whose more than 18 inches are filled with fresh, tangy vegetables and seasonings. Otherwise, many of the usual staples, like curries, are a pleasant enough way to fill your stomach, but nothing mind-blowing. Plus, there's a safety latch on the spice cabinet in the kitchen. Vindaloo is described as "Fire Spicy"—a meaningful claim on a menu, you'd think, that only appends "spicy" to a small handful of its listings—but its red sauce comes only moderately spicy, and it's heavy on the potato and onion. Undhio curry is a perfumed, yellow sauce that benefits from the flavor of lima beans, if it suffers, again, from too many starchy potatoes.

As a side dish, paratha, made with whole-wheat flour, is great when stuffed with fresh green peas; the bread is nicely charred and drizzled with butter, but the rice is separated and dry.

Ultimately, there's some hit, but plenty of miss. There's better Southern Indian in the metro area, but for vegetarian cooking right downtown, you could do much worse. –CK

# Nooshi

6.6 **Food**  6.2 **Feel**

Unremarkable sushi and bland, passable noodle dishes anchor this

## Pan-Asian, Japanese

Casual restaurant

**$25** Price

www.nooshidc.com

| | | |
|---|---|---|
| Mon–Sat 11:30am–11pm | **Bar** Beer, wine, liquor | **Farragut** |
| Sun 5pm–10pm | **Credit cards** Visa, MC, AmEx | 1120 19th St. NW |
| | **Reservations** Accepted | (202) 293-3138 |

"Pan-Asian" has become a far-too-familiar term when it comes to cuisine, and Nooshi is one of those far-too-familiar places that offer something Asian (or at least Asian-influenced) for everyone, without really shining at any one of those things. Its wide-ranging menu and generic Asian décor deliver exactly what you'd expect from a restaurant offering dishes representing an entire continent: renditions of familiar Asian classics—some solid, and some fairly mediocre.

At lunch on a weekday, the restaurant has the harried feel of many of its peer lunch spots in the Golden Triangle: lines out the door (including a separate crowd waiting for carry-out), a cluster of hostesses near the front who seem unsure about how to expedite seating, and waiters turning sideways to edge past each other in the too-narrow spaces between tables. The red-and-black lacquered décor carries the pan-Asian theme throughout the long and narrow space that amplifies the clatter of chopsticks, bowls, and glasses.

The name of the restaurant is a mash-up of "noodles" and "sushi," which are, unsurprisingly, the two major menu categories here. The sushi is unremarkable, inoffensive, and relatively inexpensive, with all the familiar players (a passable spicy crunchy tuna roll, yellowtail and scallion, and so on) and one or two more unexpected options (including the always-disastrous smoked salmon with cream cheese). Noodle dishes fare somewhat better than raw fish, with the menu running the gamut from nabeyaki udon to mee goreng. The generous portions don't skimp on the accompaniments, and you could do worse for a lunch under $10 that will almost certainly provide enough leftovers for a snack later. But seasoning is often insufficient; "Phuket Noodles" billed as "very spicy," for example, deliver no more than an average hot-and-sour punch.

Then there's satay chicken, lemon chicken, salmon teriyaki—you know the drill. Nonetheless, ingredients are reasonably fresh, and, to its credit, Nooshi certainly doesn't overreach. With reasonable prices, a central location, and a well-known happy hour offering half-price drinks from Monday through Saturday, Nooshi serves its purpose. Given the genre, it's almost part of that purpose, you might say, not to be that great. –CD

# Nora

Pricey and organic, yes, but—more importantly—
warm, romantic, and consistently pretty good

| 8.6 | 9.3 |
|---|---|
| Food | Feel |

## New American

Upmarket restaurant

| $80 |
|---|
| Price |

www.noras.com

Mon–Thu 6pm–10pm
Fri–Sat 5:30pm–10:30pm

**Bar** Beer, wine, liquor
**Credit cards** Visa, MC, AmEx
**Reservations** Accepted
Date-friendly, Wi-Fi

**Dupont**
2132 Florida Ave. NW
(202) 462-5143

This is the nation's first certified organic restaurant, but Nora features the white linens, classically trained waiters, dimmed lighting, and high prices of any other very-top-end DC establishment. Although they may not mandate that you wear a tie, you probably won't feel comfortable in a T-shirt.

It was in 1999 that Nora first won organic certification, which means that 95% of its ingredients come from organic sources. They'll even go out of their way to flag the remaining 5% on the menu (with Roger-Maris-style asterisks). Even so, and even though this is DC, the restaurant doesn't try to make carefully sourced, upscale organic food into a political statement. Rather, Nora bears the organic label without condescending to junk-food eaters or exalting health-consciousness—although, in a nod to Berkeley, the menu does note that it is printed on "Elemental Chlorine-free Paper," which is "100% Post-Consumer Recycled" with "Environmentally Sound Dyes." Thankfully, that's about the only part of a meal here that might make you a bit uneasy about the way you're living your life back home.

The 19th-century building, which once held a grocery store, conceals several intimate dining rooms. The warmest is up a half-flight of stairs, and showcases hanging Mennonite quilts in subdued tones. Tables are set close together, and conversation generally occurs in hushed tones in the early hours, although it's not unusual to see several sets of dinner guests kick back over digestifs (Calvados, for instance) and dessert, occupying their table for what might strike even the French as an eternity. But we like it that way.

The best news is that the food is honest and true to form. We love the quality and succulence of Maine Jonah crab, which is pleasantly—and not overbearingly—paired with guacamole, tomato, and ancho chile. Halibut comes out soft and buttery, but we've been even more delighted to see underappreciated fishes like sturgeon show up on the menu. Speaking of the menu, though, we wish it changed more completely and more often—and we've been underwhelmed by some of the simple dishes that organic restaurants are supposed to execute best, like a red and yellow beet salad that didn't sing as sweetly as we'd hoped. The last pear tart we tried, on the other hand, tasted as if perfectly ripe fruit had been picked that very day.

This is not one of DC's best restaurants, if only because the taste sensations rarely rise to the sublime. But we salute the effort. Restaurant Nora is a treat. As with other DC treats, bring your wallet (but leave your Birkenstocks at home). –FC

# Obelisk

Still disarmingly unpretentious, and still DC's top
Italian? Believe it

**9.3** Food  **9.1** Feel

## Italian

Upmarket restaurant  **$110** Price

Tue–Sat 6pm–10pm

**Bar** Beer, wine, liquor
**Credit cards** Visa, MC
**Reservations** Essential
Date-friendly, good wines

**Dupont**
2029 P St. NW
(202) 872-1180

You might expect DC's best Italian restaurant to feel less initially
innocuous. It's just a brownstone, almost residential in aesthetic. Inside,
tables are close and cozy, but an elegant informality dominates the scene;
white walls and simple furnishings seem merely to convey that you're in
the townhouse of a tasteful friend. Of course, your tasteful friend couldn't
cook like this.

A lot of restaurants make bold claims about seasonal artisanality;
"authentic" Italian menus and "locally sourced" ingredients are all the
rage. But there are few restaurants that work within the genre as
smoothly as Obelisk. Some ingredients simply speak for themselves, like
burrata—the creamiest buffalo-milk mozzarella you can imagine, drizzled
with an unusually grassy olive oil and sprinkled with a carefully calibrated
number of salt flakes.

But rare is the kitchen that can so consistently pull off far more complex
dishes with such seeming ease, amalgamating them into something that
is so much more than the sum of its locally sourced parts. Rare is the chef
that can so consistently elevate a marinated sardine, a fried squash
blossom, or a raviolo barely larger than a fingernail into the realm of the
sublime.

The meal will begin with a succession of small plates, followed by a
series of larger courses with a few choices. The handwritten menu
changes often enough that there's no point in seeking out a particular
dish, but pastas are a particular strength, as in delicate, diminutive duck
raviolini that concentrate an enormous amount of flavor into a few square
millimeters of pasta. Meat and fish mains—too often a weakness at the
city's upmarket Italian restaurants—have been no less impressive: roast
suckling pig with fava beans; sweet, firm branzino with Meyer lemon,
roasted cherry tomatoes and artichokes.

Obelisk is prix-fixe-only, and it's not cheap. Nor is it exorbitantly
expensive, though, especially when compared against some of lesser top-
end District restaurants. The wine list isn't cheap, either, but it's also a real
achievement: authentic, thoughtful, focused, and—unlike much of the
upmarket competition—worth the money.

What might be most amazing of all, though, is the restaurant's
longevity. To consistently set the Italian pace for more than two
decades—decades, at that, of dramatic culinary change in America—
seems an almost incomprehensible feat. –FC

# Oceanaire Seafood Room

7.4 6.8
Food Feel

Fried, grilled, or chilled, none of it's good—or professional

## Seafood

Upmarket restaurant

$82
Price

www.theoceanaire.com

Mon–Thu 11:30am–10pm; Fri 11:30am–11pm; Sat 5pm–11pm; Sun 5pm–9pm
Hours vary by location

**Bar** Beer, wine, liquor
**Credit cards** Visa, MC, AmEx
**Reservations** Accepted

**Downtown**
1201 F St. NW
(202) 347-2277

Oceanaire, an elaborately fonted, carefully conceived upmarket seafood chain shows a flashy façade—but ultimately disappoints. Its aesthetic virtually ensures a hefty bill, and given the pleasant vibe and healthy din of the room, it's one that we wish were justified. It looks nice enough; round, comfortable banquettes afford a nice level of privacy, although you should make sure you stay away from the windows, whose views of the parking garage exit aren't the most romantic in town.

If there's a wait, a bar area is nice, and you can have a cocktail and some good, fresh oysters while you wait. Ten or so different oyster appellations might grace the selection on any given day, and littleneck clams are generally available too. The cocktail list has all our old-time favorites: the rusty nail, the sidecar, and, most delightfully, the negroni (gin, campari, and sweet vermouth: the ultimate apéritif, packing a pleasantly bitter, subversively alcoholic punch).

Service can be quite neglectful. While most everyone can navigate a cocktail list, people often need some help with the wines, and the wine stewards here seem to be in short supply. There's no shame in a waiter that's clueless about wine, but a restaurant selling bottles this pricey should send out a top-notch sommelier—someone who won't just steer you toward the priciest bottles.

Oh right, the food. It's not terrible, but it doesn't exactly justify the prices. Whole fish is usually the way to go, but it has come out overdone, defeating its simple purpose. This can be especially disappointing given the general freshness of the fish. Crab cakes are good, and they don't skimp on the crabmeat. Fried seafood, like the "Fisherman's Platter," is somewhat better, but its batter could use some more aggressive seasoning; salt-and-vinegar fries, available as a side, really succeed.

Leave it to fries to save the day. –AH

# Oe Gad Gib

This hidden Korean gem is a triple threat: food, fun, and value

**9.0** Food  **9.3** Feel

## Korean

Casual restaurant  **$20** Price

Sun 10:30am–midnight

**Bar** Beer, wine
**Credit cards** Visa, MC, AmEx
**Reservations** Not accepted
Date-friendly, kid-friendly

**Annandale, VA**
7331 Little River Trpk.
(703) 941-3400

Perhaps one of the most infuriating—or thrilling—things about Annandale's Little Seoul restaurant scene is that you have to bounce around from place to place to get the best version of whatever dish you crave, but no one has the paragon of them *all*. Annan-gol's got better barbecue, Gamasot excels at seolleongtang, Light House has the best soon dubu (best tofu, in general), Seoul Soondae has everyone's favorite soondae…but who has the most dishes with a uniformly high level of execution at the best price?

You'll find the answer in the least likely of places: wedged into a strip mall between Jerry's Subs & Pizza, Austin Veterinary Clinic, River Side Hair Salon, and a karaoke recording studio.

You wouldn't notice the place from the main highway, or even the turn-off, unless you were really looking for it. The doors are of simple glass, on which is printed "Oe Gad Gib" (pronounced way-cat-cheap); there are no real windows, so you're completely shielded from the stark environs outside.

Inside, it's a cozy oasis: there's wood paneling everywhere and cute wood latticework. An open bar, bustling kitchen, and fun music makes it feel like home—if home is rural Korea. For us, this is the warmest, most enjoyable Korean restaurant in the DC area.

One big draw here is the barbecue table grilling, where the meat is cooked on hot stones instead of metal grates. It's very tasty, but Annan-gol has it beat on quality of meat cuts. Pancakes—the ultimate shared starter—are light and fluffy (we like the pa jeon); spicy codfish soup and stone seafood bi-bimbap are standouts. Spicy whole cuttlefish is, hands down, our favorite dish here; it's a rare treat, unusually tender, and paired well with the chili. There are also good hotpots, and soul-warming spicy casseroles. Even the banchan here are a cut above, and more diverse. At lunch, specials run $6-9, and you won't do much more damage at dinner, unless you go crazy and order everything. It's happened to us.

Make sure to wash it all down with dong dong ju, unfiltered rice wine—certainly not as complex as what filtered cold sakes are capable of, but it does the job. It creeps up on you, to be sure, but could your rapturous bliss be caused by the mere warmth of the food and feeling? —FC

# Olazzo

Red-sauce Italian with portions big enough to keep you out of the supermarket for days

| 3.7 | 5.6 |
|---|---|
| Food | Feel |

## Italian

Upmarket restaurant

**$45**
*Price*

www.olazzo.com

Mon–Thu 11:30am–2:30pm, 5pm–9pm; Fri 11:30am–2:30pm, 5pm–10:30pm; Sat 5pm–10:30pm; Sun 5pm–9pm

**Bar** Beer, wine, liquor
**Credit cards** Visa, MC, AmEx
**Reservations** Not accepted
Kid-friendly, outdoor dining, veg-friendly

**Silver Spring, MD**
8235 Georgia Ave.
(301) 588-2540

**Bethesda, MD**
7921 Norfolk Ave.
(301) 793-7490

Olazzo is an exercise in mediocrity, from concept to execution. The small dining room exudes coziness, but only because it's too dark to see the faux sophistication: walls rag-painted to look like marble, somber paintings, and grave black accents. Even the wood-burning fire exudes no warmth, displayed, as it is, on a television set.

The food lacks creativity, authenticity, and care. Pastas aren't homemade, and the flavor wheel stutters on "garlic" and "salt." A testament to how unabashedly far this olive has dropped from the Italian tree can be found on the "low-carb" portion of the menu. What Italian grandmother sanctioned this move?

Assuming you are here for the carbs, the bread does arrive warm—a nice touch. However, it is served with an almost-clear liquid with virtually no flavor at all. To call it light olive oil, or even oil, would be a stretch. Bruschetta features diced tomatoes blanketed with melted mozzarella cheese and seasoned with an excess of garlic powder. The penne in the "Shrimp Rosé" can be pleasantly al dente, but get lost in an oppressive tomato cream sauce; the shrimp, themselves, come unevenly cooked and oversalted. Dry chicken parmesan is drenched in tomato sauce and cheese. Cheap, tacky salads are an afterthought. And is there a law that states that every DC kitchen, regardless of cuisine, must serve a salmon-mango dish? This is about as Italian as a pagoda.

If you make it this far without falling asleep, tiramisù may be creamy, delicate and spongy, but where does bottled chocolate syrup belong in this classic dessert? Even in Bobby Flay's chocoholic nightmare world, this would never happen.

A childish martini menu—with over 25 silly names like Italian Surfer and Cotton Candy—employs the cheap, syrupy mixers you'd find in any dive bar; we'd argue they're only appropriately priced on Tuesdays, when they're $5 a pop. In the final draw, Olazzo stages a coup against great Italian wine by providing none, instead tossing a bunch of grocery-store names up there—wines renowned for missing the mark completely. So maybe it is a perfect list, after all. –FC

# Old City Café & Bakery

**5.9** Food    **5.5** Feel

Familiar falafel in a build-your-own format

## Middle Eastern

Counter service    **$10** Price

Sun–Thu 10am–11pm
Fri–Sat 10am–3:30am

**Bar** None
**Credit cards** Visa, MC, AmEx
Outdoor dining, veg-friendly, Wi-Fi

**Adams Morgan**
1773 Columbia Rd. NW
(202) 232-1322

A miniature soap opera erupted in Adams Morgan in 2006 when the chef at Amsterdam Falafel Shop refused to sign a non-disclosure agreement with the shop's owners. The owners wanted to protect (and possibly, expand nationally) their concept: a do-it-yourself falafel bar—you're served a few patties in a pita, you add your own toppings from an array of salads and sauces—based on the ones that abound in European capitals.

The chef waffled, delayed, and repeatedly refused to sign the document for a year, before announcing that he was leaving Amsterdam Falafel Shop in order to open his own place—just down the street. His concept is identical to Amsterdam's: falafel with the add-ins bar, plus some shawarma dishes, desserts, and sides. For a few weeks in the summer of '06, the controversy was on the tips of local tongues, but these days Adams Morgan has resigned itself to the fact that the two shops are pretty much interchangeable. Each eatery has its handful of die-hard patrons, but there's enough foot traffic on 18th Street to keep business pretty swift at both.

The Old City Café and Bakery (which is also known as "that falafel place on Columbia") serves up a chickpea patty that's smaller than most, but still manages to combine a crisp outer crust with a moist inside. The balls are quite nicely spiced, and deep-fried in front of you when you place your order.

You can order a "small" or "large" sandwich: the small comes with three balls in half a pita; the large is five balls in a whole pita. The bread, which is of the generic packaged variety, runs rather small, and a single sandwich can seem skimpy for a large appetite. With some engineering savvy, however, you can tear open the pita a little, pile in toppings (which are all freshly made, and include options ranging from eggplant to taboulleh to spicy chickpeas), and truly make a mountain from a molehill.

And don't overlook Old City's desserts. We haven't found a rice pudding quite like Old City's anywhere in DC—Amsterdam Falafel Shop not excluded. –CK

# Old Ebbitt Grill

## 6.9 | 8.7
### Food | Feel

Since 1856, a DC institution known for its oysters and excess

## American

Casual restaurant

### $40
### Price

www.ebbitt.com

Mon–Fri 7:30am–1am
Sat–Sun 8:30am–1am

**Bar** Beer, wine, liquor
**Credit cards** Visa, MC, AmEx
**Reservations** Accepted
Date-friendly, kid-friendly

**Downtown**
675 15th St. NW
(202) 347-4800

If a Walrus and a Carpenter were to sit down and dine, they might end up at Old Ebbitt. So, it seems, does just about every tourist in DC. They come, first and foremost, for the oysters, which come from both coasts; this may be one of the only in the area to stock Olympias. It's also where the annual Oyster Riot takes place, as well as the International Wines for Oysters competition (where Antonin Scalia has regularly been a judge). Further, being that it's a few blocks from the White House, Old Ebbitt is a remnant of a trickier Washington, where the heavy hitters met to make or break deals with a handshake, a stiff drink, and a slab of animal flesh. Though it's moved several times, and was acquired in the 1970s by the Clyde's Restaurant Group (as if it weren't touristy enough already), the interior of Old Ebbitt has preserved or carbon-copied much of its 150-year history—from the recreated mahogany bar to the oil paintings, to the (possibly Presidential) taxidermy.

The menu seems never to have evolved from the days of the hard-eating politicos you often see in portrait galleries. This could very well be how Taft got fat. The bisque in the fried-oyster soup is so rich it's like eating a bowl of cream sauce that is streaked with oil slicks from the fryer. Admittedly, it is (cardiac-) arrestingly delicious. A "Breakfast Club" puts other food to shame with its sheer audacity: parcels of French toast and ham sandwiches are mummy-wrapped in thick ribbons of bacon and then drenched in syrup. It is sweet/savory/meaty/bready, crunchy on the outside but still loose and fatty on the inside where the bacon has barely cooked. It is quite possible that you will hurl or dream about this sandwich for years to come…or both. Keep in mind that oysters and cholesterol-fests do best on this menu; some of the simpler meat and fish mains aren't up to the standard.

Servers are lovely chaps, well-mannered and a tad comic in their uniform of red bowties, braces, and Walrus pins. Cocktails are of the same syrupy ilk you find at all the Clyde's properties, but there are plenty of classics, too. Bloody Marys are ample, but surprisingly weak given the generosity of the menu. A hearty wine list is New World-heavy, but fits the Baroque bill just fine. All around, Old Ebbitt is a beloved institution of DC history and gastronomic excess. It's loud and proud. What finer place for legislators and press corps to sit and ponder why the sea is boiling hot and whether pigs have wings? –JC

# Old Glory Bar-B-Que

**6.3** | **5.8**
*Food* | *Feel*

Some of the better BBQ in DC's weak field—a big
pig in a small pen?

## Barbecue

Casual restaurant | **$30**
*Price*

www.oldglorybbq.com

Mon–Thu 11:30am–2am
Fri–Sat 11:30am–3am
Sun 11am–2am

**Bar** Beer, wine, liquor
**Credit cards** Visa, MC, AmEx
**Reservations** Accepted
Delivery, kid-friendly, live music,
outdoor dining

**Georgetown**
3139 M St. NW
(202) 337-3406

Old Glory may seem contrived, with its artfully aged detailing and rough-hewn furniture. Yet the wall mural covering the length of the staircase is touchingly sincere. The elongated figures dancing against a backdrop of unbroken fields are beautiful and sad, a poignant note of levity and contemplation amidst the gorging masses, calling to mind WPA art commissioned during the Great Depression. But really, what could represent our pioneering spirit and zest for life better than eating a plate of meat cooked over hot coals? At Old Glory, you'll come to understand the fierce pride Americans take in their barbecue.

The first indication of this national obsession is on the table. Five bottles of homemade sauce sit in a rack, each labeled with its city of origin. Waiters make introductions, detailing ingredients, viscosity, and recommended pairings. They also cheerfully warn you about the dangers of pouring too vigorously and point you to the mountain of napkins on the table. This place is serious.

You can say one thing for Old Glory: they get the texture right. Wings come steroidically plump and juicy. Brisket has a good charred edge and a nice, fattier underside. It's a good, thinly sliced showing of tough meat turned tender with time. Ribs have the right texture as well, and pulled pork is aptly stringy. The universal problem is blandness. It's the lack of a deep wood-smoke flavor that, in top-notch barbecue, renders barbecue sauce superfluous, or at least turns it into a finishing touch, not a driver of flavor. Here, instead, there are several sauces (served in measly portions) named after various US barbecue regions. Guess what, guys? Regional barbecue differences are about a lot more than sauce flavors.

Side dishes are passable but nothing special. Applesauce is indistinguishable from other homemade versions; the same goes for somewhat bland mac and cheese and soggy sweet-potato fries. Dessert is particularly sub-par. Though bread pudding is the size of Texas, its texture is too sticky and too dense, like a grainy, undercooked brownie; there is no custardy goodness. You can finish your meal with a somewhat overpriced glass of Bourbon, but at the end, you'll want to go back to the beginning. More meat please.

A $20 brunch feeds you all the smoked suckling pig, hash, caramel French toast, biscuits and gravy you can eat; $10 more gets you blind drunk. A late-night menu also caters to your midnight hankering for flesh. Ain't that America? –JC

# Old Siam

Don't waste your time—it's just more bland
coconut-gravy Thai

| 5.1 | 6.0 |
|------|------|
| Food | Feel |

## Thai

Casual restaurant

**$25**
*Price*

www.theoldsiamrestaurant.com

Mon–Thu 11:30am–3pm, 5pm–
10:30pm; Fri 11:30am–3pm,
5pm–11:30pm; Sat 11:30am–
3:30pm, 5pm–11:30pm; Sun
noon–3:30pm, 5pm–10:30pm

**Bar** Beer, wine, liquor
**Credit cards** Visa, MC, AmEx
**Reservations** Accepted
Delivery, outdoor dining

**Capitol Hill**
406 8th St. SE
(202) 544-7426

Our hopes skyrocketed when we tasted the spring rolls at Old Siam. We'd
already begun, against our best intentions, to write the place off as yet
another middle-of-the-road, risk-free, and mostly flavor-free DC Thai
restaurant. The atmosphere, after all, was Pier-One-perfect: colorful
chinoiserie-fabric pillows, mellow wooden Buddha statues, and a few
palms tastefully placed in corners. There was no striking smell from the
kitchen; the menu options looked pleasant but unoriginal.

Not that fried spring rolls are a Thai dish, really, but it's true that the
spring rolls undermined those budding impressions. The duo had a
remarkably light, crisped outer crust; the rolls were filled with vegetables
shredded finer than we've even seen vegetables shredded, and rice
vermicelli thinner than the thinnest vermicelli we'd seen. The
accompanying sauce was tangy but too sweet.

Apart from a small selection of appetizers that's done right, the fare at
Old Siam is classic DC Thai. The restaurant features dishes that are neither
extremely bad nor shockingly good: just run-of-the-mill Thai-American
food that suffers from being under-spiced, overcooked, uncreative and, in
a word, mediocre.

Most dishes are criminally under-spiced and end up tasting like very
little. The green curry is allocated three stars on the rudimentary spice-
scale (one star is mild, two is medium, and three is supposedly hot; most
dishes have no stars, which we have some evidence to believe means
"unbelievably bland"), but the curry still fails miserably in its attempts to
stir to life the hot-sensing taste buds. The result is something like warm
coconut soup, garnished with Thai basil.

The Panang curry (one star), meanwhile, has very little basil in the
broth, nor, for that matter, much meat. The pieces of chicken that do
emerge (or that you rescue from the swimming pool of broth) are tough
and flavorless. Once you've fished out the meat, you're left wondering
whether you should spoon more broth onto the remaining steamed rice,
or just quit while you're ahead.

Smart gamblers learn from hindsight (and was there ever a game as
high-stakes as the DC Thai scene?): we should have folded after the
spring rolls. –CK

# Oohhs & Aahhs

Mama's home cookin', a long way from home

**8.5** *Food*  **8.0** *Feel*

## Southern

Counter service

**$25** *Price*

www.oohhsnaahhs.com

Tue–Sat noon–10pm

**Bar** None
**Credit cards** None
Kid-friendly, Wi-Fi

**Shaw**
1005 U St. NW
(202) 667-7142

Washington, DC fluctuates between feeling like a small southern town and a much larger northeastern city. But as soon as you step into the vibrant Oohhs and Aahhs, any confusion will melt away. This is southern DC at its best. The place itself, which functions largely as a carry-out joint, but has a full dining room upstairs, is intimate, with the fryer (a key item), cooks, and side dishes in plain view. The few downstairs counter seats are privy to all the exciting action and the chatting, while the larger air-conditioned dining area upstairs has a plasma TV that, if you're lucky, is tuned in to the latest Tyler Perry movie.

Eat at Oohhs and Aahhs, and you'll be among regulars who come from the surrounding U Street neighborhood and from farther out for great soul food. Portions are huge but come conveniently in Styrofoam containers—you'll be eating leftovers for a few days. Fried chicken is some of the city's best, meaty and juicy on the inside with a crisp, well-seasoned crust. The tender blackened catfish, hot and smoky but not unbearably so, is a lighter alternative.

Side dishes are a crucial element in soul-food dining, and at Oohhs and Aahhs they are most certainly not overlooked. The macaroni and cheese is cheddary and gooey and delicious, if a touch undersalted. Fish is a touch less strong—it's cooked through, and then some—but collard greens, tart and tender, hold their own even without the traditional bacon, which can dominate their flavor in other incarnations. We would, however, have preferred them to be as warm as the atmosphere here. The over-dressed potato salad, slathered in a sweet mustardy relish, doesn't hold a candle to the other better-executed sides. A word of caution: iced tea and lemonade are sweet as your mama's love, and, like everything else, very big. As those of us from the south know, drinks as big as peach baskets are essential to surviving the dog days of summer. So are good company, good food, and a good, slow sweat to work it all out of your system again. Ya'll come back now, y'hear? –SDC

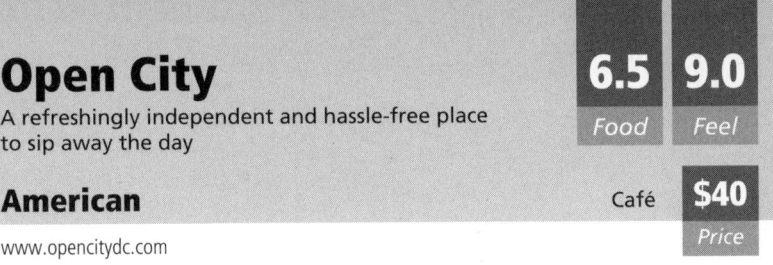

# Open City

A refreshingly independent and hassle-free place
to sip away the day

**6.5** Food   **9.0** Feel

## American

Café   **$40** Price

www.opencitydc.com

Sun–Thu 6am–midnight
Fri–Sat 6am–1am

**Bar** Beer, wine, liquor
**Credit cards** Visa, MC, AmEx
**Reservations** Not accepted
Outdoor dining, veg-friendly, Wi-Fi

**Woodley Park**
2331 Calvert St. NW
(202) 332-2331

Washington needs more places like Open City. The third in a line of successful sister cafés (its siblings are Tryst and The Diner), this joint provides a middle ground between the legions of upscale reservations-only establishments and holes-in-the-wall with hit-or-miss quality. Open City offers the convenience of a coffeeshop without the brand consciousness of a Starbucks (and this, in a city with so few non-chain cafés!): you can linger with spread-out books and notes and a single latte for hours without eliciting complaint. Or, you can come late at night for a bottle of wine and dessert. All the while, Open City serves breakfast at all hours, hearty dinner fare at most hours, and rich cakes and pastries baked in-house (the sour cherry pie leaves lasting memories). While loners are welcome, the café is, in the end, a social place.

There's so much to be said for the atmosphere that the food at Open City almost seems secondary. The café offers standard breakfast fare like eggs and pancakes. The preparation is nothing special, but some of the ingredients are top-notch—Applewood smoked bacon or quality lox, for example. On the sweet side, the brioche French toast is made with a rich, home-baked sweet roll that is almost too thick to cut, and can be topped with banana walnut sauce or nutella. Also try the croque monsieur or croque madame.

Open City's burgers are served with subtle updates: the cheeseburger, for example, can be made with one of six types of cheese. The turkey burger is thick and well salted. As a side or a main, Open City's vegetarian black-bean chili tastes as if it's been simmered for hours; unfortunately, it's served with oyster crackers rather than bread.

The staff at Open City is factory-line hip (vintage scarves in the girls' hair, vintage button-downs on the boys), but don't be put off: the servers are so kind that their hipness is forgivable, and the place is dominated by families and older couples rather than disgruntled twenty-somethings. Open City is a great space to come to see friends. But not to "be seen."
—CK

# Oriental East

A dim sum find in the Maryland suburbs

**8.9** Food   **7.0** Feel

## Chinese

Casual restaurant

**$40** Price

www.orientaleast.com

Sun–Thu 11am–10pm
Fri–Sat 11am–11pm

**Bar** Beer, wine, liquor
**Credit cards** Visa, MC, AmEx
**Reservations** Accepted
Kid-friendly, outdoor dining

**Silver Spring, MD**
1312 E. West Hwy.
(301) 608-0030

What will it take to cure the multiple personality disorder that has come to define the Chinese restaurant in America? Even in the places—like the Maryland suburbs—where Chinese communities thrive, and where good Chinese food is legion, the secret Chinese menus are kept largely out of sight unless you speak the language or are part of the ethnic ingroup. Oriental East's pink paper carry-out menu, for instance, is a roll call of Chinese-American slop: chow mein, sweet-and-sour pork, "orange chicken," combination fried rice, egg rolls, fortune cookies.

But the big round tables of Chinese customers that frequent this cafeteria-like strip-mall restaurant—whose only attempt at décor is a set of mirrors bearing cartoonish Chinese scenes in garish shades of neon—aren't eating anything from that menu. Instead, their meals look classically Cantonese: a cold salad of gently resilient jellyfish and pig's foot; a delicately steamed whole fish with garlic and ginger; a bowl of congee with pork and preserved egg; a bowl of marvelously silky bean curd or tender beef tripe; or a plate of bright, shiny Chinese greens, fired by a wok for only a moment. Some of these dishes are concealed within a section of the menu entitled "House Specialties," but many of them, including the specials of the day, don't appear on *any* menu—instead, they're discussed with Chinese customers at the table.

Weekend dim sum is the great equalizer, replacing the arm-wrestling match of trying to order "what they've got on that table over there" with a simple game of food-cart show-and-tell. Come between 11am and 1pm, and expect to wait for a while before your number is called. Among the dishes that should be snapped up as soon as they roll by are tender slices of squid, plated with pickled vegetables and tinged red by a deep marinade; chicken feet, rich and gelatinous, steeping in a profoundly flavorful soy-based sauce; pork, shrimp, and dried scallop dumplings with expertly textured rice wrappers; or sticky rice penetrated by flavor from its lotus-leaf wrapper. A sweet-savory treat rarely seen in America is the golden baked pork bun, whose sugary, slightly underdone dough envelops a soupy nucleus of salty red meat. This Cantonese feast—one worth meditating on—will rarely run more than $10 per person after tax. For all those that complain about the questionable value propositions of top DC-area restaurants, we invite you to Silver Spring. –RG

# The Oval Room

**8.5** Food   **7.7** Feel

The tony tone it down a bit at this beautifully presented—too beautifully?—restaurant

## New American

Upmarket restaurant

**$75** Price

www.ovalroom.com

Mon–Thu 11:30am–3pm, 5:30pm–10pm; Fri 11:30am–3pm, 5:30pm–10:30pm; Sat 5:30pm–10:30pm

**Bar** Beer, wine, liquor
**Credit cards** Visa, MC, AmEx
**Reservations** Accepted
Good wines, outdoor dining

**Farragut**
800 Connecticut Ave. NW
(202) 463-8700

In the past this restaurant has been guilty of the "one ingredient too many" sin that plagues ambitious kitchens. But it seems to have since tightened its focus, pairing flavors that are a natural evolution of tradition, not a cavalier nose-thumbing at it.

Although its name may conjure a stuffy Presidential feel, the friendly and laid-back atmosphere of the Oval Room proves quite the opposite. Soothing green walls, abstract paintings in reds and yellows and oranges, rust-colored leather chairs, and plenty of sunlight give this restaurant a mellow but smart vibe. On a cooler afternoon or evening, the tree-shaded outdoor patio is the only way to go.

Plates are meticulously choreographed from the flavors to the presentation, which is always beautiful—if a little cumbersome. Smoked peach purée, lime gel, and popcorn and basil powders flank a cylinder of smooth-as-flan corn custard. It takes quite an effort to put bites of this dish together, and the flavors, though generally harmonizing, become cloying after a few laborious mouthfuls. A fish dish that rotates between salmon and Arctic char is similarly attractive and takes less effort to compose—delicate, barely cooked fish sits on top of fried Chinese eggplant and thin garlic chips. Braised baby bok choy and kaffir lime leaf give the dish a couple of interesting points of brightness. The one downside: the lingering taste of fried garlic stays with you for the rest of the day. This can be a beautiful thing when paired with the right wine. Which brings us to the wine list: though diverse and well-chosen, it doesn't take nearly as many exciting risks as does the kitchen, and some revelatory pairing opportunities are missed. Their Sancerres, white Burgundies, and Sangioveses would be lovely with maybe one or two dishes, but there's a dearth of Riesling, dry Muscat, and funky light-bodied red varietals that this food cries out for.

Desserts are more recognizable than their precursors. Almost all of the homey options come with homemade ice cream as good as whatever it's accompanying. The decadent hazelnut dacquoise is served with salted caramel ice cream, helping to cut through the richness of the dacquoise's milk chocolate and peanut butter. And the presentation is once again impeccable.

It looks like Oval Room may be on the right track; we'll keep you posted. –SDC

# Oya

Waterfalls, wine, and distracted waitstaff—Oya's too cool for school

**7.1** Food · **7.4** Feel

## Pan-Asian

Upmarket restaurant · **$75** Price

www.oyadc.com

Mon–Thu 11:30am–2:30pm, 5:30pm–10:30pm; Fri 11:30am–2:30pm, 5:30pm–11:30pm; Sat 5:30pm–11:30pm; Sun 5:30pm–9pm

**Bar** Beer, wine, liquor
**Credit cards** Visa, MC, AmEx
**Reservations** Accepted
Good wines, veg-friendly

**Penn Quarter**
799 9th St. NW
(202) 393-1400

Oya is cool—perhaps too cool. White marble, white leather chairs, frosted white glasses, a waterfall blurring the view into the kitchen, and a red leather bar are all elements that one might associate with a pretentious upscale restaurant. So is the name "Restaurant & Lounge." But Oya somehow manages to make even the uncool kids feel comfortable in its presence—except, that is, when they encounter the spectacularly bad service.

An admirable wine and sake list provides playful and helpful descriptions that serve to better pair them with specific dishes and flavors. Wines cover some unlikely regions of the United States—Michigan, Idaho, Pennsylvania, Georgia—and the world, too, like effervescent Txakoli from Basque Country (a great Asian-food wine), a good Madeira selection, and Lebanon's light, earthy Château Musar red. It's exciting to see a list that ventures into lesser-known territories when it could easily get away with the usual thoughtless lineup of reds and whites, as most pan-Asian restaurants do.

Flavors on the menu, at first, seem to run unsupervised all over the playground—Mediterranean and Asian and American in one—but some of them work well. Prix-fixe lunch and dinner options are available ($18 and $28 respectively for three courses), and value-wise, these are really the way to go. Tuna tempura roll, a first-course option, is crunchy on the outside, while the tuna on the inside is rare and warm. The bold heat of a seven-pepper sauce gives it a well-deserved kick. A main course of Atlantic salmon has a too-cool description—saffron "caviar" is one of the elements (it's really infused Israeli couscous)—but once again, when it arrives beautifully composed on the plate, pretentions fade away. The salmon's crispy exterior protects a barely cooked interior, and a parade of Mediterranean flavors brings the dish together: olives, crisp snap peas, warm cherry tomatoes, mashed red potatoes, and basil oil. Among desserts, the hazelnut biscuit buried beneath a mass of mousse in "Chocolate, chocolate, and chocolate" is a bit underwhelming, but banana bread pudding delivers moist caramel goodness.

The most disappointing part about Oya is the laughably slow, inattentive service from an attractive but aloof staff, sapping a good deal of the restaurant's charm and undermining the Asian concept (Asia, after all, is known for its hospitality). When will these maverick trend-palace restaurateurs come to their senses and realize that, at dinner as in bed, indifference isn't ultimately all that sexy? –FC

# Oyamel

Sexy Mexican with some upmarket twists

**8.0** *Food*   **9.2** *Feel*

## Mexican

Upmarket restaurant   **$60** *Price*

www.oyamel.com

| | | |
|---|---|---|
| Sun–Mon 11:30am–10pm | **Bar** Beer, wine, liquor | **Penn Quarter** |
| Tue–Thu 11:30am–11:30pm | **Credit cards** Visa, MC, AmEx | 401 7th St. NW |
| Fri–Sat 11:30am–midnight | **Reservations** Accepted | (202) 628-1005 |
| | Date-friendly, kid-friendly, outdoor dining | |

With hyped-up pedigree (José Andrés) and the promise of unusual authenticity, Oyamel breathes with excitement—and not just because the concept is generally being evaluated by margarita-lubricated neural pathways. The space almost always feels colorful and lively, modern but not pretentious, equally suited to a liquid brunch or a classy dinner date.

More importantly, the eyes of anyone who's traveled in Mexico (and we're not talking Cancún spring-breakers) will light up at the sight of the menu. It dances across the country, starting in the Bajío, with sopa tarasca estilo Pátzcuaro (a satisfying black bean soup) and ending on the coast, with myriad of ceviches and huachinango a la veracruzana (red snapper with tomatoes, onions, capers, and olives), with plenty of Oaxacan moles along the way. And, of course, there's the apocryphal "Ensalada Alex-Cesar Cardini" to tie everything together.

But, as anyone who's traveled in Mexico knows, the best food is generally had on the street, at a roadside *parador*, or anywhere that you see locals. It's rarely found at the pricey places. True to that theory, the food here is a bit less exciting on the palate that its promise on the menu. But it's a really fun place nonetheless, and there are some standout items on the menu. "Gaspacho" estilo Morelia (not the Spanish tomato purée you might be expecting) is a salad whose mix of jicama, jalapeños, mango, cucumber, and orange is rather refreshing. Papas al mole might as well be served in a ballpark—presentation is sub-par (especially when compared to some of the pretty platings you see with other dishes)—but it's hard to argue with potatoes smothered in black mole, cream, and cheese. Tacos check out better on paper than on the plate; cochinita pibil comes out a bit dry, but the accompanying escabeche is a lovely counterpoint. Chapulines (grasshoppers—a very popular snack in the state of Oaxaca) come with shallots, and are a bit soggy, but a dab of guacamole helps them along.

It's the drinks that really shine. The "Oyamel Margarita" is a careful blend (made, admittedly, with Cuervo) topped with "salt air," a foamy essence—and José Andrés show-thing (we won't use the cringe-worthy word "signature")—that's a far superior delivery mechanism for savory balance than big chunks of salt.

Try ordering one of *those* at a street cart. –AH

# Palena

A hyped-up Cleveland Park showpiece whose high prices can be circumvented at the café

**8.8** Food  **8.0** Feel

## New American

Upmarket restaurant

**$100** Price

www.palenarestaurant.com

Tue–Sat 5:30pm–10pm

**Bar** Beer, wine, liquor
**Credit cards** Visa, MC, AmEx
**Reservations** Accepted
Date-friendly, outdoor dining

**Cleveland Park**
3529 Connecticut Ave. NW
(202) 537-9250

Should we mention the ten-dollar hot dog? We'll state unequivocally that it's a damn good hot dog, but it's still a *ten-dollar* damn good hot dog. Like any other hot dog, it's served in a bun, with mustard and relish—but there are some marked differences. First of all, the dog is less uniform than a frank: it's sort of rotund and even slightly lumpy, like a sausage. The outer package is burnt nicely in a couple of spots, and the meat inside is of a much higher quality. It's served on a high-class toasted bun with sourdough hints, with a grainy boutique mustard and two handfuls of thin french fries made from real potatoes. It makes a fine meal, at the end of which we're left unsure if Palena's attempting to be ironic, or just homey.

The restaurant is run by two chefs with White House tenures, and it aims at upmarket American cuisine with a fresh and whimsical twist. The ingredients are indeed top-flight, even if there is inconsistency in the resulting dishes. The dining room is sophisticated without being staid: white linens and light-toned decorations that make the small room feel spacious and airy. The wine glasses and menus are big, and the tables are ideally sized for intimate conversation without unwanted elbow interaction.

A lot of the food is up to the task: potato gnocchi, for example, are roundly viewed as the best in town, and it's extremely hard to argue with their surprising lightness and softness, whether they're paired with fava beans (sound too starchy? not here) or a sharper olive-and-hare sauce. Either way, they're unforgettable. The prix-fixe rotates frequently, but recently, we've sampled house-made cotechino sausage with silky squash raviolini, and an unbelievably moist braised New York State guinea hen with foie gras and brussels sprouts (is there anything more modern than such an aristocrat-peasant pairing?). Fish mains and desserts have been reliably well executed, too.

Here's the thing: two of Palena's best works—the roast chicken and the burger—are available at the much cheaper, no-reservations café. Given how far the prix-fixe prices have been creeping up, that is certainly the way to go. Yes, it's more casual, but we don't think that's necessarily a bad thing. We fear that Palena's dining room may be riding too much on its good looks, intelligent wine list, and elegant menu listings. Too often, some of the flights of fancy go wrong, and you wind up jealous of the burger-eaters, who are paying a third what you are. Especially these days, such a value proposition is hard to resist. –CK

# The Palm

**7.0** **8.0**
Food Feel

Steaks and chops in a cartoonish carbon copy of
the over-the-top Manhattan original

## Steakhouse

Upmarket restaurant

**$95**
Price

www.thepalm.com

Mon–Fri 11:30am–10pm
Sat 5:30pm–10:30pm
Sun 5:30pm–9:30pm
Hours vary by location

**Bar** Beer, wine, liquor
**Credit cards** Visa, MC, AmEx
**Reservations** Accepted

**Dupont**
1225 19th St. NW
(202) 293-9091

**Tysons Corner, VA**
1750 Tysons Blvd.
(703) 917-0200

Ah, the Palm. Here we have yet another player in the steakhouse scene,
but this one has the force of an entire chain behind it—locations are
everywhere, even Puerto Rico. All the outposts are styled by detail-
obsessed experts to look, feel, and smell like the storied, still-delicious
Manhattan original, the exemplar after which the chain is modeled, and—
of course—they cost as much, too. Yes, the atmosphere (wall cartoons
and magnums of California Cab, mostly) is totally contrived, but at least it
manages to feel slightly warmer and more casual than the competition,
even if the business clientele plays the rude-corporate-credit-card-
customer part perfectly.

It's not often that you'll find us raving about a salad, but the "West
Coast Gigi" here does get us excited. It's similar to a Cobb salad, rich with
avocado, egg, and bacon. What don't get us excited are the Italian
specialties on the menu; you don't come to a steakhouse for linguine with
clam sauce. We wish wallet-busting prime steaks came out as we'd expect
them to, but this kitchen seems to struggle a bit with cooking times; there
seems to be little all-around consensus over what exactly a rare steak is.
Creamed spinach, though, is excellent. The wine list, however, is
disappointing. Wines by the glass aren't great to begin with, and they're
even worse when you get a glass of oxidized wine that was opened the
last time someone ordered it, and since has been waiting around for
someone to finish the bottle. Bottle options, obviously, are better, and
you've got all your big reds on the list, but the markups are brazen.

A business lunch menu gets you a three-course meal for $22—if you
want a steak in the middle of the day. (There are other options, like fish or
chicken.)

It's a great deal, but if we find ourselves in Tysons Corner at lunchtime,
we're jumping on the Leesburg Pike and heading down to Eden Center—
where we couldn't blow through $22 even if we tried. –AH

# Paolo's

A better atmosphere than food, but barely better food than Olive Garden

**4.5** Food  **8.7** Feel

## Italian

Casual restaurant  **$40** Price

www.paolosristorante.com

Mon–Thu 11am–11:30pm
Fri 11am–12:30am
Sat 10am–12:30am
Sun 10am–11:30pm

**Bar** Beer, wine, liquor
**Credit cards** Visa, MC, AmEx
**Reservations** Accepted
Date-friendly, kid-friendly, live
music, outdoor dining, veg-friendly

**Georgetown**
1303 Wisconsin Ave. NW
(202) 333-7353

One member of this minichain is just a short walk up Wisconsin from Georgetown, so it's become that one restaurant where students take their parents when they are in town. It's perfect for this: from the décor to the service to the food, Paolo's is expertly mediocre.

Georgetown's quaint yellow house with shiny black shutters, decorated in a style somewhere between beach house and villa, exudes charm. The mishmash of styles is melded together by the coziness of dim lighting and close tables. Diners at Paolo's run the gamut from date-nighters to large parties of students, which means that it's a crapshoot as to whether it will be quiet and intimate or loud and raucous on a given night.

Whatever the atmosphere may be, the food fails in too many of its interpretations of Italian food. Paolo's version of bruschetta, served deconstructed in a mixed platter is one of the better choices here. Roasted peppers, eggplant, and mushrooms tile the plate in a mosaic of colors, and pools of sauce and fresh herbs add an extra layer of scent and flavor. Though the dish probably shouldn't be called bruschetta (there are too few pieces of gorgonzola-topped toast on which to spoon the vegetables), it is still worth ordering. The sauces include an olive oil infused with basil and a fruity balsamic reduction that is rich, spicy, and complex.

Tortellini in rose sauce is overrich; large chunks of sun-dried tomatoes and prosciutto bathe in a tomato cream sauce thick enough to obscure the pasta, which isn't necessarily a bad thing, because the noodles are gummy and thick. Pasta dishes here, in general, are all about the sauce…and full of *stuff*. The brick-oven pizzas aren't particularly brick-oveny, although the crust is thin and evenly cooked. Toppings are kind of heaped in the center instead of evenly spread.

At dessert, cannoli shells are of the thinner tuille variety (versus pastry), and the filling tries for savory, but comes off bland. It tastes more like frying oil than anything else, and rich chocolate sauce isn't enough to save it.

Paolo's isn't the place to turn if you want a meal true to the diverse regional cuisines of the Boot. But if you're a student, and your folks are of that red sauce/alfredo variety, this sure beats Olive Garden. –JC

# Park Café

The melody of this little neighborhood favorite is all grace notes

| 7.6 | 9.4 |
|-----|-----|
| Food | Feel |

## New American

Upmarket restaurant  **$60**
*Price*

www.parkcafedc.com

Mon–Sat 5pm–10pm
Sun 10am–2pm, 5pm–9pm

**Bar** Beer, wine, liquor
**Credit cards** Visa, MC, AmEx
**Reservations** Not accepted
Date-friendly, Wi-Fi

**Capitol Hill**
106 13th St. SE
(202) 543-0184

The Park Café is a true neighborhood establishment and one of the loveliest spots to dine in DC. On spring and summer nights, the floor-to-ceiling windows are opened up to the quiet streets of eastern Capitol Hill, and the smooth siena-red-tile floors assert the feel of southern Spain. The regular keyboard-bass duo pulls together a slowed down Charlie Parker tune, and the walls are covered with a tasteful series of prints by a friend of Alcione Vinet, the Café's owner.

While a debonair waiter single-handedly mans all 10 tables, Vinet himself wanders the aisles, unassuming and unobtrusive to the point of being mistaken for a busboy or host. When it comes to ordering wine, however, the affable young server defers to the hefty Vinet, who sizes up a party and its food, listens to requests and queries, then takes away the list (which, already, is extensive) and scurries downstairs to find a better match. More often than not, his recommendation is smart, and it is never more expensive than the original pick. A peek downstairs reveals an earnest wine-collector's lair, with nearly-full racks and cases piled on the floor.

A small disappointment compared to the wine, Park Café's food is uplifting but not transporting. A few dishes are outstanding: the gazpacho is made with sweet red and slightly sour yellow tomatoes, sweet balsamic vinegar and basil, and topped with fresh, soft crab meat for a mellow flavor and a superb mingling of textures. Bookending the meal on the opposite end is one of the richest dessert menus in town: the tiramisù, despite a full soaking in coffee liqueur, maintains a contrast between wet ladyfinger crumbs and creamy layers of mascarpone.

The mains at Park Café deserve praise for achieving simplicity without minimalism; however, we wish the kitchen could be a little more daring with its use of salt. Tilapia is mild—without sufficient salt, the full taste of the fish doesn't come through—and the main flavor in the dish arises from the herbed blue potatoes beneath. A poblano pepper, on the other hand, is daringly stuffed with gamy boar meat and fresh crab; here the salt is sufficient and the mix of flavors, if odd, comes to the fore. Portions are notably slight for the price, but somehow, in the face of industry-wide excess, this suits the restaurant's pleasing modesty.

The food, in short, is good enough, and diffident enough, not to get in the way of the rare warmth of the staff, the beauty of the location, and the delight of the entire dining experience. –CK

# Passage to India

**8.0** Food  **8.6** Feel

Well executed, delicately spiced, and pleasantly surprising dishes among Indian antiques

## Indian

Casual restaurant  **$40** Price

www.passagetoindia.info

Daily 11:30am–2:30pm,
5:30pm–9pm

**Bar** Beer, wine, liquor
**Credit cards** Visa, MC, AmEx
**Reservations** Accepted
Kid-friendly, veg-friendly, Wi-Fi

**Bethesda, MD**
4931 Cordell Ave.
(301) 656-3373

At our last visit, we arrived at Passage to India without a reservation, but we were assured that if we could just wait a little while, we'd get the first available table. We passed the time by asking the affable staff to tell us the stories behind some of the gorgeous Indian antiques that tastefully decorate the walls and windows. A bronze statue of the elephant-headed god Ganesh is meant to bring success to the restaurant, we learned. We don't know for sure whether Ganesh has anything to do with it, but Passage to India is certainly successful.

The warm welcome you'll receive from the decorous but gracious servers sets the tone for a surprising and delightful meal of Indian dishes spanning the country's regions. While you can stick to Brit-Indian favorites like chicken tikka masala, the diverse menu rewards a willingness to try something new. The menu is divided into quadrants representing the four corners of the nation—North, South, East, and West—with a variety of specialties unfamiliar even to the Indian-savvy Westerner. Among our favorite surprises was the salli boti jardaloo, a West Indian Parsi-style lamb stew with apricots and straw potatoes in a sweet, tangy sauce. And you won't find chena-nentrakaya kalan—a coconut curry from South India featuring sweet potatoes and bananas—at many other Indian restaurants in town.

Among the appetizers, we favor the tandoori scallops (tender and touched with familiar smoky and spicy flavors of the tandoor) and the hariyali tikka (juicy, bite-sized nuggets of chicken in a mint-and-cilantro chutney). Ask for the platter of house pickles, which include lemon-and-ajwain as well as mixed-vegetable and green-chile versions, and for the assorted chutneys, which include tomato chutney flavored with nigella seeds. The chef's samplers—khazanas—are a great way to get an overview of the options: each platter starts with a trio of assorted appetizers, followed by four curries in small silver dishes, saffron rice, raita, and salad; later, there's dessert, too.

The room is hushed and intimate, with a variety of carefully assembled photographs, prints, paintings, and antiques from across India; soft music doesn't drown out conversation. It is this attention to detail and sense of pride in its own choices that make Passage to India such an admirable project. Still, we come, above all, for the exciting regional dishes—a passage through which we pray mainstream District Indian will eventually walk, too. –CD

# Pasta Mia

Mamma mia, check out the wait on Columbia Road

| **7.8** | **8.2** |
|---------|---------|
| Food | Feel |

## Italian

Casual restaurant

**$25**
Price

Tue–Sat 6:30pm–10pm

**Bar** Beer, wine, liquor
**Credit cards** None
**Reservations** Not accepted
Veg-friendly

**Adams Morgan**
1790 Columbia Rd. NW
(202) 328-9114

What exactly is it that possesses people to wait more than an hour for a table here? And we don't mean waiting at a bar with a cocktail in hand. We mean standing out on the sidewalk along Columbia Road, rain or shine, February's cold or April's rain, August's oppressive heat or June's sticky humidity. Perhaps it's Pasta Mia's popularity among both locals and tourists that makes it doubly difficult to patronize. Perhaps it's the reasonable prices for gargantuan plates of pasta. Or perhaps people just like a good challenge. If you view the wait as part of the trials and tribulations of the experience here, you'll feel like you've paid your dues and *earned* your pasta.

Which is why it's even more insulting when your pasta is served to you at such a searingly hot temperature that, upon receiving it, you have to wait about 10 minutes before you can even attempt a bite without fear of scalding your taste buds and rendering them useless for days to come. And we're not kidding. These noodles are *hot*. We can understand the problem that limited kitchen space presents, but c'mon guys. Figure *something* out. This is unacceptable.

But once it cools down, you'll be pretty happy. The pasta is cooked to an ideal al-dente, ensuring an solid starting point for the dishes. Sauces tend to be heavy and creamy, especially so in the case of the legendary chicken ravioli with pink sauce; any meaty flavor the chicken might have is pretty much obliterated by an unbelievably deep, rich, intense blend of reduced tomato, cream, and, quite possibly, crack. But you won't mind—you'll be lapping it up like soup. Pesto is another popular option, green, herby, and pleasant, although it doesn't hew closely enough to the noodles.

Quarters are cute, with tables set close, and just enough cheesy Italian-American accents like red-checkered tablecloths. And the high rate of turnovers pretty much ensures a constant and lively buzz. Servers, while a bit harried, are friendly and accommodating.

So is Pasta Mia worth the unpleasant wait? Nope. But we're not going to let that keep us away. Our trick is to come as late as possible; there might be a short wait, but chances are you can wait inside instead of being queued up on Columbia. –AH

# Patisserie Poupon

Pastries here bring DC a little closer to France—and they're as pretty as they are delicious

**7.3** Food
**8.0** Feel

## Baked goods, Sandwiches

Café **$35** Price

Tue–Fri 8am–6:30pm
Sat 8am–5pm
Sun 8am–4pm

**Bar** None
**Credit cards** Visa, MC, AmEx
Outdoor dining, veg-friendly

**Georgetown**
1645 Wisconsin Ave. NW
(202) 342-3248

Welcome to Heaven. Maybe it's the cream-colored interior that calls to mind vanilla-scented clouds, or the two large glass cases each displaying three shelves of delicate fruit tarts, creamy pies, buttery éclairs, jewel-like truffles, and a dozen other delights. Or maybe it's the smell of expertly made espresso drinks served at the simple bar. Past an exposed brick wall in the back, there's a brick patio (actually a narrow alley), with pretty tables and a slant of sunlight, that evokes a little Parisian courtyard: on one side is a wooden gate, and on the other, windows face into the Patisserie.

Deciding where to begin can be a challenge. A compulsory light breakfast and lunch menu is offered. Refreshingly, olive oil is featured more prominently than traditional butter, and the result leaves you with more appetite for dessert. A Caprese salad, for example, is made with large, red, juicy tomatoes (a rarity in city Caprese), a chiffonade of basil, infused oil, and molehills of fresh mozzarella. Breakfast omelettes are delicate if a little boring, and butter returns to the fore in Poupon's decently cheesy, if standard, quiches. The bakery's breads are excellent by DC standards. Baguettes are crunchy and thoroughly floured on the outside, slightly sour and soft inside. If Poupon's sandwiches are a bit uninspiring, it's by no fault of the bread's.

Finally—and you may want to start here anyway—the desserts. But how to choose? Shiny berry-filled tartlets are gems to the eye as well as the tongue: the vanilla custard cream and buttery dough are enlivened by just the right amount of tart, sweet fruit. Macaroons, no easy feat for even skilled pastry chefs, are properly puffy sandwiches of almondy sweetness, not too doughy and not too dry. Croissants are some of the better ones in town. Though they are not quite as flaky as they should be, neither are they greasy, and their million layers of butter also come laced with almond paste or dark chocolate. Try the petits fours, or the refined Italian sorbet. And don't forget your friends—bringing a pricey (but oh-so-worth-it) Poupon cake to your next dinner party will ensure that you get invited back. –CK

# Peacock Café

A good-natured, if preppy, Georgetown brunch spot with a bright buzz

| 6.3 | 7.8 |
|-----|-----|
| Food | Feel |

## New American

Upmarket restaurant

**$60**
Price

www.peacockcafe.com

Mon–Thu 11:30am–10:30pm
Fri 11:30am–11pm
Sat 9am–11pm
Sun 9am–10:30pm

**Bar** Beer, wine, liquor
**Credit cards** Visa, MC, AmEx
**Reservations** Accepted
Date-friendly, outdoor dining,
veg-friendly

**Georgetown**
3251 Prospect St. NW
(202) 625-2740

All of the elements at Peacock Café seem carefully calibrated to please as many people as possible. Certainly the place pleases the preppy Georgetown crowd that comes out in droves every Sunday for brunch. It's got a great brunch vibe, as the place is aptly named: there's a definite café-gallery-like feel to the bustling, airy, sometimes loud space, and a plumage of modern artwork splays across the walls in bright blues, reds, and oranges.

Ask about the wine list, and a well-meaning server might take time to consult a more senior staff member in an attempt to fit your expressed taste preferences—but then come back and earnestly suggest an extremely unremarkable bottle of Pinot Grigio. And this points to a larger issue at Peacock: try to please everyone, and you're left without culinary focus.

The menu of American standards is similarly well meaning but inconsistently executed. Burgers are popular and possibly the best choice, displaying an unusual consistency of cooking time. Good, too, is a sweet-and-sour lobster salad, which successfully integrates fennel, avocado, grapes, and mango with a light citrus vinaigrette. Fried calamari are pleasantly crispy and soft within, but they're plopped in a pool of pedestrian, barely spiced marinara. Mini crab cakes are packed with crabmeat, but a trio of disparate sauces dotted on the plate (pungent wasabi, ordinary cocktail, and horseradish-spiked mayonnaise) suggest that the dish is designed to please any palate in choose-your-own-adventure fashion rather than making any strong flavor statement. Pepper-crusted tuna is seared to temperature, but the accompanying spaghetti squash lacks seasoning, and the tomato-corn-fava-bean relish tastes like the ingredients could have come from a can. Among desserts, a white chocolate cheesecake is creamy and rich, just as you might expect.

To add to the roster of crowd-pleasing elements, there's a flexible $35 three-course prix fixe and a half-price deal on wine with the purchase of any main course. It's hard to complain about that. But in the end, while we understand that a business must cater to its customers' desires in order to make money—and we understand, too, that Peacock's customers include some people who like predictable food—we prefer to frequent restaurants whose vision feels more chef-driven, and their finances, perhaps, more risky. –CD

# Peking Gourmet Inn

**7.7** Food  **9.0** Feel

Proof that, at least in the suburbs, great Chinese can coexist with lovely surroundings

## Chinese

Casual restaurant

**$35** Price

www.pekinggourmet.com

Sun–Thu 11am–10:30pm
Fri–Sat 11am–11pm

**Bar** Beer, wine, liquor
**Credit cards** Visa, MC, AmEx
**Reservations** Accepted
Kid-friendly, veg-friendly

**Falls Church, VA**
6029 Leesburg Pike
(703) 671-8088

Peking Gourmet Inn may just be one of the nicest Chinese restaurants in America. Despite slumming in a ratty strip mall in Falls Church, the restaurant has a beautiful interior. Oversized red lanterns hang festively over the narrow dining rooms packed with people, and the walls are tiled with framed and signed photos of just about every politician that has served a term in Washington. Elegant dinnerware and courteous servers (it may be the only time a waiter at a Chinese restaurant ever introduces himself to you before your meal) break all the stereotypes.

As legend has it, where Chinese is concerned, good décor equals bad food, and vice versa. Although it's not quite what it used to be, Peking Gourmet Inn is still reliable. The menu includes foods for both the adventurous and timid. For the former, winter melon soup with sea scallops is cheered by ginger and kissed with white pepper. The clear broth is quite thick and threaded with egg, but also cleanly and delicately flavored. It tastes touchingly authentic. Dumplings arrive with inky aged Chinese black vinegar that is spicier and more robust than its Western cousin. Whole Peking duck is masterfully carved tableside using the meat cleavers found in every Chinese kitchen. They are scraped of their fat and sliced thin, with the crackling skin intact.

Less adventurous diners will be wowed by how well familiar dishes are executed. Moo shi pork is a paragon of stir-fried goodness, with the ideal balance of egg and cabbage for bites alive with crunch and chew and hard and soft. If you like, it also comes with sweet brown sauce and doughy "pancakes." Singapore rice noodles are appropriately gritty, and spicy with curry. They're not the best around, but they're above average. We do wish the menu would focus more on what this place does best.

The prices here are just a couple of dollars more than what you'd find at any Chinese place with horoscopes on the paper placemats, but the difference in execution and ambiance is worth every penny.

If you still don't believe that the DC suburbs are hiding better Chinese food than you can find in tourist-trappy Chinatown, Peking Gourmet Inn should serve as one among many counter-examples. –JC

# Persimmon

This nouvelle destination showcases the rewards, and limitations, of effort

**6.7** Food

**7.6** Feel

## New American

Upmarket restaurant

**$75** Price

www.persimmonrestaurant.com

Mon–Fri 11:30am–2pm, 5pm–10pm
Sat 5pm–10pm
Sun 11am–2pm, 5pm–9pm

**Bar** Beer, wine, liquor
**Credit cards** Visa, MC, AmEx
**Reservations** Accepted
Date-friendly, outdoor dining

**Chevy Chase, MD**
7003 Wisconsin Ave.
(301) 654-9860

At its best, Persimmon works as a charming, unpretentious neighborhood restaurant, with knowledgeable, no-nonsense service and an eclectic, mostly affordable wine list. The warm, goldenrod-hued walls and intimately sized tables create a relaxed atmosphere that invites conversation rather than imposing a hush. The general air of welcome is epitomized in an unusual treat tucked into the bread basket: creamy house-made chicken liver pâté, rustic yet satisfying.

On the downside, the food, occasionally admirably bold, sometimes borders on chaotic and sloppy. Wasabi-crusted oysters pack less heat than you might think; a light soy broth and cooling cucumber salad make for light, complimentary accompaniments. An unusual sautéed calamari preparation balances acidic tomatoes with rosemary, pumpkin-seed pesto, and a heap of creamy polenta. Roast duck, however, is a mish-mash of too many familiar flavor partners: sweet potato, celery root, and foie gras muddle with the duck and shreds of confit in a dish that tries too hard to do too much.

We could forgive the heavy-handedness as a misguided eagerness to please, but the prices make us slightly indignant—at $50 for a three-course meal without wine or cocktails, this would-be local haunt veers toward downtown prices. The varied, affordable wine list proudly displays a 2008 Wine Spectator Award of Excellence; this would impress us more if we didn't know that the magazine would just as soon bestow the Triple Crown on a unicorn if the ads looked promising. Nonetheless, pleasant surprises include a little-known Cahors "black" wine. $14 wine "flights" are a signature flourish, three tastes of wines united by region or style.

At these prices, and with plenty of rich food already under your belt, merely ordinary desserts like cheesecake and profiteroles fail to tempt. A nice closing coffee is more in keeping with the chilled-out, neighborhood vibe, anyway. –CD

# Pesce

Good fish in tacky (or as some might say, homey) settings

| 8.9 | 7.3 |
|-----|-----|
| Food | Feel |

## Seafood

Upmarket restaurant

**$60**
*Price*

www.pescebistro.com

Mon–Thu 11:30am–2:30pm, 5:30pm–10pm; Fri 11:30am–2:30pm, 5:30pm–10:30pm; Sat 5:30pm–10:30pm; Sun 5pm–9:30pm

**Bar** Beer, wine
**Credit cards** Visa, MC, AmEx
**Reservations** Accepted

**Dupont**
2016 P St. NW
(202) 466-3474

This little P-Street hideaway is quietly serving some of DC's best seafood. Your first tip-off that this might be the case is the fact that there's not even *one* meat dish on the menu—common, perhaps, for seafood restaurants in Europe, but virtually unheard of in the US. It's a show of great things to come: an extraordinary commitment to ingredients, execution, and reasonable prices.

We don't know what to make of Pesce's general aesthetic. It's in the tacky-tourist-trap-on-the-beach school of thought, the kind of place that would be equally at home hawking glittery seashell creations or trashy shot glasses with the name of some Jersey beach inscribed on them. Even the dishware takes it over the top; plates mix bright blues and greens—with some yellow thrown in for good measure—and have giant, childishly-rendered images of fish on them. Tables couldn't possibly be any closer together; it takes some flexibility and skill to squeeze yourself in to the cramped space. Still, there's a homey, relaxed aspect to it all—the menu comes over on a chalkboard, for instance—that makes it all okay.

At midday, you'll find that the crowd comprises quite a few business lunchers. And when you think about it, it makes sense. A lunch at Pesce is upmarket enough—and considerably less high-maintenance than a lunch at one of DC's steakhouses. Anyway, who wants all that meat in the afternoon? Or to deal with the implicit pressure that accompanies stakes that high (and steaks that expensive)?

We recommend going with the whole fish when available—which it usually is. We've had a delicious branzino (Mediterranean sea bass) that was simply prepared, its white flesh tender and with that elusive sticking-to-your teeth quality that we like so much. Scallops have also been a particular strength, large and seared just so. Homemade pasta dishes display an unusual prowess for Italian technique that isn't often seen at a seafood restaurant. The wine list is balanced and fairly priced, but too short.

Servers at Pesce mean well, but it's not always the coordinated show that it should be. But no worries—it's just more time for you to strike that big deal. –AH

# Pete's Diner

This Capitol Hill odd couple of greasy spoon-and-Chinese is a welcome change from the hoity-toity

**6.5** Food
**7.5** Feel

## American

Casual restaurant

**$25** Price

Mon–Fri 5am–3pm
Sat–Sun 6am–3pm

**Bar** None
**Credit cards** None
**Reservations** Not accepted
Outdoor dining, veg-friendly

**Capitol Hill**
212 2nd St. SE
(202) 544-7335

Just across from the Library of Congress annex and practically within spitting distance of the Capitol, this humble little diner serves up its greasy spoon fare on a sunny patch of 2nd Street SE. It adds some much-needed levity (in character as well as price) to the hustle and bustle of these parts.

There are a few quirky touches that make Pete's all the more charming. Most dishes are served on plastic plates with chinoiserie themes, and none of the plastic water glasses match. Inside, the round bar stools are padded and worn, and a menu board posts the day's specials. Half the seating is at tables, the other half at hard plastic booths. In warm weather, some sidewalk tables make for great people-watching.

Breakfast is served until mid-morning, and is composed of the usual suspects. You can't go wrong with a stack of pancakes, prepared one of several ways. The blueberry and banana varieties come loaded with fruit, although the former seem to have been previously frozen; but the cakes themselves are fluffy and always golden brown (never overcooked). We're almost tempted to pull a Seinfeld and bring our own Vermont maple syrup in a flask. Eggs to order are done right, but omelettes have come a bit dry. Some appealing combinations include the Western (bacon, nice spicy sausage, green pepper, onions, cheese), and an occasional special like feta and spinach; all, of course, served with buttered toast. Skip the watery grits.

In an unusual twist, some of the Asian lunch items outshine the American stuff (with bread like this, it's hard to make sandwich miracles happen). Vegetarians are drawn to an ample selection of Chinese dishes, and Korean bulgogi has been a hit here. Although as you can probably guess, it's hardly got the deep Korean flavors and spices you'd hope for. On the other hand, what diner do you know serves the ever-addictive Thai iced tea? Milkshakes, especially, are creamy and sweet, and make up for shortcomings in the kitchen. Yes, it's just a diner, and yes, the food is prosaic and fairly industrial, but the regulars who love it do so because it's friendly, it's got character, it's Main Street, and coffee refills are free and abundant. –CK

# Petits Plats

Charming, old-school neighborhood French
without pomp or circumstance

| 6.9 | 7.8 |
|---|---|
| Food | Feel |

## French

Casual restaurant

**$45**
Price

www.petitsplats.com

Mon–Thu 11:30am–2:30pm,
5pm–9:30pm; Fri 11:30am–
2:30pm, 5pm–10:30pm; Sat
11am–3pm, 5pm–10:30pm;
Sun 11am–3pm, 5pm–9:30pm

**Bar** Beer, wine, liquor
**Credit cards** Visa, MC, AmEx
**Reservations** Accepted
Date-friendly, outdoor dining

**Woodley Park**
2653 Connecticut Ave. NW
(202) 518-0018

These days, even a lot of the restaurants claiming to be French tend to forget about the classic bistro dishes that captivated Julia Child in her culinary infancy. But Petits Plats remembers them well. Yes, they're somewhat Americanized—missing here are the kidneys, the tripe, the blanquette de veau, the old-school dishes that were left off the list when French restaurants started popping up all over America in the 1950s and '60s.

But there are escargots, the dish that once epitomized the sometimes contemptuous mystique that French cooking held for Americans, but which now eludes the menus of many upstart chefs. Here, the Burgundian snails are prepared au gratin, and served in their shells—so there's no mistaking these for mushrooms, ye of faint hearts. They're delightfully crunchy and only slightly chewy, with a light, buttery breading to which snowflakes of fresh basil and other herbs have been added. These simple refinements do wonders for a protein that's really just a platform for its dressing.

Bisques tend to be thin; the café's pesto soup is really more of a potage, a delicate blend of vegetables and herbs, rather than the soupe au pistou of Provence. Although the consistency is creamy and light (the base is mostly vegetable, rather than dairy), one wishes there were a little more of a basil kick than is provided by the meager drizzling of pesto.

This light touch is appreciated in Petits Plats' preparation of meats and vegetables. A good steak frites is thankfully made, as it should be, with hanger steak, which employs just enough salt to bring out the beef's juices. Another nice touch is the restaurant's baguette, which is baked in-house; its crunchy crust gives way to airy innards, perfect for sopping up every last drop of boeuf Bourgogne. This cooking is not marked by technical excellence, but rather a sense of honesty and comfort. There's too much garlic, sometimes, and fish mains tend to underwhelm.

The succinct, focused wine list is 99% French, and the markups are standard. With most bottles under $50, you should have no problem finding memorable matches for your meal.

A former townhouse, Petits Plats is charming and rag-painted in a Provençal light yellow, and the outdoor seating is lovely in warm weather. Brunch is perfectly suited to this atmosphere, and their famous rotisserie chickens are available for pre-order and pick up. Aside from this ample beast, the serving sizes are, as the restaurant's name would suggest, on the small side. Hey, there's a reason the French tend to be thinner. –CK

# Pho Xe Lua

The space is charming, and the menu is—you guessed it—pho

**7.2** Food

**8.2** Feel

## Vietnamese

Casual restaurant

**$15** Price

Daily 7:30am–8pm

**Bar** None
**Credit cards** None
**Reservations** Not accepted

**Falls Church, VA**
6765 A Wilson Blvd.
(703) 533-3130

Are you ready for a vaguely Bohemian treat that feels straight out of French Indochina?

How about a vaguely Bohemian treat in a mall whose Vietnamese-food spaces—even if they peddle high-quality food—are generally going for little more than white walls and a TV?

If Eden Center's atmospheres are mind-numbing, this one will transport you straight to the old-school colonial Orient. From the time-worn bookshelf lined with a curious library of Vietnamese culture and history—the dominant interior element from the moment you walk in—to the disarmingly sophisticated oil paintings that line the white walls of this airy space, Pho Xe Lua comes off as an eminently literate outpost of coffee, conversation, and, of course, delicious broth.

The menu is short, sweet, and to the point. Pho is it—refreshingly, there's literally nothing else on the menu—and all the versions cost the same, which is a couple of dollars more than the competition: at press time, it was $7.75 for a small and $8.95 for a large. That's certainly not cheap for Eden, but it's also not even the price of a mediocre appetizer at an upmarket DC joint. Free marinated onions highlight the assortment of veggies that come with the pho.

Meats come in smallish cuts, but they're serviceable, and the broth is good but not great. But on the balance, the pho is on par with most, and the one-of-a-kind atmosphere makes it all worthwhile. –RG

# Ping by Charlie Chiang's

**3.7** Food **7.3** Feel

More sugary sweet pan-Asian food from another mini-chain

## Pan-Asian

Casual restaurant

**$45** Price

www.charliechiangs.com

| | | |
|---|---|---|
| Mon–Thu 11:30am–10:30pm | **Bar** Beer, wine, liquor | **Arlington, VA** |
| Fri–Sat 11:30am–11pm | **Credit cards** Visa, MC, AmEx | 4060 Campbell Ave. |
| Sun noon–10pm | **Reservations** Accepted | (703) 671-4900 |
| | Delivery, kid-friendly, outdoor dining, veg-friendly | |

When in the course of human dining habits, it becomes glaringly apparent that traditional Chinese-American is no longer a solid business plan, some misguided restaurateurs have concluded that it is then necessary to reinvent oneself as a fusion restaurant. This is exactly what the Charlie Chiang empire has done to its 20-year-old Shirlington location: they've sexed up the look, added exotic influences to the menu, and dubbed it Ping (after a Chinese character denoting highest quality and living). The exterior mimics bamboo shades offering glimpses of the inside, where patrons choose either the bar area—lively in red and black with community-style benches and flatscreen televisions—or the slightly more austere dining room which, despite the clear acrylic chairs and stainless steel lighting fixtures, manages to look warm and inviting.

They're still doing the white bread-Chinese fare (General Tso's chicken, beef with broccoli, and so on), but Charlie Chiang's Ping now flirts with other corners of the continent, as well, and it suffers from a lack of focus. Hey, not since Genghis Khan has anyone successfully conquered all of Asia. Case in point: the half-hearted attempt at sushi. Even failsafe California rolls are only passable, seemingly made without the use of properly vinegared rice. A nigiri list without mackerel is forgiveable in a place that doesn't purport to be a serious sushi joint—but, then, why would you even get sushi there?

The xiao die, or small plates, suffer from the classic severe sweet-tooth problems that plague pan-Asian joints around the city. Dong po, steamed buns folded around pork belly cooked in a rock-candy (!!) soy mixture, are a creative twist on pulled-pork sandwiches, with hoisin standing in for barbecue sauce, but they lack seasoning. Shiny, slippery shrimp, coated in a tempura-like batter, have a pleasing crunch but saccharine sauce. That same sauce—or something identically sweet and gloopy—seems to deck out sesame chicken, too.

More impressive is the restaurant's ambitious beer selection, which offers a surprising array of imports and local award-winning brews. A less zealous wine list has more losers than winners; the cold sake list is a better bet. If the sugary dishes are any indication of the palates in charge of this restaurant, it should come as little surprise that, at the bar, martinis follow suit.

Come here only if you are craving the comfort of the old Chinese-American takeout standbys in a prettier atmosphere—or a sugar high to get you through the afternoon. When will it become glaringly apparent that oversweetened Pan-Asian isn't a solid business plan either? –CD

# Pizzeria Paradiso

Good pizza and great beer in even better surroundings—in Georgetown, at least

| 8.2 | 8.2 |
|-----|-----|
| Food | Feel |

## Pizza

Casual restaurant

**$30**
Price

www.eatyourpizza.com

Mon–Thu 11:30am–11pm
Fri–Sat 11:30am–midnight
Sun noon–10pm

**Bar** Beer, wine, liquor
**Credit cards** Visa, MC
**Reservations** Not accepted
Date-friendly, kid-friendly,
veg-friendly

**Dupont**
2029 P St. NW
(202) 223-1245

**Georgetown**
3282 M St. NW
(202) 337-1245

We're not the first to say it, but it bears repeating: Pizzeria Paradiso serves one of the better pizzas in DC. The crust is thin near the center, puffs a little on the outskirts, and is browned in just the right places by Paradiso's wood-fired oven. The toppings are plentiful. The price may be the only thing that's not just right, but we're more than willing to pay a little extra for a standout pizza, an excellent selection of draft beer, and atmosphere to match.

Both the Georgetown and Dupont locations are appointed in the classic upscale-pizzeria-or-bistro style: casual tables, wooden chairs, dried hanging foodstuffs or oil renderings of foodstuffs. But the Georgetown spot has some major advantages: better lighting; more buzz; lower, more intimate ceilings; a casual bar area, where the tables are set around a pile of wooden logs; and you'll generally see faster service with a little less pomp. As such we vastly prefer the Georgetown branch.

Upon your arrival, the table will be set with a small bowl of green and black olives; once you order, the drink service is speedy. Beyond the excellent draft selection, there's an expansive (seven-menu-page) selection of bottled beer, including some outstanding Belgian choices and a sizeable list of IPAs from smaller US breweries. At the Georgetown location, you can also order one of several specialty cocktails, as well as a white sangría that's made with plenty of wine and uses fruit juice in lieu of sugar or Sprite as a sweetener.

Paradiso's use of cheese in its pizzas is skilled, even if it's a bit more than purists would like; it rarely overwhelms or detracts from the other flavors. Our only occasional complaint is that the crust isn't quite as nicely salted as we'd like—nor, sometimes, is the tomato. The quattro formaggi (which is actually made with five, not four, cheeses and a few dashes of fresh herbs) is complemented by the flavor of roasted garlic, and the "Atomica" is a delightful exemplar of a traditional concept done up to taste right; Paradiso has taken the classic pepperoni pie and run with it. Instead of dry pepperoni, you'll find thin slices of a spicy salami, plus red pepper flakes and juicy whole Kalamata olives. More advanced concepts are also executed with aplomb: the bottarga version, for example, is a revelation, pairing a salty dried roe with salty parmesan, topped with a fried egg whose yolk is left still runny. We'll end with the obvious: this ain't paradise, but at least in Georgetown, it's pretty close. –FC

# Po Siam

**6.8** **6.0**

*Food* *Feel*

Neighborhood Thai awaits you with a few
authentic touches—but more inauthentic ones

## Thai

Casual restaurant

**$30**

*Price*

Mon–Sat 11:30am–10pm
Sun noon–9:30pm

**Bar** Beer, wine, liquor
**Credit cards** Visa, MC, AmEx
**Reservations** Accepted
Delivery

**Alexandria, VA**
3807 Mount Vernon Ave.
(703) 548-3925

With a paint store next door, a Wafle *[sic]* House across the street, and a dilapidated parking lot to boot, Po Siam has every bit the look of a sleeper restaurant.

Add to the spicy Thai-American specialties and familial atmosphere a manager who greets regulars with a handshake or hug, and a run-down of the diner's favorite dishes gratifyingly littered with possessive pronouns ("We have your crispy fish, we'll have your soft-shell crabs very soon, about a month"), and it seems hard to ask for more. Well, one could, conceivably, ask for a refreshing mango drink to accompany one's meal, but if you do so, Po Siam will deliver it with a smile.

With or without the mango daiquiri, you might begin with a soup. The tom kha gai infuses a light coconut base with lemongrass in a muted arrangement of slightly sweet (coconut) and slightly sour. Lemongrass also features prominently in the tom yum goong, but unlike at many less authentic Thai spots, both soups are made with enough chili to give the creamy bases bite.

The "Noodles of the Drunks" (a better name, we think) are thick and sweet, a dish that would be laughed out of any restaurant in Thailand. But salads go beyond the usual; we love yum pla dook foo, a crispy catfish salad with green mango that isn't seen on many American menus. Som tam is a classic green papaya salad (green papaya, for the uninitiated, bears virtually no gustatory relation to the ripe version; rather, it has the crunchy consistency of apples, but none of the sugar). Po Siam is one of the few Thai restaurants in DC to use dried shrimp, as they do in Thailand, to give the salad some crunch, and the result is a refreshing and authentic accompaniment to any main course.

Not on the menu, but available to regulars in the know, is the whole fried crispy fish, which is doused post-fry in a brown basil and chili sauce that's more Chinese-American than Thai, with sautéed straw mushrooms, bamboo shoots, and bell peppers. It's not bad; remember to snap off and eat the crisped tail. Still, the DC area is ready for Thai places to stop serving Chinese-American food. Broccoli in oyster sauce? Fried egg rolls with pineapple sauce? Haven't we outgrown this? –CK

# Pollo Campero

Not enough delivery, but still a nostalgic Central American experience

**7.5** Food
**6.0** Feel

## Latin American

Counter service

**$10** Price

www.campero.com

Daily 10am–9pm

**Bar** None
**Credit cards** Visa, MC, AmEx
**Reservations** Not accepted
Kid-friendly

**Columbia Heights**
3229 14th St. NW
(202) 745-0078

**Falls Church, VA**
5852 Columbia Pike
(703) 820-8400

**Wheaton, MD**
11420 Georgia Ave.
(301) 942-6868

**Gaithersburg, MD**
701 Russell Ave.
(240) 403-0135

Whenever restaurant chains from back home install themselves in new countries, they rarely taste the way you remember. Such is the problem with Pollo Campero. True, it is loved by many Central Americans as comfort food; alas, it doesn't strike that chord that propels people backward to their homeland when they taste and smell a childhood favorite. And a favorite it is indeed: board a flight to the U.S. that's originating in San Salvador or Guatemala City (the chain started in Guatemala), and the plane will be as full of Pollo Campero (it's a tradition to bring a big bag of it to your American relatives) as it is people.

A piece of fried chicken can be a thing of beauty when it's served right out of the hot oil; when the crusty coating is penetrated, a stinging vapor of chicken steam hits you in the face. And that's what the US branches of Pollo Campero are lacking: that sexy, exciting crunch that only fried chicken can provide.

Nonetheless, with a hint of oregano in the flour, it is a better piece of poultry than most American chicken chains are capable of frying. Unfortunately, sitting under a heat lamp for the lunchtime rush, it loses all of its self-esteem—like a girl getting stood up on prom night.

The sides at Pollo Campero are meant to play supporting roles to the famous chicken, but there are no award-winning performances here. Some locations have tostones (fried plantains), but they taste a bit too starchy. French fries are delicious, but the tortillas that come with every meal have little flavor and are sometimes hard, sometimes greasy. In the end, you'll like Pollo Campero more if you haven't experienced the real thing in Central America. As for us, our fondest memories of Pollo Campero, which we frequented in El Salvador, come from the morbid fascination of watching a grown man in a full-body chicken suit get on a scooter to make a delivery. "I've got a great new job," you imagine him stuttering to his wife. "There's only one catch." –FC

# Pollo Granjero

Rhymes and trademarks be damned—this is
damned good fried chicken

**8.4** *Food*  **4.0** *Feel*

## Latin American

Counter service  **$15** *Price*

Sun–Thu 10am–10pm
Fri–Sat 10am–11pm

**Bar** None
**Credit cards** Visa, MC, AmEx
Kid-friendly

**Adams Morgan**
1742 Columbia Rd.
(202) 464-4444

**Takoma Park, MD**
6838 New Hampshire Ave.
(301) 891-6800

The name is—or seems, anyway—a rather humorous rip-off of Pollo
Campero, the legendary fried-chicken chain that is like a religion in much
of Central America, especially Guatemala (where it started) and El
Salvador. So central is Pollo Campero to the Salvadoran identity that it's a
tradition among many Salvadorans to carry bags of Campero fried chicken
onto US-bound flights so that their extended families up north can have a
taste. Now that's brand loyalty.

Luckily for Pollo Granjero, trademark lawyers aren't generally on the
payroll of Latin American chicken shops.

Now, we love Pollo Campero too, and Campero also has a DC-area
branch—a fact that calls the bring-it-on-the-plane practice into question.
But what's amazing is that, here in DC anyway, Granjero beats Campero
at its own game.

It bears mention that the atmosphere at Pollo Granjero is not what
Campero's is. While Campero feels like a brightly lit, hygienic fast-food
joint in the KFC vein, Granjero feels like a grungy fast-food joint without
the hygienic neurosis that comes from being part of a nationally
scrutinized franchise. Instead, Granjero's rewards come on the plate,
beginning with the impossibly moist, beautifully crisped bird, which come
with complex and addictive green and white dipping sauces—frequently
the unsung heroes of the Latin American chicken restaurant. Happily,
here, they don't have to do all the work.

Where sides are throwaways at so many roast-chicken joints, Pollo
Granjero's beans are particularly good, wonderfully seasoned and
complex. There's also well-executed fried yuca—crispy and delicious—plus
lomo saltado (a bit overcooked) and pupusas (for that Salvadoran touch).

Service is merely perfunctory; speaking Spanish will get you further than
speaking English. Even if you can communicate well, waits are strangely
unpredictable; one day, your fried chicken will come out in less than a
minute, yet on another, it will take 10 or 15. We'll give this kitchen the
benefit of the doubt and take it as a sign of quality rather than of poor
inventory management and planning. After all, nobody wants chain fried
chicken. Pollo Granjero seems happy to leave that task to Pollo Campero.
—FC

# Pomegranate Bistro

Let's stop faking it and get some real dairy in here

**5.1** / **7.7**
Food / Feel

## New American

Upmarket restaurant

**$60**
Price

www.pombistro.com

Mon–Thu 11:30am–2:30pm,
5:30pm–9:30pm; Fri 11:30am–
2:30pm; Sun 11am–2:30pm,
5pm–9:30pm

**Bar** Beer, wine, liquor
**Credit cards** Visa, MC, AmEx
**Reservations** Accepted
Delivery, outdoor dining,
veg-friendly

**Potomac, MD**
7943 Tuckerman Ln.
(301) 299-9888

Nothing screams kosher restaurant like nondairy cream cheese. This inimitable ingredient features prominently in Pomegranate Bistro's beet napoleon, alongside pistachios and a balsamic vinaigrette. Because Pomegranate serves meat, they cannot include dairy products in any of their dishes. That's fine, but why must they try to fake it? Why must vegetarians insist on faking meat, kosher people on faking milk, and customers everywhere on faking pleasure? We're talking about products really only a jilted cow could love. Wherever Pomegranate's imitation dairy rears its unfortunate head, we duck for cover: in the insipid, balsamic-glaze-swirled gravy under a Portobello mushroom cap that tastes of Thanksgiving leftovers; in the "ice cream" atop the apple cobbler (soy vey!); and did we mention the nondairy cream cheese?

Sadly, Pomegranate's faux-pas extend beyond the faux milk. Moist but bland chicken satay skewers, served with a cloying peanut butter dipping sauce, are acceptable only when juxtaposed with the ribeye satay, whose supposed garlic-and-lime dipping sauce relies too heavily on Worcestershire.

When it comes to the mains, Pomegranate takes advantage of its meat license with a wide variety of beef, lamb, chicken, fish, and vegetarian selections. The braised lamb shank arrives like a king on his throne, but the huge bone with comfortingly tender meat is drowned, not crowned, by a mustard-colored mystery sauce which turns out to be puréed root vegetables. Undercooked risotto (lacking promised wild mushrooms on one visit) wallows in its murky bath, resulting in a soupy mess of lamb, rice, and gravy.

The aforementioned apple cobbler, which comes highly recommended by the hovering chef, is unfortunately salty and lacking in apple. The amaretto chocolate tart, on the other hand, is densely chocolaty, creamy, and all around satisfying. We appreciate its simplicity of flavors and presentation. Maybe kosher food is best for fressing—Pomegranate succeeds most when it appeals to our more basic culinary wishes. Lunch, for example, is a pleasantly low-key affair with a variety of deli sandwiches and streamlined main dishes, and the deli in front sells high quality meats and prepared sides.

There is no reason why Pomegranate Bistro can't be a great restaurant: the space is chic and cozy, decorated in deep earth tones and soft lighting, and the servers are enthusiastic. If all the food here shared the sensibly straightforward qualities of that chocolate tart, then perhaps we'd do a little less kvetching and a little more kvelling. –SDC

# Poste Moderne Brasserie

**9.2** Food   **8.7** Feel

Some of the city's most intelligent modern food in an escapist setting

## New American

Upmarket restaurant   **$80** Price

www.postebrasserie.com

Mon–Thu 7am–10am,
11:30am–2:30pm, 5pm–10pm
Fri 7am–10am, 11:30am–
2:30pm, 5pm–10:30pm
Sat 8am–2pm, 5pm–10:30pm
Sun 8am–2pm, 5pm–9pm

**Bar** Beer, wine, liquor
**Credit cards** Visa, MC, AmEx
**Reservations** Accepted
Date-friendly, good wines, outdoor dining

**Penn Quarter**
555 8th St. NW
(202) 783-6060

Poste Moderne Brasserie, part of Hotel Monaco, is a restaurant that feels like a village unto itself. Maybe it's the huge outdoor courtyard where well-dressed visitors, like so many townspeople whiling away time in the village square, arrive early and stay late. Maybe it's the sense that there are thriving worlds hidden around corners and behind the huge stone pots of bushy herbs that scent the air, like the little garden out back where fresh mint is picked warm from the sun to garnish your drink. Or maybe it's the rustic, old-world breads. Every visit to Poste reveals another detail worth falling in love with.

The first thing you'll notice at the bar is the impressive mosaic of glass bottles lined against the wall, each labeled with a base and an infusion: chamomile in vodka, perhaps, or cinnamon and anise in Bourbon. The colored liquids—their infused ingredients floating inside—create an apothecary aesthetic. Bartenders are masters of their craft, preparing drinks with awe-inspiring fluidity and textbook attention to detail. Although a lot of their cocktails are too sweet (pear vodka, raspberry liquor, pineapple juice, and a dash of sparkling wine), some are well-balanced, creatively fun throwbacks (a Jack-Daniels-based Sazerac, for instance).

The dining area is warm and handsome, with deep booths embellished with pinstriped pillows. A long open kitchen tends toward the rustic, with baskets of brown eggs and vegetables. Poste's seasonal menu combines complex flavors that are often earthy, sometimes haute-nostalgic, and frequently exciting. For example, "bruschetta" (tired in most kitchens' hands) is generously topped with a gloriously rich, fluffy, mousse-like liver pâté, which is punctuated by nubs of smoky bacon and deep-fried sage and sweetened by dried apricots and Port-wine sauce. A thick cube of striped bass is nestled among potatoes and topped, to a macabre and beautiful effect, with an egg poached in red wine. The combination of gooey yolk on crisp, flaky fish tangy with capers is substantial yet blessedly clean. Poste's wine list is balanced and well-composed, but also pricey, and too weak on affordable red Burgundy or Bordeaux.

Desserts are so carefully put together that your spoon feels like a wrecking ball. A fig-and-mascarpone napoleon is acrobatically staged and charmingly serious—you can dive into the generous figs, flaky pastry, and creamy cheese, but you'll find almost no sugar. A final treat of miniature cookies sweetens the bill. If it takes a village to make a superb meal, who wouldn't want to move to the country? –JC

# Posto

Post up here with a pie, a pasta, and pretty people

**9.0** *Food*  **7.6** *Feel*

## Italian, Pizza

Upmarket restaurant

**$55** *Price*

www.postodc.com

Mon–Thu 5:30pm–10:30pm
Fri–Sat 5pm–11:30pm
Sun 5pm–10pm

**Bar** Beer, wine, liquor
**Credit cards** Visa, MC, AmEx
**Reservations** Not accepted
Date-friendly, good wines,
veg-friendly

**Logan Circle**
1515 14th St. NW
(202) 332-8613

Posto's exterior is extremely efficient at concealing its contents. Literally, it's not immediately clear that you've arrived at the restaurant. No fancy awning, no eye-catching signage. (Obviously, this was a deliberate move, intended to make patrons feel special and "exclusive.") But you also wouldn't expect the inside to look as it does. In the harsh light of day it looks rather cafeteria-like. Tile floors, an airiness that can seem cold when the restaurant is emptying, and tons of four-tops (not booths) fill every bit of floor space available. (On that note, try to avoid being seated at one of the tables smack in the middle of the restaurant, if possible.)

But this would be one stylish cafeteria. It's decked out in beiges and browns, with chairs made of a visually pleasing combination of dark wood and shiny silver. There's the roar of a wood-burning pizza oven in the background. Lighting was calculated with a sharp eye. Even servers look good. It gets pretty noisy when it's full—what with all those hard surfaces that don't absorb sound, but rather reflect it—but just consider that part of the experience.

And you should start your experience by getting a bottle (or a glass, depending on what kind of night you're in for) from the well-chosen, Italian-focused list. Make no mistake; the selection is by no means limited to Italy. All the biggies—U.S., Spain, France, and so on—are represented. Look for crisp, interesting Ligurian whites. As for noshing, a salad with octopus, chickpeas, and frisée is a winner; it's cool and refreshing, a study in textures, with slightly resilient flesh blending with, but not overpowering the peas.

The kitchen definitely has a way with pastas. Meat-filled ravioli, our favorite, are savory and rich, further enhanced by their butter sauce, through which thyme cuts clearly. This is one of the best pasta dishes in DC at the moment. Amazingly, the pizzas are equally impressive, their crusts arriving with the appropriate poofiness, but also that much-sought-after char underneath. The "Bismarck" combines ricotta, spinach, and egg in an ultimately savory, but vegetarian-friendly, pie.

Meals this good give you wings. One like this might even make you feel as hip as your surroundings. –AH

# Potbelly Sandwich Works

**7.4** Food   **7.5** Feel

Yeah, it's a chain. And we love it.

## Sandwiches

Counter service   **$10** Price

www.potbelly.com

Daily 11am–10pm
Hours vary by location

**Bar** None
**Credit cards** Visa, MC, AmEx
Delivery, kid-friendly, live music,
outdoor dining, veg-friendly

**Chinatown**
726 7th St. NW
(202) 478-0070

**Downtown**
555 12th St. NW
(202) 347-7100

**Penn Quarter**
637 Indiana Ave. NW
(202) 347-2353

**Additional locations**
and more features at
www.fearlesscritic.com

Although Potbelly's official headquarters are in Chicago, DC residents almost unanimously claim the sandwich chain as their own. Locals have been known to invite visiting friends to partake of a Potbelly roast beef before even bothering with the White House or Smithsonian. To pin Potbelly's roots inside the Beltway is a lie, but it's an attractive and believable lie, and a lie with which we're willing to roll.

Because, quite frankly, with apologies to Schlotzsky's, Jimmy John's, and Which Wich?, Potbelly is the highest-quality fast-casual deli-sandwich chain around. The reasons are threefold: first, the atmosphere is a lot more fun. Second, toasting is mandatory. Third, Potbelly's ingredients are better. The last reason is really the clincher. The deli meats are painfully fresh, never dry; vegetables are uniformly crisp and fresh. The improvement in the bread has been the single most important advance in fast-casual chains over the past decade, and Potbelly's wheat is excellent: slightly undercooked, slightly chewy, almost bagel-like. Toasting transforms it into an even more blissful state.

Among quality toppings, don't miss the mushrooms, which are smothered with cheese and meat before going through the toaster. Most importantly, the hot peppers (also sold separately in a jar) lend a juicy, vinegary bite. Beyond the sandwiches, well-reduced chili, laced with cumin, comes with onions and a full triangle of yellow American cheese, and is unambitiously wonderful—like an Atkins cheese enchilada platter. Also good are not-too-sweet potato salad and well-loved Oreo milkshakes (rich, if as uselessly thick as soft-serve), although Lay's potato chips and oyster crackers are embarrassments.

Two of Potbelly's greatest strengths, relative to its competitors, are the great prices ($4.19 for a sandwich at press time) and the simplicity of the menu (not too many ingredients). Potbelly produces a delicious product with a factory-line approach. But used books, hand-painted-ish signs, and local live music (in the Dupont branch, an old-school blues often covers the Smashing Pumpkins), and antiques—the place began as an antique store in 1977—elevate Potbelly to an atmospheric league above the fast-casual model. It's a fast-casual restaurant that, in spite of the kitsch and hand-painted-ish lettering, feels real. And that, above all, might be why we're all so eager to claim it as DC's own. –FC

# Pour House

Staffers lose their ties and reputations at this
Capitol Hill hideout

**4.8** **6.5**
*Food* *Feel*

## American

Casual restaurant

**$35**
*Price*

www.pourhouse-dc.com

Mon–Thu 4pm–2am
Fri 4pm–3am
Sat 10am–3am
Sun 10am–2am

**Bar** Beer, wine, liquor
**Credit cards** Visa, MC, AmEx
**Reservations** Not accepted
Live music, outdoor dining, Wi-Fi

**Capitol Hill**
319 Pennsylvania Ave. SE
(202) 546-0779

For the closest thing to a frat house on the south side of the Capitol, head
to Pour House. Sandwiched neatly between the "Top of the Hill," where
the high rollers roll on the floor above, and Scheiss Haus, which speaks for
itself, in the basement below, this pub is where the post-college
cognoscenti come to rub elbows (and bums), drink beer, celebrate a
kickball win, and watch the election results roll in through the wee hours
of the night. It's loud, crowded, dim, and downtrodden; but spirits are
always high, and—luckily—the meaty bartenders have impeccable
patience and good senses of humor.

And you'll have to adopt the bartender's ethos if you order food here.
Especially on nights when Pour House hosts the "after-party" for one of
the many intramural teams it sponsors, it might be half an hour before
your burger arrives. And at eight bucks a pop for a big, greasy, dry hunk,
you're better off ordering a pizza and having it delivered to the bar. You'll
fare better with the appetizers, which include pierogi and pretzels as two
interesting eccentricities; the Cincinnati-style chili is also a winner.

As you're stumbling to the bathroom and wondering where you left
your beer, perhaps you'll take a moment to recall that, upstairs, past the
masses of Ultimate frisbee players and Young Republicans, past non-profit
know-it-alls and congressional aides and paralegals, just a few blocks up
the street, lies the throbbing hub of American power. You'll smile to recall
as well, as you maneuver by the dome to the metro, that its halls are filled
with the very men who used to rub elbows (and bums) at Pour House.
–CK

# Prego Delly

**3.6** **5.0**
*Food* *Feel*

An Italian sandwich shop and specialty store that's not really great at either

## Sandwiches, Italian

Counter service

**$25**
*Price*

Daily 10am–5pm

**Bar** None
**Credit cards** Visa, MC, AmEx
Outdoor dining

**Capitol Hill**
210 7th St. SE
(202) 547-8686

Yes, it's spelled that way. Like the sauce bearing the same name, this attempt at an Italian deli is somewhat one-dimensional and inauthentic, an experience only to be sought out in the most dire of circumstances. Like, if Market Lunch is packed and you're feeling a little social anxiety.

It's so easy to be drawn in by a deceptive display of Italian specialties: Plump and puckering olives line the back shelves, along with specialty crackers and potato chips, canned tomatoes, and a variety of Torani syrups. If you must succumb to anything at Prego, these goods will be the least disappointing. But the deli counter is another story.

The sandwiches suffer from a scourge of poor ingredients. An Italian sausage sandwich sounds promising (generally, sausage is always good, even when it's not). Not here: this sausage is thick-skinned and devoid of flavor, and the tomato sauce is soppy. To further worsen the texture, the onions are undercooked and the sub roll tastes cheap and stale.

Other deli options are no better. The meats look as if they've been behind the faded counter since Mussolini's day, and most of the bread is sliced and packaged. Steer clear of the rock-hard cookies in a jar by the cash register, as well. In fact, it's probably best to stick to items that are bottled and canned, with expiration dates printed on them.

Prego's service is pleasant and easy going (it seems the owners are usually there). It's funny that the best thing about Prego is that, on some weekends, a woman outside Prego's lovely patio seating area sells exquisite homemade breads, cookies, and plastic containers of pesto. Instead of a trip to Prego, you may as well have just opened a jar of some of that stuff, and made your own lunch. –CK

# Prime Rib

A steakhouse that's best when enjoyed while using an expense account

| 8.5 | 3.0 |
|-----|-----|
| Food | Feel |

## Steakhouse

Upmarket restaurant

**$90**
Price

www.theprimerib.com

Mon–Thu 11:30am–3pm, 5pm–10:30pm
Fri 11:30am–3pm, 5pm–11pm
Sat 5pm–11pm

**Bar** Beer, wine, liquor
**Credit cards** Visa, MC, AmEx
**Reservations** Accepted
Live music

**Farragut**
2020 K St. NW
(202) 466-8811

We bid pompous customs goodbye
When the last of their advocates die,
But there's still one more place
That will say it straight-faced:
Nice jacket, but where is your tie?

If you don't have one with you, you pig,
They'll wrap you with one that you'll dig—
Hèrmes might be nice,
and no matter the price;
They're positioned as that kind of gig.

Get ready to deal with the staff;
They might glare you down if you laugh.
But when check-time arrives,
They'll be trading high-fives
Over dinner's long, cruel epitaph.

Prime rib is the one thing to eat;
It's a freakily thick, fatty treat.
Don't let yourself slip
And request New York Strip,
'Cause they don't even dry-age that meat.

Now places like this are just done.
The war's over—and casual's won.
And though we might long
For the tuxes of song,
Our food is best done by the young.

The hammer on this coffin's nail
The true sign the Prime Rib would fail
Was the bittersweet end
Of the lobbying trend,
That left Abramoff's wallet in jail. –RG

# Primi Piatti

A wood burning grill and nice outdoor seating are
all this outdated Italian place has going for it

## Italian

Upmarket restaurant

**$70**
Price

www.primipiatti.com

| | | |
|---|---|---|
| Mon–Fri 11:30am–2:30pm, 5:30pm–10:30pm | **Bar** Beer, wine, liquor | **Foggy Bottom** |
| Sat 5:30pm–10:30pm | **Credit cards** Visa, MC, AmEx | 2013 Eye St. NW |
| | **Reservations** Accepted | (202) 223-3600 |
| | Outdoor dining | |

This place screams "expense-account Italian." No, really. Right on the
front page of the restaurant's website, where you can "prepay for a
guest's dinner or lunch." Does it get any more expense-account than
that? Oh yes, the optional magic show.

The font on the awning should give away how incredibly dated this
place is. It's very 1987 (the year they opened), like the iron-on lettering
from an old softball team T-shirts, across a field of powder blue. Props for
the outdoor sidewalk seating, which is preferable to the seating inside,
done up as it is with a restaurant-catalog-meets-Siena-Duomo look, all
thick stripes and diamond shapes. The website's marketing materials are
also caught in the past, full of ancient press, most amusingly a post from
July, 1987 that called the restaurant "fresh, inventive."

The food here is merely serviceable, which makes its high price point
offensive. But if you get taken here on someone else's dime, stick to the
wood-burning grill, which makes whole fish and pizzas. Go for the basic
one with roasted peppers and fontina, as the other combinations are
more questionable ("mixed vegetables and smoked mozzarella"?!) Simple
pastas won't be too bad, like green lasagne with veal ragù and dried
porcini, or mollareddus (a Sardinian shell pasta) with sausage, tomato,
and saffron. We lose confidence with some hilarious Hispanicisms in the
menu ("atonno," "Chiante") and totally ill-inspired preps, especially in the
fish area (halibut filet stewed in tomato sauce with anchovies, capers, and
black olives? Disgusting!).

Not surprisingly, desserts are cursory and feeble: tiramisù, chocolate
and hazelnut this-and-that, and they are ridiculously overpriced. $10 for
mixed berries? They'd better be served in a bowl of cognac. But in the
end, this is just a big fat disappointment, and even a magic show can't
help that. –RG

# Prince Café

Don't waste your time here...under any circumstances

| 1.4 | 2.6 |
|---|---|
| Food | Feel |

## Middle Eastern

Casual restaurant

**$25**
Price

www.cafeprince.com

Sun–Wed 11am–3am
Thu–Sat 11am–5am

**Bar** Beer, wine, liquor
**Credit cards** Visa, MC, AmEx
**Reservations** Not accepted
Wi-Fi

**Adams Morgan**
2400 18th St. NW
(202) 667-1400

**Adams Morgan**
2400 18th St. NW
(202) 667-1400

**Georgetown**
1042 Wisconsin Ave. NW
(202) 333-1500

**Additional locations**
and more features at
www.fearlesscritic.com

We weren't exactly in search of this particular needle in a haystack, but we don't think it's premature to declare we've found it: The Worst Restaurant in DC. Because we live in a world of uncertainty, and to keep our enemies at bay and hedge our bets, we'll amend that statement slightly: The Prince Café is one of Washington's 10 Worst Restaurants.

We only think it's worth writing about because it's so popular. Somehow, the café has managed to maintain several outposts of bad food and reckless service, and inexplicably, people actually seem to patronize them all. The uptown location survives, we assume, largely as a late-night joint for hookah and tea (in individual, generic teabags); the residing hipsters seem to ignore, as they puff away on apricot shisha, that the Prince's estate looks upon nothing more than a depressing commercial strip in Tenleytown, featuring Hudson Trail Outfitters and The Container Store. The other outposts of the Café are no more inspiring.

Hookah aside, the food service is abominable. The Prince's menu, which claims an "Indian and Middle Eastern" bent, whatever that means, has a variety of options that sound promising on their face. The standard items of both cuisines are featured—kebabs, curries, and mezze—but when, after an endless wait, the server finally thinks to take your order, you discover that one after another of the dishes you had planned to order is "unavailable." When you give up and ask your man, "Well, what *is* available?" he sighs and rudely—as if you should have known—mumbles a short list that is limited to shish kebab, vegetable or chicken curry, and a few appetizer dips. No lamb vindaloo, no fish masala, no dolmade.

Somewhat peeved, you ask for a recommendation. He thinks, and again, mumbles: "The vegetable curry is very good." Fine.

When, after 45 minutes (and this, in a nearly empty restaurant), your food finally arrives, the recommendation sounds at the very least laughable, and at worst, perverse. The curry tastes like no more than a defrosted bag of "mixed veggies" (carrot cubes, deflated peas, corn, sliced green beans) done up in a tomato-and-mild-chile-powder based sauce. It is insulting. The "Prince's Combo" consists of a nothing-special shish kebab and a few pieces of chicken (to their credit, the meat tastes fine and won't make you sick). *This* took 45 minutes? –CK

# Proof

This relaxed classroom-laboratory for food and wine lovers makes dining out fun again

**8.4** Food
**8.5** Feel

**New American**

Wine bar

**$55** Price

www.proofdc.com

Mon–Wed 11:30am–2pm, 5:30pm–10pm; Thu 11:30am–2pm, 5:30pm–11pm; Fri 11:30am–2pm, 5:30pm–2am; Sat 5:30pm–2am; Sun 5pm–9:30pm

**Bar** Beer, wine, liquor
**Credit cards** Visa, MC, AmEx
**Reservations** Accepted
Date-friendly, good wines, outdoor dining, veg-friendly

**Penn Quarter**
775 G St. NW
(202) 737-7663

America is experiencing a dining boom the likes of which it has never seen. If you don't believe us, Google any restaurant and see how many people have devoted precious time and energy to talking about it online. Cookbooks dominate best seller lists, the Travel Channel has more shows about food than resorts, and the word (shudder) "foodie" is officially part of the mainstream lexicon. Couple this with an increased eco-consciousness, and you've got the perfect storm—one that has been bringing a wave of talented chefs exercising a philosophy of eating seasonally and locally.

Proof is the result of aforementioned perfect storm plus a wheelbarrow of money. Done up in French pewter, Jerusalem stone, Italian leather, and walnut floors, this place certainly appreciates the finer things…but is it *sincere*? Here's the proof (sorry):

1. A 65-page wine list of (some worthy, some not so much) red-carpet celebrities like Didier Dageuneau (rest his soul), Angelo Gaja, and Screaming Eagle, but more importantly, plenty of exciting wines under $50.

2. Despite needing a black AMEX card to purchase more than half the wines on this list, the mark-ups are restaurant-reasonable.

3. Tables are customized with extensions just for your bottle, decanter, and glasses.

4. Robotech-like wine storage means a hefty list of 40 wines by the glass will stay fresh and lively; 2-oz pours encourage playing and learning.

5. An on-floor sommelier and well-trained staff guide novices beyond the "critter wines."

6. Local, sustainable and organic ingredients are emphasized, and assembled with a careful regard for balance.

7. One word: fromagère.

8. Many culinary treats like veal sweetbreads (perfectly crispy outside, creamy inside; paired with dates, spinach, and bacon in a delicious balance), as well as sustainable swimmers like tilefish and sablefish.

9. A wide array of small plates (simple and delicious roasted beets with goat cheese and honeyed black walnuts; a terrific crispy cauliflower with lemon-tahini dressing) invite experimentation and sharing.

10. A late-night menu ensures no one need eat poorly after 11pm (but only on Fridays and Saturdays).

Not a "concept," nor trendy, nor stuffy, Proof is a place to celebrate one's inner *bon vivant*, whether one has extravagant means or not. –FC

# PS 7's

The feel's a lot more waifish than the food

## New American

Upmarket restaurant

**7.1** Food

**8.6** Feel

**$60** Price

www.ps7restaurant.com

Mon–Thu 11:30am–2:30pm, 5:30pm–9:45pm; Fri 11:30am–2:30pm, 5:30pm–10:45pm; Sat 5:30pm–10:45pm

**Bar** Beer, wine, liquor
**Credit cards** Visa, MC, AmEx
**Reservations** Accepted
Date-friendly, outdoor dining

**Chinatown**
777 Eye St. NW
(202) 742-8550

A restaurant with a painfully trendy name has to deliver on the food, or else it is just begging for ridicule. Thankfully, the southern-tinged food and the inviting dining and lounge spaces at PS 7's (an amalgam of chef-owner Peter Smith's name and the restaurant's street number, 777) allow for a tasteful playfulness that goes beyond nomenclature.

Walk in and you'll be swallowed up in a sea of chocolate brown and blue. Huge windows flood the room with natural light, and the contrast between the white tablecloths and the rich color palette resonates throughout. You may feel a bit too swallowed: even on a weekend night, the spacious but sparsely furnished bar/lounge area can take a surprisingly long time to warm up. The rather well-heeled crowd that does eventually show up to fill in the empty corners seems to enjoy PS 7's ritzy wink-and-nod at more plebian pleasures, happily sipping cheeky cocktails (sweet potato pie, for instance) and munching on the cute, addictive tuna sliders on Parker House rolls, mini hot dogs, or half smokes. Prices, however, are more suited for pols than proles.

The menu follows the lounge's tongue-in-cheek lead. It offers more high-end send-ups of down market classics. In a somewhat deconstructed wedge salad, iceberg lettuce slices are topped with thin slivers of red onion, crisp bacon strips, tomato confiture, pepper vinaigrette, and buttermilk blue cheese aioli. This is much easier to eat than a classic wedge, and the condiments are top-notch; the tomato confiture, cloyingly sweet when eaten on its own, cuts through the sharpness of the onion and dressing and pares down the saltiness of the bacon.

In a hot brown main course described to us on our last visit as a "turkey sandwich," turkey breast was pan-seared, served over a slice of toasted bread, and topped with slightly floury béchamel, slices of juicy tomato, bacon, and cheese that unfortunately began to congeal after a few minutes. It was a heavy, decadent satire on a bland staple.

For dessert, moist and rich chocolate soufflé cake—not a soufflé at all—sits next to a scoop of thick Bourbon cream and on top of a smear of chocolate sauce and neon green droplets of mint gel. We could have done without the creepy green stuff—a sense of humor is great, so long as the joke's not on us. Speaking of which…

P.S. Why was 6 scared of 7? Because 7 8 9. –SDC

# Pupusería San Miguel

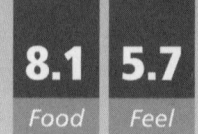

**8.1** Food   **5.7** Feel

This hole in the floor makes pretty good pupusas and even better Mexican food

## Salvadoran

Casual restaurant

**$10** Price

Daily 8am–10pm

**Bar** None
**Credit cards** Visa, MC, AmEx
**Reservations** Not accepted

**Columbia Heights**
3110 Mt Pleasant St. NW
(202) 387-5410

Down a set of stairs in a small, ugly Mount Pleasant basement lies one of Washington's prime purveyors of the pupusa, a round little Salvadoran corn pocket that's stuffed with cheese and, sometimes, meat. San Miguel is a find—if not so much for its pupusas, which are average, as for its Mexican food, which is well above the mean.

We'd call the restaurant hidden but for the large, homemade sign at street level announcing the place in bold red typeface. Inside, there's a meager first dining room with fake-wood tables, a jukebox (selections tend to favor upbeat Mexican pop or ska), a television blaring Spanish-language news, and maybe a couple of men with beers and pupusas. The second dining room is slightly more formal, at least relative to the first: here, you get red checkered plastic on the tables, a couple of posters, and a generally quieter atmosphere.

Either way, the service is bound to be a bit slow, a mystifying and frustrating feature of a restaurant that's usually nearly empty (carry-out, which is quicker, is a popular option). We can't see behind the tall metal divider in the first room, but we suspect there's just a single cook in the kitchen. There's something trustworthy about this, especially when compared to the million-man kitchens of bad Mexican restaurants like Lauriol Plaza.

San Miguel makes a very good taco, even if its varieties are few: the res (beef) is moist and just a bit oily, with plenty of salt and spice. The tortilla is a small, thick flour or corn number with grill marks on both sides, and each taco is garnished with a dusting of queso fresco, a few thin slices of pepper, and a delicate avocado wedge. Also noteworthy is the chicken tamal, made with finely ground masa and stuffed with a potato wedge or two and plenty of spicy, shredded chicken. San Miguel also offers a decent plate of fried yuca and roasted chicken. Its pupusas are really nothing special relative to others in Salvadoran-rich DC (but then, it's hard not to adore a fried ball of dough with cheese melting out from all edges), but even if the pupusería is a false front for a taquería, we like this place. –CK

# Quarry House Tavern

**8.1** Food    **9.3** Feel

Artisanal burgers, bar food, and beer-nerd beer in an underground speakeasy-like space

**American**      Casual restaurant    **$25** Price

| | | |
|---|---|---|
| Mon–Thu 5pm–1am | **Bar** Beer, wine, liquor | **Silver Spring, MD** |
| Fri noon–2am | **Credit cards** Visa, MC, AmEx | 8401 Georgia Ave. |
| Sat 2pm–2am | **Reservations** Not accepted | (301) 587-8350 |
| Sun noon–1am | Date-friendly | |

The closest thing Silver Spring has to a speakeasy, this hidden haunt is an unexpected dose of subterranean fun—and it's tasty, too.

A lot of people sneak down to the Quarry House just to drink. If you're in the laid-back school of dating, it's a great choice—in part because of the easy, divey, tavern-like feel and lively crowd, but also in part because your date will be seriously impressed by the you-must-be-in-the-knowness of the joint. But those who know, *know*; they come back again and again. They come in ones, twos, and big groups for an easy evening of revelry and good, old fashioned eatin'. The only thing that's not easy, on a busy night, is getting a table.

The practically unmarked entrance to the Quarry House is on the corner of Georgia Ave. and Bonifant, tucked in beneath the high-school-kids-must-not-be-able-to-handle-themselves-when-they-see-the-name-and-even-our-adult-gay-friends-can't-stop-giggling-at-it Bombay Gaylord. You make your way down a narrow staircase, you open a creaky door, and you step into an alternate, windowless universe of clinking glasses, sizzling burgers, and hearty laughs.

What's surprising, given the whole dive shtick, is the artisanal angle of the nouvelle-comfort-food menu and the impressive breadth of the beer list. Fried pickles, house-made potato chips, Pabst-Blue-Ribbon-battered chicken tenders, tater tots, half-smokes, and wings are good sideshows to the main bar-food event: well-executed burgers made from up to a pound of high-quality meat. We're particular fans of the patty melt, which allows the cheese to play a more central role in the taste/texture combination.

Speaking of PBR, they've got it on tap too (no snobbery here), rubbing elbows with crazy, little-known microbrews—and, of course, Dogfish Head, the beer that will get you drunk faster than any other. Beyond that, the extensive "beericulum vitae" is extremely strong in Belgium and Germany, with some overhopped American IPAs and nice English porters thrown in. Particularly nice to see is the dry cider from France: Christian Drouin Pays d'Auge, Etienne Dupont Bouche Brut de Normandie. These are underappreciated gems even in a mainstream beer world that is getting increasingly sophisticated.

And how about a Lindemans Framboise float?

Cheers to that. –RG

# Queen Makeda

Regal Ethiopian, served in a place that's actually
pleasant to spend time in

| 8.1 | 8.9 |
|-----|-----|
| Food | Feel |

## Ethiopian

Casual restaurant

**$30**
Price

www.queenmakedadc.com

Sun–Thu 11am–2am
Fri–Sat 11am–3am

**Bar** Beer, wine, liquor
**Credit cards** Visa, MC, AmEx
**Reservations** Accepted
Delivery, live music, veg-friendly

**Shaw**
1917 9th St. NW
(202) 232-5665

On the restaurant-lined block of Ninth Street—DC's Little Ethiopia—the ambiance generally takes a back seat to what's on the plate. Queen Makeda is a notable exception, setting itself apart with an unusually welcoming environment, particularly on the second floor, whose ceilings are covered by elaborate hangings, whose chairs are cheerily woven and outfitted with red cushions, and whose tables are fashioned from African drums made with stretched cowhide. Over at the bar, a roof descending from above aims to create a faux-outdoor feel, and brass lanterns add yet another evocative element.

The cooking technique at Queen Makeda seems to differ slightly from surrounding Ethiopian kitchens in that the kitchen manages to achieve an unusual degree of tenderness from the stew meat. This tenderness reaches its apex with lamb alicha, colored yellow from turmeric. Ground beef is excellent, too, but pot-roasty gored gored, made with red pepper, is less impressive. The flip side is that, perhaps due to a combination of cooking at an appropriately slow simmer and a lack of skimming, the stews are also fairly oily. This isn't necessarily a bad thing; the injera (a good version, appropriately soft and spongy with just a whisper of sourness) quickly absorbs the brightly colored pools of beef and lamb fat, turning it into a mess of soppy deliciousness from which your fingers will definitely need a wet nap to recover. The oiliness might not be for everyone.

Kitfo, the iconic steak tartare, is more aggressively herbed than usual, and it can be substituted into the lunch combo special if you ask really, really nicely; request it raw, as you should, and you'll get the standard raised-eyebrow-plus-smile response. The menu is more pared-down than most in the area, but veggie dishes like shiro (yellow split-pea stew) and collard greens are successful too.

In a departure from the norm, the exceptionally friendly staff will bring out the big silver tray lined with injera first, and then bring your stew dishes in separate metal containers, dosing them onto the bread as you go for a more elegant effect than usual. It's just another of the many little touches that elevate Queen Makeda above the pack. –RG

# Rainbow Restaurant

**8.3** **7.2**
Food  Feel

Ghanaian goat that's some of the best around

## Ghanaian

Casual restaurant   **$20**
Price

www.rainbowrest.com

Daily 11am–9pm

**Bar** Beer, wine
**Credit cards** Visa, MC, AmEx
**Reservations** Accepted
Kid-friendly

**Gaithersburg, MD**
312 E. Diamond Ave.
(301) 947-0099

The cuisine of Ghana is little known to most Americans, but some of the elements—fufu (that irresistible potato starch), jollof rice, goat meat, peanut-butter soup—are shared with other West African cuisines. But there's something totally unique about the Rainbow Restaurant, the cuisine's foremost practitioner in the DC area. Maybe it's the atmosphere, which is several notches more festive than you'd expect in a blank-walled, white-tiled, office-ceilinged room; there's live Ghanaian music, for instance.

Or maybe it's Rainbow's singular proficiency in marketing. These folks seem uniquely well connected to the who's-who of Ghanaian culture, be it Embassy events or catering events for visiting dignitaries from back home, so you'll often see an array of Rainbow's steam-table buffet dishes showing up within the District.

There are many good goat dishes in the DC suburbs, but several at the Rainbow Restaurant are among the best anywhere, including goat-and-pepper soup, bright orange in color and gentle in flavor; a stew of meltingly tender goat with eba (a smooth boiled starch made from cassava flour), spinach, and egusi (ground melon seeds); or omotuo (steamed rice balls in a goat soup made from palm-nut butter, spinach, and egusi).

The kitchen has a way with spinach, and with collard greens too; it would be irresponsible to complete a meal here without a leafy-green stew of some sort. There's a version of jerk chicken, subtler and less spicy (this is not necesarily a good thing) than the Jamaican version. Oxtail, rich and fatty, is another overlap with Jamaica—the West Indies are not so far away—but the "Ghanaian style," stewed with tomato, is more unusual than the curried Jamaican version. Both are good, though, and both require a willingness to gnaw.

Some shrimp and fish mains can come fairly dried out; accompanying them with rice and fufu certainly doesn't help cure the dryness. Tilapia filet is unimpressively cooked—forming a relatively tough skin around the flesh—and the taste is not the freshest. Other weaknesses include useless salads of iceberg lettuce and underripe tomato. When will the suburban ethnic restaurants realize that it's not necessary to serve iceberg-lettuce salads to make people happy?

We're happy, nonetheless, once you set us up with some spinach and egusi. –RG

# Raku

Another pan-Asian concept that underestimates its audience by dumbing down its food

**4.4** Food

**7.2** Feel

## Pan-Asian

Upmarket restaurant

**$35** Price

Mon–Thu 11:30am–10pm
Fri–Sat 11:30am–11pm
Sun noon–10pm

**Bar** Beer, wine, liquor
**Credit cards** Visa, MC, AmEx
**Reservations** Accepted
Outdoor dining

**Logan Circle**
1440 P St. NW
(202) 332-4300

**Dupont**
1900 Q St. NW
(202) 265-7258

**Bethesda, MD**
7240 Woodmont Ave.
(301) 718-8680

We're not sure exactly how "Asian" modifies "Diner" to create "Raku"—perhaps there's some formica hidden away in the kitchen. The space is self-consciously decked out in red and black, with all the minimalist balsa wood and wide open space of a typical upmarket Dupont spot. The waitstaff is also far from diner: no one here is about to call you "sweetheart" (not by a long shot). Nor is there a malt in sight.

In this age of insufferable fusion, it could theoretically be even worse. Still, this is one confused concept. After an introduction of paltry sides ($2.50 for pickled ginger, a condiment that usually comes free of charge?), the menu lists Raku's selection of "Pan-Asian Tapas." Come on, can't a restaurant just call its small plates "small plates"? Does a fancy foreign name make paying $10 for a dollop of dough and sliver of tofu more palatable? Either way, the restaurant's verbiage adds yet another axis to the now three-dimensional dining landscape: tapas-diner-Asian.

And Asia's a pretty big place to tackle. Just ask anyone who plays Risk. At Raku, the chief factor that unites the dishes from disparate Asian cuisines is their impressive blandness. Vietnamese summer rolls are mostly filled with flavorless vermicelli (rice noodles)—only a few sprigs of cabbage and mint can't compete—and the rice paper is dry. The accompanying peanut sauce tastes disturbingly like low-sodium Skippy. As for Raku's Hunan Chicken Salad (whose misleading name just sounds disgusting: Hunan chicken and mayo?), the dish entails a few bland slabs of barely-spiced meat on a bed of greens. The sushi here is of grocery-store competence. It's meant to be a moneymaker, not any sort of artistic feat of excellence. In fact, this is true of the entire concept. Dumbed-down Asian food. Skip Raku. You can find much better Japanese, Chinese, and Vietnamese nearby. –CK

# Rasika

Chutneys, curries, nibbles, and naans, all dressed up for a perfect night out

**8.6** Food

**9.0** Feel

## Indian

Upmarket restaurant

**$70** Price

www.rasikarestaurant.com

Mon–Thu 11:30am–2:30pm, 5:30pm–10:30pm; Fri 11:30am–2:30pm, 5pm–11pm; Sat 5pm–11pm

**Bar** Beer, wine, liquor
**Credit cards** Visa, MC, AmEx
**Reservations** Accepted
Date-friendly, veg-friendly

**Penn Quarter**
633 D St. NW
(202) 637-1222

First impressions are totally underrated. When you venture into a new restaurant, your first impression—what and whom you see upon entering—is an essential part of your meal. After all, when we go out to eat, we don't go only for the food—we go for the ambiance, the company, and for the delicious feeling that, unlike at home, we don't have to do a thing. And when a place ranks highly in these regards, we are more likely to be receptive to that which is served on our plates. But when the food is also good enough to make you mutter to your companions, "forget home, I'm moving in here," you know you're at a great restaurant.

Rasika deserves this title. The décor at this nouvelle-Indian hot spot is cool without being aloof—oranges, browns, and reds set a warm tone that is further highlighted by soft lighting emanating from bold fixtures. It's comfortable and hip at the same time. The service is impeccable, if cold and a bit impersonal—water glasses are always full, plates are delivered and cleared smoothly. If you can't get a reservation at one of the dining-room tables (the best ones are along the windows), there's seating at the bar and at low lounge tables.

The attention to gorgeous detail is beautifully reflected on the plates. In both taste and appearance, the kitchen has successfully merged traditional and modern elements of Indian cuisine, as others have failed to do. The shikampur kebab, for example, is a short stack of pillowy and smooth lamb patties layered with crème fraîche, pickled onion, and aromatic, faraway fragrances. Even better is palak chaat, ethereally crispy spinach whose texture is addictive, and whose tamarind, date, chutney, and sweet yogurt are matched with enough salt to keep the dish in balance.

We've suffered through tough lamb among main-course stews; bone-in dishes are better, as is moist, tender duck breast with a hot smoky chili-saffron-cashew sauce. You must order the bread basket to sop up the amazing sauces.

It's true, first impressions are underrated. But the warm glow that stays with you long after leaving the lovely Rasika—that's an unparalleled pleasure that anyone can appreciate. –SDC

# Ray's Hell-Burger

**9.0** Food
**6.8** Feel

A gutter-sprawling food coma of near-religious ecstasy

## American

Counter service

**$15** Price

Mon 5pm–10pm; Tue–Thu noon–10pm; Fri–Sat noon–11pm; Sun noon–10pm

**Arlington, VA**
1713 Wilson Blvd.
(703) 841-0001

**Bar** None
**Credit cards** None
Kid-friendly

**Arlington, VA**
1713 Wilson Blvd.
(703) 841-0001

Carnivores of DC rejoice! Ray of Ray's the Steaks has rented the next room over in an Arlington strip mall and opened a burger joint. Not only does it share the sparse décor and down-to-earth vibe of Ray's, it also uses the same meat. Holy cow—that means the possibility of enjoying your ground beef *bloody*.

Like its steakhouse neighbor, Ray's Hell-Burger is not an aesthete's hangout. Vintage horror movie posters lend a macabre touch to the institutional fluorescent lighting and cheap plastic furniture. The grill station in the back is what you'd find in high-school football concession stands across America with baskets of potato chips and chalkboard menus vibrating to the hum of an ice cream freezer.

Yet devotees of Ray's will tell you that this sparseness is the point; there is a clear mission here, and it is meat. And what a joy it is. Diners can choose mounds of toppings (mostly free) to festoon their burger, from grilled vegetables to various cheeses. If you really want to pimp out your sandwich, you can opt for a $4 designer cheese (nice, stinky Époisses, for instance, or aged Danish blue), or dress the thing up like steak au poivre. We're partial to the Diablo burger, with chipotle sauce, grilled onions, sautéed mushrooms, and blue cheese; it's a sensory barrage of full-bodied flavor. Still, it's hard to argue that anything does a better job of burrowing straight to the pleasure centers of your brain than simple bacon and Vermont cheddar.

Regardless, what will arrive at your table is a concoction of heroic proportions, with freshly ground meat that falls apart at the touch. It will be sensuously soft and impossibly juicy, a sloppy, delicious, lustful mess that can magically be consumed without feelings of sickness. You will notice the absolute silence descend upon diners as all consciousness is focused on the masterpiece before them.

Some quirks to beware of: Ray's Hell-Burger only accepts cash, and is annoyingly deficient in French fries. Furthermore, their greasy, overly rich mac and cheese preparation is not very good, and it's often impossible to find seating. But for a burger like this, you'll be willing to squat in the street. If you can handle it, a pitcher of root beer (on tap) or a float will immediately send you into a gutter-sprawling food coma of near religious ecstasy. All hail the Hell-Burger. –JC

# Ray's the Classics

Retro American dining: our new guilty pleasure

**8.2** Food   **7.6** Feel

## Steakhouse, American

Upmarket restaurant   **$45** Price

Sun–Fri 6pm–9:30pm
Sat 5:30pm–10pm

**Bar** Beer, wine, liquor
**Credit cards** Visa, MC, AmEx
**Reservations** Accepted

**Silver Spring, MD**
8606 Colesville Rd.
(301) 588-7297

Ah, America. Land of big plates filled with big food. What happened to eating this way? It's been villainized and defamed by snobs like us who insist on loving farm-to-table concepts and hole-in-the-wall Chinese joints. Places like this are now exotic to us, and so maybe it's with those rose-tinted glasses that we admit we really, really like Ray's the Classics.

While not quite as good as Ray's the Steaks (har), it does have more atmosphere. We think both places are quite nice for not trying too hard and avoiding that gross corporate thing, and the service does a good job of supporting the constant, bustling crowds. This Ray's is more minimalist—simple lighting dangles from the ceiling—but it still manages to be fun and cool. Seating is also more comfortable here than at the original.

The menu also cuts a wider swath through Americana retro dining. Crab is the way to start: both the crab fritters with Maryland crab; and the "Crab Royale," which is a mess of lump crabmeat with Old Bay and sherry butter. Delicious. You almost feel guilty eating it without cracking and peeling and stabbing yourself in the thumb…this is like *mainlining* crab. The steaks are similar to those at the steakhouse: wet-aged, not dry-aged, soft and tender but missing the funkiness that we seek in a top-notch steak. They're well charred, though, and ideal at medium rare. The brandy mushroom cream sauce doesn't really add much; it just masks the beefiness. "Cajun" spices—another option for the steak—aren't really all that spicy. Hanger steak is never tough, a feat considering the lean cut. Their work with spinach is good, both creamed and in a soufflé.

If you don't feel like glutting it up, the bar menu has smaller versions of many of the menu items, including steaks. And they have these addictive little spiced nuts that go great with a martini. Just don't fill up; you've still got a long way to go. –FC

# Ray's the Steaks

A steak house where the focus is on the bull, not the B.S.

| 8.4 | 7.4 |
|-----|-----|
| Food | Feel |

## Steakhouse

Upmarket restaurant

**$45**
Price

Sun–Thu 5pm–10pm
Fri–Sat 5pm–11pm

**Bar** Beer, wine
**Credit cards** Visa, MC, AmEx
**Reservations** Accepted
Kid-friendly

**Arlington, VA**
2300 Wilson Blvd.
(703) 841-7297

Ray's the Steaks is a quirk of DC dining that is too wonderful to miss. In a city abundant with steakhouses (what is it with politicians and their love for red meat?) created to flaunt shady expense accounts and encourage epically ostentatious meals, Ray's is a curmudgeonly breath of fresh air. It is uncompromising, self-righteous, and, even if these aren't the very best steaks in town, absolutely worth it.

Ray's is unique because of its value proposition: simply put, it will serve you great meat at low cost by cutting overhead from everywhere else. In practice, this means diner-like service, hurried meals, few niceties, and a monastic cell of a dining area, although the new location has dressed things up a little. If ever you're confused, the menu will defend Ray's ethos by cheekily reminding you about what you're paying for. And while the old location only took reservations in person—so that you needed to show up senior-citizen early or arrive in advance to put in your name— you can now saunter in like a civilized person, having called ahead to ensure your spot.

But any rough edges in Ray's presentation are emphatically smoothed over by the arrival of the meat. Huge cuts of beef are butchered and wet-aged in-house and cooked at properly high temperatures with a careful eye to doneness. Ribeye is inches thick, pillow-soft, and exuding juice, but it's got enough chew to make your mouth feel like it's doing something. Horseradish sauce is a weak excuse, but you don't need it. In fact, we don't quite get the emphasis on sauce here. None of them—not the weak horseradish, not the boring mushroom, not the rich au poivre, not even the famous-but-distracting diablo—add much. Our other, ahem, beef is that the wet-aged meat doesn't achieve the funky tang of the city's best dry-aged steaks. So Ray's is not quite in their league, and at least on that axis, Bobby Van's and the Prime Rib are easy winners. We do get more funk from Ray's hanger steak, however.

It helps that the meat is brilliantly cooked. A guide on the paper menus details temperature, color, and char. Mid-temperatures are allowed and encouraged by the staff. What's so excellent is the care they take to get it just right. Meat can be blushingly, mooingly rare but warmed through and just cooked enough to lose any toughness. Ray's makes your meal even easier by supplying skillets of so-so mashed potatoes and better creamed spinach for free.

If you want to go show off your red-blooded manliness in front of your peers, there are many steakhouses in the District that will strive to outdo you. If you want to wine and dine, wheel and deal, and be robbed at the point of a steak knife by the prices, this city will be happy to oblige. –JC

# The Red and the Black

A New Orleans-style tavern that offers food just
edible enough to keep drinkers functional

**6.0** Food

**8.0** Feel

## Southern

Bar **$25** Price

www.redandblackbar.com

Mon–Fri 5pm–2am
Sat–Sun 7pm–2am

**Bar** Beer, wine, liquor
**Credit cards** Visa, MC, AmEx
**Reservations** Not accepted
Live music, Wi-Fi

**Northeast DC**
1212 H St. NE
(202) 399-3201

We can't be the only ones confused about why a New Orleans-themed tavern decided to pull its name from a novel about 19th-century France; we suspect it has something to do with the French Quarter, but the connection is loose, at best.

What we do know, however, is that you can get a decent bottled beer here, even though there's nothing on tap. The atmosphere is fun, and bands play most nights of the week, but the food could really use a little work.

Red and the Black offers the same five dishes night after night, which are scribbled on the wall menus and served, cafeteria style, out of large crockpots. The contents are gumbo and red beans and rice. The food bears more resemblance to a kind of casserole your grandmother might whip up after returning from a tourist's visit to New Orleans, rather than the kind of food you'd find in the town itself. The jambalaya isn't properly spiced, and any flavor of meat is hidden away behind the mushy rice and other starches. The "chunk of French bread" that's appended to it, moreover, is nothing more than a long boring roll of white bread, straight out of the bag (the staff makes no attempt to hide this). It's insubstantial, flavorless, and bad. There's also a decent muffaletta and something like a Cuban sandwich, though it's tricked out with Emmentaler. But it's nothing special.

Even without the paltry attempt at food, we have a hard time knowing what the Red and the Black is going for. The place strikes a few too many poses to be credible: on the one hand, it's an edgy tavern in an edgy part of town. Seen another way, it's a neighborhood spot with nothing-fancy bottled beer and a lovely outdoor patio. Or perhaps, it's a well-known destination to hear indie bands. While we like the intimacy of the bar, and the red diner-style booths are appealing, it's certainly not the place to get good New Orleans food. –CK

# Red Hot & Blue

Reliable, fast, and cheap barbecue that doesn't suck

| 6.9 | 5.5 |
|-----|-----|
| Food | Feel |

## Barbecue

Casual restaurant

**$15**
Price

www.redhotandblue.com

Sun–Thu 11am–9pm
Fri–Sat 11am–10pm

**Bar** Beer, wine, liquor
**Credit cards** Visa, MC, AmEx
**Reservations** Not accepted
Kid-friendly, outdoor dining, Wi-Fi

**Nationals Park**
1500 Capitol St. SE

**Arlington, VA**
1600 Wilson Blvd.
(703) 276-7427

**Fairfax, VA**
4150 Chain Bridge Rd.
(703) 218-6989

**Additional locations**
and more features at
www.fearlesscritic.com

While local chains may not provide the most thrilling culinary experience, they have their place. Red Hot & Blue—with its many locations throughout Maryland and Virginia—is like the Old Navy of barbecue: cheap and reliable, the favorite of few but enjoyed by most. Each branch has its own Yankee take on the Southern theme (Blues music, mass-produced posters for said music, photographs of makers of said music) and emphasizes either carry-out, catering, and/or dine-in service. Still, nothing beats a picnic table in your park of choice.

RH&B's best work is with the classics, but they tend to overreach, reading like a Congressional roll call. Representatives from Texas (beef brisket), St. Louis and Tennessee (pork ribs), and North Carolina (vinegary chopped pork) convene on platters of two, three, and five meats. Ribs fall from the bone in tender shreds full of juicy pork flavor (we prefer the "dry" version, rubbed with RH&B's own secret blend of spices). Pulled pork is moist and equally flavorful with a soft, utilitarian bun and crisp, creamy cole slaw. We've encountered chunks of bone in the mix, which is a no-no—yet also reveals that it's actually pulled. Ask for some of the "Hard Luck," a Carolina-style, vinegary hot sauce, to complement its sweetness. "Grandma's Potato Salad" is of the familiar mayonnaisey variety, but exalted by red-skinned potatoes, eggs and whole-grain mustard. The sweet BBQ beans are a little soupy but sufficiently smoky and savory. Collard greens tend to be bland, and desserts are pre-fab, but hey…Banana pudding!

You have a basic choice of beers here, the most exotic being Heineken and Corona, though RH&B has its own "award-winning" ale, micro-brewed in PA. (When pressed for the specific award, we couldn't get an answer, nor much enthusiasm for it.) Regardless, it's bound to be a better choice than the gas-station wines and goofy cocktails (Sour-Pucker appletinis, margaritas, and hurricanes).

In a pinch, on a short lunch break, or for a family gathering where there are no good cooks, you could do better than RH&B, but you could also do worse—and you could hardly get more convenient. –CD

# RedRocks

Rockin' brick-oven pizzas on the patio

## Pizza

Casual restaurant **$35**
*Price*

www.redrocksdc.com

Mon 5pm–11pm
Tue–Thu 11am–11pm
Fri–Sat 11am–1am
Sun 11am–11pm

**Bar** Beer, wine, liquor
**Credit cards** Visa, MC, AmEx
**Reservations** Accepted
Date-friendly, kid-friendly, outdoor
dining, veg-friendly, Wi-Fi

**Columbia Heights**
1036 Park Rd. NW
(202) 506-1402

With Columbia Heights gentrifying like crazy, it was only a matter of time before an ambitious pizza place dropped anchor in this up-and-coming neighborhood. RedRocks serves brick-oven pizza in a cozy, brick-lined dining room and on their popular, picnic-table-studded outdoor patio. Young couples and groups of friends, mostly from the surrounding area, abound, enjoying the pizza and beer or waiting around to take their food to go. In the summers, there is a comfortable, lazy buzz on the patio, which is perfect when the stretching hours of evening have sapped the sun of some of its energy.

The host and waitstaff at RedRocks are friendly, if at times a bit frazzled. Plates can come out at random times; and in the cramped interior, trays of food swing in wild orbits around the tables and waiting patrons' heads on their way to their destinations, like some strange solar system run amok. Just duck, and go with the flow—RedRocks doesn't stand on ceremony, but neither will it leave you standing long. In just a few minutes you'll be enjoying your own assertively seared, generously adorned pie.

But RedRocks' menu goes beyond pizza, and we recommend you take advantage of the kitchen's sophistication. To start, order the wonderful burrata mozzarella, served on a bed of dressed arugula and grape tomatoes; it is fresh and creamy but could use a sprinkling of salt. The pizzas, which are sized, Italian-style, for individuals, with a thin, chewy, and (aggressively) charred crust, have good-quality toppings that can seem a tad skimpy. Favorites include the "Toscano"—salty black olives and salami, a welcome alternative to the usual pepperoni—and the "Salsiccia," which beautifully marries smoky, homemade fennel sausage with roasted peppers and Parmigiano-Reggiano. A highlight of all of the pizzas is the use of fresh mozzarella in able moderation, which lets the mild tomato sauce and yeasty crust speak for themselves.

Although the wine selection at RedRocks is limited, there are plenty of bottled domestic beers and a few imports, along with six beers on tap. Beer drinkers will be happy to see both familiar and unfamiliar faces on this impressive list.

A weekend brunch complements a variety of breakfast pizzas (potato and egg, anyone?) with cheap bottomless mimosas. Get a few of those in you, and the pies that emerge from RedRock's red rocks will send you over the moon. –SDC

# Regent Thai

**7.0** Food   **6.8** Feel

This may not be Bangkok street food, but that won't bother you too much

## Thai

Casual restaurant

**$35** Price

www.regentthai.com

Mon–Thu 11:30am–3pm, 5pm–10pm; Fri 11:30am–3pm, 5pm–11pm; Sat noon–3pm, 5pm–11pm; Sun 5pm–10pm

**Bar** Beer, wine, liquor
**Credit cards** Visa, MC, AmEx
**Reservations** Accepted
Delivery, outdoor dining

**Dupont**
1910 18th St. NW
(202) 232-1781

If you can't make it to the suburbs for Thai food, Regent Thai is one of your better bets within district limits. With thick-legged chairs and cherry wood tables, the restaurant's interior seems far removed from the 18th Street traffic just outside. Even on Regent's busiest nights, it's possible to conjure the sense that the world ends just beyond your table. Luckily, your table is subject to some infiltration (albeit gentle) from rice-and-curry-bearing servers.

The litany of menu options at many Thai places is long enough to make Martin Luther (with a mere 95 propositions nailed to the cathedral door) look positively concise, but Regent limits itself to six or eight options per course. The restaurant offers all of the expected fare—red, green, and panang curries, pad Thai, and drunken noodles—as well as some more daring specials and a couple of dishes that look simple on the menu but are full of unexpected flavors (the basil fried rice, in particular, is chock full of its fragrant namesake herb, and peppered with meat and vegetable additions).

A sure sleeper is the drunken noodle dish: Regent's version entails thick noodles, a slightly-smoky soy-based sauce, fine vegetable matchsticks, and meat that truly tastes as if it's been fried within the sauce with extra basil, rather than thrown on top of the noodles as garnish. Given, this is just another Americanized Thai dish—you won't find a lot of kaffir lime or dried shrimp paste in this restaurant—but it tastes good.

Another of Regent's strengths, again in the Thai-American genre, is its intelligent use of fruit. Both traditional (pineapple) and edgy (lychee) flavors are integrated into curries and stir fries in a manner that complements, but doesn't compete with, the meat. And although the result is sometimes a tad on the sweet side, Regent's dishes come off as balanced rather than cloying. The duck main, for instance, is made with stewed lychee fruit and pineapple in a light sauce infused with cherries, which lends an unusual and muted tanginess to the meat; the dish is much less sweet than it sounds. Fruit and fowl blend seamlessly, and the pieces of each are large enough to take on the character of a stir-fry rather than a stew. Pineapple is again employed with success in the dipping sauce that accompanies some appetizers.

In these parts, you could easily do a lot worse for dinner. We're lucky to have Regent. –CK

# Rice

Contemporary Thai with more emphasis on looks than substance

## Thai

**4.4** Food
**8.8** Feel
**$30** Price

Upmarket restaurant

www.ricerestaurant.com

Mon–Thu 11am–2:30pm, 5pm–10:30pm
Fri–Sat 11am–11pm
Sun 11am–10:30pm

**Bar** Beer, wine, liquor
**Credit cards** Visa, MC, AmEx
**Reservations** Accepted
Date-friendly, delivery, outdoor dining

**Logan Circle**
1608 14th St. NW
(202) 234-2400

The best way to describe Rice is as an average Thai-American restaurant that, had it never attempted to be upmarket, may have turned out all right.

Sure, the minimalist décor puts you in a state of zen-like ease: we like the teak tables and simple place settings, and the narrow, white brick dining room feels airy even on the stickiest of summer days, and at night it's warmly lit, a romantic hideaway. On the other hand, the place packs guests on top of each other, and looks like it could house any trendy cuisine.

This lack of personality extends to the service staff, who appear unable to answer any questions about the food and act principally as couriers for your order. This is especially distressing because many menu descriptions necessitate follow-up queries; the abundance of adjectives like "unique" and "special" before sauces makes you curious to know how they're made, a topic on which the staff is mute.

Good luck going it alone. Rice's menu is a postmodern incomprehensibility. First, the card is split into four separate sections, each of which lists appetizers, soups, salads, and mains. Each section is named something esoteric and unhelpful, like "green," "Thai," or "ginger." It's true, most of the dishes in the ginger section include the root in some form, but so do dishes in other sections. Was this menu designed by Derek Zoolander?

A beverage program is a terrific indicator of an upmarket restaurant's understanding of its own cuisine, so it's fitting that the selections here are gas station-terrible; not one of the few varietals offered pairs well with Thai food. Aside from that, there are syrupy stripper drinks and the usual beers.

This is the part where we'd love to pop up and say, *But guess what? It's surprisingly good!* Sigh. Contrary to all the hubbub and fuss (the website lists a production crew easily half the size of a low-budget film), the food falls flat. It's shockingly substandard for these prices—heck, for most casual spots, never mind a hip one like this. "Unique" chicken satay is actually ordinary satay with a weaker sauce. Even that embarrassing American habit, pad Thai (icky, ketchupy), is below average. Lo, the restaurant's eponymous starch is the best thing here: well-cooked, a little sticky, and with a delicate jasmine aroma. At least we can't cry false advertising. –CK

# Rocklands

The hunt for good barbecue in the Mid-Atlantic continues—this isn't it

**5.6** Food  **7.5** Feel

## Barbecue

Casual restaurant  **$15** Price

www.rocklands.com

Mon–Sat 11am–10pm
Sun 11am–9pm
Hours vary by location

**Bar** Beer, wine, liquor
**Credit cards** Visa, MC, AmEx
**Reservations** Not accepted
Kid-friendly, outdoor dining

**Glover Park**
2418 Wisconsin Ave. NW
(202) 333-2558

**Arlington, VA**
3471 Washington Blvd.
(703) 528-9663

**Alexandria, VA**
25 S. Quaker Ln.
(703) 778-9663

**Rockville, MD**
891 Rockville Pike
(240) 268-1120

The hunt for good barbecue in DC, or anywhere near, has taken on the high-anxiety tambor of the scene in *Jaws* where Roy Scheider (rest his soul) says, in what may be the understatement of all time, "we're gonna need a bigger boat." Hordes of food bloggers have taken on this very quest, only to become palpably jaded as the pursuit ebbs out to an eventual declaration that "Rocklands is okay." You would think that in a place where seersucker suits are encouraged, there would be more places to find hunks of smoked meat slathered in tangy sauce. Rocklands does indeed fill in this smoky lacuna—if not by being the best, then at least by being in your face: there are branches in DC, Maryland, and Virginia.

The décor is encouraging right away. You'll find yourself comforted and piqued by the tubs of peanuts waiting by the menus, and a huge kettle of barbecue sauce begs to be pilfered. White-washed walls and rustic accents are hokey but sincere, and an equally sincere staff puts you at ease.

The food tends to be greasy and a little dull. Pulled-pork egg rolls are an interesting concept, but frying an already rich meat results in a heap of (tender) meat drenched in oil. Traditional favorites are no better. Both varieties of ribs are on the tough side and even with ample sauce taste pretty bland. A bottle of homemade barbecue sauce labeled "scream your head off hot" barely causes a whimper.

Stick with grilled chicken, served tender, moist, fatty and with the skin on. They smoke it first, so the flavor permeates the meat, reminding you that even boring ol' chicken can still hold its own under the right circumstances. Cornbread is a guilty pleasure here. It doesn't taste deeply of corn, but it's still sticky and sweet, more cake than bread, good enough to treat as dessert. Other sides, like cole slaw and potato salad, are mayonnaisey and underseasoned.

Despite being not so great, Rocklands has been a popular staple since 1990. Are we that desperate? –FC

# Roger Miller Restaurant

**8.9** Food | **7.4** Feel

A cozy little place that will whisk you away to West Africa on your lunch break

## Cameroonian

Casual restaurant

**$30** Price

www.rmrestaurant.com

Sun–Thu 11am–11pm
Fri–Sat 11am–1am

**Bar** Beer, wine
**Credit cards** Visa, MC, AmEx
**Reservations** Accepted
Delivery, outdoor dining, Wi-Fi

**Silver Spring, MD**
941 Bonifant St.
(301) 650-2495

This isn't the Roger Miller, Country Music Hall of Fame inductee, whose dedicated museum lies in Erick, Oklahoma. Rather, this restaurant is named after the legendary soccer striker, listed in Wikipedia as "Roger Milla," who came out of retirement at age 38 to play in the 1990 World Cup, scored four goals, and led the Cameroon side to the quarterfinals.

The food, too, hails from Cameroon, but if you're familiar with West African cuisine, you'll find some things you recognize: egussi, for instance, is a mild, rich, nutty sauce made from ground melon seeds. Here, it might be served with chunks of beef that are stewed to extraordinary tenderness; a cylinder of fufu, that ubiquitous African yam-based starch that, here, has a grainy consistency more like grits (as opposed to the smooth, gnocchi-like Nigerian version); and an aromatic side dish of spinach.

Speaking of aromatic, the superb goat pepper soup sings with faraway fragrances, reducing goat's gaminess to a mere whisper. Every sip from the spoon seems to yield new facets of flavor. It doesn't end there. Cassava leaves; sauces with subtle hints of smoked fish and beef; ndolle; eru; deep, rich goat curry; sweet, tender fried plantains; and a fresh, tender whole roasted fish, rubbed with yet another set of unique spices.

Aside from the TV playing bizarre world programs (generally having nothing to do with Cameroon or Africa), the interior—just a few tables, really—is actually cuter than you'd expect from viewing the place from outside. The feeling is enhanced by exceedingly friendly service from a staff that gets particularly excited if you demonstrate a real interest in the food and make it clear that you're not just a lunch-bargain-seeker. For this kitchen deserves reverence; to act perfunctorily toward your meal would be to do Roger Miller (or Roger Milla) a disservice. The restaurant is a revelation, a welcome apparition from another time and place, a re-affirmation of the wondrous culinary diversity of the DC area. –RG

# Rosa Mexicano

**5.8** **8.3**
Food  Feel

This East Coast upmarket Mex chain may have pioneered the genre, but it's spread too thin

## Mexican

Upmarket restaurant

**$55**
Price

www.rosamexicano.com

Mon–Wed 11:30am–10:30pm
Thu–Fri 11:30am–11:30pm
Sat 11am–11:30pm
Sun 11am–10pm

**Bar** Beer, wine, liquor
**Credit cards** Visa, MC, AmEx
**Reservations** Accepted
Kid-friendly, outdoor dining

**Penn Quarter**
575 7th St. NW
(202) 783-5522

"Since 1984 we have been serving freshly made guacamole with avocado, jalapeño, tomato, onion, and cilantro (prepared tableside)," reads Rosa Mexicano's menu.

Who can name the crucial missing ingredient? (Hint: it's what supplies the guacamole with its much-needed acidity and keeps it from tasting like mild avocado-flavored mush.)

Lime! A guacamole without lime is simply too one-dimensional.

And why is "prepared tableside" in parenthesis? This is the feature that has people going wild. Nowadays, even your mom is making tableside guacamole for you when you're home for Thanksgiving, but Rosa Mexicano pioneered the million-dollar scam. It's as if the level of control afforded by picking one's spice level (give us a break...there is minimal variation between mild and hot) is enough to negate the importance of the outcome of the how-does-it-taste test. And boy, you are paying a premium to watch your server—as opposed to a trained chef—prepare your food. It's like $12 for one avocado—an unheard of food-cost markup. It's bonkers.

So bonkers, in fact, that a Friday night will generally finding you waiting, tableless, for at least 30 minutes at the packed bar. Margaritas can only carry you for so long—especially margaritas of this quality. They're by no means the worst in town, but they're definitely on the sweet side. Get the pomegranate version and you might need to check your insulin. But they are strong, and they'll have you ready to devour your food. The digs are nice, too. High ceilings amplify sound, giving the space a lively buzz. Bright colors help the cause.

"Zarape de pato" comes with dry duck sandwiched between dry corn tortillas. Its not-dry-at-all habanero cream sauce has some binding and moistening properties, but not enough to save the dish. Enchiladas suizas come with a sauce that more resembles tomatillo than the rich sour-cream-based indulgence we dream about, and the spice warning of "two peppers" is laughable. Tacos with carne asada disappoint, their skirt steak a little, well, dry.

We wish service were more attentive, too. We've gone far too long with empty glasses or empty bellies. But when servers are spending half their time making guacamole, what can you expect? –AH

# Rosemary's Thyme Bistro

**6.2** **8.7**
Food   Feel

A lovely neighborhood haunt with a confusing
menu—stick to the Middle Eastern section

## American, Italian

Casual restaurant   **$40**
Price

www.rosemarysthyme.com

| | | |
|---|---|---|
| Mon–Thu 5pm–11pm | **Bar** Beer, wine, liquor | **Dupont** |
| Fri 11am–midnight | **Credit cards** Visa, MC, AmEx | 1801 18th St. NW |
| Sat 10am–midnight | **Reservations** Accepted | (202) 332-3200 |
| Sun 10am–10pm | Kid-friendly, outdoor dining, | |
| | veg-friendly | |

Touting itself as a "friendly neighborhood restaurant," Rosemary's Thyme
is quaint, welcoming, and gay-friendly, but the food is hit or miss. The
menu suffers from a bit of ADD, trying its hand at too many dishes from
too many parts of the world. Still, the kitchen pulls off a few Middle
Eastern dishes that are worth coming back for. And the service—
amicable, helpful, and knowledgeable—is a big plus. So is the lovely array
of outdoor tables, which almost merge into the sidewalk in one of DC's
most pleasant walking neighborhoods, although the brightly lit gas
station across the street does little to enhance the ambiance.

The menu, because of its length and variety, can be difficult to
navigate. We suggest skipping any dishes that seem too mundane or out
of place, such as ceviche, bruschetta, "Mussels Chardonnay," Caesar
salad, pasta Bolognese, and classic pizzas. Instead, try the "Trio Med"
appetizer, a sampling of hummus (speckled with sundried tomato), baba
ghanoush (smoky, authentic, and just plain great), and domatesli (tangy,
refreshing, and tomatoey). The dish is confusingly served with both soft
pita wedges and tortilla chips, as if it were Arab-Mexican fusion.

Although Rosemary's seems proud of its homemade pasta, we
recommend avoiding spinach ravioli, which are heavy and lack seasoning.
More refined and flavorful is timballo: fresh sheets of pasta rolled with
spinach, roasted peppers, and cheese, and then cut into wheels, two of
which are served over a rich, oniony tomato sauce. But pide (Middle
Eastern pizzas) are this kitchen's best work. Our favorite is the pastirma
and cheese pide, stuffed with strips of cured beef (which tastes like a
combination of pastrami and beef jerky), cheese, fresh spinach, and
tomatoes. It's elegant but rustic, balancing flavors and textures—salty,
sweet, earthy, chewy, crispy, meaty, creamy—quite nicely.

If you order well, a meal at Rosemary's Thyme can be great; otherwise,
it can be a roller coaster of mediocre and geographically misplaced dishes.
Still, it's hard to argue with those beautiful sidewalk seats. –SDC

# Round Robin Bar

Schmoozing and boozing for the old boys

| 7.6 | 9.5 |
|-----|-----|
| Food | Feel |

## American

Bar **$40**

Price

www.washington.intercontinental.com

| | | |
|---|---|---|
| Mon–Thu 4:30pm–1am | **Bar** Beer, wine, liquor | **Downtown** |
| Fri 3pm–1am | **Credit cards** Visa, MC, AmEx | 1401 Pennsylvania Ave. |
| Sat noon–1am | **Reservations** Not accepted | NW |
| Sun noon–midnight | Date-friendly, Wi-Fi | (202) 628-9100 |

The lobbyists who so ably grease the rusty wheels of Washington got their name, it is said, from lingering in the lobby of the great Willard Hotel, frequented by politicians and thus by their parasites. It is only fitting, then, that the Willard would have a bar like the Round Robin: the outer leather booths allow for optimal schmoozing, and the inner circular bar lets regulars cozy up to the bartender. The carpets are red and the walls plush. In the back, what one might call a "ladies' lounge" has been appended; here, marble and natural light prevail, and brandies and fizzes are assumed to be the drinks of choice.

The Round Robin claims to have introduced DC to the mint julep (and Congress never looked back). Sampling one is requisite for Washington diners and history buffs alike. In the fall and winter, the Robin's menu also includes seasonal cocktails, drawing on apples, cinnamon, and the like.

Even though the Willard Room (the hotel's restaurant) has closed, Round Robin is still going strong. The kitchen manages to pair its work well with the bartender's concoctions, although none would claim that inventiveness is the cuisine's key feature. Rather, the chefs turn out dishes of classic competence. The excellent crab cakes are served with a woodsy mix of sautéed mushrooms and bacon, all topped with crisped hairs of red onion.

The Robin's pizzas fare weakly aside those of the better Washington spots, but the paper-thin crusts offer a delicate snack during (or after) cocktails. We can only assume the small-plates lobbyists had their way at the Round Robin, as they have at most of DC's upscale establishments. Let's see if the new, stricter lobbying rules change the gam here. The Willard doesn't exactly seem to believe in new rules. –CK

# Rustico

Pizza and beer...and beer popsicles

| 7.0 | 7.8 |
|-----|-----|
| Food | Feel |

## New American

Casual restaurant

**$40**
Price

www.rusticorestaurant.com

Daily 11:30am–midnight

**Bar** Beer, wine, liquor
**Credit cards** Visa, MC, AmEx
**Reservations** Accepted
Date-friendly, kid-friendly, outdoor dining, Wi-Fi

**Alexandria, VA**
827 Slaters Ln.
(703) 224-5051

Rustico, a cozy, beer-centric Alexandria hideaway, tastes like someone cares. Don't let that fool you into thinking someone does. Despite the warm atmosphere, the service at this popular restaurant-cum-bar can be atrocious. Rumors of two-hour lunches and large parties with reservations being made to wait for long periods for a table abound.

Fortunately for Rustico, and for its customers, the food goes a long way toward comforting the neglected clientele. Generally speaking, the earthy dishes are at once homey and innovative. A wood-fired pizza oven turns out chewy but bold pies loaded with spectacular ingredients like house-made sausage, duck confit, pressed ricotta, and marinated anchovies. They also have a chickpea crust if gluten isn't your thing. This isn't the best pizza in town, but it's still fun to eat. Other successful dishes include a decadent mac and cheese—loaded with mushrooms, pancetta, and peas, and tuna tartare that's spiked with chilied brown butter jam. Butcher-block items are novel and worth sampling, especially the salmon pastrami and duck ham; although these selections may not fit into the comfort-food theme, the deli counter lies just near enough in their collective memories for them to be undemandingly satisfying.

The beer obsession at Rustico comes out in several of the menu items, including a hearts-of-romaine salad, whose red onions are marinated in Framboise before being tossed with a creamy buttermilk dressing. Rustico's extensive collection of well-known favorites and anonymous brews with unpronounceable names really stands out, with more than 300 bottled beers and 30 draught beers. Have no fear: if you do manage to flag down a server, he or she will amicably suggest a few that will pair beautifully with your meal.

The hottest things at Rustico are their summer beer popsicles. Banned for a few months but now (quite thankfully) back, they are charmingly playful, and delicious. Just don't let the kids get to them. Rotating flavors including plum, banana, chocolate, and raspberry are made with stouts, lambics, and Framboise. What carefree fun! –SDC

# Ruth's Chris Steakhouse

**7.8** Food   **7.5** Feel

A Louisiana-based steakhouse chain, yes, but a loveable one

## Steakhouse

Upmarket restaurant   **$90** Price

www.ruthschris.com

Mon–Sat 5:30pm–10:30pm
Sun 5:30pm–10pm
Hours vary by location

**Bar** Beer, wine, liquor
**Credit cards** Visa, MC, AmEx
**Reservations** Accepted

**Downtown**
724 9th St. NW
(202) 393-4488

**Dupont**
1801 Connecticut Ave. NW
(202) 797-0033

**Arlington, VA**
2231 Crystal Dr.
(703) 979-7275

**Additional locations**
and more features at
www.fearlesscritic.com

There's something very specific about the pleasures of a good steakhouse. You walk in knowing exactly what you want. A shrimp cocktail, perhaps, or an iceberg wedge with blue cheese dressing. An expensive steak, aged and buttery, with a big California Cabernet. It's self-indulgent capitalism, and for a long time, it was impossible to find at a chain. Enter Ruth's Chris, which got started in New Orleans in 1965, and in the years since, daringly challenged the notion that a chain restaurant had to be mediocre—and, in the process, added a nuance to the Great Chain Debate that simply could not be ignored.

Bread comes fresh and well heated. The chopped salad, touted as a classic, sports a little spill of fried onions on top that adds texture but steals thunder from the tasty blue cheese. Steak arrives as refreshingly rare as ordered, with a bewildering, peppery sizzle, and extra melted butter on request (do it!). Creamed spinach is like a dream, with the pepper and béchamel and spinach leaves all blending together into an irresistible pile of fatty goodness.

Being the chain that it is, you can rest assured that you'll feel equally at home at all locations. There is an equalizing dark, clubby feeling and impeccable service. It's one of the only places in town where businesspeople can waltz in at 10pm on a weeknight and have a proper meal. And they *pay* for it: with appetizers up to $17.95 and mains into the $40s, this ain't a cheap proposition.

Then again, does anybody who comes here care? –RG

# Saigon Saigon

Superb pho to be eaten with all the tourists

**7.1** **6.0**
*Food* *Feel*

## Vietnamese

Casual restaurant

**$25**
*Price*

Mon–Fri 11am–10pm
Sat–Sun 11am–11pm

**Bar** Beer, wine, liquor
**Credit cards** Visa, MC, AmEx
**Reservations** Accepted
Outdoor dining

**Arlington, VA**
1101 S. Joyce St.
(703) 412-0822

It's easy enough to be put off by Saigon Saigon's Pentagon City mall location. The restaurant sits just beyond the spot where tour buses offload, spilling their captive sightseers into the cornucopia of Pentagon City to cap off a day of touring with The Gap and food-court meals.

Thankfully, Saigon Saigon is not actually within the mall but beside it, thus saving it from this bustle of visiting humanity. It still sits smack between Sur la Table and Chico's in the more upscale "Pentagon Row" section behind the mall, but after just a few seconds in the palm-and-fountain-filled dining room, you can, at least temporarily, forget this fact.

And Saigon's amazing pho abets this erstwhile memory loss. Its broth is rich enough that a sip tastes almost like biting into a strip of the beef itself, and the meat comes in razor-thin slices, along with ample noodles, vegetables, and a separate plate of bean sprouts, Thai basil, and sauces for topping.

Bargain hunters will be tempted by Saigon's pricing scheme: the "large" pho is only a dollar more than the "small." But be forewarned: the portions here are enormous. A small could easily feed two people (or one very hungry person), and finishing off the large in one sitting is unfathomable for all but the most jaded of professional eating champions.

Saigon is a wonderful instance of a non-dive Vietnamese restaurant that serves an earnest pho while maintaining an upscale menu of meat and seafood dishes. That said, the remainder of the menu has trouble living up to the superior soup. A gingered salmon is a rather quotidian take on a rather quotidian fish. The sautéed vegetables are delightfully crisped and the vermicelli noodles are properly cooked, but somehow the combination amounts to significantly less than the sum of its parts. Saigon could push itself to go beyond the risk-free (and under-spiced) options so typical of spots where people "do lunch." But maybe they don't have to. If the tourists don't keep you out, the pho alone will bring you back. –CK

# Sakana

Fresh fish finds you snug as sardines in a tin can

**8.4** *Food*   **7.5** *Feel*

## Japanese

Casual restaurant

**$35** *Price*

Mon–Thu 11:30am–2:30pm, 5:30pm–10:30pm; Fri 11:30am–2:30pm, 5:30pm–11pm; Sat 5:30pm–11pm

**Bar** Beer, wine, liquor
**Credit cards** Visa, MC, AmEx
**Reservations** Accepted
Kid-friendly, outdoor dining, veg-friendly

**Dupont**
2026 P St. NW
(202) 887-0900

Every neighborhood needs—or at least covets—a decent, moderately priced, intimate sushi bar. Sakana satisfies that wish—especially the part about intimacy, with tightly squeezed tables that make it easy (and almost inevitable) to strike up a conversation with the couple or group sitting next to you. No pretentious artifacts adorn this restaurant, but a few choice outdoor tables provide the opportunity for a relaxed Dupont Circle dining experience.

Sakana has none of those new-age trendy maki—you won't find mango, micro-cilantro, or green-apple jelly here. Instead, you'll find fresh fish (ask the sushi chefs what's freshest) atop expertly vinegared sushi rice. We've been equally impressed by the basics—yellowtail, scallop, fluke—and by the flopping-fresh prestige items like sea urchin and fatty tuna.

On the other hand, miso soup, usually a shoo-in at Japanese restaurants, is a bit disappointing at Sakana. The cubes of tofu, which should be silken and smooth, are distractingly firm. The vegetable-and-shrimp tempura appetizer, crispy and not too greasy, sports a gratifying crop of vegetables: crunchy green beans and broccoli, thin slices of Japanese eggplant, sweet tender shrimp. We've also enjoyed eel and egg over rice. Sweet, warm, creamy, and salty, it's Japanese comfort food at its best.

Most notable about Sakana, perhaps, are its cheap prices and quick (but not pushy) service. The table of Japanese businessmen sitting in a back table sipping green tea and eating vast quantities of sushi, sashimi, and hot Japanese dishes on our last visit was a sign that the place has been discovered in some circles, anyway; but, in general, we're baffled by how this place has remained mostly unknown, while neighbors like Sushi Taro (under renovation at press time) have gained such renown. Maybe Sakana just isn't good at self-promotion—which is a good thing for your wallet. –SDC

# Sala Thai

Stay away from here...even sweet tooths will be overwhelmed

| | |
|---|---|
| **3.2** Food | **6.5** Feel |

## Thai

Casual restaurant

**$25** Price

www.salathaidc.com

Mon–Thu 11:30am–3pm, 4pm–10:30pm; Fri 11:30am–3pm, 4pm–11pm; Sat noon–11pm; Sun noon–10:30pm

**Bar** Beer, wine, liquor
**Credit cards** Visa, MC, AmEx
**Reservations** Accepted
Delivery, live music, veg-friendly

**U Street**
1301 U St. NW
(202) 462-1333

**Dupont**
2016 P St. NW
(202) 872-1144

**Arlington, VA**
1100 S. Hayes St.
(703) 415-2400

**Bethesda, MD**
4828 Cordell Ave.
(301) 654-4575

It is astounding and a tad insulting that a place like Sala Thai can persist in a place like DC. Although the Thai options are far from ample in this town, there are enough good restaurants that it's hard to justify eating somewhere as bad as Sala Thai. And with five locations in the mini-chain, it's clear that the insult is not limited to a single neighborhood but that it's equal-opportunity in its reach.

Although Sala Thai's menus differ slightly across locations, most of the offerings are the same, or similar, at all five. Each begins by listing the vegetarian options—salads, appetizers, soups, main courses—and then does the same for the meat and seafood dishes. Thus, if you are undecided between a vegetable and a meat soup, be sure to consider both sections. Luckily for vegetarians, the meatless menu at Sala Thai is extensive.

Let's start, as is customary, with the appetizers. It's difficult to mess up chicken satay (which is not Thai, by the way), but the Sala manages to overcook it to such an extent that it doesn't taste like anything, not even charcoal residue. It's then coated in a sticky sauce that has no distinguishing feature beyond its sweetness, and accompanied by a peanut dipping concoction that would be too sweet for the chicken even if the chicken weren't already sweetened.

For a place that specializes in vegetarian dishes, the Sala should really manage a better tofu. The pad pik king (sautéed tofu and green beans in chili sauce) also suffers from hypersweetness, and the tofu is cut into chunks that are far too big to fry correctly. The result is a set of cubes with a watery inside and an improperly browned exterior. The rice, we suspect, is reheated: the grains are dry and stick together.

Can the restaurant at least be redeemed by that old Thai-American standby, drunken noodles? Nope. The noodles are too thick, and there are too many noodles relative to peanuts, bean sprout, and meat. And—surprise!—the dish is too sweet. We can't come up with a single sweet word—never mind five—for Sala Thai. –CK

# Sam & Harry's

A classic steakhouse that's starting to wear down

**7.5** Food    **5.8** Feel

## Steakhouse

Upmarket restaurant    **$85** Price

www.samandharrys.com

| | | |
|---|---|---|
| Mon–Fri 11:30am–2:30pm, 5:30pm–9pm | **Bar** Beer, wine, liquor | **Dupont** |
| Sat 5:30pm–9pm | **Credit cards** Visa, MC, AmEx | 1200 19th St. NW |
| | **Reservations** Accepted | (202) 296-4333 |

Sam & Harry's must have lost an extraordinary amount of business due to all the construction on 19th Street obscuring its storefront. In spite of the sign, somewhere or other, announcing the steakhouse's continued existence to the world, it has always been a bit depressing to peer inside and see the sad faces of the waiters peering out, and to see the rows of empty tables behind them.

But you can't blame Sam & Harry's empty tables on the scaffolding alone. Aside from a little boost for restaurant-week participation, there's no real reason to frequent this once-proud steakhouse anymore. Service is deferential and attentive, but you have to wonder why the décor still looks like a bland old boys' cigar club that's wearing around the edges. Even the lobbyists don't really cherish these types of environments the way they used to.

Not that there's any better reason to frequent the Palm across the street, part of the massive chain, whose steaks are slightly inferior and equally pricey. For some reason, the Palm still does a swimming business. We'd urge you to support the little guy, but it turns out that Sam & Harry's is a chain too—it's got branches in Newport Beach, CA, and Schaumburg, IL (as well as DC's Caucus Room)—and, anyway, its prices are much too high for the "little guy" designation.

That goes doubly true for the seafood starters, which include an excellent lump crab cake that you'll pay through the nose for the privilege of eating. Seared scallops are less memorable, and the "Cajun-spiced jumbo shrimp" is really nothing special—especially given the price. As for the steaks, they're wet-aged—not dry—which makes us less excited about the splurge. They're good, but not great, and certainly they don't do much to distinguish themselves from the other local players' steaks. The wine list is competent, but little more. 25% off a $12 spinach-and-crab dip or a $14 shrimp cocktail isn't exactly a happy-hour special that people are going to flock to.

We have no beef with a good steak. But this feels like a restaurant that time has simply left behind. –RG

# Seoul Soondae

If you're here for an ice-cream sundae, you're
pretty far off

**9.0** **7.0**
Food  Feel

## Korean

Casual restaurant

**$15**
Price

Sun–Thu 10:30am–10pm
Fri–Sat 10:30am–2am

**Bar** Beer, wine, liquor
**Credit cards** Visa, MC, AmEx
**Reservations** Not accepted

**Annandale, VA**
4231 Markham St.
(703) 642-2220

If you're not Korean, here's a good game to play: tell one of your Korean
friends that you love soondae. She probably won't believe you at first, but
once you convince her that you're for real, you'll probably be greeted by a
combination of incredulity, newfound respect, and the sense that you're a
slight freak—but in the best possible sense of the word "freak."

That might be what happens, too, with the staff at this simple,
pleasant, gently upmarket restaurant. They'll certainly consent to bring it
out, but they might at first do so skeptically. But once they're witness to
your obvious pleasure in devouring it—and, trust us, the pleasure will be
obvious—you'll all be one big, happy family.

Until you try to order the jok bar (steamed pig's feet), that is.

Seoul Soondae definitely has more atmosphere than much of the local
competition. There's a hilarious collection of cartoonish wall art, soju
(Korean rice-wine) specials, the Korean pop/rap medley piped through the
speakers, and the requisite huge-screen LCD flat-panel.

By this point, you must be wondering what soondae is. It's a type of
blood sausage, made from pig's intestine and congealed pig's blood,
that's actually not all that different from the British black pudding, the
French boudin noir, or the Spanish or South American morcilla. However,
it's also more exotic than those two versions, stuffed with glass noodles,
redolent of sweet spice and black pepper. It's best on its own, served in
the soondae platter (which also comes with tripe, hearts, and kidneys)
rather than in a soup, because it holds it texture better.

That's not to say that you shouldn't try the soup, too—Seoul soondae
jung shik, which integrates soondae plus the above innards—because it's
extraordinary. The steaming bowl, which contains enough for two to
three people, takes at least 15 minutes to cool to the point of edibility,
during which time you can snack on your soondae platter. Once it's cool
enough, the broth is deep and spicily delicious.

The starters are decent, three varieties of kimchi, but we've seen better.
And skip the "American style dishes," which are breaded fried meats. Big
casseroles (e.g. sausage, bacon, ham, and kimchi casserole, or spicy pork
rib and potato casserole) are good, too, and they can feed a whole party
for a few bucks a head. Jjol myun (spicy cold thick chewy noodles) is a
classic, and young yang taang (rarely seen spicy goat soup). But none of
this is the point. If you don't order the soondae, the joke's on you. –RG

# Sequoia

Location, location, location....and little else

**3.9** Food  **8.3** Feel

## New American

Upmarket restaurant

**$50** Price

www.arkrestaurants.com

Mon–Thu 11:30am–10pm
Fri–Sat 11:30am–11pm
Sun 10:30am–10pm

**Bar** Beer, wine, liquor
**Credit cards** Visa, MC, AmEx
**Reservations** Accepted
Date-friendly, kid-friendly, outdoor
dining

**Georgetown**
3000 K St. NW
(202) 944-4200

The elevated terrace at Sequoia may be one of the most pleasant pieces of real estate in the District of Columbia. On long summer days, you can watch the sun make its way over the Kennedy Center as skulls, paddleboats, and kayaks cruise by on the Potomac.

The interior, on the other hand, has all the fresh flowers, polished wood, and floor-to-ceiling glass of the nicest lido deck. It feels like money. Like starchy, soulless money. Like any minute, a tuxedoed butler is going to appear at your table and announce that the "chimmy-churry" is simply divine.

Sequoia's tome-like menu commands respect, as does its full bar and equally formidable wine list. However, for all its variety and fuss, the food is extremely disappointing. In general, dishes tend toward the bland and prosaic. Shrimp tacos are plump with corn relish and chipotle, but they have an unfortunate sandwich-shop lack of imagination or seasoning. The accompanying fries are skinny and mealy. What you would expect to be a luxuriant Maine lobster ravioli in a thick, pink tomato sauce (was there chervil? We didn't notice) is only as flavorful as its asparagus, which is to say, not very. Handfuls of teeny Gulf shrimp have a taste that's so far from their sweet potential, that it turns them into a negligible garnish rolled off of some "restaurant concept" conveyor belt and tossed with a bit of "local" this and "fresh" that.

Desserts are not much better. Cinnamon sorbet sounds exciting but tastes artificially sweet, like Red Hots. A decadent-sounding chocolate-hazelnut tart has a chalky center.

The prices aren't bad; they're just not appropriate for the execution or concept. It's clear that what you're paying for is the extraordinary location, and the right to dine among DC glitter. On a sunny day, it still might be worth it, but we prefer to head straight for the bar for oysters.
–FC

# Sesto Senso

**5.9** **7.4**
Food  Feel

It's got a great location, and superb design, but the Italo-fare falls by the wayside

## Italian

Upmarket restaurant

**$55**
Price

www.sesto.com

Mon–Thu 11:30am–3pm, 5:30pm–10:30pm; Fri 11:30am–3pm, 5:30pm–11pm; Sat 5:30pm–11pm

**Bar** Beer, wine, liquor
**Credit cards** Visa, MC, AmEx
**Reservations** Accepted

**Dupont**
1214 18th St. NW
(202) 785-9525

Given Sesto Senso's connectedness and similar aesthetic to the throbbing nightclub beneath, Andalu, it might surprise you that the restaurant's look works. It works in a way that you wouldn't expect it to. It's decked out in full-on faux-regal style. Dark reds and deep blues have the potential to sink the whole place into heavy gloom. Light fixtures that could be macabre are instead retro-hip. Blue, yellow, and beige seat cushions have vertical stripes; they're as boring as a JCPenney suit, but they blend in well. Evenly spaced mirrors help make the place feel bigger than it already is, and a loft area means that ceilings are quite high. Dark woods at the bar make you feel comfortable. It all sets the stage for the food.

Too bad the food here is only mediocre. Fried calamari, that comfort food for the ages, come with a thick but underseasoned breading; their accompanying spicy marinara could use some more kick. The squid rings, at least, aren't too chewy. Pizzas come without a properly seared crust—which pretty much ruins the party. And some combinations are mind-boggling. Take, for instance, the "Scoglio," which puts scallop, shrimp, and red onion on the same pie. Bad idea.

Pastas fare slightly better, though. Cavatelli come with sausage and a rapini pesto (a lovely combo that seems to be ubiquitous these days) and...truffle oil (something that is *unmistakably* ubiquitous these days). The oil is, luckily, used in moderation, so noodles aren't totally overwhelmed in earthiness. Lasagne is made with béchamel (yay!), but spinach gnocchi with peeled tomatoes and asparagus is another attempt at innovation gone awry.

So stick with the simple classics. They won't wow you, by any means. Perhaps the best way to do Sesto Senso is to get waylaid at the bar and take in the surroundings. It's the visual attempts at creativity that ultimately succeed. Otherwise, just look at it as pre-gaming for a long night at Andalu. –AH

# Sette Osteria

Cooking of the poor, or just poor cooking?

**6.6** *Food*  **8.3** *Feel*

## Italian, Pizza

Casual restaurant

**$40** *Price*

www.setteosteria.com

Sun–Thu 11:30am–11pm
Fri–Sat 11:30am–1am

**Bar** Beer, wine, liquor
**Credit cards** Visa, MC, AmEx
**Reservations** Accepted
Outdoor dining, veg-friendly

**Dupont**
1666 Connecticut Ave.
NW
(202) 483-3070

In the Italian tradition, the word "osteria" usually refers to a humble, tavernlike dining establishment. It implies food and wine that is simple, rustic, and honest: "cucina povera," often, or cooking of the poor. From its appearance, Sette Osteria matches that description. Warm tiles, a wood-burning brick oven, and huge crockery jars are inviting and unpretentious. Especially at the see-and-be-seen outdoor seats, a young Dupont Circle crowd looks comfortably at home here, casually dressed and casually mannered. The smallish patio is relatively unadorned, the wine list exclusively Italian, the prices all below $21. At one recent visit, the joint was teeming with Italians snacking on wood-grilled pizzas while watching soccer on the two televisions above the bar. That's always a good sign.

Beneath its appearance, however, the osteria loses its spirit with the food and the service. Courses feature basic thin-crust pizzas, soups, and pastas: the basics of slightly evolved Italian-American cooking. But here, simple and honest becomes sloppy and bland. A meal might begin with affettati tipici, a mediocre platter of "Italian specialty meats" (translation: cured meats) and grilled bread, served with a small dish of olives and preserved beans. Prosciutto di Parma comes out with a grayish tinge, instead of that happy, bright pink-red, and it's missing the intense porkiness we love; instead, it just tastes of salt. Mortadella—Italy's legit version of "baloney"—is better, with a garlicky kick, but it's nothing special. Butternut squash soup is a massive disappointment, with a gritty texture, a tepid temperature, and a soggy, underdone, roasted tomato marooned at the center of the bowl. Mealy tomatoes are the downfall of several of the salads.

Mains don't tend to fare much better. Pizzas are light enough, but they have other problems, like sometimes coming out lukewarm. A salsiccia e rapini version tastes mostly bitter from charred garlic, with greens that merely add sogginess and sausage that's shockingly absent of any flavor whatsoever; it's remarkable for a sausage-and-melted-cheese combination to actually taste *bland*. A few pasta dishes save Sette somewhat: bucatini alla amatriciana, for example, sports a straightforward, well executed sauce of pancetta slivers, onions, tomatoes, and pecorino that's thick enough to heartily coat the noodles.

Otherwise, Sette Osteria needs to go back to the basics; the outdoor tables, the lively crowd, and the crackle of wood can't rescue this recipe. "Cucina povera" it may be, but poor cooking is never okay. –FC

# 701

Passé décor and mediocre, uninspired food—some
of the 701 reasons to stay away

**4.8** Food

**5.8** Feel

## New American

Upmarket restaurant

**$70** Price

www.701restaurant.com

Mon–Thu 11:30am–3pm,
5:30pm–10:30pm; Fri
11:30am–3pm, 5:30pm–
11:30pm; Sat 5:30pm–
11:30pm; Sun 5pm–9:30pm

**Bar** Beer, wine, liquor
**Credit cards** Visa, MC, AmEx
**Reservations** Accepted
Good wines, live music, outdoor
dining

**Penn Quarter**
701 Pennsylvania Ave. NW
(202) 393-0701

Are you ever in the mood for a mediocre meal, the kind where the
ambiance makes you gag and the food is completely unremarkable? If so,
head over to 701. Here you'll find lilac walls and chairs, tired carpeting,
and retro (not in the cool way) red leather couches. You'll also find nightly
jazz piano which adds to the sort of kitschiness that you would expect in a
seedy '70s hangout. The back-corner bar and outdoor patio add a touch
of redemption to this otherwise dull space.

The food is slightly more inspired and original than the restaurant's
name, but that's not really saying much. A decent crispy ahi tempura roll
lacks the sort of innovation that we've come to yearn for when it comes
to tuna preparations. Dull sautéed shrimp scampi are boring and
effortless—they're smallish; sautéed with garlic, onions, and tomatoes;
and perched atop golden crostini.

For dessert, a warm apple napoleon (layers of puff pastry and cooked
apples) is uninteresting and often out of season. The unifying theme:
sloppiness in the composition and execution of dishes.

The best way to go, if you must, is to stick to the bar menu which
provides smaller dishes at smaller prices—sea bass tostadas or a baby
croque monsieur. At least these dishes are more casual and creative (in
the good way) than their main menu counterparts. But this centrally
located restaurant needs a lot more than that to realize its potential. For
example, the kind of facelift that would make a Beverly Hills plastic
surgeon proud. –SDC

# 1789

A stuffy, unjustly famous sinkhole for your wallet

**7.9** Food  **5.9** Feel

## New American

Upmarket restaurant

**$100** Price

www.1789restaurant.com

Mon–Thu 6pm–10pm
Fri 6pm–11pm
Sat 5:30pm–11pm
Sun 5:30pm–10pm

**Bar** Beer, wine, liquor
**Credit cards** Visa, MC, AmEx
**Reservations** Accepted
Good wines, live music

**Georgetown**
1226 36th St. NW
(202) 965-1789

One almost must resort to conspiracy theories to explain why this palace of stuffiness is thought of as one of DC's best restaurants—and, perhaps even more bizarrely, as one of DC's most romantic restaurants. These preposterous notions seem to have taken on a life of their own and spun out of control, becoming increasingly unrelated to the realities that await within this restaurant: tired pottery, pretentious service, overframed artwork, and underwhelming food.

Some rooms are more tolerable than others—it's luck of the draw—but we pity the date of any fool that's awkward and bumbling enough to think that a couple of hours stuck in one of these great-aunt's-house, you're-not-allowed-to-touch-anything drawing rooms would actually make for a romantic evening out. For that unlucky couple, we forecast a long and sexless few decades.

Your greatest amusement—unless you find pricing like $15 for a simple, decent raw yellowtail appetizer (well salted, at least, and well oiled)—might be watching the crowd around you: dads and grads at one table; at another, a solo group of teenagers, looking very uncomfortable in their jackets and ties; next to them, a would-be 50-year-old playboy, smooth gray hair and tanning-booth skin, wining and dining his slutty, prestige-impressed date.

It's not that the food is bad, exactly. It's just so much less impressive—in both conception and execution—than the whole world would have you think. Homemade pastas tend to be the highlight: nicely resilient cavatelli, for example, with duck confit, caramelized onions, cracked black pepper, and sage. It's hard to go wrong when you stuff homemade pasta with duck; this much, at least, the 1789 kitchen knows. As for a much-heralded rack of lamb for almost $40, it comes in a terribly boring preparation, a notch or two overcooked, with cannellini beans that are undercooked—as if to overcompensate with another wrong.

Much better, at our last visit, was delicately fried soft-shell crab with grilled vegetables and a vinegary Asian sauce that, happily, wasn't too sweet. But desserts often fall flat, which is especially unacceptable at such a special-occasion-geared place. The bitter truth is that our favorite part of a meal at 1789 is going downstairs to the Tombs afterwards and getting wasted with the college kids. –RG

# Shanghai Village

Good Peking duck and off-the-menu specials hide
behind a banal Chinese-American façade

| 7.4 | 7.0 |
|---|---|
| Food | Feel |

**Chinese**                          Casual restaurant   **$35**
                                                          *Price*

Sun–Thu 11:30am–10pm
Fri–Sat 11:30am–11pm

**Bar** Beer, wine, liquor
**Credit cards** Visa, MC, AmEx
**Reservations** Accepted
Kid-friendly

**Bethesda, MD**
4929 Bethesda Ave.
(301) 654-7787

The wine "list" is a choice between supermarket white and supermarket red. The first two pages of the plastic menu offer the classic umbrella-adorned cocktails: piña coladas, scorpion bowls, and something called "Navy Grog." But the chef—a genuine Shanghai native—is the real deal. White-haired and slightly stooped, he's always eager to greet his regular customers—in large part an older crowd that has followed this chef over the last 25 years, from his original restaurant in DC to the newer suburban location. The reason is plain: the Peking duck at Shanghai Village is worth the journey into deepest, darkest Bethesda.

Order a whole duck, and your dinner comes with free entertainment. The chef will bring out the prepared bird on a platter, don a pair of plastic gloves, and wield a razor-sharp Chinese cleaver with what looks like reckless speed; in fact, it's actually an incredibly skilled, practiced, and choreographed set of moves. He begins by slicing off strips of the shatteringly crisp, dark-caramel-colored skin. Using the dull edge of the cleaver, he'll scrape off the excess fat before slicing off the duck meat into tender, bite-sized pieces.

The result is one plate full of crackling skin, one plate full of sliced duck, and the drumsticks, which the chef will cut off the carcass for a lucky diner to unceremoniously gnaw to the bone. If it's your first time at Shanghai Village, the chef might even help you put together your first bite by spreading hoisin sauce on the pancake, topping it with duck and skin, adding a few shreds of scallion, and rolling it up into a perfectly-enveloped package of sweet, savory, crunchy, and juicy. Insiders will ask to take home the duck carcass from which to make soup at home (make a basic duck stock; add bean threads, Chinese cabbage, ginger and scallions to taste).

Spring rolls exhibit a similarly fine balance—in this case, between a greaseless, perfectly crisp exterior and a delicately flavored filling of shredded cabbage and pork. In fact, the chef seems to have a gift for all things fried. Salt-and-pepper shrimp come crisp and golden (not heavy or oily) on their bed of slivered jalapeños and scallions.

The Chinese-American dishes here—Orange Beef, General Tso's Chicken, and so on—aren't *worse* than they are elsewhere, but you know better than to order these flawed recipes. Instead, inspect the chalkboard specials; ask the waiters what's good; and if possible, flag down the chef to ask for his recommendations. We have enjoyed eggplant in spicy garlic sauce, as well as a traditional Shanghai-style dish of pressed-then-shredded bean curd, stir-fried with strips of pork in a slightly sweet, slightly spicy sauce. It's not on the menu, though, so ask nicely. –CD

# Shashemene

This is love that we're feeling in Little Ethiopia

**8.8** / Food

**7.0** / Feel

## Ethiopian

Casual restaurant

**$25** / Price

www.shashemenedc.com

Sun–Thu 11am–2am
Fri–Sat 11am–3am

**Bar** Beer, wine, liquor
**Credit cards** Visa, MC, AmEx
**Reservations** Accepted
Live music, veg-friendly

**Shaw**
1909 9th St. NW
(202) 328-2223

We very nearly wrote this review as lyrics to the tune of Bob Marley's "Is This Love?" but it made us sound really, really lame. Instead, we'll just listen to *Legend* as we tell you about Shashemene. It's a relative newcomer to 9th Street's burgeoning Little Ethiopia, whose identical 19th-century row houses—many of them bearing Ethiopian restaurants—can at first seem difficult to distinguish from each other. The joke in Manhattan's (vaguely analogous) Indian Row is that all the restaurants tunnel into the same kitchen and vary only by their degrees of garish tinsel and Christmas lighting in the dining rooms. There's no danger of that at Shashemene; there's a lot of great Ethiopian food on this block, but some of the achievements in this kitchen aren't matched nearby.

The interior is dominated by a large Bob Marley tapestry, in which he smiles over diners like their patron saint (Shashemene is the name of an Ethiopian town given as a gift to Rastafarian Jamaicans in the '60s). Otherwise, it's just white walls and simple, new wood furnishings.

When it comes to the food, though, well...this is love. There's a sensational luxuriance to the kitfo, the Ethiopian version of steak tartare. Ask for it raw and you'll get a grin; more importantly, it will come at a proper room temperature—not too cold, as is often the problem with minced raw beef—with treble notes of butter and lemon that are subtle but bright. We also love Shashemene's treatments of the classic vegetable dishes, among which a buttery-beyond-belief stew of brown lentils stands out; it's one of the best Ethiopian veggie dishes we've ever had.

Alicha, a cooked beef stew, was the central weakness of our last Shashemene meal. Its cubes were neither gently simmered nor carefully seared—just roughly overcooked, ruining an otherwise pleasant, spicy onion stew. Doro wat sees much more tenderness in its chicken, though, whose meat seems gently placed on—rather than attached to—the bone.

You owe it to yourself to explore 9th Street's entire range of options, but Shashemene is a good place to start, with its great food, irie friendliness, and live music Thursday through Saturday nights. It's jammin'. (Okay, seriously, knock it off). –FC

# Singapore Bistro

A pretty place, but the attempt to do everything
Asian overstretches the kitchen

**5.1** Food **7.5** Feel

**Pan-Asian**                    Casual restaurant    **$25** Price

Mon–Thu 11:30am–10:30pm
Fri–Sat 11:30am–midnight
Sun 4pm–10pm

**Bar** Beer, wine, liquor
**Credit cards** Visa, MC, AmEx
**Reservations** Accepted
Delivery, live music, Wi-Fi

**Farragut**
1134 19th St. NW
(202) 659-2660

Like its namesake country, the Singapore Bistro is small, tidy, and a place that—in culinary terms—offers a taste of everything. There is one major difference, however: at a Singapore hawker center, the chance to experience the country's culinary diversity—Malaysian, Indonesian, Chinese, and more—is a special treat, in part because each food stall generally just covers one specific category, and does it well. At Singapore Bistro, instead, one kitchen jumps between Americanized versions of some of these cuisines, plus many more—Thai and Japanese, to name two—without the culinary skills or kitchen resources to do any of it, never mind all of it, well.

This menu hops from Malyasian Gado Gado to General Tso's Chicken, from a Tsunami roll to Thai green curry to Vietnamese lemongrass beef to a cross-cultural fried banana dessert. You can have your fried rice in the supposed style of any of five different countries. The best things in a weak field are Indonesian-style noodles and nasi campur, which includes tender satay chicken, crispy anchovies and rich coconut rice. Less exciting is the Malaysian wonton soup, which consists of a lot of fried dough floating in a lukewarm broth. Other appetizers, such as the edamame and shrimp or vegetable gyoza, are standard-issue, and sushi is extremely dubious.

The rather subterranean-feeling digs are modern and a little sexy, with what looks like giant Tibetan prayer flags swaddling the ceiling. Diners have their choice of padded booths, tables or the sushi bar. Happy hour runs unusually long (from 4pm to 7:30pm daily) and features discounts on beer, an acetone-like hot sake, syrupy martinis, and nigiri sushi, which goes as low as 99 cents. We'd warn you against the latter. Does close-out sushi sound like a good idea to anyone?

The conclusion is clear: the Singaporean theme is a clever disguise for pan-Asian. Yet it's not even true to that concept: you can finish your meal with carrot cake. Or better yet, don't start a meal at all. –FC

# Skewers

At this late hour, we'll take it, and like it

| 4.3 | 7.0 |
|-----|-----|
| Food | Feel |

## Middle Eastern

Casual restaurant

**$30**
Price

www.skewers-cafeluna.com

Mon–Wed 11:30am–10pm
Thu–Sat 11:30am–midnight
Sun noon–10pm

**Bar** Beer, wine, liquor
**Credit cards** Visa, MC, AmEx
**Reservations** Accepted
Live music, outdoor dining, Wi-Fi

**Dupont**
1633 P St. NW
(202) 387-7400

Nestled in an old DC townhouse above the equally mediocre Café Luna, Skewers offers mediocre Mediterranean food with two distinct advantages: late hours and cheap prices. As one of the few places in town where you can continue to get food (and drinks) when most restaurants kitchens are long closed, and even the pubs are scraping the last remnants of french fry from the bottom of the fryer, Skewers fits a particular niche in DC and fills a particular hole in our collective belly.

The appetizers are the restaurant's raison d'être, it seems, an appropriate move for a Mediterranean place. Foole, or bean salad, is deliciously enhanced by lemon and salt, and the baba gannoush is smoky and good. Skewers' hummus, unfortunately, is overly creamy and bland, and the addition of poorly seasoned lamb and pine nuts doesn't aid the affair.

Steer clear of Skewers' salads: these vast fields of lettuce might surprise you with peperoncini or cherry tomato, but they are hardly thrilling. Steer clear, too, of the Caesar Salad (really, what business does a Caesar with blackened salmon have here?), and the equally-out-of-place Filet Mignon Kabob.

For a restaurant that purports to specialize in kabob, the skewered dishes are not terribly impressive. The shawarma and chicken are dry, which sort of misses the whole marinated wonder of the Kebab concept.

If you can forgive all of this, as well as the weird beaded curtains and low-slung seating, Skewers may be the place for you. If you can't, and it's late, and you're hungry: well, then you're, um, let's say...stuck. Maybe you'll have to make Skewers the place for you. The wee hours have a way of making even the sharpest foodie mellow out. –CK

# Skye Lounge

Have karmic mishaps led to what this place is today?

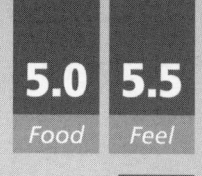

**5.0** Food | **5.5** Feel

## Middle Eastern, American

Casual restaurant

**$40** Price

www.skyedc.com

Mon–Thu 11am–midnight
Fri 11am–3am
Sat 7pm–3am

**Bar** Beer, wine, liquor
**Credit cards** Visa, MC, AmEx
**Reservations** Accepted
Live music, outdoor dining

**Farragut**
1919 Pennsylvania Ave. NW
(202) 331-5800

If there is divine retribution, then the bar Karma did not lead a virtuous life. Despite a decent following in the downtown business district, it has been reincarnated into a lesser being. The loftily named Skye Lounge held on to many characteristics of its predecessor: an outdoor deck still seats throngs of happy hour revelers, drinks persist in being small and expensive, and food retains a somewhat Middle Eastern vibe, although dishes have been renamed with new-age abandon.

Unfortunately these dishes seem to function more as an accompaniment to alcohol than as a pleasure unto themselves. This is disappointing, because the drinks, for starters, are far from exceptional. Skye has no beers on tap, so the focus is clearly on the bar's menagerie of cocktails (steeply priced even during happy hour). Drinks look and taste like sorority-house concoctions during a Sex and the City marathon: syrupy, colorful, and girlishly named. While mojitos are well balanced, there is so much leaf in the glass it feels like you're poking into a mulch pile. Some drinks are horrors of adolescent mixology: the cream and Baileys in the "Milky Way" actually separate and form distinct curds when they mingle with acidic, low-grade vodka. It begs the question if anything in a martini glass is ever meant to be chugged.

Luckily, the food menu avoids any serious mishaps. A mezze platter includes a well-seasoned chickpea salad that is playfully crunchy, and a peppery, unexpectedly complex baba ghanoush. The rice in the dolmade can be overcooked, but not egregiously so. The "Neptune" main of mixed skewers is barely related to the sea, but the meat is well-charred and decently seasoned. Chicken is gingery and moist, if unexciting, and the beef tangy, sweet, and lean. Shrimp are milder than their trident-wielding maker, but they're generally plump and juicy.

Dessert is even more of an afterthought than the rest of the food; the selection is small and featureless. With its expansive deck and nice nibbles, Skye Lounge isn't the worst place to pass an evening. But, karma or not, it's hardly heavenly. –JC

# Smith & Wollensky

Stick with the steaks, and relish the good life and the good ole times

**8.3** Food
**7.0** Feel

## Steakhouse

Upmarket restaurant

**$85** Price

www.smithandwollensky.com

Mon–Thu 11:30am–11pm
Fri 11:30am–midnight
Sat 1pm–midnight
Sun 5pm–10pm

**Bar** Beer, wine, liquor
**Credit cards** Visa, MC, AmEx
**Reservations** Accepted
Live music, outdoor dining

**Farragut**
1112 19th St. NW
(202) 466-1100

As of 2009, this New York-based steakhouse chain had nine US branches, though none of the latest eight boast the nostalgic patina of the Midtown Manhattan branch, which dates to 1977. That one alone has the distinct air of an old, top-end steakhouse, but the entire chain generally delivers a decent to good dry-aged Prime steak at high cost and circumstance. The environment exudes that contrived brand of refinement, more Disneyish than exclusive, with a lot of touches that evoke the American Adventure pavilion at Epcot Center: vintage clocks, copper-shaded lamps, latticework, marble, and lots of brass. Even in tough economic times, the chain still seems to manage a decent fat-cat draw, especially at the bar area.

Even if the out-of-the-oven pan of bread that comes out in advance of your meal is a cheap trick, it's a good cheap trick. It's cooked in a bath of butter, rendering it more tart than bread, and it's intentionally slightly undercooked and doughy—a good call. Add in the delightfully soft tub of butter and dare to see how much fat you can possibly ingest in one bite of bread. The "Wollensky Salad" is less impressive, done with boring Romaine, aggressive slab bacon, mushrooms, and out-of-place potato cubes that get cold and gross in about four seconds. A nicely balanced Dijon vinaigrette lacks the acidic bite of a French vinaigrette, but, refreshingly, doesn't overemphasize the mustard.

Smith & Wollensky's dry-aged Prime steaks are hard to argue with. These are well-marbled, well-prepared pieces of meat—even the filet mignon (which can so often be a disaster). On the plate, they're absolutely drowned in butter—another good cheap trick—and can (should, actually) be accompanied by a dreamily textured creamed spinach. The pricey wine list is strong in California cabs, and glasses often come from bottles that have been open too long—there's no excuse for this at a top steakhouse.

Desserts are marginally acceptable. Cheesecake is competent, though with a lower graham-cracker-crust-to-cream-cheese ratio than we favor. Whipped cream is a granular farce, and strawberries and blackberries are underripe and no fun. Come for the steak, though, and it's hard to go too far wrong. –RG

# Sonoma

A wine bar and restaurant that celebrates
California more in concept than in approach

**5.7** Food  **7.6** Feel

## New American

Wine bar  **$65** Price

www.sonomadc.com

Mon–Thu 11:30am–2:30pm,
5:30pm–10pm; Fri 11:30am–
2:30pm, 5:30pm–11pm; Sat
5:30pm–11pm; Sun 5:30pm–
9pm

**Bar** Beer, wine, liquor
**Credit cards** Visa, MC, AmEx
**Reservations** Accepted
Good wines, outdoor dining

**Capitol Hill**
223 Pennsylvania Ave. SE
(202) 544-8088

More well-heeled Napa than understated Sonoma, this Pennsylvania
Avenue hotspot caters to an increasingly trendy clientele. As soft techno
music plays in the background and hip white benches adjoin group tables,
it becomes difficult to believe that wine is the focus here. In fact, your
server will likely accept your first request without considering your meal or
suggesting a better pairing. At times like these, we almost miss the old
"selling you up" wine list game: if we wanted our wine without an
opinion, we'd buy it from, gee, just about any other restaurant.

Among the most popular items on the menu are Sonoma's cheese
plates, which offer a mix of two, three, six, or twelve cheeses. The
selection is well-chosen, regional and artisanal. There are also some
excellent charcuterie options; try the sleek bresaola or woody duck salami.

Beyond this, things begin to turn south. Strangely, there's very little
"California" in the cuisine at Sonoma. It's difficult to fault the restaurant
for extending the bounds of "local" up and down the East Coast; after
all, we don't have California's Central Valley at our doorstep. Sonoma
makes a good effort to source ingredients on its menu, but the real
divergence from what we've come to know as California cuisine is in the
execution of the dishes, which at Sonoma is rather heavy-handed.

The pizza crust is thick and dry, and the red sauce completely devoid of
personality or natural tomato flavor. There's no attempt to pair
ingredients creatively, or even to pick seasonal toppings. Alice Waters this
is not.

Much better is the delightfully smoked Carolina trout, which is served
with an eclectic mix of chive cream, egg, grapefruit, microgreens, cheese,
and pumpernickel croutons. But most of this menu really eludes us. Penne
with "pulled Amish chicken" is presented as a bowl of naked noodles
(perhaps this is what they meant by "Amish") with a few slithering pieces
of meat below. The promised tomatoes are few, and there is no sauce of
which to speak.

The wine list is bountiful, not epic; it's fitting and well-chosen (which is
a good thing given the lack of advice). The wines are mostly domestic
(there's also a bit of an Italian fetish); these are some respectable names,
not flashier ones. Sonoma would have some potential if it toned down
the self-conscious hipness factor and turned up the taste. Until then, we'll
be in the bar. –CK

# Sorriso

Pizzas that will put a smile on your face—especially if you're on the red line

**7.4** Food  **7.5** Feel

## Italian, Pizza

Casual restaurant  **$40** Price

www.sorrisoristorante.net

Mon–Thu 5:30pm–9:30pm
Fri 5:30pm–10:30pm
Sat noon–10:30pm
Sun 5pm–9:30pm

**Bar** Beer, wine, liquor
**Credit cards** Visa, MC, AmEx
**Reservations** Accepted
Outdoor dining, veg-friendly

**Cleveland Park**
3518 Connecticut Ave. NW
(202) 537-4800

We're not sure if Sorriso's location is its virtue or simply its burden to bear. The restaurant sits literally at mouth of the Cleveland Park metro station. The escalator steadily spits out riders a few feet from a smattering of outdoor tables. We suppose the seeming urbanity of it could be a bit fun—if terribly distracting. On the other hand, it's got to drum up some business; consider the unsuspecting and famished WMATA patron, happy to eat the first thing in sight.

Not that said red-line rider needs to be suspicious of Sorriso. We've had some solid pizzas here. A classically simple margherita hits all the right pleasure points. Its cheese is evenly spread (not too thick, not too thin), not dispersed in a few gob-like mounds, as you often see. (It's not that one method is necessarily preferable to the other—we just find that the former creates a more consistent flavor profile.) Tomato sauce, the crucial ingredient that has the power to make or break the pie, plays sweetness off acidity, and the result is flavorful and balanced. Aah. (Thank God there were no raw tomatoes on this margherita—the hallmark of inauthenticity.) Other permutations are more or less equally successful.

But do keep in mind that it's the pizzas that are the focus here. Execution on pastas, while not bad, is not on the same level as that of the pizzas. And other Italian-American mains (think veal saltimbocca) aren't too exciting either. But, for better or for worse, you won't find anything that's overstretching on the menu. Preparations are kept largely simple. (For more fancy-schmancy, ambitious, or delicate fare head elsewhere in town—Palena, perhaps?)

Those outdoor tables are nice if you can get past the fact that the metro is *right there*. But indoors is even cozier, more like the living room and kitchen of a home in rural Italy (all right, maybe there's *some* Disneyification going on...). Service, however, can be a bit rushed and distracted, but these guys' hearts are in the right place.

And that just about sums it up here. It's not the best, but hey, the price is right. And is it ever convenient... –AH

# The Source

CEOs chillin' California-style at this high-end eatery

**8.8** Food  **8.4** Feel

## New American

Upmarket restaurant **$120** Price

www.wolfgangpuck.com

Mon–Thu 11:30am–2pm, 5:30pm–10pm; Fri 11:30am–2pm, 5:30pm–11pm; Sat 5:30pm–11pm

**Bar** Beer, wine, liquor
**Credit cards** Visa, MC, AmEx
**Reservations** Accepted
Date-friendly, good wines, outdoor dining

**Penn Quarter**
575 Pennsylvania Ave. NW
(202) 637-6100

Wolfgang Puck's first foray into DC is a far cry from the chain nouvelle-pizza places and airport food-court stalls that have, with some exceptions, defined the last phase of his career. This is the good old ambitious side of the first true celebrity chef (in the Hollywood sense of celebrity), and the ingredients and meticulous techniques showcased here are nothing if not ambitious. It is pricier than you would expect, with ambitious ingredients meticulously presented. It's inside the gleaming modern Newseum—the museum devoted to the history of the (transitional) news industry—and as such, it's bigger and cleaner in its sleek design than the usual club-chair DC fine dining. From the glass paneled stairway and dining areas to the stainless-steel accents, it feels almost too chic and glossy to be DC. The clientele is heavy on the corporate-expense type, all nice suits and loud voices preening and basking amongst their flocks.

Waiters at The Source are as competent and self-assured as the clientele. They are the sort who recommend the best temperature for meat and fold your napkin when you leave the table. The timing of service is impeccable. Food arrives at the table at precisely the right temperature.

Dishes bounce around the globe, but they all seem to have entered the country through Southern California. Pizza (still a Puck signature) and hummus live easily next to dumplings and roast duck. Small bites at the bar are thoughtfully executed, and offer a better value than their larger counterparts. Tiny crab cakes are a dainty mouthful, as if designed for the company cocktail party. They're rich with thick strips of loosely packed crabmeat bound together magically by air. A tiny dab of tangy mayo is a finely balanced counterpoint to the meat. Pork-belly soup dumplings are liquid and oozy, gushing hot liquid and paired with a surprisingly authentic, pungent, and vinegary dipping sauce.

Some dishes seem like they contain too many elements. Kobe beef short ribs seem to have gotten rather ropy after their long bath, and their beef flavor is obscured with a thick, overly tangy sauce. A 15-layer mocha cake has the soft density of the spongy rolls at Asian bakeries. And though it does have all 15 layers (count 'em), the fancy sauces that accompany it are artful smudges that are too meager to lift off the plate.

If your wallet is similarly meagerly supplied, you may find that the Source is above your pay grade. If you can swing it, it's definitely worth trying once. Otherwise, you can always try Puck at the airport, we suppose. –JC

# Spezie

Modern Italian that has reinvented itself—but not quite enough to justify these prices

**7.3** Food  **7.5** Feel

## Italian

Upmarket restaurant  **$80** Price

www.spezie.com

Mon–Fri 11:30am–2:30pm,
5:30pm–10pm
Sat 5:30pm–10pm

**Bar** Beer, wine, liquor
**Credit cards** Visa, MC, AmEx
**Reservations** Accepted

**Farragut**
1736 L St. NW
(202) 467-0777

This expense-account Italian restaurant was fading, fading, fading, and seemed about to disappear…

…And then it was rescued—for the time being, anyway—by an ex-Tosca chef who came in and re-energized the menu, and by a simultaneous redesign of the restaurant's interior. This included the setup of a more casual wine-bar area up front, which, so far, doesn't seem to be attracting many patrons. Still, we like the new look, and not just because the walls are now a brilliant shade of Fearless Critic orange, warming up the atmosphere.

Prices are, to put it mildly, high; at press time, appetizers ran $15-18. A trio di crudo di pesce, a plate of three raw fishes, when available, is perfectly fresh, even if nothing really sings. Ricotta gnocchi with tomato is a simple dish that requires a silky texture from the dumplings to succeed, but Spezie's version doesn't pull that off; they just feel like ricotta balls in a chunky, underreduced red sauce.

But the homemade stuffed egg pastas can be glorious. Agnolotti stuffed with roast veal, spinach, and prosciutto (all puréed together) and smothered with a buttery red wine sauce isn't subtle, but it's a beefy blockbuster, one of the best pasta dishes we've tasted all year. Spezie has also done a version of this dish with ravioli, and it's just as good.

Whole grilled branzino—prepared simply, with olive oil, lemon, and herbs—is all the rage in 2009-2010 DC, but Spezie adds a haute touch by sending your waiter out to fillet the fish at the table—doing your dirty work—while you drool. It's a fresh, competent version, if not particularly notable, and it's served with a "seasonal vegetable" side dish that, at our last visit, was terrible cauliflower, underseasoned, rubbery, and generally inedible. Fairly incompetent, too, are some of the other protein mains, which just come off like bumbling old Italian-American banalities. Seared salmon filet with porcini mushrooms? Fillet of beef with gorgonzola sauce?

Sadly, the menu doesn't change often enough, either. The wine list is as overpriced as the food, but otherwise, it's really quite serious, with thick coverage of northern Italian reds (Barbera, Dolcetto, Nebbiolo, and so on) and wines from lesser-known Italian regions. There are some good finds from Emilia-Romagna, Friuli, Umbria, Molise, and Sicily. But it's not quite enough to justify an evening here, given the prices. Neither are the agnolotti, good though they may be. –RG

# Spices

Middle-of-road pan-Asian that happens not to be better than middling

| 5.2 | 6.8 |
|-----|-----|
| Food | Feel |

## Pan-Asian

Casual restaurant

| $35 |
|-----|
| Price |

www.spicesdc.com

Mon–Fri 11:30am–3pm, 5pm–11pm
Sat noon–11pm
Sun 5pm–10:30pm

**Bar** Beer, wine, liquor
**Credit cards** Visa, MC, AmEx
**Reservations** Accepted
Delivery, kid-friendly, veg-friendly

**Cleveland Park**
3333 Connecticut Ave. NW
(202) 686-3833

Spices is just another pan-Asian joint. If this one succeeds slightly more than some, it's because the setting is a little more elegant and the service a little more cheerful. The lighting is bright but not harsh, and the space is subdivided into manageable alcoves that make the restaurant feel less vast. The sushi bar runs the length of the restaurant, with a regiment of tall stools; blond wood furnishings accented with black lacquer pieces give the place a modern feel that, thankfully, doesn't try too hard to costume itself as Asian.

The kitchen's dishes are familiar ones, although there are a few items beyond the normal self-conscious recitation of American-Asian favorites. The sticky-sweet General Tao chicken and caramelized shrimp are available for those suckers who crave it, but there is also a better-than-average green curry, which is served in a stylish brass wok, rich with coconut and studded with creamy eggplant pieces. The sushi won't win any accolades for innovation, but it's fresh enough—and the chef's special rolls feature enough spicy sauces and crunchy tempura bits to distract you from the unremarkable fish. It's that kind of sushi place. The restaurant even seems to acknowledge its own gimmicks with a wink, serving its gigantic sushi combination platter on the decks of a lacquered platter shaped like a Chinese junk. (We prefer to give them the benefit of the doubt on the wink part.) There's a wine list that's so average it's hardly worth mentioning.

Granted, the point of a pan-Asian restaurant like this isn't to be particularly authentic or ground-breaking. You walk into Spices knowing that you're going to get the familiar Americanized versions of pad Thai, mee goreng, and fried rice. Sometimes, that's what people crave—a dish that's rich in umami (or at least MSG), salty, spicy, sweet, and tangy all at once. But we're food critics, and to us, this menu is profanity. –CD

# Starfish Café

Casual Caribbean cuisine in cute quarters

| 6.8 | 7.3 |
|------|------|
| Food | Feel |

## Seafood

Casual restaurant

**$55**
Price

www.starfishcafedc.com

Sun–Thu 11am–10pm
Fri–Sat 11am–11pm

**Bar** Beer, wine, liquor
**Credit cards** Visa, MC, AmEx
**Reservations** Accepted
Live music, outdoor dining

**Capitol Hill**
539 8th St SE
(202) 546-5006

Imagine a Caribbean island within the confines of a historic, shotgun-style DC building, and we'd venture that it will look a lot like Starfish Café. The first-floor dining room features a bar of ocean-blue tiles, exposed brick walls hosting oversized colorful paintings of fish, and white-linen-topped cherry wood tables. An identically aquatic scene is just a steep climb upstairs. It hits that elusive note between sleek metropolitan bistro and laid-back tropical bar, without being too kitschy.

Things get much sillier at the bar, where classic mojitos lead a pack of other rum- and vodka-based drinks with names like "Kiss My Bass" and "Groping Grouper."

Yowzers. Mojitos do enjoy a refreshing restraint in the sweet-and-sour department, with a balanced snap of fresh, muddled mint. During happy hour, these (and caipirinhas, too) are a steal at under $5, and half-price oysters with flavorful corn poppers sweeten the deal.

The focus, naturally, is on seafood, though it's not limited to Caribbean-influenced seafood (nor Cajun, nor Creole). While the crab cakes ("best in town"—at least according to Starfish Café) are packed loosely and without much spice, the fresh crab flavor comes through. San-Francisco-style cioppino offers fresh scallops, mussels, and giant shrimp in a rather ordinary spicy tomato base, with crispy garlic bread. It's a dish to be avoided. In general, the food here is hit or miss. Be forewarned that fried food is seriously fried; none of this is gentle touch stuff. The oyster bar won't disappoint, but we can't understand why on earth anyone would pay almost $5 for a Blue Point oyster as a shooter drowned in cocktail sauce and vodka; you don't taste the pricey, reputable oyster, and there's not enough vodka to get you buzzed. In the end, Starfish's goals seem relatively modest: the place just wants to feed its neighborhood some fish, and for that, it's fine. –FC

# Station 9

Highs and lows that really need to even out on the high side

| 6.3 | 7.0 |
|------|------|
| Food | Feel |

## New American

Upmarket restaurant

**$45**
Price

www.station9dc.com

Wed–Sat 5pm–10:30pm
Sun 11am–3pm

**Bar** Beer, wine, liquor
**Credit cards** Visa, MC, AmEx
**Reservations** Accepted
Date-friendly, kid-friendly, live
music

**U Street**
1438 U St. NW
(202) 667-1661

Behind grand columns, in what at the turn of the last century was a post office, lies a red-hot restaurant and even hotter nightspot. The interior of Station 9 is gorgeous. Cavernous ceilings are accentuated by floor-to-ceiling drapes and dim lighting—it's nice to be in a restaurant that gives the energetic eater plenty of elbow room. Long joined tables make it the ideal place for a large party or banquet; raised seating along either side gives those areas the voyeuristic feel of nightclub balconies. Beige booths, sleek leather pod chairs, and somber tones of magenta and teal are stylish but still austere. Spherical chandeliers made out of plastic cups add a touch of the avant garde to the restaurant's mood.

But Station 9 needs to get its kitchen under control. The menu—let's generously call it "eclectic"—is supposed to be an homage to the ragbag of cultures on U Street, but the restaurant seems to muddle it as much as mix it up. On one visit, a reception upstairs slowed the kitchen down so much that by 6:30pm, servers were hopelessly delayed. The same trend continued late into the evening—even plating a brownie sundae took more than 45 minutes. In what universe does it take that long to scoop ice cream on a brownie and drizzle it with chocolate and chopped nuts?

Many dishes have displayed some basic technical errors. Oodles of noodles come in richly spiced broth, heavy and deep with acid. The soup is tasty, but the vegetables have been sandy. The sauce on peanut chicken is a pretty poor rendition of Asian—salty and gritty instead of sweet and spicy. Jasmine rice is a further mockery. You probably would do well not to order Asian here.

Yet when the kitchen delivers, it really delivers. We especially recommend the southern American dishes. "Big Bob's Bass" exemplifies this strength. It's a whole fried fish that graces the plate like a crown, circling a jewel-toned bed of greens. The meaty flesh, deeply scored, juts out like segments from a macabre, rusted sunken treasure. It is rich and gloriously fishy, and it will make you want to pull off pieces of crispy, breaded skin and nibble on fins and tails.

It is that kind of populist grandeur for which the soaring spaces of Station 9 seem to cry out. Too bad the cries are so often left to echo through the void. –JC

# Sticky Fingers Bakery

**5.8** Food   **6.0** Feel

Vegan pastries that earn our respect, and savories
that don't feel like punishment

## Baked goods, Sandwiches

Counter service   **$10** Price

www.stickyfingersbakery.com

Mon–Thu 7am–7pm
Fri 7am–9pm
Sat 8am–9pm
Sun 9am–6pm

**Bar** None
**Credit cards** Visa, MC
Delivery, kid-friendly, outdoor
dining, veg-friendly, Wi-Fi

**Columbia Heights**
1370 Park Rd. NW
(202) 299-9700

Good. Vegan. Bakery. Three words we may never put together. The best
you'll get from us is "decent," said with a lilting tone of respect. Sticky
Fingers Bakery, located in the up-and-coming Columbia Heights area,
attracts vegans and non-vegans alike. The dessert case holds beautifully
frosted cupcakes, layer cakes, sticky buns, little devils and on and on. And
the savory case holds pre-made vegan delights, like barbecue seitan,
peanut noodles, sandwiches, hot wings with blue cheese dressing, and
chili. All vegan, all the time.

Sticky Fingers does manage to avoid the cardboard texture rampant in
vegan desserts. Cowvin cookies, vanilla frosting sandwiched between two
buttery oatmeal bar cookies, have a hint of salt and plenty of oats.
Chocolate-frosted chocolate cupcakes are decadent: the frosting is deep
and chocolaty and smooth. The chocolate cake, which features more
prominently in the little devils, is moist but...there it is...that slightly off
taste. It's not bad (especially when it's slathered in frosting), but it lacks
the chocolaty depth that would make it stellar. Chocolate chip cookies—
of the large and flat variety—somehow taste buttery, and are studded
with small chocolate chips. Other baked goods include rocky-road
cupcakes, peanut butter fudge cake, and brownies.

The savory stuff is self-serve (there's a microwave in the condiment
section should you choose to heat anything up). These items tend toward
that destitute taste we've come to expect from vegan fare that uses meat
substitutes, even though they're spiced boldly and carefully. The sesame
peanut noodles offer a hot kick that is balanced by sweet peanut butter
and tender tofu. Although dressed well, some of the faux-meats are just
undeniably depressing. It's like being promised Black Sabbath and getting
Yanni. We don't know if there's any way around that missing-meat
conundrum, but this comes from a group of people who are trying to see
if we can legally marry bacon.

Sticky Fingers does nearly take the scary out of vegan. It's replete with
Wi-Fi and good coffee and espresso (soy milk only), and the pastries here
are almost good enough to make us drop the snarky quotation marks we
usually resort to when describing dairy-free "chocolate," "blue cheese"
dressing, "buttery" cookies, and "food". Almost. –SDC

# Stoney's Bar & Grill

It no longer dives, but this sports bar sure gives us that sinking feeling

**6.2** Food  **7.3** Feel

**American**  Casual restaurant  **$40** Price

Mon–Thu 11am–12:45am; Fri 11am–1:45am; Sat 11am–1:45am; Sun 11am–12:45am

**Bar** Beer, wine, liquor
**Credit cards** Visa, MC, AmEx
**Reservations** Not accepted
Outdoor dining, Wi-Fi

**Logan Circle**
1433 P St. NW
(202) 234-1818

Stoney's isn't the kind of place that spells "Grill" with a silent "e" at the end. Nor is it the kind of place that harbors any qualms about installing multiple television screens to blast the same sports channel from six different angles. Nor does the staff at Stoney's really seem to care what its customers think.

Which probably helps to explain why you'll be left to stand in the cold in mid-January, while a shrugging bouncer tells you he has no idea when your table will be ready. You're free to hover at the back of a three-man-thick bar crowd, he might add, and try to get the attention of the equally surly bartender.

There's something to be said for the atmosphere of a dive bar, and Stoney's, in the old days at a different location, was once a legitimate dive. But with its move to new digs on P Street across from Whole Foods, Stoney's has taken the "dive" concept corporate. With its former life a mere memory, Stoney's today is little more than a slick sports bar with overly polished dark wood and an outsized attitude.

The food, too, has been cleaned up, and it doesn't clean up well. Moreover, where the menu has tried to retain the dive frame of mind, it's failed completely. The too-thick fries, for example, are not crisp enough, and the skins are quickly overtaken by condensation. A turkey club claims to be served on Texas toast defeats its thin, unbuttered bread.

The best thing to have here is the burger; it's correctly prepared and, in general, not overcooked. Some other sandwiches, especially after a few beers, are palatable, and while the "Pastrami Delight" falls somewhat short of delightful, the combination of good meat, properly melted Swiss, and nutty toasted rye is satisfying. Steer clear of the chili, on the other hand, which is watery and under-spiced.

It is miraculous that Stoney's continues to enjoy such popularity when it's neither a place to eat well, nor, comfortably, to eat. Granted, a fine set of brews on tap helps redeem the spot, but with this slick attitude and bad food, full redemption remains a distant dream. Now this former dive's just taking a dive. –CK

# Stoupsy's

Food court-Greek prepared and served by a loveable one

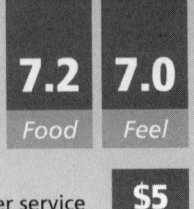

**7.2** Food
**7.0** Feel

**Greek**

Counter service

**$5** Price

Mon–Fri 7am–4pm

**Bar** None
**Credit cards** Visa, MC, AmEx
**Reservations** Not accepted

**Farragut**
1825 Eye St. NW
(202) 223-1169

The exaggeration of cultural stereotypes is considered integral to the success of some ethnic cuisines in America. (How else can we account for the success of mediocre behemoth Benihana?) The centuries-old notion of the boisterous, mercantile Greeks as middlemen of the Mediterranean (an area well stocked with other merchant cultures as well—the Venetians and Turks, to name two) is embodied in the larger-than-life owner of Stoupsy's.

"I'm George the Greek," he might announce as you approach his counter at the International Food Court on K Street. "I make the best Greek food in Washington." A bold claim, unless you give him the benefit of the doubt: recall that it's George's job to cook up hyperbole alongside his gyros. Both are done well.

Down a set of skinny escalators just off of Farragut Square, International Food Court shares in common with its namesake in the Hague the capacity to inspire remorse (at the IFC, however, you're only punished for the sin of gluttony). The Food Court is an inspiring reconsideration of the depressing fast food-filled courts of shopping malls, featuring a number of pretty solid international food stands (and a Five Guys shop serves to remind patrons that America still boasts a national foodstuff, thankyouverymuch). Stoupsy's is surely the highlight of these.

Put another way, Stoupsy's, at the ripe old age of 22, is the "anchor of the food court" (or as George pronounces it, its "uncle"). Eating here certainly feels like being fed by a member of the family, if an overbearing one. The portions are enormous, and the meats are terrific: large chunks of chicken souvlaki, well-browned and tender, are soaked in an aromatic lemon marinade; the meat is nicely salted. And here is a place that does eggplant right: the vegetable is smoky and full, with just enough oil, pepper, and tomato to add character.

Fear not, for the tired homages to Greek-American cookery remain at Stoupsy's: that clichéd Greek salad, for instance, and (an admittedly terrible version of) baklava, in which the walnut pieces are large, the pastry is dry, and the scant sauce doesn't pack much flavor.

But for its few errors, and especially for an unassuming food-court stop, Stoupsy's sells itself. As backup, George sells it pretty well, too. –CK

# Straits of Malaya

Head straight here—not across the street...

6.9 7.6
Food Feel

## Malaysian

Casual restaurant **$35**
Price

www.straitsofmalaya.com

Sun–Thu 5:30pm–10:30pm
Fri–Sat 5:30pm–11pm

**Bar** Beer, wine, liquor
**Credit cards** Visa, MC, AmEx
**Reservations** Accepted
Date-friendly, delivery, kid-friendly,
outdoor dining, veg-friendly

**Dupont**
1836 18th St. NW
(202) 483-1483

On a warm summer night, the rooftop patio at Straits of Malaya is more appealing than its Mexican competitor across the street (we won't name names). The food here is authentic and unpretentious, the drinks are strong, and the service is friendly. The space isn't elegant—the table-tops are vaguely grimy, the narrow staircase to the roof is precarious—but it's welcoming in its own way. Start with a mai tai or Singapore sling, the house specialty cocktails made with tropical fruit juices and rum or gin. We must admit to having a certain fondness for these two drinks.

We can't even begin to identify all the spices in the tasty laksa, but we've licked the bowl clean of the rich, savory coconut and curry broth. Also unfamiliar but surprisingly delicious is the combination of hot and sweet spices in the cinnamon-and-nutmeg-scented five-spice rolls of ground meat wrapped in a thin sheet of crispy tofu. You'll realize quickly, and just as quickly come to enjoy, that Malaysian cuisine is heavily influenced by both its Chinese and Indian neighbors.

Main courses are served family style, and a wide variety of curries and noodle dishes is available. The "chef's favorite," cha kway teow, comes off like your average Chinese-American dish: it consists of wide, flat rice noodles served in a dark brown sauce flavored with mushrooms and spicy chili paste. Another signature dish is a vivid-yellow curried Chinese eggplant with chicken—the warming coconut-based sauce includes cumin and fennel seeds, and is worth lapping up with whatever rice or noodles you've got. Don't come here expecting the real-deal flavors of Malaysia. The preps here are definitely dumbed down for Americans—less spicy, less fish sauce, fewer real animal parts.

The wine list is a total afterthought, consisting of fewer than ten basic wines in categories labeled "premium" ($25 per bottle) and "adventurous" ($35 per bottle). The wines are really neither premium nor adventurous, so stick with the tropical cocktails.

The restaurant has great service, though, courtesy of a casual but friendly waitstaff that's happy to recommend dishes, keep the cocktails coming, and pack up your leftovers. The roof deck manages to project a spirited, party-like atmosphere without loud music or deafening chatter. Don't hold it against the place that the best dessert on offer is fried bananas served with ice cream. Just enjoy the home-style (if Americanized) Malaysian food and the friendly environs, and go ahead and feel superior to the suckers packing the roof deck across the street. —CD

# Sunflower Vegetarian

**5.7** Food    **6.4** Feel

The herbivore's dilemma, solved by the Japanese

## Chinese

Casual restaurant    **$20** Price

www.crystalsunflower.com

Mon–Sat 11:30am–9:30pm
Sun noon–9:30pm

**Bar** None
**Credit cards** Visa, MC, AmEx
**Reservations** Accepted
Kid-friendly, outdoor dining,
veg-friendly

**Falls Church, VA**
6304 Leesburg Pike
(703) 237-3888

Why are so many vegetarian restaurants notoriously below average? Often even their own clientele feels resigned to going just because there are so few other options around that don't require legwork ahead of time. Either they smell musty, or they produce dish after dish of paper towel-textured sorrows. ("But," someone's always telling you, "they make a good salad!" Zzzzz.) At Sunflower, diners are treated to a little of both offenses. A persistent waft of sour, soyish air advertises the main ingredient, and perhaps also foreshadows the queasy feeling you could get from consuming too much of it. Vegetarians revolt! You deserve better than this!

Occupying a squat strip mall hut deep in Falls Church, the entire restaurant is festooned with a bizarre array of sunflower-themed tchotchkes and odds and ends (be on the lookout for the stuffed reindeer and plastic animal figurine collection). The menu, with its classification system of sections and genres and poorly described dishes, is even more confusing than the decoration.

You may be tempted to overorder, with dirt-cheap prices and whimsical names like "hot hot shabu shabu." Besides, aren't we all quaking with anticipation to see what new vegetarian creations will free us from the shackles of carnivorous cynicism? The Japanese influence helps, as this is already a cuisine that's done quite well without meat. Aromatic curry is mild and subtly flavored—perhaps too subtly. It's just not enough to compensate for a thoroughly monotonous texture. You'll want to keep eating in the vain hope of finding just a little more flavor and just a little more satisfaction.

Soup dumplings (a rare sight, even in Chinese restaurants), made with cabbage and mushrooms, are delicate but substantial, squirting hot broth at the first bite. They are delicious, though not a revelation. But for heaven's sake, avoid any "meat without the meat" preparations. This goes for the fried "chicken" made from soy. Formed into popcorn-sized nuggets, the crunchy novelty wears out its welcome rather quickly. This is a treat that needs the naughty succulence of bird fat; without it, or without a suitably flavored take, it just tastes like fried breading and ketchup.

Sunflower's not a bad vegetarian option in a pinch, but if you have the time, a better one is this: hit the farmer's market, crack open a cookbook, and make some unforgettable dishes of your own. –FC

# Super Pollo

The best birds in town have those in the know flocking to this Arlington rotisserie

**7.4** Food **5.5** Feel

**Latin American**

Counter service **$10** Price

Daily 11am–10pm

**Bar** Beer
**Credit cards** Visa, MC, AmEx
Delivery, outdoor dining

**Arlington, VA**
607 N. Randolph St.
(703) 525-0999

Housed in a huge and ramshackle cafeteria off of Glebe road in Arlington, Super Pollo is a fascinating operation, efficiently delivering some of the most delicious Latin-style rotisserie chicken in DC to the masses.

If you're driving down Glebe and can't recall the precise location of the Pollo, you can attempt this proven trick: roll down your windows, drive slowly until you catch the faintest smell of roasting bird, and stop. Turn left or right, repeating as the smell gets closer. It really works! We wouldn't claim the same shenanigans success at any other place, but this is some powerful-smelling chicken.

Once you're inside the cavernous room, make your way to the back, where the service counter just barely blocks a view of the kitchen and its rotating birds. You then face a very simple decision: how much chicken to order (a quarter bird, half a bird, or a whole one). The typical meal comes on a three-compartment plate with slaw and fries, but you can accessorize with jazzed-up chickpeas or red beans. For us, the crunchy, creamy slaw and golden, salty fries do the trick, but the fried yuca also has a serious following.

The chicken here is often nearly charred on the outside. Don't let this skin fall off. It is, as is customary with chickens, the best bit. But unlike with some pollo wannabes, the meat inside these birds is tender and well-spiced. Your meal comes with a trio of sauces: one red, one white, one green. The green tomatillo sauce is spicy and satisfying. Guard these little plastic containers carefully; the staff can be sticklers about replacements, and extra sauce will put you back a few dimes.

These days, Super Pollo's main competition, the similarly-conceived Pollo Rico, seems to have been overtaken by migrant herds of youth, who seek the chicken cure to carry them over the hump of afternoon beers and into a second evening round. By contrast, Super Pollo continues to attract the same demographic as before, which consists mainly of lunching construction workers during the mid-afternoon, and families with children starting around 5pm. At peak hours, the cafeteria is bursting and noisy, and it can sometimes be difficult to get a seat. Trust us: you'll happily eat these fair fowl anywhere.

What? There's nothing wrong with eating in the parking lot! After all, it smells just dandy there. –CK

# Sushi-Go-Round & Tapas

How do you make cheap sushi taste better? Put it in motion! Not!

## Pan-Asian, Japanese

Casual restaurant

**$45**
Price

www.sushigoroundatverizon.com

Mon–Thu 11am–10:30pm
Fri 11am–11pm
Sat noon–11pm
Sun noon–10:30pm

**Bar** Beer, wine, liquor
**Credit cards** Visa, MC, AmEx
**Reservations** Accepted
Delivery, live music, outdoor dining, Wi-Fi

**Chinatown**
701 7th St. NW
(202) 393-2825

This is about as good an idea as a helicopter ejection seat.

Think about it. Raw fish, which are already terribly high maintenance due to their propensity for carrying parasites and their, you know, *temperature-sensitive* state, are placed on conveyor belts and allowed to peruse about at 75 degrees for an unknown amount of time. Grand idea.

People love to point out that the Japanese, themselves, have sushi conveyor belts. Yes, and we had McDonald's. Now they do, too. Isn't this global exchange of terrible food neat?

At Sushi-Go-Round, the sushi does—you guessed it—go round, on a small conveyor belt that circles the bar. If you pick a seat close to the chefs, you can observe the fish-slicing in action (you'll also be well-positioned to make special requests, and you can keep an eye on how long stuff's been in rotation). Assuming you dig the conveyor belt beyond all reason, the onus is on you to know exactly what is on each plate before you grab it. No give-backs!

If you can live without the riveting drama of motorized maki, eschew the bar's tall, uncomfortable stools in favor of the slightly more comfortable IKEA cafeteria tables. True to its fast-food format, the restaurant offers only paper menus, which are full of rather adorable linguistic stumbles such as: "All item are none refundable due to high seafood cost." Tee-hee! But wait, why would they need such a disclaimer? Has this been much of an issue in the past? Hmmm.

The food performs about as well as you'd expect. In one roll, crab is tasteless and the eel sticky-sweet. In general, spicy rolls are made with too much mayo and too little fish. The spider roll is below average (and that's saying a lot), because the soft-shell crab is tooth-shatteringly crunchy. And a seared salmon with asparagus is too dry. Whatever you order, fishes are almost indistinguishable from each other in thick, chewy texture and slightly sour taste that begs for soy and wasabi.

Benihana-like gimmicks, mayonnaise-y rolls and fish that needs disguising. This is sushi for people who hate sushi. –FC

# Sushi-Ko

Cutting-edge innovation—for the 1970s, anyway—
and good, fresh fish

| 8.5 | 7.2 |
|-----|-----|
| Food | Feel |

## Japanese

Upmarket restaurant

**$60**
Price

www.sushikorestaurants.com

Mon 6pm–10:30pm; Tue–Thu
noon–2:30pm, 6pm–10:30pm;
Fri noon–2:30pm, 6pm–11pm;
Sat 5:30pm–11pm; Sun
5:30pm–10pm

**Bar** Beer, wine, liquor
**Credit cards** Visa, MC, AmEx
**Reservations** Essential
Delivery

**Glover Park**
2309 Wisconsin Ave. NW
(202) 333-4187

**Chevy Chase, MD**
5455 Wisconsin Ave.
(301) 961-1644

In a city that celebrates tradition and longevity—monuments are never razed and long-serving Congresspeople are spoken of highly even by the other party—it is no wonder that its first sushi restaurant, Sushi-Ko is still so venerated. While others force edgy fusions upon sushi or insist on serving it to thumping club music, this 30-year institution has kept it simple and classic, if not exactly cutting-edge. The idea here, in décor and presentation, is simplicity. The minimalist space can feel boring, and the lighting too bright, but the constant crowd makes for a fun, convivial atmosphere. If you can, sit at the sushi bar, and order omakase (chef's choice).

The menu is a hybrid of white-bread American Japanese (teriyaki, dragon rolls); more traditional dishes (age-tofu, smoked mussel soup); and a host of Nobu-inspired modern fusion dishes that often employ raw fish, and are surprisingly good. The quality of the sushi, too, is better than most places in town; a board changes daily letting you know if the sushi chefs have uni, toro, aji, or live scallop. Ama ebi is delicious here; it's sweet and succulent.

The website goes into a florid description of ikebana, which dictates that all the chef must do is whittle away the excesses that stand in the way of the natural flavors. This is best exemplified by a tuna tartare with sesame seeds and slivers of green apple, which are kissed with sesame oil and formed into a pretty red bloom. A spicy scallop roll sees more elaborate dressing, but a refreshing restraint comes in the form of a soft-shell crab roll whose spicy sauce is on the plate, allowing the diner to decide how much (if any) is needed.

If you want to stray from raw fish, asparagus-and-rock-shrimp tempura is a pillowy treat; a crisp, salty, lightly oily skin gives way to a flavor enhanced by the steam treatment within. Duck breast is surprisingly also first-rate. But under no circumstances should you miss the marinated, crispy eel. It is delicate, sweet, and smoky.

The wine and sake list makes more of an effort than do other Japanese restaurants, with some unoaked white Burgundies that will pair nicely with the food. It's nothing spectacular—little here is—but it's also one of the city's most reliable tables, night in and night out. –FC

# Sweet Mango Café

We're thankful for how the food makes us feel, but we'd like a warm place to hang out, too

**7.7** Food
**6.4** Feel

## Caribbean

Casual restaurant

**$25** Price

www.sweetmangocafe.com

Mon–Thu 11am–10pm
Fri–Sat 11am–midnight
Sun 11am–8pm

**Bar** Beer, wine, liquor
**Credit cards** Visa, MC, AmEx
**Reservations** Not accepted
Outdoor dining, Wi-Fi

**Petworth**
3701 New Hampshire Ave. NW
(202) 726-2646

We associate Jamaica with colors, warm smiles, and exotic flavors, so the bare-bones setting at Sweet Mango is off-putting and a little frustrating. Yes, we constantly tout the importance of a dumpy and depressing atmosphere when in search of the Authentic Asian Holy Grail, but *man*, who among us isn't dreaming of Caribbean escapism when they stroll into this neat, clean Jamaican dive? We have screen savers and calendars that are more evocative than the inside of this place. That said, its three levels teem with amenities designed to keep you there, including a covered rooftop patio with a view, a full bar, HDTVs, and free Wi-Fi. The walls are a cheery bright green and yellow, with sophisticated-looking black and white photographs, but it still feels like a cafeteria, the lights inside too bright and the lights up top nearly nonexistent. For this reason, most people get take-out, which is ordered at the ground-level counter (there's table service on the next two floors).

The food is more successful. Beef patties are delicious, although they're not homemade (they're culled from Royal Caribbean Bakery in NYC). Curried goat is always a good choice, tender and rich, but—sorry, vegetarians—the tofu version doesn't hold up as well. Brown oxtail soup is a deep and nourishing choice when seeking a recovery of any kind, as is gelatinous cow's foot.

Their biggest seller, jerk chicken (choose dark meat, not white), is good and juicy, and absorbs some nice charcoal flavor, although we like it even spicier. Dirty rice is well seasoned but can be slightly dry, depending on where you are in the batch. An escoveitch of red snapper is a touch overcooked by the vinegar. Eggy ackee and saltfish runs the gamut of sweet, salty, savory, and spicy, and makes a good breakfast. Try it with a cup of excellent, mild Blue Mountain, something of an appellation d'origine contrôlée for Jamaican coffees. Or you can wash it all down with homemade ginger brews, black cherry lemonade, and coconut water.

Sweet Mango was destroyed by a fire a few years ago then rebuilt, which we are thankful for. So we can pick up tasty Caribbean flavors and take them back to our cubicles, where an iPod and a 1680 x 1050 resolution makes us almost *feel* the ocean breeze. –FC

# Sweetgreen

A salad shop and yogurt bar that's full of yuppie
virtue: healthy, fresh, and overpriced

## American, Ice cream

Counter service

www.sweetgreen.com

Mon–Fri 11am–9pm
Sat–Sun noon–9pm

**Bar** None
**Credit cards** Visa, MC, AmEx
Kid-friendly, outdoor dining,
veg-friendly

**Georgetown**
3333 M St. NW
(202) 337-9338

Opened by Georgetown alums, Sweetgreen is an exemplar of yuppie
virtue. All self-admitted members of the bobo clan might too make their
pilgrimage to the tiny shack on M Street in search of food that will fill
stomachs but not consciences. Indeed, Sweetgreen is a model of
righteousness: the space is lined with reclaimed wood planks, and the
menus (recycled), containers (biodegradable), and silverware (both) all
bear the stamp of sustainability.

Like the design, the food at Sweetgreen is also guilt-free; organic and
local ingredients are combined in that most virtuous salad. Visitors are
offered the choice to make their own creation (constructed from an
extensive list of greens, cheeses, vegetables, meats, crunchies, and
dressings) or to sample a chef-designed combo.

"Deconstructed guacamole" (a pricey but justifiable $9) is a mix of
mesclun, artfully mashed avocado, grilled chicken, tomatoes, onions, and
crushed tortilla strips. The proportions are generous and you'll thank
Sweetgreen for understanding that salads as meals require a little more
oomph. Though it's hard to taste all of the elements of the lime-cilantro
jalapeño vinaigrette, the amount strikes a happy balance between coating
the salad and drowning it. The salt of the chicken and bite of the onion
cut through the fatty avocado, and hunks of warm bread will fill you
without fear of global warming or arteriosclerosis.

Dessert will not curb your self-satisfaction. Developed by the owners,
Sweetflow yogurt follows Pinkberry to create true frozen yogurt. It is fluffy
like fresh, albeit frozen, whipped cream, and the flavor is tart, tangy, and
not at all sweet. For $4, you are allowed three toppings that include fresh
fruit and a granola scented with spicy ginger. It is a testament to
Sweetgreen's commitment that you will find no M&Ms, caramel sauce, or
Oreos anywhere on the premises.

Customers eat their meals sitting squashed in an alley with their fellow
diners. All will most-likely be wearing do-gooders' looks of clarity and self-
assuredness. The draw of Sweetgreen is so strong that there is often a line
around the corner of devotees waiting to take their turn at the little green
shrine. This is a wonderful place for worship. In a street filled with heavy
options and frilly cuisine, Sweetgreen is a refreshing place to experience a
bit of paradise. –JC

# Tabaq Bistro

Satisfying small plates in the hippest heart of U Street

**7.1** Food   **8.0** Feel

## Middle Eastern

Upmarket restaurant   **$45** Price

www.tabaqdc.com

| | | |
|---|---|---|
| Mon–Thu 5pm–11pm | **Bar** Beer, wine, liquor | **U Street** |
| Fri 5pm–midnight | **Credit cards** Visa, MC, AmEx | 1336 U St. NW |
| Sat 11am–4pm, 5pm–midnight | **Reservations** Accepted | (202) 265-0965 |
| Sun 11am–4pm, 5pm–11pm | Date-friendly, outdoor dining | |

With DC practically drowning in small plates as the mediocre tapas trend surges relentlessly across the city, we light with some relief on a restaurant that actually does it right. Tabaq offers a range of excellent Mediterranean mezze in about as light and stylish a setting as you could wish for.

From its bright color palette to its wonderful open-air roof deck hung with airy linens and lit by candles, Tabaq deftly delivers on its refreshing promise. The diners and waiters are as slick and pretty as the mixed drinks. Young and fresh, they form a pretty picture of U Street at its finest. While we've heard frequent complaints of shoddy service (missed drinks and dishes, long waits, rudeness), we've never experienced it—although during a busy brunch, you may have to be patient as the friendly but bare-bones staff can get a bit overwhelmed.

Though many know of Tabaq as a lounge, its menu is quite capable. To begin, the bread is amazing. Soft, dark grained ropes are served warm and fragrant, with big pools of olive oil that are cloudy and rich and courageously infused with garlic. You will make baskets disappear without realizing it.

The Mediterranean staples are deservedly popular, too. Hummus is spiked with smoky paprika, while muhammara brings out the oft-forgotten sweetness of red peppers. The texture of both is wonderful: the former is pleasantly coarse, while the latter is creamy and thick. Beef kofte is dressed with lively tangy soft yogurt and nutty pips of pinenuts—an ideal balance of tart and sweet.

More substantial dishes are also a delight. The sautéed calamari prove that squid can be a tender meat. Lamb chops are delicious celebration of culinary restraint: a smoky carbon crust gives way with a snap to fatty strips of meat and bone on the inside. Place bets on who at your table will break down and gnaw on the bone.

Our only major complaint about Tabaq is dessert; most of the options do their names a disservice. Profiteroles are among the worst in the city, with thick, unforgiving dough that is so tough it needs a steak knife. Chocolate cake is indistinguishable from what you might conjure out of the box at home.

But these do little to put us off Tabaq, which charms so where others have failed. Apparently, some nice things do come in small packages. –JC

# Tabard Inn

**7.6** Food  **9.6** Feel

Soft-spoken class prevails at this genteel brunch hotspot, but the food's a bit uneven

## American

Upmarket restaurant  **$55** Price

www.tabardinn.com

Mon–Thu 7am–10am, 11:30am–2:30pm, 6pm–9:30pm; Fri 7am–10am, 11:30am–2:30pm, 6pm–10pm; Sat 8am–9:45am, 11am–2:30pm, 6pm–10pm; Sun 8am–9:15am, 10:30am–2:30pm, 6pm–9:30pm

**Bar** Beer, wine, liquor
**Credit cards** Visa, MC, AmEx
**Reservations** Accepted
Date-friendly, kid-friendly, live music, outdoor dining, Wi-Fi

**Dupont**
1739 N St. NW
(202) 331-8528

The Tabard Inn, which has been a functioning, if creaky, small hotel for over a century, invokes the seasons in its restaurant menu, but also in its atmosphere. The seasonal variation in the dishes is creative but not overwrought (a refreshing gesture in an age of formulaic restaurant rhetoric: pea shoots in spring, butternut in autumn). In complementary fashion, the Tabard's spaces adapt to changing temperatures. A fireplace and close-knit sofas warm the sitting room in winter; come spring, the windows are thrown open, and the bricked-in patio is a fine place to catch a summer breeze.

This has long been one of DC's favorite brunch spots; the spring brunch menu might feature a smart balance of spring ingredients and breakfast staples: omelettes, pancakes, and poached eggs are not squeezed off the menu by caperberries and arugula, but congenially share the space. If anything, it's the preparation of some dishes that's still a bit green. While a pair of poached eggs, at one visit, was both pretty on the plate and rich on the tongue, and the accompanying veal and Toulouse sausage pleasantly spicy, little effort was made to bring it all together; a giant clump of watercress had to be wrestled apart with fork and knife and manually added to the rest.

Similarly, pan-fried soft-shell crab has come tough, and its underlying salad almost creamy with soft mango, mustardy mizuna greens, and cilantro; the textures never united to form a dish. Halibut with Jerusalem artichoke caponata, on the other hand, was a paragon of incorporation; the basil, caperberries, and potatoes mixed in seamlessly, even if the resulting flavor combination was a little bland. We highly recommend starting your meal with the sweet corn soup, when available, which tastes of a dozen cobs of buttered corn packed mercilessly into a six-ounce cup.

While the Tabard's mimosa is markedly chic (the orange juice is fresh-squeezed and foamy), the restaurant retains a feel that's quiet and unassuming; with this location and pedigree, the Tabard could easily be a much more pompous place. Although the raw components are almost there, the food preparation could stand a few renovations. To that (depending on the season), we'll raise a fresh mimosa or a warming glass of port. –FC

# Tabeer

Great Pakistani in an unlikely (or is it likely?) Maryland location

**8.7** **6.5**
*Food* *Feel*

## Pakistani

Casual restaurant **$25**
*Price*

www.mytabeer.com

Sun–Thu noon–9pm
Fri–Sat noon–9:30pm

**Bar** None
**Credit cards** Visa, MC, AmEx
**Reservations** Accepted

**Hyattsville, MD**
1401 University Blvd. E.
(301) 434-2121

How spectacular is Maryland's diversity?

This spectacular: one of the best, and most authentic, Pakistani Muslim restaurants in the mid-Atlantic United States is in a mall called "La Unión," presumably (though not verifiably) named after a coastal city in a humble corner of El Salvador. This is no accident: this is just another in-the-course-of-everyday-business reflection of the overlap of two of the area's cohabitating ethnic groups—and just another little token of the everyday miracle of the American experiment.

Tabeer, attached to the Bismillah Halal Meat Market, is an expansive, brightly lit space that's dominated by an aggressively extensive buffet table that sits right in the middle of everything. Unusually, the buffet operates both for lunch and for dinner, and the Pakistani stews take well to sitting around—perhaps even gaining complexity as their flavors meld throughout the day.

The thing to have here is the mutton (in this case, used synonymously with goat) korma, a rich, creamy, deeply goaty but not really gamy preparation that pairs excellently with some of the area's best fresh-baked naan, always a signature of a true Pakistani place. There's also a great off-the-menu goat soup that regulars tend to order. Don't expect much help from the menu on stew flavors; almost every one is described as spiced with "coriander, ginger, and green chilies." No matter; try the lamb- or goat-brain masala ("no brainer, this is the best," quips the menu), the biryanis, or achaar gosht (a lamb stew that brandishes the surprising brightness of pickle). Weekend-only specials include a subtle and complex dish called haleem, which is beef simmered with several different varieties of lentils for so long—overnight—that the whole thing turns into a rich, addictive purée.

Here's how authentic Tabeer is: you're expected to eat with your hands. In fact, the only seemingly inauthentic thing about the place is its marketing prowess, which shows in a flashy web site (which, incidentally, doesn't come up in a Google search) and a proactive effort to reach out to squeamish American eaters. "In order to be able to satisfy all our patrons," explains the site, "we offer different levels of spicing for almost all the items on this menu." (You know better than to order things mild, right?)

And in case the hand thing weirds you out: "Just like eating with chopsticks in a Chinese restaurant," Tabeer reassures its germophobic would-be customers, "feel free to switch back to utensils if you are not enjoying the experience."

Trust us: you'll be enjoying the experience. –RG

# Taberna del Alabardero

A 20-year tradition of tapas and aristocratic romance

| **8.7** | **8.7** |
|---|---|
| Food | Feel |

**Spanish**

Upmarket restaurant

**$75**
Price

www.alabardero.com

Mon–Fri 11:30am–2:30pm,
5:30pm–10:30pm
Sat 5:30pm–10:30pm

**Bar** Beer, wine, liquor
**Credit cards** Visa, MC, AmEx
**Reservations** Accepted
Date-friendly, good wines, live music, outdoor dining

**Farragut**
1776 Eye St. NW
(202) 429-2200

Despite its blah storefront exterior, Taberna del Albardero is hiding one of the most romantic dining rooms in the city. Once you get past the tiny lobby, the space blossoms into deep rose-colored baroque splendor. Shades of red and gold run through heavy, brocaded linens, and both a wall-sized tapestry of various flora and fauna and an open kitchen hung with brass pots make a side room feel particularly old-world historic. It's more fun than stuffy, though, and you'll get a kick out of the very old-school service, which is attentive and charming. The Spanish embassy types that frequent the place add to the effect—and to the expectation that you, yourself, speak Spanish (at the very least, you'll get some adorably broken English from your server).

Not surprisingly, Taberna boasts one of the best tapas menus in DC. This is where the best value is to be had, as several small plates provide a three-ring circus for your mouth. Try patatas bravas, crisp from the fryer, with just a whisper of breading; spicy aioli brings a different kind of heat to the already invigorating dish. The Spanish tortilla is satisfying, too, with slices of potato layered between fluffy eggs. Croquetas burst open with ham-spiked steam.

More substantial dishes are also good. Whole quail stuffed with earthy pork trotters, served on a bed of sweet potatoes, is succulent and rich. Inexplicably, even paella "mixta" doesn't include the trademark chorizo; if you ask for it to be added, it might come out on the side instead of being cooked together with the seafood. However, at least it will be free: when this happened to us, we were reassured at the end that "we invite the sausage."

The wine list is a split between Spanish and Californian, but we suggest using this opportunity to expand your vocabulary to include Bierzo, Rias Baixas, and Ribera del Duero (your dollar will go a lot further here than in America…for a change!). Or refresh with a crisp white sangría, brightly perfumed with citrus and tasting like spring. Then relax and enjoy the slice of aristocracy around you, and the distinct lack of thumping club music.
–FC

# Tachibana

Some of the most authentic Japanese food in suburbia

| 7.0 | 5.5 |
|-----|-----|
| Food | Feel |

## Japanese

Casual restaurant

**$45**
Price

www.j-connections.com/dc/blog/tachibana.php

Mon–Thu 11:30am–2pm, 5pm–10pm; Fri 11:30am–2pm, 5pm–10:30pm; Sat noon–2:30pm, 5pm–10:30pm; Sun noon–2:30pm, 5pm–9:30pm

**Bar** Beer, wine, liquor
**Credit cards** Visa, MC, AmEx
**Reservations** Accepted

**Tysons Corner, VA**
6715 Lowell Ave.
(703) 847-1771

Tachibana certainly looks like the real thing. Marooned on an island in the middle of a McLean parking lot and surrounded by a large veranda, it's like a red brick interpretation of a Japanese house upon a misty hill. You almost expect to see snow cranes dancing under the lampposts. The interior is surprisingly spacious and encouraging: waitresses are actually Japanese, and tables and the multiple sushi bars are filled with Asian diners. It's only natural that the food at Tachibana sees more authentic flavors than those you'd find at similar restaurants elsewhere in the area.

Take, for example, a fish soup (hooray for a restaurant that has something other than miso). The light, briny broth is studded with bitter carrots, flowering radishes, and wilted greens, and is suffused with fishy redolence. If it weren't for the clod of over-boiled chicken stowing away in the bowl, it would be an ideal start to a meal. Bitter hot tea in ceramic mugs further demonstrates that Tachibana hasn't been entirely Westernized.

Main courses bring moments of beauty. Pieces of sashimi unfold like little flowers in a bowl of chirashi. Eating it is like a treasure hunt or a game of he-loves-me, he-loves-me-not. Each petal removed reveals yet another fragrant layer—tawny pickled mushrooms, blood-bright tuna, smooth and fatty salmon. Slivers of fresh ginger add spicy-sweet thorns of heat to random bites. There's a much more expansive list of nigiri choices than at other suburban Japanese places.

Salmon marinated in sweet soy, though, is something of a bust. The lower quality fish is obvious, and the big, hacking cuts are incongruous with a chopstick culture. Noodle dishes are charmingly rustic in their heavy clay pots. There are moments of further authenticity (like eggs floating in the chicken broth) and moments of disappointment (said chicken broth tastes like it came from a can). It may be red brick, but the food and the humble interior are closer to Japan than is customary. –JC

# Tackle Box

The house of eternal summer

**8.2** *Food*  **7.0** *Feel*

## Seafood

Casual restaurant  **$25** *Price*

www.tackleboxrestaurant.com

Mon–Thu 11am–10pm
Fri–Sat 11am–11pm

**Bar** None
**Credit cards** Visa, MC, AmEx
**Reservations** Not accepted
Delivery, kid-friendly, live music

**Georgetown**
3245 M St. NW
(202) 337-8269

Displaced citizens of New England rejoice! For here in our nation's capital you can relive the summer shacks of your rocky beaches and sunburnt youth!

Situated next door to its elegant sibling, Hook, casual, shabby Tackle Box channels New England's coast all the way. Poured concrete floors, rough-hewn picnic benches, and hanging colorful buoys drive the point home, but what gives Tackle Box its soul are the anachronistic touches: boom boxes that blare Jimi Hendrix, singing in the kitchen, and touching eco-consciousness (check out the "good fish, bad fish" map next to the register).

Like summer-shack fare, the food isn't sophisticated or beautiful. Apart from some baked sides, there are only two cooking techniques: crispy (fried) and wood-grilled. Customers happily wolf down red cafeteria trays full of scallops (sweetish with a just the right amount of chew), calamari (salty and soft), sweet potato fries (gloriously blackened on the edges), and homemade blueberry pie (mandatory, if only for the fresh, tart filling). It's refreshing also to see a high-profile restaurant group focus on fishes that are delicious but still plentiful: tilapia, rainbow trout, bluefish (whose grilled form we highly recommend), and catfish. Lobster pots to go are also available for $40, filled with seafood and vegetables that you can cook up in your own kitchen—great for Hamptons beach parties without the beach.

Some Southern touches also shine: crispy fried oysters with the right pop of brine, crumbly sweet corn muffins scented with garlic and studded with kernels, house-brewed sweet tea, and downright hospitable service that does not (sorry) exist in New England. Hush puppies are a bit thick and mealy, though; better leave those guys to the Deep South. Also underwhelming is a bland cole slaw and slightly anorexic clam chowder.

It bears mention that infighting has led to some shake-ups in the kitchen, which has sometimes affected consistency. Still most of the time, this is a good restaurant. It's not just good for what it is—it's good in its own right. And it's affordable. At $13, the Maine Meal will get you two sides, a decent portion of fish and your choice of sauce. You may leave with that fried-food-sitting-in-the-tummy feeling, but isn't that, too, part of the nostalgia? –JC

# Tai Shan

A miserable Chinatown dump, cleaned up a little, is still a miserable Chinatown dump

**4.0** Food   **5.0** Feel

## Chinese

Casual restaurant

**$15** Price

Sun–Thu 8am–2am
Fri–Sat 11am–4am

**Bar** Beer, wine, liquor
**Credit cards** Visa, MC, AmEx
**Reservations** Accepted
Delivery, kid-friendly, live music,
outdoor dining, veg-friendly

**Chinatown**
622 H St. NW
(202) 639-0266

With a glass awning that opens out into onto the street, Tai Shan is one of the more prominent restaurants in Chinatown. Compared to its peers, it's bright and clean and garishly overwrought. Multi-colored Christmas lights clash fantastically with red lanterns, pink posters, orange walls and western chandeliers. Nothing matches, but an earnest effort is apparent. Sadly, the décor may be the best part about it.

Tai Shan's menu is a battlefield. Cheap lunch and dinner specials compete for space with no fewer than seventeen categories of food. It's hard to tell what you're getting because dishes are poorly labeled and include some odd adjectives (what could they possibly mean by "ball egg"?!). This is no great loss, as it turns out, because none of the options is particularly good, and you'd be far better off taking your business elsewhere.

Sha cha pork, named for the thick, gritty Chinese barbecue sauce, has great potential. It's a huge disappointment. The smoky-spicy-sweet sauce is diluted down until it barely has any flavor and the overall effect is slickly oily. The bite from green peppers is too strong to let the sweetness of the sauce come out and completely overwhelms the dish. Pineapples, thrown in as an afterthought, only add to the mess. It could have been a wonderful, homestyle dish, but instead, it's a disaster.

Another potentially exciting dish pairs fried grouper with stir-fried vegetables. But the batter turns soggy and flat almost immediately and the texture of the fish is dense instead of flaky—kind of like a dry, flavorless fish stick. Though the dish is advertised as having Chinese broccoli, the actual vegetable selection is a terrifying mix of giant stalks of celery and overcooked beans. It doesn't taste the least bit Chinese.

Even the mundane "special thick noodles" don't clear the bar. The stir-fried noodles have a good chewy texture, but cause slimy mouth-feel and aftertaste typical of awful Chinese food. Plump slivers of shiitake mushrooms might help, but more anemic, overcooked green beans completely cancel out their positive effect. An odd remnant of thick, dry, shredded seafood flesh adds flavor, but awful texture to the dish.

Tai Shan may have spruced itself up a little, but with Chinese food, we say the divier, the better. With such ponderous, gloopy, grisly fare on offer, we have only one question: Why eat here? –JC

# Tako Grill

A simple sushi joint that's fresh and fairly priced, with some of the fish flown in from Japan

**7.8** Food   **5.5** Feel

## Japanese

Casual restaurant   **$45** Price

www.takogrill.com

Mon–Thu 11:30am–2pm, 5:30pm–10pm; Fri 11:30am–2pm, 5:30pm–10:30pm; Sat 5:30pm–10:30pm; Sun 5pm–9:30pm

**Bar** Beer, wine, liquor
**Credit cards** Visa, MC, AmEx
**Reservations** Accepted
Kid-friendly, veg-friendly

**Bethesda, MD**
7756 Wisconsin Ave.
(301) 652-7030

The clattery, brightly lit interior of Tako Grill is an unlikely setting for some of the freshest sushi available in the Maryland suburbs. Look inside the laminated menu for a piece of printer paper listing the day's specials, which are generally flown in from Japan. This piece of paper is also where you'll find out if there are whole fish available grilled and served with a light ginger-and-scallion soy sauce. We've thoroughly enjoyed everything we've ordered from this informal typed list, including excellent toro and creamy king salmon.

The familiar à-la-carte sushi menu renders favorites such as spicy tuna and scallion-yellowtail rolls. While there aren't many Japanese sushi chefs behind the counter these days, the guys rolling the sushi are competent and friendly. Most importantly, Tako's offerings are fresher than those of most competitors in the area, and they're reasonably priced, too. Well-seasoned seaweed salad bunches up four or five different kinds of sea greens in an appropriately light sesame-flavored dressing. Equally pleasant appetizers on the hot side include negimaki—bundles of scallions wrapped in thinly-sliced beef and served with a slightly sweetened soy sauce. Tempura dishes are ably executed, too, arriving crisp and hot, if more thickly battered than we'd like.

Service is polite and generally expeditious, though occasionally servers' inexperience shows in overly long delays between courses and too-long-empty water glasses. The atmosphere here is more of a family restaurant than a fine-dining establishment; young couples with or without children dine in casual attire, elevating the noise level to chatty rather than subdued. Furnishings are utilitarian, and a large flat-screen TV in one corner generally shows soccer or sumo wrestling.

Nonetheless, the long, shiny, black-topped bar at Tako Grill is sleek and pleasant, extending the length of the room and concealing a wide selection of sakes that merit a menu of their own. While not quite at the level of DC's finest sushi spots, Tako Grill is an affordable and reliable stop in Montgomery County for fresh fish and reasonable value. When possible, stick to the specials, supplement with sushi à la carte, and enjoy a fuss-free meal among local families and repeat customers. –CD

# Tallula

A restaurant that plays with its food, to mixed but
generally amusing results

| 7.8 | 9.0 |
|-----|-----|
| Food | Feel |

## New American

Upmarket restaurant

**$55**
Price

www.tallularestaurant.com

Mon–Thu 5:30pm–10pm; Fri
5:30pm–11pm; Sat 11am–
2:30pm, 5:30pm–11pm; Sun
11am–2:30pm, 5:30pm–10pm

**Bar** Beer, wine, liquor
**Credit cards** Visa, MC, AmEx
**Reservations** Accepted
Kid-friendly, outdoor dining, Wi-Fi

**Arlington, VA**
2761 Washington Blvd.
(703) 778-5051

Tallula is often touted as one of Arlington's culinary highlights. Funky, out
of the way, and filled with its own unique spirit, it's a justified icon to
many citizens of Northern Virginia. Inside, brassy bronze detailing and
purple upholstery clash spectacularly with orange gauze curtains. This is a
place that is well aware of its quirkiness.

The pride is reflected in the Tallula dining experience. More than 70
wines are available by the glass, suggested by expert waiters and drawn
from a non-traditional list. Rotating selections of artisanal cheeses
complete the pairing. If nothing else, it's a great place to go and drink.
Though known for its wine, Tallula is also the home of quite possibly the
most charmingly named cocktail in the universe: "Gnome's Water," a
whimsical and deliciously fresh and fragrant combination of Hendrick's
gin, lavender, English cucumber, and lime. It's enough to make you rub
noses with your neighbor and consider riding through the countryside on
a fox named Swift. (At which point your neighbor will surely ask to be
moved to another table.)

In line with its playful spirit, Tallula's menu advises you to "amuse
yourself" with seasonal small bites that are easily the highlight of the
menu. They're bigger than just one bite (let's say two to three for the
average-sized mouth) and let you experience the childish glee of ordering
one of everything. Permutations can include duck tacos (nicely spiced with
the surprising texture of soft, stewed pork), croquettes made from mac
and cheese (jazzed up by cilantro), and an excellent slider made with
truffle butter and onion marmalade (sweet, earthy, tenderly moist, and
wonderfully cooked). Other small bites, such as a lime-obliterated ceviche,
and a fishy crab potsticker, are less amusing, and should be avoided.

Sadly, regular menu items are hit or miss, often on the same plate.
Porkchops tend to be tough and overcooked but are paired with smoky-
sweet-briny cornbread pudding and an unbelievably arresting sauce that
tastes deep and rich like the color purple. Broccoli rabe ravioli are
excessively bitter even for lovers of the green. Occasionally, Tallula's wit is
its undoing, as with a decadent foie gras dish oddly accompanied by a
strawberry pound cake. Hummingbird cake is shaped into a tiny, spongey
house—perhaps inhabited by an inebriated gnome—but also a bit boring.
It tastes like a moist, lemony muffin.

But there are few reasons not to visit Tallula. Between the wine and
your amused bouche, you'll find yourself more than just smiling. It's nice
to find a restaurant good-natured enough to make you out-and-out
laugh. –JC

# Tandoor Grill

Standard Indian fare that doesn't rise too high
above the norm

| **6.3** | **6.9** |
|---|---|
| Food | Feel |

## Indian

Casual restaurant

**$30**
*Price*

www.capitolhillgrill.com

Mon–Thu 11am–3pm, 5pm–
10pm; Fri 11am–3pm, 5pm–
11pm; Sat 11:30am–11pm; Sun
11:30am–3pm, 5pm–10pm

**Bar** Beer, wine, liquor
**Credit cards** Visa, MC, AmEx
**Reservations** Accepted
Delivery, kid-friendly, outdoor
dining, veg-friendly

**Capitol Hill**
419 8th St. SE
(202) 547-3233

Indian places tend to resort to a somewhat limited repertoire of restaurant nomenclature, as if drawing from a baby-names book with various combinations of Indian-like terms that ring familiar to American ears: Sitar, Nirvana, Bombay, Tandoor, or Karma. Although some hidden gems are to be found in restaurants with boring names, a place like "Tandoor Grill" raises the immediate suspicion of mediocrity.

And dining at Tandoor confirms this suspicion. The restaurant manages to look upscale: the tablecloths are a pristine white, and the place settings are adorned with deep-blue-stemmed goblets for water. But as the reasonable prices indicate, the place is far from high-end; rather, Tandoor is an ambitious ruffian trying to keep afloat with neither dazzling style nor compelling flavor (although in a neighborhood with options like the revolting China Wall take-out and the thick, greasy mess of Today's Pizza, the argument can be made that Tandoor's done pretty well for itself, relatively speaking).

There's not too much we can pick out to diss or praise at Tandoor. The restaurant makes a fine tandoori chicken, with good-quality meat and a bright, hot skin, and its saffron-tipped rice is a pretty dish to behold. The dal is not quite creamy enough, but the flavor of the lentils is hearty and sweet. Some of the curries hold together better than others: in general, the saag dishes are nicely integrated and rich.

We would have preferred more adventurous naan from Tandoor, as well as more attention to the hot spices and smaller pieces of meat in the curries. But even with dedicated reflection, it's hard to highlight a single poorly prepared dish, only general room for improvement.

If you're not too bored (see above) or too full (the portions are large) to order dessert, Tandoor's rice pudding is worth a try. Here, a dish finally rises to the fore, with a silky constitution, a gentle sweetness tempered by the taste of cardamom and milk, and a few softened pistachio nuts thrown in for color and flavor. But it's too little, too late. –CK

# Taquería Distrito Federal

**8.0** Food  **6.0** Feel

Marvelous meats for modest prices, just like in
Mexico's great capital city

## Mexican

Casual restaurant  **$20** Price

www.taqueriadf.com

Sun–Wed 8am–9pm
Thu–Sat 8am–11pm

**Bar** None
**Credit cards** Visa, MC, AmEx
**Reservations** Not accepted
Delivery, live music, outdoor dining

**Columbia Heights**
3463 14 St. NW
(202) 276-7331

**Petworth**
805 Kennedy St. NW
(202) 421-8240

Taquería D. F. is run by two smiling Salvadorans who seems to feel no particular compunction about serving food from a country other than their own. In fact, unlike most of Washington's Mexican-Salvadoran hybrids, D.F. is without a doubt a big-city kid (that's Distrito Federal, Mexico City's greater metropolitan area). Although a few things are off, the taquería gets so much right that it's hard to believe the little shop is actually situated within the bounds of our very own District.

You enter D.F. down a set of three stairs. The slightly buried room is nevertheless brightly lit, and small, with a dozen small tables and undersized chairs. Even during slow times, the taquería seems busier than it is, with some lively telenovela action on the tube, and two or three people intersecting to bring your order. With large groups, the line-order nature of D.F. becomes transparent: dishes are brought to the table, one by one, in the precise order they were taken and written down by the waitress (she's almost always female).

D.F. offers tacos, burritos, and tostadas with any of over ten types of meat, including carnitas, lengua (tongue), chorizo, tripa, and chivo (goat). The packaging is almost immaterial—because the meat is so exceptional—but a few things do bear mention. First, the burritos are small and squat. They fall apart easily, and are clearly not the taquería's strong suit.

The tacos, by contrast, are the trump cards. Made with six-inch doubled-up corn tortillas (rather than with the three-or-four-inch tortillas sometimes found in taquerías in the Mexican capital), they're big enough that three tacos will usually suffice for one person. Each is garnished with fresh cilantro and a thin slice of avocado: an attractive presentation in a restaurant whose last concern—in terms of décor, at least—seems to be with appearances.

The meats of D.F. are outstanding: the chorizo is superbly spicy, the beef al pastor tastes warm and earthy, the chicharrón is served in a tangy salsa verde, and D.F. has done the best it can do with the chicken, although carne asada can be dirt dry. Vegetarians will be unhappy here, but the staff is accommodating (if perplexed) and will whip up a meatless burrito with small cubed white cheese and plenty of beans.

Be sure to order the "Coca-Cola Mexicana"—small glass bottles sweetened not with high fructose corn syrup but with the real deal—sugar cane. Maybe D. F. stands for Delighted Foodie. –CK

# Taquería El Poblano

Stick to the more traditional, simply made dishes to avoid a white-bread disappointment

| 7.2 | 6.5 |
|---|---|
| Food | Feel |

## Mexican

Casual restaurant

**$15**
Price

www.taqueriapoblano.com

Mon 5:30pm–10pm; Tue–Fri 11:30am–3pm, 5:30pm–10pm; Sat 11:30am–10pm; Sun 10:30am–9pm
Hours vary by location

**Bar** Beer, wine, liquor
**Credit cards** Visa, MC, AmEx
**Reservations** Not accepted
Kid-friendly, live music

**Alexandria, VA**
2400 Mt. Vernon Ave.
(703) 548-8226

**Arlington, VA**
2503 N. Harrison St.
(703) 237-8250

Every city has a few silly Tex-Mex restaurants that seem to take their design cues from the desert in Road Runner cartoons. Taquería El Poblano is one of those restaurants, from its sunset-colored walls to the corrugated-tin roof over the bar, to the proliferation of cacti, chile peppers, coyotes, and sombreros. In short, it rocks the kitsch. Admittedly, the hokiness is a little fun, but when the décor screams "gringo expectations of Mexico," doesn't the food usually follow suit?

The menu is a mish mash of Mexican, Tex-Mex, and Cal-Mex. It takes great liberties with authenticity, which can be construed as poetic license in the right hands, but here these liberties are not executed with the sort of confidence and prowess that successfully reinvent regional cuisine. If you're going to substitute anything for pork (why on earth would anyone do that?), duck can be appropriate, so long as it's fatty enough. Carnitas made with such fatty duck are perked up by tangy pickled onions, but their unevenly cooked flesh is tough and dried out here and there. A taco featuring battered and fried fish is wonderfully flaky and moist, but it lacks much flavor, other than oil. After a few seconds, it quickly turns to mush. Grilled pineapples in tacos al pastor are a delightfully spicy treat, but they can't improve the tough pork. And tacos al carbón wear a suspicious coating of cheese. Which distracts attention from the moist meat, fresh onions, cilantro, and a squeeze of lime in homemade corn tortillas.

There are some moments of beauty: cebollitas are grilled green onions, the textural equivalent of nesting dolls, where charred crispy layers give way to softer, more transparent inner layers, each petal marked with a different degree of onion-sharpness. The retinue of tacos is followed by plates of enchiladas, mole, and mammoth burritos that fare as well.

There seems to be a dearth of good Mexican in the District, but the standard adage of "the farther out you go, the better it gets" doesn't necessarily pertain to Taquería El Poblano. But even if it doesn't live up to the potential that's reached in some more traditional kitchens, this place is well above average. It's also popular for Sunday Mexican brunch—and it's hard to argue with that. –JC

# Taquería Nacional

Authentic, delicious tacos and more from the least
likely of places: one without wheels

**8.2** Food  **7.0** Feel

## Mexican

Counter service  **$15** Price

www.taquerianacional.com

Mon–Fri 7am–3pm

**Bar** None
**Credit cards** Visa, MC, AmEx
Outdoor dining

**Penn Quarter**
400 N. Capitol St. NW
(202) 737-7070

"Tacos for the Boho Masses!" may well be the rallying cry of Taquería
Nacional, which serves up some of the closest facsimiles of true Distrito
Federal cuisine in one of the poshest locations of our own little federal
district. This paradox—local food brought to you by The Establishment—is
further vexed by the proletariat-friendly prices at Nacional, as well as the
exquisite side dishes, baked goods, horchata, and aguas frescas.

This just may be one of the oddest places to eat in Washington:
Taquería Nacional shares a kitchen with Johnny's Half Shell—an expensive
meeting place for the suits of Capitol Hill and their K Street patrons,
complete with white cloth and grand piano tunes at noon—but the
similarities between the oyster shop and taquería end with this shared
space. Like Johnny's, Nacional is clean and kempt, and those who believe
that good tacos can only come from rusty trucks or dirty hovels may be
tempted to turn back at the door.

But don't go! The tacos here are very similar to what you'll find in
Mexico—two small corn tortillas full of spiced beef, pork, sometimes
tongue, topped with the traditional cilantro-onion-lime mix—served out
of a location that's pure Capitol Hill. The spot is take-out only, and each
taco is presented individually in a recycled cardboard hamburger box
(another nod to the upscale surroundings). Be sure to grab a container of
fresh salsa, available in green, red, or chipotle iterations; spicy or mild, it's
some of the freshest stuff around.

You're likely to be eating your meal on a park bench or in your living
room, but these tacos will transport you to a south-of-the-border
taquería: lardy, wet beans, tender beef, or lightly battered snapper topped
with shredded cabbage and a tangy white crema. Well-travelled taco
lovers may notice that, here, the meat is a touch less greasy than the real
deal, but it doesn't take away from the experience in the slightest.

A board out front changes daily, offering American specials with a flair:
pimento cheeseburgers sometimes, a spicy jambalaya others. These are
every bit as delicious, and a nice break from a daily taco habit. Wash it all
down with the world's most refreshing beverage, agua fresca, or a
Spanish-style horchata (nutty, cinnamony), and you'll find Nacional to be
one of the district's finest affairs. –CK

# Tara Thai

We like to be, under the sea, when predictable is just what we want

**5.9** Food
**6.8** Feel

## Thai

Casual restaurant

**$25** Price

www.tarathaiexpress.com

Mon–Thu 11:30am–3pm, 5pm–10pm; Fri–Sat noon–3:30pm, 5pm–11pm; Sun noon–3:30pm, 5pm–10pm

**Bar** Beer, wine, liquor
**Credit cards** Visa, MC, AmEx
**Reservations** Accepted
Delivery

**Upper NW**
4849 Massachusetts Ave. NW
(202) 363-4141

**Bethesda, MD**
4828 Bethesda Ave.
(301) 657-0488

**Falls Church, VA**
7501 Leesburg Pike
(703) 506-9788

**Additional locations**
and more features at
www.fearlesscritic.com

Somewhere along the line, a particular brand of Americanized Thai food became a reliable, affordable, standard cuisine, its execution epitomized by this kind of small local chain. Tara Thai, with a few locations scattered around the DC metro area, builds its solid reputation on able renditions of those faux-Southeast Asian dishes that have become familiar to the American palate: satay, pad Thai, green curry. And in its Bethesda location, at least, Tara Thai sets itself apart with an under-the-sea decoration scheme and friendlier-than-average service.

If you're used to Thai-American food, nothing on this menu will surprise you, although we're always happy to see green papaya salad. Tiny icons depicting hot chili peppers denote which dishes are "hot," "hotter," and "incendiary." Of course, even the "hottest" dishes are toned down for the American palate, so don't be afraid to try the nicely tangy larb gai, in which minced chicken is seasoned with fresh red onion, scallions, cilantro, and piquant spices. "Kapow" beef (or chicken or pork or seafood) is genuinely spicy only if you bite directly into one of the tiny green bird chilies. The seafood specials are generally a livelier choice: whole rockfish, flounder, or soft-shell crabs are market-priced and available in your choice of sauces—our favorite is the chili-pepper-and-garlic version.

More notably, Tara Thai offers the most extensive and interesting dessert selection of any Thai restaurant in town. Sure, oldies-but-goodies like mango sticky rice and mango sorbet are available, but so are a dish of coconut ice cream mixed with jackfruit and a sticky rice pudding studded with starchy taro root and fresh coconut.

At the Bethesda location, constant foot traffic means that an outdoor table, or even a table by the windows, offers close-up views of the local sidewalk culture. Tara Thai is a mainstay here, as elsewhere, and it does its job competently. But as food critics, we wish that some of these neighborhood Thai restaurants would actually dare to try serving authentic food. –CD

# Taste of Morocco

**8.0** Food · **5.0** Feel

At last, Moroccan food that's more spice than spectacle

## Moroccan

Casual restaurant · **$35** Price

www.atasteofmorocco.com

Sun–Fri 11:30am–2:30pm,
5pm–10pm
Sat 5pm–11pm

**Bar** Beer, wine
**Credit cards** Visa, MC, AmEx
**Reservations** Accepted
Kid-friendly, live music,
veg-friendly

**Arlington, VA**
3211 Washington Blvd.
(703) 527-7468

Don't confuse this Arlington restaurant with a better-known Moroccan joint with an identical name in SIlver Spring. And don't confuse it with the bigger and fancier Moroccan restaurants in the area. This Taste of Morocco is something smaller and subtler. Despite advertising weekly belly dancing, Taste of Morocco shirks common pretentions to focus on the food. With its small storefront and relatively staid décor, it feels more like a family-table place. The change of pace is welcome.

Food at Taste of Morocco is what you might expect from a nice, home-cooked meal. Potions are huge, and there are fewer bells and whistles than you would normally associate with restaurant food. Menu items are pretty traditional and generally well cooked. Standouts include an eggplant purée that is deeply smoky and a touch bitter—a dish that is much more intensely flavored than other versions. A couscous dish with mixed vegetables and meats is a treat: dense, dry merguez sausage is full of punchy spices and tastes almost cured, while the addition of winter melon to the vegetable mix adds a new texture to a familiar dish.

Bastilla, a kind of pie that combines sweet and salty flavors, is also excellent. The chicken filling is rich and dense, and ground almonds add an extra layer of flavor on top of the cinnamon and sugar. Once again, flavors here are more vibrant and concentrated than at other Moroccan restaurants. Every table even proffers tiny tagines full of spices: you can add cumin, cinnamon, turmeric, coriander, or salt and pepper to your heart's content—a welcome addition that celebrates how colorful North African cuisine can be.

At Taste of Morocco, it's not uncommon to be served by the owner himself—a man who is full of advice (to the point of being a tad pushy). Like a fussy parent who urges you to finish your plate and have seconds (shades of Italian mothers protesting "what, you don't like my cooking? See how skinny you're getting!"), he leaves you worrying that each leftover spoonful will be seen as an insult to the chef. In fact, he may get so carried away that he'll bring you extra dishes for free.

And just like in Mama's kitchen, you'll be reluctant to refuse. Taste of Morocco is the kind of restaurant that helps you grow up big and strong.
–JC

# Taverna the Greek Islands

**7.5** **6.8**

Food  Feel

Authentic whole fish in dull surroundings—bring
on the drunks and the raki!

## Greek

Casual restaurant  **$35**

Price

www.greekislandsgrill.com

Daily 11am–9:30pm

**Bar** Beer, wine, liquor
**Credit cards** Visa, MC, AmEx
**Reservations** Accepted
Delivery, live music, outdoor
dining, veg-friendly

**Silver Spring, MD**
15410 New Hampshire
Ave.
(301) 879-7600

You can't blame Taverna the Greek Islands (whose name we won't try to diagram gramatically) for failing on the count of authenticity. Down to the surly waitstaff and abundant rounds of bone-dry white bread, this place has almost every mark of the small tavernas and watering holes of the Greek isles.

Well, maybe a few things are missing. For one, even on a Friday night, the place is quiet as death. There are few empty tables, but all conversation occurs in a hushed whisper. Couldn't the owners import a few Greek drunks along with the phyllo dough and special feta? (Admittedly, during the summer months the patio fills up with another variety of rowdies.) And although the Taverna strives to replicate island menus, and does a fair job of it—offerings include octopus and taramosalata—there remain some gaps: no raki (a Greek apéritif), for example; and no fava purées, anchovies, or halva semolina cakes.

The Taverna's main courses and specials, however, truly shine. If it's available, try the whole fish main, an exquisite specimen that the kitchen cooks gently with herbs and leaves unadorned but for a touch of lemon and oil. A Greek salad has much more in common with its island counterparts than with the outsized mess of iceberg typically found in American Greek diners. Its sole shortcoming is also Washington's: we're simply not blessed with succulent tomatoes year-round. But the salad overcomes this handicap with fresh lettuce, boutique capers, full-bodied olive oil, and a unique and not-too-salty feta. The Taverna's vegetarian offerings go far beyond spanakopita. Try the melizanes imam bayildi, for example; it's eggplant stuffed with tomatoes and herbs and smothered in a mozzarella-like cheese.

The Taverna fills an important place in the area's Greek landscape. Although Zaytiyna's food may be better overall, Taverna does the most justice to the Greek island cuisine. –CK

# Tavira

Portuguese seafood shines in this hard-to-find find

| 7.9 | 7.7 |
|-----|-----|
| Food | Feel |

## Portuguese

Upmarket restaurant

**$60**
Price

www.tavirarestaurant.com

Mon–Thu 11:30am–2pm, 5:30pm–9pm; Fri 11:30am–2pm, 5:30pm–10pm; Sat 5:30pm–10pm; Sun 5pm–9pm

**Bar** Beer, wine, liquor
**Credit cards** Visa, MC, AmEx
**Reservations** Accepted
Date-friendly, delivery, live music

**Chevy Chase, MD**
8401 Connecticut Ave.
(301) 652-8684

Getting to Tavira can be quite a challenge. It seems as though it's trying for this Holy Grail status. *If you can find it, you can have it.* Head to the suburbs of Chevy Chase, and locate the seemingly random bank building with inconspicuous signage. Once you descend a spiral staircase to the basement and continue past a dermatologist's office, you are greeted by a charming subterranean restaurant. Portuguese-themed artwork adorns the walls of four cozy dining rooms in which the tables are set with elaborate china and faux-crystal glasses; in a move that is at once goofy and adorable, fake grapevines hang from the low ceiling. To avoid a cavernous feeling, the walls are painted in light colors and lighting is ample, without being the least bit glaring.

One of the many highlights of eating at Tavira is the exceptionally gregarious waitstaff, who marvel diners with their ability to recite the myriad nightly specials from memory (the brief regular menu is always supplemented by an endless list of varied specials). We definitely recommend paying close attention to this portion of the presentation; nightly specials make a meal at Tavira a memorable experience, not only because the specials are often the best dishes here, but because hearing your waiter say them is also quite a treat, especially if said waiter has a particularly thick and charming accent.

The best way to go is to share various plates among your fellow diners, sampling the fresh seafood, salads, and meats. When they have it, tender, barely cooked baby squid come delicately flavored with garlic and a healthy dose of olive oil. Incredibly fresh fried sardines are terrific, crunchy little bones and all. And the winner: a pan-seared red snapper with hearty sun-dried tomatoes. (The name of the dish might just be described to you with extra verve—and extra volume.)

None of these dishes will knock your socks off, but the briny, maritime food pairs especially well with the acidity of the Vinhos Verdes and Alvarinhos abundant on the wine list. The only real downer here are the desserts—we would much prefer an extra portion of earthy roasted red peppers stuffed with goat cheese and bathed in a sherry vinaigrette. We do insist on closing your meal with a glass of Port for the most complete and authentic experience. –SDC

# Teaism

The united nations of tea strut their stuff at this popular café

| 6.2 | 7.0 |
|-----|-----|
| Food | Feel |

## Pan-Asian

Café **$20**
*Price*

www.teaism.com

Mon–Thu 8am–10pm; Fri 8am–11pm; Sat 9am–11pm; Sun 9am–10pm
Hours vary by location

**Bar** None
**Credit cards** Visa, MC
Outdoor dining, veg-friendly

**Penn Quarter**
400 8th St. NW
(202) 638-6010

**Farragut**
800 Connecticut Ave. NW
(202) 835-3827

**Dupont**
2009 R St. NW
(202) 667-3827

Using the culture of tea as a point of departure, this café-cum-tea-shop two blocks north of Dupont Circle offers dishes from both the Eastern and Western worlds. A salmon bento box and palak paneer sit side-by-side on the chalkboard menu…kebabs, curries, and soups round out the options.

Amid this cosmopolitan bazaar of foods, it's the Asian-inspired dishes that speak our kind of language. "Thai chicken curry" features matchstick-sized pieces of bamboo, green beans, and chicken in a spiced yellow broth with a coconut base. It's not particularly spicy, but it feels healthful. The "Asian Gazpacho" resembles its Spanish counterpart, but adds a kick of sesame and soy. And a tea-cured salmon handroll ably demonstrates the virtues of steam. None of this fusion food really passes serious culinary muster, but somehow, when you're drinking warm, nourishing tea, all is forgiven.

Except, perhaps, for the sandwiches: although the whole-wheat bread is nicely nutty, the contraptions come pre-wrapped and somewhat dry, with limp ingredients. But the pinnacle of Teaism's culinary geography is the "Salty Oat Cookie"—a surprising take on oatmeal-raisin in which butter, salt, and the rich oat flavor dominate rather than the sweet raisins.

The other zenith of the Zen-ish locale is, of course, the tea. The small chain, which has two food locations in DC plus a shop (two doors down from the downtown location) dedicated entirely to tea and its accoutrements, sells several dozen black, green, oolong, herbal, and white varieties in two-ounce packages, about twenty of which are available by the pot to accompany a meal. Our favorite is the delicate, complex Silver Needle. There are refreshing cold options as well, including a not-too-sweet ginger limeade.

With its thoughtfully appointed interiors, Teaism could make a delightful stop for a meditative brew or a filling dessert; the Japanese décor adds to the relaxed and contemplative atmosphere. Beware, however, the mellow masses—if they're busy, you might get unceremoniously booted from your seat if you linger too long, which is an even more offensive move for a tea shop than for a normal restaurant. But on a cold DC weekday afternoon, a steaming cuppa with a nice cookie can make Teaism tea-cozy. –FC

# Teatro Goldoni

There's more tragedy than comedy at this confused high-end Italian restaurant

| 6.1 | 6.7 |
|-----|-----|
| Food | Feel |

## Italian

Upmarket restaurant

**$90**
Price

www.teatrogoldoni.com

Mon–Thu 11:30am–2:30pm, 5:30pm–10pm; Fri 11:30am–2:30pm, 5:30pm–11pm; Sat 5:30pm–11pm

**Bar** Beer, wine, liquor
**Credit cards** Visa, MC, AmEx
**Reservations** Accepted
Live music, outdoor dining, Wi-Fi

**Farragut**
1909 K St. NW
(202) 955-9494

Teatro Goldoni is a baffling restaurant. Even those who frequent the place often comment that they can't quite piece together what it's about. We love the warm orange glow, the interesting lamps, the playful Venetian carnival masks, and the five round banquettes. Yet the restaurant's odd business-district location throws the mood off somewhat; the bar tends to have a loud, fratty after-work feel that de-romanticizes the atmosphere, and the pleasant outdoor deck puts you in the path of hurried businesspeople hustling past.

Alas, the food at Teatro is just as confused as the atmosphere. Teatro's new star chef has vaulted the restaurant into DC's culinary firmament with his six-seat Chef's Table, where a meal of up to twenty courses (for the reasonable price of $125) is groundbreaking, sometimes molecular; it might begin with branzino smoked tableside in a cigar box, and close, in a playful echo, with a cigar-shaped dessert of lit spun sugar smoke.

But dine off the regular menu with the proletariat, and you'll have a very different meal. Focaccia with tomato paste evokes a pizza bagel, flaccid and cold with a cracked skin of tomato reminiscent of wounded flesh. Olive oil is wimpy and tasteless, the kind you'd only really consider for cooking. And some dishes just don't make much sense. Salad with shaved fennel, oranges, goat cheese and nuts has so many sweaty elements that the entire mass is soggy within minutes.

Pastas are generally homemade; their preparations range from glorious (a fishy, flashy display of black squid ink served with a luscious lobster ragù) to thoroughly uninspiring (cream sauce with barely visible flecks of pancetta). Worse still is a dry, unbalanced, chewy, underseasoned prosciutto-wrapped chicken breast that's perhaps the worst dish we've sampled in an Italian restaurant in the past year. The value is poorer still; although there's a cheaper bar menu, the dining-room à-la-carte options are unbelievably overpriced. The $32 price tag on a plate of risotto with gorgonzola, candied beets, and pistachios might give it the highest price-to-ingredient-cost ratio of any single dish in the city.

Teatro's service is even more inconsistent than the food. Depending on which waiter you get, you'll have either a perfectly refined, courteous meal, or one with which you'll have to hunt for menus and ask, repeatedly, for your food. Meanwhile, at the Chef's table, the lucky few are waited on by a whole cadre of staff, and doted on by the chef himself. He would do well to pay more attention to what's going on out in his dining room. –FC

# Teddy's Roti Shop

Roti, roti, roti...what more can we say?

**9.0** Food    **6.0** Feel

## Caribbean

Counter service    **$15** Price

www.teddysrotishop.com

Daily 9am–9pm

**Bar** None
**Credit cards** Visa, MC, AmEx
Wi-Fi

**Takoma Park, MD**
7304 Georgia Ave. NW
(202) 882-6488

When you like roti—that griddled flatbread of unequalled richness, served with potato curry—it can become a craving.

We admit to being sufferers. It seems to be universally acknowledged, within the West Indian community of DC and the suburbs, that this Trinidadian place up Georgia Avenue makes the best roti around—and we wholeheartedly agree.

Certainly Teddy's is a plain-walled dive, but would you expect to get good roti anywhere else? And certainly the service is brusque; fail to finish your food, and you might get yelled at—but lovingly. The other roadblock is that the place keeps moving around, from the District to Silver Spring and back. The latest location is a block north of Walter Reed Hospital, but you should call first to make sure they haven't moved again since press time.

When you do find Teddy's, you'll quickly discover that the roti, delicious though it is, is merely a platform for a sensational array of rich, protein-based gravies: deeply aromatic goat curry, tender bone-in chicken curry, and oxtail stew. Some in the West Indian community complain that the prices have gotten out of hand—$12 for a platter—but by downtown DC standards, to get this level of flavor and careful execution at that price is a steal. That's doubly true given that each meal includes several side dishes like callaloo (a Caribbean leafy green), rice and peas (the Caribbean version of rice and red beans), macaroni pie, and so on.

The salad is rather sorry, but otherwise, the wonders here seem endless: house-made pineapple juice. Curried conch, bull joll (salt cod), and coconut bake (fried shark fillet in a coconut bun). On Saturdays, there's cow heel soup. Don't miss dhalpourie, a thin, yellow-split-pea-filled pancake, or the classic buss up shut (a derivation of "burst-up shirt"—the idea is that the bread looks like torn fabric). Teddy—the namesake, original partner, and brother of the owner—is back in Trinidad, but we have no doubt that he'd be proud of what's going on here. –RG

# TenPenh

Nudging your brain towards something beyond
the norm

| 7.4 | 8.4 |
|-----|-----|
| Food | Feel |

## Pan-Asian

Upmarket restaurant

**$70**
Price

www.tenpenh.com

Mon–Thu 11:30am–2:30pm,
5:30pm–10:30pm; Fri
11:30am–2:30pm, 5:30pm–
11pm; Sat 5:30pm–11pm

**Bar** Beer, wine, liquor
**Credit cards** Visa, MC, AmEx
**Reservations** Accepted
Date-friendly, outdoor dining,
veg-friendly, Wi-Fi

**Downtown**
1001 Pennsylvania Ave. NW
(202) 393-4500

In a downtown dining district that is best characterized by a propensity for expense-account lunches, TenPenh is a cornerstone of the professionals' meal circuit. And in a manner fitting to its clientele and its reputation, the restaurant is impeccable. From its sleek design to its accommodating and efficient service, TenPenh exceeds expectations and outclasses many of its competitors.

The most deserving thing about TenPenh is the remarkable thoughtfulness with which it has combined East and West. While other attempts have relied on cliché or novelty, TenPenh's fusion is principled and considerate—even down to the décor. The bar solidifies Zen minimalism, with broad, bold stokes and geometric weight, while the high-backed seats of the dining room evoke carved imperial chairs without being hokey. Artifacts like T'ang horses and paper lanterns are chosen with an editorial mind. Even the embroidered coats and mandarin collars of the waiters are fitting.

The same thoughtfulness is often reflected in the food. Little details belie a deep understanding of the spirit of the dish. For example, seared tuna served over a bed of rice studded with peanuts is deeply reminiscent of the bowls of congee eaten for breakfast in Asian households around the world, and cilantro sauce adds an unexpected but welcome dimension (and an acidic bite) to the dish. Desserts also tickle the memory. Coconut panna cotta mirrors the milky almond jelly served atop shaved ice in the summer. Blondies are made exotic by cardamom and the throaty zing of lemon zest.

On the other hand, traditional dishes are less exciting. Lettuce wraps, though competently crunchy and moist, are too salty, with gristly chicken. Lumpia are oily and boring—and a little disappointing. If you're expecting the meatier and more substantial Philippine version, don't hold your breath. What you'll get are three substandard spring rolls that you could get at any mediocre Chinese dive, saved only by a delicate sauce that features a dark, woody, and deeply astringent Chinese black vinegar.

Despite some flops, TenPenh is a pleasant dining experience with shining moments of insight and creativity. In a business where wasabi is thrown into anything that moves, it's refreshing to find a fusion restaurant that mixes cultures with the wit and attention of someone who actually knows them, instead of with reckless abandon. An innovative dish that nudges you into the recognition of something familiar is hard to pull of, and worth quite a lot. –JC

# Thai Chef

Another sad casualty of the ridiculous add-a-sushi-bar trend

**5.6** Food

**7.4** Feel

## Thai, Japanese

Casual restaurant

**$40** Price

www.thaichefsushibardc.com

Mon–Thu 11:30am–10:30pm
Fri 11:30am–11pm
Sat noon–11pm
Sun noon–10:30pm

**Bar** Beer, wine, liquor
**Credit cards** Visa, MC, AmEx
**Reservations** Accepted
Delivery

**Dupont**
1712 Connecticut Ave. NW
(202) 234-5698

We're not sure there's a single "Chef" behind this fusion operation just north of Dupont Circle; in fact, the hybrid sushi-Thai menu leads us to suspect the name's a generalized concept, rather than a placeholder for a single chef's name (perhaps inserted to ease the pronunciation path of the restaurant's somewhat-intoxicated American clientele). But it certainly appears that there are multiple cooks spoiling the broth at Thai Chef.

While some dishes get spicing spot-on, others taste like bland versions of the real thing. Not surprisingly, Thai food is the Chef's main attraction: in fact, the sushi chefs seem to be asleep at the wheel. This restaurant got on the disastrous add-a-sushi-bar bandwagon in 2003, right around the time a lot of other mediocre Chinese or pan-Asian places did. The results should offend anyone who's serious about sushi. You can do much better than the dry cuts of salmon and tuna inhabiting the sashimi platter, and although the menu proposes some creatively or even disturbingly named maki options (a "Pearl Harbor roll," anyone?), you can find the same creativity along with better quality elsewhere.

On the Thai front, however, the restaurant is better than many places in the Dupont Circle area, anyway. While still far from authentic, the curries have more character than the Coconut Soup Avec Boiled Veggies that passes for curry at some of the Thai chains peppered along Connecticut Avenue and throughout downtown. Even here, though, the chicken dishes can be bland, bland, bland, and asking for "extra spicy" curry has little effect. This place is catering to the lowest common denominator of spice tolerance.

Larb gai, a cold salad with minced chicken, boasts a nice use of red pepper and the authentic flavor of kaffir lime leaves, and the result is spicy and fresh. "Thai Chef dumplings," on the other hand, are a rather standard affair: the little suckers are too doughy, and filled with uninteresting meat to boot; the resulting texture unnervingly evokes greasy banana chunks.

We were happy to see the crispy whole fish offered on the menu, and while the result is decent, the sauce is too sweet and the preparation pedestrian; it's not really worth its "market price." In the end, this Chef demands discipline and focus: the menu's too large of a minefield to allow for reckless ordering. Tread carefully here. –FC

# Thai Market

Dig deep, and you'll find some delicious gems

**8.3** Food  **6.0** Feel

## Thai

Counter service

**$20** Price

Mon–Sat 9:30am–7:30pm
Sun 9:30am–6:30pm

**Bar** None
**Credit cards** Visa, MC
Veg-friendly

**Silver Spring, MD**
902 Thayer Ave.
(301) 495-8936

There are several barriers to enjoying the authentic Thai cuisine at this hidden Silver Spring gem.

The first barrier is just finding and noticing the place. The name seems to be simply "Thai Food," and it's part of what just looks like an Asian grocery store on a side street just off downtown Silver Spring's main drag. Wander around the store—which is attached to the plain, white-walled, slightly grungy dining room—and you'll immediately realize that you're in no ordinary pan-Asian grocery. Nearly everything on the shelves comes directly from Thailand. There are dozens of varieties of Thai coconut milk and cream, fresh galangal, and Thai basil. The place functions like a community center; in the back, there's even a Thai video library. Any place that rents videos in Thai must make authentic food, right?

The second barrier to dining, however—and this is all too common with authentic Asian—is ordering. It's not that there's no menu, or that the staff isn't friendly; there is one, and they are. It's that the menu is studded with things you don't want: Chinese-American atrocities like sliced chicken breast with cashews and onions in brown sauce, or shrimp fried rice; and Thai-American atrocities like chicken-and-noodle soup, deep-fried spring rolls, and vegetarian pad Thai.

That said, you will find *some* of what you want on the menu: som tam poo, for instance—to our knowledge, this is the only place in greater DC where you can get the lesser-known version of som tam, found mostly in Laos or the very northern edge of Thailand; it's made with crushed crab shells instead of dried shrimp. There's gaeng pa moo (country-style curry with ground pork, bamboo shoots, and vegetables), and a version of tom yum goong (sour lemongrass soup) that actually employs kaffir lime leaves, as few in the area do.

But most of what you want isn't on the menu. Behind the scenes, there's larb moo, the delicious minced-pork salad with red onion, salad, fish sauce, and lime (only the chicken version makes an appearance in print). There are slices of grilled pork, wonderfully marinated, kissed by charcoal, dosed with chili, fish sauce, lime, palm sugar. There's a whole steamed fish (it takes 20 minutes) for $7.75, served with a searingly delicious sour curry, that's nowhere to be found on the list. Yet you'll see the local Thais carrying them out routinely (most people carry out). Sometimes infiltrating the squeamish-farang-diner-generated gauze of purposeful inauthenticity can yield tremendous dividends. –RG

# Thai Roma

It takes skill to get a truly good meal here

**4.0** Food | **4.6** Feel

## Thai

Casual restaurant | **$35** Price

www.thairomarestaurant.com

Daily 11:45am–10pm

**Bar** Beer, wine, liquor
**Credit cards** Visa, MC, AmEx
**Reservations** Accepted
Delivery, outdoor dining,
veg-friendly, Wi-Fi

**Capitol Hill**
313 Pennsylvania Ave. SE
(202) 544-2338

It might not come as a surprise, given the unappetizing name of the place (one imagines penne Thai), that Thai Roma is eminently mediocre. The restaurant, located on a strip of Pennsylvania a few blocks from the Capitol, is—appropriately—a ghost town at Sunday dinnertime, when both the lunching Hill staffers and the Friday-Saturday-dining Hill residents have other places to be. What is surprising, however, is that the place is so popular on weekdays. Chalk it up to a limited selection of sit-down lunch options close to House offices, or to a generalized Thai food disorder in DC. Whatever the explanation, Thai Roma's popularity is outsized compared to the hit-or-miss quality of the food.

And there's plenty of hitting and missing to be done: the restaurant's menu is dizzyingly long, even when compared to the menus of other Thai places. At more than four pages, Thai Roma's list is exhaustive or at the very least exhausting. Many dishes are simply minor variations on ones listed elsewhere.

Also exhausting is Thai Roma's décor. The interior feels overly dark, even on a sunny day, and is cluttered with wood paneling, house plants, and posters of Southeast Asian landscapes. In the back of the restaurant is a seemingly unaffiliated bar, replete with neon tubing and graying men (exiled scandal scapegoats, perhaps) getting drunk alone. If the weather permits, you're much better off outside; Thai Roma has annexed a nice patch of Pennsylvania sidewalk with tables and umbrellas.

Unfortunately, there's precious little to enjoy in their shade. Spring rolls are pedestrian, curries are weak, and the beer and wine list is pitiful. A few small points of light include shrimp hot pot, which includes plenty of spicy broth, and a sample of delicate, glassy rice noodles to accompany the shrimp. The dish is a little cabbage-heavy, but the vegetable blends nicely with the other flavors. Thai Roma also does a good job of adding chili to its dishes. Vegetarian mains, especially, benefit from this proclivity, and there is nothing bland about the pak raum: a mix of fresh vegetables is sautéed in hot chili oil, with plenty of garlic.

But ultimately, the menu is a minefield. With so many options, picking dishes can become an exercise in negotiation—perfect, perhaps, for Hill staffers. –CK

# Thai Square

Join the native Thai crowd to enjoy this fiery, diverse, sometimes authentic menu

**7.5** Food

**4.5** Feel

## Thai

Casual restaurant

**$35** Price

www.thaisquarerestaurant.com

Mon–Thu 11:30am–10:30pm
Fri 11:30am–11pm
Sat noon–11pm
Sun noon–10:30pm

**Bar** Beer, wine
**Credit cards** Visa, MC, AmEx
**Reservations** Accepted
Delivery

**Arlington, VA**
3217 Columbia Pike
(703) 685-7040

These days it's all too easy to find mediocre Thai-Chinese-American food in the kind of restaurant that serves sugared versions of pad Thai and peanut-sauced satay to the timid and gullible. Those kinds of things certainly have their place (drunk, starving), but Thai Square is one of the few places around DC that goes beyond that level.

That's not to say it's not also playing a secondary role as a bad Chinese-American restaurant, like almost every Thai place in the greater DC area seems to feel the need to do; as such, Thai Square's menu includes steamed dumplings with soy sauce, pork fried rice, chicken with garlic sauce, beef with broccoli, shrimp with baby corn, and "sweet and sour assorted seafood."

But if you navigate your way around such wastes of calories, you can have a good meal here, beginning with a fragrant, herby pig's knuckle stew. Pad ped pla dook (catfish sautéed with chili and Thai eggplant) is spicy and complex, as is the crispy whole flounder in a pork-and-ginger sauce whose balance far outstrips the standard sweet-chili sugar-fest that's overrepresented in Thai-American fried-fish dishes. The green chilies dotting a dish of crispy squid with basil add a refreshing dose of heat. Spicy roast-duck salad, nam sod (minced-pork and pork-skin salad), and yum pla krob (a limey salad of shredded tilefish) are unusually authentic options, as is the simple kai yang (grilled, marinated half-chicken with sticky rice). We encourage you to ask for everything "Thai hot," but you must do so at your own risk—the natives of that country tend to have palates of steel.

Some other dishes aren't exactly authentic Thai, but they're not the standard Thai-American or Chinese, either; hot-pot dishes, noodle soup with fish ball and minced pork, and salt fish sautéed with Chinese broccoli evoke, you might say, the sort of more authentic Chinese food you'd expect to find in Thailand, which does have a significant Chinese immigrant population (including a major Chinatown in Bangkok).

Don't be distracted by the somewhat dingy surroundings, highlighted rather than camouflaged by the fading tourism posters on the walls. The atmosphere here is familial and friendly, and the homey feel is bolstered by the low prices. Nothing on the menu is more than $14, and generous portions are amenable to our preferred strategy of delving into the unfamiliar, sharing among our friends, and taking home the leftovers.

So while we're not claiming that little-known restaurants without the trappings of fine dining are *always* better and more authentic, in this case the faded awning and clattering interior just happen to be reliable indicators. –FC

# Thai Tanic

Fresh, accessible Thai food that doesn't give you that sinking feeling

| 6.8 | 6.4 |
|-----|-----|
| Food | Feel |

## Thai

Casual restaurant

**$30**
Price

www.thaitanicrestaurant.webs.com

Mon–Thu 11am–10pm
Fri 11am–11pm
Sat noon–11pm
Sun noon–10pm

**Bar** Beer, wine, liquor
**Credit cards** Visa, MC, AmEx
**Reservations** Accepted
Delivery, kid-friendly, veg-friendly

**Logan Circle**
1326 14th St. NW
(202) 588-1795

Walking down 14th street looking for Thai Tanic, you will probably think that it is impossible that a decent restaurant is to be found on that block. Or, for that matter, with that name.

And then you arrive at a clean, bright, and cheerful Thai-American restaurant that brims with a veritable crowd of Logan Circle inhabitants. The dining room is playful, with sparkly red chairs, plenty of light, and shiny tables. There's also a plasma TV front and center which can be distracting if you're with a group of people who expect you to be more interested in their conversation than in the home improvement show. Then again, if you're dining alone, you might end up with a newly lacquered bureau along with your standard array of Americanized curry gravies.

Although some people go to Thai restaurants craving the same few dishes every time, Thai Tanic offers enough variation that it's quite possible to venture into other waters. Som tam (green papaya salad) is made with dried shrimp, as it should be but too often isn't, and soups employ real kaffir lime and galangal. A delightful panko-crusted fillet of salmon, for example, is crisp yet not greasy, hot and smoky, and its yellow curry is coconutty and good—if nothing new. The abundant vegetables tend to be just cooked through, which is good for most of the vegetables, but too harsh in the case of the pearl onions. Spicy Japanese eggplant, another favorite, has basil leaves and a hot chili garlic sauce, although its bell peppers are useless (as bell peppers almost always are in curries). We like the whole steamed rockfish with garlic, chili, and lime juice, but the choose-your-meat curries are boring. Where the innovation strays further from the Thai-American spirit, the results are more foreboding. The "shrimp in a blanket" appetizer is simply too greasy, and seems heavy enough to take down, say, a large ocean liner. The heart, so they say, will go on, but eat enough of these, and we're not so sure. Stick with the brighter options. In season, Thai Tanic offers soft-shell crab, and it's beautifully fried.

Fresh ingredients, elegant presentation, and precise execution offer a welcome change from some of DC's more mundane Thai options, even if, like everyone else, they just can't stay away from the bell peppers. Now if only we could do something about that blasted movie. –SDC

# Thai X-ing

Conversation, curries, and curiosities intrigue you
at this one-of-a-kind Thai venue

| 8.3 | 8.0 |
|-----|-----|
| Food | Feel |

## Thai

Casual restaurant **$30**

*Price*

www.thaix-ing.com

Tue–Sun 4pm–10pm

**Bar** None
**Credit cards** Visa, MC
**Reservations** Accepted
Outdoor dining, Wi-Fi

**Shaw**
515 Florida Ave. NW
(202) 332-4322

If you're looking for Washington's quirkiest restaurant, here you have it. Housed in the basement of a large creaking townhouse in Shaw, Thai X-ing is a one-man operation run by the singular Taw Vigsittaboot, who can be heard in the kitchen and found, eventually, attired in a sleeveless athletic shirt, a rolled and faded bandana, stained apron, and ponytail.

Outside the house, a hand-painted wooden sign bearing the name "Thai X-ing" is the only indication you've arrived, and enormous potted plants nearly obstruct entry to the tiny sitting-room-cum-kitchen. The inside is crammed with large books, hanging plants, and a birdcage. There are a few piles of rumpled carry-out menus, a tapestry thrown on a decomposing armchair, three wood chairs and a small table, on top of which sits a mango that's a few days past ripe.

Even on a slow night, Thai X-ing's service is, well, painfully slow. A half-hour wait is several standard deviations from a mean around fifty minutes. However, rumor has it that on occasion, after several successive half-hour estimates, Taw has informed a famished, furious take-out customer (most people get take-out; there's only one table with four chairs) that his order would have to wait until morning. We give you fair warning. If you're eating in house, the larb gai appetizer is a serviceable (if unspectacular) way to pass the time, plenty spicy, and prepared with generous lime and cilantro. While you eat, observe as your cook fields bottles of sauce, chopped veggies, spices, and oil with frenetic but confident grace.

Even with extreme commotion as a proxy for progress, you may begin to doubt that your meal will ever arrive. Luckily, the X-ing's curries are restorative. The "Udon Pork" is a fragrant red curry livened by small sweet tomatoes and whole young peppercorns; the pepper brings the soft rich pork to life. Also excellent are the pork ribs in Thai-basil-filled green curry, which, if ordered spicy, comes spicier than you're liable to taste within a radius of a couple hundred miles. The menu isn't particularly authentic (there's fried rice, veggie pad Thai, and such), but the curries are better executed than they are almost anywhere else, employing kaffir lime leaves and plenty of chili.

While you're eating, the clatter in the kitchen continues, punctuated, perhaps, by very loud classical music from a rusty stereo. One of the best parts of the meal? No matter how late it is, you're never under pressure to depart (and if he's finished cleaning, Taw will sit for a brief chat). That alone, we'd venture, is well worth the wait. –CK

# Thaiphoon

Psychadelic Thai that's nothing special

| 5.9 | 6.8 |
|-----|-----|
| Food | Feel |

## Thai

Casual restaurant

**$40**
Price

www.thaiphoon.com

Sun–Thu 11:30am–10:30pm
Fri–Sat 11:30am–11pm

**Bar** Beer, wine, liquor
**Credit cards** Visa, MC, AmEx
**Reservations** Accepted

**Dupont**
2011 S St. NW
(202) 667-3505

**Arlington, VA**
1301 S. Joyce St.
(703) 413-8200

Walking into Thaiphoon is a shock, although it's a shock you may have anticipated given the restaurant's name. You're first greeted by a swirl of green and turquoise and a topsy-turvy bar lit up by neon cords in ocean tones. Walk further into the dining room, and you'll begin to feel as if you're inside a Disney version of a tropical storm, with swirling waves along the walls, slanted tops to booth benches, and glittering tables embossed with shiny aquamarine plastic.

Color scheme notwithstanding, the "Thai" remains in the title to alert you to the kind of cuisine you're about to consume, lest you've forgotten in the midst of all the visual stimulus. And some of the culinary cues are as in-your-face as the décor. Lemongrass, for instance, dominates in many dishes, and wedges of lime are so omnipresent as to risk clashing with the light green tables.

Basically, Thaiphoon is your typical mid-sized-city Thai-American joint, with healthy if subdued fare, catchy décor and exciting mixed drinks, and a witty name to boot. At times, the restaurant even waxes American on the Thai-American spectrum, with such offerings (under "daily specials") as fried calamari. These rings are outsized monsters, much bigger than the typical 1-inch rings in greasy seafood places, and sealed in a smooth coating, instead of the more crumbly breading that sometimes covers calamari. The rings remain tasteless and oily, qualities which the sweet and sour dipping sauce (an attempted nod East, but an overly sweet one—like too much at this restaurant) does little to remedy.

Other appetizers are more successful: steamed dumplings, for example, are doughy little beasts, replete with ground, spicy pork, and crabmeat, and served with a generic light brown sauce. Thaiphoon soup is, again, filled to the brim with lemongrass, as well as with a rather ordinary (and likely once-frozen) medley of seafood. The pad pik khing is made with unusually crisp green beans, but the chicken in the dish is ordinary.

At Thaiphoon, your eyes will feast, even as your mouth and stomach find themselves deprived. –CK

# Thanh Tong

The best bun bo hue in the Eden Center, which is
like saying "in this whole book"

| **9.0** | **4.5** |
|---|---|
| Food | Feel |

## Vietnamese

Casual restaurant

**$15**
Price

Daily 9am–9pm

**Bar** None
**Credit cards** None
**Reservations** Not accepted

**Falls Church, VA**
6795 Wilson Blvd.
(703) 532-1476

Vietnamese food lovers, rejoice! The Eden Center is a bazaar paradise of
All Things Vietnamese, from shops to bakeries to restaurants. If you mean
to make your way through every eatery in this plaza, you'll have your
month pretty well booked up. Where to start? Thanh Trong is a safe bet.
This simple, bright, exceedingly popular hole-in-the-mall epitomizes
what's great about Eden Center: it's cheap, it's straightforward, and its
kitchen peddles some of the most authentic Vietnamese food in America.

We especially like bun bo hue, the classic beef noodle soup, whose
show-stopping broth displays unusual richness and depth of spice. Plenty
of fresh greens are served on the side for you to add in. Though bun bo
hue is the runaway winner here, rice soups are good, too, as are banh,
especially banh hoi thit nuong. It's the textural heaven banh should be,
from the baguette's easy brittleness, to its warm fluffines, then the crunch
of pickled vegetables and creamy spread. Green papaya salad is also a
fresh, tart treat. Such unusual specialties as hen xuc banh da show up as
well. That dish is described somewhat enigmatically on the menu as
"baby clams sheet" (we assume it's referring to the traditional rice
crackers meant for scooping). And then there's a salad of duck and
bamboo shoots, which is also a real crowd-pleaser.

Thanh Trong does set the bar kind of high, but this whole plaza is
perfect for venturing around and mining your favorites. Perhaps that's the
subject for another book: Fearless Critic Eden Center. –RG

# Thomas Sweet

A sweetly deceitful Ivy League rivalry smooshed into a scoop of premium ice cream

## Ice cream                                         Counter service

www.thomassweet.com

| | | |
|---|---|---|
| Mon–Sat 10am–midnight | **Bar** None | **Georgetown** |
| Sun 10am–11pm | **Credit cards** None | 3214 P St. NW |
| | **Reservations** Not accepted | (202) 337-0616 |
| | Kid-friendly, veg-friendly | |

According to the Thomas Sweet web site, the "Blend-In®" was invented in 1980, in Princeton, New Jersey, when fudgemakers Tom Grim and Tom Block founded their first ice cream shop. Apparently, Harold, Tom Grim's father, "found a mechanical contraption in upstate New York in someone's barn." Then, Tom "came back with it, fiddled with it, and the Blend-In® was born."

At least, that's what they've led generations of Princeton students to believe. The problem is, the concept was actually invented seven years earlier, in Somerville, MA, by a man named Steve Herrell, who named it the "smoosh-in." He still runs a few modest Herrell's ice cream shops around the state, including one in Northampton, where he now lives; and a shop in Harvard Square that has been fanatically patronized by generations of students. Some of Herrell's many copycats have graciously acknowledged his influence, like Amy's Ice Cream of Austin, Texas ("Crush'ns," 1984). Others have taken the Sweet route and trademarked their own names for the borrowed idea, including Dairy Queen (the "Blizzard®," 1985) and Cold Stone Creamery ("Creations™," 1988).

In 2002, the *New York Times* wrangled the real story from the Thomases: "Tom Block...can't help reminiscing about the weeks in the winter of 1980 when he traveled to Massachusetts to learn the ice cream trade at the feet of one of its masters, Steve Herrell...who was then something of a cult figure among ice cream aficionados. 'Everybody wanted to know Steve's secret,' Mr. Block said. 'They all loved him up at Harvard.'"

Fudgemakers, indeed.

The DC outpost of Thomas Sweet plays host to tired Georgetown shoppers, students, and people who have accidentally wandered too far and been lured in by the intoxicating smells. The space is a bit dumpy, but not necessarily in a bad way. Cases of fudge jockey for space with tubs of ice cream and piles of candy, and little troughs of toppings form a mosaic in the counter. In summer, the humming freezers, chalkboard-scrawled menus, and bare plastic furniture evoke a beachside town; in winter, all of this feels more bare and less charming.

Sweet's ice cream isn't bad; it's frothier and lighter than some of the premium competition. In a way, it's like soft serve without the beloved swirl. Flavors range from the traditional (chocolate, vanilla, strawberry) to the mildly playful (cake batter, sweet cream, tiramisù). Cookies and cream is a lovely choice, with a texture that is integrated and luxuriant. And, of course, there's the Blend-In® option. All rights reserved. –RG

# To Sok Jip

**8.5** Food **8.7** Feel

Huge portions of nourishing, authentic Korean food are totally worth the wait

## Korean

Casual restaurant **$15** Price

Daily 10:30am–10:30pm

**Bar** Beer
**Credit cards** Visa, MC, AmEx
**Reservations** Not accepted
Veg-friendly

**Annandale, VA**
7211 Columbia Pike
(703) 333-2861

The law of supply and demand tells us that if 1) a place is making terrific, authentic Korean food in an area that has very little of that, and 2) there are only about 10 tables, then it follows that there will be a wait time. Bring a book or a friend to talk to and get right with your patience—you won't be sorry. Squeezed between Cha Hair Salon and Fairfax Auto Parts is this tiny, sparse and, yes, very crowded little gem. (Claustrophobes and basketball players: be forewarned, the ceiling is low clearance.) A couple of efficient waitresses scuttle between tables and help keep turnover high enough so as not to lose any waiting customers who need to get back to the office. This is *not* the time for you to get out your list of dietary restrictions, and you'd better know what you want when you sit down, but that won't be hard, as anything you choose will be delicious.

The menu is pretty typical. And by "menu" we mean a collection of scribbled specials and dishes on chalkboards and paper signs. In Korean. May we make some suggestions?

You're going to fill up fast, between the generous portions and the swarm of free banchan dishes that accompany them. Kimchi (in all of its forms) is excellent here, as are ge jaang (addictive marinated, raw crab) and spicy winter melon. Koreans, along with Mexicans, have the market cornered on nourishing food. It's all the tripe and bones, you know. Starving? Steamed pork hocks, tosok jokbal, are a rich indulgence that have that smoky-sweet pork flavor with beads of savory fat. Hungover? Try hae jang guk (it even translates roughly to "hangover soup"), whose spicy broth will help you sweat out the booze while getting nutrient-rich marrow molecules in you. In a mood for seafood? The seafood pancake is right on, as are the fish specials. You can trust it—the wait time suggests it's made to order.

The common wisdom goes, you know an ethnic joint is a good bet if lots of natives eat there. Well, what does it say when we've noticed more white people here than you'd expect, given the neighborhood? History says "manifest destiny," but here's hoping To Sok Jip doesn't change or expand much. There's just the right amount of mojo going on. –RG

# The Tombs

The best four years of your life lie buried in this bar; perhaps you should let them rest

| 4.6 | 8.5 |
|------|------|
| Food | Feel |

## American

Bar **$25**
Price

www.tombs.com

| | | |
|---|---|---|
| Mon–Thu 11:30am–1:15am | **Bar** Beer, wine, liquor | **Georgetown** |
| Fri 11:30am–2:15am | **Credit cards** Visa, MC, AmEx | 1226 36th St. NW |
| Sat 11am–2:15am | **Reservations** Not accepted | (202) 337-6668 |
| Sun 9:30am–1:15am | Date-friendly, live music, Wi-Fi | |

When Georgetown students talk about their "dive bar" they almost always mean The Tombs. That said, it's hard to see what is so divey about the place. Maybe it's the prison reference in the name, or that the bar is underground. Maybe it's merely in comparison to the prices and pomposity of its upstairs neighbor, 1789. But once you walk under the macabre name over the door, you'll likely be a tad confused, especially since the bar's inside is a cramped homage to the gentlemanly sport of rowing. The walls are festooned with oars, prints, photos, and paintings of strapping young lads in skinny boats.

The bar's menu closely resembles that of its parent company, Clyde's, from which the Tombs has imported a good many dishes and and the greater part of a cocktail list (including a disturbing penchant for using half-and-half in mixed drinks). But while Clyde's reaches for more upscale cuisine, The Tombs focuses on those hearty and not-so-healthy dishes that will bring you back to your collegial days of dining out: food best enjoyed in the throes of booze, study, and youth. It is nostalgically underwhelming.

Take for example, the well-recommended crab dip. It tastes heavily of cream cheese and lightly of crab, and it oozes over with stringy, bubbly-burnt cheese. Floating chunks of artichoke and little pieces of vegetables say "Super Bowl" more than "out to dinner" and the overall effect makes you want a beer, which is probably its intent. Beer there is: a decent classy-for-college selection in frosted mugs that become less frosted and more sloshily served as the evening progresses.

The fancier the dish, the worse the effect. While the burgers and giant brownie sundaes are fine, and the Southwest Chicken salad is barely passable (think piles of iceberg, not-so-fresh salsa, and chicken on a big round of flatbread), some of the heftier mains are out-and-out mistakes. "Tombs Gumbo" does the name no honor: it is a mess of soupy gray-brown that's light on both spice and flavor. The satisfying pop of skin off andouille sausage is ruined by the blandness of the meat inside. Tiny shrimp in the stew are so overcooked that they have the consistency of paper pulp.

We have fun here, but if you plan on eating, there are better places in the city to relive your college years. If you do decide to pay The Tombs a visit, we recommend that you eat as the students do, and try your best to adopt their standards. –JC

# Tono Sushi

The fish flops too often—and we don't mean
freshness—at this popular spot

| **5.7** | **6.5** |
|---------|---------|
| Food | Feel |

## Japanese

Casual restaurant

**$40**
Price

www.tonosushi.com

Mon–Thu 11:30am–10:30pm
Fri–Sat 11am–11pm
Sun 11am–10pm

**Bar** Beer, wine
**Credit cards** Visa, MC, AmEx
**Reservations** Accepted
Delivery, outdoor dining

**Woodley Park**
2605 Connecticut Ave. NW
(202) 332-7300

Tono does a good job of catering to its audience. Unfortunately, on any given night, much of the audience in question is usually fanning out from a convention at the behemoth Hilton across the street, or trickling down Connecticut after touring the National Zoo. It tends to be a very hungry, often indiscriminate audience (with the wisdom to pick the cute sushi place over the Hilton vending machine, at least), and Tono does an excellent job of feeding it quickly and efficiently.

But Tono's food is hardly excellent. After water (which is refilled religiously) and drinks (which arrive quickly) are served, the first thing to hit the table is a set of small bowls of watery, wilted bean sprouts in sesame oil. Even if the salt nicely whets your appetite for beer, the sprouts are distinctly unappetizing, and no sooner have they arrived than you begin to really wish they'd go away.

Luckily, they do. In fact, everything at Tono comes and goes quickly, if not so quickly that you ever feel rushed (the check, for example, doesn't come automatically, but rather only when requested). The service is efficient and neat, and servers are responsive to questions and last minute changes.

Before 7:30pm, a happy hour special pegs most nigiri at a buck a pop; maki are not much more lest you get excited (keep in mind that bargain sushi is rarely an actual bargain). Although the restaurant is sometimes out of sea urchin (better than keeping it around, we suppose) and some other fishes, the specials board announces daily features. Mackerel has been brinily irresistible, but the same can't be said for the tuna, which comes in paltry, tasteless slices. A dragon roll is thin and low on eel. It's worth trying some non-sushi offerings, though, such as the homemade, doughy gyoza, which are nicely fried to a sweet golden brown.

If it's summer, you're likely to be consuming your meal on Tono's lovely patio, which is adorned with wooden trellises and hanging plants. At the end of your meal, you're given a comment card along with the check (the former elicits your impressions; the latter, alas, is non-negotiable). Our notes? "Nice place, spotty fish." –CK

# Tony & Joe's Seafood Place

**3.9** Food    **8.5** Feel

An old-school seafood joint that's faded far over the years

## Seafood

Upmarket restaurant    **$55** Price

www.dcseafood.com

Sun–Thu 11am–10pm
Fri–Sat 11am–midnight

**Bar** Beer, wine, liquor
**Credit cards** Visa, MC, AmEx
**Reservations** Accepted
Date-friendly, kid-friendly, live music, outdoor dining

**Georgetown**
3000 K St. NW
(202) 944-4545

Stepping into Tony and Joe's on the Georgetown's waterfront is like taking a step back in time. It's a place that is swanky by a definition, a place that came of age several decades ago, and has since aged, and aged, and aged...and possibly died. There's a nostalgic, nautical theme to it all; from the blue striped iron rings on cream smokestack columns strategically placed about the restaurant to the stubborn adherence to a set color scheme, the décor screams "cruise ship"—but in a fading, Tom Jones kind of way. The swank coefficient goes down considerably in the outdoor part of the restaurant, where a slightly stale beer, plastic cup, frat-boy vibe can sometimes take over. Still, this is the restaurant's most compelling feature—with sweeping Potomac views, it's like a summer vacation just steps from M Street.

The ship is old, but it's still got its dignity. They do take care with the little things. Bread baskets teem with hot corn muffins that are sweet and moist and water glasses never go below half full.

But the generically American food falls flat on its face. In what has almost become a culinary cliche, tuna tartare serves faithfully as the token "Asian" element on the menu. The roughly diced tuna is drizzled with creamy chili-lime sauce that's light enough, and a plum sauce that's artificially sweet. Texturally, the tartare is a bit too mushy, especially when eaten with big chunks of avocado.

Things get much worse when you progress to the fish mains. Petrified salmon or tuna cooked to a sad shade of gray might come next to hospital-food steamed vegetables and potatoes. If the fish were fresh it would be impossible to tell.

Sandwiches are much better, and almost too big to eat: mammoth rolls of bread might be layered with cornmeal-battered oysters, for instance, and then cross-hatched with thick strips of bacon. The bread-to-meat ratio is too high, but picked apart, the inside of the sandwich is fattily delicious. Mounds of fries are crisp, golden, and lightly seasoned with Old Bay, and cole slaw is tangy and invigoratingly cool.

Tony and Joe's is a throwback to an older, tamer, and...yes, worse...kind of seafood restaurant. But those views are fun, and hey, some people like steamed veggies and overcooked fish. –JC

# Tony Cheng's Mongolian

**4.0** Food    **3.7** Feel

Watching the preparation of your food is far more exciting than eating it

## Pan-Asian

Casual restaurant    **$35** Price

www.tonychengrestaurant.com

Sun–Thu 11am–11pm
Fri–Sat 11am–midnight

**Bar** Beer, wine, liquor
**Credit cards** Visa, MC, AmEx
**Reservations** Accepted

**Chinatown**
619 H St. NW
(202) 842-8669

Even if the Mongolian Grill concept was stillborn when it launched in the 1980s and early 1990s, at least it was popular and trendy back then. Now it's just old and depressing—like the room at Tony Cheng's Mongolian Grill, which manages to feel antiseptic and grimy at the same time. As for the food, it actually seems to have gotten worse over time—whether for lack of attention or for the mere fact that an increasingly food-savvy city has outgrown the more-is-better, throw-it-all-on-the-grill-together school of cuisine.

The basic idea, for the uninitiated, is that you select a bunch of proteins, vegetables, and sauces all by yourself, and the grill man cooks it all together, right in front of you, with much pomp and circumstance, in one mass of oil and steam. (The original incarnation of this restaurant involved do-it-yourself grills at each table, a concept we've actually seen in some parts of Asia; but it's been scrapped for a more Benihana-like setup.)

The punch line is that you wind up spending more than twenty dollars per person for a selection of ho-hum meats, vegetables—which includes such Mongolian hum-dingers as tomatoes and broccoli—and sauces, which seem straight from the Joyce Chen's section in the supermarket aisle—and without a bit of culinary expertise, or assistance as to recipes, provided by the kitchen (with the exception of the recommended serving size for each sauce). The sesame bun—a possible receptacle for your plate full of goopy stuff—is a nice touch, but it's not quite nice enough. The alternative is hot pot, more like fondue, where you dip meats, fishes, and such in broth; it's an equally bad deal, and the flavors are equally wimpy.

Whatever it is that we Americans love so much about Benihana and Mongolian grill eatertainment concepts—the interactivity of it all, perhaps—we seem consistently willing to forfeit a lot of taste, and pay a lot, to get our fix. But when the fix comes in this kind of run-down, bright-white, depressing package, it starts to seem a bit less difficult to kick the habit. –RG

# Tony Cheng's Seafood

You've got to be stealthy to manage to order food that's actually Chinese here

**4.5** Food   **3.9** Feel

## Chinese

Casual restaurant   **$35** Price

www.tonychengrestaurant.com

Sun–Thu 11am–11pm
Fri–Sat 11am–midnight

**Bar** Beer, wine, liquor
**Credit cards** Visa, MC, AmEx
**Reservations** Accepted

**Chinatown**
619 H St. NW
(202) 371-8669

It can be such a challenge to get the real food at Chinese restaurants. When you're brought the lunch menu at the famous Tony Cheng's Seafood, for instance, the only hint that the kitchen might be capable of producing any actual Chinese food is the appearance of jellyfish salad and BBQ roast pork among the starters. The rest of the pages are lists of those dishes—beef with broccoli, lo mein, and so forth—with which it's almost impossible to order well, because the recipes are American, not Chinese, and they're fundamentally flawed. Now, it's one thing to highlight soggy, gloopy General Tso's and underseasoned broccoli for the Americans-who-lunch. But it's another thing for such a renowned restaurant to choose not to include *any* of the real Chinese dishes on that menu, and to force real Chinese food lovers to order off the dinner menu, where they'll find the good stuff: hot pot of sizzling flank skin with white turnips, pig's belly with preserved mustard greens, and steamed ground pork with salted fish.

But getting the real menu is one among many uphill battles here. Another is getting the attention of the distracted servers, who might or might not decide to grace your table with teacups. There's a pleasant bustle to the big, open room, whose only décor is self-congratulatory news articles (most from the 1980s) and celebrity photos. But indifference kills that buzz pretty quickly. Certainly it's hard to argue with the fresh seafood from the tanks: Dungeness crabs with "house spicy salt," live tilapia steamed with ginger and scallion. But this kitchen's execution is way off, even for authentic recipes. Roast duck has musty off flavors, and its bath tastes like nothing but soy sauce. A simple plate of sautéed Chinese watercress is awfully prepared: the flavorless greens are tough as weeds, more burnt than wok-seared, and at more than $10 for the lunchtime portion, it's remarkably overpriced—like everything else.

So why does Tony Cheng's continue to thrive? Is it just a reflection of the paucity of options in the neighborhood? Of customers who don't know the difference, or who continue to convince themselves that the lofty 1980s reputation is still relevant today? Regardless, with so many better options for authentic Chinese food in the area, it's hard to see what keeps the crowds coming back here—and paying a premium. This is the kind of place that gives DC's Chinatown a bad name. –RG

# Tortilla Café

Cheap pupusas are why it's worth coming here; skip the tortillas altogether

**6.0** Food

**6.4** Feel

## Salvadoran, Mexican

Casual restaurant

**$20** Price

Mon–Fri 9am–7pm
Sat–Sun 8am–7pm

**Bar** None
**Credit cards** Visa, MC, AmEx
**Reservations** Not accepted
Outdoor dining

**Capitol Hill**
210 7th St. SE
(202) 547-5700

This pint-sized Salvadoran eatery hasn't taken much of a cue from its Eastern Market neighbors, which have all inched upscale as the neighborhood has gentrified. Rather, Tortilla has left on its walls the amateur (and unframed) magazine photos of fishing boats and smiling villagers, as well as the yellowing (but framed) clipped review of the restaurant from the Spanish-language "El Tiempo Latino." Along the opposite wall, opened cases of juices and sodas are piled high.

But it needn't worry much about décor: the Café competes strictly on price. This is one of the cheapest places to eat in the neighborhood—and, in fact, in town. Four dollars buys you a burrito; for five, you can have a pupusa or quesadilla "platter." Of course, under these circumstances, you expect (hope) to hear that, in addition to being cheap and in simple digs, the food is great.

Well, that's certainly true of the pupusas. For $1.50, you get one of the cheesiest, gooiest, and greasiest rounds of fried dough in DC; this isn't a snack to undertake without a plate. Five dollars entitles you to two (choose cheese and/or chicharrón) plus a scoop of rice, a scoop of beans, and curtido.

All else here is lost, primarily because they rely on a substandard version of the namesake foodstuff. The burritos are wrapped in industrial-tasting flour tortillas; the rice, beans, and meat inside are somewhat dry and unsatisfying. Similarly, the tacos come on a pair of old-tasting corn tortillas that begin to break once folded.

After the tortillas, one of the café's most egregious errors is its rice, which resembles a Yankee attempt to make "Spanish" rice: it's basically just bland rice colored yellow, with no hint of stock. The rice makes the undersalted pile of refried beans with disconcertingly crunchy chunks of onion almost look good.

It would seem, from the quality of the food, that the real reason Tortilla Café has resisted the trend toward upscale is not to keep it real, but to cut corners. Stick to cheap pupusas. –CK

# Tosca

Go for the tasty and thoughtful pastas

**9.1** *Food*

**6.7** *Feel*

## Italian

Upmarket restaurant **$75** *Price*

www.toscadc.com

Mon–Thu 11:30am–2:30pm,
5:30pm–10:30pm; Fri
11:30am–2:30pm, 5:30pm–
11pm; Sat 5:30pm–11pm

**Bar** Beer, wine, liquor
**Credit cards** Visa, MC, AmEx
**Reservations** Accepted
Good wines, veg-friendly

**Downtown**
1112 F St. NW
(202) 367-1990

Are you skeptical of whether Tosca is as good as it's cracked up to be, given that the restaurant is so deeply representative of the Washington power-meal scene? Given that it's a place with a cheesy name, a place defined most clearly by the jacket- and bowtie-clad servers that scurry about the room, deftly timing courses to allow ample time for lingering (i.e. negotiating)? That the management seems to be as interested in networking as many of their customers?

Well, free your mind, because the kitchen is turning out homemade pastas on a level that would be taken seriously in Italy—and there are precious few Italian restaurants in DC about which you could say that. The emphasis here is on seasonal ingredients and fresh homemade pastas. Plump ravioli pillows, homemade and cooked for just a few moments, to an ideal texture, ooze with spot-on buffalo ricotta and evocative herbs. Ribbons of pappardelle, orange from a barely discernible dose of carrot, a magisterial rabbit ragú, deeply developed and subtly sweet, with whispers of white wine and thyme.

We like to build our meals here around pastas; mains are a bit over-focused on dark, syrupy sauces of red wine, fortified wine, balsamic vinegar, and such. Nonetheless, a whole grilled branzino (Mediterranean sea bass) or other fish of the day, deboned at the table, is first-rate—sweet and delicate—and fried, breaded veal chop Milanese, one of the most gently delicious of northern Italian classics, is expensive but extremely delicate. Salads can sometimes miss the mark; greens sometimes get slicked in oil rather than lightly dressed. Desserts are another weak spot—more style than substance—a fact that might be charitably interpreted as yet another sign of Tosca's Italian authenticity. Amaretto-and-chocolate custard, for instance, comes out with a gelatinous texture that warrants prodding rather than indulging, and it's surrounded by decorative spun sugar that looks more like scaffolding than an artistic culinary endeavor. The sugar's failure to melt in the mouth results in near impalement when swallowing, rendering the dessert all but inedible. But Italy has never been a country of desserts. Order grappa instead.

It's not particularly pretty, Tosca's office-building-ish room, decked out in muted yellows and whites—elegant, maybe, but even that's a bit of a stretch. But if you can get past the bland formality and the corporate-expense-account-tailored bill, you can have one of DC's very best Italian meals here—networking not necessary. –RG

# Trader Joe's

Come and play in foodie paradise

## Groceries

Market

www.traderjoes.com

Daily 9am–9pm

**Bar** Beer, wine
**Credit cards** Visa, MC, AmEx
Good wines, veg-friendly

**Foggy Bottom**
1101 25th St. NW
(202) 296-1921

**Alexandria, VA**
612 N. Saint Asaph St.
(703) 548-0611

**Bethesda, MD**
6831 Wisconsin Ave.
(301) 907-0982

**Additional locations**
and more features at
www.fearlesscritic.com

The folks at TJ's have their heads and hearts in exactly the right place. Their business model represents a much-needed return to simplicity: cut out all the fat. Trader Joe's makes a concerted effort to buy most of their products directly from producers themselves. This means that your vegetables haven't changed hands five times before they end up on your plate—and it also means that you're not paying each of those hands to pass them along the chain. Buyers are an elite group, with well-trained eyes for the best stuff out there, be it wine, cheese, coffee, tea, olive oil, chocolate; the list goes on and on. The best deals of all are usually the private label (TJ's brand) products.

The wine sections at Trader Joe's are like playgrounds for wine geeks. Carefully chosen bottles come from tiny estates the world over. But you'll also find quite a few of the big names. And we can't forget about Charles Shaw ("Two-Buck Chuck"—we know that no one on a budget possibly could). The value wine to beat all value wines, it's made from surplus juice, so it's bought at a very low cost. In a series of blind tastings conducted in 2007-2008, one batch of Charles Shaw Cabernet Sauvignon was actually preferred by tasters to a $40 bottle of Beringer Founder's Estate Cabernet Sauvignon. (For more on this, see *The Wine Trials*, another Fearless Critic Media title.) In fact, Trader Joe's features a remarkable number of winning bottles form *The Wine Trials*. Beer is chosen with an equally keen eye. Microbrews from all corners of the earth converge on the shelves here, and staff are über-knowledgeable.

There's a definite focus on organic goods, and all products have slickly designed and super-easy-to-understand labels. Low-sodium, heart-healthy, and kosher are just a few of the indications you might run into. Stores are well laid out and easy to navigate. The aesthetic is nice, with natural woods set against bright colors. It's a visual wonderland.

It's no wonder the place has such a cult following. We can't thank Trader Joe's enough for all it does to bring some of the world's best products to our fingertips at great prices. But we'll try anyway.

Thanks, TJ. –FC

# Tragara

Upscale, overpriced, French-inflected Italian food
in a self-consciously elegant setting

**6.5** Food **5.8** Feel

## Italian

Upmarket restaurant **$80** Price

www.tragara.com

Mon–Fri 11:30am–2:30pm
Sat 5:30pm–10:30pm
Sun 5pm–9pm

**Bar** Beer, wine, liquor
**Credit cards** Visa, MC, AmEx
**Reservations** Accepted
Wi-Fi

**Bethesda, MD**
4935 Cordell Ave.
(301) 951-4935

Bethesda is a neighborhood of high turnover, so it's impressive for a
restaurant to last more than 10 years. According to its website, this Italian
institution has been in action since 1994. The restaurant certainly shows
its age: the décor features airbrushed floral paintings and a warm burnt-
sienna color scheme that probably felt "modern, yet elegant" back in the
'90s. Today, the atmosphere reads as a little stuffy, like it's trying hard to
feel expensive enough to support a menu with main courses averaging
$28 and soaring all the way up to—believe it or not—$40.

Another surprise at Tragara is the provenance of the chef: he's French.
This is perhaps why many plates here are executed with the kind of
finesse and precision that's traditionally associated with French cooking: a
neat arrangement of vegetables accompanying a veal scaloppine, for
example, or carefully formed agnolotti with sharp, clean edges and a
precise quantity of filling. The menu cuts a wide swath down the boot,
from a Milanese osso buco to Sicilian swordfish.

Ultimately, though, Tragara seems more focused on looks than taste.
Those agnolotti are some of the kitchen's best work: light pillows of
delicate pasta filled with an intensely flavored spinach stuffing, served in a
decadently creamy parmesan sauce. Many other dishes here underwhelm,
including an appetizer of baked artichokes that has been served
refrigerator-cold with no trace of artichoke taste.

The rather chilly and ceremonious execution of dishes extends to the
service, which is as impersonal and florid as the décor. The staff is
tuxedoed and curt, and never misses a beat. You'll be in good hands,
even if they are a little anesthetized.

If it's a show you're after, the desserts won't disappoint; they're flashy,
photogenic, and frequently coated in a glossy sheen of chocolate. The
wine list tends toward pedestrian Italian. Fittingly, a Wine Spectator
Award of Excellence is proudly displayed on the website (alongside a AAA
award). WS awards are given out freely to nearly anyone who shovels
over the cash for them (for more on this subject, visit
http://osterialintrepido.wordpress.com). It's a hollow prestige, much like
an experience here. –CD

# Trattoria Alberto

Don't fall for the antics—this unexciting Italian-
American won't have you doing backflips

## Italian

Casual restaurant

**$45**
Price

www.trattoriaalbertodc.com

Mon–Fri 11:30am–2:30pm,
5:30pm–10:30pm
Sat–Sun 5:30pm–10:30pm

**Bar** Beer, wine, liquor
**Credit cards** Visa, MC, AmEx
**Reservations** Accepted
Outdoor dining

**Capitol Hill**
506 8th St. SE
(202) 544-2007

Like play-actors in a terrible farce, the waitstaff at Trattoria Alberto don
the costumes and mannerisms of servers at a restaurant with a wholly
different caliber of food. These middle-aged men with Italianate
complexions and brooding compositions make sure to seat the ladies
before gents, recite a litany of specials, patronizingly come over to the
table to grate fresh pepper (which has never been done within the
borders of Italy during recorded history), and urge the host to inspect the
cork before the wine is served (a practice that even wine aficionados
acknowledge to be an exercise in pointless pomposity).

There is little in Alberto's décor to contradict this theater: small vines
snake around the wrought-iron staircase and up the white plaster walls of
the building, and the outdoor patio is a delight on summer evenings. The
clientele is generally well dressed and well behaved, and the menu
categories include the non-English "Zuppe" and "Antipasti". It's possible
to spot a crack or two in this façade even before the food quality utterly
undermines its foundations: for example, most waiters are hard pressed to
answer substantive questions about the contents or preparation of a dish,
or to offer anything beyond perfunctory recommendations.

And when the food does arrive, the final veil is flung from Alberto,
revealing the tragic reality: despite all pretense and prices, you're not
going to eat well. This fact is evident from the first glance of the Caprese
salad, which comes on a bed of dingy iceberg lettuce, inspiring the acrid
aside: "Have they no decency!" Atop the "greens" (and who ever heard
of lettuce in a Caprese, anyway?), the tomatoes are dry and the cheese
bland; a first taste confirms your first impression.

Many pasta dishes look like the kind of thing you'd be proud to have
concocted in the fifth grade. The "Penne alla Arrabiatta" [sic] is best
described as noodles in salty tomato sauce with red pepper flakes. Plain,
dry spaghetti with oil accompanies a plain grilled fillet of salmon. The
"zuppe" are made with not-so-fresh kidney beans.

When the curtain finally goes down, it's difficult to muster applause.
But we should have looked more carefully at the Playbill: "Garlic Bread" is
listed as one of two "Vegetali." –CK

# Trusty's

The team might have a new home, but Nats spirit remains here

**6.8** Food  **7.0** Feel

## American

Casual restaurant  **$35** Price

www.pourhouse-dc.com/TrustysHome.php

Mon–Thu 4pm–2am
Fri 4pm–3am
Sat 11am–3am
Sun 11am–2am

**Bar** Beer, wine, liquor
**Credit cards** Visa, MC, AmEx
**Reservations** Not accepted
Outdoor dining, Wi-Fi

**Capitol Hill**
1420 Pennsylvania Ave. SE
(202) 547-1010

Looking for a hipster-free, leprechaun-free neighborhood bar with cheap beer and amazing chili? Look no farther than Trusty's. In the back are dominos and a 1980s version of Trivial Pursuit; apparently, they're not for "ambiance," but rather because someone brought them in years ago and no one's bothered to chuck them since.

Not sufficiently entertaining? How about the big buck hunter arcade game, rusty license plates pinned to the walls (okay, those are there for "ambiance"), and a scrappy front "patio" of roped-off sidewalk, from which you can hear the sweet music of gunned engines on Pennsylvania Avenue.

Trusty's food menu diverges from the traditional array of pub grub. Instead, the cuisine is somewhere between nouvelle-dorm-room and Sunday afternoon ballgame: a big plate of nachos factors in largely, but here, the cheese is real, even if the beans come from a can. The chicken-and-white-bean chili is excellent, with big, tender beans that definitely don't come from a can. The ubiquitous accompaniment of dry corn chips does get old, however. Trusty's half-smokes are a reliable standby.

When the Nationals still played at their old stadium near the Armory, game days would bring a sporting time to Trusty's, and it remains to be seen how the bar will fare now that the Nats have a new home. –CK

# Tryst

DC goes grunge at this 18th Street icon

**5.1** Food
**9.0** Feel

## American

Café **$25** Price

www.trystdc.com

| | | |
|---|---|---|
| Mon–Thu 6:30am–2am | **Bar** Beer, wine, liquor | **Adams Morgan** |
| Fri–Sat 6:30am–3am | **Credit cards** Visa, MC, AmEx | 2459 18th St. NW |
| Sun 7am–2am | Date-friendly, live music, veg-friendly, Wi-Fi | (202) 232-5500 |

One of the central icons of the transformation of Adams Morgan from dangerous neighborhood to twentysomething scene, Tryst defies being branded a "café" as much as Starbucks commandeers it: you can order breakfast at dinnertime, wine by the glass or tea by the pot, and more than half the sandwiches include cheeses that Safeway doesn't stock. The couches are clean but dingy, or at least faux-dingy. Almost everyone here during the day has a laptop, but it's a diverse mix of Macs (hip, artsy types), PCs (IR geeks), and computers so unrecognizably beat up that it's hard to tell what OS they're running (humanities grad students).

Even mid-morning, when its big picture windows afford a pretty view of Adams Morgan without the accompanying Saturday-morning stench, Tryst manages to pull off a chilled-out evening vibe. But as the real evening arrives, the Macs and PCs snap shut, the live jazz kicks in, and the "Coffeehouse * Bar * Lounge" gently transforms from a communal home office into a community of offers to take people home. Whatever you think of the place, it's hard to deny that it's truly one-of-a-kind in DC.

The food isn't the main event here, but at any time of day, sandwiches are an okay choice. The ingredients are thoughtfully composed (Norwegian salmon, watercress, and cheese come on a sour, thin baguette, for example), and each is accompanied by a whole-bean salad lightly dressed in olive oil and herbs. Tryst's quiches are plenty cheesy, although its croissants tend to be outsized and a bit greasy. Don't get anywhere near the meatier proteins—they taste like they're prepared by vegetarians. At least the place doesn't do burgers.

In addition to its coffeehouse, bar, lounge (and even restaurant) shticks, as the headquarters of Adams Morgan's new guard, Tryst embraces its role as a hookup scene, too: there's an "I saw you at Tryst" missed-connections-type service on its website. The posts are predictable, addressed longingly to "cute girl with curly hair and dark shirt who caught me staring and smiles," or "the dude reading 'Buddhism for Dummies.'" Honestly, do you really want to see that guy again? —FC

# Tunnicliff's Tavern

Old-school excellence sets the agenda at this neighborhood pub

**6.9** Food

**8.0** Feel

## American

Casual restaurant

**$40**
Price

www.tunnicliffstaverndc.com

| | | |
|---|---|---|
| Mon–Thu 11am–2am | **Bar** Beer, wine, liquor | **Capitol Hill** |
| Fri 11am–3am | **Credit cards** Visa, MC, AmEx | 222 7th St. SE |
| Sat 10am–3am | **Reservations** Accepted | (202) 544-5680 |
| Sun 10am–2am | Outdoor dining, Wi-Fi | |

If DC's Eastern Market neighborhood has a town hall, it's Tunnicliff's Tavern. Although it has the feel of a sports bar, with dark, well-worn wood and a perpetual view of the Game, the spot appeals to a much broader population than the typical baseball-watching crowd. Be advised, however, that seats can be hard to find if the Nats happen to have a home game.

Tunnicliff's is further differentiated from the typical pub by a menu that would thrill even a teetotaler. You don't have to have a beer in hand to enjoy the homemade pizza, which feeds at least two and is, at seven bucks a pie (from the bar menu; more in the restaurant), one of the last deals left in town. The crust is thin and a bit sour, the pepperoni extra spicy, and the sauce mild.

The tavern's sandwiches look like national monuments, with meats and vegetables pilled high atop thick bread that's further thickened with mayonnaise. Melted Swiss cheese envelops the top of the pastrami sandwich, and Tunnicliff's crab cakes are big and fresh, if underseasoned and over-greased. Also enormous are the desserts, which range from a too-sticky bread pudding to an extra-chocolately brownie to a rather dull apple pie, all served a la mode. This is America, after all.

It's a pleasure to sit at Tunnicliff's bar and chat with the friendly tenders; of course, conversation can take a backseat to sports. The back of the tavern is oriented more like a restaurant, with dark wooden tables and somewhat rickety chairs. Outside, the front patio is a delight in the summer, and plastic coverings and heat lamps keep the area toasty in the wintertime, too. We the citizens approve this measure. –CK

# 2941 Restaurant

**8.0** Food  **7.8** Feel

Do it up at the bar with an exciting wine and great artisanal cheeses, but stop there

## New American

Upmarket restaurant  **$100** Price

www.2941.com

| | | |
|---|---|---|
| Mon–Thu 11:30am–2pm, 5pm–9:30pm; Fri 11:30am–2pm, 5pm–10pm; Sat 5pm–10pm; Sun 5pm–9pm | **Bar** Beer, wine, liquor<br>**Credit cards** Visa, MC, AmEx<br>**Reservations** Accepted<br>Good wines, outdoor dining | **Falls Church, VA**<br>2941 Fairview Park Dr.<br>(703) 270-1501 |

Going to a restaurant named after its own address is like dating Jimmy from Seinfeld, who refers to himself in the third person: you really can't get angry when it turns out the way it does. 2941 certainly looks impressive in its glass and glimmering white, like a Mormon temple designed by Howard Roark. Koi ponds, waterfalls, and uplit fountains evoke Vegas. The chefs hearken from NYC's twin darlings, Daniel and Café Boulud. And yet with all this, people have the darndest time feeling that their visit was worth the 200 bones you might well drop. These same people reminisce about a time when 2941 was cutting edge and inspiring. Now, it seems to be heading towards hotel-banquet-hall disaster.

One clue is inside, where a stuffy and generic décor comes off as over-formal—too many flowers and too much stemware and flatware fuss up the tables. Any sexy thoughts inspired by the exterior are neutered by all that beige. Another clue is the menu, which is late-'90s-fancy: pan-Asian dishes, crusted fish, and Wagyu beef. The latter is priced at $55, a conceit that plays upon American fantasies of a mystical beef species that enjoys daily massages and a diet of beer (not here). A modest Colorado lamb loin gets a price tag of $44. Is it smothered in uni? For a few bucks more, we could get a one-way flight to Denver and gnaw on the whole flock.

These dishes do look lovely; the kitchen succeeds in artfulness…but not so much in flavor and innovation. A beef trio (dry aged, American Wagyu, braised shortrib, marrow) as the centerpiece of a $95 tasting menu? Boring. No interesting animal parts. The closest we get to offal is a $26 appetizer of seared foie gras (which is executed properly). Tuna tartare is boring, not particularly silky or anything.

One thing that does turn us on: the wine list. Given all the ambient drama and astronomic prices, we expected the wine list to be little more than a promenade of blousy New World celebrities, but 2941's list is a beauty: over 45 pages of well-chosen wines from the geeky (Blaufränkisch) to the culty (Dagueneau), and—rarely—to the obvious (Silver Joke). There's something for everyone in every price range, and whatever your selection, it might be the most exciting thing about your visit. –FC

# 2 Amys Pizza

Some of the best pizza in America is hiding in
Cleveland Park

**9.6** *Food*  **8.8** *Feel*

## Pizza

Casual restaurant

**$35** *Price*

www.2amyspizza.com

Mon 5pm–10pm
Tue–Thu 11am–10pm
Fri–Sat 11am–11pm
Sun noon–10pm

**Bar** Beer, wine, liquor
**Credit cards** Visa, MC
**Reservations** Not accepted
Kid-friendly, outdoor dining,
veg-friendly

**Cleveland Park**
3715 Macomb St. NW
(202) 885-5700

2 Amys is not a romantic restaurant. The lighting is bright; the service is
fine, no better; loud kids often dominate the soundtrack; no reservations
are taken; and you might have to wait a while for a table.

And none of this matters. This is the best authentic Italian pizza in DC,
and some of the best in America. The many neighborhood- and city-wide
accolades are insufficient to describe 2 Amys' uniqueness within the DC—
and American—pizza landscape. The membership of 2 Amys in the
Neapolitan appellation, "Vera Pizza Napoletana," is not mere puffery; the
19 certified restaurants in America are serious pizza places. There are
other restaurants in DC with wood-fired brick ovens; but it is a much rarer
thing to find a staff that operates such a wood-fired brick oven correctly,
searing a pizza at extremely high heat in no more than a couple of
minutes, creating those telltale ink-black bubbles of singed crust.

It is a rare thing, too, to find a kitchen that applies so judiciously little
tomato and cheese to the pizza, allowing them to serve as wonderful
backups to a crust that sings the lead. If you're not schooled in this brand
of pizza, open your mind to fewer toppings and more taste: on the simple
Margherita DOC—the crowning achievement here—the layer of fragrant
sauce on the red pizza is almost translucent, while deep, rich buffalo
mozzarella is dotted onto the pie like clouds across the Arizona sky. If you
must get more elaborate with toppings, you might consider fresh cockles
with a chewy touch; prosciutto di Parma sliced, for once, as thinly as it
needs to be; broccoli rabe lightly sautéed in olive oil; or soft eggplant
confit that's just a touch sweet.

Pizzas are all personal-sized, so we recommend a family-style plan of
attack: each person orders one pizza and they're all passed around. And
save some retroactive room for one of the many deliciously authentic
Italian appetizers, like the refreshing Venetian sarde in saor (a vinegary
dish with sardines, raisins, and pickled onions), which is plated more
artfully here than we've seen it in Italy. As a result of all of this
deliciousness, the queues outside and flurry within show no signs of
subsiding.

And none of it matters. –RG

# Two Quail

**8.0** Food   **8.8** Feel

A deliciously comfortable place, where the focus is on the food, despite the lovely feel

## French

Upmarket restaurant   **$60** Price

www.twoquail.com

Mon–Thu 11am–9:30pm
Fri 11am–10:30pm
Sat 5pm–10:30pm
Sun 5pm–9:30pm

**Bar** Beer, wine, liquor
**Credit cards** Visa, MC, AmEx
**Reservations** Accepted
Date-friendly

**Mt. Vernon Square**
320 Massachusetts Ave.
NE
(202) 543-8030

This modest establishment doesn't put up much fuss about itself. No photos of the celebrity chef are plastered on the walls, the menu is free of "foam," "frappe," and "fricassée" (in fact, "stuffed with" is the most common phrase), and the birthplace or pedigree of an ingredient is always left unspoken.

Even before you can be enchanted by the Quail's cuisine, or by the demure waiters that flit about with menus and wine, you will be enchanted by the restaurant's layout. The dining room is spread over the walk-up story of three connected Victorian rowhouses. Each table—and the accompanying pair of overstuffed parlor chairs—is situated in its own nook or cranny, and the whimsy of candles, curtains, and Victorian knick-knacks give the place an intimate, hushed air.

The restaurant's signature dish is, not unexpectedly, an order of two quails, which are served rain, snow, or shine. When it snows, the birds might be filled with pumpkin and apple and braised in a Jack Daniels cider sauce, while the spring version might be topped with grapes and stuffed with boursin cheese. Either way, the quails are delightfully moist and flawlessly presented.

The golden trout stuffed with spinach and artichokes seems to be served across seasons: a thick fish is softened with just enough butter, cut in half, and filled with full, flavorful artichoke leaves that complement the trout without masking its texture or taste. In a rare misstep, most dishes come with matchstick vegetables and rather ordinary wild rice; Two Quail could go much further in pairing its main courses and sides.

The wine befits a place this refined, but the wine choices and prices, like the meals, are accessible. At lunch, the Quail draws a small crowd of Hill staffers for its "Senator's Lunch," a reasonably-priced soup-and-sandwich or pasta combination. The evening crowd is, as might be expected, couple-heavy. It goes without saying (and it's no big secret) that Two Quail is a wonderfully romantic spot for a night out. Without the fuss. —CK

# Udupi Palace

A South Indian mini-chain that serves satisfying vegetarian food

**7.1** Food    **5.5** Feel

## Indian

Casual restaurant    **$20** Price

www.udupipalace.com

Daily 11:30am–9:30pm

**Bar** None
**Credit cards** Visa, MC, AmEx
**Reservations** Accepted
Kid-friendly, veg-friendly

**Takoma Park, MD**
1329 University Blvd. E.
(301) 434-1531

South Indian vegetarian is one of our favorite culinary categories—and one that's been arriving to US cities with increasing frequency. Although we're generally buffet naysayers, we appreciate South Indian buffets for their capacity for exposing even small dining parties to the kitchen's entire range. And unlike their non-vegetarian counterparts, the vegetarian buffets don't generally leave off the most exciting dishes to be ordered separately.

At Udupi Palace, which sits along a Takoma Park strip center (and has two sister restaurants in Illinois), the lunchtime buffet runs an extremely fair $8.95 and stays out until a refreshing 3pm. You'll join a healthy mix of Indians, local office workers, and hippie vegetarians on pilgrimages in a space that's bright yellow—too yellow. The music is Indian down the line; strange art deco chandeliers hang from the ceiling; a take-out dessert and juice bar is glass-walled-off in a corner. It's hardly a romantic spot, but it's actually a decent escape from the parking-lot surroundings.

We don't find Udupi's food quite worthy of all the accolades the place seems to have received, but it's a nice break from non-veg Indian. You'll do best with dosai (e.g. a very competent masala dosa), along with chats and such that are ordered from the menu rather than taken from the buffet. Seasoning is good across the board, from the forward chili pepper in rasam (a hot, clear soup with surprising complexity for a vegetarian broth) to a nice depth of flavor in pav bhaji (a soft dish of peas and potatoes) to layers of subtlety in the all-important sambar, in which some of the starches are meant to be dipped.

Speaking of starches, however, Udupi Palace suffers from a systematic problem with their execution. Paratha is made with white flour and improperly integrated butter; medhu vada (deep-fried doughnuts) have a skin that's a bit tough; idli (rice-flour dumplings) are fluffy but too crumbly; and yellow dal, a vegetarian staple, is unusually watery. There are other problems, especially with the little things. Iceberg-lettuce salad is a throwaway; some chutneys are missing from the buffet; tea is bagged, not home-brewed. This is not South Indian vegetarian cuisine at its best, but South Indian vegetarian food is pretty tasty and satisfying even when it's not at its best. –RG

# Ulah Bistro

## 7.5 Food | 7.8 Feel

A hip U-Street eatery that plays on the border between upscale and casual

## American

Upmarket restaurant

## $45 Price

www.ulahbistro.com

Mon–Thu 11am–1am
Fri 11am–2am
Sat 10am–2am
Sun 10am–1am

**Bar** Beer, wine, liquor
**Credit cards** Visa, MC, AmEx
**Reservations** Accepted
Date-friendly, Wi-Fi

**U Street**
1214 U St. NW
(202) 234-0123

For a self-described "neighborhood bistro," Ulah is pretty fancy. A quaint black awning leads to a cozy dining room dim alight with rows of tea lights, deep with mahogany wood, black leather, and red brick, and artfully hung with stylish prints. Sprays of seasonal blooms rest in large vases in window nooks, and the air is alive with conversation and softly pulsing music. If ever there was a face of U Street society, this might be it. Ulah is a restaurant you'll want to come back to over and over again.

The menu at Ulah ranges from updated American classics to less formal fare. Throwbacks like a dessert of milk and cookies, and the sweetly attentive waiters wearing bistro-issued baseball tees, make elaborate dining at Ulah feel more casual than at other places. The kitchen carries this joke out at the expense of its more pretentious competition, serving, for example, a meatloaf dish under the moniker "American Pâté." Sadly, like at many neighborhood places, much of the charm is about the atmosphere rather than the food.

Some dishes are quite competent. French onion soup is light but fulfilling, and playfully garnished with fried onions. Its broth, though looped with stringy cheese, isn't oily, and the croutons maintain a nice crisp edge despite a good soaking in the middle. As the colder months settle into DC's bones, this could very well become the dish you crave. Fries are also pretty grand. It's unclear whether it's the grown-up feeling you get from eating crisp fries from a cone or the whippily playful dollops of garlic mayonnaise that make them so addictive.

Less exciting dishes include mushroom ravioli and wood-fired pizza. The former is not bad, but not good either; the mushroom filling is dense and dry, and the cream sauce congeals quickly into a dishwasher-ready streak. Pine nuts, though interesting from a textural point of view, add an incongruous flavor that overpowers the mild dish. "Ulah pizza" has so much cheese that you feel like you're biting into a rubber mat. And Ulah's upscale perks don't always pay off. The addition of crabmeat to the more traditional basil, though luxurious-sounding, just makes the pizza taste vaguely fishy.

Still, Ulah has enough charisma to convince us to overlook these shortcomings. It's worth a lot to have a restaurant whose main goal is to make you feel comfortable. –JC

# Uni

Keep movin', folks...there's no good sushi to see here

| | 4.6 | 4.9 |
|---|---|---|
| | Food | Feel |

## Japanese

Casual restaurant

**$40**
Price

www.unisushi.net

Mon–Thu 11:30am–2pm, 5pm–10pm; Fri 11:30am–2pm, 5pm–11pm, 11:30am–2pm, 5pm–11pm; Sat 1pm–11pm; Sun 5pm–9:30pm

**Bar** Beer, wine, liquor
**Credit cards** Visa, MC, AmEx
**Reservations** Accepted
Delivery

**Dupont**
2122 P St. NW
(202) 833-8038

It's got a dark, haphazard, trying-too-hard-to-be-trendy look, but Uni runs like a well-oiled sushi machine. A clear and concise menu leaves no room for confusion. Tables are seated in an efficient and orderly manner. Waters are brought to the table, orders taken, plates delivered, taken away, checks paid, and diners sent on their way. Rest assured, your meal here is going to go without a hitch. Unless you try to come in at a time that's within a half-hour or so of the closing time. We were once sternly rebuked in our attempt to have lunch here at 1:38pm. When we mentioned that the web site said they served lunch until 2, they responded: "It's 2:00 according to our clock." Touché.

"All of our seafood and meats are individually sliced to order and prepared," Uni's website brags. Um, isn't that the point of sushi? Nonetheless, we've had some cuts of fish here that didn't seem so fresh. They've come out a bit on the dry side, as if they had been sitting out for a while. Rice lacks adequate vinegar and leans toward the undercooked side of the spectrum. Miso soup is competent, but we would like a bit more depth to the flavor of the broth.

Beyond the lowest-common-denominator items like chicken teriyaki, there are some slightly more interesting options like...ceviche. Or mussels with jalapeño sauce (eek). Well, at least there are sakes and beers. That will help get you through any meal. At a minimum, perhaps you could rely on the waitstaff to point you in the direction of the hidden sleepers on the menu.

But then again, on a recent visit our waiter was wearing a Yellow Tail shirt. (Yellow Tail is the world's largest producer of cheap, mass-produced, over-extracted wine.) Do you really think he can be trusted in matters of taste? –AH

# Union Pub

Boy, is it ever convenient—if only it were good

**3.8** Food   **5.0** Feel

## American

Casual restaurant   **$25** Price

www.unionpubdc.com

Mon–Fri 11:30am–11pm
Sat noon–11pm
Sun 5pm–11pm

**Bar** Beer, wine, liquor
**Credit cards** Visa, MC, AmEx
**Reservations** Not accepted
Outdoor dining, Wi-Fi

**Capitol Hill**
201 Massachusetts Ave.
NE
(202) 546-7200

Hill staffers complain that the only reason they go to Union Pub—and they go there a lot (as they did when it used to be called Red River Grill)—is the dearth of other reasonably priced lunch options in the area.

We feel for them: for such a popular place, this one really doesn't have a lot going for it. We've rarely had anything good to eat here, but somehow, we still find ourselves stuck here when meeting our politico buddies. It's liveliest for after-work happy hour.

Although the joint has clearly got location down, the atmosphere doesn't have much going for it. The only plus is a patio out front, where you can pretend you're not in the Union Pub; otherwise, inside, you'll be stuck in what basically feels like a slightly trashy sports bar with a mix of TVs as giant as 100" and a ready schedule of major sporting events with an arbitrary focus on the Nebraska Cornhuskers. At least there's WiFi.

Just as we went to press for this edition, a new chef had come on board at Union Pub. As a rule, we don't invalidate restaurants' reviews based merely on staff turnover—after all, turnover in the restaurant business is almost more the norm than the lack thereof—but we will hypothesize that this could only improve things. Thankfully, the new guy seems to have euthanized such atrocities (experienced on our last visit) as an "Asian chicken salad," which was drizzled with a sweet, gloopy orange sauce evocative of the worst of Chinese-American take-out; and a muddy-tasting fried-catfish-feta-and-veggie wrap that was so devoid of moisture that we were tempted to dip the thing in our water glass.

Speaking of texture, at our last visit, Union Pub's were some of the worst, soggiest French fries we've tasted anywhere. Burgers, however, were passable, and are likely still the best way to go, although we'd caution against straying too far down the "Burgers of the World" list. To wit: the "American Indian burger," with ground turkey, chili, and apples. Just as the Native Americans prepared it, no doubt. –RG

# Union Station Food Court

Bringing back the romance to train travel, one food stall at a time

Counter service

www.unionstationdc.com/dining.aspx

Mon–Sat 10am–9pm
Sun noon–6pm

**Bar** Beer, wine
**Credit cards** Visa, MC, AmEx
Kid-friendly, veg-friendly

**Union Station**
40 Massachusetts Ave. NE
(202) 289-1908

This is one of America's great train stations, a throwback to the glory days of the romantic rails. While Union Station's upstairs area now has a few more upscale restaurants, it is the food court below—in the bowels of the station—that's still at the heart of its culinary scene. Don't overlook the noble past of Union Station's food court: in the early 1990s, its offerings were positively cutting-edge among American train stations—certainly the one in America where you could get sushi. The following are our favorite picks (in order of preference) in the current incarnation of the food court:

**Kabuki**: Interestingly, all these years later, it's still the sushi that stands out. Kabuki goes above and beyond the call of food-stall duty with nigiri assembled to order by actual sushi chefs, spicy tuna rolls with well-chopped fish and integrated hotness, and surprisingly reasonable prices.

**Vittorio's Gelato Bar**: The Italian ice cream is solid, but Vittorio's also makes sandwiches from well-chosen ingredients that, thankfully, don't try to do too much. Chicken salad is good; the fresh bread's even better. For a bright, sandwich-based lunch, it's hard to do better than this.

**The Great Steak & Potato Company** (American): A real griddle for making real griddled sandwiches in the food court? Respect! The steak and cheese and the Reuben are both well-executed versions. If you're hungry before your train ride, this is definitely a satisfying approach.

**Häagen-Dazs**: The granddaddy of the "gourmet ice cream" (i.e. extra butterfat) movement in America, this chain has been selling its rich, smooth ice cream—in waffle-cone, sundae, and shake format—for more than 40 years. They've resisted fads and kept the product consistent.

**Johnny Rockets**: The only table-service restaurant in the downstairs food court is a branch of this nostalgic, Disneyish, 1950s diner chain whose Coca-Cola kitsch and paper-hat-topped waiters appeal particularly to kids. Burgers are properly griddled in the diner style, and cheese fries and malts are done right, too.

**Paradise Smoothies**: The concept is simple and lovely—fruit shakes, made right in front of you, from fresh fruit: ripe bananas, oranges, lemons, and frozen raspberries and strawberries. If you're just in the mood for a sweet sip, these are an unexpected pleasure. –FC

# Urban Bar-B-Que Company

**7.3** Food **6.8** Feel

This well-meaning Q is some of the best around DC—but that's not saying much

## Barbecue

Counter service **$25** Price

www.urbanbbqco.com

Mon–Sat 11am–9pm
Sun 11am–8pm

**Bar** None
**Credit cards** Visa, MC, AmEx
Delivery, outdoor dining

**Silver Spring, MD**
10163 New Hampshire Ave.
(301) 434-7427

**Rockville, MD**
2007 Chapman Ave.
(240) 290-4827

The walls are decorated with silly bumper stickers ("Be Nice to Your Kids—They'll Choose Your Nursing Home"; "I Love Animals—They Are Delicious"), and the staff greets you with a smile. Urban Bar-B-Que manages to feel friendly and un-fussy, transcending its one-room strip-mall environs. In many ways, this is our favorite kind of restaurant: modest, inexpensive, and not pretending to be anything other than what it is—in this case, an accessible take-out barbecue spot.

While there are some eat-in seats available, these are best used for biding your time and enjoying the free unshelled peanuts available while you wait for your food. Don't forget to help yourself from the collection of bottled hot sauces along a back wall, in addition to the house-made barbecue sauces (a sweet red version, and a more exciting vinegar-and-mustard yellow rendition).

The main attraction here is obviously the barbecue, and all the usual suspects are here—pork, chicken, sausage, brisket—served with your choice of side dish and bread (flour tortilla, corn bread, white bread). None of it has that deep wood flavor we really seek, but pulled pork is appropriately moist and smoky, and the sausage casings snap open to yield a nicely spiced and juicy interior. Brisket, while unfailingly tender, lacks seasoning.

Nonetheless, you can put together an altogether pleasant platter here. Choose any combination of one, two, or three meats, or have a sandwich instead. As for sides, the cole slaw is chopped rather than shredded, and vinegary rather than mayonnaisey; other Southern standards like collard greens, mashed potatoes, and baked beans are also available. Cornbread is some of Urban's best work, almost dessert-like, sweet, crumbly, and studded with fresh corn kernels.

Texans, Carolinians, and other opinionated barbecue connoisseurs will have strong opinions—mostly negative—about the authenticity and worthiness of these incarnations of regional cuisines. And they're not wrong. But at least we can say that here, for not a lot of money, you can get a hearty plate of good, all-American food. Even if the genuine article is still mysteriously missing from this part of America, the unpretentious Southern hospitality and good humor seems to have made the trip just fine. –CD

# Urbana

Good things *can* come in trendy packages

| 8.5 | 8.3 |
|-----|-----|
| Food | Feel |

## New American, Pizza

Upmarket restaurant

**$55**
Price

www.urbanadc.com

Mon–Thu 7am–10:30am,
11:30am–3pm, 5:30pm–10pm
Fri 7am–10:30am, 11:30am–
3pm, 5:30pm–11pm
Sat 8am–3pm, 5:30pm–11pm
Sun 8am–3pm, 5:30pm–10pm

**Bar** Beer, wine, liquor
**Credit cards** Visa, MC, AmEx
**Reservations** Accepted
Date-friendly, good wines,
veg-friendly

**Dupont**
2121 P St. NW
(202) 956-6650

The first impression you might get upon walking into the Hotel Palomar's hot, happening wine bar is that it's a velvet-rope Vegas nightclub with a Blade-Runner-meets-wine-cellar theme. Only the thugs and the preening supermodels seem to be missing. On weekends, the bar area absolutely hops with the twenty- and thirtysomething in-crowd.

As such, you'll probably be pretty shocked when you sidle up to the bar, ask your knockout bartender about whites by the glass, and are treated to a lesson on the differences between Verdejo and Albariño.

The entirety of the wine program is as down to earth and well-informed as these bartenders. As many as 35 wines are poured by the glass, yet—remarkably—every one we've sampled has been in good condition (i.e. not open too long). The focus is on lesser-known artisanal producers, with an excellent balance between New World and Old—and that's no small feat in DC, either.

Better yet, the wine prices are unusually accessible, closer to double retail than the standard triple. On a recent version of the list, for instance, a bottle of Sèvre et Maine sur Lie, a snappy Muscadet, went for $24, and a delightful Lagrein "Castel Turmhof," a light red from Tieffenbruner in Alto Adife, was priced to move at $41.

We've only spent this long talking about the wine because it makes us so happy—not because the Italian-influenced food menu isn't worthwhile in its own right. Baby zucchini salad with manchego is a model of restraint, balancing crunch with softness, acidity with salt. Crispy pork belly with cannellini purée and "parsley pesto" (why can't they just call it parsley?) isn't a subtle dish, but the belly is properly crisped and the white beans match well. Unlike the manchego, it's definitely a winter dish.

Which brings us to our biggest criticism of Urbana's menu: it's not seasonal, and it doesn't change often enough. That said, the crispy, salty margherita pizza—which brandishes the deeply evocative tang of buffalo mozzarella—is a dish for any season. Roast chicken is often an overlooked main, but this version is juicily successful; on one night, it came with chanterelles, watercress, and sweet, well-textured brown-butter gnocchi—inspired, perhaps, by the sweet cjalsons (dumplings topped with brown butter and a sprinkle of cinnamon) that you might find in Friuli-Venezia Giulia (northeastern Italy) or western Slovenia.

The dessert wine's great, too. We're duly impressed. –RG

# Vace

A delicious little place where the pasta abounds
and the pizza pies rule

| | |
|---|---|
| **8.0** | **6.2** |
| Food | Feel |

## Sandwiches, Pizza

Counter service **$30**
Price

www.vaceitaliandeli.com

Mon–Fri 9am–5pm
Sat 9am–8pm
Sun 10am–5pm
Hours vary by location

**Bar** Wine
**Credit cards** Visa, MC, AmEx
Veg-friendly

**Cleveland Park**
3315 Connecticut Ave. NW
(202) 363-1999

**Bethesda, MD**
4705 Miller Ave.
(301) 654-6367

Vace is a local institution, accompanied by its share of neighborhood
hype. In this case, the enthusiasm is well deserved. This Italian-deli-cum-
pizzeria-cum-provisioner serves up fresh, homemade pizza by the slice and
by the pie; more importantly, the store has saved many a Sunday dinner
from canned purgatory with its expansive supply of fresh pastas, sauces,
cheeses, and sides.

The pizza is made with the cheese integrated into, rather than on top
of the slightly sweet, tangy homemade red sauce. The medium-thick crust
is an excellent middle ground between the too-crisp Ella's and the too-
thick Armand's, boasting edges and stray cheese that are well crisped but
still soft. The classic array of toppings is complemented by choices such as,
during the season, fresh tomatoes (which are truly fresh), and prosciutto.

Craftier patrons can also purchase a bag of refrigerated dough, red
sauce, and imported mozzarella to recreate the experience at home. The
latter option seems well suited to the burgeoning class of IKEA
"carpenters" who like to cook from pre-assembled scratch; for the rest of
us, it's actually cheaper to order an already-made pie, which comes with
neither bragging rights nor clean-up.

Vace's collection of fresh pastas is so expansive that one wonders if, on
the afternoon of the fifth day after finishing with the beasts of the sea,
God didn't devote a half hour or so to crafting a menagerie of noodles to
populate Vace's shelves. The ravioli are especially delicious: the pumpkin
variety requires little more than butter and fresh sage to sate both
appetite and palate. It seems as if we discover something new every visit:
spinach lasagne, a surprising flavor of Torentoni syrup, even Argentine
alfajores. Most likely, once the smell of cooking pizza has drawn you to
Vace, we'd be surprised if you left empty-handed. –CK

# Vegetate

Vegetarian food that varies between healthful and heavy

| 5.8 | 7.6 |
|-----|-----|
| Food | Feel |

## New American

Upmarket restaurant

**$45**
Price

www.vegetatedc.com

Tue–Sat 6pm–9:30pm

**Bar** Beer, wine, liquor
**Credit cards** Visa, MC, AmEx
**Reservations** Accepted
Live music, veg-friendly

**Mt. Vernon Square**
1414 9th St. NW
(202) 232-4585

Vegetate takes on the challenge of exciting the vegetarian palate with inventive and tasty concoctions that move far beyond begrudging attempts by the chef to dress up rabbit food, resulting instead in a first-rate all-veg meal.

Despite its nondescript row-house exterior, Vegetate channels a chic, trendy vibe with locally sourced artwork hung on bright green walls and sleek metallic seating on each of its two floors. A hipster twenty- and thirtysomething crowd sips microbrews or cocktails mixed with homemade herbal simple syrups, while owner Dominic Redd's alter ego, DJ Dredd, spins trip hop from the second story DJ booth. Service is often slow and distracted, taking away from the fun.

American classics get a vegetarian, or even vegan, makeover here. Some of these are successful, such as soy-based mini burgers, which get dressed up with pickles and chimichurri. Biting into the crisp outer shell of the risotto croquettes reveals a warm, tender filling that, when combined with a sundried tomato tapenade, feels like mozzarella sticks done vegan-style.

Nut butters play a large role in Vegetate's kitchen, providing depth of flavor, and in some cases replacing animal fats, to allow for vegan options.

Golden beets marinated in balsamic vinegar and coriander oil pair deliciously with a coarsely ground almond butter, resulting in a refreshing departure from the tired beet and goat cheese combo. For a unique take on risotto, the kitchen uses cashew butter rather than more traditional dairy products to create a surprisingly rich and creamy base. When paired with pattypan squash, heirloom tomatoes, and a drizzle of truffle oil, this nutty and hearty dish stands out as one of the restaurant's best.

Unfortunately, Vegetate suffers from too many missteps to be worth recommending. Liquid smoke overpowers any essence of tea in the smoked black-tea polenta, and the side of chard gets drowned in salt. A lot of plates are starchy and heavy—isn't veggie/vegan food supposed to feel healthful? Seasoning is uneven, and blandness is rampant. The graver misfires mostly fall on desserts, where what tastes like grass clippings spoil an otherwise creamy mound of bittersweet chocolate ganache. If dessert is a must, stick to the gelato options. Or better yet, go somewhere else. —FC

# Veranda

**4.6** Food  **5.4** Feel

A small-time venue where both the food and the atmosphere seem like afterthoughts

## Greek, Italian, American

Casual restaurant

**$40** Price

www.verandaonp.com

Mon–Fri 5pm–12:30am
Sat 10:30am–2:30pm
Sun 10:30am–2:30pm, 5pm–12:30am

**Bar** Beer, wine, liquor
**Credit cards** Visa, MC, AmEx
**Reservations** Accepted
Live music, outdoor dining, Wi-Fi

**Logan Circle**
1100 P St. NW
(202) 234-6870

The name "Veranda" is a total misnomer when it comes to Logan Circle's Mediterranean-themed restaurant. Conversely, the restaurant makes few attempts to evoke any sort of open-aired isle aesthetic, and the only "veranda" involves an exposed block of concrete out front, where two cramped tables face the not-so-scenic oncoming traffic. Uncomfortably stiff red-and-green-striped pleather seats line the perimeter of the lackluster beige dining room, where grainy black and white photos depicting crumbled ruins serve as the one reminder of the restaurant's culinary theme.

The struggle with ambiance extends to the kitchen. Thick tzatziki tastes like a container of sour cream mixed with white onion chunks, something even less desirable when served with stale pita wedges. It's anyone's guess as to why the lamb shank with winter vegetables can be ordered mid-July, but it's the waiter's description of the shank's "Vegas style" preparation that makes us do a horrified double-take. What is Vegas style, exactly? Is the shank wearing pasties and snorting coke? Although certainly tender, the lamb seems to be missing any of the anise, cinnamon and coriander flavors described on the menu, and a miserable heap of gritty, musty mashed potatoes ruins the savory meat drippings.

It's fitting that the only winners here are the gelatos from local favorite Dolcezza (Greek yogurt, lavender, spicy chocolate), but get them by themselves; Veranda's cakey white-chocolate bread pudding just brings it down.

At this point, it's almost expected, but a terrible list of supermarket wines is inexcusable when there are so many exciting and lovely affordable producers from Greece, Lebanon and…hello? Italy?

The food presentation and execution here feel largely reminiscent of a corporate cafeteria, so anteing up anything close to the average $20 per main course may leave diners feeling cheated. Yes, the physical space is cozy, but a neighborhood ethnic spot this is not: the lack of atmosphere and the extremely mediocre (and overpriced) food render this more of a destination of last resort than anything else. –WS

# Veritas Wine Bar

Veritas Wine Bar is a little more lax than lux

| 6.5 | 8.5 |
|-----|-----|
| Food | Feel |

## New American

Wine bar

**$40**
Price

www.veritasdc.com

Daily 5pm–midnight

**Bar** Beer, wine
**Credit cards** Visa, MC, AmEx
**Reservations** Not accepted
Date-friendly, outdoor dining,
veg-friendly

**Dupont**
2031 Florida Ave. NW
(202) 265-6270

Wine bars are to the naughties what sushi bars were to the nineties; they're springing up everywhere these days. And the analogies are legion: the abundance of mediocrity, the dilution of quality, and the incorrect assumption that if you build it, they will come.

Although it's as hard to find a good wine bar as it is to find a good sushi bar, at least the phenomenon has had one positive influence on the restaurant scene: it discourages the too-long menu, one of the most objectionable pitfalls in the industry. It stands to reason that a kitchen focused on fewer things executes them better.

Veritas almost takes this philosophy too far: the only edible items on its menu are cheese, charcuterie, and chocolate. We approve of the fruity Garrotxa, a goat cheese from Spain; the mousse truffée, made with chicken livers, Madeira, and black truffle; and the terrine of braised rabbit, dates, and Cognac. But the cheeses are generally a bit predictable, and the cured meats are generally sort of lame. And while some of the chocolate creations are interesting, the dessert wine selection isn't (although we do appreciate the Madeira selection).

As for the rest of the wine cellar, while markups are fair, and there there are a couple areas of Old World strength—Alsace whites are well represented, for instance—there's a glaring problem: the selection is offensively tilted toward the New World. At last count, there were 71 red wines from California, but just 10 red wines from France (and none under $40). And how could a serious wine bar have just one German Riesling and one white Burgundy, arguably the world's two most important white wine regions?

Interesting, although we're often skeptical of wine-tasting flights, they actually seem to be the best work of the wine program here, with much better balance of New World to Old World than the list as a whole. The "Tour de France," with a Languedoc Mourvèdre, a fairly obscure Bordeaux, and a Châteauneuf-du-Pape, goes beyond predictable French reds; and the "Iberia," with a Loureiro, an Albariño, and a Verdejo, is cool, crisp, and pairs beautifully with a warm DC night.

We can sign off on the atmosphere, too. It's got more the vibe of a neighborhood bistro than a trying-to-be-trendy wine bar. Veritas is cozy and elegant without pretense—the ideal setting for a low-key night out. But without a better wine program, the minimalist food offerings seem even less compelling; atmosphere alone just isn't enough to rescue Veritas. –RG

# Vermilion

The pride of Old Town seems to get better with every season

| 9.2 | 8.8 |
|---|---|
| Food | Feel |

## New American

Upmarket restaurant

| $65 |
|---|
| Price |

www.vermilionrestaurant.com

Mon–Thu 11:30am–3pm,
5:30pm–10pm; Fri 11:30am–
3pm, 5:30pm–11pm; Sat
11am–2:30pm, 5:30pm–11pm;
Sun 11am–2:30pm, 5:30pm–
10pm

**Bar** Beer, wine, liquor
**Credit cards** Visa, MC, AmEx
**Reservations** Accepted
Date-friendly, good wines

**Alexandria Old Town**
1120 King St.
(703) 684-9669

One of the most sweetly shining stars of Old Town, Vermilion sets itself apart from its King Street neighbors with more style, a swankier clientele, higher prices, and—yeah, we'll admit it—more pretense, too. Adjectives could be used less on this menu; that said, the staff is about as unpretentious as anyone could be who's serving dishes with names like "trumpet mushrooms 2 ways, parmesan froth & winter herbs," "path valley kaleidoscope carrots," or—on an otherwise English menu—calling tomato "pomodoro" for no reason.

But here's the kicker: unlike at some of the overpriced, trying-too-hard New American trend-fests all around the greater DC, Vermilion backs its claims up with legitimate sensory mastery of the palate, beginning with simply masterful raisin bread and butter, an element of the meal that is so often merely perfunctory.

The menu changes often enough that we'd merely be torturing you by lavishly describing much of what we've had here, but one really notable preparation has been a cream-of-cauliflower soup, with a whisper of curry, that would have been a bit bland on its own—but was elevated to greatness by its totally unpredictable mix of sweet-savory accoutrements: raisins that added sweetness, expertly fried oysters that added salt, and fried cauliflower that added crunch. And out of nowhere came a treble note of anise.

Fish is handled with extraordinary patience, care, and expertise in this kitchen, whether it's seasonal shad roe—in a star-crossed threesome with smoked bacon and Meyer lemon brown butter—or grilled whole fish, served as simply as it should be, with olive oil and lemon. Prices have not gotten out of hand here; the four-course tasting, $45 at press time, is one of the city's most reasonably priced.

Brunch is an unexpected delight at Vermilion; in fact, it's one of the best in the city. You might be treated to a loose, ground-pork-shoulder version of scrapple—the mystery breakfast meat of the Pennsylvania and Delaware small-town working class. We surely thought we'd never seen an haute version of *that*. (Just when you thought the fashion of fetishizing the native cuisine of America's rural poor couldn't go any further.)

Cocktails are excellent, too, and the wine program is unusually thoughtful, with good amounts of attention paid to underappreciated white wine regions like Austria.

Oh, and as if all of that weren't enough, they call main courses "mains," not entrées. Respect. –RG

# Vidalia

Going for many things, and achieving most of them

**9.0** Food

**7.2** Feel

## Southern, New American

Upmarket restaurant

**$70** Price

www.vidaliadc.com

Mon–Thu 11:30am–2:30pm, 5:30pm–10pm; Fri 11:30am–2:30pm, 5:30pm–10:30pm; Sat 5:30pm–10:30pm; Sun 5pm–9:30pm

**Bar** Beer, wine, liquor
**Credit cards** Visa, MC, AmEx
**Reservations** Accepted

**Dupont**
1990 M St. NW
(202) 659-1990

Vidalia is one of those restaurants that has been around long enough to be overlooked. This isn't the hottest ticket in town, but the restaurant is quietly putting out great food that is impossible to categorize. It's known for its Southern roots, but when you descend the stairs from the street to the subterranean space—past a boastful wall of accolades dating back to 1993—you'll discover a brightly lit, restaurant-cataloggishly modern dining room that suggests anything but pork fat and pecan pies.

These, days the menu reads as if it was put together by Mad Hatter: homey macaroni and cheese and roasted Vidalia onions share space with contemporary dishes like slow-poached duck egg and blue-corn polenta. It all might feel disorienting until the first few dishes arrive at the table—beginning, perhaps, with a refreshing amuse of not-entirely-Southern chilled cucumber soup. Soon, things suddenly fall into place. If you are adventurous enough to order a soused shad, you are rewarded with one of the finest raw fish preparations anywhere, built around warm shad roe, cipollini, yellowfin potatoes, and a touch of acidity from the bacon-apple vinaigrette. The buttery fish fillet wouldn't be out of place at a top sushi bar, but what's most surprising, perhaps, is the use of sousing—a technique used to lightly marinate herring in some European countries and almost unheard of in the US.

This kitchen has a way with offal—and a way with carving it, too. Tender pig's trotters have their meat scooped out, chopped, and placed back into the neatly cut cylinders, preserving their original shape. Chicken livers come out in perfect geometric shapes, as if to mimic foie gras torchon. Pig's tails are picked of bone and cartilage, stuffed into casings, and deep fried; the end result looks and feels a little like a rubbery egg roll, but the tail-meat filling is like pornography to a self-respecting pork fanatic.

Vidalia has the capacity for unevenness. We've sometimes been disappointed at lunch, when service has been clueless, rockfish has been overcooked, and shrimp and grits have come out with a surfeit of salt.

But come for dinner and get the tasting menu, and by its conclusion, you will have given up on trying to categorize Vidalia. But perhaps that's why it feels so comfortable in this city. Like the District itself, it is Southern, and also Northern. And like the District itself, it is nostalgic, and also modern. –RG

# Vietnam Georgetown

**4.3** Food    **4.2** Feel

Pass on this poor performer; there's much better
Vietnamese across the bridge

## Vietnamese

Casual restaurant    **$30** Price

Sun–Thu 11am–10pm
Fri–Sat noon–11pm

**Bar** Beer, wine, liquor
**Credit cards** Visa, MC, AmEx
**Reservations** Accepted
Outdoor dining

**Georgetown**
2934 M St. NW
(202) 337-4536

Here's a restaurant that's wasted no time on such a frivolous matter as a
title: it's simply compiled the name of the country (Vietnam) from whence
its cuisine derives with that of the city-state (Georgetown) whose
residents will consume its dishes. "Vietnam Georgetown," two strung-
together proper nouns, doesn't even make sense grammatically, but, well,
it gets the point across.

Here's wishing the restaurant had devoted the same sense of utility to
its prices. Alas, you're stuck with the typical Georgetown fifteen: up to
fifteen bucks per main course, even though the setting is decidedly
downscale compared to that of its neighbors (inside, anyway; outside,
there's a patio that becomes rather romantic at night with strings of
lights). Plus, the food comes in clunky helpings (the upside is a lot of bang
for a lot of buck; the downside is leftovers you'll avoid in the fridge).

Although Vietnam Georgetown does, at times, seem to harbor some
desire to serve authentic food—there are sour soups, Hue grilled beef,
and caramel pork with lemongrass—this is ultimately more of a Chinese-
American restaurant than anything else. With some of America's best
Vietnamese food lurking over in Falls Church, just a few miles past the
Key Bridge, it is embarrassing to the District that this place should be
taken seriously serving tossed salad, sweet-and-sour shrimp, and chicken
fried rice.

Among the dumbed-down dishes, we favor the crêpes, which are very
large, but cooked to the ideal golden brown. Their fillings aren't up to
snuff, though. A "Vietnamese Crispy Crêpe," for example, is filled with
shrimp and pork in peanut sauce that is somewhat weak, and many of
the ingredients (e.g. mung beans) seem thrown on as an afterthought,
rather than integrated in any meaningful way.

Another disappointment is the "Five Vegetables Rice Noodle," which
comes not only with five vegetables (dominated by broccoli) but also with
three types of meat: shrimp, scallop and pork. While the scallops are soft,
fresh and plump, the oversized shrimp taste as if they've been sitting too
long in the fridge or freezer. The various versions of pho are pretty bland,
too, lacking that rich beefy goodness and herbaceous aroma.

Keep walking—or, better yet, metro-ing, taxi-ing, or driving—because
there's far better Vietnamese just around the corner. Here's a start: keep
going all the way down M Street, and take a left at the big bridge. –FC

# Vinoteca

**7.3** | **8.8**
Food | Feel

A happening place where the food is on, and you'll find all the cool kids here

## New American

Wine bar | **$45**
Price

www.vinotecadc.com

Tue–Thu 4:30pm–2am
Fri–Sat 4:30pm–3am
Sun 11am–3pm, 4:30pm–2am

**Bar** Beer, wine, liquor
**Credit cards** Visa, MC, AmEx
**Reservations** Accepted
Date-friendly, good wines, live music, outdoor dining, veg-friendly, Wi-Fi

**U Street**
1940 11th St. NW
(202) 332-9463

Vinoteca feels like the joint where cool kids hang out. Tucked into the corner of 11th and U, the non-descript restaurant is largely unadvertised. Even so, Vinoteca is always a party. Whether it's the pounding of flamenco heels, the strumming of flamenco guitars, or the buzz of many conversations in a small space, the entire restaurant feels and sounds alive. Just being there is a rush.

The tapas-esque menu at Vinoteca is quite fitting for the atmosphere—with all of the bustle and the noise, Vinoteca is better suited for small bites and many libations than it is for a big meal. It's too deafening in here for lazy table-wide conversations. Happily, the wine list is balanced between the New and Old Worlds, including a fair number of lesser-known craft producers, at reasonable prices, although France is more or less dismissed. All selections are available by the taste, the glass, and the bottle.

The significant selection of meats and cheeses are from all over the world, too. The meats are well sliced and a wonderful find. Soppressata is salty and meaty—all the best things in a cured meat. Duck prosciutto is so rich that it's moist and slick, with a hint of sweetness and a velvety smooth texture. Fiore sardo cheese is dense and bitter enough to induce a surprising rush of saliva and a quick cheek pucker when it hits your mouth.

More substantial dishes are delightful. Homemade chorizo is soft, loose, and subtly spiced. A bison steak is bloodier and more metallic than beef. Its accompanying dill-laced chimichurri is intriguingly acidic and just a tiny bit sweet. The bison is served with giant potato croquettes that hold together surprisingly well for their size. Placed on a bed of ketchup, they bring to mind oversized, rotund tater tots.

Dessert is one of the more pleasant surprises here. Cheesecake made with goat cheese sets a light, fluffy texture against a powerful flavor. Fig compote adds a dusty sweetness to the dish that suggests dessert rather than screaming it. The cake toes the line between savory and sweet and makes you stop and consider. If only all dishes were this thoughtful.

Not so for the service at Vinoteca, which is uncharacteristically careless. Food is served at a snail's pace (even though most dishes don't require much cooking) and the wait staff is sloppy. Yet despite it all, you'll be happy to be there. If slower service means more time at the table, then revel in it. Vinoteca can't remain an in-crowd secret for too long. –JC

# W Domku

You'll feel at home here, no matter where home really is

**7.7** Food **9.5** Feel

## Scandinavian, Polish

Casual restaurant **$40** Price

www.domkucafe.com

Tue–Wed 5pm–11pm
Thu 10am–11pm
Fri–Sat 10am–midnight
Sun 10am–10pm

**Bar** Beer, wine, liquor
**Credit cards** Visa, MC
**Reservations** Accepted
Date-friendly, kid-friendly, outdoor dining, Wi-Fi

**Petworth**
821 Upshur St. NW
(202) 722-7475

W Domku is a rare bird indeed. The Petworth eatery falls far outside the three Linnaean kingdoms of DC: It's not a turbo-charged place to lunch, nor does it have a toe-tapping happy hour, nor (despite its name) is it a cheap ethnic hole-in-the-wall for immigrants and hipsters.

But Domku is rare in the more usual sense as well. It's uncommon enough to find a restaurant serving Polish or Latvian or Swedish specialties; to have a single joint dish out all three is, quite frankly, a bit frightening. To top it off, on a recent winter night Domku proposed a "sunny getaway" specials menu with eight dishes from the Subcontinent. You can't know for sure that herring and saag paneer don't mix until you try—but unfortunately, once you do, the evidence against such crass cross-culturalism is damning.

Domku offers self-consciously mismatched décor as well. The loft-like space features exposed brick, unassorted chairs and sofas, vintage lamps and other accoutrements of the bohemian-hip. The servers are young and interestingly dressed, and even the location, in the backwaters of Petworth, can seem premeditated. Despite its various affectations, however, the floorplan is so welcoming and the menu so interesting that you're inclined to forgive (and even become enraptured by) Domku's mild pomposity.

The food isn't bad, either. We cringed at paying $5 for a thin slice of rye bread spread with spiced mayonnaise and an even thinner layer of sprat, but in terms of taste (if not volume), Domku is an excellent value. The pickled herring three ways showcases the flavor of this northern staple, and the carrot-ginger soup is expertly spiced and filling. Domku has gravlax, bison burgers, and eggs and bangers. You can order Swedish meatballs, pierogi, kielbasa, or goulash.

Whatever you decide on, the aquavits—including black currant, lemongrass and ginger, and cardamom—are not to be missed: in fact, hard alcohol may be the only thing to unite the hodgepodge countries whose flags Domku flies. –CK

# Weenie Beanie

Sometimes, the best half-smokes happen where you least expect them

| | |
|---|---|
| **8.0** | **6.0** |
| Food | Feel |

## American

Counter service

**$5**
Price

Daily 6am–6pm

**Bar** None
**Credit cards** Visa, MC
Kid-friendly

**Arlington, VA**
2680 S. Shirlington Rd.
(703) 671-6661

The half-smoke is, by many accounts, DC's one truly native food, and one of the best half-smokes in the area can be found at this little drive-up-or-walk-up stand, which sits unassumingly along Shirlington Road. The place is not far from the District, but it's in a sort of no-man's land; across the street is an area where some day laborers hang out, looking for work, and they love the half-smokes here. You will too.

The place is strictly order-at-the-counter—low prices, no frills—and you'd better know what you want by the time you get there, because patience isn't up there with short-order-grill and half-smoke expertise on the list of talents of the Weenie Beanie staff.

The thing to have is a half-smoke with chili and cheese. It's beautifully charred, served on a super-absorbent white hot-dog roll, and has in every sense mastered the delicate balance of fat, salt, sugar, and starch that's required for all-out, straight-up pleasure.

Even more treats await if you travel down the menu a bit. Fried-fish sandwiches are surprisingly good, as are the basic egg-plus sandwiches (like bacon, egg, and cheese on toasted white bread), and the vinegary North Carolina-style pulled pork sandwiches (not up to smoky Carolina standards, but not bad for the DC area). Skip the soggy fries, though.

The *Urban Dictionary* defines "weenie beanie" as follows: "A condom. A party hat for your hot dog. One size fits most. Usage: *I brought a pack of weenie beanies in my pocket to the yacht party.*"

Might get a bit messy, with all that chili and cheese oozing out of your jeans, but it still sounds like a good yacht party to us.

# Wellness Café

There's little done well at this hippie haven;
vegetarians deserve better

**3.1** Food  **3.0** Feel

## Sandwiches, Sweet drinks

Café  **$20** Price

www.wellnesscafedc.com

Mon–Fri 9:30am–6:30pm
Sat 10am–6:30pm

**Bar** None
**Credit cards** Visa, MC, AmEx
Outdoor dining, veg-friendly

**Capitol Hill**
325 Pennsylvania Ave. SE
(202) 543-2266

The Wellness Café will very likely deal a shock to your senses, but perhaps not in the way you'd expect. This Pennsylvania avenue hovel-in-the-wall is one of the most visually stimulating places around, and it's packed to the brim with potions and products claiming to cure what ails and ward off all that menaces to ail.

When its outdoor chalkboard boasts fresh and healthy lunches within, we can't help but suspect that their claims are nothing short of boldfaced lies. Take the panini, which aren't really panini at all so much as regular toast with stuff on top. There's very little that's particularly healthy (or good) about generic, sliced wheat bread topped with oily (even slimy), under-roasted vegetables, soy cheese, and rock-hard tomatoes. The sandwich seems to have been put through some kind of tabletop toaster-press, or otherwise branded, to emerge with a few parallel brown lines that are supposed to substitute for toasting. The resulting mess is soggy and gross.

Wraps, which come in equally generic flour tortillas, are no better. The homemade soups are decent but ordinary: the selection is usually limited to some mix of cubed vegetables in a pretty good broth. Wellness' smoothies, meanwhile, are too sweet: you're better off opting from one of the juices in its admittedly excellent collection. Strangely, Wellness Café also serves Coke. Wellness, indeed.

And the service is mind-bogglingly slow. If it offers any consolation, Wellness is a rather interesting place to have an excuse to poke around while waiting, if only to shed light on the disturbing nature of our "culture of wellness"; beyond the basic bran and flax, you'll find such remedies as desiccated liver, amino fuel, muscle milk, and Arctic cod liver. We located (and love) the raw honey, but we're still searching for the raw truth.

Wellness may have garnered a certificate from the "Forrest Friendly 500," but it won't get any praise from us. The café's hippie ethos has gone without its deodorant for too long (in other words, this place stinks). —CK

# Westend Bistro

Sometimes greatness is more about moderation than flash

| **9.4** | **8.6** |
|---|---|
| Food | Feel |

## New American

Upmarket restaurant

**$65**
*Price*

www.westendbistrodc.com

Mon–Thu 11:30am–2:30pm, 5:30pm–10pm; Fri 11:30am–2:30pm, 5:30pm–11pm; Sat 5:30pm–11pm; Sun 5:30pm–10pm

**Bar** Beer, wine, liquor
**Credit cards** Visa, MC, AmEx
**Reservations** Accepted
Date-friendly

**West End**
1190 22nd St. NW
(202) 974-4900

Unlike some of the world's other great chefs, Eric Ripert has not franchised his name. Yeah, he's got the requisite cookbooks and the web site; he seems to do some Cuisinart toaster-oven promoting; he collects his honors and awards. But considering his culinary achievements and his rock-star potential, it seems as if the man actually avoids attention.

When Ripert puts his name on a new restaurant—and, beyond his New York flagship, Le Bernardin, he's only done it for three Ritz-Carlton restaurants, including this one—you can bet that it's not going to be a glorified casual-dining concept, and it's not going to be a margin factory trying to do 500 covers per evening.

Westend Bistro is the restaurant that you would have him open in a fantasy world. It's casual, it's accessible, and it's about as close as you can get in the United States to Le Bernardin's level of execution at this price point.

The secret is in how wisely the great "Culinary Director" seems to have allocated his costs. Instead of filling his menu with complex show-off recipes that demand a line full of superstars and an MBA managing inventory—frequently the mistake of a brash young chef—he's spent his money on high-quality ingredients and a well-trained, competent staff that executes consistently on an immensely satisfying menu of great balance and sophistication.

It might begin with melting, eye-rolling jamón ibérico with grilled country bread, arugula salad, and white beans with a whisper of truffle; an assortment of clean, bright oysters; or a rosy tuna carpaccio that's pounded into a thin film over the plate, probably unlike any you've had unless you've been to Le Bernardin. An extraordinarily delicate salmon fillet goes brilliantly with lentils, pickled mushroom, and black truffle butter. And then there are two of the city's greatest under-$20 dishes: a beautiful fish burger, with fennel, oven-roasted tomato, and saffron aioli, on a sweet brioche; and—surprise!—perhaps DC's best tagliatelle alla bolognese. This, from America's greatest seafood spokesman?

Chocolate caramel cream with sea salt, one among many excellent desserts, is yet another creation that demonstrates elegance through balance and restraint. The wine list is a bit short and limited given the power of the kitchen, but there are some decent Alsatian whites.

Horizontal fluke tastings and acrobatics with lobster in New York might have earned Ripert his high profile, but perhaps, in this latest phase of his great career, a magnificent sort of moderation is the quality from which we can learn most. –RG

# The Wharf Seafood

| 7.7 | 6.8 |
|-----|-----|
| Food | Feel |

Take in all the fish and oysters you can get...just
ignore the dirty water you're near

## Seafood

Counter service

**$25**
Price

www.captainwhitesseafood.com

| Daily 7am–9pm | **Bar** None | **Southwest DC** |
|---|---|---|
| | **Credit cards** Visa, MC, AmEx | 1100 Maine Ave. SW |
| | Outdoor dining | (202) 314-5759 |

Whatever wise-guy city planner decided that DC's fresh fish market should be placed along the water must have either had a raging sense of irony, or no sense at all. One look at the water—actually a dirty dead-end channel of the Anacostia river that seems little more than a repository for beer cans, parked motorboats, and seagull droppings—might actually convince you to renounce eating fish altogether, the buzz about Omega-3 acids notwithstanding.

Luckily, the fish at the Maine Street Fish Market does not come from Washington (latest Potomac advisory: pollution causes male fish to lay eggs), but is shipped in from the crab kingdom of the Chesapeake. As you'd imagine, crabs feature prominently at the fish shacks, as well as on the menus of the several establishments that serve prepared foods, but you can also find oysters, clams, shrimp, various white fish, and other Atlantic goodies.

If you're in the mood for appetizers, begin on the windward side of the Wharf, where a separate counter offers fresh oysters or clams, shucked in front of you and served three at a time. The quality of the dish depends heavily on the quality of the oysters that day, but you can count on them being good in general. The Wharf provides a shelf of sauces and lemon juice, but little else in the way of condiment or utensil; the custom is to eat the oysters in situ while chatting with the shucker.

Moving down the long counter of the Wharf (the Wharf is but one of many seafood vendors in the fish market, but only two others—including Jimmy's next door—offer prepared food as well as fish), your next stop is the main food counter. Here, you can order any of a number of soups, seafood salads, sandwiches, plates, and sides. If the seafood gumbo special is available, it's well worth a try: although it's a little soupier than most gumbos, the integration of several types of seafood and hot chile is incredible.

For a true value, try the pupusas—a Salvadoran specialty with no affiliation to seafood whatsoever. –CK

# White Tiger

An Indian joint that goes just a bit above and beyond the pack

**6.7** Food   **7.5** Feel

## Indian

Casual restaurant   **$35** Price

www.whitetigerdc.com

Sun–Thu 11:30am–2:30pm, 5pm–10pm; Fri 11:30am–2:30pm, 5pm–10:30pm; Sat 5pm–10:30pm

**Bar** Beer, wine, liquor
**Credit cards** Visa, MC, AmEx
**Reservations** Accepted
Kid-friendly, outdoor dining, veg-friendly

**Capitol Hill**
301 Massachusetts Ave. NE
(202) 546-5900

It's not easy to find a decent Indian restaurant within the District itself. We're known for a cadre of solid Ethiopian and Salvadoran places, but South Asia isn't a specialty that shines. Our general advice to those pining for matter paneer is to head to the Maryland or DC suburbs, but if you're stuck in the District when the itch for tandoor becomes intolerable, the White Tiger is a decent bet for ordinary curries.

This Capitol Hill restaurant is fancy enough for an evening out, with thoughtful décor, excellent service, and the lights dimmed just short of just-so levels. Creative additions to Indian classics set White Tiger apart from its counterparts: a traditional tomato soup, for example, is topped with a fried-okra garnish. Along with the usual retinue of samosa and skewer appetizers, the restaurant offers a tangy papri chat salad—essentially chips atop a chutney-accented yogurt sauce—and a set of mystifying Indian crab cakes. The major disappointment of the early meal—at least for those who expect a certain routine from Americanized Indian—is the absence of a plate of papadam and its three accompanying sauces.

The remainder of the menu offers a good selection of lamb, chicken, beef, and seafood choices, plus tandoor specialties and a good set of vegetarian specialties. White Tiger is consistently decent and on occasion creative; but no dish we've tried has been particularly remarkable in terms of preparation. Vindaloo is spicy and refined. Saag is appropriately creamy. Chicken is well-prepared but on the dry side. Of the vegetarian options, kofta, a set of fried dumplings served in a yellow curry sauce, is the most interesting.

White Tiger also boasts an above-average wine list, a fair selection of beers including Indian brews, a weekday buffet lunch, and Sunday brunch. One of its finest assets may be its outdoor seating overlooking Union Station and Massachusetts Avenue, making it an ideal spot for people-watching on a warm day. Throw in a decent menu and a strong kitchen, and you've got a fine combination. –CK

# Whitlow's on Wilson

An old neighborhood bar that rose from the ashes to reappear in Arlington

**6.9** | **7.6**
*Food* | *Feel*

## American

Casual restaurant

**$35**
*Price*

www.whitlows.com

Mon–Fri 11am–2am
Sat–Sun 9am–2am

**Bar** Beer, wine, liquor
**Credit cards** Visa, MC, AmEx
**Reservations** Accepted
Kid-friendly, live music, outdoor
dining, Wi-Fi

**Arlington, VA**
2854 Wilson Blvd.
(703) 276-9693

When Whitlow's re-opened in Arlington in 1995, there was a distinct air of triumph over "the man." Despite being forced out of downtown DC in 1989 by rent increases, the neighborhood bar would rise again—this time in the suburbs. Sitting in Whitlow's is like being in a funky museum of Americana, surrounded by a patchwork of doodads and whosiwhatsits that showcase 60 years of history through the lens of a neighborhood bar. Pieces of detritus have attached themselves like barnacles to the walls of Whitlow's over the years, each with its own story. Note the old stove, church-trimmed booths, transplanted stained windows, and bowling lane-turned-bar.

There is something about Whitlow's that brings you back in time. Looking at the menu, it's not hard to imagine lone bachelors coming to the original every night for dinner specials. Though it may have introduced some international flavors, deep down inside, its root is still in the America of the '40s and '50s, where Campbell's soup was a legitimate base for a dish.

Take for example the signature meatloaf. A log of meat the width of a fat corgi is sliced inches thick and slapped on the plate and festooned with fried onions. Titanic mounds of mashed potatoes cratered with gravy and a veritable forest of collard greens complete the dish. The plate weighs as much as a backstreet boy and probably tastes kind of like one too—frivolously light, "spongy," and loose, with a surprisingly garlicky edge. The gravy is some of the thickest you'll ever encounter. This is an epic recreation of a classic dish.

Less traditional dishes are not authentic, but can be surprisingly good. "Caribbean Shrimp," while a terrible excuse for ethnic food, is thoroughly crave-worthy. Crispy, floury chips are topped with giant shrimp and tons of tangy mango salsa, sour cream, and guacamole. This is food designed for the really drunk, really tired, or really stressed—but it's actually executed well enough to cure those disparate ills and then some. Whitlow's even manages to add salsa-ranch dressing to the dish in a way that is appetizing instead of sickening. It's the platonic ideal that TGI Friday's menu will forever reach for and always miss.

Within the walls of Whitlow's, whether downtown or on Wilson, you'll feel easy-going, well taken care of, and very, very full. You'll be glad, in short, that Whitlow's has survived the passage of time. –JC

# Whole Foods Market

The show-stopping foodie and wine-geek
wonderland to end all arguments

## Groceries

Market

www.wholefoodsmarket.com

Daily 8am–10pm

**Bar** Beer, wine
**Credit cards** Visa, MC, AmEx
**Reservations** Not accepted
Good wines, veg-friendly

**Logan Circle**
1440 P St. NW
(202) 332-4300

**Georgetown**
2323 Wisconsin Ave. NW
(202) 333-5393

**Arlington, VA**
2700 Wilson Blvd.
(703) 527-6596

**Additional locations**
and more features at
www.fearlesscritic.com

Whole Foods is the homegrown health-food market gone national—a
hippie, food-obsessed Austin, Texas local boy made good. It is no small
praise for the American consumer—a glimmer of hope?—that Whole
Foods has been such a success story. This is not just because the stores are
gorgeous, but they are; the produce, cheese, and seafood are all
beautifully displayed, and the overall experience is quite simply
overwhelming, in part because there is just so much to choose from.

Yet in an America that is all about breadth of choice, Whole Foods has
chosen wisely—with one eye on the environment and another on good
taste—yet its scope is so vast that the global research magic happens
behind the scenes, leaving the shopper more choice than ever—but the
right kind of choice.

Sprinkled throughout most stores are several mini-restaurants and
buffet stations, which display seafood, sandwiches, barbecue, pizza, sushi,
salads, "living foods," and more. Foods from around the world
(sometimes different parts of the world at different times of day) can be
boxed up or plated, eaten inside or outside or taken home. Wander
around until something piques your interest, but find it fast before
sensory overload completely incapacitates you.

Equally staggering—yet chosen with magnificent care—is the wine
section. It is an operation that's equally concerned with quality, savings,
and supporting independent, small, sustainable producers—yet also
gently exerting enough influence on the buy side that they get the best
prices from producers and reflect those savings back to the customer. It's
like having a brutally honest, personal expert wine agent represent you in
the marketplace, and find you the best deals. –FC

# Wok & Roll

**3.8** | **6.5**
Food | Feel

Wok, don't roll, at this Chinese-sushi hybrid—or
better yet, forego both and just grab a bubble tea

## Chinese

Casual restaurant | **$20**
| Price

www.wokandrolldc.com

Mon–Thu 10:30am–10:30pm
Fri–Sat 10:30am–1am
Sun noon–10:30pm

**Bar** Beer, wine, liquor
**Credit cards** Visa, MC, AmEx
**Reservations** Accepted
Delivery, live music, Wi-Fi

**Chinatown**
604 H St. NW
(202) 347-4656

Forks are the default utensil at this Chinatown eatery, whose ambitions
tend to favor kitsch over taste. With a (cringe) sushi bar in back, a regular
bar in front, and plants and turquoise hues in between, you might feel as
if you're in some kind of psychedelic aquarium.

As is becoming the money-hungry, flavor-poor norm, Wok & Roll is a
Chinese-and-sushi hybrid restaurant. As a way to bridge the cultural
divide, perhaps, a pot of rather ordinary tea is provided free of charge.

The "Chinese" side of things consists of all the American favorites:
orange beef, sweet and sour pork, Peking duck, Singapore rice noodles,
and so on. In terms of taste, the food is passable; it's a cut above much of
the Chinese fare on H Street, and this elevated quality is reflected in
somewhat elevated prices relative to its neighbors (only about $1-$2 more
per main). Although the moo shu pancakes are somewhat dry, the rice
and sauce are competent, the filling a classic mix of crunchy water
chestnuts and tender mushrooms.

The sushi, on the other hand, leaves much to be desired. The wasabi is
a disturbingly neon green, and the tuna's too red to be credible. Mackerel
(addictive when it's good and sickening when it's bad) is tough here, and
unpleasantly funky. All of the nigiri are about half the size of those at
comparable sushi restaurants, but then, do you really want more fish
when it's this bad? At happy hour, nigiri is priced at only a dollar a pop,
which might be closer to what it's worth.

Grab a milky bubble tea from the long list; there's also a full bar and
desperate cocktail list. Nothing goes better with General Tso's chicken
than a blended daiquiri (barf!) The truncated sake and wine list is only
good for a giggle ("*Chablish*?" Cooking-wine alert!)

Wok & Roll is not without its touch of rock and roll: the speakers seem
to always carry tunes well-suited to American karaoke. There's the Dixie
Chicks, some Elvis. But we'll sing no praises for the food. Our chorus, in
brief, might be: more wok, less roll. –CK

# Yee Hwa

Yee Hwa, not yee haw-style barbecue at one of the
only true Korean options in the district

| 7.0 | 6.0 |
|------|------|
| Food | Feel |

## Korean, Japanese

Casual restaurant

**$40**
Price

Mon–Fri 10:30am–10pm
Sat noon–10pm
Sun noon–9:30pm

**Bar** Beer, wine, liquor
**Credit cards** Visa, MC, AmEx
**Reservations** Accepted
Kid-friendly

**Downtown**
1009 21st St. NW
(202) 833-1244

For the best Korean food in DC, you have to leave DC, and make the drive
to Annandale, Virginia. However, if you ever develop a desperate craving
for bibimbap, there are a couple places in the city that aren't so bad. Yee
Hwa, unobtrusively settled in the Downtown district, is one. Clean,
spacious, and orderly, it feels like a replica of a higher-end, informal diner
in Asia. Down-to-earth service and endearingly faded napkins add to the
mom-and-pop feel.

Like many Asian restaurants in DC, Yee Hwa's menu has caved and
offers "pan-Asian" cuisine, mixing a sushi bar and Chinese appetizers
with traditional Korean fare to attract as many clients as possible. Given
their quality, you would do best to stick with the traditional offerings.

Meals at Yee Hwa begin with the standard complimentary banchan
(small dishes). This includes ubiquitous pickled vegetables (kimchi—sharp,
pungent, bitter, acidly spicy; cucumber—mild at first bite but filled with a
long, slow heat; radish—tangy and clean) and less traditional dishes like a
lost-looking pasta salad (?!). The dishes are a welcome and (mostly)
authentic touch, but ultimately underpowered. Kimchi, when done well,
should burn off the lining of your mouth and overpower you with its
gloriously stinky aroma. Yee Hwa's version is nowhere close.

That being said, some of the other dishes are very well executed. Hae
mul pa jeon, a Korean version of a scallion pancake, is looser and eggier
than its Chinese cousin, and laced with bits of various seafood. It is served
piping hot, and the chunks of vegetables and fish in the batter are
incredibly crispy yet soft inside. Bulgogi (marinated beef) is sweet, gritty,
and cut thin for maximum marinade absorption. If you sit at one of the
tables with the built-in barbecue grills, you can cook it to chewy, juicy
tenderness. You'll get treated to the smell of charring meat, which is
deeply reminiscent of the street food sold in Asian open-air markets.

Your meal at Yee Hwa will end with another traditional offering: a
teacup full of cinnamon-spiced punch. As you leave, the earnest smiles of
the servers will make you feel like coming again. Which, given the
lackluster local competition, you probably will. –JC

# Yuan Fu

The faux-fowl may be mostly good for a laugh, but we're good natured enough to say "l'chaim!"

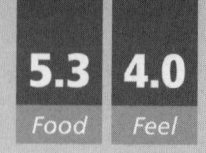

**5.3** Food

**4.0** Feel

## Chinese

Casual restaurant

**$25** Price

Sun–Thu 11am–10pm
Fri–Sat 11am–10:30pm

**Bar** None
**Credit cards** Visa, MC, AmEx
**Reservations** Accepted
Kid-friendly, veg-friendly

**Rockville, MD**
798 Rockville Pike
(301) 762-5938

With a menu that's entirely meat-free and dairy-free, it's no wonder that Yuan Fu spotlights in its entryway a framed copy of a positive review from a local Jewish newspaper—it's kosher, too. But that's where the potential appeal ends. Although elaborately specific mock meats are popular in China, this is hardly authentic Chinese cuisine. But diners here aren't in search of authenticity: quite the opposite, really. It's the spectacularly artificial that they crave.

Yuan Fu has a truly impressive repertoire of fake flesh—everything from squid and shrimp to beef and duck is one hundred percent man-made. For vegetarians who revel in the kitsch factor of squid impressions and General Tso's chicken, hold the chicken, Yuan Fu is quality eatertainment. Spam fans: Fu's for you; for us, it's just about worthless.

We just can't bring ourselves to recommend the meat substitutes concocted from tofu in various forms, or wheat gluten, or rice noodles. We prefer not to squint at our food, wishing it were something else. Devotees will tell you to think of these not as poor stand-ins, but as new and exciting textures and protein sources. Vegetarians will justly laud the food's ethical and constitutional advantages.

Is it really ethical, if you don't believe in eating animals, to fool yourself into thinking you're eating animals? Kant, anyway, would say no. Plus, we think they're simply selling vegetables way, way, short. The vegetable is a glorious thing, easily able to stand up, flavor to flavor, with the best of meats. So why not simply serve it? Real Chinese vegetable dishes are amongst the best in the world. The best thing we ate at Yuan Fu—steamed vegetable dumplings, straightforward and traditional—is a dish you can get at any respectable Chinese place. Likewise, the vegetable stir-fries are widely available and far superior elsewhere—Yuan Fu's asparagus-and-shiitake-mushroom version seems sapped of flavor by its glossy sauce.

You will not, however, easily find the "roast duck" appetizer, essentially a deep-fried stack of wide, flat rice noodles, at your corner take-out. Inoffensive enough, it is to duck what Log Cabin is to real maple syrup. Or perhaps to real log cabins.

The restaurant occupies a nondescript space in a strip mall marooned in the ocean of a desolate parking lot. The drab interior is redeemed by extremely friendly, if not always efficient, service. The warmth here, at least, is the real deal. –CD

# Zaytinya

Well-polished, hipped-up Greek with the
calculated power and glory of an "it" club

| 8.5 | 8.9 |
|---|---|
| Food | Feel |

## Middle Eastern

Upmarket restaurant

**$65**
Price

www.zaytinya.com

Sun–Mon 11:30am–10pm
Tue–Thu 11:30am–11:30pm
Fri–Sat 11:30am–midnight

**Bar** Beer, wine, liquor
**Credit cards** Visa, MC, AmEx
**Reservations** Accepted
Date-friendly, outdoor dining,
veg-friendly

**Chinatown**
701 9th St. NW
(202) 638-0800

Although Zaytinya has become quite a scene lately, the restaurant still offers some of the finest mezzede in Washington. On most evenings, the enormously popular, soaring space—which has big plate-glass windows onto the street, making it feel very much a part of the city—gets louder and busier than some can tolerate. At lunch, it's more sedate, and, for many, more enjoyable. Either way, Zaytinya is, of course, a concept, and, no less, a concept of mega-chef Jose Andrés (Café Atlantico, Minibar). The "small plates" formula is not unfamiliar to Andrés; luckily, it's also a familiar tenet of Greek cuisine, and one that hasn't been botched in its journey West.

There have been a few alterations, however. Gone is the taverna food doused in a bath of olive oil (though oil laced with pomegranate paste might come out, to start, with a warm but uninspired pita, which gets very chewy as it cools). In its place are whimsical and even effeminate renderings of familiar Greek (with some Turkish and Lebanese thrown in) foods in which some of the oil has been replaced by more attentive spicing and teensy garnishes.

The results are totally unique in DC. On the permanent menu, falafel balls are wonderfully raw and spiced inside. Mavrofassoula me loucaniko is a pork sausage with orange rind whose flavor really shines through—an effect a bit like pâté with orange marmalade or aspic—and comes with a competent, if underseasoned, black-eyed-peaish bean stew. In general, look to the night's specials for the best results. We've tried a subtle, delicious feta-stuffed zucchini blossom, whose fried batter had a certain lightness; mint and an almond-and-red-pepper purée added further color, although some inedibly tough onion pieces were in the mix, too. The execution isn't always perfect. And some dishes just fall flat, like a somewhat moist but very bland swordfish kebab with a meaningless sauce of herbs.

The restaurant's knowledgeable, shockingly attractive waitstaff is a plus: they maintain incredible composure and rarely act rushed. More than anything, Zaytinya is an industrial-age engineering marvel: it's amazing to see such a busy operation run so smoothly, especially with the addition of belly dancers. Now if only their valet partner would lower its insulting $15 valet fee. But that's probably calculated exactly, too; this is the kind of restaurant group that would probably run pivot-table models on valet elasticity of demand. Sometimes competence has its downside. You've got to take the bitter with the sweet. –FC

# Zed's Ethiopian Restaurant

## 3.6 | 6.0
### Food | Feel

*Yesterday's Ethiopian hotspot is mostly bread and dozes*

## Ethiopian

Casual restaurant

### $30
#### Price

www.zeds.net

Daily 11am–11pm

**Bar** Beer, wine, liquor
**Credit cards** Visa, MC, AmEx
**Reservations** Accepted
Outdoor dining, veg-friendly

**Georgetown**
1201 28th St. NW
(202) 333-4710

While Zed's may win the Most Action Shots with Celebrities award, it certainly won't garner any accolades from us for its food. We're not sure what Clint Eastwood, Hillary Clinton, and Mike Tyson are all smiling about in the framed photos hanging in Zed's entryway and up the stairs to the second dining room, but we doubt it's the beef tibs.

Georgetown seems to have exerted its gentrifying influence on Zed's. This might be a good thing with regard to décor; when it comes to the food—well—suffice it to say that this is no 9th Street. We generally like our tibs hotter and our lentils creamier than Zed's, and on the whole, the restaurant's food is too dry and sanitized to taste any good.

Worse still, the service is utterly patronizing. After being seated, your party is asked if everyone has previously eaten at an Ethiopian restaurant. If anyone at the table demurs, the entire party is subjected to a pedantic introduction to cuisine and etiquette (psst...you don't use utensils), delivered with the mindless automation and bored listlessness of a flight attendant reciting evacuation instructions for the umpteenth time. By the end of the speech, you're apt to find yourself looking around for a parachute.

Zed's food does show one surprising strength: its bread. The restaurant's injera is a bit browner than usual, and is so full of tang that it seems to get up and hop about in your mouth. Would that the same held for what went on top. Instead, shrimp tibs are made with old-tasting shellfish and a weak sauce. Doro wat contains but a slim offering of dry chicken meat, although the sauce, to its credit, is nice and red and spicy. We'll leave it to the manners experts to decide how to handle the whole boiled egg.

Zed's vegetarian options are mostly spiceless; you almost can't even taste the collard greens. So why are the celebrities smiling? With apologies to Pulp Fiction, it must be "Zed's bread, baby... Zed's bread."
—CK

# Zengo

Exciting Latinasian fusion or expensive confusion?

| 6.7 | 7.4 |
|:---:|:---:|
| Food | Feel |

## Pan-Asian

Upmarket restaurant

**$65**
Price

www.modernmexican.com

**Bar** Beer, wine, liquor
**Credit cards** Visa, MC, AmEx
**Reservations** Accepted
Live music

**Chinatown**
781 7th St. NW
(202) 393-2929

Sometime in the '90s, someone put chipotle sauce on salmon and—voila!—Latinasian fusion was born. It's a pretty natural marriage when you consider the cuisines' shared inclination toward aromatics, fish, and spicy peppers; but these notoriously assertive ingredients require very careful balancing.

Zengo is trendy, to be sure. Décor is restaurant-group zen-chic: red-and-rust walls dotted with artfully random arrangements of driftwood and fake rocks, hardwood floors, and modern furniture. There are some mind-boggling design choices—like a semi-exposed bathroom, narrow passageways, and little acoustic insulation—but the balance between vivacious Latin and minimalist Asian mostly works here.

This balance varies in the food. Though ahi tuna, mango salsa, and chipotle are more overplayed and dated than Amy Grant's "Baby Baby," they work together nicely inside wonton tacos, where a light char is complemented by sweet heat. In ceviche, tuna does an appealing textural dance with mashed avocado, its rare flesh gently cooked by citric acid. But black cod is overpowered by hyphen-happy elements like lemon-togarashi aioli and chipotle-miso. Shrimp is held hostage by an abusive tomatillo sauce. Peking duck is rendered greasy and gritty.

Despite the errors, there is a stimulating attention to detail that shows through small things like pickled ginger spiked with hot peppers (a creeping, slow burn), or rum sauce that somehow manages a throaty, musty aftertaste of banana without the initial punch.

The bar downstairs is usually packed with flashy folks sipping fresh mango mojitos—which strike a fine balance with muddled mint and puckery lime—and sake sangría with Asian pear and Fuji apple. There are also a few decent cold sakes and the most basic citizenry of beers from Mexico and Japan.

Service ranges from snooty and cold to over-explanatory and untimed. A pointer: when asked if you've dined there before, just say yes. A menu of shareable plates isn't that complicated, is it?

At lunch, Bento boxes are available for a whopping $20. For this, you get what is essentially a deconstructed teriyaki bowl and a basic roll. Which brings us to a critical point: prices at Zengo are extremely conceited. $5 for salted soybeans? Are they using fleur de sel or something? How about $12 for a ceviche in which you see more jicama than mahi-mahi, or $18 for tofu? There are restaurants that warrant this kind of pricing, but Zengo isn't quite there. –JC

# Zola

A gourmet destination cleverly disguised as a museum restaurant

**8.3** *Food*  **9.3** *Feel*

## New American

Upmarket restaurant

**$60** *Price*

www.zoladc.com

Mon–Thu 11:30am–3pm, 5pm–10pm; Fri 11:30am–3pm, 5pm–11pm; Sat 5pm–11pm; Sun 5pm–9pm

**Bar** Beer, wine, liquor
**Credit cards** Visa, MC, AmEx
**Reservations** Accepted
Date-friendly

**Penn Quarter**
800 F St. NW
(202) 654-0999

Who would have thought that the delightfully entertaining Spy Museum would also have a great restaurant? Yet here it is, with a scarlet-lipstick smear of a name and a film-noir interior. It's like stepping into a spy movie, all black leather chairs and sleek design, right down to the huge tubs of chilling wine that are scattered across the restaurant. Frosted-glass frames hold etched silhouettes of mysterious trenchcoated figures. The theme is playful, but the overall effect is surprisingly tasteful and relaxed.

Décor aside, Zola is an immaculate restaurant. Service is well informed and comfortable, and food is adeptly prepared and discerningly presented. Meals begin with a surprise amuse-bouche, which, at one visit, was a pair of tiny endive boats carrying little loads of peanutty pork. It was a cheek-squeezing punch of flavor that sent us straight to the extensive cocktail list.

For such a concept restaurant, the food at Zola is surprisingly focused. Ingredients are cooked straightforwardly and well, and the results are wonderful. Tortelloni, raggedly hand-formed from fresh pasta dough, are filled with sheep's-milk ricotta, manchego, and truffle oil. The filling is salty enough to break through both the pasta dough and the mild, frothy sauce, turning your attention where it ought to go. The belly button of the pasta catches a sprinkle of melty shallots and just enough sauce to moisten the entire bite.

A fat round of pork loin leaks pan juices when you cut in. Each bite is a combination of thick, chewy muscle and smooth fat. A seemingly negligible pesto of broccoli, gouda, and pine nuts imparts an excellent balance of acid to the plate. Mashed potatoes are lusciously thick, and honey-glazed baby carrots and turnips are soft but not mushy.

In case you're wondering, Émile Zola wasn't just a writer—he turned into a big-time political activist when he published a risky newspaper article defending a French artillery captain named Alfred Dreyfus, who stood accused of spying. As a result of his writings, Zola wound up being arrested and had to flee to England—and helped get Dreyfus exonerated. Here's to the power of the great intellectuals—and to the power of great restaurants to stimulate not just our palates but our brains, too. –FC

# Zorba's Café

A Greek restaurant whose menu globetrots a bit too much for its own good

**6.4** Food
**8.0** Feel

## Greek, Sandwiches

Counter service

**$25** Price

www.zorbascafe.com

Mon–Sat 11am–11:30pm
Sun 11am–10:30pm

**Bar** Beer, wine
**Credit cards** Visa, MC, AmEx
Outdoor dining, veg-friendly

**Dupont**
1612 20th St. NW
(202) 387-8555

The infinitely popular Zorba's may be named after a hero from Crete, but its cuisine isn't limited to the island's (or even Greece's) dishes; in fact, the restaurant serves falafel, subs, and pizza, and its staff is mostly Mexican (instead of tahini, oil, or flakes of red pepper, the condiments table holds ketchup and Castillo-brand hot sauce). There's very little that's Greek about it. In other words, Zorba's seems to fall easily into the "typical Greek-American place" category.

But upon closer examination, Zorba's is a little more difficult to pin down. Few of the Greek-style dishes are oversized, as they tend to be in many Greek-run American diners, and many are rendered quite tastily. Carafes of table wine, a cramped interior with painted scenes of fishing villages, and equally tight-knit outdoor seating seem to add to the island taverna effect, and make the term "diner" seem altogether inappropriate. Although the interior and exterior décor is café-style, with patio seating and umbrellas, there's no table service at all—you place your order at the counter, and receive your meal and drink on a blue plastic tray.

And unlike Crete's tavernas, Zorba's features no fish dishes. Its menu choices are limited to the traditional street fare of falafel and gyros, all of which are wrapped in small, unremarkable pita bread—the pita tends to be soft but not particularly flavorful. When filled with falafel—the patties are on the mushy side, but the taste of herbs and chickpeas is fresh—and doused in tahini sauce, the pitas sometimes do fall apart, leaving you no choice but to stab at your food with a plastic fork and hope the paper plate does not fall entirely to pieces.

But what most people order—and what you should, too, probably—is the gyro sandwich or salad; the gyro meat is extraordinarily flavorful and well-tended here. Zorba's lentil soup is also remarkably good: it is creamy, a little bit spicy, and served with a wedge of fresh lemon, whose acidic bite offers due complement to the more woody lentil flavor. Less successful are the French fries, which are little more than chubby, soggy, and under-salted wedges of potato.

Is Zorba's just a pleasant spot to gather outside over inexpensive drinks and middling pan-Mediterranean fare? Clearly, it's more than that. Clearly, its inordinate popularity is not arbitrary. Clearly, there's something about this place—and it's not the seasoning on the gyros, or the paintings on the walls—that strikes a nerve with the culinary consciousness of the city. Sometimes, after a long day at work—or 600 pages of food criticism—all you want to do is sit down for a cold beer and an okay gyro. Sometimes there's just an ineffable placeness of a place that seems to mock the notion of trying to quantify its food, its feel, its ranking. Sometimes the food critics don't have all the answers. –FC

# Fearless Critic
## Index